J M Turner.
1958.

1933 - the Year Hitler came to power but his Name does Not appear in the Index!)

This is a fairly rare book Now)

CHRISTIANITY AND THE CRISIS

Edited by **DR. PERCY DEARMER** Canon of Westminster

CHRISTIANITY AND THE CRISIS

CONTRIBUTORS

THE ARCHBISHOPS OF CANTERBURY AND YORK

PROFESSOR W. G. S. ADAMS   F. R. BARRY

N. BERDIAEFF   J. S. BEZZANT

THE DEAN OF CANTERBURY

THE BISHOP OF CHICHESTER   THE BISHOP OF CROYDON

LORD DICKINSON   THE DEAN OF EXETER

PRINCIPAL GARVIE   E. N. PORTER GOFF

DR. A. HERBERT GRAY   DR. HUNKIN   S. E. KEEBLE

P. T. KIRK   THE BISHOP OF LIVERPOOL

DR. ALBERT MANSBRIDGE   THE BISHOP OF PLYMOUTH

PROFESSOR RAJU   PROFESSOR RAVEN

MAURICE RECKITT   PROFESSOR J. MORGAN REES

THE BISHOP OF RIPON   R. ELLIS ROBERTS

SIR C. GRANT ROBERTSON   DR. MAUDE ROYDEN

MALCOLM SPENCER   SIR W. BEACH THOMAS

E. C. URWIN   H. G. WOOD

A very formidable group indeed

LONDON
VICTOR GOLLANCZ LTD
14 Henrietta Street Covent Garden
1933

Printed in Great Britain by
The Camelot Press Ltd., London and Southampton

CONTENTS

PART II: WHAT CHRISTIANITY IS

PREFACE

By THE EDITOR

Exactly a hundred years ago, Christianity succeeded in defeating two giant evils which were but two forms of the same immorality—the oppression of the weak by the strong. They were sometimes called the Black Slavery and the White Slavery : in 1833 Wilberforce and Clarkson accomplished the last stage of their life-work, and the Great Emancipation Act registered what is perhaps the chief Christian triumph in history. In the same year Lord Shaftesbury, whose attacks upon the horrors of unrestrained industrialism had already produced two measures of factory reform, saw the climax of his crusade, in the chief Factory Act, of 1833, by which children and young women were rescued from oppression, and inspectors were appointed. It is perhaps more than a coincidence that in the same year the work of popular education, which had been begun by the Church in Anglo-Saxon times and was now systematically spread over Great Britain by three great religious organisations, was recognised by the State, and the first Government grant made for national education. The vast religious movement of the eighteenth century which sprang from John Wesley (in whose dominating personality Churchmanship and Nonconformity were combined) had changed the heart of England ; and therefore moral triumphs, impossible in the world before, were accomplished.

Yet the years that followed Waterloo had been years of dearth, depression, and calamity, when the chief actors in the drama were, as is noted on p. 42, on the brink of despair. The parallel with our own moment is remarkable : a period of post-war exhaustion had begun, in 1815, as in 1918, with its social antagonisms and moral confusion, and civil disturbances more violent than anything we have known this time in England or America. Yet the religious accumulation of moral power had been so ample that the foundation of civil and religious liberty had been already laid, and the establishment of democratic government begun, at the time when the two slaveries were abolished.

It is the belief of those who are contributing to *Christianity and the Crisis* that the same moral power is with us to-day, because the same religious spirit is at work—is, indeed, as most close observers believe, emerging now with greater strength from the confusions and disloyalties of the post-war decade. Each contributor naturally writes for himself, and is responsible for his own opinions alone ; but the fact that we have not conspired together, or even met in hasty conference, makes the convergence of opinion the more remarkable, now that the result is printed. Other people may still welter in confusion, but those who take their religion seriously seem to know what they want.

The issue, indeed, is simple. The motives and methods of human life are not sufficiently moralised : it was to moralise the machinery of production, to limit the power of selfishness, that Wilberforce and Shaftesbury were working a century ago ; and the whole world now enjoys what Christians then won : but in many ways industry and business, and family life, and civic and political activity, need further moralisation. Money—the necessary use of tokens of exchange—has been overlooked in its moral aspect (in spite of what Christ said about it) and treated as machinery, working by what are euphemistically called laws, as if the desire of the natural man to snatch what he can, inherited from his animal ancestors (for whom in their small intelligence there was no other way), cannot be now shaped and controlled for the common good.

And, alas, there was one aspect of human life which was not understood a hundred years ago ; and to this our present miseries are mainly due. The very word " international " had then only just been coined by Jeremy Bentham. The whole conception of moralising international relations was in its infancy. So the world went on to its doom. So, because the nations and their representatives have not yet learnt the elements of international behaviour,

we stand at this moment of writing on the brink of irretriev-
able disaster. It is in a very real sense true that only Christ
can save the world from ruin to-day. Are we prepared to
let his spirit save the nations from themselves ?

The community of nations is the most difficult lesson for
mankind to learn, because atavism is here at its strongest.
Yet enormously difficult sides of the problem have already
been mastered : there is no cause for despair. Again we can
look back a century, and see that the federal principle, for
lack of which the American Colonies had separated from
Britain, had been thereafter triumphantly brought in, to
form those Colonies into the United States. In 1839 Lord
Durham's famous report applied the federal principle to
Canada ; and to-day the British Commonwealth, like the
United States, is one because its Dominions are free, and is
in fact a federation of federations ; and this way of federation, already that of nations like Australia and South
Africa, of Germany and Switzerland, is now being sought
for the huge territory of India, and surely offers the one
principle through which throughout the world nationalism
may be merged in internationalism, and liberty combined
with order. That is, after all, an ancient Christian principle :
the early Church consisted of self-governing Churches
which for centuries remained in unity ; the ancient Churches
of the East have never ceased to be " autocephalous "
and at the same time united : it is the principle of the
Anglican, Presbyterian, and other great communions
to-day ; the Church of England, for instance, the Church
of Ireland, the Protestant Episcopal Church of America,
that of Canada, and the rest, are perfectly free and self-
governing, while all belong enthusiastically to the Anglican
Church. Just as the Christian religion is one of intense
individualism holding the infinite equal value of every
human soul, and yet is not less an intensely social religion,
so also it is the religion of perfect freedom, working out the
ways in which liberty can be combined with commonwealth, endeavouring, as St. Paul says, to keep the unity
of the Spirit in the bond of peace. That enormously

difficult problem has only been partly solved in our nine-teen centuries. It is still before us. But there is no reason to despair : we shall solve it, unless Christianity perishes.

And by Christianity we mean, I think, in this book a very large thing, larger perhaps than any of us can yet know. We mean—I at least certainly do ultimately mean—the religion of all good men. To the Christian principles of charity and co-operation all the prophets and philosophers had been shaping, when Jesus Christ came to unite the highest aspirations of Hebraism and of Hellenism, to show what God is in his character and essence, and what man can be in the image of God. Since Christ came, all wise and good men have followed in the same way, with increasing understanding. Christians, of course, were frequently false to the name they bore, and from age to age the Light of the World has been shuttered ; monstrous things have been done by Church officials and institutions ; and the pages of Gibbon and Lecky are a warning against any attempt to idealise the past. Often the spirit of Christ has been re-covered by those who stood outside the Churches. But the crimes and failures of Christian history only prove how far Christ was above the ways of average men, how far in advance of his age, and of that brief succeeding period which we call the Christian era : during that fraction of his fifty thousand years of development man has in fact made a remarkable advance ; and Christ would not be the saviour of the world if he were not still far ahead and only just in sight of our extremest vanguard.

Meanwhile " at sundry times and in divers manners " the testimony has increasingly converged, till at the present time the educated classes of Asia itself are sharing increas-ingly in the fellowship of the Christian ethic. There is a unity of ideal such as the world has not known before, a unity in which there is indeed neither Greek nor Jew, Barbarian, Scythian, bond nor free. The world is sick from eating sour grapes : but the wise and good men, all the world over, know the cure. Against the insanities of self-seeking, ignorance, hatred, cruelty, and fear, they will proclaim, more audibly and insistently than ever before, the resistless principle of universal charity. And we have to go in and help them.

That audible proclamation was most insistently made eighty years ago by Frederick Maurice, Kingsley, and their friends ; it has persisted ever since, and has increased, with notable results ; for social evils have been enormously reduced, good citizenship and good government have improved to the remarkable extent that Professor Adams illustrates, and the Christian public is more ready to act on Christian principles than ever before. The writers in this book, representative and distinguished as they are, form but a fraction of the philosophers and statesmen, theologians and economists, who agree with their diagnosis and share their faith. They are just a few who have managed, in the midst of other work, to contribute at very short notice some part of their special knowledge and experience.

THE SCHEME OF THE BOOK

Our plan is simple. After an Introduction by the Bishop of Ripon and Dr. Mansbridge, speaking for the Oxford don and the " ordinary man " respectively (though the parts might be reversed), we proceed to what in correspondence between ourselves we have generally called " *The Mess*." This is *Part I.*, and begins with a chapter by a distinguished philosopher, Dr. Matthews. From his description of the moral and intellectual confusion of the moment we pass to one who reads every book that is published, and has reviewed a large proportion of them— Mr. Ellis Roberts, who shows how the post-war confusion threw up its strange signals in the literary world. The social and economic distress is analysed by a critic who, as secretary of the Industrial Christian Fellowship, has peculiar opportunities for knowing the various aspects of the situation—Mr. P. T. R. Kirk ; and Dr. Masterman, the Bishop of Plymouth, with a historian's judgment, describes the international condition into which humanity has reduced itself.

Part II, What Christianity Is, begins with two chapters by Dr. Raven and Dr. Herbert Gray which endeavour to set forth the actual teaching of Christ ; and in the third chapter Dr. Hunkin brings the early documents of the Church to show how Christianity began as a religion of fellowship. After a chapter by Mr. Bezzant on the Christian conception of man, Mr. Malcolm Spencer, the Secretary of the Christian Social Council (without whose help this book could not have been made), Dr. Garvie, and the Bishop of Chichester discuss the history of recent movements for social and economic reform in Christendom. The Bishop of Croydon then describes the way in which the Churches are coming together on a principle akin to that of federation between States ; and Mr. Keeble supplies a much-needed reminder of the enormous amount of work for humanity that is already done by the Church. We are never grateful enough for the untrumpeted service of thousands upon thousands of devoted men and women, which prevents humanity from sinking to a lower level and steadily raises the standard of human life.

Part III deals with the problem of reconstruction, the *Christian Solution* for our present distresses. The Bishop of Liverpool, beginning with the unit of the family, hands on the torch to Sir Charles Grant Robertson, the Vice-Chancellor of Manchester University, who sets forth the ideals for education. The next section, the Social and Economic Order, is divided into five chapters : the Dean of Canterbury, who might have been an engineer or a financier if he were not a parson, writes on Money, the basis of exchange ; Professor Morgan Rees presents a mass of relevant facts to illustrate the need of Civic and Industrial Reform ; Mr. Urwin deals with the central problem of the Individual in relation to the Community ; Dr. Maude Royden relates Leisure with Labour ; and that most far-seeing of experts on the countryside, Sir W. Beach Thomas, tells us how the rebuilding of village life has already begun.

Still broadening in scope, Part III proceeds to give us a chapter on the State by Professor Adams. After this comes the International section. Lord Dickinson, who is so prominent a figure in combining the Christian forces of the different nations for the solution of international misunderstandings, writes on the League of Nations, and an Indian expert, Professor Raju, on the spiritual aspects of the Racial Problem in the East. The sermon delivered by the Archbishop of Canterbury in December 1931 at St. Paul's Cathedral, before an audience that included most of the foreign ambassadors then in London, as well as the leading members of the Government, adds here a weighty pronouncement on the crucial question of disarmament. Mr. Porter Goff writes on the way to secure peace. The three alternatives before the world are next discussed : secular Scientific Humanism by Mr. H. G. Wood ; the " religion " of money-making, or material success—Industrial Secularism by Mr. Maurice Reckitt; and Communist Secularism by the well-known Russian professor, Nicolai Berdiaeff. After a stimulating chapter on the Church and the World by Mr. F. R. Barry, who has an intimate knowledge of both, the Archbishop of York sets out the conclusion of the matter.

There is unflinching diagnosis in this book, but there is also the record of a steady progress in fundamental principles, and the evidence of an intense and widespread determination at this moment of crisis to seek the Kingdom of God and his justice, and to secure the good life for all.

INTRODUCTORY:
"CHRIST OR CHAOS?"

I. VINDICATION

By Dr. E. A. BURROUGHS, Bishop of Ripon

The world which for its Babels wants a scourge,
And for its wilds a husbandman, acclaims
The Crucified that came of Nazareth.
                                        GEORGE MEREDITH

The meaning of history is not Cæsar but Jesus :
history tends not towards Cæsar but towards Jesus.
                                        PRESIDENT MASARYK

I

THIS BOOK seeks to suggest in detail the practical relevance of Christianity to the complex of connected problems —personal, political, financial—which we call " the world crisis." The organic relation of Christianity to life has probably never been more obvious, nor illustrated on a wider stage : though the illustrations are, unhappily, mostly negative—the consequences of ignoring what should, in a Christian era, have been obvious long since. And experts in one part of the field or another will show how solutions and remedies may still be found in the principles of Jesus Christ.

But it must be made clear at the very threshold that Christianity as a social programme stands or falls by its truth as a religion—a theory of the nature of God and of his relation to man and the universe. Christianity meets us as a form of theism : the completest and (as Christians claim) the highest form of the conviction that the First Cause of this universe must be conceived of as, in some sense, personal. Theism can be developed into a philosophy : it begins with an act of faith. The theist claims that this hypothesis answers more questions and raises fewer difficulties than the only alternative, *viz.* the faith that the universe has an impersonal origin.

We of to-day no longer think in terms of spirit and matter as contrasted " substances," but rather in terms of personality and process.

The ultimate question is, and always has been, " Which comes first ? " Is personality the source and starting-point of process, or only something that in course of time emerges from it ? Theism, for reasons which it is beyond the scope of this Introduction to discuss, says, with the writer of Genesis, " In the beginning—GOD ! " And it has good modern ground for saying so. After ingenious efforts by scientific materialism to explain personality as an epipheno-menon or non-significant by-product of the evolutionary process, followed by such non-rational compromises as the " Stoicism in plus-fours "[1] of the Humanists and the eclectic pessimism of Bertrand Russell, we have reached a point in the development of thought, even in the region of the natural sciences, at which the theistic hypothesis is stronger and more respectable than ever.

When Sir James Jeans writes :

" From the intrinsic evidence of his creation, the Great Architect of the Universe now begins to appear as a pure mathematician,"[2]

he states a conclusion based on premises which equally allow men impressed by other no less valid bits of intrinsic evidence, to see as the source of process the Great Lover, the Great Artist, and the Great Philosopher as well. The recognition by modern physics of an element of indeter-mination at every stage of the world-process, from the atom up, is also evidence for the freedom and therefore the transcendence of personality. And all the arguments for this hypothesis focus in two facts of human experience. First, it is precisely with the emergence and development of person-ality, the reign of man, that creativeness appears again on earth, and the steady rhythm of the world-process is modified by happenings which, but for human activity, would never have been known. The scientific advance of the last hundred years is a case in point. Secondly, this new

[1] F. R. Barry, *The Relevance of Christianity*, p. 129.
[2] *The Mysterious Universe*, p. 134.

handling of the powers wrapped up in the world-process by beings who find within them the creative urge depends on a new appreciation of the plan which the process increasingly reveals : an appreciation only possible to personal intelligences. But the plan, with its strange symmetries, is only discovered, not invented, by man. What to the modern mind is the most characteristic feature of this universe—its absolute coherence and " mathematical " lay-out—is a feature that could only be revealed to a speculative and creative mind. And the emergence, late in time, of just such minds from the seemingly impersonal process is clinching evidence for Mind as the background of the process too.

Hence the new strength of the theistic hypothesis at the end of a period of scientific progress which, in its early stages, threatened even to sweep it away. And Christianity, as a form of theism, is entitled to claim its share in this accession of strength. Christianity says, in effect, " Come and meet, on your own level, in a form which you can at least partly understand and get to know, the Mind behind the world-process : God, in whom you live and move and have your being." This Introduction seeks to give a preliminary bird's-eye view of the vindication of Christ's view of God and man in contemporary experience, which others will develop in detail. Later on, my emphasis will have to fall on the need to get theory put into practice, if the key which Christianity offers is to turn the stubborn lock. And others will have to discuss the justification, historical and philosophical, for the Christian equation of " God in relation to man " with " Jesus Christ." (" My Father is greater than I," yet " He that hath seen me hath seen the Father.") At this stage the point to emphasise is that we can, rightly and reasonably, adopt Christ's key-word, " The Father." It does correspond with reality, as reality reveals itself to the best contemporary thought. Others, in a word, will have to consider whether our key is of the right shape and size. We are entitled, here and now, to say that it is, at any rate, good metal.

There is, however, another reason for emphasising at the outset that Christianity meets us as a form of theism, a belief about the nature of God and his relation with the universe. Many at the present day find it easier to believe in Jesus Christ than in a Personal God. They acknowledge the beauty of Christ's plan, its relevance to human need, its provision for a progressive emancipation of the human spirit. But the hard facts of the universe do not encourage the belief that his plan can ever be realised. To such people the Christian idealist is working against, not with, the grain of reality. His master may be the greatest of the sons of men : but he is not the Son of God—he is a stranger in a hostile universe. We shall see reason to dispute this view, and to recognise, with President Masaryk of Czechoslovakia, that " the meaning of history is not Cæsar but Jesus : history tends not towards Cæsar but towards Jesus." Meanwhile it is important to get clear (1) that belief in a Personal First Cause is more than defensible in the present state of human thought ; (2) that, if it is a question of alternative conceptions of the Divine Personality, the Christian conception has already driven all rivals from the field, so much so that non-Christian theists have, in effect, to dress their God in the attributes of Jesus Christ ; but also (3) that, if the Christian hypothesis is the truest, its truth can be established only by action based on real acceptance of it. We must, in Luther's phrase, " let God be God," if we are to be able to apply the gospel of Jesus Christ. The pathos of the present deadlock lies in the synchronising of a new (though largely negative) experimental vindication of the world-relevance of that gospel with a " deep depression " of scepticism—a bewildered sense that " the foundations are removed." As there is, for a Christian, only one foundation—the belief that Jesus Christ speaks for, and touches, and enables man to touch reality (" No man cometh unto the Father but by me ") —it is vital to establish this foundation as valid if we hope to realise the Christian programme. Its practicability depends on the existence of God, and on God's likeness to

" the Father of our Lord Jesus Christ." And it is only a new conviction of this that can " let God arise and let his enemies be scattered."

It is easy to find in quite unlikely quarters a new conviction that Christ's way is the one way out of the present chaos, though not so easy to find men ready to follow it. I have referred to the eclectic pessimism of Mr. Bertrand Russell. Let me couple with it the eclectic optimism of Mr. Winston Churchill and illustrate my point from both.

Mr. Churchill gave the world some years ago a candid survey of his spiritual experiences and his religious creed : Referring to his Boer War days, " I found," he wrote, " that, whatever I might think or argue, I did not hesitate to ask for special protection when about to come under the fire of the enemy, nor to feel sincerely grateful when I got home safe to tea. I even asked for lesser things . . . and nearly always in those years, and indeed throughout my life, I got what I wanted."[1] Yet he sees no point in efforts to reconcile such experiences with " modern science and historical knowledge," and sums up : " I therefore adopted quite early in life a system of believing whatever I wanted to believe, while at the same time leaving reason to pursue unfettered whatever paths she was capable of treading."[2] It is a convenient creed, reflected interestingly in Mr. Churchill's political career. As a statesman he has not usually been on the side of the angels of idealism. In India, for instance, he has seemed to prefer the big stick to the helping hand as a method of persuasion ; and his normal political bias is not towards respect for moral factors. But lately, if one may judge by a newspaper article from his pen, he has come to appreciate the political necessity of just what faith in Christ does bring. Calling for a halt in material progress and scientific discovery—no new call, but new from such a source—he writes : " Without an equal growth of Mercy, Pity, Peace, and Love, Science herself may destroy all that makes life majestic and tolerable. There never was a time when the inherent virtue of human beings required

[1] *My Early Life*, p. 130.   [2] *Ibid.*, p. 131.

more strong and confident expression in daily life ; there never was a time when the hope of immortality and the disdain of earthly power and achievement were more necessary for the safety of the children of men."[1] One can but ask, " Is Saul also among the prophets ? "

And then Mr. Bertrand Russell. Listen to these words from his book *The Conquest of Happiness*, and, remembering all he stands for, ask if you could have a more direct plea for the way of Christ as the way of salvation ?

" Whenever you happen to take your children to the Zoo you may observe in the eyes of the apes, when they are not performing gymnastic feats or cracking nuts, a strange strained sadness. One can almost imagine that they feel they ought to become men, but cannot discover the secret of how to do it. On the road of evolution they have lost their way ; their cousins marched on and they were left behind. Something of the same strain and anguish seems to have entered the soul of civilised man. He knows there is something better than himself almost within his grasp, yet he does not know where to seek it or how to find it. In despair he rages against his fellow-man, who is equally lost and equally unhappy. We have reached a stage in evolution which is not the final stage. We must pass through it quickly, for if we do not, most of us will perish by the way, and others will be lost in a forest of doubt and fear. . . . To find the right road out of this despair civilised man must enlarge his heart as he has enlarged his mind. He must learn to transcend self, and in so doing to acquire the freedom of the universe."

Anyone familiar with the New Testament will recognise the parallel here with the Christian plan of salvation : the sense of failure, of missing the mark, which is sin ; the poignant counterpart, the sense of " something better than himself almost within his grasp," which is the glory and kingdom of God ; the need " to forget the things that are

[1] In the *Sunday Graphic*, December 18th, 1932.

behind, and press on," which divine forgiveness makes possible ; progress by enlargement of the heart rather than of the mind—the widest sympathy being always the highest wisdom in a world where the last word lies with love ; last, and most significant, the claim that " to acquire the freedom of the universe "—that is, to be at home and happy in God's world as a son of the house—man " must learn to transcend self "—to " cancel self out, and take up his own cross daily, and follow "—not Cæsar, but Christ. Could you have a more complete capitulation to the Christian wisdom by one who is by way of excluding religion altogether ?

But then Mr. Russell is pointing out a way which neither he nor humanity can follow. He asks, in effect, for a new, divine humanity without God as the means of producing it. And Mr. Churchill's eclectic optimism is equally remote from Christian faith in God. God cannot be an Occasional Expedient. He must be all that the word implies. It is here that everything turns, for our present purpose, on whether we are prepared to accept, and act on, Christianity as rightly interpreting reality, and " let God be God " that its social programme may be realised. My aim so far has been to show that we not only can, but may and must. Apart from experimental evidence—and here the fruits of Christian evangelisation in all parts of the world might be laid under tribute—the philosophical case for theism is to-day immensely strong. It is far stronger than when, just before the war, Mr. Arthur Balfour (as he then was) gave his Gifford Lectures on *Theism and Humanism.*" And even then so detached a mind as his could confess and plead for faith in God in the full sense of personal religion. " When I speak of God, I mean something other than an Identity wherein all differences vanish. . . . I mean a God whom man can love, a God to whom men can pray, who takes sides, who has purposes and preferences, whose attributes, however conceived, leave unimpaired the possibility of a personal relation between himself and those he has created." [1]

[1] *Op cit.*, p. 21.

II

" A God who takes sides, who has purposes and preferences." If that be so, then the neglect (for whatever cause)
—still more, the defiance—of these purposes and preferences is enough to explain such cosmic breakdown as the
world is conscious of to-day. If " in his will is our peace,"
any other will is a will to chaos. And developments, which
have made many shallow persons cry out upon a universe
which has betrayed them, only prove how law-abiding
God's universe is. " Be not deceived ; God is not mocked :
whatsoever a man soweth, that shall he also reap." And
it is usual for the crop to yield more than the seed sown ;
he who sows the wind must expect to reap the whirlwind.

" A day of crisis," someone has said, " is a discovery of
God." And when, in the war, the Church of England
launched her " National Mission of Repentance and
Hope," the words chosen for its keynote were : " When
thy judgments are in the earth, the inhabitants of the world
will learn righteousness."[1] The very events which drew this
country into the war focussed clearly the moral and spiritual
issue behind it. If " Might " is not " Right," as Prussianised
Germany was thought to be claiming, the only alternative is
that " Right is Might " ; that " righteousness exalteth a
nation " ; that " Society is based not on science but on
conscience " ; that therefore religion, on which the functioning of conscience depends, is the key to sociological
progress ; but that, for the right functioning of conscience,
the religion appealed to must be right itself. " Rightness "
in a religion includes three things at least : truth to fact,
faithfulness to the highest in man, and appeal to what is
best in him—to love, not to fear.

If what most prominently leapt into prominence, in the
light of the war, was the extraordinary relevance of the
Hebrew prophets, with their insistence on righteousness,
there was also a sense in which the Cross of Christ above
all came into its own. Though post-war novels have hardly

[1] Isaiah 26 : 9.

ever touched this side of the war, it was made much of at
the time by Mr. H. G. Wells in his own way : good proof
that what not many spoke of was working in the minds of
all. What it meant to some at least at the Front is suggested by this paragraph from a letter written by a chaplain—an Oxford colleague of my own—when serving with
the 51st Division in the summer of 1915.

" A boy who had seen his brother's body broken before his
eyes crept back into his dug-out and fixed a little drawing on its wall. He drew a cross and a sunrise, and wrote
the simple inscription, ' God is love.' So he reassured
himself, and incidentally his friends who happened to
see what he had done. That is the kind of reassurance
we need here in defiance of the daily challenge of faith,
and, thank God, it is not denied."[1]

In a variety of ways this war seemed like a rough apprentice-
ship in practical Christianity, as men discovered that " a
man's life consisteth not in the abundance of the things which
he possesseth," that he does " find " himself by " losing "
himself, that even the most mixed lot of mortals, when
bound together by this joyous indifference to self, enter into
a comradeship which more than makes up for all they
sacrifice to reach it, and that " man's extremity is God's
opportunity " in far more ways than one. The meaning
of God and of the Cross did thus stand out with a new
clearness for millions, though many, through sheer ignorance, failed to recognise what had come to them, and far
more soon forgot. But at least this new illumination and
training lay behind and justified that belief in " a new
world after the war," which was another significant feature
of the war years.

[1] Quoted in *The Valley of Decision*, by the present writer, a book published in 1916 which went through six impressions before the end of
1918, and was an attempt to work out in detail the moral and spiritual
significance and challenge of the war. The chapter in question, " The
Vindication of the Cross," gives other first-hand illustrations. I venture
to mention this because it seems sometimes now to be forgotten how
clearly this aspect of the war was recognised at the time.

What did happen after the war, we know but too well. The point is that the then backsliding was a revolt against lights that multitudes had really seen. If economic dislocation and breakdown as well as continuing political unsettlement have been chiefly due to culpable blindness on the part of statesmen, public opinion should have guided politics better. Disillusionment, and the loss of moral courage to stand up to adverse conditions when they came, represent the penalty of widespread sinning by individuals everywhere against our war-time " discovery of God." " The decay of faith in a nation is a moral fact, the stigma or the scar of sin."[1] The words bear closely on post-war psychology. Already in the summer of 1919 this was noted by Mr. J. M. Keynes, whose study, then so startling, now so fully vindicated, of *The Economic Consequences of the Peace* ended thus, with a sombre quotation from *Promotheus Vinctus* : Unbound .

" The events of the coming year will not be shaped by the deliberate acts of statesmen, but by the hidden currents, flowing continually beneath the surface of political history, of which no one can predict the outcome. In one way only can we influence these hidden currents—by setting in motion those forces of instruction and imagination which change *opinion*. The assertion of truth, the unveiling of illusion, the dissipation of hate, the enlargement and instruction of men's hearts and minds, must be the means.

" In this autumn of 1919, in which I write, we are at the dead season of our fortunes. The reaction from the exertions, the fears, and the sufferings of the past five years is at its height. Our power of feeling or caring beyond the immediate questions of our own material well-being is temporarily eclipsed. The greatest events outside our own direct experience and the most dreadful anticipations cannot move us.

[1] Principal R. T. Forsyth.

In each human heart terror survives
The ruin it has gorged : the loftiest fear
All that they would disdain to think were true :
Hypocrisy and custom make their minds
The fanes of many a worship, now outworn.
They dare not devise good for man's estate,
And yet they know not that they do not dare.
The good want power but to weep barren tears,
The powerful goodness want ; worse need for them.
The wise want love ; and those who love want wisdom ;
And all best things are thus confused to ill.
Many are strong and rich, and would be just.
But live among their suffering fellow-men
As if none felt : they know not what they do.

" We have been moved already beyond endurance, and
need rest. Never in the lifetime of men now living has
the universal element in the soul of man burnt so
dimly."[1]

Men had talked of " the inevitable reaction " after the war,
so of course it came ; and the cost of that reaction has been
greater than that of the war itself. For it robbed us of the
power, or will, to profit by the one really good gift which
the war years brought—their moral and spiritual lessons.
And the new " discovery of God " was forgotten just when
needed most.

Yet from the first there were some, on both sides, who
set their faces the right way, and, even before the war was
over, knew what a vast repentance would be asked of the
post-war world. Professor Zimmern, in his *Europe in Con-
valescence*, relates how Friedrich Naumann, a great leader of
German idealism, but once a believer in " Machtpolitik "
for all that, readjusted his mental furniture in 1918 and
told German parents that their sons " had fallen to close
an epoch, and that a new age demanded new tasks and
a new outlook." From a very different angle, the late Professor Wildon Carr in 1920 told a London audience that

[1] *Op. cit.*, pp. 278–9.

" the era in which we were living was only comparable to the time of the Copernican revolution, when people first realised that the world was moving." Professor Gilbert Murray, who, in a pamphlet published shortly before the war ended, spoke of " the common man and woman, the workman and peasant and teacher and civil servant and tradesman," as " wearying for a return to love, crying out, each man in his loneliness, for the spirit that is called Christ,"[1] described the situation as he saw it in 1920 in these words :

" The present world order, if it survives the present economic crisis, has a wonderful opportunity, such an opportunity as has never been granted to any previous order in the history of recorded time. . . . We have the power and we know the course. . . . We have been given everything except a certain necessary greatness of character."[2]

Lord Hugh Cecil, in *The Times* in August 1918, warned people not to hope too much from the League of Nations, then already in prospect, " unless it is associated with a profound conversion of opinion and affection. . . . Such a change as this cannot be effaced by the experience of war, however terrible, or by any treaty, however solemn. It must be the work of moral and religious influence, and probably of a long period of time." And, again passing on to 1920, we find a writer in the *Round Table* thus expressing himself :

" The attainment of a world-commonwealth is the inexorable condition of world-freedom—of life, that is, in the highest form which this planet can offer. . . . This final freedom, with all its blessings, is not in sight, for the spiritual basis of the world-commonwealth is as yet lacking."

[1] *The League of Nations and the Democratic Idea.*
[2] Article in *Contemporary Review*, April 1920, p. 476.

One might go on quoting from a store of similar quotations, illustrating the slow growth of spiritual consciousness in the years since then, and the gradual recognition of where the real post-war problem lies. Our real task is to assert the supremacy of the moral factor in politics, in economics, in finance, in every field of human activity ; and, that we may be able to do so, to appeal at once to the spiritual nature of man and to the spiritual power for which the word " God " stands—the " Power, not ourselves, that makes for righteousness." Is there any adequate moral standard short of the Christian standard, with its equal emphasis on individual conscience and on that Human Whole to which national sovereignties have now to be subordinated, and its exorcism of cosmic selfishness and fear by " infinite love in ordinary intercourse " ?[1] Is there any adequate power to lift men to this standard but the Spirit of Christ ? To-day it seems as though the light which shone in the war and was then rejected were coming back, refracted through a variety of judgments on that disobedience, and is again focussing itself gradually upon the figure of Jesus Christ. Again men are saying " It is Christ or Chaos."

III

In particular we are being forced to see the economic no less than moral rightness of Christ's idealism, and its bearing on the international problem which dominates economics to-day. For, by common consent, the one thing that would really revive trade the world over would be an assurance that peace was secure, such as a really sweeping measure of disarmament all around might have given. Yet it is precisely the half-hearted perversity of the Disarmament Conference which precipitated the new international crisis of 1933 in consequence of which disarmament has almost become impossible.

At a critical moment in the war, when the late Lord Lansdowne published a letter which only one big London

[1] The phrase is Harnack's, to describe what gave the Church of the first centuries its rapid triumph over the forces which set out to crush it.

newspaper would print, urging that the time had come to speak with our enemies of peace, Prince Max of Baden (afterwards the last Imperial Chancellor of Germany) made a speech in answer—which probably no English newspaper reported. In it he said :

> " Everywhere men are growing weary of the moratorium on the Sermon on the Mount. Humanity longs for notice of its repeal even before the war ends. Sir William Byles, that true Christian who died the other day, when he coined this awful phrase, a ' moratorium on the Sermon on the Mount,'[1] was thinking not of the unavoidable horrors of the battlefield but of the heathenish attitude of mind in which so many men of outstanding intellect in all countries almost prided themselves in war time."[2]

Going on to refer to that one of our Lord's precepts which is, perhaps, most difficult in time of war, he added : " Even in war, to love your enemy is the mark of loyalty to the Lord. And I would add : It is also the mark of loyalty to Germany."[3]

Prince Max would not, I think, have suggested that the Sermon on the Mount had in any true sense been applied in peace-time either. But the war did represent a special and violent suspension of the attempt to put the ideal into practice. It is well in the present bitter phase of the consequences of not thus " loving our enemies," and especially with Germany in her present tragic state, to recall that, even during the war, and on both sides of the great line of cleavage, there were those who still strove to be loyal to Christ, and who saw, even then, that loyalty to him is also the truest loyalty to one's country. For, seeing (as we can now) the immense difference it would have made if, in the light of the war, Christian idealism had been allowed at least to shape the peace settlements, we may be the more ready to-day to look to Christian idealism to point the way

---

[1] In the House of Commons, May 26th, 1916.
[2] *Memoirs of Prince Max of Baden*, p. 191.   [3] *Ibid.*, p. 192.

out of the economic penalties of war and peace alike. To quote Prince Max of Baden again, " We ought never to leave off reminding the world of the blessings that were lost to it when the belligerent nations spurned their great opportunity."[1]

If, instead of the old preoccupation with economic prospects and ambitions, the treaty-makers had " sought first the kingdom of God and his righteousness "—aimed at a settlement according to moral principles, which would be " right " from the divine point of view—it would have saved us, at any rate, from the great underlying mistake of all that pitiable peace-making, the consequences of which lie so heavy on victors and vanquished alike to-day : the perpetuation of fear.

We should have remembered that fear and faith are incompatibles ; that prosperity depends on confidence, and confidence on good-will ; that, in the words of an eastern proverb, " Hatred ceaseth not by hatred at any time, hatred ceaseth only by love " ; and that the only way of rendering an enemy harmless is to treat him as, and so turn him into, a friend. We should have remembered that even God, the source of all man's sense of justice, could not work this world on a basis of retributive justice, but, after men had learned from long experience that law alone is not a sufficient moral lever, took the risk of a policy of free forgiveness, and set himself to save the world by love. " Forasmuch as they had not wherewithal to pay, he freely forgave them both." And, remembering this, we should not have sought peace in ways that, on the pretext of retributive justice, gave fear and resentment a new lease of life just when we were by way of banishing war by organising the nations as a family.

Still less, when in 1919 we had linked the disarmament of Germany and her allies with a pledge to go on as soon as possible to the limitation and reduction of armaments all round, and in 1925 had renewed that pledge at Locarno, should we ever have let the General Disarmament Conference, when at last it met, become for Germany the final

[1] *Op. cit.*, Preface to English edition.

Bc

proof that she would never get a fair deal. The revival of
Hitlerism last year, when it was already a discredited and
waning force, was largely due to the disarmament deadlock. Its present dominance in Germany is the nemesis on
post-war policies fundamentally un-Christian and therefore
politically short-sighted and economically unsound. The
Allies have destroyed not only the old Germany that (as
we hold) plunged Europe into war but the new Germany
of 1918 which should have been a main bulwark of European peace.

Again, with some respect for Christian principles, we
should have been more ready to follow those who, merely
on economic grounds, told us that in the whole effort
permanently to handicap our ex-enemies we were getting
ready to cut our own throats ; that, if the post-war world
was ever to recover, it must be by recognising the economic
interdependence of all the nations—all of them " members
one of another " ; and that, after such wholesale orgies of
destruction, moral and material, there could be no real
" reconstruction " which was not reconstruction *all round*,
no real progress or prosperity which was not prosperity
and progress *for all*. We should have seen then, what now
we see too late, that " prosperity is not something which
can be enjoyed in small compartments," and that economic
nationalism is a blind alley. But why wait so long and suffer
so much to learn what was already in the Sermon on the
Mount, and familiar to all in the Lord's Prayer ? To have
meant, as well said, " Our Father," and to have " sought
first the Kingdom of God and his righteousness," would
have saved us from the huge self-stultification which has
overtaken our rich, emancipated, scientific age, and
incidentally have provided conditions for confidence,
prosperity, and progress which economists and statesmen
are now compassing land and sea to find. For it would
have made easy the coming of that " new spirit," in all the
contacts of men with men, on which the return even of
material prosperity depends. " Seek ye first the Kingdom
of God and his righteousness, and all these things "—the

wherewithal for food and raiment, as typical of man's economic needs—" all these things shall be added unto you." In the Christian perspective, economic prosperity is a by-product of right human relations—of that human brotherhood which flows from the all-Fatherhood of God.

The question is whether so much contemporary vindication of the economic rightness of him whom Christians call " Our Lord " will make the nations even now begin to adopt the Christian perspective. Have we suffered enough from the present *reductio ad absurdum* of our traditional secularism and Mammon-worship to " let God be God " all along the line ? If statesmen and financiers alike have come to see (in the words of a director of the Bank of England[1]) that " the healing word for which the world is waiting is this, which was first spoken so long ago, ' Forgive us our debts as we forgive our debtors ' " ; and that " in the sphere of Reparations and War Debts those words teach us . . . the wise, and indeed the only practical, economic policy," then why should we not accept elsewhere that " foolishness of God " which is " wiser than men " ? May it not even be in the interests of business to move of its own free will towards that Christian revolution for which the Christian Church is supposed to stand, and which we call the coming of the Kingdom of God ? It follows, not from Christianity merely but from any belief in a holy and righteous God that, in his universe, you cannot ultimately prosper except by making his will yours. He has (as Lord Balfour said) his " purposes and preferences " and " takes sides." And it did not need the present breakdown of our modern economic system, with its worship of profit at all costs, its resentment of moral interference, and its frequent indifference to human factors, to suggest that it at least can claim no divine sanction as being in harmony with the will of God.

Here, as we gaze on the self-stultification of the modern " economic man," there rises the spectre of a new nemesis yet to come. Just as at last men begin to see that we need

[1] Mr. Alexander Shaw, in *The Times*, January 11th, 1932.

Christianity to save us, a new world-religion sets up its banners in all lands to drive the Cross out of the field. The power of modern Communism lies in the failure of political and economic systems which have claimed to be Christian and are not, and which the Christian Churches have not clearly enough condemned. And Communism is winning converts not because of its economics, but because of its missionary enthusiasm, resourcefulness, and courage. Its first principles are diametrically opposite to ours. It denies God and denatures man. But it seems to be able to call out something like the spirit of the early Church, and, like it, does not shrink from the pains and risks of revolution where reform has failed. Its " plan of salvation " for the world has, apart from its starting-point and goal, far more in common with our plan than Christians readily recognise who have only seen Christianity in the cramping framework of a Capitalist society. " The relative truth of Communism is its longing for real community."[1] . . . " Communism cannot be opposed by ideas, but only by religious reality. . . . We need nothing else more than a fundamental re-thinking of the Christian message . . . [Communism] has taught Christianity what it never ought to have forgotten, namely, that real faith is asking for everything in the life of man. There will be no ' private affairs ' left."[2]

If this is so, our duty is plain. Spiritual force must meet spiritual force. Unless somehow we of Christ's Church can wake up living, corporate enthusiasm for his " plan," on the same scale as that with which young Russia has watched and worked for the Soviet's " Five Years' Plan," there are already signs that we shall see (and deserve to see) many of the best of our younger folk go over to the Communist banner. And the persecution of Communism will, of course, only strengthen its appeal.

Here we come back to the point from which we started. The social programme of Christianity is useless, impracticable, unless its doctrine of God is true, and the power of

[1] Dr. Hanns Lilje, in *The Christian Faith To-day* (S.C.M.), p. 52.
[2] *Ibid.*, pp. 50-1.

God can (as the Doctrine of the Trinity sets forth) both redeem and inspire human nature and raise it to a new power. " To as many as received him, to those gave he the right to become children of God." " The creation stands on tip-toe with expectancy, waiting for the sons of God to be revealed." And the claim of the Christian Gospel is that this new humanity can anywhere and everywhere be multiplied by contact with the Cross and Spirit of Jesus Christ. He is thus " the Second Adam," the Source of a new race of saviours, and so the Saviour of the world. Communism despairs of humanity as it is ; and, finding it already half-mechanised, completes the process. For it Economic Necessity plays the part of God. Jesus Christ finds man torn and frustrated between the old tyranny of the beast within and the new tyranny of the slave turned master—the machine. He emancipates him by humanising every human relationship as the result of " the taking of the manhood into God." So " in Christ " the cash nexus (for instance) is subordinated to the bond of brotherhood, and racial divergences are harmonised within the Human Whole, the sense of which is part of the Divine Image in the heart of man.

> *Why should I strive, why should I cry,*
> *And press my case and claim my right,*
> *While deep in mine own heart doth lie*
> *A kingdom of such rare delight,*
> *Where none dispute my sovereign right ?*

> *It is not true that Love is blind,*
> *But fear and hate. Love has an art*
> *In every land his way to find ;*
> *Nor alien speech avails to part*
> *Where love interprets heart to heart.*[1]

In effect, Christ offers man the quality of moral genius, " the innate or acquired power of feeling more sensitively

---

[1] Canon Peter Green.

for and with other people, of making wider, deeper, more vivid connections,"[1] coupled with the courage of moral conviction, with which (as history repeatedly shows) lies " the victory which overcometh the world." These qualities, developed on a large enough scale, would quickly reverse the present desperate drift of things and " guide our feet into the way of peace." And the Christian doctrine of the Holy Spirit provides for the divine self-incarnation *in any individual*, in such wise that in him, however partially and gradually, the Eternal Christ appears and works. " If God dwells even in me, a sinner," writes Toyohiko Kagawa, whom future generations will recognise as the St. Francis of twentieth-century Japan, " and God's Power enters me, I myself change into a wonderful existence. I have the experience of the Holy Spirit. In this human flesh dwells Jesus Christ, the Image of God. . . . I am not the one who is working. God works through me. This is the experience of the Holy Spirit, and it comes through prayer, if we seek it."[2]

" It comes through prayer, *if we seek it*." Christian prayer as the condition of moral genius : worship (in Ruskin's phrase) " in some manner the source of intellect " : fellowship with the Creator and Redeemer of men the means of " overcoming the world " and " moulding it closer to the heart's desire " ; so that " the saviour of the community is the community of the saved." The theory fits the world situation perfectly : it only needs to be put into practice. If one-tenth as much thought and money had gone to the humanisation of humanity as has gone to the mechanisation of industry, the latter would have been the blessing it should be and not the curse it has largely proved so far.

True, humanity can only be humanised one by one. There is no mass production in the Kingdom of Heaven. But this method need not be so slow as we imagine. The New Humanity, once it came to birth, would propagate rapidly

---

[1] Dr. Jane Harrison, *Alpha and Omega*, p. 66.
[2] *The Religion of Jesus*, ad fin.

in a world prepared by disillusionment for God. The mention of Kagawa suggests the evidence provided by even the meagre missionary efforts of the Church so far to prove that Christian sainthood will grow in any racial soil, and that Jesus Christ is already a world-power.[1] His Kingdom is the one possibly happy issue out of the afflictions which indifference to his principles has brought upon mankind. And all men are at heart his soldiers.

> *The kingdoms of the earth go by*
> *In purple and in gold :*
> *They rise, they flourish, and they die,*
> *And all their tale is told.*
> *One kingdom only is divine,*
> *One banner triumphs still :*
> *Its king—a servant, and its sign*
> *A gibbet on a hill.*

But even God cannot save man without his own co-operation with God's plan. He too " waits for *the sons* of God to be revealed."

[1] See *Kagawa*, by Wm. Axling (S.C.M. Press, 6s.), a recent biography. Toyohiko Kagawa began life as the illegitimate child of a dissolute petty nobleman and a geisha, came under Christian influence as a boy, and, while still a student, plunged into the slums of Shinkawa (Kobe) where, despite a tuberculous constitution and then the almost complete loss of his eyesight through contagious disease contracted in a pestilential as well as criminal district, he lived Christianity for fifteen years in a room six foot by six, wrote numerous books, organised the first Japanese trade union, and emerged as one of the most influential forces in Japan, alternately used and imprisoned by the Government, and, in the winter of 1930-31, called by the Mayor of Tokyo, which to cope with the prevailing depression was spending £1,000,000 a year on relief, to be chief of the Social Welfare Bureau with plenary powers. Here he began by refusing the salary of £1,800 a year, and, in five months, put through the City Council a scheme of unemployment insurance which set the whole problem on a sound modern basis, as well as starting new social settlements in all the worst districts. This but indicated one side of his relevance to the problem faced in *Christianity and the Crisis*.

The reference is the more in point as no special chapter in this book is devoted to Christian evangelisation in non-Christian lands.

2. THE DEMANDS OF THE ORDINARY MAN

By Dr. ALBERT MANSBRIDGE, C.H.

JUST AS the body of the individual contains parts or organs, created or evolved for special purposes, which, functioning rightly, minister to the good of the whole, so it is certain that humanity, whether it be regarded as one body or not, is served by men who are endowed with diverse gifts, even though they live and move in the same environment. The bulk of men are ordinary. This does not mean that they are inferior, but simply that they have no recognisable special gifts. They are as important in the scheme of things as the limbs of the body of man are in relation to his eyes, ears, nerves, and brain. If they are not healthy in body, mind, and spirit, the extraordinary men—those, roughly speaking, of ascertainable special ability—are handicapped in their functioning. " God must have loved ordinary people ; he made so many of them."

To-day, the ordinary man is beset on all sides, particularly by those who expect him to have clearly thought-out ideas, not on one main subject only, but on all.

Whether it is agreeable or not, there can be no doubt that only a small percentage—not more than 20 per cent under the best conditions—have the power to think on matters, abstract or concrete, which do not come within the range of their everyday experience.

Yet all are urged to do so, and knowledge is flung before their eyes and in their ears. They are inevitably confused. If they were not impervious, they would be ruined.

All men respond, consciously or unconsciously, to the forces which operate in their natural life. They also respond in greater or less degree to the motions of their spirit. The big things in life come unsought to men.

The important thing is not that they shall understand with their minds, but that they shall live their life to the full, and that, so living, they shall do their work in the world, whether it be mental or manual, writing books or ploughing fields, and do it all in healthy relationship with their fellows. But such a healthy relationship is only created as the inevitable outcome of love and worship, the primary instincts of normal men.

It is essential, therefore, that a consideration of Christianity in relation to a state of affairs in England and in the world so acute as to justify the term " crisis " should be preceded by an attempt to express the demands of the non-specialist ordinary man. He represents the vast bulk of humanity. His point of view is necessarily of immense importance, for it at once affects, and is affected by, the researches and efforts of those experts—theologians, philosophers, historians, or economists—who have set forth their own specific analysis of the nature of the problems and their own approach to solutions.

It may be urged that ordinary men who are not Christians have no right to make demands ; but this can only possibly carry weight if it is confined to the content of faith. All men are potentially Christians, and they are justified in demanding that Christians shall so think and act as to bear compelling witness.

There is a world hunger for all that Christianity claims to give, as a tree gives its fruits.

Thus from the point of view of the ordinary man the position and place of Christianity in its relationship to the crisis may be examined, and reasonable demands made upon those who proclaim " that the application of Christian principles is the way by which the world can recover and move forward."

I. THE CRISIS DEFINED

" Civilisation is at the crossroads." If this recurrent platitude has any truth in relation to the present time, it is that one road, with material and superficial promise, may lead to decline and perhaps ruin ; the other road, through spiritual and deep happiness, may lead to increasing health and power. The title of this volume, *Christianity and the*

Crisis, suggests that there is an eternal and spiritual force to be brought to bear upon a temporal and material condition.

The feeling of crisis is accentuated by the widespread consciousness of it. The unending reception of bad news tends to depress even the most optimistic minds. It damps the spirit of adventure, wears confidence away, and induces mass paralysis.

The evil of it all would be diminished, if the sources and background of life were kept in mind, and if good news were circulated as readily as bad.

" Who will show us any good ? Oh, for a Prince in Israel ! "

It is easy for us to imagine that there has never been such a crisis before. " The hungry forties " is no more than an ugly phrase. The Napoleonic Wars and their effects are viewed through the visions of a final dramatic victory and a prosperous later Victorian age.

A modern novelist has collected utterances of outstanding men and women of the last century which show that they too were burdened with a sense of impending crisis no less heavy than ours. " There is scarcely anything round us but ruin and despair," said William Pitt. Queen Adelaide had only one desire—" to play the part of Marie Antoinette with bravery in the revolution that is coming in England." Wilberforce dared not marry because the future was so dark and unsettled. Lord Shaftesbury prophesied that nothing could save the British Empire from shipwreck. Disraeli thought that in industry, commerce, and agriculture there was no hope, and the Duke of Wellington said on the day before he died : " I thank God I shall be spared from seeing the consummation of ruin that is gathering about us."

It would seem that the present crisis has been in part precipitated by man's power to invent instruments and machinery which, because he gives himself up to them, he is unable to control.

The problem is an ancient one. Invention is good in

itself. " I, wisdom, dwell with prudence and find out knowledge of witty inventions."[1] But when inventions get out of
their proper place in the life of man, then only are they to
be deplored. " Lo, this only have I found, that God made
man upright ; but they have sought out many inventions."[2]
The result is inevitable. " Thus they provoked him to anger
with their inventions : and the plague brake in upon them."
The Old Testament writers had different inventions in
mind. " They made a calf in Horeb and worshipped the
molten image." To-day the images are different but the
golden calf still stands on its ancient pedestal. As a result,
the crisis breaks in upon us.

Man has largely solved the problems of mass production,
but has made no corresponding advance in the problems of
mass distribution. The trouble goes deeper. The nature of
man demands that he shall occupy himself in healthy toil
which has a reasonable objective. By so doing he keeps his
body right and his mind awake. He generates power. High
mental and spiritual enterprise depends for its strength and
inspiration upon the right living of all men. But mechanisation and urbanisation force too many men from the work
they would do in the place they would occupy.

The dilemma is real, yet it ought to be resolved. " Wisdom
should dwell with prudence " and " witty inventions "
should minister to the development and sustenance of
healthy human beings. Our day is being tested and tried,
and the incidence of judgment will rest upon the kind of
men and women we are, not upon the piles of elegant and
inelegant material we have collected.

Nothing less than strenuous effort on the part of individuals and nations who recognise the unity of all men will
enable man to manage his material. Wisdom and not
cleverness will serve men best.

There are now, as always, certain types of clever people,
relying unduly upon their own brains, and out of touch with
reality, who say that " Life is short and tedious " ; " We
are born at all adventure " ; " Let us enjoy the good things

[1] Proverbs 8 : 12.   [2] Ecclesiastes 7 : 29.   [3] Psalm 106 : 29.

that are present " ; " Let none go without his part of our voluptuousness."[1]

They accentuate the " crisis " while they help it to continue. Happily, their influence will spend itself, since they deal with superficial things. The realities remain in their deeps untroubled. Yet such men can spoil human life both in individuals and nations, even to the destruction of health and happiness.

If an increasing number of men will think of the good of all men and forget their " voluptuousness," the channels of just and equitable distribution now blocked by the masses of production will be gradually freed, and a growth of confidence among men will dismiss the " crisis " with rapidity.

Meanwhile much encouragement may be derived from the effect of Christian action already on English life. In spite of the glaring defects of mal-distribution, social life and relationships are more in harmony with the highest and best interests of man than they have ever been in the centuries of recorded history. It is not merely developed humanitarianism but the ethic of Christ, translated into the terms of the community by men avowedly working in the power of the Holy Spirit. This ethic and this power have been kept, in word and teaching at least, consistently before men by the Churches.

Great and outstanding reforms have almost without exception been initiated by Christians. This present year is the centenary of the abolition of slavery in the British Empire and of the chief Factory Act. Wilberforce and Shaftesbury were inspired by their faith in Christ. The Churches also were the begetters and the nursing mothers of education, not only in universities but in the nineteenth-century rise of schools for the children of the poor.

It is beside the point to deplore that Christians, in the face of great need, with the vision of the City of God on earth before their eyes, were slack and slow, much too concerned with their own comfortable lives. They did move ; and their force was irresistible ; the facts are clear.

[1] Wisdom of Solomon 2 : 1, 2, 6, 9.

No one can imagine what the present state of the English community would be if Christianity had never found foothold in Britain. Ghastly things have been done in its name, but it is certain that no higher or better force has ever entered or been expressed in the whole story of English life. Every ethic that is worth while either derives from it or is in harmony with it. But the English community is not what it should be, and could be, if an increasing number of sincere Christians trained themselves for service in its behalf.

II. THE PLACE OF CHRISTIANITY IN ENGLISH LIFE

Corporate bodies of Christians united in great Churches are so numerous and powerful as to justify great demands being made on them. The Churches are certain that by the grace of God they are wells of living water in a thirsty land. Those who drink go out refreshed, courageous, devoted, loving, to face and deal with the problems of daily life in the community.

Looked at from any point of view, the Churches are the most widespread institutions in the national life. They have been, and still are, the most powerful. The population of England and Wales was nearly forty millions in 1931, of whom about sixteen millions were children or adolescents. At least seven million adults are duly enrolled members of Churches. The electoral rolls of the Church of England contain three and a half million names, and vast numbers besides have never claimed the franchise. In the country villages, for example, they are shy of signing papers. There are certainly not less than two million adult members of Nonconformist bodies and roughly one and a half million adults in the Roman Communion. These figures are sufficient to reveal that there is a real heart of Christian belief in England.

After all allowance has been made for those who regard Christian worship as little more than a respectable and desirable amenity, it is clear and certain that Christianity is in a position to exercise a powerful influence on human affairs and relations, whether individual, national, or international. Apart from the membership of the Churches, it may be confidently asserted that the temper of ordinary men is at bottom religious. There is no court of appeal more readily admitted than the teachings of Jesus. At critical moments the majority of men turn to religion for sanction or consolation.

Older men have seen positive atheism become negligible, either replaced by reverent agnosticism or sometimes by belief. At the same time family prayers in workshop or home have almost died out, while the family Bible is regarded almost entirely as an heirloom. Sunday observance is now not insisted upon, except in limited circles or in special areas. But co-operators and trade unionists are always ready to attend special services arranged for them. Books dealing with religious subjects are often good sellers, and sometimes best sellers. There is an increasing demand for classes in religious subjects, and would be more if it were not for the retarding influence of sectarian difficulties. Such difficulties are steadily diminishing in schools owing to concordats between the Churches.

On the other side is a group of " intellectuals " who combine an attitude of contemptuous, or at best indifferent, scepticism towards the Christian faith with a determined attack on the Christian moral standard. They make a strong appeal to many young men and women in universities who are not rooted and grounded in the Faith. For the rest, apart from the widespread reverent agnosticism that is expressed by those who realise the place of spiritual force in human life, the bulk of people more or less outside the Churches are where they are because of preoccupation with the affairs of this world, a preoccupation forced upon some by poverty and others by riches. " Give me neither poverty nor riches."

III. THE DEVELOPMENT OF THE ORDINARY MAN AND HIS DEMAND

At present the sound of many voices is heard in the land, and it is difficult for any one of them not to be lost in the welter of noise. In many ways the experts cancel one another out. Those who have no special knowledge listen in bewilderment. The ordinary man's demand is not, " Give us more knowledge," but " Give us a good will and heart to use knowledge and material aright." It is misuse that has made our chaos.

The ordinary man is the product of the working of many forces. He is in part the creature of his environment, which nowadays may be said to include the whole world. Yet his thought is English, not perhaps in its content but in its method and quality. His forerunners stood firm on this island and absorbed the qualities of diverse races, both conquerors and conquered. In the English land they evolved the English character, compounded of the characteristics that were in many nations. The climate and the position helped ; but that character had for its dynamic force the motion and rhythm of Christianity. It is impossible for ordinary men to ignore this force either in their lives or work. In untroubled days they may forget it for a time ; but it is in their make-up, and one day or another it will assert itself. The ordinary man is potentially, even when not actually, religious.

By the power of the Spirit, Christianity entered the lives of his forbears, expressed and revealed to them by the missionaries of Christ. It gradually became the dominant fact in the land. When the Romans left it in A.D. 443, " The Christian missionaries," writes G. M. Trevelyan, " alone among the emissaries of civilisation did not desert the Britons in their day of trouble." The hordes of the Northmen poured into the land ; they came in allegiance to Odin, and they grew into that of Christ. As the centuries passed, Christianity continued to mould English life. It gave birth to characteristic institutions whilst it covered the land with its churches. Clergy were to be found in the midst of every national happening. They stood always in word and teaching, if not always in deed, for the rights of the poor and oppressed. But the importance of the Church declined in the eyes of men as the institutions it had created increased their power and sought uncontrolled liberty. This is clearly exemplified in the story of the Universities of Oxford and Cambridge and also in the history of Parliament.

During the last century or so, the Church has still continued to create institutions for amelioration, education, and reform ; but its essential task has been to ensure that all the institutions of modern civilisation shall be infused and permeated with the Christian spirit. " The impetus which drove me first of all into the Labour Movement," wrote Keir Hardie, " and the inspiration which carried me on in it, has been derived more from the teachings of Jesus of Nazareth than from all other sources combined. Many of the best workers in the movement are men who know their New Testament almost by heart but," he adds, " they have been driven out from the Churches by the travesty and burlesque of the gospel which there passes for truth."

This " travesty and burlesque," to which Keir Hardie refers, had in his mind no connection with doctrine. It referred to glaring insincerity, to the willingness to oppress employees and to the worship of material position in those who at the same time uttered the high things of God. To him " the Kingdom of God meant the establishment right here upon earth of a condition of things in which human life would be free to develop on God-like lines." He voiced the demand on Christians of all clear-sighted, ordinary men as they make it in time of crisis. The general demand may be analysed in many ways, but in the main it is for sincerity and radiance. It is not concerned with doctrine, but with true and right living based on the example of Christ.

The demand—the challenge to the ministers of Christ— is to strive, and to induce their flocks to strive, for conformity with the spiritual in life, and to place diminishing reliance on material things—on all that is not essential for right living. It is not indeed their function to attempt the solution of economic and social problems, but it is their duty to inspire men to approach them in a right way, without ulterior motive, to combat evil by the insistence on and practice of good, and in their radiant faith and confidence to welcome all genuine efforts of thought and discovery. It is for them to show that effort on man's part to create things that are pure and lovely is in reality a part of his worship, and should be accepted and hallowed by ·the Church in her work of building the Kingdom of God. This is no time for half-heartedness. " Is not my word like as a fire ? saith the Lord ; and like a hammer that breaketh the rock in pieces ? " A fire that burns all that is false, a hammer that breaks rocks in the path. The earth is designed for the right living of all men, using their bodies and minds happily and well in the power of the Spirit. Christians are challenged to work in the power of their faith to see that the intentions of God are carried out.

It may be said that this demand is too simple, too platitudinous ; but it *is* the demand, and just in so far as it is answered, so the wisdom from heaven will have way made for it, and will lead men to the haven where they would be.

For Christianity, in the record of the Gospels, is absolute actuality incorporated into human life. It stands revealed both in the witness of history and in the urge of the present. The expression of its creative force among men, in the terms of the righteousness, justice, and love of God, has been effective or non-effective in so far as Churches and men have yielded themselves to it. The mission of the Churches and of individual Christians is, by intensifying their own faithfulness, to extend the area of the operation of this force of God in the world. Wherever and whenever they succeed, order will replace chaos in human life and affairs.

The struggle of Christians to be faithful has never been without witness. At a time of crisis the demand is that they shall increase their efforts to make actual among men that wisdom and love which they derive from God. It is theirs to bring the force of reality to play upon that misdirection of human effort, and that mal-distribution of human necessities, which have produced the present crisis in human affairs.

PART I

THE PRESENT CHAOS

1. THE INTELLECTUAL AND MORAL CONFUSION

By Dr. W. R. MATTHEWS, Dean of Exeter

IN THIS chapter an attempt will be made to sum up the intellectual situation of the present day and to estimate the nature of the " crisis " at which it has arrived. It is generally agreed that some profound change has taken place and that our ideas in the spheres of religion, philosophy, science, and ethics are undergoing a development which promises to lead to a new outlook in all these departments of human thought. If we could discover why there is a crisis we should have made the first step towards its resolution. It is difficult to give an accurate account of the intellectual tendencies of any period ; and the difficulty is enhanced when that period is the present, at which the inquirer must look out rather than back. But there is an additional perplexity confronting us in our present task. In most of the great periods of intellectual and moral change it is possible to discern a dominant trend, a prevailing wind of the spirit, so to speak, but to-day there is no such definite movement. In this incoherence of modern knowledge and thought, it will be maintained in this chapter, lies the essence of the crisis. Our minds seem to be led in directions which are not only inconsistent with one another, but even opposites. No doubt some of the confusion from which we suffer has arisen from the bewildering rapidity with which discoveries are being made in all the chief branches of science, but this is not the main source of trouble. We might be content to leave much knowledge unco-ordinated if we were assured that it was capable of co-ordination, but this assurance is precisely what we lack. The latest conclusions of physics are definitely inconsistent with materialism ; but that is understating the case, they make materialism unmeaning. The progress of biology appears, in much the same way, to be leading away from the theories of evolution which were akin to materialism. But, on the other hand, the psychologists are experimenting with ideas which have close affinity with materialism. The physicists appear to be discovering that matter is thought or mind, while important groups of psychologists are eliminating mind. It is not surprising that, in these circumstances, the philosophers have little to show in the way of constructive work on which there is any considerable amount of agreement. They have been partly directly affected by the uncertainty of the fundamental concepts of science, and partly seem to have imbibed the incoherence of the age on their own account.

We shall defend and elaborate this thesis in the remainder of this chapter, but we may pause here to reflect on the peculiar difficulties of the religious teacher or theologian in a time such as ours. He is exhorted to translate his message into the terms of modern thought, and he is eager to do so ; but when he asks what is modern thought, what is the world-view held by modern science and philosophy, there is no answer.

THE END OF MATERIALISM

The picture of the universe which was given by natural science at the end of the nineteenth century was, in principle, clear and definite. The basis of the world-view was a refined materialism. Though materialism as an ultimate philosophy was held by few competent thinkers, and the prevailing outlook on first principles was an agnosticism of the type of Herbert Spencer's, the cosmological theory which was almost universally accepted was that of a provisional materialism. It was supposed that, given a few assumptions—the existence of atoms among them—the fundamental axioms on which all scientific explanation could be based were known. The scientific mind was, on the whole, indifferent to the criticisms which were brought against its concepts by the metaphysicians. To-day the scene has been completely transformed. The physicist has been compelled by the progress of his own science to raise the very questions of philosophy which he formerly ignored.

The nature and reality of substance, the status of time and space in reality, the meaning of causation, these are burning questions in natural science. They have stalked out of the text-books of philosophers and demand to be considered by science.

It is, of course, a commonplace that the old conception of the atom as an indivisible and real piece of stuff has been abandoned, and the atom is now conceived as a complex entity. But the elements which, in the current view, enter into the composition of the atom are not, in any ordinary sense of the word, material. They are charges of electricity or they are waves. But there is nothing which has the charge of electricity or in which the waves exist—the electrons are the charges or the waves. It is obvious enough that we have here a complete refutation of materialism as a world-view. Matter is resolved into something which, whatever it may be, is certainly not material.

But the situation is even more perplexing than this. According to some of the most competent authorities, the result of the scientific analysis of the material world is to reduce it to a series of symbols which do not correspond in any degree to anything in our experience. " If to-day you ask a physicist what he has finally made out the æther or the electron to be, the answer will not be a description in terms of billiard-balls or fly-wheels, or anything concrete ; he will point instead to a number of symbols and a set of mathematical equations which they satisfy. What do the symbols stand for ? The mysterious reply is given that physics is indifferent to that ; it has no means of probing beneath the symbolism."[1]

Another foundation of the older scientific materialism has been seriously called in question by the advance of physics—the principle of causation. Until recently it was assumed that the universe throughout was determined by causal laws, so that " chance " was simply a term indicating our ignorance of the determining factors in a given instance. It seems that this is probably untrue when we penetrate

[1] Eddington, *Science and the Unseen World*, p. 20.

to the foundations of the material world. The consequence of the " uncertainty principle " of Heisenberg has been formulated by A. Haas in the following words : " If a precise description of atomic events in the classical sense is impossible in itself, the causal principle naturally loses its meaning for physics. For this principle, according to which the exact knowledge of the present allows an exact calculation of the future, ceases to have any object when an exact knowledge of the present cannot be acquired. According to quantum mechanics, causality must be denied for the elementary processes of physics, and can only be confirmed for the probabilities which are ascribed to these processes for statistical reasons."[1] The implications of this astonishing development are disturbing, and it is perhaps too soon to be sure that the " uncertainty principle " will be confirmed by subsequent research, but it is at least clear that the conception of nature as a rigidly determined system has been shaken to its foundations. We have to consider the possibility that indetermination, even " chance," is at the heart of the physical universe, and that science always works with " continuous successions of probabilities."

It is not surprising that, in view of these developments, many physicists have reacted against materialism to the opposite view—that of idealism—and have inferred from the facts as now known that the ultimate reality is mental or spiritual. Among these writers we may reckon Eddington and Jeans. It may be doubted whether the arguments in favour of idealism have really been strengthened, except in a negative manner, by the revolution in scientific concepts. One alternative to idealism has been manifested as untenable ; but philosophers thought that they had refuted materialism long ago.

We must also mention, though space forbids us to do more, the effect of the theories of relativity on the scientific outlook. The established conception of a fixed spatial framework of events and an endless, evenly flowing time

[1] A Haas, *Wave Mechanics and the New Quantum Theory*, p. 102 ; quoted by B. Bavink in *The Anatomy of Science*.

has been undermined, and, though science does not yet admit the relevance of the mind of the observer, it cannot get on without the point of reference at which an observer stands. The assumption that space and time are thoroughly " objective " and independent of mind is less plausible than it was, and there are scientific authorities who would be prepared to admit that space and time are " mind-dependent," if not " mind-created."

LIMITATIONS OF SCIENCE

Of more ultimate importance than the end of materialism is the beginning of a more accurate conception of the nature and limitations of scientific knowledge. Here again the conclusions to which men of science have come were anticipated by philosophers who had pointed out the abstract nature of scientific truth. This has now become evident and its importance is widely admitted. Science abstracts from the full concrete reality of the world given in experience. It selects the most general aspects of what is given, and ignores individuality ; and it deals with the quantitative aspect of the world while letting the qualities slip through its net. In the last resort, its results may be a series of " pointer readings," or of equations which sum up pointer readings. As we have seen, it may be that science deals with symbols which cannot be translated into any terms of concrete experience. The consequence of this view of the limitations of the scientific method have as yet been understood only by a minority of scientific men, but they are rapidly becoming recognised, and must have the most important results in the attitude of the science of the future towards " values " and religious insight. We cannot sum up the position better than in the words of Mr. Joad : " Science does not tell us the whole truth about things. . . . Science is competent to tell us something about everything ; but it cannot tell the whole truth about anything. Moreover, in regard to many things, the information which it has to offer is not the kind of information which matters."[1] Thus

[1] C. E. M. Joad, *Guide to Modern Thought*, p. 106.

there is no reason to suppose that science gives us a better means of approach to the reality of the universe than other avenues, such as art and religion. Indeed, it may be held that only in art and religion do we come into contact with reality in any full sense at all. Professor Schrodringer is quoted as saying, " In the new universe, it appears, our religious insight is granted as great validity as our scientific insight. Indeed, in the opinion of the greatest creator of them all (Einstein), our religious insight is the source and guide of our scientific insight."[1]

THE BIOLOGICAL CONCEPTS

The tendency of physics to raise some of the most profound problems of philosophy is, to a certain extent, paralleled in the sphere of biology, though perhaps the situation is not quite so clear. The effect of Darwin's theory of evolution by natural selection was, undoubtedly, to give support to a materialist or mechanistic view of the world. Darwin seemed to have propounded a principle which explained the development of new forms of organism without any reference to a creative mind or any purposive tendency. The theory, of course, presupposed the existence of " variations " ; but these were supposed to be minute, and it seemed no unreasonable lacuna in the theory to assign these small divergences to " chance." But the importance of variation in the theory of evolution has become more evident as time has passed, and it has been discovered that they are by no means always " minute," but are sometimes considerable and sudden " mutations." Just as in physics the concept of mechanism has become useless, so in biology it is widely recognised as insufficient.

The question what concepts shall take the place of mechanism is in debate at the present time and provides one of the most important points of contact between science and philosophy. A return to the ideas of Aristotle is prominent among the suggested solutions. Professor Driesch, for example, supposes that an immanent principle,

[1] *Observer*, April 13th, 1930 ; quoted Joad, *op. cit.*, p. 107.

" entelechy," informs the organism and determines its growth. But the most important problem is that of the coming into existence of qualitatively new forms of life, and it is here that the older materialistic or " naturalistic " theories of evolution seem most obviously insufficient. The old idea of a " life-force " has been revived to explain the creative aspect of evolution, and in the hands of Henri Bergson has formed the basis of a complete philosophy. A closely related but quite distinct conception is that of " emergent evolution," which, expounded first by Professor C. Lloyd Morgan, has been adopted and worked out in diverse manners by Professor Alexander and General Smuts. According to this theory, the evolutionary process has the property of producing new types of being which are not the mere " resultants " of what went before. It may be doubted whether the idea of " emergence " is anything more than a useful descriptive device. It certainly does not furnish us with any explanation of the peculiar quality of the evolutionary process to which it calls attention.

Among those who admit the fact of " emergence " there is the widest difference of opinion with regard to the reason of the fact. It may be referred to the activity of a Life-Force, or to the existence of an Absolute Mind, or to the organic structure of the universe. The important point, however, is that biology seems to be tending towards the view that its problems can only find a solution by relating them to some higher category of existence and not by reducing them to the more abstract categories of mechanism.

PSYCHOLOGICAL THEORIES

There can be little doubt that the recent developments of psychology have had a wide influence on the contemporary mind. To say " psychology teaches " this or that, or to regard it as consisting of a generally accepted body of truth, would be misleading. In fact, psychologists are divided into almost as many sects as Christians. But it is unfortunately the case that the most influential schools of psychology have been, on the whole, inimical in their tendency to religious faith. Whereas the results of natural science have been contradictory of materialism, the most generally known theories in psychology have lent support to a view of life which reduces it to the lowest terms.

The Behaviourist school of psychologists has had a far greater vogue in America than in England, but it has had repercussions throughout the intellectual world. It may be regarded as the most extreme form of materialism as applied to the study of the mind. In fact, it denies that the aim of psychology is to study the mind, and that the mind is capable of being studied. The suggestion is that traditional psychology has been mistaken in its emphasis on introspection as the ultimate source of psychological data. The proper study of mankind is not man as a rational being, but human behaviour. It is asserted that consciousness may be neglected ; doubtless it exists in some sense, but it is irrelevant to science. Human behaviour can be explained as a series of reflexes and " conditioned reflexes " without any reference to the influence of conscious will or thought. It must be observed that the hypothesis is all-embracing—including every form of human behaviour, not excepting rational thought itself. It is, of course, obvious that Behaviourism, when it is put forward as the final truth, is open to potent philosophical objections and can be convicted of self-contradiction, since the theory of Behaviourism itself would on its own assumptions, be nothing more than a series of conditioned reflexes. But this has not prevented it from making important contributions to the study of behaviour, and probably it has reinforced the widespread revolt against the supremacy of reason.

The many groups of psychologists which are vaguely brought together under the title " psycho-analysis " differ considerably from one another in fundamental principles, but agree in one tenet—that man is governed by his instinctive tendencies. The picture of human nature which is given by Freud, Adler, Jung, and their followers is strangely different from that which the classical tradition had made current. So far from being a " rational animal," man is carried forward by impulses which, working in the unconscious depths, determine the contents of his consciousness. Much at least of what we had thought was the calm deliverance of reason is nothing but " rationalisation," the finding of reasons for what we do by instinct. It would be impossible here to give an outline of the psycho-analytical theories, and it may be assumed that their general character is sufficiently well known. The important question for us is their effect on the general intellectual situation. There can be no doubt that this has been profound. It has been almost entirely an influence against rationalism, against religion, and against the recognition of absolute value and good.

It is an easy inference from the principle that the instinctive nature dominates the intellectual life that the philosophies which have professed to be founded on the unbiassed search for truth are really the expression of unrecognised desires. Religion is naturally represented as a collection of phantasies which hide the face of reality from those who dare not contemplate it as it is, while the idea of God is facilely dismissed as a " father fixation," fulfilling perhaps, some useful function for neurotic individuals, but nothing more than an illusion. In much the same way, art is deprived of any significance for reality. It is the pleasing veil which phantasy throws over the grim features of the actual world. Nothing is more remarkable in the psycho-analyst theory than the unconscious assumption that the real world is known, and that it is very much what the materialistic science of the nineteenth century supposed it to be. The intuitions of the poet or the prophet are simply misleading projections of the unconscious desires.

There can be no doubt that this type of psychology has had a far-reaching effect on the attitude of the educated classes of Europe and America to morals. In the first place, the theory of human nature which it presupposes leaves no room for the hypothesis that man by his reason or conscience is able to grasp and formulate principles of action of universal validity. Moral judgments, like all others, must be traced, in the end, to instinctive needs which are below reason. In the second place, the real services which Freud and others have rendered in psychiatry have been connected with the solution of problems of conflict and repression in the unconscious. The danger of repression has become a commonplace, and in some circles " thou shalt not repress " has taken the place of all the ten commandments.

It would be far from accurate to describe the whole of psychology as tending in the direction of irrationalism. Together with these theories which make much noise in the world and are reflected in current literature, there are others, which have a different inspiration. The so-called *Gestalt* psychology has introduced the conception of organism into the study of mental life and could not justly be accused of undermining the reason. Representatives of the philosophical tradition in psychology, such as Professor Stout, Dr. William Brown, Dr. Spearman, and Professor F. Aveling, probably show the way in which psychology will develop in the future better than either Behaviourist or Freudian.

SUMMARY

Enough has been said, even in this brief sketch, to show that the leading ideas of the chief branches of science are at present inconsistent with one another. The ideal of one unified science proceeding from common principles is further off than it was in the days of Herbert Spencer, and, at the moment, the sciences appear rather to be diverging from one another. It is impossible, by putting the results of science together, to obtain any coherent view of the universe. This is one of the difficulties of our time ; but we need not suppose that it is more than a temporary phase. The trouble arises, in part at least, from the fact that the various sciences are at different stages of development, and psychology, being much the youngest, is passing through the confusions of adolescence. But however we may explain the phenomenon, it remains true that science at present helps to make the intellectual crisis, but does very little to solve it. We turn with some anxiety to the philosophers, whose business has been supposed to be to find order in chaos.

CONTENDING PHILOSOPHIES

The intellectual confusion of the present generation is reflected in the current philosophies rather than resolved by them. It would be impossible to select any particular system or method and treat it as the representative philosophy of our time. We are reduced to a catalogue of the most influential theories without, of course, attempting here either to defend or criticise them.

One of the most notable characters of current philosophy is the distrust of systems. It is widely held that the day of systems of philosophy is over, and that the philosopher must confine himself to a critical study of the nature of knowledge and some special problems of existence. The attempt to grasp, in principle, reality as a whole must be abandoned. This attitude, of which the most distinguished exponent is Mr. Bertrand Russell, is the modern form of agnosticism. We shall clearly gain no help towards a coherent conception of life from this, and it is, in fact, difficult to see what important function remains for philosophy if it be prohibited from the attempt to think systematically about the universe as a whole. But even those who would, on principle, repudiate the accusation that they had a system have often a view of reality which has wide implications.

The revolt against reason which we have already noticed is well represented in philosophy. Pragmatism as a theory of knowledge is really a theory that no knowledge, in the older sense of the word, is possible. For the pragmatist, truth is what " works "—that is to say, what has value for life, what is life-furthering. The older pragmatism applied this theory chiefly with regard to the individual ; the newer pragmatism has interpreted it with reference to social life. Thus, in Professor Dewey's opinion, philosophy is a function of social evolution, and that theory is " true " which corresponds most effectively to the needs of society at any given moment. This is, so to speak, Platonism standing on its head. According to the classical tradition, we can remake our social order to good effect only when we have understood the truth about man's nature and his good ; according to this later view, we must let our society make our truth. It would appear that we can gain little guidance towards a better order from a thought which waits upon events.

The most important representative of the irrationalist strain in modern thought is Bergson, to whom we have already referred. The reason, according to him, is incapable of bringing us into contact with reality. It is evolved with a purely practical function and is utterly incompetent to grasp the really existent, which is life. We have contact with reality only in an intuition in which we are immediately aware of the Life-Force which constitutes our being. Reality is not static or rational, it is movement and life. There is, according to this view, no overruling purpose in the course of evolution, and the Life-Force moves towards no consciously apprehended goal. The philosophy of Bergson has done real service to the spirit of man by making it possible to hold fast to the reality of freedom against the determinist view of scientific philosophers. It might be claimed that the recent developments of science have been, in part, a vindication of Bergson's intuitions. But it must be confessed that, so long as we remain at Bergson's standpoint, we can find singularly little help towards the construction of a reasonable life, either for ourselves or for the world. If the Life-Force is going it knows not whither, but somehow towards greater freedom and higher types of existence, our best course would seem to be to " let it rip," and engage, not in controlled effort, but in unthinking adventure.

Other philosophies of evolution do not employ the conception of the Life-Force, but that of " emergence." In Professor Alexander's impressive work we are presented with an attempt to build up a theory of evolving reality out of the assumptions of Space—time plus a " nisus " within it. But, different as the leading ideas are, the philosophy of Alexander has affinities with that of Bergson. The effort of life and the aspiration of religion are directed towards the next step in the evolutionary process. But the nature of the being who will constitute the " next step " is wholly unknown.

It would seem, then, that we are in the same dilemma as before. The existence of the " nisus " may, perhaps, give us encouragement, but is not able to give us direction.

The idealist tradition in philosophy has been infected by the same dynamic spirit. It might have been expected that the philosophy which held mind or thought to be the sole reality would have been the inexpugnable stronghold of the belief in the rationality of the universe. The " new " idealism, however, in the writings of Croce and Gentile has made a departure from the idealistic tradition which brings them nearer to Bergson. The Thought, which, in their opinion, is reality, is not static, completed thought, but the act of thinking. Reality is a " pure act " of thinking, and hence there are no principles of thought or conduct which are not created by the act of thinking. History is the life of the spirit, which is in no sense transcendent of the process.

In all these types of philosophy, so different from one another in most respects, we may hear the same ground-note. It is that of life, energy, movement ; and there goes along with it the despair of finding any fixed and eternal standpoint, or even the joyous recognition that such fixed standpoints are unnecessary.

But, concurrently with this philosophy of movement and flux, there is developing another line of thought which is, in many respects, a return to Platonism. The nature philosophy of Whitehead has certainly not neglected the fact of evolution and change, but it has employed two concep-tions which have constructive value—that of organism and that of " eternal objects." The " process," for Whitehead, is not all. There are the " eternal objects " which by their " ingression " into the process give it definite character. The return of Platonism to a world wearied of constant change is to be observed in other writers in England, America, and Germany.

THE ETHICAL THEORIES OF TO-DAY

The contradictory character of our current thought is reflected in the most striking way in the ethical theories

Cc

which are popular. As we have already seen, there are powerful currents in psychology and literature which sweep people away from the fixed moorings of the past. The right of the instinctive desires to find expression and satisfaction is the basis of some ethical theory. In Mr. Aldous Huxley's *Do What You Will* we have the literary expression of an ethical attitude which is common and which claims support from psychology. Every aspect of the individual should have its turn : not one should be suppressed. The ideal of " self-realisation," which was the watchword of the idealist ethics of T. H. Green, has been given a new turn. In the ethical theories of the idealists of the previous generation self-realisation was understood as meaning the development of a harmonious personality. It required sacrifice of the lower impulses, and rational control of all. In the thought of the present time it means often the satisfaction of impulses in turn, without regard for consistency or harmony, which, indeed, is dismissed as impossible. Mr. Shaw has said that the golden rule is that there is no golden rule ; the ethical theory, if such it can be called, which we are now considering might be summed up by saying : It is our only duty not to let ourselves be hampered in self-expression by duty.

The most remarkable development, however, in the sphere of ethical speculation in recent years has been the attention given to the general theory of value. The nature and validity of value-judgments have been the centre of much discussion. This is in itself significant. Man finds that some current views of the universe and of his own nature afford little support for his judgments of good and evil ; he turns to the judgments themselves to discover whether they carry their own guarantee within them. The great controversy has turned on the question of the " objectivity " of value. On the one hand, it is maintained that value-judgments are subjective, the expression of the needs of the individual or of the convenience of the social group. On the other hand, it is maintained that the judgment of value implies an objective standard, it is the recognition, and not the creation, of a good. Here, again, we may note as a sign of the times the strong support which is given by distinguished thinkers to a philosophy which has close affinity with Platonism. It must be added, however, that the view that there are absolute or objective values does not necessarily go along with a defence of religion or of belief in God. In the case of von Hartmann, at any rate, the opposite is the fact—it is argued that the moral standpoint, with its recognition of absolute obligation, is in contradiction with the religious consciousness.

The intellectual crisis has some analogy with the economic crisis. We are told that the world is suffering from overproduction and under-consumption. Something of the same kind is true in the realm of thought. There is an excess of material which the constructive intellect has not yet succeeded in mastering, and, in consequence, one-sided and imperfect theories hold partial sway. The intellectual and moral confusion is reflected in the political situation. In Russia we have a social order based on the old-fashioned abstract rationalism of materialism. The other great force is that of nationalism, which in Germany, Italy, and elsewhere has gained the dominant position. The romantic and enthusiastic mythology of nationalism is inspired by the philosophy of the Life-Force and its adventure into the unknown. In the meantime there is struggling into existence an organisation to direct and harmonise nations through rational methods and in the light of rational principles. The idea represented in the League of Nations is that of the power of reason to find a reconciliation of opposite interests and ambitions in a system of co-operative movement. In the same way, we may believe that the constructive power of reason is not exhausted in the theoretical sphere, and that the new synthesis is on the way to birth.

RELIGION

It would be easy to suggest that the cause of the present intellectual and moral crisis is the departure of large parts of the civilised world from the Christian faith, and that the way out of crisis is a return to religion. If the present writer did not believe that this was, in one sense, true he would not be a contributor to this book ; but it would be quite futile to contend that the way out is simply the way back, and that the path of safety is that of reaction. A contributory cause of the crisis has been the decay of institutional religion, and this has been due to the incoherence of the Christian message and its apparent contradiction with modern knowledge.

Roman Catholic controversialists are accustomed to make use of this argument. The modern world began to depart from the *philosophia perennis* when it followed Descartes, and has been astray ever since. There is, of course, some truth in this contention. The synthesis of the Middle Ages was based upon a philosophy which has claims to our respect, and there are signs that the constructive philosophy of the future will not be so far removed from the positions of Aristotle as was that of the nineteenth century. But we cannot return to the old formulations of the faith precisely as it was. The new knowledge will not fit into the old framework. We are really living in a new world.

It is no part of the purpose of the present chapter to indicate the solution of the problem. We are concerned here simply with a diagnosis of the nature of the crisis. It will be relevant to ask why the Christian religion is at this time in the midst of a crisis.

The answer to this question appears to be twofold. In the first place, the basis of the Christian religion is questioned. Much modern knowledge has seemed to make belief in God less reasonable than it formerly appeared. The theory of evolution, even in its less materialistic forms, has thrown doubt upon the most obvious and powerful of the traditional arguments—that from design. Psychology has been fruitful in suggestions of how the belief in God may have grown up as the product of illusion. The first need is a formulation of the grounds on which we believe in God.

But, secondly, the progress of knowledge has involved a complete change in the idea of revelation. Christianity claims to be a word of God ; to be more than a philosophy. The study of the Bible and the critical account of its growth, the study of comparative religion and ancient history, have undermined the old conception of the Bible as the unique word of God, and we have nothing equally clear to put in the place of the traditional doctrine of revelation.

Within the Christian Church there are represented the two main divisions of the intellectual world which we find outside it—the distrust of reason and the return to reason. There are several important schools of Christian theology which would lay the chief stress on the religious experience. Theology, in the ancient sense of the word, in their opinion, is not possible. The basis of religious certainty is not to be sought in the coherence of its doctrine, but in the unique character of its impact on the human soul. The important work of Dr. Otto has been responsible for the prevalence of the word " numinous " in religious literature. It expresses the idea that religion is a feeling of a unique character, and that the revelation of the Divine comes in an experience which is non-rational. To suggest that there is any considerable agreement between Otto and Karl Barth would be false, but they have at least this in common, that they consider revelation to be a gift apprehended by some faculty other than the critical reason. In the theology of Barth it is asserted that the Word of God is quite other than the words of men, and that the divine revelation cuts across history and human knowledge. In religion, no less than in philosophy, we encounter the revolt against reason, and the search for some different avenues of approach to reality.

The crisis of religious thought manifests itself also in the discussion of the nature of Christianity. What was the original gospel ? And what is its relation with historical Christianity ? The conflict between different conceptions of the meaning of Christianity is sharp, and is not confined to the familiar dissensions of religious denominations. Was the gospel an apocalyptic message of the approaching end of the age, and, if so, is Christianity essentially an other-worldly religion ? If we reject this conception there are still several others open to us. It may be conceived as in essence a " mystery religion," a cultus, and a sacramental system centred upon a " hero God." Or, again, it may be regarded as primarily a " way of life," an ethical impulse based upon a simple belief in the Fatherhood of God. Shall we find the Christian religion in the history of the Church, or must we look for its significance in the original preaching of Jesus, if we can discover what that was ? All these questions are matter of acute controversy, not only between Churches, but between members of the same Church, as may be seen, for example, in the discussion which is now proceeding between Professor Heiler and the Barthians in Germany. Again there is no agreement concerning the kind of ethical guidance or inspiration which we may expect from Christianity. On the one side are those who maintain that there is a " Christian ethic " in the sense that there are principles peculiar to Christianity which constitute a special kind of valuation of life, while on the other side it is held that Christianity gives us only an " attitude " towards life. It is obvious that this divergence of view must extend itself to the social implications of Christianity. It is held that the Kingdom of God has a direct relation to the political and economic situation ; but it is held no less strongly by other Christian thinkers that the Kingdom is other-worldly in its reference and has only an indirect bearing on the problem of social life.

This very brief and extremely imperfect statement of the fundamental controversies which rend enlightened Christianity is sufficient to show that the crisis has invaded religion, and perhaps also that it is the same crisis. There is a cleavage in all these questions between those who distrust reason, and seek some other foundation, and those who cling to the hope that reason, working upon a wide induction of experience, will prove once again to be the guide to coherence and security. The difficulty about all proposals to go behind reason is that you seem by so doing to cut yourself off from the possibility of communicating your discoveries to the world at large. If a man tells me that he

" feels " a truth or a reality, I need not doubt his word, but I am at a loss to know what truth or reality he feels and how he knows that it is truth or reality. I cannot share his feeling : it is only thoughts that can be shared. The Christian religion, when it entered on the career of world-conquest, was soon compelled to formulate itself in a system of more or less intelligible notions. So it always must do, it would seem, if it is to be a world-religion or to have anything to say in a time of intellectual and moral crisis. " Uplift " by itself is not only futile, it is positively dangerous. This does not mean that a Christian philosophy of reality and value would leave out all reference to religious experience. It must start from that experience as its datum : but it must not stop there. The constructive reason has its part to play in building up a coherent teaching which will be comparable with other systems of philosophy, though richer than they because of the wider range of experience with which it deals.

Perhaps no intelligent Christian is blind enough to suppose that the intellectual and moral crisis has left his religion untouched and that he can sit untroubled in a peacefully riding ark while he contemplates less fortunate persons battling with the waves. It may be that the most important contribution which the Church can make towards the solution of the crisis in the world is to set about clearing up its own mind, so that the critic may have no ground for the taunt that we should put our own house in order before we rush with offers of help to those outside. Some progress has been made towards the new Christian synthesis ; and Christian philosophy, as interpreted by Professor A. E. Taylor and the Archbishop of York—to mention only two of a distinguished company—can justly claim to be worthy of any candid man's respectful attention. We need to show that the inspiration which we derive from Christ can be made the basis of a world-view and a conception of human life and its end which are more reasonable than any alternative.

2. THE CONFUSION IN LITERATURE

By R. ELLIS ROBERTS

I

It seems an impiety to trace the present confusion in literature to old and now venerable authors, yet, if we are to find the first beginnings of the movement which has given us the Dadaists, Miss Gertrude Stein and Mr. James Joyce, we must go far from our own day. The two sayings—for I will not blame the authors, who said much beside and are not guilty of what others make of an epigram—on which modern error has chiefly flourished are Montaigne's *Que scais-je ?* and Descartes' *Cogito, ergo sum.* Most of what is wrong with modern art, and especially with modern literature, can be attributed to two main tendencies—the supersession of philosophy by psychology, and the substitution of individualism for authority. Of these two tendencies the famous sentences are the key-words, the excuse, and the defence : and they relate to each other, not by precise logic, but by that kind of loose popular thinking which itself becomes the foundation of impressive, if unexamined, mental edifices. The scepticism of Montaigne is not the subject of this essay, nor is Descartes' theory of existence and thought. What I am concerned with is the effect made in the world of literature by the popularisation of the points of view for which Montaigne's scepticism and Descartes' hypothesis have been responsible. In our own time we, too, have seen the stricter thought of the workroom and the study degenerate into the popular opinions of the fribbles of the drawing-rooms, and the newspapers. Many of the people who use lightly such words as " repressions," " inhibitions," " Œdipus complex," " neuroses," and " censor " are quite unacquainted with the works of Dr. Freud except as the meaning of some of them has drifted into easily read textbooks. Yet Freud in one way, as the American Behaviourist,

Dr. Watson, in another, must be held responsible for the axiomatic authority now given to the psychologists, and for much popular inability to distinguish between speculation and discovery, between evidence and a verdict.

When Montaigne poses himself with his sceptical inquiry he is not in intention or in result subscribing to a complete Pyrrhonism ; yet he led the way for others to do so. For his question suggests the answer—which he was very far from giving—that if *he* did not know, then a thing was not, could not, be known. So Descartes far more dangerously risked man's existence on man's self-consciousness : and the Cartesian formula has been used, though he did not so use it, to expel from the world of human existence the only real grounds for man's being, and the definite and necessary condition of the thought which proves that man is. The real ground of man's being is not his thought, but God's being and God's thought. The Cartesian formula has, since it was first made, been used to expel God from the world of thought : and the disappearance of God has meant the degradation of art, especially of literature. (Specifically atheist literature—for example, *The City of Dreadful Night*— is dependent on the idea of God.) The importance of God in literature can only be understood if we investigate the alternatives which have been offered for him—and the history of the effort to find these alternatives, and their failure, is the history of a literary movement of which the present disorderliness is only the culmination.

When we are confronted with the absurd extravagance of Dadaism—of which a leading exponent declared, " If you know what da-da means you are not a da-da-ist ! "—there is a tendency to think that we have here a completely new phenomenon. It is a common human ambition to make the most of our own diseases : hence the affectionate manner in which some people will always refer to " my rheumatism," or " my influenza," as if affirming the sacred particularity and maleficent uniqueness of a common complaint. If we read certain writers on the distress and agony and disaster of the last war, we might believe that there had never been a war before, and never the disorganisation which follows a state of war. Yet that powerful German novel, *Simplicissimus*,[1] gives a picture of European suffering under the Thirty Years' War, a picture as ghastly as any given of modern war ; while the subsequent economic distress was even more devastating : the only way in which we suffer more to-day is by the presence and the prognostications of economists, from which our ancestors were comparatively free.

The student of literature, then, will not be unduly alarmed at the muddle of our own day. The fiction in which sexual interest is as prominent as its treatment is trivial has its parallel in preceding centuries ; the experiments with language of James Joyce, Gertrude Stein, and E. E. Cummings are our equivalent of Euphuism, of Gongorism, or even of the forgotten and neglected Spasmodics of last century. That the prophet-artist, as he is acclaimed in D. H. Lawrence, should have been greeted as a phenomenon startlingly new and defiantly modern meant, not that his disciples necessarily over-estimated Lawrence, but that they were apparently ignorant of Rousseau, of Carlyle, of Tolstoy, of Whitman. The road on which our innovators in the arts are marching in a condition of discreetly advertised accidie is not a new road : the new fact is that they may have come to the end of it.

II

In *The Faith of a Moralist*, Professor Taylor writes thus of Shelley :

" From the moralist's special point of view . . . it is Shelley's most obvious intellectual defect that he never seems to have been able to understand the value of a moral tradition, supported by the practice of generations of civilised men and the approval of the most eminent reflective thinkers, as witness to its own fundamental soundness. The very fact that a practice or a

[1] By Grimmelshausen ; published 1669.

belief had been a permanent factor in shaping the civilised society of Western Europe actually seems to have operated on him as a reason for suspecting its validity. Theoretically, indeed, he maintained only that a belief may be false, or a custom baneful, in spite of its apparently universal acceptance ; but in practice, when he came to deal with specific beliefs or customs, he habitually tended to assume that what all men accept must be false or pernicious just *because* everyone accepts it."

With the few necessary changes, that passage might stand as the conservative critic's summary of the advanced rebel movement in literature. The mere force of tradition, the mere fact of general acceptance, aggravates your rebel into a furious disagreement. Great artists rarely start as rebels. Shelley, the rebel in morals, was a traditionalist in literature, and all our greatest creative artists have begun traditionally—often by imitation. This is as true of Shakespeare as of Blake, of Tennyson as of W. B. Yeats. It is true of James Joyce. Successful imaginative innovation in art needs experience—just as seminal, productive innovation in thought needs intuition. No man of genius—perhaps Rimbaud is a doubtful exception—attempts innovation in art until he has tested his wits and his material by practice along traditional lines. After that experience in tradition, an artist may become an innovator from one of two motives. He may have a genuine desire to experiment ; he may feel that for him the old methods have become exhausted ; he may believe that it is only by the discovery of a method more specifically his own that he can do what he wants to do. These are all varieties of the one determining motive, which is, of all artistic motives, the strongest and the most reputable, the passionate desire of the artist to say what he means, to communicate his vision of truth and beauty in the best possible way. A conspicuous instance of such development in our time is W. B. Yeats.

The other motive is very different. There have always

been—the Silver Age of Latin poetry alone contains many examples, of whom Silicus Italicus is the most conspicuous —men of considerable æsthetic power but of small creative genius or inventive talent. Such men have felt the need to write ; but, lacking intense imagination and weak in invention, they busy themselves with variations in method or style. These men are usually responsible for the more eccentric experiments in art. They have more time and more space for such work than have the great creative artists. It is obvious that Balzac or Dickens, with an imagination perpetually fired with new ideas, with a memory weighed down by a multitude of people, can have had little time or energy to do anything but transfer to paper, as quickly as possible, the world which these people must inhabit, which these ideas must inform. Occasionally an artist of this rank, not in his first youth, by dint of iron self-control can find the mental energy for considering the claims of new craftsmanship as well as the rights of his unborn children. Ibsen did this when he limited himself— the rule was only once broken—after he had deserted poetry, to the writing of one play every two years. But, to do this, Ibsen had to allow the creatures of his dramas to occupy his mind and his imagination for long months : and, in order to make that great series of plays from *The Doll's House* to *When We Dead Awaken*, he practically made and murdered a novel for each play he wrote. As a rule we may say safely that the greatest, most abundant, most prolific artists are not innovators, unless they find innovation necessary for the proper presentation of their vision. And even then they may fail, or fail comparatively ; for few admirers of Blake would admit that he ever found the form most suited to the vision mirrored obscurely in the prophetic books ; or that, among those books, the later are the more successful.

Innovation in literature, then, comes from one of two causes : (1) the artist's dissatisfaction with traditional forms, because he believes that they cannot hold his vision ; (2) the artist's superfluous energy seeking an outlet in formal innovation, because he lacks inventive power and creative imagination.

Innovation of the first kind is probably as old as literature. Whether she invented it or not, we may suppose that Sappho found the lyric stanza to which she has given her name more suited than other lyric measures to the emotional content of the poems she wrote in that form. Then it is evident that the changes—though they are always not *of* the form but *within* the form—which Euripides made in the iambic metre are more suited to his spirit than the form of Æschylus and Sophocles. To-day, I suppose, most lovers of Latin literature would take the opposite view from that which was held, when I was at school, by schoolmasters and dons ; they would assert that Ovid's less lively and less irregular elegiacs are inferior to the form of Propertius and Catullus ; but it is evident that the close, more elegant Ovidian form does suit better the spirit of that poet. It is not his fault that he became the model for the world. Similar changes and experiments in traditional forms can be found throughout classical literature ; but they are all changes *in* form not changes *of* form. There is no alteration in the structure, but only of articulation. Nor, I think, can the Elizabethan experiments in the use of classical metres be called so clear a change in structure as, for instance, Mr. Cummings's change in English verse. When Sidney, Spenser, and Gabriel Harvey were trying to adapt the hexameter and pentameter to use in English, Latin was still a living language. The classical experiments of these poets were an effort to adopt for English poetry forms which were familiar to them in Greek and Latin, at a time when English, owing to the lack of a strong Chaucerian succession, was still an unformed and tentative language. It would not be false to say that there is no modern English, nothing which was at once traditional, authoritative, and alive, until Shakespeare, especially in his magnificent prose, made the language of life the language of literature. The experiments of the classicists were not anti-traditional ; they were not a rejection of anything already established ; they were endeavours to make a tradition. The men who tried them were not men, weary of a long journey, abandoning an old road ; they were men who, at the beginning of an adventure, took the wrong turning. They erred, not about the genius and purpose of literature, but about the genius of the English language.

It is with the other kind of innovation that I am concerned : the kind which originally springs, not from excess of invention, not from the passion to discover a more appropriate method, but from waste energy, the need to use in some way the powers which, by a congestion in the artist's mind, cannot be used in the finding of fresh content, in the making of new and abundant life. Why is it that this need has taken the form it has ? Why should Mr. James Joyce, that martyr of a tormented memory, having so little creative imagination, and so few ideas—I do not deny him almost infinite fancy—take refuge from the satiety of *Ulysses* in a world of new words, no words and per-verbs ? Anciently, when an author was exhausted he went on decorously enough saying little in familiar ways : a man, alas ! did not stop writing Latin verse because he had nothing more to say. He wrote still ; and his work might have the faint pleasantness of recollection, be a not ungraceful shell, in which one could hear echoes of Virgil or Ovid or Horace, or even of the poet's own more impetuous past. He belonged, as it were, to the Academy : and long after he had painted his diploma picture he would go on repeating it or the masterpieces of greater men. To-day the equivalent of that minor artist—and far greater men than he follow his example—prefers to stay in the courtyard outside and scribble—very freely—on the walls of the precincts. What is the reason of the change ?

III

Some say that it all came in with Rousseau—the first proletarian artist, the first individualist, the first free man, the Prometheus of Romanticism, the precursor of the Revolution, the heart of that movement of which Voltaire was the spear-head. This is all nonsense. Rousseau was bourgeois, not plebeian. He was no more of an individualist and far more of a " gentleman," with genteel vices and genteel fears, than François Villon. He was not so free as Francis, the poor man of Assisi. He did not make the Revolution, but merely misled the revolutionaries. It should not be necessary to-day to say this ; but recently Mr. Leonard Woolf repeated the old errors in an essay on Rousseau as " A Maker of the Modern Spirit," a title to which he certainly has some claim, if we believe that anything can be made by mutilation and falsehood. To Rousseau's less influential contemporary, Restif de la Bretonne, author of *Monsieur Nicholas*, is due much of the praise given to Rousseau ; for Restif was a plebeian, and in his book one can see the causes of the Revolution. One must, however, go behind the time of Rousseau and Restif to find the reasons which have led to the making and marring of modern literature. Rousseau merely crystallised an idea which was in Europe before he was born, an idea which can be seen in Luther's reformation, in the scepticism of Montaigne, in the philosophy of Descartes, and which in English literature first found expression tentatively in Richardson and definitely in Laurence Sterne.

Briefly one might say that the idea is this. The soul is supplanted by the ego : that which is made by that which makes : that which is dependent by that which is independent : that which is by that which dreams : the social by the solitary. That this idea reached its greatest expression in the magnificent literature of the Romantic, post-Revolution periods of England and France has obscured the fact that the Romantics were merely developing something which became a part of European life when the theses were nailed to the door of Wittenburg cathedral, something which had been adumbrated in snatches of song, Latin and vernacular, long before that ; though in the Middle Ages the idea was but the expression of a mood, not the statement of a conviction. The mood belongs to the mental life of everyman, especially of every artist ; but it is by the civilised man and the traditional artist so controlled that it works with, and not against, the social order ; and, by being subjected to his intellectual and spiritual convictions, adds richness to the artist's expression and vision, and variety to his acceptance of the order which he believes to be imposed by God upon the universe and which he endeavours to impose upon his work. It is only by recognition of limitations, and by respect for the material, that great art is born.

There is, so far as I can find, no statement of anti-traditional technique before the nineteenth century. As is generally the case, the artists precede the theorists. Just as the great tragedians of Athens made the plays on which Aristotle founds his theory of the poetic, so the romantic, sentimental, expressionistic works of art long precede any theories which justify their manner.

The first modern author is the Reverend Laurence Sterne, Prebendary of York, perpetual curate of Coxwold, master of Shandy Hall. He was born in Ireland in 1713 ; the first two volumes of *Tristram Shandy* were published in 1759—a year before Rousseau's *La Nouvelle Héloïse*—the last in 1767. *A Sentimental Journey through France and Italy*, written between 1765 and 1768, was published in 1768, the year of its author's death. I call Sterne rather than Montaigne the first modern author, because Montaigne, who is in spirit perhaps more akin to us, is not so modern in his tradition or method. He is still within the Academy of European culture, as much as Erasmus or Rabelais ; or, to vary the metaphor, Montaigne and Rabelais have not forsaken the great Gothic cathedral which was France's contribution to the art of the world. They may behave oddly in it ; they may, at times, be grossly individualistic ; but they are definitely inside the building, and aware of it. Sterne is outside and insensitive to its appeal, except when it is an appeal to his sentiment. He has abandoned the world of tradition and conviction : he does not deny it, or abuse it—he ignores it. Evidence of this abandonment, this profound indifference, abounds in both his books. It can be

found, for instance, in the episode at the opening of
A Sentimental Journey which ends in his exchange of snuff-
boxes with the Franciscan friar. The friar has become to
him, not the representative of a religion or of an order, not
an object either of reverence or repugnance, but a quaint
individual for whom his pity is moved as it is moved by the
dead donkey. It is, however, in the very tones of his prose
that he anticipates our modern rebels. This is more evident
in *Tristram Shandy* than in *A Sentimental Journey*, yet it is in
the latter book that we find distilled the modern spirit. For
in that book Sterne proclaims the subordination of content
to self, a proclamation on which hundreds of authors have
subsequently based their writings. There were before
Sterne, as there have been after him, many writers whose
personality rather than their subject excites the reader : but
Sterne is the first considerable author who deliberately
trusts to his own interest in his own character and his own
idiosyncrasies to awake and sustain the interest in his
readers. You cannot read Sterne with enjoyment unless
you are attracted by his personality. This is what differentiates him from authors such as Montaigne, or Charles
Lamb, or Thackeray of the *Roundabout Papers*. In reading
them, the reader's enjoyment is enhanced, often very considerably, by a liking for the author ; but those who are not
under the sway of those authors' personalities can still obtain pleasure from their writings. This is not so with Sterne.
If you find him antipathetic, what he writes has, apart
from its technical curiosity to the student of style, very little
to engage the attention. There is no world in *A Sentimental
Journey* except Sterne's world ; there are no people, only
Sterne's sentiments about people. He is not an author who
claims attention because he persuades us that his people and
his incidents have the virtue of intrinsic merit—as Addison
does in his portrait of Sir Roger de Coverley. He is also
apart from such later Romantics as Byron, who exploits his
self and his adventures, of the mind or the body ; who, if you
like, is often an exhibitionist. Byron, however, exhibits
himself because he believes he is a symbol. In his world,

Byron—(Childe Harold, or The Corsair, or Cain, or
Manfred, or Don Juan)—occupies the position which a
poet like Shelley gives to his opinions. He is at once the
object and the subject of his poetry. Sterne demands more
from the reader than this. Sterne invites our interest in
whom he meets and in what he suffers, not because we may
meet and suffer the same people or the same incidents, but
merely because he, Sterne, has met and suffered them. He
is the father of self-expressionism. He is the first author to
write as if it were the purpose of an artist to express himself, without reference to God or his neighbours.

IV

While Sterne may be claimed as the first apostle of self-
expressionism, it is not easy to discover when and by whom
it was first stated that the object, or the main object, of art
is self-expression. There is a sense in which self-expression
is the right object not merely of the artist, but of all men.
In so far as the keeping of one's soul, the preservation of
spiritual and intellectual integrity, can only be achieved by
self-expression, self-expression is a duty. It is, indeed, only
on such lines that certain forms of art can be defended
philosophically. Unless we believe that the artist has a duty
to his own kind of self-expression, it would be hard to
defend the art of the actor : Plato's attack on the poet—and
all arts can be brought under the ensign of poetry—is
difficult to rebut except by those who believe in the Christian doctrine of the importance of the individual soul, and so
are prepared to defend any form of self-expression (artistic
or otherwise) not demonstrably anti-social, which the
individual may find necessary for the making of his life. We
have no right to put obstacles in the way of our fellows'
self-realisation. The emphasis here, however, is on *fellows*.
Society can have no duties toward the pure, self-exiled
solitary ; and his duty towards society must always be a
matter of purely capricious definition, extraordinarily dependent on circumstance and temperament. There is no
need to demonstrate here that, in origin, all arts are social—

that is, they are means of communication as well as of expression : and what we have to consider in the literature of recent years is the gradual decline or abandonment of the communicative element in art.

There were self-expressive artists—men, that is, in some of whose works the main object was self-expression—before Sterne or Montaigne. There is Catullus, there is St. Augustine : but in each the purpose of self-expression was to establish a truer communication. They ask us to take an interest not merely in them, but in their principles and their experiences. The author is not merely anxious that the reader should observe him ; he is also anxious that the reader should understand and, by understanding, share. There is no demand for a sentimental absorption of the reader by the author. It is here Sterne is a true innovator—when he journeys he expects you to journey, not with him, but in him. Rousseau advances Sterne's position ; and he had far wider influence because of the greater scope of his writing. He was, I suppose, one of the greatest liars in literature ; by which I do not mean that he frequently twists facts, but that there is something false, not merely deceived, in his self-knowledge. It is one of the oddest ironies that this man, whose own conduct was both false and cruel, should believe, and induce others to believe (old-fashioned agnostics can still be found to subscribe to it), that all men are naturally kind and good. He transferred Sterne's sly, half-honest sentimentality into the world of ethics and philosophy, and induced a confusion of thought from the consequences of which the world is still suffering. In *The Confessions* he was a great artist ; and *The Confessions* were the soil from which the later Romantics drew their strength. Much of the literature of the early nineteenth century bears witness to the fact that the old Greek apothegm has been disastrously remodelled. The measure of all things is no longer man—it is I. We pass from the judgment of the created, social, worshipping individual to the rule of the dreaming, rebellious, defiant solitary, which may mean a passage from sanity to madness. (The type, and this dangerous progress, are admirably portrayed by Ibsen in Peer Gynt.)

A great deal of romantic literature is, of course, free from this falsehood. Other springs contributed to that gigantic river—and the excitement of the discovery of nature (here Rousseau's influence was beneficial) and Gothic produced much of the greater work—the novels of Scott, the novels and plays of Dumas, some of Hugo, the best of Wordsworth, Keats, Coleridge are free from the exaltation of the ego. The extremist statements of the importance of self-expression are found, as one would expect, in the minor artists. It is implicit in Amiel, and it can be found directly in Senancour's *Obermann* :

" Whatever happens, I must remain always the same and always myself, myself as I am in this interior life, the only refuge of the affections. I question myself, I watch myself, I listen to my heart, persuaded that a man is never right except when he is following his own nature ; and I have decided never to encourage anything in myself that might tend to alter my original form."[1]

One might compare with this Emerson's defiance : " If I be the devil's child, I will live then from the devil. No law can be sacred to me but that of my nature " ; and the mood expressed is to be found in most of the early Romantics—Hugo, Madame de Staël, George Sand, Benjamin Constant, and Alfred de Musset. None of these authors, however, were content to write only of themselves, or to subdue entirely the content of their books to the need of self-expression. It is with a later movement that we enter on the last phase of the decline. It comes with the French naturalists and symbolists.

When Flaubert insists that the artist writes to please himself, his challenge can be defended. What the artist writes

[1] I owe the reference to Senancour to Miss Enid Starkie, Fellow of Somerville College, Oxford.

and how he writes are his concern primarily—not exclusively, unless he desires to forbid communication, and such forbidding prevents the making of art. That he should write at all can never be only the artist's concern : the mere fact of practising an art assumes an audience. I can find no trace in the French innovators of the eighties and nineties of the error that self-expression is enough. The doctrine of art for art's sake never led to such stupid and sterile excesses as the doctrine of self-expression. It never reduced art to self-abuse. Indeed, a keen sense of the futility of Rousseauism drove the acutest intellect of that period, Charles Baudelaire, to his more extravagant statements— such as the universal superiority of art over nature.

" If you examine and analyse what is natural, the natural
    man's activities and desires, all of them, you will find
    nothing that is not horrible. All beautiful, all noble
    things spring from calculation. Crime, the tendency to
    which the human brute contracts before birth, is in
    origin natural. Virtue, on the other hand, is artificial,
    supernatural. . . . Evil is committed without effort,
    naturally and of necessity : good is always the product of
    art."

It is, however, to Baudelaire and to Mallarmé that we owe one of the most insidious elements that have assisted the deliquescence of literature : it is to them that we owe the degradation of content, the assertion that sound is above sense, the effort to approximate literature to music. When a novelist of the rank of Flaubert can say that a beautiful poem without meaning is to be preferred to a beautiful poem with meaning, or regret that he could not construct a novel of form only, one can hear behind these theories the lament of a man who has exhausted his talent for invention, but not his appetite for writing. Mallarmé and Baudelaire derived their appetite for poems that should subordinate sound to sense or even exclude sense, from Edgar Allan Poe. Unfortunately for the theory, it is not possible entirely to deprive a word of its meaning ; and even such practitioners of disassociation as Tristran Tzara must rely on associative recollection in their readers to make the effect of disassociation. It is presumably in an effort to combat this difficulty that James Joyce has invented a new language, and is writing his latest work in it. His is certainly the greatest natural talent, and by far the most influential, concerned in the new movement ; and it will be best to give a specimen passage from *Work in Progress*.

" My long farewell I send to you, fair dream of sport and game and always something new. Gone is Haun ! My grief, my ruin ! Our Joss-el-Jovan ! Our Chris-na-Murty ! Tis' well you'll be looked after from last to first as yon beam of light we follow receding on your photophoric pilgrimage to your antipodes in the past, you who so often consigned your distributory tidings of great joy into our nevertoolatetolove box, mansuetudinous manipulator, victimisedly victorihoarse, dearest Haun of all, you of the boots, true as adie, stepwalker, pennyatimer, lampaddyfair, postanulengro, our rommanychiel. Thy now paling light lucerne we ne'er may see again. But could it speak how nicely would it splutter to the four cantons praises be to thee ! For you had—may I dare to say it ?—the necleus of a glow of zeal of soul of service such as rarely if ever have I met with single men. There are a dozen of folks still unclaimed by the death angel in this country of ours to-day humble indivisibles in this grand continuum, overlorded by fate and interlarded with accidence who while there are hours and days will fervently pray to the spirit above that they may never depart this earth of theirs till in his long run from that place where the day begins, on that day that belongs to joyful Ireland, after decades of longsuffering and decennia of brief glory to mind us of what was when and to matter us of the withering of our ways, their Janyouare Fibyouare wins true from Sylvester (only Walker himself is like Waltzer, whimsicalissimo they go murmurand) come marching ahome on the summer crust of the flagway. Life it is true will be a bank without you, to nomore cares from nomad knows, a slip of the time between a date and a ghostmark, rived by darby's chillday embers, spatched fun Juhn that dandyforth, from the night we are and feel and fade with the yesterselves we tread to turnupon."[1]

That is rather more intelligible than much of *Work in Progress*, and so not quite representative ; also it contains no occluded indecencies ; but it will serve. I have no space here for detailed criticism : but a few comments must be made. Joyce proceeds by association of sounds as well as of sense (for a non-sense association is logically made by sense) ; he also gets an effect through occasional rhymes and assonances, and also relieves the strain of sophistication by a sudden descent into commonplace, as " may I dare to say it ? " While the content of his new work is very slight, it *has* a content. He is still an Irish novelist, loose in a paddyock of new shoats, if I may venture on a modest experiment in his own manner.

Here is a passage from Gertrude Stein's *An Instant Answer or a Hundred Prominent Men* :

" The twenty-ninth neglects the history of a mute. Mute and unavailing. The twenty-ninth does not add considerably to his expense. He is not needed there. Where is he needed. He is needed here and there. Drive me there.

" The thirtieth manages to be lavish. He washes land and water, washes them to be green, wishes them to be clean, his daughter merits her mother and her sister her brother. He himself witnesses this himself and he carries himself by special train. A train of cars. Will there soon be no trains of cars. Did you hear me ask that. Will there pretty soon be no bridling.

[1] transition, summer number, 1928.

" The thirty-first remembers that a pump can pump other things than water, and because of this he says miles are astray. They have proof of this. Can you solidly measure for pleasure."

There is some similarity between this method and James Joyce's ; but as Gertrude Stein ignores altogether, or cannot achieve, the rhythmical effects which Joyce can, it is hard to know why she stops where she does. There seems no reason for the limits she puts to her childish game of sound-association and of playing on the variation in the meaning of the same word. In the last paragraph why should not the second " pump " be " pomp " or even " pimp " ? And why should leisure be left out of the final sentence ?

v

I have taken the extremest exemplars of the new literature for two reasons. One is that they are acclaimed as great figures in literature, engaged on a new task of high importance ; and the other is that, if I can show that they are lost in a desert, and that the claims made for James Joyce by his admirers can find no support from his *Work in Progress*, it will not be necessary to deal with the small army of disciples and imitators. The making of new words, of sense or nonsense, is not a novel thing. Rabelais did it, and Shakespeare. It is a favourite device of humorists, such as Lear or Lewis Carroll. The effort to subordinate or banish sense from imaginative literature is not new ; but it has never been practised with such patient industry or on so large a scale as that shown in *Work in Progress*. Mr. Stuart Gilbert, who wrote a commentary on *Ulysses*, says that " the ' romantic ' sees in *Work in Progress* a revolutionary art, an impassioned reversal of all values and a challenge to the past ; the classicist discerns, behind the spinning flux of words and symbols, the steel frame of unalterable law "[1] ; while M. Louis Gillet of the *Revue des Deux Mondes*, while far more cautious in his praise, speaks of the book as containing

[1] transition, No. 21.

" some of the most exquisite cadences which have charmed the ear since the prose of Shakespeare."

It has been said that the non-sacramental religions rely on the sacramental religions for much of their strength. So James Joyce, in his effort to escape from the thraldom of the English language, could produce nothing without the living influence of English literature. Nothing is more mistaken than the endeavour to represent Joyce's latest experiments as giving us any freedom, or as initiating a livelier, less academic literature. *Work in Progress* is bound by the tightest of chains to the past of English literature. It can be enjoyed only by those who are very familiar with that literature. It is full not only of local and moderately recondite references, but also of allusions that are journalistic in their appositeness, journalistic in their predestined dismissal to oblivion. How many readers of the passage I have quoted will " get " the allusion in " Our Chris-na-Murty " ? Still, many great works of the past are handicapped, or enhanced for the scholiast and the pedant, by references to things and persons forgotten. That is not my objection to *Work in Progress*. My objection is that the book, while revolutionary in intention, and innovating in parts of its technique, is in effect rather scholastically traditional. It is not traditional in the good sense of carrying on the great tradition. It is traditional in the way of the more ingenious and time-wasting poems in mediæval and renascence Latin. Joyce is kin to the men who re-wrote the Iliad, and left out " epsilon " ; or composed a long poem in hexameters in which every word began with C (" Cattorum canimus certamina clara canumque ") ; and his use of other languages than English is in the line of the macaronic poems which combined Latin with the vernacular. Technically, *Work in Progress* is a typical silver piece ; decadent not affluent ; a typical schoolmaster's task, undertaken, however unconsciously, to impress and impose rather than to excite and exhilarate. I must be careful to insist that I speak here only of the technical side of the work. I yield to no one in my admiration for James Joyce's gift of fancy, his

sombre satiric genius, his astonishing power to put places
and atmospheres into words, his occasionally wonderful
rhythm. I can only lament that he has used these powers in
the writing of a work which, as his expositor Mr. Gilbert has
proudly declared, " has made the world—of intellect—
unsafe for democracy."

And Gertrude Stein ? Can anything but impolite
imitation meet her ?

" There is Stein. And Wine. There is Stein-wine. I asked.
For wine why Stein. There is no wine stain in stein-
wine. There is wine. Why whine ? There is always
Château Haut Brion. Literature has no lines but line
o' type. Stein's. Linoleum is a side line."

VI

The writer expresses, he does not communicate.—Proclamation
in transition, 16–17.

*The creative artist writes because he cannot help it. He is constrained
to express himself. At this stage, there can (if he is a sincere creator)
be no idea of " communication." When God created the world, He
surely acted on an impulse which had no ulterior motive ; He saw it
was good, but good for Him alone ; He was not playing to a gallery
of angelic harpists or canvassing the celestial proletariat.—The
artist claims as of right . . . " a freedom to play by himself."*—
Stuart Gilbert, transition, 19–20.

*I don't care about the rhythm of phrases and all this calculated
boring mechanism. Nothing matters to me but Expression.*—Paul
Valéry in a letter to André Gide.

*The creative artist's chief aim is to express himself regardless of
the consequences.*—Eugene Jolas, transition.

*In attempting to convey a metaphysical state of mind, the poet does
not ask himself if such and such an expression is precise and clear
to the reader. It is enough that it is to him.*—Eugene Jolas,
transition.

I do not wish to consider the work of many others who, in the popular view, represent a modernist tendency in literature. Work such as Hart Crane's is too remote from literary achievement—his verses are poetic notes, not poems ; and it is sufficient to name Mr. T. S. Eliot, for whom the classical tradition is a romance ; Mr. Ezra Pound, who when he forsakes poetry (derivative but pretty) hesitates between pastiche and self-parody ; and D. H. Lawrence, who wandered over the world seeking uneasy release from a prison of his own and his age's making, of which he was the self-tormented gaoler. What is important to us, as we investigate causes, is not the men, but the fashion in thought which has produced and fostered their governing opinions, which has used them, often in their own despite and to the spoiling of their genius, for its own purposes. We come back to what our age has made of Descartes' brag and Montaigne's question. The evidence of my existence is my self as I think of I. What, then, do *I* know ? And if I know nothing, not even that I can think, can I be ? And if *I* am not, is there anything in the world, or out of it ? Is there more than doubt or dust or dreams of which patterns are made, patterns I may dream that I control ; but while I dream of control comes the nightmare that there is no control, no dream, not even the nightmare.

Hundreds of modern novels, though their authors may not know it, express that mood. The novels in which sex and cigarettes form a chain of trivial futility are of this kind. Yet in so far as they have, in their slight way, any entertainment or force for their authors or their readers, these depend on a philosophy which the novelists explicitly or implicitly reject. They all depend on the assumption either that they are mildly shocking, or mildly exciting ; but, if there is nothing but an outmoded bigotry in the idea that chastity is a virtue, that virginity is of positive value, that fidelity is lovely, and that loyalty has power, these books lose the slight interest they have. Slack as our young people are supposed to have become about these virtues, it is evident that they still believe that in the denial of them something is transgressed ; or they would obtain no kick out of the recital of these transgressions. Imagine a modern novel written around a series of falls of a different kind. Thora Quirk leaves her flat in Fitzjohn's Avenue. As she goes out of the door, she stumbles on the last step. She walks to the railway-station in the Finchley Road, and three times stumbles from the kerb into the gutter. As she enters the train she trips over the edge of the door. When she arrives at Tottenham Court Road she balks badly as she gets off the moving staircase. She muffs the return of the revolving door as she enters the restaurant. As she goes upstairs she has to clutch the banister to save herself another tumble ; and when she sits down at the table she collides with one of its legs. All of these actions have as much moral significance, from the standpoint of Determinist science and Behaviourist psychology, as the lapses from virtue retailed so patiently by popular novelists. But it would be difficult to make an exciting entertainment out of them. Why ? Because, however unlicensed our popular novelist may be, he still relies for his effects on the existence of standards he has ceased to treasure. The old poet urged that his mind was chaste, though his page might be lascivious : the modern novelist may claim that though his story perforce is moral, at least he has a dirty mind.

At present, that is, all those authors who depend, for the making and appreciation of their books, on the behaviour of human beings have to tap in themselves and in their readers the old tradition that there is such a thing as the soul, that man really is, and is really responsible. They depend on the tradition they have discarded, on the power of sanctions which they profess to think meaningless. Just as the agnostic thinkers and artists of last century believed that they could keep Christian morality while they rejected Christian theology, so these are for the moment relying on imaginative and emotional effects which have no meaning and no authority except when nourished by the philosophy to which they owe their origin.

The history of human culture and of human art is

inseparably associated with the growth of the belief in the importance of the human soul, in the indefeasible separateness of each individual. That is now being denied : it is being denied by some—many of the ardent admirers of Soviet Russia, for instance—in great relief, for they are freed so from the damning weight of responsibility which the Platonic-Christian theory of the soul brings with it. Great artist as he often was, D. H. Lawrence is guilty of that cowardice : his passionate desire for comradeship, for freedom from mental tyranny, for recognition of something in men of greater singleness and simplicity than the mind springs from a longing to evade responsibility. His comradeship has not that generous commonness of Whitman's. He does not, as Blake did, seek for a singleness which shall include the mind. His teaching does not lead to the noble herd of fine creatures, living in splendid freedom from frittering self-consciousness : it leads—how horrified and disgusted he would have been at this absurd reduction !—to Mr. Gerald Heard, and to the cult of the sad, self-consciously conscious Group. From Lawrence's Pisgah can be seen no Promised Land, no Garden with the twin sword of Sex and the Soul, but only the crowded forms in the class-rooms of the Garden City. Lawrence, however, was never a slave to the new solipsist æsthetic. He longed for a strange, obscure life, below the life of the mind, behind even the life of the body—a sort of vegetable existence ; but he did at least desire some kind of social life, some kind of communication. The grave evil of modern art is the doctrine that expression is enough—or as Mr. Ducasse, an American writer on æsthetics, has said, " art is consciously objective self-expression."

What exactly anyone means either by expression or self-expression is hard to discover. Mr. Stuart Gilbert agrees with the *transition* group, which declares the artist does not communicate. Frankly, what surprises one is the apparent ease with which a gigantic bit of bluff has been put across. When Paul Valéry writes, " expression is all that matters," it is evident from the context that he is writing of æsthetic method only. I dislike the word " expressionism "—it is at once too narrow and too vague—but it has a meaning. The method displaced impressionism, and those who follow it endeavour to paint or describe, not what a thing looks like, but what a thing is. That this can only be done either by representing or distorting the thing's appearance need not now concern us. Expressionism of this kind need have nothing to do with the nonsense about the non-communicative artist. Valéry wishes to communicate, just as Verlaine did : but he wishes to communicate a different object and in a different way. " Self-expressionism " is a very different affair. Its prophets, so far as I have read, have lacked either the time or the power to think what they mean. " The writer expresses, he does not communicate." It has apparently occurred to nobody to ask what " express " means : whether a man can express without communication ; how, if he can, is anyone, in the absence of communication, going to know that the writer has expressed. What evidence of dispatch can be accepted, unless the express message is received ? Again Mr. Gilbert writes : " the individual and living thing in an artist's personality is his power of self-expression." Mr. Gilbert is a hot-gospeller, not a thinker ; but this statement is surprising even from him. Self-expression is not peculiar to the artist : it is a normal human duty. The artist differs from the ploughman, not by expressing himself, but by the way in which he does so. You might as well distinguish an artist from other men by saying that he has back teeth as by saying " the individual, etc." Of course, Mr. Gilbert may have meant " quality " or " kind " when he wrote " power " of self-expression. Even so, his argument is still as hopeless : it does not differentiate the artist from other men more than it differentiates artist from artist. Indeed, Dr. Johnson, as an artist in his books, in his life, and in his conversation, has far more of the true Shakespearean quality of self-expression than Miss Stein would ever have if she wrote a wilderness of compositions.

I am, however, grateful to Mr. Gilbert, for, in his comparison of the artist to God, he exposes the whole modern cult. It is really a cult of despair. Gradually the idea of theism has been abandoned—first under the assaults of scientific determinism, then under the less obvious insinuations of the psychologists. Of all men the artist needs God most. He is trying to render the absolute ; he has his home in eternity ; he is more quickly wearied of time, more easily discontented by appearances. The factual non-utility of his work demands sanctions ; and the sanctions of philosophy and theology have been, for those infected by the modern heresies, removed from him. Even if the artist be of that class " for whom the visible world exists," he knows, if he can think at all, that the existence of that world must depend on the existence of another ; that if there is no world, no reality back of time and space, then there is NO thing for him. It is only relatively that he can create : to use that word of the artist cannot be justified, can indeed have no sense, unless there be a Creator and a creation. And this science and psychology deny.[1] There is nothing but natural law, determined and discoverable, and perhaps an odd law that in some way over some phenomena there may be caprice, which is also determined. In such a world the artist can work only by his recollection of an older universe in which he has ceased to believe, and his readers ; but he and they both have to assume its validity if they are to work or to appreciate work. Some admirers of the more modern artists become aware of this inconsequence. They see that the works they admire must either inhere in a philosophy which is denied, or in nothing. So they must make a new God. And they offer us the artist himself. I will not stay to discuss whether Mr. Gilbert's account of the Creation will bear investigation, nor what he means by " impulse " as applied to the divine. What is important is this. He deliberately intends to put the artist and his work on an equality with, or in place of, God and his work. The artist

---

[1] I am not forgetting such scientists as Jeans and Eddington ; but the young modern acclaims Hogben, who writes : " The new school of psychologists has come into being with the express object of . . . relieving Man, the celestial pilgrim, of his burden of soul."

has " a freedom," he says, quoting Mr. Max Eastman, an acute critic of the extremists, " to play by himself."

Has he ? And, if he had, has he the power ? The power, that is, to play by himself in the wilderness which men have tried to substitute for the garden of God.

One of the greatest of living poets, who is also a novelist and short-story writer of extraordinary subtlety and distinction, was once discussing D. H. Lawrence with me. He was at once amused and slightly astonished at the enormous importance which was attached to Lawrence's vehement exhortations on sex. " Is it," he said, " any evidence that Lawrence was especially expert or wise on this subject because he seemed unable to let it alone ? Why do his admirers never think that those of us who do not write with the ' frankness ' of Lawrence, refrain not from indifference but from choice ? " One of the oddest things about modern criticism is its readiness to accept what men claim to be, instead of making investigation into what they are. It is nearly always true that the powerful man finds no need to boast or to advertise his strength. It does not occur to him to protest violently that he is virile. Some to whom I have expressed my conviction that the specific disease of modern literature is this claim to self-expression have disputed the diagnosis because of its unreasonableness. They point out that the most distinctive thing in modern psychology is the emergence of that school of psychologists which deny human personality. There is no man, only " reactions," observed phenomena : how, then, can the cult of self-expression be the typical gospel of those whose work shows an adherence, often, no doubt, unconscious or involuntary, to that psychology ? I answer : *For that very reason.* Only those who doubt the reality of self need to emphasise it. Such emphasis is the last struggle of the despairing soul against its self-decided dissolution. There is a parallel to this in the life of the body. A man, as he grows older, accustoms himself, whatever his faith, to the thought of death. There is nothing of great unhappiness, nothing of despair, in this expectation of death. He accepts it, while he is still feeling himself, with resignation, even with cheerfulness. Then a lingering illness seizes him. He becomes bed-ridden. He is moved by others, fed by others, relies upon others for his contact with the world of affection and incident outside himself. Month by month he grows weaker, and his hold on bodily life becomes less. The senses begin to fail. He cannot hear as he used, and has to suffer the torment of half-hearing the discussions of those who are nursing him. His taste gets less and less acute. His eyesight is feeble, his speech low and stumbling, even his touch is uncertain and deceitful, so that he may not be sure of his own hand. The accustomed service of memory grows treacherous, and he cannot control the wandering pilgrimage of his thoughts. As all this—which is but the disorderly process of dying—overcomes him, the sick man often becomes more eager for this narrowed and shrinking existence than ever he was for the life he had in health. It is a debt to our animal nature, to what is mechanical in us : the thin strands which bind him to life have a greater weight to support, and he is more aware of it. What he resents is not that death will come, but that death has chosen this way : and it is desperation, not desire, which binds him to the existence that is ending.

So in an age when the soul of man is denied, and his identity taken away from him, man will exalt the self which he is losing. At present no great artist has, in his art, accepted that decree of abolition. In *Ulysses* there are passages where James Joyce comes near it : often while reading in that book I am reminded of the old patristic doctrine that the fires of hell give out extreme heat, but no light. The heat of the senses remains, though the light of the will is extinguished. Not even in *Ulysses*, however, is there any definite acceptance of the non-existence of the self, for Joyce is too much the child of memory for that abandonment : and to the artist that which remembers, and that which is remembered, for ever is. Unless, however, this false determinism is destroyed ; unless we can bring mankind back to philosophy and theology from this barren bypath on which self-pretension drives men to self-destruction, we may see—

Dc

not an art which accepts the unreality of self, but no art at all. At present, all who write of their fellow-creatures as if they were flies or imposthumes on the carcass of a dead and mindless world ignore in their art the mental and emotional attitude they declare to be true. There must come an end to that. They cannot always continue to enjoy this dishonest division. They must finally write as they believe. The ancient mirror, as they think it, in which they have seen reflected traditional truths, becomes fogged and blurred with their despondent breath. They are left to their determined task. Express nothing, communicate nothing, symbolise nothing, and then they will enter, lamentably sterile, into the possession of that kingdom of which the freedom is perfect servitude.

3. THE SOCIAL AND ECONOMIC CONFUSION

By P. T. R. KIRK

THE PRESENT troubles of the world are partly our fault and partly our misfortune. The fault can be traced easily to such perversity of spirit as made the war possible, and brought the aftermath of international squabbling and refusal of co-operative reconstruction. The misfortune lies mainly in our ignorance. Placed as we are in an age of unprecedented opportunities, no one seems to have any coherent idea of what to do next. The state of our leaders in politics and finance suggests the predicament of a referee who has swallowed the pea of his whistle, and can neither direct nor stop the game. We trust to conferences, and are disappointed ; thereupon we plan new conferences, destined to end as abortively. Schemes fondly believed likely to save society at last are heralded with the ringing of bells, but they are shelved almost as soon as formulated. Never did the race of men more completely answer the description given of our Lord's contemporaries ; for we are " harried and distraught."

A dead weight of depression rests upon the shoulders of the whole of civilisation. Economic nationalism, the Black Death of the twentieth century, has caused such a decline in international trade that unemployment has steadily increased in volume and intensity in almost every industrial country. The International Labour Office at Geneva estimates that there are now thirty million unemployed people in the principal nations ; with their families and dependants this means that something like a hundred millions have no current income of their own, and are living on a standard of consumption below the bare physical efficiency level.

Ours is a time when more goods can be produced, and are produced, than ever before ; and with greater ease than in any former century. Wheat-growing areas are being pushed up nearly to the Arctic line. Heavier harvests are yielded

per acre. Transport was never more efficient. The life of
the worker might almost be leisured, so greatly has machinery minimised his toil. A sufficiency of everything
necessary to existence, and of most things essential to comfort, could be provided for every human creature on each
continent, so plentiful are our resources.

Yet, because we cannot get consumers and producers,
buyers and sellers together, houses stand empty and men
in thousands walk the streets without a roof to call their
own ; they go ill-clad and ill-shod, though the stores do not
know how to dispose of their stocks ; they are hungry, while
food, which has been amassed in unbelievable quantities, is
destroyed or otherwise withheld from the market. Could
anything be more tragically silly than the fact that one
child in six in the British Isles lives below the poverty level,
at a time when wheat-stacks are being burned in America,
and wool is trampled into Australian roads ? Our workless
queues return disappointed to homes uncheered and
pantries unstocked, while cornland is allowed to lie fallow,
and cotton is thrown into the sea to get it out of the way.

The perfection of modern mechanical appliances has
been allowed to contribute to our distress. Machines and
methods have improved to such an extent that each individual's output is considerably greater than it was even a
few years ago. We have moved from the time when a man
could produce enough for his family's requirements and
leave a margin of goods to market, into an age of such astounding productivity that, if an exchange of goods were
possible, all might live in comfort with a minimum of
manual toil. What has been lacking is a control of machinery by which the rhythm of life might have been kept,
with a balance between the material and the spiritual
needs of men, and between the benefits of mass production and the joy in arts and crafts. The rapid nature
of the evolution, unaccompanied by a sufficient sense of
moral opportunity, is responsible for many of the world-
causes of want. A heightened understanding of spiritual
values is needed to redress the balance. Meanwhile, machines

of uncanny ability and prodigious capacity have turned multitudes adrift, many of whom can hardly hope to be employed again ; and the most up-to-date factory is the one that can dispense with the greatest number of workers.

Machinery has enabled the modern mill to make three thousand barrels of flour per man per day, where only one barrel in the same time was possible by primitive methods. The miner of to-day can dig twenty thousand tons of iron ore per year against eight hundred a century ago. All the coal normally required per annum can be brought to the surface in six months by the men employed at present. Six months only are necessary for the manufacture of all the boots and shoes the world uses ; and all the window glass could be blown in seventeen days. Such examples might be multiplied many times. There is hardly an industry not involved.

Our present hard times are not due, therefore, to any failure of raw material or inability to produce ; quite the reverse. Nor have they come because our planet is so over-populated that there is not enough to go round. The trouble is simply one of distribution and exchange. These are " financial " hard times, and our penury has nothing to do with the means of supply. It is merely a question of purchasing power. Money, which was meant to be a medium of exchange, making the obtaining of goods more convenient, has become a dictator telling us to go without things.

The way in which this works out is seen if we examine the heavy fall in prices. During three recent years, wholesale prices dropped by roughly one-third ; in the case of some primary commodities, the fall was even greater. Wheat has touched a lower level than was recorded anywhere in the previous four centuries. This fall has upset the business of the producer, who cannot get a satisfactory price for his goods. One of two courses is generally suggested. He may reduce his output and increase the amount the purchaser must pay. But this increases unemployment, and the man with a fixed income cannot then buy what was within his reach before. Or an expansion of the currency is proposed by those who believe that by the issue of paper money in large quantities nominal prices could be raised.

The experience of the U.S.A. seems to show that inflation within the present system is no longer effective to raise commodity prices. If, however, prices could be raised to the 1928 level, and wages could be similarly restored to the level of that year, the burden of fixed contractual obligations would certainly be eased.

Together with the state of trade and employment must be noted the appalling condition of public finance in most lands. Different Governments for a time increased their expenditure in the hope of relieving unemployment. The result generally was a deficit in the national budget, and this had to be met by an increase in the taxes of an already overtaxed public, and by " economies " which still further reduced the purchasing power of those needing goods that unemployed workmen might have supplied. In short, in a world in which the pressing need is increased purchasing power in the hands of consumers, taxation is merely able to take purchasing power from one citizen to give it to another, without increasing the total amount available.

This is a gloomy survey, only slightly relieved by the underlying absurdity of it all. We grow food in certain parts of the world and then burn it, though people in other parts are lean and hungry, all because of a complicated game played with metal discs, bits of paper, and entries in ledgers. Every now and again we fly at each others' throats because we cannot find a mysterious something called a " formula." With all this earth to enjoy, we condemn millions to a cheerless existence because of artificial values and codes. There must be something fundamentally wrong, morally unsound, and socially insecure in such a condition.

I. THE ECONOMIST AND THE BANKER

The economic methods we employ depend upon assumptions and theories inherited from the pre-industrial era, an era of intense individualism. Although many of the so-called

" economic laws " have been long exploded, our social system still revolves around them, as if they still existed. The principle of *laissez faire*, that self-interest and free competition are sufficient guides in industry, has broken down completely. The vast abundance, due to scientific invention, has made a farce of Ricardo's " iron law "—that the tendency of population to increase rapidly as soon as wages rise above the bare necessaries of life causes wages to be fixed by a " natural law " to that level. Most of the treatises on economics printed before the war are as out of date as the science books of a century ago. Yet we blandly assume their authority, or order our lives by their dictates.

We have left the interpretation of economic principles to experts, whose characteristic it is to follow one line of thought wherever it may lead, irrespective of all human values.

An instance of the working of the " expert mind " was seen in the Land Commission of the Disarmament Conference, where many representatives deliberated in subtleties and split hairs for weeks, in an attempt to discover what artillery might be deemed " offensive." They droned out commonplaces, with never a hint of any desire to check the competition in armament-building. They embroidered their A B C , and succeeded in making it unintelligible ; but they never used the alphabet in words that might offer constructive propositions.

In the same way, the economists have made finance a thing of mystery, with vague and hidden meanings. They invent a vocabulary of their own, string words together in a semblance of grammatical order, and then proclaim a " law," by which, they say, our economic life must be ruled.

The amazing callousness to which such abstract reasoning can lead is evidenced by the economists' regret that " such vast strides have been made by power-production during the past twenty years that never again will there be a sufficient scarcity of goods to cause a prosperity-breeding boom." Notice the implication that scarcity in the larders of the world is necessary if there is to be prosperity in money circles.

Banking is similarly in the control of men whose mentality is divorced from questions of human need. Time was when the conflict in industry was between the workers and many scattered capitalists, who sought their wealth without regard for the welfare of those they employed ; but the power has been removed from these " captains of industry " and is vested now in a " headquarters staff," equally irresponsible, but the more sinister because even remoter and more powerful. The aim of these men is to prevent money from getting into the hands of the consumer. The very idea of financing consumption is inconceivable to them, because no trading return on the creation and issue of money can be got that way. They trade in debts, and strenuously oppose Governmental issue of paper money. An official circular issued by the American Bankers' Association to its branches contained this extraordinary warning : " To restore to circulation the Government issue of money will be to provide the people with money, and therefore seriously affect your individual profits as bankers and lenders."

This individualism is particularly pronounced in the case of the Bank of England—an essentially undemocratic institution. It has an issued capital of £14,553,000, and its stock is held by investors in the ordinary way. The total number of holders is now 14,370, but of these more than half only own stock of £500 or less. Even the larger holders, however, have no voice in the policy of the bank. This is decided solely by the Governor, in conjunction with the Court of Directors. The twenty-four directors are selected by the existing court, and are largely the personal choice of the Governor. Not only have the stock-holders no effective part in their appointment, but neither the Government nor industry, though so closely concerned, is represented. Thus, bank control is kept in the hands of a small, powerful group, which works strictly in accordance with certain rules designed to protect and strengthen the power of the money-interest not only in this country, but throughout the world. The money-power is international. Its interest in trade and industry closely resembles that of the spider for the fly. As Mr. Montagu Norman said in his speech at the Mansion House in 1932 : " The time will come when great opportunities for investment, speculative investment included, will be offered in many places. . . . What we need, and shall need when that time arises, is a robust and rationalised industry and commerce which here can offer the same attractions by way of investment as will assuredly be offered in those other countries. I look forward, knowing very little about industry, to the near future, to a growth and development and improvement in the industry of this country on which in large measure the business of bankers depends, and on which we can again rebuild the eminence which we enjoyed and received from our fathers. . . ."

Such an arrangement fits in ill with a Governmental order which is avowedly that of a democracy. The consequence can be seen when it is remembered that it is the banker who sets the wheels of industry turning, or stops them. The operations of the central banks, the fixing of the bank rate, the raising and lowering of general price-levels, the decisions on war debts, reparations, and the gold standard, determine the social condition of the nation ; and these are settled, not by the Government, but by the money-power behind it.

The minds of financiers still fondly turn to thoughts of gold, but the relationship of gold to the requirements of world industry is now almost farcical. Bullion is stored up in safe places and never heard of again. The Federal Reserve Bank of New York has the largest collection of bars of solid gold in the world. They are guarded, with almost mediæval care, behind moats and bars ; only very important people, after very considerable difficulty, are allowed so much as to look at them. Between December 1929 and December 1930, says the MacMillan Report, the American gold stock rose from £880,000,000 to £944,000,000 ; that of France during the same period rose from £336,000,000 to £431,000,000. It does not seem even lack of gold that causes our economic troubles ; as a matter of fact, the last year was reported as that of the heaviest gold-production in history. Moreover, the outflow of hoarded gold from India during the year 1932 equalled approximately a year's South African production of new gold.

But the idea that the quantity of available money is dependent on the gold reserves in the bank can no longer be held. During the past twenty years, the quantity of gold in the Bank of England, for instance, has varied from £130,000,000 to £150,000,000 ; but the value of the notes in circulation has reached treble that amount, and the clearing-house returns of cheques—the real money of industry— is in the region of £60,000,000,000 per annum.

One by one these old idols of a pre-industrial age are toppled over by the sheer force of events, like fetishes in a typhoon ; but our witch-doctors still hold to their faith in pathetic loyalty. It would be an occasion for quiet scorn if so much did not depend upon it. But it is lack of the tokens of purchasing power in the hands of the people, forbidden them by those who still profess the vaunted necessity of abrogated economic " laws," which is responsible for the workless, houseless, foodless condition of millions of the children of God. Something is needed to put human values in the forefront of the policies which control our common life.

2. SUGGESTED REMEDIES

The confusion of thought which pervades the minds of economists is evidenced by the various suggested means of reform. Through the disguise of the new vocabulary they have invented it is possible to see an utter bewilderment as to how they may save their top-heavy structure from falling in to complete ruin. Those simple folk who had imagined that the Bank of England had reserves of wisdom and foresight unknown to ordinary people had a feeling as of a tremor beneath their feet when the Governor confessed that the present economic confusion was " too great " for him. " One step enough for me," he said : " that is as far as, on the whole, I can see."

One of the most significant political events of recent years has been the Protectionist revival—a game in which each nation tries to erect a higher tariff barrier than any other. There is not one Tower of Babel now, but almost as many sets of them as there are nations, all arrayed along the coast-line and the customs lines. This sport of " Beggar my Neighbour " has many forms, all with the purpose of reducing imports to the lowest possible amount, and all working for the restriction of trade.

a. *Tariff Barriers*

The post-war tariffs are at least fifty per cent. higher than formerly, and a new kind has been instituted—that of absolute prohibition of certain imports. Where no further bricks can be put on the wall, the " psychological tariff " is introduced, and people are told with strident tones, from all the hoardings and every journal, that it is unpatriotic to purchase any goods not made within their own border or their own empire.

Every nation recognises the disastrous consequences of this policy, but none is able to break away from it. On the contrary, Great Britain, in sheer self-defence, has been compelled to join in. There must, then, be some profound and basic vice in the system which impels all nations to take measures to avert immediate and complete national collapse—measures which they nevertheless recognise must ultimately result in universal disaster. Each nation would like to shorten working hours, but none can do so for fear of being undercut by the rest. Although useful and desirable commodities are the only real wealth, each nation is passionately anxious to force this wealth upon its neighbours and to receive nothing of any use to anybody in return. The neighbours, however, are equally determined not to receive this wealth, but, on the contrary, are set upon thrusting their useful and desirable products upon others. They are even prepared, if necessary, to go to war in order to find what they strangely describe as an outlet for this wealth—some country where they can dump it undisturbed.

The brilliant notion of dumping its surplus into the middle of the ocean has occurred to one or two nations, and is now being practised. There can be no doubt that, if done on a sufficiently large and enterprising scale, a considerable measure of prosperity could, in this way, under our present system, be enjoyed.

It will be found, on consideration, that the root factor in producing all these apparently ludicrous situations is the failure to distribute through wages sufficient purchasing power to absorb the nations' production. This, in its turn, will be found to be the outcome of an international monetary system which, by monetary stringency in one or two countries, can drive down the standard of living there, and then use those countries to undercut the rest in the world's markets, and so bludgeon them into coming down to the same level. It is this international monetary system which compels the debtor nations of the world to trade, not for goods and services, which are cheap and plentiful, but for gold, which is dear and scarce. International trade, which should be a mutually advantageous exchange of commodities, has become a savage struggle, with bared claw and tooth, to get possession of a comparatively useless metal, of which there is an insufficient supply. If, therefore, one nation gets enough to meet the demands of the taskmaster, others are necessarily short in their tally.

Here, then, at the very root of the economic life of the world, lies the canker which, unless cut out, will destroy modern civilisation. It is utterly hostile to the spirit of Christ. It is based upon a fallacy which holds that the only motives which can move men are power, fear, and greed ; and, until the nations are prepared to denounce it as anti-Christian, all attempts to deal with the other social ills which arise from it, and which, being nearer the surface, are more easily apprehended, must be foredoomed to failure. It is clear that those who control the international money system control the world, and it is hardly surprising, therefore, that any and every explanation of the world's troubles, rather than the true one, is avidly seized upon by them ; or that, in so far as statesmen have any policy, it should be for an ultimate return to the gold standard system. To acquire a claim to gold a nation must export more than it imports : it must, in fact, acquire a " favourable " balance, and this necessarily involves " unfavourable " balances on the part of other nations. In this struggle for " favourable " balances the nations, finding themselves unable to increase their exports, which others, in the same predicament, are unwilling to take, are driven to curtail their imports. This they do by means of tariffs, quotas, exchange restrictions, and the rest. These phenomena are merely effects of a root cause—the right of the creditor nation to demand payment in gold, instead of in goods and services. Until that right has been abolished, there is as much likelihood of persuading the nations to abandon these economic weapons, or, for that matter, military ones, through the use of which they can alone hope to survive, as there would be of persuading a drowning man to let go of his lifebuoy. If the drowning man is lifted from the water and placed in safety in a boat, he will presently begin to wonder why he is clinging to a lifebuoy, and will of his own volition leave go of it.

It is this fundamental vice in the system which has been clearly recognised by the London Chamber of Commerce. As Sir Basil Blackett said in his book *Planned Money* : " It is not far short of the truth to say that the whole modern system of protective tariffs throughout the world owes its origin to the attempt to combine national economic policies with the existence of an international monetary standard which was not a stable measure of value." And again : " The central banks would no longer be in competition with each other for gold and would not be continually driven unwillingly to take measures to contract or expand their internal currency for reasons not arising out of the needs of the situation at home, in order to meet conditions forced on them by the action of other central banks."

b. *Rationalisation*

Meanwhile, the policy of the moment, which appears to be most authoritatively supported, is that on which Mr. Montagu Norman laid great stress before the MacMillan Committee—the rationalisation of industry.

Rationalisation, in the words of Lord Melchett, is " simply the rational control of industry to ensure as far as possible that you do not produce more than your market can absorb." This involves inevitably, and of set purpose, the closing down of plant and machinery, and the use of every labour-saving and every fuel and power-saving device which, with the elimination of every unnecessary link in the chain of distribution, may result in a saving in the cost of output.

This means the displacement of labour not only from production, but also from distribution. It results in a further limitation of the money in the hands of possible purchasers ; and how it is hoped to cure the disease by a further injection of the germ that caused it is one of the mysteries concealed under the current economic jargon. This method, in addition to its blind confusion, plainly merits disapproval from any ethical standpoint.

c. *Communism*

In the experiment of Communism there is an approach from a diametrically opposite position. All Socialistic criticism, from Karl Marx onwards, has protested against the inequality of economic power between the different sections of the community. Under the Soviet regime, an attempt is made to face the situation by the abolition of all private property, the national ownership of industry, and the communising of all social activities. Its aim is the removal of all incentive and opportunity for individual and business saving on a competitive basis, and the increased efficiency of industry by its methods over all methods which involve private enterprise.

The first moral objection to Communism, apart from all

question of its workability, is its dependence upon force, not only in its inception, but for its maintenance. Setting out to destroy the capitalistic order, it sees no hope of success in any other means than compulsion. Revolutions necessarily involve a certain ruthlessness, and the Communists believe that force must be used, since the possessing classes will never voluntarily surrender their privileges. In answer to the objection that force is not a desirable way by which to secure their ends, they retort that force is equally used in the capitalistic system. They can see nothing but hypocrisy in those who use force, as they say, for the maintenance of social inequality and then profess themselves horror-stricken at its use for the maintenance of social equality. But however they may return the *tu quoque* on us in this matter, all history is a declaration that a foreshortened view of life, with a man-centred and man-determined world, cannot give an abiding social order. Communism's false ends and false motives, with the confining of ideals to this life's span—ignoring such things as reverence for human personality—can only work out a greater evil than it tried to remove. A large part of our case is that our present troubles have come through our failure in moral idealism ; we cannot therefore hope for better results from a system which even more definitely sets such idealism aside. After nineteen centuries, it is still true to say that no society based upon Christian principles has ever been tried. The choice before the world now is Christ or anti-Christ, and not, as the Communist would have us believe, between his system and our old one, which is in any case doomed.

Some whose sympathies towards Communism have been aroused by the degree of success attending the Five Year Plan have spoken of the " passionate humanism " it contains. The phrase seems ill-applied. For the Communist, a man has no higher value than that of social membership. His value to the rest is expressed in the amount and quality of the work he can do, not in anything inherent in him as a man. Everything must be subordinated to the interest of the whole, and no delicacy of feeling makes allowances for age or sex or invalidity. The religion which professes a care for man as man, however poorly its exponents may have lived their creed, is ostracised. The religion of Communism is the self-deification of humanity, not the recognition of the worth and claims of any individuals, even though it be that of a workman at the same bench or the woman who promised a life-long companionship. If this is passionate humanism, it is curiously shown.

But every advance in social reform, apart from the present inconclusive experiment, has been motivated by earnest care for man as man, whether that has been under the auspices of the Church or in spite of her indifference. If it is granted that misery has been caused by the over-riding of everything that made for individual well-being, the remedy is not more ruthlessness of the same sort. If Western nations, by their tacit ignoring of moral values and callousness to the rights of personality, have brought the state of chaos we deplore, a more outspoken denial of God and his will is not likely to bring anything finally better.

Nor is the Communistic Utopia, by whatever means secured and however well established, one that the Christian could regard as desirable. The enjoyment it offers is too much like that of the child on the sands who was threatened with a hiding if he didn't have a good time. Happiness imposed by tyranny is a poor substitute for that natural outflowing of a full life which, from the words of Jesus, seems human nature's highest right. Mere salvation from actual privation is not the highest good a man can have. Many have suffered such privation voluntarily for the sake of some truer joy. The sublimest delights of life are those of the spirit, and the regimentation of material conditions no more secures those than a decent suit of clothes helps one to appreciate the wonder of a sunset.

3. POPULAR CONFUSION AND THE PRESS

If there is confusion of mind among the experts, how great is that of the people themselves ! The majority have barely the vaguest knowledge of the forces that control their lives. When disaster comes, it is as out of the blue, like a thunderbolt from a mysterious sky. How many of the myriads constituting our electorate are qualified to give an answer to the simplest question concerning the social order ? The conversation on the 9.15 indicates an ignorance upon the influences which sway the world, even on the part of business men, which is nothing less than appalling ; and that vast host whose interests are confined to the chances of backing the winner of the 3.30 shows little sign of caring for anything that may help their fellows and themselves to a well-rounded life. When the pinch comes, they either grouse or display a truly pathetic patience ; but of knowledge of causes, or of how to change what they deplore, there is no sign.

Their ignorance is fostered by the Press. Our popular newspapers help hardly at all in the quest for a better order : their vision is perverted by political partisanship, the spirit of class, the domination of wealth, and the desire to please rather than to inform. Through what a jungle of misrepresentation one must thrust a way in order to learn the facts of things in their simple and transparent state ! They offer a view of the world as remote from reality as the palaces of Hollywood are from the homes of the vast majority of picture-goers.

The sense of unreality is deepened by the proportion of space given to amusements and sport ; and many journals either maintain a precarious existence, or enhance their already adequate profits by appealing to the " something for nothing " craze which is ousting honest toil as the daily interest of multitudes.

When pictures of modern life are given, they are usually of the activities of Society lions, of whom the average reader had never heard until that moment, and whose contribution to the welfare of humanity seems to consist in a safe removal of their persons to remote spots where they can sun-bathe or ski. Take almost any of the newspapers—particularly perhaps those issued for the delectation of readers on their

Sunday rest-days—and see what percentage comes under these headings.

Where serious topics are approached, it is in the same spirit of catchwords and headlines. From time to time, religion is judged by editors to be " good copy " ; but the contributors to such symposia as on " What I Believe In," " Life after Death," and so on, are generally novelists, comedians, jockeys, and others who have won notoriety. These, it seems, must be heard with respect, however little their previous training or interests have qualified them to write. In days of national or international crisis, all the attention is fixed on certain personalities, either hailed as heroes one day to be cast out as traitors to-morrow, or as fit subjects for the scorn of pungent cartoons. Nations are grouped together, and praise or blame is awarded as though all their millions were adequately represented by the speech of some possibly misreported statesman. And memory is so short-lived that there is nothing to prevent these moulders of public opinion from urging us to kick hard those to whom we were recently bidden to doff our hats. Emotion, and that of the most purblind kind, rather than reason, is made the criterion by which we are led to judge matters of mighty importance.

In times of political election, the mind of the newspaper-reading masses is stirred by side-issues, and equally by hero-worship, or by contempt for those who please or oppose the magnate-owner's cast of thought. Since the provincial Press is coming more and more under the direction of the great London dailies, the views of a comparatively few men are expressed in the millions of copies of the various journals that circulate over the country. How is it possible, in such a welter of sensationalism, to discover the way to better things ?

Broadcasting offers more promise ; for talks by qualified authorities are frequently given on matters of current concern. Generally these are in popular language ; and some at least listen. But here again the control of the views expressed is still somewhat rigid, and the average thoughtful listener can hardly be sure, in the circumstances, that he is hearing all sides of the case, or all the information which might be brought forward. Not unnaturally, he suspends his judgment, under the impression that he is only being told what the authority in power at the moment wishes him to believe. He may be wrong in this, but at least he has some cause for suspicion.

The result is bewilderment worse confounded, or an even more regrettable carelessness about what is going on in the world of affairs, for good or ill.

4. THE ELECTORATE AND ITS REPRESENTATIVES

Fifty years of compulsory education and cheap literature in England have produced strange and ironical results. In the main, we have been more anxious to teach jingoism to the children than citizenship ; and, though there are notable exceptions, it is still generally true that anything they learn about the way the world is governed comes after school-leaving age. This is not to suggest that political economy be added to the already crowded curriculum of elementary and public schools ; but if citizenship is important, some reference should be made to it before its responsibilities are entered.

When he leaves school, the ordinary Englishman picks up what knowledge of politics he can. He wants to take his part in conversations with men who seem to know things, and presently he is using terms of whose meaning he has only the vaguest idea. The notion that if a thing is in print it is true, persists through youth into early manhood. He accepts, therefore, the point of view of his favourite newspaper ; or, if he inclines to a certain independence, opposes it because it is the popular one. In either case, his judgment is not stable. Where he has inherited a family political tradition, he will stand by his party, " right or wrong," and assimilate all the facts of the present situation so that they increase his certainty that he is on the right side.

Misled by catchwords, and prevented from discerning clear issues, the electorate sometimes appoints to Parliament representatives as bewildered as those who vote, whose

fitness for the place of legislation has little or no reference
to the titanic questions which come before them for decision.
It has seemed a feature of democracy worth retaining that
a man shall be elected as a man, and not as a student of
public affairs. No test of his ability even to read a Blue
Book or White Paper is required, providing he can quote
the party hand-book well enough to make a decent show
of it on the hustings.

There is a disposition to-day to appoint young men chosen
for their excellence of university manner and speech and for
their general bonhomie in election times. An impartial
observer of a typical campaign would be equally amazed
at the irrelevant matter put forward as qualifications for
candidature, and at the careful avoidance of those subjects
which affect the critical questions of the hour. Surely the
time has come for a more reasonable method of selecting
the representatives of democracy.

Our Parliamentary system has become a rule by Cabinet,
with a band of permanent officials untouched by election
results. The majority in the House takes away all point
from the discussions ; it rarely affects the vote that follows.
The private deliberations of Ministers, from which these
effects proceed, are so carefully guarded that information
as to the reasons for certain policies only seeps out at discretion. Occasionally, one Minister or another will hold up
hands in despair ; but usually the bewilderment shared
with the rest of mankind is couched in grave words, befit-
ting the dignity of eminence, but contributing nothing to
the solution of the moral problems which are at the root
of all our difficulties.

It would be hard to find any Government in recent history which at any moment made pretence of facing its task
with the inspiration of a high moral ideal. The best it can
do is to put forward policies of expediency. When definitely
social issues seem important—such questions as affect the
drinking or gambling habits of the people—it will appoint
a commission to hibernate for several months, and then
bring forward a report which is received and shelved.

Deputations from vested interests and social reformers alike
—selected at the discretion of the Minister concerned—are
introduced and heard ; vague promises are given ; and
there the matter generally ends. It would be a portent of
the gravest of emergencies if a statesman rose in his place
and said that a certain course must be pursued because it
was right. The kindliest historian would be hard put to it
to find a case in point. Any moral reason that may exist
for projected legislation is smothered in considerations of
what will affect the standing of the Government, and its
likelihood of being returned to power at the next election.

It might be thought that the Government of a Christian
nation would sometimes find occasion to express its Christian motives. The nearest we have come to this in recent
years was the Prime Minister's reply to a Church deputation, when Mr. Ramsay MacDonald urged his visitors to
take every opportunity of approaching responsible Ministers
with the viewpoint that seemed to them to be that of Christian ethics. The Church has missed an opportunity in closing its pulpits to the laymen who govern. If a Prime Minister
or Leader of the Opposition could sometimes stand in Westminster Abbey and affirm his moral reasons for the attitude
he adopted, he might remember more easily that expediency
is not the rôle his followers expect of him, and his recorded
words on such occasions might control his subsequent
actions. As things are, we are governed by bewilderment,
the more confused for the absence of any obvious moral
reasons for the policies introduced.

Democracy has yet to find its soul. While it is possible for
power-seekers, title-purchasers, and a financial oligarchy to
rule, on the condition that their fantastic " economic laws "
are never questioned, it is unlikely that notable advance
to a better order will be made. There is need of a new vision
which can only come by a clear re-statement of the principles concerning righteousness.

The hope of the nation is in better Parliaments, elected
by better methods, by better electors. The world needs not
so much men of energy, zeal, eloquence, charm, power, or

even of ability, as men of fine moral and spiritual sensibility. The Spirit of Wisdom is available for whatever is so complicated that it baffles human ingenuity. Those who are informed of the divine plan for society are the more likely to work out that plan, using their authority not for private profit but for the public weal. In the widely extended franchise, we have the chance of sending men and women to represent us who stand pledged to enthrone righteousness in our communal life. We need not wonder that we move so slowly by political action to the Golden Age when the God of the Golden Age is left so sedulously out of our reckonings. No man can help any other man to real and lasting good without loyalty to the divine purpose, and no Parliament is likely to lift us to our highest hopes unless it is composed of those whose idealism has a religious basis.

5. THE DUTY OF THE CHRISTIAN CHURCH

The financial structure of Western civilisation is shaking because it is not founded on a moral basis. Apart from Christianity, if we can keep it apart, the need of the world to-day is a new sanity. At the present stage of human progress we could do with less speed and more sense. Material mastery has broken loose from spiritual control. The popular perspective is wrong, for the true pathfinders for the modern world are not the experts but the moralists. Of them all, still undethroned though spurned, the greatest is Christ. We live in a sick old world which cries from its soul, out of its deepest need, for healing. We are looking for a master-word to control our life. We want power to heal our divisions, to free us from servitude, that we may build ordered peace and true prosperity upon the earth. That master-word is found in Christ, whose economic wisdom and power are at our service if we will but seek them. The Spirit of Jesus, found still in some of our institutions, is available in its sanity and kindliness for the distresses which cannot be relieved apart from him.

It is of little use our making a new economic vocabulary, putting together formulæ consisting of high-sounding terms ;

what is needed is the discipline of Christian thought, which will issue in patient inquiry into the facts. Without that, we are unlikely to get anywhere. The problems confronting us are, as we have seen, well-nigh insoluble ; the statesmen and economists of the world are baffled. No attempt to restore the conditions of the past can be successful ; or, if successful, satisfactory. Our social life must be rebuilt from the bottom, with full cognisance of the new resources of this age, and with a fresh moral impetus. When the primacy of the material over the spiritual has failed, as it has failed signally in every instance, it is time for the primacy of the spiritual over the material to be asserted. If the world is not to suffer a permanent disorder, there must be a new insistence on the divine principles we have ignored already, to our loss. Where all other authorities have broken down, the authority of God must be declared. We are witnessing a crucifixion of human life, a tragedy only less than the crime of Calvary ; resurrection can only come by the power of God.

We shall certainly not be controlled by men better than ourselves. An electorate of blind men would have none but blind men to rule them ; if in that electorate there should be some who saw, there might be a hope of a minority in the council having vision. When all see, the country will be ruled by far-sighted statesmen. We cannot expect to have a Government pledged to the plans of God until we have a population willing for an era of righteousness.

While we rail at Governments, parties, and policies, we must not forget that our representatives represent us ; that is the pity of it ! They represent the fickleness and the foolishness, the dishonesty and the mistaken ideals of us all. They must do so, for they are of us. The method of reform is not the successive testing of different parties and schools of thought, but the lifting up of the moral energies of the whole nation. The times call us, not to trials of new and unexpectedly promising policies, but to an effort to lift the whole of society to a new level of life, which can then be represented in our senates.

Occasionally an S.O.S. is sent from the economic to the spiritual world, as some publicist or banker admits that the terrible game of international barriers, hatred and exclusiveness, is up, and that Christ and his spirit of forgiveness and peace must be appealed to at last. Christ, however, promised peace on earth to men of good-will, and, whilst the world is greatly clamouring for the reward, it is not prepared to pay the price. It wishes to retain a financial and economic system based upon power, fear, and greed, and is not yet ready to adopt a system founded upon good-will, free-will, and justice. But the Church is normally refused any part in the possible awakening to new life. Her leaders are told that their duty is to preach principles, and to stand quite apart from the application of the Christian message to business life.

In the main, they have consented to the limitation. An instance of this is seen in a recent review of the history of Britain since the war, where the pitiful story of our social and economic chaos was recorded, with barely a mention of the Church in all its pages. A single passing reference to the treatment of the Archbishop of Canterbury, when he attempted to interpose in the General Strike, a counter-statement of Cardinal Bourne's more popular pronouncement on the same issue, with a few scattered quotations from parish magazines whose editors objected to mixed bathing and so on, are all there is to indicate that there even was a Church in England during the last critical years.

Admittedly, this is not a fair picture. Another contributor to the present volume will indicate many forces which the Church has called into being for the spread of righteousness and good-will among the sections of industry and the contending nations. But it can hardly be denied that there has been a practical non-intervention in an hour of intense bewilderment ; and here must be found a reason for the loss of influence over the lives of the people which the Church has to confess. We have left economic and social reform to many who desire a different order from the wrong reasons. Some tacitly ignore God in their attempts to secure better

advantages for their own class ; others declare quite
blatantly that they are seeking a revolution because they
are anti-God. We have too rarely indicated in the Church
that we have a duty in these respects because we are pro-
God. Our leaders in religious thought must come to a
common mind, and speak fearlessly on the moral values in
modern economics.

Unhappily, our inactivity has to be attributed in large
measure to a confusion of thought like that of the rest of
men, a confusion that extends even to the social implications
of the Christian message. We have emphasised those views
of the person of Christ which did not involve active combat
with unethical systems, and have made religion synony-
mous with religiosity. To that extent we have limited the
glory and range of Christ's power.

There is no department of life in which the teaching and
meaning of Christ are not vital ; and on economic and
social problems he has much to say. He laid down fundamental principles and, as I have attempted to show earlier
in this article, the financial and economic, and consequently
social life of the world, is founded and based on principles
diametrically opposed to those he taught. It is the duty
of the Church to point out specifically where Christ's
principles are being defied, and point the way to a new
financial, economic, and social order which would be in
accordance with them.

It is not enough to preach principles. If we confine ourselves to this, we have by no means fulfilled our vocation.
A doctor may be expected, not unreasonably, to outline
what may be called the laws of good health ; but to go on
repeating those laws, as it were in the air, when a patient
shows the first signs of an internal growth, and to do nothing
more about it, would be to fail in the very purpose of his
calling. The followers of Christ have certainly to preach
his principles, but there are times when they have to
diagnose, and others when they must use the scalpel. The
symptoms of ill-health in the body politic must be traced to
their cause. Nor is it good healing to deal with the symptoms

alone ; the knife must go down to the root of the trouble.

It is a false view of political economy that regards it as dealing with things and not with persons ; and all that concerns human beings is a fit subject for action on the part of those who follow the righteous and compassionate Christ. To change our metaphor—where the Church intervenes, it must not be merely as philosopher and friend, but also as guide. The position must be clearly understood that intervention is not that of political or economic partisanship; but nevertheless there must be intervention. If the Church is qualified to hold casualty-clearing activities at the foot of the economic precipice—a task unanimously assigned her—has she not also the occasion and energy to erect a stout fence to cut off the supply of those who fall ? While religious leaders remain befogged, they do disservice to the world they were commissioned to save. The fog is soon dispelled by devoted study of the teaching and implications of the Son of God. We have no reason to be as confused as the rest of men. We must, as a nation and individuals, pray for guidance, and, having received the answer, be prepared to act upon it. " I will yet for this be inquired of by the House of Israel, to do it for them. . . ."

The Church cannot stand aside and say that economics are not her concern, and at the same time hope to win men to her allegiance. Unless we, as Christians, can show that Christ has something to offer the world to-day to make it a fit place for men, not merely to live in, but in which to develop their whole personality and to get nearer to God, she cannot hope to win humanity to Christ. It was those things Christ came into the world to do, and when men say they will have none of him, it is simply because they have not understood. It is, therefore, one of the duties of all Christian thinkers so clearly and unambiguously to enunciate the principles laid down by our Lord, and so earnestly to strive to remove the causes of our distress, that they may have an effective part in the re-ordering of the life of our times. And this must be done with such boldness and purity of conscience that we cannot be suspected of compromise with elements that are of their very nature incongruous with Christ's teaching. It is in the arena of economics that the next battles for Christ must be fought. We have carried the Cross into many fields, but the one where our greatest victories for humanity may now be achieved is where bankers and leaders of high finance, pursuing their own interests instead of planning to meet the needs of the world, have evolved the insane policy of destroying goods already grown or manufactured, together with the policy of restricting output, with the object of keeping wrongful power over the bodies and souls of men and nations. Can we doubt what the comment and action of Christ would be in such a situation ; and can we be content to avoid what he would have done ?

If we are to be allowed to speak on " moral issues," we must also be given the right to determine where and when those issues arise. When we are faced, for example, by the question of whether financial advantage or human ends should be the dominant factor in industry, we are compelled to assert that the right lies with those who contend for the human values ; to deny that would be to cut many vital pages out of the Gospels. Jesus was constantly saying that the right to live a full, well-rounded life must not be forbidden for the sake of gaining merely material things. We cannot remain complacent while millions are unemployed and while hosts of little children suffer from malnutrition.

The economics of reconciliation belong to Christianity. That is generally allowed in the case of disarmament. As representatives of the Prince of Peace, we are permitted to speak on the need for good-will, as that may be spread so as to make war impossible.

But if, as many state, the root cause of war is economic, are we merely to concern ourselves with taking arms away from the nations, whilst leaving to grow and flourish the hidden root which must one day bring forth war, however ill- or well-armed the nations may then be ? Are we not merely once more laying ourselves open to the charge that we are dupes engaged in bolstering up the system, by enabling the nations to maintain such a level of armaments as may be financially supportable ? If wars arise from a struggle by the nations to acquire a reasonable share of an utterly inadequate world purchasing-power, so inadequate that, if one nation is successful, others must go without, is the Church to ignore this state of affairs ? Whilst the most enlightened business men have always recognised the principle that the only business which is satisfactory is where both parties to the deal are well content, is the Church to be satisfied with a world-system which results, not in the exchange of goods between nations, to their mutual advantage, but in a fierce struggle for gold, culminating sooner or later in war ?

The Christian community has a responsibility for economic change. Its task is not only that of proclaiming an ideal. It exercises its functions rightly in examining the reality and effectiveness of those policies which control the material life of men, and it has been raised up that it may so order human relationships that the principles of Christ may be built into the life of the world. Christ had much to say about money, and the false view of it that he exposed underlies all our present dilemma. Money is not a commodity ; it is essentially a title to goods and services, a social mechanism for their orderly production and distribution. It has no intrinsic value apart from the function it performs, and to regard it as wealth in itself is contrary to reason and to the whole philosophy of Christ. If money-tokens must be distributed in such a way that they are commensurate with the limit of production, so that everyone has enough for their material needs, and according to their needs, we have to say so. If this is the way by which the way out may be found from the present position—a position which combines the fantastic absurdity of *Alice in Wonderland* with the horrors of a Grand Guignol play—and if this is, as it seems to be, consistent with the ideals of Christ, then the Church must demand that no private interests be allowed to stand in the way of its accomplishment.

Since, on all evidence, a diminishing amount of human

effort will be needed to produce the goods that satisfy material needs, the Church must insist on a far greater place being given to service in its widest connotation ; to the advancement of those arts and crafts, of those spiritual and intellectual adventures, which make in every realm for the good of the whole.

Moreover, since the coming age is to be one of greater leisure, the Church must recognise its duty in educating the people in the use of their spare time, that this be not used for waste but for the upbuilding of all the faculties with which human beings have been endowed.

Spheres of influence possibly transcending those of any other time are open to the servants of Christ. To fail in our duties and opportunities now would be to renounce all our heroic past, and to merit the rejection at the hands of the world that would inevitably follow.

The future of the world seems to lie either with secular Communism, with the Church a mere hobby for the aged and sick ; or with a re-baptised Church, preaching its message with fearlessness and a real understanding of social and economic questions. The message such a Church would give would deal with the fundamental facts of personal religion in language that all could understand ; but it would need to be taught in the profoundest application of its gospel and ethic to the intricacies of modern life. Such a Church might be hated, might have to suffer persecution ; but it would know itself true to its calling, and the opposition it evoked would be a worthier distinction than the badge of scorn and indifference it has to wear to-day. We shall remain in chaos until one or other of these forces captures the imagination of the majority.

When it ignores these duties, and timidly consents to an authority which denies that they are duties, it is failing in one of its supreme purposes. Christ's words, " If any man follow me, he shall not walk in darkness but shall have the light of life," are applicable to the Church to-day. It is walking in darkness, and the implication is obvious that this is because it is not following the way of Christ.

6. THE SOCIAL PROBLEM A RELIGIOUS MATTER

It falls to other contributors to suggest definite means by which deliverance from the present chaos may be sought. The present writer's task is to describe the situation as it is. We are therefore left for the moment with problems unsolved ; but to clarify a problem is a necessary stage in its solution. The problem of our age has many facets.

There is primarily its financial side : the fact that we have a financial system inadequate to its task of distributing the produce grown and the goods manufactured. We have to discover what means there are, since some means there must be, of bringing into being an economic order in which advantage can be taken of all the material wealth that floods upon us from the fields and factories. It is left to this decade to find a more satisfactory way of equating effective demand with available supply.

There must be a world view of the need that exists. Even though prosperity returned to this or that country in the West, if it still remained true that hundreds of thousands in India lay down at night hungry, as indeed they do, we could not feel that we had reached the end of the matter. Nothing but our incompetence prevents us from seeing that all citizens of the world are well housed, well fed, and well clothed. There is shipping enough, or could soon be, and the act of distribution only waits upon a settlement upon the means by which it is to be arranged. To feed the whole world is as Christian a duty as to preach the gospel to it ; but we lack either the will or the ability, or both, to plan the sufficient distribution of the means of life.

Thus the problem reaches out until other nations are included. International settlements have to be made. A way of working together has to be found, treaties to be agreed upon, and safeguards instituted to ensure their honourable observance. So long as one nation is working against the rest, the full programme of reconstruction is hindered.

It by no means follows, however, that a united mind

can best be achieved in a uniform system. The experience
of the British Empire in the political and constitutional
sphere seems to point to the possibility of greater good-
will and mutual confidence where there is no superimposed
centralised force to compel uniformity. Each nation
has its own peculiar characteristics, its own cultural
development, and its own contribution to make. When
that right is unreservedly recognised, and no attempt
whatever is made to interfere with it, suspicion and fear
disappear and willingness to co-operate to the mutual
advantage of all manifests itself. The contrary view that
co-operation is only possible where there is a superimposed
centralised force to compel uniformity has been proved
right through the ages to be definitely mistaken. Whilst
the British Empire has not attempted to set up any such
centralised superimposed force in the political sphere, and
has relied upon good-will, free-will, and justice, it has been
prepared, hitherto, in the financial sphere to accept the
continental view that such a centralised superimposed
force was necessary. The international gold standard
system was such a centralised force. By putting gold into
a country or taking it out it raised and lowered the general
price-level, causing injustice as between citizens and as
between nations by varying the burden of all contractual
obligations. It may very well be that a system under which
each nation owned and controlled its own currency, and
voluntarily entered into agreements with the other nations
by which its currency would have a fixed exchange relationship with theirs, may prove a solution. There would, in this
way, be no fear of financial and economic domination. In
order that a family may be united, it is not necessary that
they should live in the same room.

At bottom, it is a moral and religious question. The compassion which recognises the need of the world, the good-
will which strives in fellowship towards its supply, the
unity of spirit that oversteps racial bounds, the wisdom to
devise something more successful than has ever been attempted—all are at one point or another concerned with

religious impulses and experience. So the problem is how to appeal to the moral mind of the world that the things desired may be so accomplished. How may a change of the world's heart be induced ? Fear must be removed, and all illusions and fictions designed to disguise facts must be exposed. " The Truth shall make you free."

The conviction of this contributor is that this may be attained by faithful preaching of the essential content of the gospel, by the denunciation of any financial or economic system which gives to one nation tyrannical dominance over others, and by an insistence on the fact that real wealth consists in the power of the people to produce and consume. The dignity of labour must be declared : that to gain riches by positive disservice to the community, and, at the other end of the scale, to be compelled to suffer impoverished idleness, is demoralising. Nature has more to yield than we have ever taken, and no man should be denied a share in the good things of God's world through man's mismanagement.

We must announce the obligation of rendering mutual service. There is sacramental value in labour when it is understood that Christ shares the benefit of what we do, in the persons of those who receive the products of our toil. The contributions to the world's well-being offered by earnest workmen may be of most varied kinds, but when service has been accepted as the cause for our going forth until the evening the task will be the better done, and a real gift to the community will result.

It is in fine character alone that a nation is great. We are in the world for the sake of souls. It is by work and sharing, and by the association of both with the supreme object of worship, that a fine quality of life is attained. Where there is poverty of spiritual experience there is inevitably bad statesmanship and bad citizenship.

But as we preach these things as means by which solutions may come, we have to oppose whatever obstructs ; and, when we hit it, to hit it hard.

4. THE CONFUSION IN INTERNATIONAL RELATIONS

By Dr. HOWARD MASTERMAN
Bishop of Plymouth

THE FACT that at the beginning of the twentieth century the world was plunged into four years of war is a sufficient evidence that the whole system of international relations needed to be reorganised. There was no desire for war among the peoples of the world, and the consciousness of economic and cultural interdependence had been growing. Rivalries in Colonial expansion had proved capable of adjustment, and though the dominance of Europe in the world-system was no longer unchallenged, it was not seriously menaced. But, politically, the relations between the European Powers were still regulated by diplomatic assumptions that were out of date. The idea that every sovereign State was the sole judge of its own rights and claims, and owed no allegiance to any common moral ideal, was incompatible with any secure and lasting peace, for it involves the recognition of offensive war as a legitimate instrument of national policy instead of being, as we now know it to be, a crime against humanity that must be outlawed by the moral judgment of all civilised peoples.

The centre of the *malaise* of Europe was the Austro-Hungarian Empire, where the tradition of racial dominance was in conflict with the claims of subject peoples to self-determination. Most of the wars of the nineteenth century were connected, directly or indirectly, with the struggle of Austrians, Magyars, Italians, and Slavs in this cockpit of central Europe. Nearly a hundred years ago, Mazzini, whose prophetic foresight we are now at last beginning to recognise, wrote : " In Austria there is a Slav movement which no one troubles about, but which one day . . . will wipe Austria off the map of Europe." Whether a generous recognition of racial equality could have held together the

Ec

Hapsburg dominions it is impossible now to decide, but in a Europe where sores left by ancient wrongs were still festering, international co-operation was impossible, and the interdependence which might have localised, if it could not prevent, the *débâcle* of central Europe, only made it universal.

The end of the long struggle left the world morally exhausted, and the treaties that closed the war raised almost as many political problems as they solved.

POST-WAR EUROPE

In the redistribution of territory that followed the war, it was inevitable that alien minorities should be left within the borders of States intoxicated with the idea of nationalist self-expression. The method of " exchange of population," by which about a million Greeks who had escaped from massacre in Asia Minor, were transplanted to their mother country, could not be applied to the Germans in Czecho-slovakia and Poland, or to the Hungarians in Transylvania, or to the non-Serbian population of Macedonia. In the treaties that resettled the frontiers of Europe, a genuine effort was made to protect these minorities. " They stipu-lated for protection of life and liberty, and free exercise of religion, as rights common to all ; they conceded to all residents in a land where the treaty came into force the privilege of nationalisation ; they insisted on equality before the law and in admission to public services, on free use of the mother tongue in social and business life, in religious services, in the Press and public meetings, and in courts of law : on the liberty to maintain, at their own expense, schools and charitable institutions ; on the right to instruc-tion in their own mother tongue in the State primary schools in localities where minorities were a large element in the population, and to a fair share in any grants given by the Government or by municipalities for educational, religious, or charitable ends." So far as paper safeguards could go, the interests of minorities were safeguarded. But the enforcement of these safeguards has been a matter of great difficulty.

There are, according to Hungarian calculations, 500,000

Magyars in Yugoslavia, nearly two millions in Roumania, and over a million in Czechoslovakia. Poland includes within its frontiers two million Germans and four million Ruthenians. In the Southern Tyrol, nearly 200,000 German-speaking people have been transferred to the Italian kingdom. None of these Powers have adopted a very generous attitude towards the minorities within their borders, whose resentment is kept alive by Irredentist agitations across the frontiers. The " Little Entente " alliance of Roumania, Czechoslovakia, and Yugoslavia was formed to resist any revision of the frontiers of Hungary. The mere transfer of a mixed population from one State to another would not solve the problem, for no rectification of frontiers can prevent Transylvania or Macedonia from being a land of mixed races.

In Switzerland, and in Canada, peoples of different language and creed have found it possible, at long last, to dwell together in unity ; and though South Africa presents at present a spectacle not altogether unlike that described by Lord Durham in Canada—" two nations warring together within the borders of one State "—there is reason to hope that race antagonisms may give place to a political co-operation founded on mutual respect. Is there any hope of a similar abatement of race hatred in eastern Europe ?

In western Europe, Germany has, if the Locarno treaty means anything, renounced any hope of recovering Alsace and Lorraine, but the creation of the " Polish Corridor," and the loss of the overseas territories of the Empire, have fostered a resentment that shows no sign of abating. Germany cannot be permanently denied a " place in the sun," and a territorial arrangement that separates East Prussia from the rest of the Reich can only be maintained at the cost of permanent estrangement between Germany and Poland. Italy also resents her restricted opportunities for Colonial expansion, and regards the control of the Adriatic, to which Yugoslavia aspires, as vital to her security. All these causes of friction are tending to restore the pre-war alignment of Europe into two groups—France and Poland, with the " Little Entente," standing for the maintenance of the *status quo*, as against the desire of Germany, Italy, Hungary, and Bulgaria for a revision of the peace treaties. A *pro rata* reduction of armaments will not, by itself, mean a corresponding increase of security, and neither the poverty of the nations, nor the desire for peace that undoubtedly exists, can be relied upon to avert an outbreak which, if once it occurs, will almost inevitably involve all Europe, and leave Soviet Russia and America as heirs to the leadership of the world.

The only hope for Europe lies in the awakening of a consciousness of common interests stronger than the racial and economic antagonisms that grow out of exclusive national loyalties. The political doctrine expressed by Canning : " Every nation for itself and God for us all," dominated the Europe of the nineteenth century ; its repudiation affords the only hope for the future.

The war itself showed the interdependence of the peoples of the world. It was " the first event in human history in which all the peoples of the earth were not only involved, but knew that they were involved." It was a turning-point in world-history because it showed that, for better or for worse, the human race had become one family. But it is as certain as anything can be that the other members of that human family will never again be drawn into the rivalries and contests of Europe, and that unless the European Powers can adjust their differences, their claim to the leadership of the world will no longer be accepted.

NATIONALISM

During the last hundred years Nationalism has been the strongest force that has challenged the existing State system. It represents the instinctive desire to find a unit of common loyalty smaller than humanity. As a protest against a merely material conception of life it has a spiritual value, but this spiritual value is lost when it substitutes the idea of dominance for that of service, and denies to other peoples what it demands for itself. No one saw the value and danger of Nationalism more clearly than Mazzini. As Mr. Griffith, his latest English biographer, sums up his teaching, he bade his followers " beware of mere pithless cosmopolitanism— the individual sprawling in mere humanitary welter. There must be, for effective action, a middle term between the individual and the race : the Pact of Humanity could be signed only by free and equal nations. They must beware, too, of the mere materialistic Rights-and-interests pro- pagandism now being elevated into a universal gospel, a propagandism that took account only of this world and was therefore powerless to transform it. And they must beware no less of the toy Nationalism of kings, with its false, egoistic, rival " patriotisms," defiant of the one true principle of progress—the association of free peoples in the family of mankind."

Nationality was, to Mazzini, the divinely appointed means to international unity. He even foresaw that in the future evolution of the world-order, " distinctions of coun- try, sacred now, may possibly disappear." He deplored the failure of Christianity to break down the barriers of exclu- sive Nationalism. " In the heart of Humanity which calls itself Christian there is absolutely nothing *collective* to re- present the consolidation of Humanity."

The lines of division in mediæval Europe were horizontal, nobles, knights, ecclesiastics, and burghers sharing common interests across the variable frontiers of States. The fellow- ship of scientists and men of learning, the Marxian idea of the universal class war, and the drawing together of the Christian Churches, are signs of a tendency to a stratifica- tion that may challenge the supremacy of the vertical divi- sions of national separation. As a corrective to the exclusive- ness of national loyalty, these other loyalties have their value. But the nation is more closely akin to the family in that it is a natural unit of mutual service and obligation through which human personality grows by what it gives. " The nation-state," says Professor Bosanquet, " as an ethical idea is a faith or a purpose—we might say a mission were not the word too narrow and too aggressive. . . . The modern nation is a history and a religion rather than a clear-cut idea. Its power as an idea-force is not known till it is tried."

Three things follow from this conception of nationality. In the first place no nation liveth to itself. The claim of a nation to existence must be founded on the special contribution that it is able to make to the many-sided life of humanity. The political organisation of a community is only the shell that it develops for the protection of its cultural life, and it is not only as States, but also as units of cultural, ethical, and social life that nations, in the modern world, come into contact with one another. Then, secondly, it is in the interest of the human race that every nation should be guaranteed against interference with its own cultural development. A nation despised by its neighbours is liable to develop an " inferiority complex " that prevents it from taking its place contentedly in the family of nations. It is significant that the smaller nations of Europe have shown a special loyalty to the League of Nations, seeing in it a new guarantee of their independence. Lastly, it is only in view of the idea of a nation as a unit of service that Christianity can co-exist with a world of nations. To a Christian man, his duty to his nation can never be the first claim on his allegiance. Loyalty to the Christian ideal may oblige him to repudiate the authority of the State, though he can never do so without deep searchings of heart. But in every act in which his nation seeks to serve the cause of humanity, he can find a channel for the exercise of the Christian law of service.

Behind the economic and political problems that represent the chaos of international European relationships, a struggle is in progress between the aggressive Nationalism that finds expression in the efforts of each nation to seek its own prosperity in entire disregard of the welfare of other nations, and the idea of the nationality of service that finds in the diversity of national character a way to a richer unity of interdependence than can be found in a vague cosmopolitanism which leaves the individual homeless in a world-order too vast to evoke his powers of loyalty and sacrifice.

THE "UNITED STATES OF EUROPE"

This nobler ideal, if it can win its way to acceptance, will ultimately find expression in some kind of United States of Europe—not as a rival of the League of Nations, but as a smaller unit of political co-operation. The constitution of the League of Nations takes too little account of the fact that Europe is an association of nations with common traditions and a distinctive cultural background. Mediæval Europe was a Christian commonwealth, inheriting its political and intellectual ideals from the Græco-Roman civilisation. The disintegration of this Christian commonwealth was perhaps an inevitable stage in the progress of humanity, but to-day it is the integrating forces in European life on which the future of the world depends. The war has shaken, if it has not destroyed, the claim of Europe to the moral leadership of the world. Gandhi speaks for more than India when he writes, " The last war has shown, as nothing else has, the satanic nature of the civilisation that dominates Europe to-day. Every canon of public morality has been broken by the victors in the name of virtue. No lie has been considered too foul to be uttered. The motive behind every crime is not religious or spiritual, but grossly material." We may think this impeachment too unqualified, but it represents the considered opinion of most of the leaders of thought of the Eastern world.

The repudiation of the moral leadership of Europe has almost inevitably discredited Christianity, except in the minds of men like Sun Yat-Sen and Gandhi, who are able to recognise that " Europe to-day is only nominally Christian."

The re-Christianising of the public life of Europe is not only the necessary condition of that moral disarmament, without which material disarmament is valueless as a security for world-peace, it is also urgently needed to enable the peoples of Europe to stand together in defence of values that are menaced by modern industrialism and Marxian Communism. Mass production and Communism both challenge the doctrine of individual self-determination which (however inadequately applied) has been an essential factor in the Christian tradition of Europe. The battle for the spiritual values of life—for art and culture, and the quest of knowledge for its own sake—must be fought and won in Europe, and only a Europe conscious of its common trusteeship can hope to win.

CHINA

It may be that the age of self-determined Nationalism is actually passing away, and that the struggle of the future will be between groups of peoples held together by common traditions and interests, and each representing some ethical ideal. China and India are more than nations, they are federal groups that have found a bond of union in historical associations and the desire for self-expression. Under conditions of extraordinary difficulty, the political leaders of China are trying to build up a new order on the basis of Sun Yat-Sen's " Three Principles of the People "— national independence, democracy, and economic security. Meanwhile the National Government in China is confronted with difficulties that might well make even brave men despair. For seventeen years rival war lords have marched and countermarched over the northern provinces of China, while the Soviet Government has made every effort to foster Communist enterprise, which often takes the form of incursions of hordes of bandits on peaceable districts. Besides all this, the Government has had to face the open hostility of Japan, and the failure of the Great Powers to give their disinterested support to its efforts to build up a Chinese State strong enough to control its own destiny. In this welter of confusion, we may find some ground of hope in the fact that several of the ablest political leaders are, like Sun Yat-Sen, Christians by sincere conviction. Under the leadership of men like Chiang-kai-sheh and C. T. Wang, the National Party will not be content to build up the material resources of China without regard for the things of the spirit.

The redemption of China will be a long process—" The

Revolution is not yet complete "—and the best service that the League of Nations can render is in insisting that China shall be left free to work out its own destiny. Probably a large measure of provincial self-government will ultimately create in China a federal republic akin to the United States of America. The restoration of order and the improvement of communications will enable the immense natural resources of the country to be developed. When it is no longer associated with foreign exploitation, Christianity will find a powerful ally in the ethical traditions that have held the Chinese people together for two thousand years.

INDIA

In India, as in China, the demand for self-government arose first in the student class, who had gained a superficial knowledge of Western political thought, and resented the exclusion of natives from the higher ranks of public service in India. Though more than ninety per cent. of the population of India lives in village communities, " it is in the towns that there are to be found the barristers and journalists who predominate among the leaders of Indian political opinion, and from whose ranks for the most part are drawn the propagandists, candidates, and public representatives of all political parties and communities." A new chapter in Indian history was opened by the demand of the Indian National Congress, in 1918, that the same principle of self-determination that was being applied to the settlement of Europe should be accepted for India. This was followed by the Montagu–Chelmsford Report—a State document that deserves to rank with Lord Durham's Report on Canada. The Preamble of the India Act of 1919, founded on that Report, asserts in the clearest terms that " it is the declared policy of Parliament to provide for the increasing association of Indians in every branch of Indian Administration, and for the gradual development of self-governing institutions, with a view to the progressive realisation of responsible government in British India as an integral part of the Empire." The hope that this declaration would bring about loyal co-operation in the working out of self-government has unfortunately been disappointed. The Khalifat agitation among the Muslims of India was followed by the non-co-operation movement, which, in spite of Gandhi's efforts, sometimes took the form of active violence. By the appointment of the Indian Statutory Commission, under Sir John Simon, and by calling together two Round Table Conferences, the British Government has shown its genuine desire to implement the pledge given in 1919.

It is not the reluctance of the British Government, but the complicated nature of the problems involved, that has prevented self-government from developing as rapidly as impatient Nationalists desire. India is not a nation in any sense in which we habitually use that word. The common desire for self-government co-exists with religious and racial divisions that are at least as strong, and any withdrawal of British authority would, in the opinion of those who are best qualified to judge, plunge India into a state of anarchy and disintegration more complete than that of China. In any scheme for self-government in India, British statesmen are obliged to keep three problems in view. The sixty million Muslims in British India must be guaranteed adequate representation ; the rights and interests of the forty million outcaste " untouchables " must be protected ; and the approval of the rulers of the Indian native States, with a population of sixty-seven millions, must be secured. This last consideration precludes any surrender of British suzerainty in India, for only under the British Raj will the native Princes be willing to enter a Federal Empire of India.

There are two elements of weakness in the outlook of the Nationalist parties in India. In the first place, they want to " foreshorten history " and blend in one conceptions which have followed a certain sequence through a century of Western history. " The growth of national self-consciousness is retarded by communal separatism. The movement towards Western industrialism is countered by the return to the spinning-wheel. The equality of Asiatic and European is proclaimed, while the clash of Brahmin and non-Brahmin, or caste and outcaste, is intensified. Ultra-democratic constitutions are propounded, although the long process which was a necessary antecedent to democracy in Europe, viz. the breaking down of class and communal and occupational barriers, has only just begun."

The other element of weakness is what Dr. Edwyn Bevan has called " Backward-looking Nationalism." The indiscriminate rejection of Western civilisation, of which Gandhi has made himself the leader, is associated with an equally indiscriminate idealisation of Indian history. But a large body of Indian reformers is looking to the future rather than to the past. They have seen Turkey, Persia, and Soviet Russia, break with their own past, in order to incorporate so much of Western civilisation as might strengthen the new order of national independence. We may recognise the significance of Gandhi's protest for the spiritual values of Indian life as against the soulless materialism of mass production and industrial exploitation : but self-government will not, by itself, afford any guarantee against these evils. The truth is, as the Simon Report points out, that Indian reformers are inclined to attribute all the evils that they attack to the absence of self-government. " In our view, the most formidable of the evils from which India is suffering have their roots in social and economic customs of long standing, which can only be remedied by the action of the Indian peoples themselves. They are much less likely to be remedied if the blame for their continuance can be put, however unreasonably, on others."

The report closes with the rather grim warning : " It is only when the difficulties of constructive policy are really faced, that the inadequacy of general phrases begins to be realised."

SOVIET RUSSIA

The Union of Socialist Soviet Republics (U.S.S.R.) constitutes a third supernational group within the world-order. The Soviet State consists of the Russian Republic, and six other Republics with local autonomy. Within this system nearly two hundred nationalties are included, the Russians forming about fifty per cent. of the whole. The tremendous constructive experiment on which Soviet Russia has embarked is the greatest new fact in the post-war world. Russia alone, of all the peoples of the world, has definitely broken with the past, and started on the creation of a new economic and social order. Measured by actual achievement, the Russian Revolution is a menace and a challenge. Only in Russia could so complete a repudiation of historic traditions be possible, for the cultural ideas of western Europe had never penetrated into the life of the Russian people, whose political system had deteriorated into a faded and ineffective Byzantinism. The war, accepted without enthusiasm and carried through in an atmosphere of muddle, corruption, and blind sacrifice, left Russia in a condition verging on anarchy. On this disillusioned world there descended a small group of men endowed with clear purpose, ruthless determination, and a passionate hatred for what they deemed the injustice and cruelty of the existing economic order. They brought to Russia a new gospel in the " dictatorship of the proletariat," a new Bible in Karl Marx's *Das Kapital*, a new patron saint in Lenin—more powerful in death than in life—and a new mission in the world-war against Capitalism.

The price for these things was the repudiation of all religions claiming supernatural authority, and the building up, as rapidly as ruthless discipline could do, of a new industrial system that should make Russia independent of the Capitalist nations of the West. The Soviet system, like Fascism, is the negation of democracy : its ruling force is a kind of Communist aristocracy that is prepared to terrorise when it cannot persuade. This is regarded by the Communist leaders as a passing phase, pending the time when the ideals of Communism have penetrated the life of the people, and the " collective man " dominated by common interest, and wholly subordinate to the purposes of the community, shall have superseded the individual man with his claim to self-determination and economic independence.

The weapons by which the Soviet leaders hope to achieve

this end are, first, their complete control over education and the Press ; then the Red Army and the secret police, both dominated by the Communist Central Committee ; and, lastly, the State control of industry and foreign trade, through which the very means of livelihood can be denied to those who will not subscribe to the Communist creed. Like the Fascist movement, Russian Communism is concentrating on the effort to inspire the young with a religious fervour and discipline that it cannot hope to evoke in a generation in which traditions of personal liberty and " superstition " still linger. The Soviet doctrine involves the substitution of the cosmopolitan for the national ideal, but it may be suspected that much of its strength lies in the desire of the Russian people for economic and cultural self-expression. The idea, assiduously fostered by every method of propaganda, that the Capitalist nations are preparing for an organised attack on Soviet Russia, exercises a powerful influence over the mind of the people.

What is the future of Soviet Russia ? All impartial observers are agreed that the present rulers are too strongly entrenched to be overthrown, either by external attack or internal revolution. Russia is far too deeply committed to the Communist experiment to turn back. But no community can maintain itself in permanent isolation from the civilised world, and, when the fear of European aggression has abated and the dream of world-revolution has given place to a more realistic view of things, the rigidity of the Communist doctrine may be modified, and the meaning of life may cease to be interpreted wholly in terms of material values.

AMERICA

Across the Atlantic we find two other supernational groups. The United States is supernational, not only because it is a federation of partly autonomous States, but also because it includes within its borders many millions of people of diverse races, some of whom, like the Germans and Scandinavians, are assimilated without difficulty, while others, such as the Irish, Latins, and Slavs, retain more obstinately their own culture and traditions. The Negro population of about ten million lives in cultural isolation— an insoluble racial problem. In the West, the Chinese and Japanese also constitute a detached racial unit. As time is reckoned in the life of nations, America is still hardly more than adolescent. Till fifty years ago the supremacy of the Anglo-Saxon Puritan element in American life was not seriously challenged, but from about 1880 the proportion of Latin and Slav emigrants grew steadily, amounting in the decade 1910–20 to seventy-seven per cent. In the 1920 census the " hundred per cent. Americans " only numbered about fifty-five per cent. of the total population. The war helped to awaken the leaders of American life to the composite character of the community and the extent to which national sympathies still persisted under a veneer of Americanism. America felt herself threatened with the reproduction in her soil of the racial and religious problems of Europe. In self-protection, the inflow of foreign immigrants was checked by the Immigration Laws of 1921 and 1924, which left America dependent for a supply of unskilled labour on Mexico, Canada, and the Negro population. The repudiation of President Wilson's effort to draw America into the world-system was partly due to the feeling that America must be free to build up a national consciousness, unentangled by the problems of the Old World. If America has turned her back on Europe, it has been, partly at least, in order to save her own soul. Unquestionably, the American people feel themselves more closely akin to the British people than to the rest of Europe ; but it is easy to over-stress the idea of the " cousinship " of the English-speaking peoples. " The American people are now creating on a vast scale an entirely original social structure, which bears only a superficial resemblance to the European." The problem that America has set herself to solve is that of combining the highest standard of productive efficiency with the conservation of the spiritual values that find expression in the free initiative of the individual. The most conspicuous feature of American life is its concentration on material well-being, but we form an entirely false idea of the " American spirit " unless we recognise the idealism that finds expression in philanthropic enterprise and social service. Perhaps energy rather than devotion is the characteristic note of American religion. But America is seething with a life that has not yet found its channel of expression. The day may come when America takes over from Europe the leadership of the world : but that day is still far distant.

South America is escaping from the tutelage of the United States, and is slowly drawing together into a confederation. Even more than the United States, it is dominated by material interests, and its cultural background is Latin rather than Anglo-Saxon. Its supernational consciousness is still nebulous, and, in view of the vastness of its area, and the mixed character of its population, its consolidation into a sixth star in the constellation of humanity will be a slow process. Yet no prophet who attempts to forecast the future of the world can afford to ignore the economic and cultural possibilities dormant in the South American continent.

THE BRITISH EMPIRE

Among these supernational groups Great Britain occupies a special position. As the mother of the British Empire, she is the leading member of a seventh supernational group of peoples, with clearly marked political and administrative traditions. But she is also, inevitably, a member of the European family of nations ; and has a responsibility, of which she cannot divest herself, for guiding the development of India. She is also the " daysman " between America and the European peoples, for this generation at least. The reconciliation of these functions is a task that calls for the highest and most disinterested statesmanship. With their admission to the League of Nations, the self-governing dominions of the Empire " came of age," and the mother country can no longer claim to direct their policy, though the main burden of the task of defence still rests on her. The right of the Dominions to exclude alien immigration from large areas of sparsely populated land may be challenged by nations like Japan, faced with the problem of finding an outlet for its surplus population and the extent to which Great Britain controls the supply of raw materials of industry raises complicated problems, especially now that she has abandoned the policy of Free Trade.

The British Empire was built up on sea power, and remained invulnerable while the British Fleet kept the control of the seas. Now that this control is passing out of British hands, can the Empire be defended against attack from a combination of powers ? " A nation that is both very rich and comparatively weak for war is almost certain to be attacked and plundered." The very existence of the British Empire depends on the building up of securities for world peace.

As Mr. Ramsay Muir points out, Great Britain has done more than any other nation to bring about the interdependence of the world by the world-wide extension of Western civilisation. " She was, during the critical period when interdependence was being established, the very pivot of the world's economic system, its central market, its chief carrier, its financier, its money-lender, and the manipulator of its monetary system. . . . In short, Britain has been, in a very remarkable degree, the source of most of the factors which have contributed to produce the interdependent world of to-day." As the outcome of this interdependence, Great Britain has now lost her insular security, and become peculiarly vulnerable to blockade or air attack. " The island that was a fortress has become a trap."

THE LEAGUE OF NATIONS

The idea of a " United States of Europe " has led us to a cursory examination of various supernational groups within the world-order, which make the national rivalries and jealousies of Europe seem parochial. But the world-order itself has common interests and needs, and the one real gain of the peace treaties was the creation of a machinery through which these might find expression. In his message to Congress in 1918, President Wilson formulated his plan for " a general association of nations, under specific convenants, for the purpose of affording mutual guarantees of political independence and territorial integrity to great and small States alike." It would have been wiser to dissociate the Covenant of the League of Nations from the Peace of Versailles, and the other peace treaties in which it was incorporated, in order that it might be clear that the League was not an alliance of nations for the maintenance of the *status quo.* The difficulty with which Europe is confronted is that for centuries war has been the only way of modifying the existing political order, except in those rare cases in which a nation has recognised changed conditions by voluntary concessions. If war is ruled out as a legitimate instrument of national policy, as is done by the Pact of Paris, how can legitimate grievances, arising from changed political conditions, be dealt with ? By Article XIX. of the Covenant, " The Assembly may from time to time advise the reconsideration by members of the League of Treaties which have become inapplicable, and the consideration of international conditions whose continuance might endanger the peace of the world." The claim that the recent treaties of peace should be sacrosanct from this possibility of revision can hardly be maintained permanently. Its abandonment, by dissociating the League from the late war, would do much to meet the objections of America and Soviet Russia. America has also found the problems of " Sanctions " a reason for dissociating herself from the League. Among the supporters of the League there is a clearly defined difference of opinion on this question. Is the League, in the last resort, to be empowered to bring pressure on any recalcitrant nation, through economic boycott, or, if need be, through hostile action : or must we trust to the moral judgment of the civilised world to restrain nations from violating their solemn undertakings ? And, if the first alternative be accepted (though without the co-operation of the United States and Soviet Russia it would in fact be impracticable), should the League have an armed force of its own, or have the right to call upon its constituent nations to levy war on the offender ? It is difficult to contemplate without repugnance the idea of a League, whose *raison d'être* is the preservation of world-peace, bombing the cities and destroying the commerce of one of its members ; yet can any community preserve order without a police force ready, if need be, to meet violence with violence ? The only way of escape from this dilemma lies in the development among the peoples of the world of an abhorrence of aggressive war as a crime of which no self-respecting nation can be guilty. The whole position has been changed since 1914 by the establishment of the League, and the setting up of a permanent Court of International Justice for the adjudication of international disputes.

The League of Nations is important not only in virtue of what it does, but also in virtue of what it symbolises. It is the outward and visible sign—imperfect, as all outward and visible signs are—of a new ideal of international relationships, in which frankness and co-operative action take the place of secret intrigues and international rivalry—" the first organ ever created to serve the needs of the whole human race." Only in so far as the peoples of the world are prepared to welcome this new ideal can the League function successfully. By equality of representation in the Assembly, and the need for unanimity in all vital decisions, the Covenant avoids the infringement of national sovereignty and averts the danger that the League may deteriorate into an alliance of the Great Powers, like the Quadruple Alliance that followed the Napoleonic wars. But while America and Russia remain outside the League the difficulty of building up a consciousness of unity transcending national egoisms is greatly increased.

The actual activities of the League have a twofold purpose. They encourage agreements and methods of conciliation designed to delay, and if possible to avert, the outbreak of war. And they also tend, by co-operation in various humanitarian enterprises, to foster the habit of common action among the peoples of the world. The statesmen of the world cannot justly be charged with disloyalty to the Covenant, and if the League has failed to achieve all that its advocates hoped, the cause must be found in the persistence among the peoples of Europe of the pre-war mentality that interprets international relations in terms of rivalry and mutual distrust. The instability of governments —an ominous disease of democracy—hinders the work of the League by endangering the continuity of foreign policy, and delays the ratification of proposals that can be carried out only with the assent of the constituent States of the League. It is not easy to see how the general body of citizens can exercise any effective control over the details of the foreign policy of the State, but the steady pressure of public opinion in favour of international goodwill must affect the attitude of statesmen towards the issues with which the League has to deal. Gestures of goodwill not supported by public opinion may, as has been the case more than once in France in recent years, lead to the fall of the Minister who makes them. It cannot be said that democracy, in modern Europe, has proved as strong a safeguard for peace as men once supposed it would be.

The idea of a World-State, charged with the task of organising the economic resources of the world and maintaining peace, has attracted some thinkers who are dissatisfied with the cumbrous machinery of the League of Nations. But any attempt so to gather the human race into one political system is both impracticable and undesirable. It is impracticable because the diversity of interests and of stages of cultural progress among the peoples of the world preclude the possibility of any uniform body of regulations imposed by a sovereign authority on their relations with one another ; and undesirable, because the mastery of the world would almost inevitably produce what Dr. Hodgkin, in writing of the Roman emperors, has called " spiritual vertigo." There is only one Claimant to world kingship who could successfully resist the temptation to do homage to the forces of evil. The supernational groups that we have been examining probably represent the largest aggregations of

area and population that can be held together within one
political system, even if the federal character of that system
provides for a large measure of local autonomy. The British
Empire has developed into a permanent alliance of States
with no central machinery for deliberation or action—a
League of Nations with no Assembly, and only the germ
of a Council in the periodical conferences of the Prime
Ministers of the constituent States.

There is one direction in which the League of Nations
already exercises something like sovereign authority. The
administration of the former German Colonies and the
liberated provinces of the Turkish Empire was entrusted to
various Powers under a system of Mandate, as " a sacred
trust for civilisation." The Permanent Mandates Commission of the League receives an annual report from each
Mandatory Power, which is supplemented by a *questionnaire*. These Mandates are of three kinds. Mandate A. refers
to Iraq, Syria, and Palestine, and entrusts to the Mandatory Power " the rendering of administrative advice and
assistance until such time as these communities are able
to stand alone." The British Mandate for Iraq has already
ended, and it is expected that the French Mandate for
Syria will soon be finished. Six of the German Colonies are
entrusted to Great Britain, France, and Belgium under
Mandate B., which provides for the administration of the
territory under conditions that guarantee freedom of
conscience and religion, and equal commercial opportunities for all nations. There remain a few less-developed
territories that are entrusted, under Mandate C., to various
powers, to be administered under the laws of the Mandatory Power as an integral portion of its territory. In all
cases the welfare of the inhabitants is to be the first consideration of the Mandatory Power. The mandated
peoples have the right to petition against any infraction of
the terms of the Mandate, and such petition the Mandatory
Power is obliged to transmit, with its observations thereon,
to the Permanent Commission. The importance of all
this is that certain territories are recognised as under

international control, to be protected against exploitation by the vigilance of the League. I have already said that a subordinate tribunal for dealing with specifically European questions would strengthen the League by leaving it free to devote itself to world problems. The people of China or of Peru are not really interested in the problem of the Polish Corridor or that of the frontiers of Hungary, and the Manchurian crisis illustrates the dangers that arise from the disproportional attention that the League has given to European affairs. If the League Assembly could sometimes meet elsewhere than in Geneva—and the improvement of communications may ere long make this possible— a meeting at Delhi or Nanking or Ottawa would give imaginative expression to the universal scope of the mission to which the League is consecrated. It is a profound mistake to underestimate the value of symbolism and " colour " in an organisation that depends for its success on romance and high adventure. At present the League Assembly presents the somewhat uninspiring appearance of a meeting of shareholders in a moderately successful international banking business ! Nationalism, with its flags and anthems, has inspired much of the greatest poetry of the world ; and even the sombre spectacle of the House of Commons in session has a romantic background of historical associations. Need the " Red Flag " be the only marching-song of human brotherhood ?

ECONOMIC INSECURITY

It may be said that before we can build up a new world-order, we must leave time for the after-swell of the war to subside. But is there time ? The danger of the present situation is that if one nation loses patience it may throw a bomb into Europe that may set the world ablaze again. It is this feeling of instability that is undermining confidence and leading to a *sauve qui peut* that finds expression in the effort of every nation to build up barriers of economic isolation. The economic confusion of the world is dealt with in another essay, but in its bearing on international relationships it belongs to the inquiry in which we are engaged. In eastern Europe, tariffs have become the weapons of political animosities, and in the West they represent the desire of each nation to safeguard its economic stability in entire disregard of any injury that it may inflict on other nations. It is claimed that our present tariff system will enable us to bargain with other nations for a general reduction of tariffs, and in so far as this is the case, we may accept the reversal of our traditional policy as a contribution to the economic recovery of Europe. The economic interdependence of the world ought to be an asset for world peace, for, next to military rivalry, what Dr. Starr Jordan calls " the tyranny of the frontier " is " the heaviest burden borne by exhausted Europe." " The United States represents the greatest trade area in the world ; her federated States can impose no tax or tariff on imports from other states and her cities no *octroi* at their gates. Hence her internal commerce is open and friendly, no State uprising against another, because all have common interests."

State-controlled education may prove a powerful instrument for perpetuating ill-will and international disunion. Even before the war, historical text-books often distorted the facts of history in the interest of patriotic self-aggrandisement. It is right that children should be taught to love their motherland, and honour the memory of the men and women who have served her, but the exclusive patriotism that regards all other peoples as potential enemies is out of place in a world that is facing towards a future in which service, not domination, shall be the measure of national greatness.

SECURITIES FOR PEACE

The difficulty of providing adequate safeguards for peace is illustrated by the fate of the Geneva Protocol of 1924, presented to the League by the Prime Ministers of Great Britain and France. " The object of the Protocol was to point a certain way of determining the aggressor in any international dispute and closing up every gap in the mechanism of the pacific settlement of international disputes. For this purpose it had to assign to the Council of the League of Nations powers over the heads of the States and make available for the carrying into effect of the mediatory or judicial decisions coercive measures which were tantamount to a collective warlike employment of force."

From various Powers, and especially from the British Dominions, objections were made to these proposals, and in the United States they were regarded with disfavour. In their place, Mr. Kellogg proposed what was afterwards called the Pact of Paris, in which the signatory Powers declared that they renounced war as an instrument of policy against one another. But the reservations made by various Powers in adhering to the Pact greatly weakened its value as a security for peace.

In criticising the Protocol, American publicists pointed out that the American Supreme Court had no power of enforcing its decisions on the States of the Union, yet the States had (except at the time of the Civil War) accepted those decisions. The greater part of the system of international law that has grown up in the last century rests on no sanction except the general moral sense of the civilised world. At present a somewhat precarious security for peace is provided by the recognition that war does not pay. The economic poverty and confusion from which the world is suffering, and the failure of the peace treaties to solve the problems of Europe, have brought home to men the futility of the idea that even a successful war can be anything less than a disaster. This does not mean that no good has come from the late war. The creation of Czechoslovakia, the restoration of Poland, and the liberation of Iraq, Syria, and Palestine from Turkish rule, are among the gains to be set against the destruction of human life and resources that has left Europe impoverished and embittered. One thing at least is certain : in view of the war debts and reparations fiasco, no nation is likely in the future to be able to borrow money for war, or obtain credits for armaments.

No inquiry into international relationships can be

complete without some attempt to consider the moral assumptions on which they rest. Ever since the religious wars of the seventeenth century were followed by wars for territorial aggrandisement, the foreign policy of the European nations has been frankly realistic. What this realism means may be seen from Sir Raymond Beazley's recent book on *The Road to Ruin in Europe*. However clumsy and unscrupulous we may regard the policy of the statesmen of Germany, the attempt to throw upon them the whole responsibility for the war will not be ratified by the impartial judgment of history. In a world where every nation was exclusively occupied in the promotion of its own interests, distrust in any other security than armed force created a situation of which war was the inevitable end. It is not just to lay the blame for all this on the diplomatists and political leaders ; any Government that adopted a more generous attitude towards the aspirations of other nations would have been condemned by the public opinion of its own nation for betraying the interests of the country. International policy is one of the departments of public life in which religion neither played, nor claimed to play, any part. Yet, in the long run, a frank disregard of Christian moral principle in public life is bound to react on the standards of conduct of personal relationships. No doubt every nation finds excuses for the tortuous character of its foreign policy. Some years before the war, I said to a German student of politics that we in England regarded our foreign policy as rather stupid but entirely honest. His reply was : " I think you are quite wrong ; we think your foreign policy brilliantly clever and entirely unscrupulous ! " The only real security for peace is a change of heart. Meanwhile, some subordinate securities may be mentioned. If the peoples of the world are sincere in their desire for peace, it ought to be possible to secure an international agreement to refuse to recognise any territorial or other advantages won by war. The difficulties in the way of this suggestion might be very great, but they would not often be insuperable. Another acid test of the sincerity of the desire of the nations for peace is the prohibition of the export of arms to prospective belligerents. The traffic in arms ought to be as much under international control as the traffic in drugs. It is something like hypocrisy for the nations to use all the available methods of conciliation to avert the outbreak of war between two nations, who, all the while. are being supplied with weapons of war by the armament firms of these same nations.

GROUNDS OF HOPE

Our chief ground of hope is that men are beginning to recognise that the real problem of the age is not political or economic but spiritual. The distrust of organisations, which is characteristic of the outlook of the younger generation, is not necessarily a sign of despair, it may be a sign of the recognition that the redemption of the world-order will be achieved not by the readjustment of institutions but by the regeneration of the human heart.

> *We may not hope from outward forms to win*
> *The passion and the life, whose fountains are within.*

There is a danger in this, for if new wine is wasted in the effort to pour it into old wineskins, not less is it wasted if no wineskins are ready to hold it. Perhaps our greatest need is that our political and religious organisations shall become flexible enough to welcome and express the spiritual ideals of the new generation. In their relation with the individual, States, like Churches, are liable to become rigid and unadaptable, and to regard passive obedience as the first duty of the citizen. Governments are generally, though perhaps only half consciously, jealous of voluntary organisations that challenge their monopoly of public service. Yet surely Thoreau was right when he said, " There will never be a really free and enlightened State until the State comes to recognise the individual as a higher and independent power from which all its own power is derived, and treats him accordingly." Humanity is not a community of nations, but a community of individuals, with many points of contact outside official national relationships. Closer intercourse between the peoples of the world is bringing home to men a new consciousness of the unreality of the barriers of separation that national antagonisms have built up. Even during the war individual contacts between enemies constantly counteracted mass hatreds. The truth is, men cannot share common experiences without being drawn together. It is the antagonisms, not the friendships, of men that are unnatural. The *Zeitgeist* does not discourage fraternisation, though the brass-hats of political tradition may regard it with disfavour. It is in this larger world of human relationships that nationality will find its true meaning. In the words of Professor Zimmern : " This is the true function of the nation, to make men conscious of the nature and quality of their inward heritage and powers, to help them to know themselves and to find themselves, and so to win faith and strength to spend themselves for their fellow-countrymen and the world."

It is only the doctrine of the inalienable value of the individual, growing in worth as he finds a way of self-expression in voluntary associations that rest on a broadly human basis, that will enable Europe to meet the challenge of Bolshevism with its almost oriental denial of the inherent right of every man to be himself. While we think of men in masses, moved by common impulses of distrust and rivalry, the best that we can do is to devise means to avert collisions. But the atoms that make up these masses are also in contact with one another within a larger system, and every man is a citizen of the world as well as of his own country. The Mussulman religion owes much of its success to the fact that it has been able to develop this sense of a larger fellowship that transcends national limitations, but its static character precludes it from ever becoming a world-religion. Christianity still remains the only religion that is able to consecrate all human relationships, reaching through family, civic, and national loyalties to the Catholic loyalty of a universal brotherhood of all men in the incarnate manhood of the Son of God.

PART II

WHAT CHRISTIANITY IS

I. THE SECRET OF CHRIST

By Professor CHARLES E. RAVEN

IN FACING the crisis which now seems to forebode the collapse of our civilisation the Christian has one ground for confidence denied to all those who do not share his faith : his fellow-believers have been through a similar experience in the past and have not only survived it but been the sole means by which the glory of the previous age was preserved and Western culture eventually rebuilt. Mr. Chesterton is not as a rule a reliable historian : if he does not deliberately sacrifice fact to epigram, he very certainly distorts it in the interest of dogma. But he is more than justified in his insistence that, whereas the " new " fads and philosophies are old and discredited by failure, Christianity has triumphed over one cataclysm and may well triumph over another.

It is indeed no small testimony to the supremacy of religion that when " the captains and the kings depart " it is the prophet and the saint who alone possess survival-value. The inhabitants of Babylon or of Memphis would have found it hard to believe that out of their imperial pomp the only living relics would be the utterances of an obscure tribe upon their frontiers ; that Nebuchadnezzar's name would be lost to all save expert archæologists but for its mention in the Hebrew scriptures ; that Jeremiah and the unnamed prophet of the exile (of whom they had certainly never heard) would live eternally when fortresses and hanging gardens were unidentifiable dust.

In the fall of the Roman Empire there is not only the same significance, but, from its similarity to our own crisis, and thanks to the aseptic influence of Christianity, a far clearer lesson. The treasures of Greece and Rome have not shared the fate of Egypt or Assyria because the scholars of Islam and the monks of the Church Catholic saw fit to perpetuate the knowledge of them. Had there not been schools and monasteries created by the faith of barbarian fisherman and camel-driver, Greek philosophy and Roman law, all the splendid humanism in which we are now bidden to put our trust, might well have perished without memorial. Thanks to the religious, we can study, for our warning and comfort, the causes of the downfall and the influence of the communities by which it was partially retrieved.

There is warning in the story, for pagan and Christian alike. Moral corruption, such as neither Stoic virtue nor mythic cult could cure, was as evident in the world of Petronius as in that of Mr. Wyndham Lewis : " Their women did change the natural use into that which is against nature : the men burned in their lust one towards another, men with men working that which is unseemly "—the apostle's rebuke is strong, but its justice can hardly be denied. Economic folly, the exploitation of enslaved populations, the creation of an urban proletariat, the crushing out of farmers and the middle class, the trustification of wealth, the loss of civic idealism and political interest—these things undermined the stability of the Roman Empire as they are imperilling the empires of to-day. Art that apes the primitive in its sculpture and the degenerate in its music ; philosophy that swings from scepticism to superstition ; ethics that confuse licence with liberty and lust with love ; these are powerless to lift the courage or restore the resources of mankind. There is no vision—and the people perish ; no confidence—and co-operation becomes impossible ; no hope—and man's only course is to eat and drink, for to-morrow we die.

Yet for the Christian there is warning also. When in the first splendour of their new life the early disciples went out into the world, their influence ran " like sparks through the stubble." Here were men who had passed from death into life because they loved their brethren ; men who had found a clean joy, an inward peace, and an outward fortitude ; men who could rise above the changes and chances of mortality into the realm of worship by way of sublimation, not of escape, who were everywhere at home because they had broken the thraldom of material possessions, who went forth conquering and to conquer because they had passed beyond death and been set free from fear and pride. For a little while they came near to transforming the character of the times and renewing the youth of the world. But circumstances proved too strong for them. Gradually they experienced the fate of the dyer's hand, alive still but saturated with the materials in which they worked ; and the dye was corrosive and paralysing. In the effort to overcome moral corruption an unhealthy prominence was given to sexual abstinence ; Tertullian the Sadist and Augustine the convert from debauchery and Manicheism voice for us the morbid horror not only of lust but of wedded love. In the attempt to formulate a Christian philosophy the emphasis was transferred from the ethical to the physical, from God as Father to God as the Absolute. In striving against the kingdoms of the world, a hierarchy and a kingly Church were as useful for the warriors of Christ as for those of Israel in the time of Saul ; and the prophet's voice of Montanus or of Origen was less effective than that of Samuel. When the pagan State ceased to persecute, Ulphilas the Arian might risk martyrdom as evangelist of the Goths, but Anthony or Simeon sought it rather in solitude or on a pillar. Fauns and virgin goddesses, festivals and pilgrimages, relics and thaumaturgy, the law of nations and the speculations of the schools were incorporated into Christianity, renamed but not christened. The Church stood up against the deluge and was not swept away : but its character was sadly altered in the struggle.

Here then is our comfort. One single institution, itself the greatest creative force in our world, remains out of the last collapse of a civilisation. We can see why its success was only partial and by what steps its original influence was distorted. If we can study these matters open-eyed, it ought to be possible both to recover the essential quality of the Christian faith and to secure that if the Church is to undergo another dark age it shall profit by past experience and avoid those compromises and lapses which of old dissipated its regenerative power and impaired the value of its achievement.

What then is Christianity ? What the secret of abundant life to which the *graffiti* of the Catacombs, and the poetry of the *Ad Diognetum*, not less than the fortitude of saints and martyrs bear evident witness ?

There is a symbolic episode in the Fourth Gospel which may serve to indicate an answer. Jesus in Galilee at the social meal which we call the Feeding of the Five Thousand had initiated his followers by that simple rite into avowed discipleship. They acknowledged his leadership even if misunderstanding its character, and wished to make him king. To them he gives a warning and two explicit commands— utterances which, as is the evangelists' habit, epitomise the long process of training described in the other records : " Ye seek me not because you understand the meaning of my ministry but because you desire its material advantages." The Kingdom is " not eating and drinking, but righteousness and peace and joy in the spirit of holiness " : you must not exploit religion in the interests of human welfare, or " make of God a tame confederate, purveyor to your appetites." That is a danger against which apostles and churchmen had constantly to be on their guard : when Constantine's conversion gave riches and power, the warning went almost unheeded.

He follows the warning by precept. " Labour not for the meat that perishes but for that which endures on into eternal life," enforces the same lesson in positive form. As a lesson it is not new. Aristotle, earth-bound as he often is, had bidden men live to the uttermost of their power for deathless ends. His great forerunners had set in contrast the phenomenal and the real, the passing and the permanent ; and had laid down clear definitions by which man could discriminate between them. Still more explicit had been the teaching of the Hebrew prophets ; for in them the service of God had taken the place which the great Greeks gave to enlightenment and justice, and the emphasis had been rather upon moral worth than upon intellectual discipline.

The lesson had not been new : but Jesus had given it a new significance. For he had followed the method rather of the poet than of the philosopher or even of the prophet. His aim had been not to define the eternal or to proclaim it, but to reveal it and infect men with the experience of it. He bade men open their eyes to the beauty and the meaning of the ephemeral that in it they might apprehend the divine ; he disclosed to them the presence of the Father amid the suffering and splendour of his creatures ; by the quality of his own life he drew them beyond the prison of the senses to a realm in which selfishness and cowardice shrivelled away. Knowledge of God, manifested not by argument nor by admonition, but by example and in the doing of simple acts, came to his followers as a way of life. They grew sensitive to the reality of God's reign ; found themselves living within its dominion ; were liberated by it from snobbishness and slavery into fellowship and an energy of power. Those who under the inspiration of a great love or through the nearness of their own deaths have been set free from self-regard will know the exaltation alike of detachment and of sympathy with which for a time they return to earth—how contempt gives place to pity, and envy to appreciation, and the common is no longer the unclean. With us such moods pass with what occasions them : with his disciples Jesus sought to make them a possession for ever.

His second precept shows the mode by which this quality of permanence was attained. Faced with the call to live for the eternal, his hearers made inquiry : "What shall we do ?" They, like ourselves, perhaps supposed that religion consisted in particular actions, in church-going or alms-giving, fasting, and prayers. Those who think the eternal a subject fit only for mystics or philosophers will gladly echo their question. Let us at all costs be practical.

To them the reply must come with something of a shock : " This is the work of God that ye believe on him whom he hath sent." Does it seem a piece of pious platitude such as generations of liturgical convention have made familiar ? Or of unbounded egoism, as the contrast between God and

Fc

man, however noble a man, strikes home ? How can the
quest of humanity for religion be so simply and immediately
accomplished ? Who is this Messiah, who claims not only to
have been sent but to express the very quality of God ? Such
a claim was blasphemy even to the Jew of the first century :
can it be less to us, so much more clearly aware of the infinite scale and complexity of the universe ?

Yet it is this precept, far more than the other, that is the
essential novelty of Christ's religion. Men before him had
found eternal worth in beauty or in the moral law or in the
majestic order of creation. They had set up symbols of the
divine in sacred tree and sacred beast, in statue and emblem;
they had striven to control it by magic and cultus, to pro-
pitiate or to adore ; they had mythologised and speculated
and defined and codified. God must be given form by
imagery and rites, by creeds and systems of conduct :
man's artistry, his intellect, his conscience must each play a
part in the expression of religion. Jesus, using all of them in
their appropriate places, yet goes far beyond them. For him
reality is not impersonal but living, not first cause nor
creative force but Father. If so, then in nothing can he be
fully known to mankind save in the person of the Son of
Man. Life, the life of a person, is the whole, of which art
and reason and goodness are but parts. It is in the whole not
in its aspects and derivatives that the living will find their
fullest interpretation of the eternal. We may not choose for
our concept of God anything lower than the highest that
we know : that is idolatry ; it is the error of those who explain God in terms of starry heavens or moral law or any
impersonal or sub-personal concept. We cannot choose anything higher than personality ; for it is from persons that all
our knowledge, art, and ethics are derived. It may be that
for other beings or in other worlds God in Man is not
enough : we are men, and being such must treat the suggestion as irrelevant. We are on secure ground when we
assert that, being what we are, we can best know God in the
most exalted of our fellows, and that not only or chiefly in
his words or works but in the quality of his person.

Such a claim could be argued philosophically : so to state it is the business of the theologian. For our purpose a simpler indication of its validity will suffice.

It is a true instinct which induces mankind to personify the objects of his interest ; in his childhood to impute life to his playthings and to populate the garden with elves and ogres ; and in maturity to represent his country as a gracious woman and his city as a queen crowned with towers. He expects to find himself in a fellowship of persons : only in adolescence does he consent to solitude among the inanimate, and, if his development is arrested, comes to prefer dead stuff to living friends. Always there is a sense of imprisonment ; he cannot find on the material plane any full satisfaction ; he yearns to escape from it, and, in his highest moments, becomes suddenly aware that it is indeed not dead but pulsing with a tense and joyous life. In the full-grown man this conviction of the vital, organic, and personal quality of the universe is widely different from the naïve animism of child or savage : nor is it akin to the so-called pathetic fallacy which sees nature as ministering to his individual needs and vanities. It is rather an overwhelming experience of a presence not identifiable with clouds and mountains, but manifested in them, and bearing the same relationship to the physical order as a man's personality bears to the cells of his bodily structure. Those moments when the world comes to life and we find ourselves in communion with its indwelling deity are no fantasy of poetic imagination—though it is to the poets that we rightly go for the plainest evidence ; they are native to every human being who has grown up through a normal range of activity and suffering. St. Francis, and Wordsworth, Shelley, and Browning interpret them for us : but multitudes of simple folk, battered but not subdued by the clamour of the senses, have entered the presence-chamber and found themselves at home with God. It is a curious inconsistency in a great thinker that Professor Whitehead, who appeals from the mathematicians and philosophers to the poets for testimony, should still perversely claim that religious experience gives no secure ground for belief in the personality of the divine. He would seem to ignore the fact that if the Buddhist attitude towards nature is valid against the saints of the West it is not less valid against its poets.

It is this conviction that the essential character of the universe cannot be described in lower than personal terms which underlies the basal claim of religion that man is made in the image of God. No one who has experienced the communion which underlies that claim will suppose that it involves any belief that God is an individual, whose ways are those of humanity, or that in itself it deserves the taunt of anthropomorphism. What it maintains is that any concept of reality in lower categories is an idolatry ; that materialism is as foolish as fetish-worship and the *élan vital* a fit companion for the bull or the seraph; and that man, for whom some symbol of the infinite is inevitable, will find it not in a mathematical formula or by biological analogy but in the highest region of our human experience, the region of personality. The whole cannot be less than its parts, nor God lower than the highest known to us of his creatures.

It is this poet's sense of the presence that Jesus, as we have seen, possessed supremely and revealed to his followers. But he went further. Having trained them to see the eternal in flower and bird, sowing and harvest, he submitted to them the parable of himself ; and accepted their confession that God, partially manifested in nature and the works of man, was supremely and uniquely present in his Christ. Such confession, wrung from them by the evidence, and despite their fiercest prejudices, involved not only the discovery of a worthier " sacrament " of deity, but a vast enlargement of the possibilities of worship and communion. So long as God is pictured in non-human terms, worship falls short of love, and communion is a poorer thing than fellowship. It can possess none of that intimacy and power of inspiration which only the contact of person with person can attain. The discovery of God in his Christ raised religion to a level hitherto wholly unknown ; that which had been imagined of

Moses, that he spoke with the Lord as a man speaks with his friend, was now no dream ; adoration which could always elevate could now transform.

Here then is the secret. Mankind had previously learnt to fear God, to contemplate and study and obey : but his highest energy, the love that can only be given by person to person, had never been confidently exercised in religion. For man cannot love the infinite, nor such symbols of it as had hitherto been offered—calf of gold or mythical hero, celestial potentate or metaphysical abstraction. Very small acquaintance either with one's fellows or with history demonstrates that those whose ideal is embodied in a person find in it a power that transfigures and inspires. That we dramatise and personify abstractions like country or city, that we claim to love the inanimate, be it a flag or an arm-chair, these are indications of the bent of our desires : only in love for a person can the highest human devotion be expressed. That is why every community must have its figurehead, and why, when a Lenin or a Mussolini arises, his followers astonish the world by their dynamic achievements. It is only when man's two noblest endowments—his quest for perfection and his capacity for love—can be united, that he can reach fullness of life. Incarnate deity, evoking and satisfying both of these, can give and has indeed given to us opportunity to integrate and sublimate our own imperfect natures, and to recognise and fulfil and transcend our highest aspirations for individual and social life.

It lies beyond the scope of this paper to set out the arguments for the divinity of Christ or to outline the effect of such belief upon philosophy or sociology. Two points may be briefly made.

The experience which led the earliest disciples to claim and the patristic Church to formulate the faith that Jesus was incarnate God has been repeated in successive ages and very notably in our own day. His own challenge : " What think ye of Christ ? Whose son is he ? " must be answered. The first century might reply with a variety of descriptive titles—supreme prophet, giver of the new law, lord of the true mysteries, word and wisdom of God, first-born of all creation, image of the eternal : each had its value ; each was proved insufficient. Our own age has seen a similar succession of honest attempts to categorise and classify : Harnack and the Ritzschlians, Schweitzer and the students of Apocalyptic, Montefiore and the Rabbinists, Bousset and the students of the Mystery Religions—these and many others have striven to set Jesus in an appropriate frame. Often it has seemed (for a moment) as if the final word had been spoken, as if at last a true definition had been fixed, as if (since to define is to transcend) Jesus was now laid in a grave. Always fuller study has proved the frame insufficient : he is too large to be so disposed of : he rises from the dead, and the search begins again.

Secondly, if this uniqueness of quality links him with the infinite and constrains the confession, " My Lord and my God," that belief cannot leave unaffected any department of the believer's thought and life. A universe, a humanity, which can contain Jesus, cannot be what it might be if he had no existence. Our judgment upon the creative process, upon the physical world and the laws that govern it, cannot be the same if we acknowledge him. We cannot cut up our thinking into departments and discover any final truth about the several parts without reference to the whole. The test of truth in any branch of study consists ultimately in the discovery that such truth is valid over the whole range of the knowable. In that range the fact of Jesus is a vital datum ; and so must eventually enter into every department of our activity. Men have argued that there can be no such thing as Christian economics, that to talk of Christian mathematics or Christian physics is absurd. Such argument involves a belief in the permanence of watertight compartments, a denial of the unity of truth. No doubt the isolated phenomenon is a convenience for study : no doubt we must analyse and delimit and concentrate. But it must be remembered always that such isolation is fictitious, and that if we would see reality as it is we must strive to see it as a whole. The world of thought is strewn with the wreckage of theories formulated upon too narrow a selection of evidence : the world of human affairs is in its present chaos for want of a wide enough synthesis.

Subsequent chapters will illustrate the contentions here outlined, and present an ordered attempt to demonstrate the relevance of Christ to the ideas and actions of to-day, to expand our appreciation of what faith in him involves, and to trace its influence upon the practical issues of the age. The present essay aims only at indicating the primary reason for the survival-value of Christianity and at maintaining that, if it is man's joy and duty to live eternally, he can best do so by believing " on him whom God hath sent."

2. CHRIST'S CONCEPTION OF THE KINGDOM OF GOD

By Dr. A. HERBERT GRAY

I. THE FAILURE TO UNDERSTAND CHRIST

Jesus Christ claimed to have a message of Redemption which would save the world. Yet it is plain that Christianity as Europe and America know it has not saved the world. The crisis that now confronts us has revealed a certain instability in the whole structure of our society. Millions are threatened with starvation in a world of plenty. For great multitudes of mankind the way into any full and satisfying life is not open. Misery and perplexity overcloud our existence. Assuredly we are not saved.

Christianity has been preached for nineteen centuries. If it has saving value for mankind it should in that period have done its work. It has been on trial for a long time. The Churches that claim to represent it have attained to great size and have gained considerable power and authority. Christ, as men have conceived him, has been offered to the world. And yet chaos and acute suffering confront us on every hand. In the worlds of commerce, industry, and finance confusion reigns. It is hardly better in the world of morals. There is much to be said for the proposition that the human race is astray. Men in general lack a clear sense of the significance of our existence, and confess that they know not what they do nor why they do it.

And yet Christ claimed to know the way that leads to life, both for men and for nations.

Some will take the view that Christ was deluded, and that the centuries which have passed since his day have simply exposed the fact that his teaching is unsuited to real life.

Others will insist that mankind has been confronted with Christ's offer, have so far understood it, and yet, because of the hardness of their hearts, have deliberately rejected it.

But though in any case there is an element of truth in that second position, there is a third view which must be faced. Perhaps Christ has throughout these centuries been very largely misunderstood. Perhaps the Churches have misrepresented him. Perhaps what men have rejected was not the real Christianity of Christ, but something partially counterfeit.

This third view is undeniably true in large measure. No one has ever fully understood Christ. Obviously the disciples themselves failed in part to understand him. Though St. Paul had such a profound experience of Christ, it is yet beyond all question that he has in some measure misrepresented him. And of the Churches it has to be admitted that at times they have so pitifully failed to be true to him, that they have come very near to apostasy—and that again and again. What has been offered to mankind in many countries and at many times has been only a caricature of the saving truth that is in Christ. Christ has never yet come into his own.

Yet the very pressure of our present distress might well constrain us to a fresh effort to understand him. We have such need to find the true way of life, and he claims with such strange persuasiveness to be able to tell us of it. We needs must try afresh. We may know that we shall not completely succeed. We are too small for his greatness. But we must try, for we are far astray.

II. WHY WE SHOULD BELIEVE HIM

If we are to reach the real truth that is in Christ we must go back—back from our present-day conventions—back through Protestantism with its complicated theologies—back past the Middle Ages—past the apostles—past even St. Paul, till we come to the Man of Nazareth. It is not the Christ of the Creeds we seek, it is that peasant prophet, who speaks with a voice that constrains attention.

This is not the place to deal thoroughly with the question, " Why should we believe him ? " But one thing must be said. The only sufficient answer is that he himself creates

belief in those who listen to him. He is his own credential.
No argument which tries to compel belief in Christ by dwelling on his miracles, or on the special manner of his entering
the world or of leaving it, can really establish him as an
authority over men's hearts. Even supposing the facts
could now be clearly ascertained, they would not carry the
conclusion aimed at. The fact that Christ could perform
what men call miracles would not prove him a reliable
guide for practical life, unless the secret of those special
powers lay in his goodness, which brings us back to the
fact that we believe in Jesus of Nazareth because he was the
kind of person who compels belief—because we cannot
resist the moral and spiritual power which is so manifest
in all his words and acts.

Those who go to him to listen are conscious of a strange
difference between the world that he created about himself,
and what we know as the religious world. Jesus conducted
no services. He gave out no hymns. Stranger still, we do not
read that he led his friends in audible prayer. He taught no
metaphysical theology. He built up no organisation. He did
not create a solemn air about himself. Men who were with
him were not conscious of any restraint or fear, except
perhaps on one or two special occasions.

For the most part, what we would have found, had we
been there, was a group of friends and one in their midst
who talked with a quiet voice. He used the language of the
people, because he was determined to reach them, and in
his illustrations he never left the familiar world of everyday
life. He spoke to them of God, and of the unchanging truths
on which life depends. Yet he thought so clearly that his
talk seems quite simple. And the intense and penetrating
power of his speech, which has made his words immortal,
all came from the intense dynamic quality of a perfectly
harmonised personality. Being entirely sincere and selfless,
he saw the truth with such clarity that his words are like
wireless waves of high potency which reach to the inner
regions of human hearts everywhere.

III. WHAT DID JESUS TEACH?

a. *That God is Love*

What, then, did Jesus say? First of all that God is love. The great religious geniuses of his nation had come very near to that truth, so that Christians use with gratitude for devotional purposes some of their psalms, and great prophetic utterances. But the nation as a whole had never discarded the primitive ideas of God which are in other parts of the Old Testament. The sacrificial system was still in operation. The idea still lived that God is pleased with the blood of sheep and oxen, and that by such sacrifices his just anger may be averted. He was, to the Jew, a God who needed to be propitiated, and a God who would accept substitutes. More definitely still, God was conceived as a great law-giver who demanded an absolute obedience to a ceremonial law, so elaborate that only specialists could master it, which worked out into details that were petty and even ridiculous. This law was not obeyed by the mass of the people, but it was conventionally believed in, and the unfulfilled obligation to obey it overclouded life and caused the thought of God to be an unwelcome thought. Jewish religion in fact was bringing neither joy nor liberty into life. It did nothing to disperse men's natural fears, but tended rather to increase them.

Into that dark world, Jesus brought the simple and liberating message that God is love—that he loves and values all men, not merely collectively but one by one, regarding even a child as of infinite worth. The truth is not that God will love us if and when we become good, but that he loves us now and as we are. He never had needed to be propitiated. He asked for neither sacrifices nor substitutionary victims. He did not make it a condition of his favour that the law should be obeyed. He loved men even while they were uncontrolled sinners. He had been waiting from all time with unconditional forgiveness ready for men so soon as they should turn to him. The only doctrine of atonement that Jesus preached is in the parable of the

Prodigal Son. God is like a father, who, having two sons, one a prodigal and the other a prig, yet " went out " to them both and won them by love.

Many of the prophets, like many preachers of later days, had tried to compel people towards virtue by first frightening them. Lurid doctrines of hell fire were common in Christ's day, and have had recurrent popularity ever since. For the delusion still lingers that people can be made good by fear. But Jesus did not attempt to achieve conversions by the way of terror. He never indulged in wholesale condemnations of men and women. The preachers who delight to call us all " hell-deserving sinners " may be right, but Jesus was not among their number. To the scandal of the religious people of his day, he insisted on making friends of the loose profligates he met. He could be infinitely tender to women who had made sad mistakes in the world of passion. He even loved a rich aristocrat who had some of the poison of covetousness in him. He saw some divine value in social outcasts. For the ordinary men whom the priests condemned, and society despised, he had words of appreciation and hope. By his whole daily conduct, as well as in explicit words, he declared that God is not a terrible spirit at all. Only the word love even suggests the truth about him. He is a love that seeks men and waits to set them free.

And so the timid began to take courage, and the depressed began to hope. From that whole sense of inferiority and self distrust which the world had induced in most people, Jesus set them free. Even the weak souls who had let themselves become stained and defiled learnt to believe that clean and happy life was still possible for them. That was the method of Jesus in redemption. He used love to drive evil out of men, and those who responded to him really were saved ; for love was kindled in them in turn, and thus they found their real life.

Those who listen to Christ to-day are apt to be surprised by the prominence in his recorded sayings of words about the sabbath. The issue raised is apt to seem a little unreal to us. We are not shocked because the Pharisees held Jesus to be a sabbath-breaker. But there was a vitally important point involved in that controversy. The ceremonial law about the sabbath had developed until it was in open conflict with the law of kindness. So the Pharisees held it to be irreligious of Jesus to heal on the sabbath. And that kindled the indignation of Jesus because it seriously misrepresented God. The law of kindness was to Jesus, who knew God, the supreme law. That the sabbath law or any other ceremonial law should be allowed to challenge its working was a thing intolerable. In the name of God such profanity had to be exposed and denounced. For the operations of love override all other interests.

For the same reason Jesus did not call for a revision of the Jewish law so much as simply neglect it. It belonged to a different world from that in which he moved. It was irrelevant to life as he saw life. His attitude really declared, concerning the law and all the meticulous controversies it excited, " There is a complete mistake behind all this. God is not like that. He is a father and you are his children. He invites you to share a family life with him, and in his family love rules—not legal requirements." The instinct of the scribes, Pharisees, and Sadducees concerning Jesus was quite correct. If he should prevail, their day was over.

This truth that God is love and nothing but love has never been fully received, rejoiced in, and acted on. St. Paul knew it and lived in the power of it. But so strong was the hold on his mind of pre-Christian ideas of God that he could only arrive at the conclusion that he was free to trust the love of God, by first thinking out an elaborate doctrine of atonement expressed in the old terms of sacrifice, propitiation, and substitution. He set himself an impossible task, for the truth about love can never be truly expressed by the use of terms which belong essentially to the law courts.

No doubt St. Paul's doctrine must have helped others who shared his presuppositions to arrive at a belief in the free grace of God. To others it has proved a serious stumbling-block. To us to-day it is in part offensive, and in part superfluous. It is offensive because, as the logicians work it out, it implies a God who would not forgive until a substitute for guilty man had been found, and so suggests a God profanely like Shylock. And it is superfluous, because if God is love of course he forgives, for forgiveness is the divine prerogative of love.

In the process of forgiveness love pays a great price. It cannot rescue sinners by condoning sin, for that would mean leaving sinners in their bondage. It can only deliver by first sharing the shame of sin, which must mean facing agony, which is surely the explanation of the bloody sweat in Gethsemane. But, by enduring that agony, love gains its victories. It attains the power to draw sinners into its cleansing and life-giving fellowship. It wins by proving itself stronger than sin. It can outlast and out-suffer the most violent and offensive assertions of evil.

For those who understand love even a little, and who believe that God is love, there remains no need of any explanation of how God is able to forgive. He does it because he is love. It is this truth in its simplicity and its majesty that is needed to save the world. No other can rescue a world cursed by greed and passion. Christianity has not saved us, because this central truth of it has always in some way or other been obscured. Men have been afraid to believe anything so perfect. It has seemed too good to be true ; even though the suggestion that ANYTHING can possibly be too good to be true is the most profane which can possibly be made.

It would be a good thing if only graduates in the school of Christ were allowed to read the Old Testament. I would like to have it forbidden to children, except in some severely expurgated edition. For though the development of the idea of God does in the Old Testament attain to sublime heights, yet the earlier parts of it present ideas of God which are quite shocking. Once such ideas have possessed the mind of a child it is almost impossible to escape from them. Even Mr. Bernard Shaw does not seem quite to have escaped from the God of Noah, who liked the smell of burning venison. At least, he still thinks it worth while to ridicule him.

The God whom Jesus revealed has been offered to minds already poisoned by stories of the god of battles, or by the conception of a law-giver, very fussy about details, or by the horrors implied in a doctrine of everlasting punishment. And the result is that many people never escape from that poison, and so fail to find the Father. With their conscious minds they may repudiate all pre-Christian or sub-Christian ideas of God, and yet in fact they remain haunted. Many are so puzzled by the whole matter that it seems to them the best way of escape would be to believe in no God at all. Therefore they set themselves to find ingenious reasons for resting in that impossible position, and so enter on the dry places of agnosticism, where they wander seeking rest and finding none.

If the world is to be set free to find its true life, this truth about the love of God must be fully and simply received. Our essential need is to have creative joy released in our midst. While we remain partially paralysed by gloomy and terrible thoughts of God, we cannot find our true happiness, cannot be reconciled to each other, cannot attain to our true power. For fear always depresses. Joy alone creates energy. The arts demand the free airs of a joyous world if they are to escape from their present stagnation, and become truly creative. All the elements of superstition, and all the many kinds of fear which still cheapen our lives and induce cruelty will disappear when men know God as Jesus showed him ; but not until then.

It may be objected that Jesus was stern towards the Pharisees. There was certainly a passion of indignation in his heart as he dwelt in thought on many of their ways. Some of his denunciations ring in the world to this day with a note of iron severity. It has therefore been suggested that Jesus did not love the Pharisees. But real love can be stern. Love that is never stern has not got redemptive quality in it, and sinks to the level of something sentimental ; for the counterpart of true love is hatred of "wickedness that hinders loving." Those who wish to be loved with a love that is never stern but always merely gentle are asking to be spoilt by love. When real love rebukes we are far more deeply moved than by any bitter sayings of our enemies, but we cannot miss the love that is behind the rebuke. There was a VERY evil thing at work in Pharisaism—a thing which most deeply misrepresented God. And Jesus had to denounce and expose that evil thing as much for the sake of the Pharisees as for the sake of the people to whom they misrepresented God. But he was always willing to meet the individual Pharisee, such as Nicodemus, with his usual penetrating understanding, patience, and helpfulness. The " thing " called Pharisaism could not be too strongly denounced. But the individual Pharisee remained a son of God's who might be won for true life.

b. *That Forgiveness is the Way to Overcome Evil*

Let us pass to another of the great teachings of Jesus. He declared that the only way to overcome evil is to forgive it. We have already seen that he declared that to be God's method of dealing with evil. We have now to face the fact that he called on men to adopt that method (cp. Matthew 6 : 14, 15 ; 18 : 21–35 ; Luke 17 : 3 ; 6 : 37). It was the most original and startling of all his teachings. It has never been to any considerable extent believed or practised. Men have been afraid to do so. It has even seemed to them that it would be wrong and immoral to do so, and as a result they have gone on trying in all sorts of clumsy ways to end evil by force and in consequence being defeated by it.

A very deep misunderstanding of the nature of forgiveness in part explains this. It has been assumed that to forgive an evil is to condone it. If that were so, no man with a moral sense could ever forgive a real evil. God himself could not do so. It has also been assumed that forgiveness means " doing nothing more about it," and so leaving evil unchallenged. But forgiveness is really a great positive and creative art. It means resuming relations of fellowship with the offender, and so refusing to allow the wrong done to disrupt the family of God. It means in fact meeting wrong with the weapons of love.

Man's instinctive way of reacting to evil and injury is to meet them with indignation expressed in forcible efforts to punish. On the moral level to which most of us have attained, it seems the righteous and just thing to impose severe penalties on the wrongdoer. We say, " He ought to be made to suffer." It is often said, " If he is made to smart, it will teach him not to do it again." And so the whole method of retaliation seems to acquire a moral sanction. It is so that individuals have acted towards other individual wrongdoers. It is so that the State has acted towards its erring citizens. It is so that the nations have acted towards one another. And in all three cases the procedure has been declared to be morally right. The Church has endorsed it with vehemence.

What is not claimed, because it cannot be claimed, is that the method overcomes evil or tends to make bad men good. Private retaliations develop into feuds which poison society. Mere repression of wrongdoers by the State manufactures criminals. The method of meeting international wrongs by war has entrenched war in the world till it now threatens to destroy us all, and has drenched the world in hatred.

Over against all that stands the truth that when men " do Christ's sayings " in this respect they end evil. When it is forgiven it has no more poisonous power to bring forth new evil, and produce legacies of hate. Nothing is more certain than that there is no hope for Europe or indeed for the whole world until the legacies of hatred which have come to us from the past are abolished by the healing power of forgiveness. Our only chance of life consists in leaving the things which are behind, and in the clean atmosphere of good-will learning how to help each other.

It may be true that such forgiveness as many of us can achieve is only a poor and weak thing. Our love is not strong enough fully to master our resentment. Our fellow-ship has little attractive power, and, even for those who accept it, little redemptive power. Yet, even so, our forgiveness is the best thing we can contribute to a situation spoilt by evil. It at least tends to lessen evil and not to increase it.

c. *That Divine Ends Cannot be Achieved by Compulsion*

From this teaching about forgiveness we may well pass on to the further truth that Jesus would seem to have attached no value to the ends which can be accomplished by mere compulsion. To compel any man to such outward manners as would conform to received standards did not seem to him of any special value, though we are largely content with such meagre results. Jesus wanted to see evil itself cast out of men's hearts, and for that end only the methods of love avail. Force is in that connection powerless.

In his age the ambition to " exercise lordship " (Mark 10 : 42 ff.) over others was universal among men of vigorous nature. To achieve domination seemed the obvious proof of superiority, and to be superior seemed the equivalent of success in life. But in plain words Jesus forbade the ambition to dominate. " It shall not be so among you." He measured the value of a life by the amount it contributed by way of service to the common good, not by the amount of compulsion it could achieve. " Whosoever will be great among you, let him be your servant." And he himself was among them as one that served.

It was thus that he came to say, " Blessed are the meek." Nothing he ever said has been more entirely repudiated by natural men and women. Because we are still much more Roman than Christian in mind, we would despise ourselves if we became meek. We feel that it would be the same thing as being poor spirited or even craven. But the meekness which Jesus commended was something wholly different from weakness. It merely meant selflessness.

He himself was meek in that he claimed and sought nothing for himself. For others he could be unbending, strong, and even stern. There is no suggestion of meekness in the ringing words he used to denounce the rich because they had seized upon plenty at the cost of making others poor. Those who have realised his utter fearlessness can never again confuse Christian meekness with either lack of energy or lack of courage.

Here, as always, the key to the interpretation of Christ's scheme of life lies in the law of love. First of all a follower of Christ can have no enemies, for to love one's enemies is to destroy them as enemies. And towards those he loves such a follower will show only the desire to serve, and never the will to compel. His service is sure to call for qualities of endurance and courage. Christ's people will always have to be as unbending as he was before the challenge of evil. They may have to endure, as he did, violence, injustice, and cruelty. They will indeed have need of strength—of such strength as the word meekness does not usually suggest.

e.g. By War

It was by this positive teaching about the way to end evil, and to treat other people, that Christ undermined the whole institution of war. He never spoke in the abstract about war. He merely led men into an attitude of mind and heart which made it impossible for them to serve as soldiers. For a man or a community imbued with the spirit of Jesus it would be impossible either to attempt to force a controversy to a decision by brute force, or to plan to kill others for any reason. Jesus and war belong to different worlds. And in the early days, when the influence of Jesus was fresh in men's lives, his followers did refuse to serve in armies. It was not until the State conquered the Church by adopting Christianity as its official religion that that fatal confusion arose which led men to identify the service of the State with the Service of the Church, and so to become willing to be enlisted. The sword and the cross were then fatally confused as symbols. It is even said that later on knights would take their swords—their killing instruments—and hold them up before altars, believing that the Lord of those altars would bless their weapons. Truly the aberrations of Christ's followers must have kept him on the cross ever since he lived.

War plainly involves the surrender of the methods of justice and reason, and an appeal to crude primitive forces. It has, indeed, in these latter days, yoked to its chariot the achievements of distinguished scientists, and has learnt to employ mental powers of a high order for organisation and strategy. But, in its essence, it is still an appeal to brute force or mechanical force. It offers no security that its decisions will be in any sense righteous. It rouses in the mass of mankind passions which nearly always mislead them, should they achieve victory, and which poison their nature should they suffer defeat. Arrogance on the one hand, and bitterness on the other, are its inevitable fruits. It is powerless to end evil. It arouses great passions, some of which may be generous, but in the end it deludes and betrays its agents. It is indeed wholly incompatible with the mind of Christ.

There is no respect in which this tortured world needs more tragically to be taught of Christ than this one. We shall never end war merely by disliking it, or having conferences about it attended by people who retain a war mentality. When Christ's view of it is accepted it will die, and, in its dying, set us free from one of the most cruel of the tyrants who have impoverished our lives.

d. *That Life Does Not Consist in Having Things*

Money

A further outstanding feature in the teaching of Jesus is his insistence that money is not the good thing men have believed, and still believe, it to be. The delusion that if he could but get enough money he would really live was firmly implanted in the mind of the ordinary man of Christ's day. And Christ insisted that it is a delusion. Possessions breed anxiety, jealousy, and fear of others, so they antagonise men who otherwise might live in fellowship. The lust for them necessarily produces rivalries, which in turn embitter life. Those who have possessions have always withdrawn from the common life, and constituted themselves a clique or exclusive class. Possessions thus become an offence against brotherhood and are productive of inequality.

Jesus recognised that we all have need of food, clothing, and shelter, but he tried to open men's eyes to the fact that, so soon as the accumulation of possessions becomes the aim of life, we at once lose life. We may have much, but we become little.

Do we here come upon the heart of the whole matter ? Do we touch something deeper even than the war lust ? Is the massive delusion about money which has gripped Western civilisation with a grasp of steel the ultimate cause of our present distress and the present crisis ?

If we could but sit loose to possessions, we should find that there is plenty for everybody, and our past rivalries and jealousies would come to seem but evil dreams. We all want to find life. We want freedom of spirit. We want to live victoriously and creatively. And we have gone astray by believing that money is the way to such life. It has been proved a hundred thousand times that it is not. The world has seen the rich dehumanised by avarice, hag-ridden by anxiety, wearied and tormented by satiety, and incited to cruelty, contempt, and arrogance till they have lost all true humanity. It has been demonstrated that wealth is a misleading and rather vulgar vanity. Yet still the West stubbornly believes in possessions. The pursuit of them has become so keen, that sordid slums, sweated workers, and disinherited millions have become its by-products, and were until lately accepted without shame.

We live to-day in a ridiculous situation. The advance of applied science has so increased our productive capacity that plenty for everybody is within our reach. We are already witnessing the deliberate destruction of wealth in order to keep up a symbolical and artificial thing called

" price," although poverty is still in our midst and life is a bitter and cruel thing for millions. What is needed is a new financial system under which consumption shall keep pace with production. Yet we remain in the shackles of an obsolete and discredited system. And the real reason for all this lies in the delusion about wealth. Those who have are so eager to keep, and so afraid lest they should lose, that they cannot think freely. The tyranny of vested interests prevents rearrangement. The rivalries which are out of date, and which belong to the past age of scarcity, still set up numerous barriers to free living. By tariffs, and currency schemes, and the attempt to maintain industries in places inherently unsuitable for them, we complicate the situation till to many it seems quite unmanageable. There is real danger that we should take to killing each other because we cannot or will not learn to live together. And in the background of this situation, which would be farcical if it were not tragic, there is the stubborn force of that delusion which Jesus sought to kill. We refuse to trust each other—refuse to serve each other—in the end impoverish one another, all because we are so set upon grasping immediate material advantages. We cling to a system which has produced dividends and profits for the few in the past, and are in danger of clinging to it till the dividends and profits have disappeared. If we would let Jesus teach us to regard life more than meat, and service more than gain, we should at once enter on a freedom of movement which would make our problems soluble.

e. *That Race and Nationality are to be Transcended*

It hardly needs to be said that Jesus was colour-blind before distinctions of race, and was entirely without the spirit of nationality in any aggressive or exclusive form. That was the inevitable outcome of his central conviction that God is the Father of all men, and that in reality we compose one family. Jesus always dealt with essentials. We complicate life by fussing over accidentals. In any human being Jesus saw a personality of absolute worth—

a brother or sister in the family of God. And he was so concerned about that fact that he seems to have been unconscious of the differences of which we make so much. He was as ready to help a Samaritan woman (John 4 : 7) or a Syro-phœnician woman (Mark 7 : 26) as to serve any daughter of Abraham. His utter refusal to endorse the exclusive national ambitions of his people was one cause of that hostility which ultimately killed him. His belief in a God who loves all men equally deeply offended the religious people among the Jews, even as it still offends many members of the Nordic races to be found in Great Britain and America. Jesus thought in terms of the whole human race. To his mind's eye " all nations " were to be gathered before the throne of God's glory, and not only the Hebrews. Though some scholars question the authenticity of the words in Matthew 28 : 19, " Go ye therefore and teach all nations," they form a perfect epilogue to all that he had taught. He had meant this always. He had been leading his own followers, firstly beyond themselves, then beyond mere family life, then beyond the limits of any one class, and finally beyond the barriers of race and nation. He could not do less than point them to " all the world." The real citizens of the Kingdom are citizens of the whole world, and though that attitude may seem so all-inclusive and therefore vague as to be almost meaningless, it does in practice mean that the citizen of the Kingdom will always be ready for friendship with any man of any class, nationality, or colour. Words like " nigger " or " dago " or " Chinks " will drop out of his vocabulary. He will literally feel that there is something profane about them.

All this means that if the teaching of Jesus were to be honestly accepted the result would be to draw from modern society one of the poisons which now produces deadly results. How much the arrogance behind the belief in " white superiority " has done to create problems which now seem insoluble cannot be measured. We have acute problems on our hands in India and Africa, which are due to its influence. Our friends in the United States have one facing them within their own borders. There are disruptive forces at work which threaten the stability of the whole world. So long as we retain the evil emotions associated in the past with the idea of race, we work for the peace of the world on hopeless terms. And so long as organised Christianity endorses those emotions by regulations which discriminate against men of any colour it denies its Lord.

On the other hand, the application of the mind of Christ would in time solve all the problems caused by racial differences. That there are acute and intricate problems cannot be denied. But they are insoluble, and therefore both dangerous and explosive, in an atmosphere poisoned by contempt on the one hand and resentment on the other. They will only disappear when faced with patience in an atmosphere of determined good-will. Those who live in real loyalty to our common Father will always in the end find ways of living together in peace. A fresh and vital religious movement in South Africa did lately surmount a racial problem which had first terrified and then defeated those who had faced it in a cold and prejudiced atmosphere. Those who understand the present situation in India would probably say that till some similar movement of the spirit towards a Christian view of the situation takes place, that situation is certain to remain both dangerous and cruel.

There is no connection in which the phrase "The Kingdom or Chaos" has more ominous truth in it than this one. The development of events in many directions has brought us to a point where we must either follow or reject Christ as our Leader. And if we reject him—if we cling to the passions and prejudices of the past, only disaster awaits us. The words "race war" conjure up possibilities which are horrible beyond all others. And they will become actualities unless race antagonism ceases in the realm of the spirit. There are those who would have the white races fight, if need be to the death, for a dominating and exclusive position in the world. It would be literally "to the death." No future awaits the human race on such terms.

We should die, because we had refused the leadership of the Lord of Life.

f. *That the Way of Life for Sex is a Narrow Way*

Jesus did not say much about sex. But he said enough. He made clear what is to be that standard in sex which is to rule in the Kingdom.

He did not need to assert the rule of monogamy. It was already accepted in the society in which he lived. He did assert that it belongs to the divine plan that man and wife should be one flesh, and in so doing he broke entirely from the fatal view that there is something sinful or shameful in those intimate experiences through which the life of the race is continued. To conserve that relationship in beauty and integrity was to him a vital concern. Therefore, he forbade men to desert their wives for selfish reasons. By implication he forbade men and women to enter on marriage except with the intention of lifelong fidelity. It can hardly be claimed that he said anything to give us final guidance in the difficult situation which arises when a man and a woman, having entered on marriage with the intention of lifelong fidelity, yet find that they have made so complete a mistake that they both desire to end the relationship. But though we may wish that he had given us more guidance for dealing with failures in marriage, he was plainly anxious to conserve the integrity of it. He condemned all forms of adultery, and was concerned with more than outward acts. The lustful look and the adulterous desire were to him roots of evil which must be guarded against.

He made great claims for children (Matthew 19 : 14). He first displayed and taught an attitude of reverent regard for them. We cannot be wrong in believing that he would have insisted that a regard for their rights must be a determining consideration in all questions regarding marriage. He would have condemned marriage divorced from the intention of parentage, and most surely the thoughtless bringing of children into the world regardless of whether or not adequate provision can be made for them. Though he declared that for an adult the claims of the Kingdom may at times have to be put before those of the family, yet his influence has always been felt to be a family conserving one.

How fundamental all this is, many do not realise. The sex factor in human life is of permanent importance. It is rich in beautiful possibilities. Those who attain a harmonised sex life, and discover the spiritual values that attach to true sex experience, are released for creative effort, and live with energy and joy. On the other hand, sex mishandled is a destructive force. It has disrupted many societies. Its aberrations paralyse the true life of individuals, and make harmonious and happy social life an impossibility. It is not too much to say that only men and women who have discovered the true way in sex can build the Kingdom of God. Calls to the joyous labours of Kingdom building may evoke a response in the hearts of many who will yet fail to achieve anything because of an unsolved sex problem in their own lives.

And Christ's exacting standard of conduct in connection with sex, coupled with Christ's infinitely tender way of dealing with all the failures due to passion mishandled, offer us the one reliable guidance for this part of life. His teaching is not primarily negative. The narrow way in sex is a way that leads to life. Only when the strong sex urge that is in us is held in check, and then coupled to love, loyalty, and service, does the individual attain to true adjustment, and become inwardly harmonised.

It is perhaps hardly worth while to take any more notice of the challenge offered to the Christian standard, and the open advocacy of sex licence which come from a group of people of whom H. G. Wells and Bertrand Russell are the chief spokesmen. The world to-day contains so many men and women whose hardened natures and unhappy hearts, due to following the false guidance of that school, are a demonstration of the nemesis that overtakes sex licence, that further argument is hardly necessary. If it is, the reasoned, balanced, and yet devastating criticism of that whole theory of life given us, in *The New Morality*, by Dr. Newsom is a final and unanswerable handling of the matter.

But the Christian way in sex is a matter of central importance for the Kingdom of God. One condition of its coming is that the sex urge in our humanity should be accepted gladly as a gift from God, and then understood, controlled, and yoked to the uses of the family and the development of personality. If it is disruptive when uncontrolled, it is also creative and enriching when truly fitted in to the whole of life. We need, and we shall always need, to employ its driving power for the labours of the Kingdom.

Life in the Kingdom is to be abundant life, and one element in its abundance must consist of happy, enriched, and harmonious relations between men and women who, having mastered and understood sex, know how to use its power to bring colour and joy into daily life.

IV. THE KINGDOM OF GOD

In all that has been written in these preceding sections, it has been assumed that Jesus did not merely reveal to individuals the terms on which they might one by one find their true life, but that he called on them to create a new society based on the truths which he revealed. It has been assumed that he was concerned about the age-long effort of the human race to achieve an ordered civilisation, and to solve the problems of our corporate life. It has further been assumed that he expected the coming of the Kingdom of God in this world, and that he looked for a day when the Kingdoms of this world shall have become " the Kingdom of our Lord."

And yet, curiously, that is one of the main points concerning which there exists acute difference of opinion among people of Christian outlook. Those who work for peace, or for industrial reconstruction, or better housing, or education, etc., are often confronted by devoted spirits who say to them, " The one thing that matters is to get people converted one by one, and when that has been achieved all the problems of the world will solve themselves." As a result of this attitude many ardent Christians are doing nothing meantime to help towards social reconstruction.

" Conversion " is not enough

Now, if " being converted " meant being brought into harmony with the mind of Christ—coming to share his values—his reverence for personality—his belief about the way to overcome evil—his tenderness for all who are oppressed, then nothing could be more obvious than that the first necessity is to get people converted. Moneylovers and believers in force will always resist the coming of the Kingdom. And if, further, such converted people always realised the necessity for working together, and for corporate efforts to achieve what individual effort can never achieve, then indeed the Kingdom of God would begin to draw nigh. But, in fact, " being converted " has often not meant any such thing. It has often merely meant going through a process of personal readjustment which has left the men and women concerned still self-centred and still dominated in mind by the received ideas about money, and war, and the claims of the dispossessed.

It was ardent evangelicals who preached contentment to the sweated workers of England last century, and who showed themselves still possessed of the instincts and prejudices of the exploiting classes (cp. *The Town Labourer*, by J. L. and B. Hammond). " Converted " people have accepted war as an inevitable and irremovable feature of human life, have held it right that there should be a few rich and many poor, have opposed popular education and the reform of the Poor Law. Some of them to-day are sceptical about the League of Nations, and lukewarm about disarmament. Every social and political worker who is trying to set up a part of the Kingdom is liable to be heard exclaiming at times, " If only the Church would wake up, this piece of Kingdom building could be carried through at once." But the Church contains many " converted " people who care for none of these things. Emphatically, it is NOT enough to get individuals converted according to the conventional meaning of the word. Many converted people seem to be chiefly concerned to meet with other converted people and discuss with them the inner movements of their souls, though the evils which Christ challenged go on unrebuked at their doors.

It has of course been openly maintained that Christ did not propose to his followers the establishment of a Kingdom in this world at all—that he meant by the Kingdom something that was to come into being in another world and another life—that he regarded this present world-order as something about to come to an end, and utterly incapable of redemption—in fact that he did not come to save the world, but only individuals out of the world.

It is probable that St. Paul held that view, at least at the time when he wrote his earlier Epistles. It was probably widely held during the Apostolic Age. It might even claim for itself some support from the sayings of Jesus, if we were to accept as his certain passages of an apocalyptic nature which have been incorporated in our Gospels. But no one who accepts Jesus as a teacher with divine authority can accept all those sayings as authentic—for the simple reason that, if Jesus uttered them, he was wrong. There is a familiar passage in all the first three Gospels which speaks of a time coming when the stars shall fall from heaven, " and they shall see the Son of Man coming in clouds with power and great glory. And then shall he send forth his angels to gather his elect from the four winds " (Matthew 24 : 30–31). And then, a few verses later, come the definite words : " This generation shall not pass away until all these things be accomplished." But no such things came to pass in the lifetime of that generation—nor have they happened since.

To me it is impossible to conceive Jesus as having uttered these words, because their general character is so utterly out of keeping with his real mind. He was not of the spirit that talks or thinks about riding on clouds in great glory.

And, clearly, the only view that leaves us a Jesus with the consistency of mind of a great thinker, is the view that regards these apocalyptic passages as intrusions—intrusions gathered from that mass of apocalyptic speculation which was rife in the first century.

It is in these same sections of the Gospels that we come upon words which lend support to the idea that Jesus taught the doctrine of everlasting punishment, even though that conception is finally inconsistent with the whole truth about the love of God which Jesus taught and incarnated in his own person. Christian instinct has of late quietly but definitely discarded any such view. It has not been argued out of existence. It has simply been rejected by minds trained in the school of Christ. God cannot be both the Father of our Lord Jesus Christ and an unmoved spectator of the unending torments of men and women whose sins, however great, were at least finite. The God whom Christ revealed could not inflict any punishment in which there was no redemptive purpose.

Belief in the eternal damnation of the wicked is notoriously the product of persecution. Hunted and harried bands of believers have again and again sought and found some compensation amidst their pains in dwelling in thought on the tortures awaiting their enemies. But if that reaction to persecution may be called very human, it is also and certainly entirely unchristian. We know what Christ's attitude was to the evil and violent men who tortured him to death. It was expressed in that saying—the most sublime of which history anywhere gives a record—" Father forgive them for they know not what they do." When some of the disciples wished to call down fire from heaven upon some Samaritans who had behaved as enemies, they were told that they knew not what spirit they were of.

This whole matter of finding the true solution to the dilemma created by the apocalyptic passages in the Gospels, and especially in Matthew's Gospel, was ably and finely dealt with in a book—which has never received the attention to which its importance entitles it—called *The Lord of*

Thought, by Miss Dougal and Professor Emmet, and to that book the reader is referred for further discussion of the matter.

When we turn again to the real Jesus, whose main concern it was to teach men to understand and seek the Kingdom, there can be no question at all that he was thinking of a Kingdom to come in this world. He did not expect any sudden and dramatic appearance of the Kingdom—any coming with outward show—because the foundations of the Kingdom lie in a spiritual change which must be effected in the hearts of men. But he declared that he had planted in the soil of human society a seed of such dynamic value that it must in the end grow till it controlled all life. It was as leaven hid in meal which ferments " till the whole is leavened." It was like the least of all seeds which yet grows till it becomes a tree wherein all the birds of the heavens may lodge. He even bade us pray that the Kingdom might come " on earth as it is in heaven."

That real conversion on which Jesus insisted as a necessary preliminary to effective discipleship consists in such a complete surrender of self as leaves a man free forthwith to give his whole energy to the work of the Kingdom. If he remains self-centred, even though he be centred on the development of his spirit, he is not of Christ's company. The people who cultivate spiritual experiences as their conscious aim are sometimes found gathered in circles which become hothouses for the forced growth of strange exotic forms of life. Their religion does literally become a kind of " dope "—a narcotic influence which produces pleasing sensations, but which induces indifference to the wrongs, confusions, and sufferings of the real world.

To escape from such circles into the company of Jesus is like getting out into the fresh air. He was intensely concerned to set captives free, to come to the rescue of the poor, and to challenge the strongholds of Mammon. Following him is an adventure—dangerous and exhausting. But it also is an occupation for free spirits, and induces perfect spiritual health. To be converted in Christ's sense

leaves a man with little time for thinking about himself.
He is apt to forget he has a soul. His soul will very likely
in such circumstances be perfectly healthy. Men in perfect
bodily health often forget that they have bodies.

V. THE KINGDOM AND COMMUNISM

The only serious rival to the idea of the Kingdom of God
in the modern world is the conception of society known as
Communism. The very word induces a sort of terror in
many minds. Capitalists shake in their shoes because of it,
and men of wealth dream dreams of horror in which they
envisage it as some new monster threatening to deprive
them of their goods. The " Red Flag " is considered the
most wicked of all human songs, and the word " Moscow "
stands to many minds for some stronghold of atheism,
immorality, and rapacity.

On the other hand, very large numbers of the unprivileged
people of the world regard Communism as the one really
serious effort of our time to bring justice and liberty to the
average man. That average man is becoming weary in
spirit through long delays. The great things which Liberal-
ism used to promise him have not arrived. The Socialism
of the Labour Party has turned out, so he says, to mean in
practice nothing more than a variety of rather small
attempts to mitigate the harshness of the Capitalistic
system, and has left the present financial system unchallenged. The Churches, he says again, evidently do not
intend to do anything really drastic about it all. They have
no doubt produced a certain number of heroic men and
women who have given sacrificial expression of their
devotion in working for social change. But, on the whole,
the Churches are too deeply involved in, and with, the
present social structure to be able to lead any movement of
revolution, however peaceful in method. The people in
those Churches are able to endure the sight of the waste of
life, the cruel inequalities, and the unmeasured sufferings
which still continue ; or, if the sight of them becomes too
painful, they know how to become blind. And finally,

philanthropy, which has proved very generous and gracious, at least at times, has also failed ever to contemplate any serious or fundamental changes.

But Communism deals in no half measures. It proposes a really different kind of society. The Capitalist, as such, is to vanish and to take his place in some national service designed to serve the common good—not to create profits for individuals. The wasteful rivalries which are so familiar are to end, and one nationally organised unit is to take the place of all the existing separate firms. Society is to be " classless " in the sense that no one section is to be on a different economic level from any other. Pride of purse is thus to become impossible. The common aim is to bring a sufficiency for all his normal needs within the reach of every citizen.

In such a scheme the dispossessed see hope at last. Here is a proposal which really gets down to the roots of things ; here are enthusiasts who, in pursuit of their ideal, are willing to face opposition, often to devote all their time to further their chosen end.

It is useless to attempt to disparage this Communism or to lessen the regard in which it is held by pointing to failures in its development in Russia up to date. The remarkable thing about the Five Year Plan is not that it has partially failed, but that any men had the audacity to suggest so short a period for its execution, and that in part it has succeeded.

It is equally futile to attempt to discount it by declaring that in Russia morality has been abandoned, and sex licence encouraged. The real facts are hard to get at. The Soviet régime would seem in some respects to have a Puritan tone in it, even although it has countenanced revolutionary changes in sex practice. But whatever be the truth about such things, the retort is relevant and inevitable that they have no necessary connection with the fundamental social theory of Communism.

Nor is Communism likely to be discredited by bringing a wholesale charge of atheism against Communists. They

Gc

accept the indictment quite willingly. They refuse to allow their members to belong to any religious organisation. But it turns out that the attitude of the Soviet régime to the Russian Church was in the first place due to a perception that a new organisation of society could not be carried out in face of a highly organised and powerful Church determined to oppose it. Politically it was necessary to end the Russian Church as a political force if Bolshevism was to succeed. And, in the second place, the antagonism of the new régime to the Russian Church was in part merely antagonism to a formal, official, and often irreligious Church which encouraged and fostered many forms of superstition in the peasant mind, and prevented the free use of intelligence everywhere.

What then are we to say about Christ's conception of the Kingdom and Communism? Firstly, that they have much in common. A classless society is only one way of describing the kind of society Christ was suggesting when he said, " Neither be ye called masters, for one is your master, even Christ, and all ye are brethren." The abolition of a class that is selfish, proud, and arrogant because of its wealth, is, from a Christian point of view, greatly to be desired, both for the sake of the people in that class, and for the sake of those whom they exploit. Among the " social evils " of our time, perhaps the greatest is great wealth in the hands of individuals.

The " Red Flag " is not more extreme than the *Magnificat*. Communists say nothing more extreme about " you who are rich " than Christ did. An organisation of industry on the basis of service and not for private profit is entirely in accord with the mind of him who taught that all greatness lies in service. A serious attempt to bring health, and education, regular employment, and social opportunity to every individual, and to bring to an end all institutions and customs which would prevent the success of the attempt is an entirely Christian purpose. It has often seemed to me that the eager, devoted, and alert Communists in some districts I have known were, though they knew it not, more Christian than the complacent and mild individuals to be found in such numbers in the Churches, for the reason that those Communists had really risen above self, and were passionately concerned to win justice for the common people. I often wonder at the small measure of success which they achieve. I would have thought that they must seem to the suffering masses the only people who are taking their wrongs seriously.

What, then, is the difference between the Kingdom and Communism ? It lies in the matter of method and spirit. Communism, as we know it now, preaches hate and is prepared to use force ruthlessly in order to attain its ends. In Russia the Communist Party did not hesitate to kill large numbers of the supporters of the old régime, and does not now shrink from eliminating by forcible means any groups of persons who seem likely to endanger the success of the new order. Humanity is to be clubbed and beaten into the new pattern, and intractable human material is to be scrapped. The most recent instance of this is the avowed policy with regard to the Kulaks. In countries not Communist, the apostles of Communism preach hate, and preach it with passion. They advocate plans which involve bloody revolution. They would if they could inflame the existing bitterness till it becomes ready for destruction. Communism does not believe in the creative power of love. It has no patience with slow methods. It cannot wait for the inevitable collapse of the present system. It is eager to compel, and it would use the power of naked hatred in carrying out its plans.

That is what stamps it as, after all, fundamentally unchristian, and fundamentally different from Christ's proposal of the Kingdom. That Kingdom is to be set up by good-will, and if need be by sacrifice. It involves a respect for personality which stamps hatred as wrong and makes killing impossible. Its servants have need of all the courage, and all the self-forgetfulness which many Communists so markedly display ; but it is not courage to kill, but courage to suffer that they need. It is true that the coming of the

Kingdom would mean the end of the era of financial tyranny, and that men of wealth would no more exist. No longer will industry produce a few who have superfluities while the many have bare necessities.

But always for individuals of any and every class the servants of the Kingdom will have tenderness—desiring not merely their overthrow, but their entrance on true life. The coming of the Kingdom will mean in reality a very complete revolution. When Christians were described as people who desired to turn the world upside down, it was a perfectly correct instinct which inspired that definition. But the coming of the Kingdom cannot be a violent, a dramatic, or a sudden matter. Christ demands for it an indestructible foundation of good-will, and that cannot be laid in a day. Its servants will have need of divine patience.

It might probably be said, with some painful truth, that in the past Christian people have had far too much of such patience and far too little of the courage and daring which are also needed. We have exalted the virtue of moderation to such a pitch that along that road we have come very near to apostasy. Whether we have much right to criticise Communists is an open question. We SAY that our method of sacrifice is a far far better one than their method of violence. But to what extent do we practice such sacrifice ?

This at least must be said. Christians are to-day on their trial at the bar of mankind, as perhaps they have never been before. The world has come to a crisis. Communists insist they can show us the way to surmount the crisis and find real life. Christians, on the other hand, deny the Communist claim, and declare that its plan has fatal flaws in it. But are we going to prove ourselves as much in earnest over building the Kingdom as those others are about building their Communist State ?

Are we going to pay the price of loyalty to our Leader ?

3. THE ORIGINAL FELLOWSHIP IDEA OF THE CHRISTIAN CHURCH

By DR. J. W. HUNKIN

THE NEW VITALITY

THE SURVIVING correspondence of St. Paul, slight as it is in bulk, brings before us a vivid and arresting picture of the birth of a new people, the new race of Christians.

It was a time when the world, as Professor Bury and others have shown us, had rather lost its nerve. But St. Paul and his readers had not lost their nerve. What strikes us most is their astounding vitality. Mark how the apostle rains down his sentences like quick, sharp blows : " Let love be without hypocrisy. Abhor that which is evil ; cleave to that which is good. In love of the brethren be tenderly affectioned one to another ; in honour preferring one another ; in diligence not slothful ; fervent in spirit ; serving the Lord ; rejoicing in hope ; patient in tribulation ; continuing stedfastly in prayer ; communicating to the necessities of the saints ; given to hospitality. Bless them that persecute you ; bless and curse not. . . ."[1] What a very high standard of practical morality these plain words imply ! But St. Paul is not in the least conscious of asking too much. " I can do all things," he says in another characteristic passage,[2] " in him that strengtheneth me " : and so, he assumes, can his readers.

" In him "—that is, of course, " in Christ " : it is one of St. Paul's favourite expressions. It connotes the surrender of the whole personality to Christ. Christ has taken possession. " I will stand between you and yourself "—St. Paul would have accepted Bernard Shaw's phrase as expressing Christ's claim upon the entire loyalty of the individual soul.

---

[1] Romans 12 : 9–14 ; cf. I. Thessalonians 5 : 14–22, etc.
[2] Philippians 4 : 13.

These are the Christians, the true Christians : men and women who in this sense are " in Christ."

WITHIN THE FAMILY

These Christians are all members of one family. They form *the household of the faith*[1] : the new society to which they belong is felt as *home*. Within the home circle, at all events, the law of Christ is recognised : *Bear ye one another's burdens.*[2] The name of this new home was taken from the Old Testament : *ecclesia*, the word regularly used by the Greek translators of the Old Testament from Deuteronomy onwards to render a Hebrew word which means " assembly." The *ecclesia* was the assembly of Israel, and the word was regularly used, not only for an assemblage of the people, but for the whole people considered as a unit—" the congregation of Israel." The word, of course, survives in the French *Église*, but not in our word *Church*, which has a different origin.

The Jewish nation had long regarded itself as, in a special sense, the *ecclesia* of God. But the Jewish nation *as a nation* had rejected Christ, and in the New Testament that rejection is regarded as an act of national apostasy. It is true that individual Jews had, in considerable numbers, become Christians. They could be regarded as the genuine stock of Abraham, and distinguished as such from the rest of the nation. If so, then into that stock had been grafted a new branch consisting of the Gentiles who had embraced the Christian faith. The two together, Jewish-Christian plus Gentile-Christian, formed a new tree : or, to abandon the metaphor and to return to the original word, a new *ecclesia* of God.

For the Jewish members of this new *ecclesia* the distinctive feature which marked it out from the old was to be found in the fact that it had the *Christ*, the long-expected *Messiah*, God's anointed king, as its head. To the Gentile members the idea of a Messiah was not so familiar. The title under

---

[1] Galatians 6 : 10 : *the household of God*, Ephesians 2 : 19.
[2] Galatians 6 : 2.

which they thought of the head of the *ecclesia* was not *Messiah*, but *Kurios*, i.e. *Lord*. It is from this word *Kurios* that, through an early West-Germanic loan word, we get the word which for us is equivalent to *ecclesia*, viz. *church*. Our own word *church* thus reminds us by its very derivation of the fundamental importance from the first of the connection between the new society and its *Kurios*, its *Lord*. The Church is the Lord's society.

THE RELIGIOUS CLUB

Clubs, formed for various purposes, of which religion was often one, had for generations been a characteristic feature of the social life of all this part of the world. Twilight was falling on the Olympian deities, Apollo, Artemis, and the rest, as Dr. W. W. Tarn has pointed out.[1] They belonged to, and fell with, the city State. Philosophy was killing them for the educated, individualism for the common man. This individualism showed itself in a great outburst of private associations after 300 B.C. Each association commonly recognised some deity as its special *Kurios*, and in honour of that deity sacred rites were performed. New members were admitted by initiation under oath not to divulge the ritual. " Communal meals and banquets, at which the deity was conceived to be present as guest, formed a principal element in the life of these associations."[2] Most of the cities of the Mediterranean area were by this time to some extent cosmopolitan, and these voluntary associations would be found scattered about in them. In most of them, too, there would be a *ghetto*, a Jewish settlement—generally, no doubt, small, but in cities like Alexandria and Antioch, very large ; and there was no lack of Jews in Rome. Synagogues were the centres of the Jewish organisations, and their worship was open, not secret, and definitely permitted by the law. At first the new Christian associations must have appeared to the general public as a kind of club which had some connection, or at least affinity, with the synagogue.

---

[1] *Hellenistic Civilisation*, pp. 277 f.
[2] E. Bevan, *Later Greek Religion*, p. xxx.

We have now to consider the inner life of these associations, their relations with one another, and with the world outside.

LIFE WITHIN A CHRISTIAN ASSOCIATION

The Church was the Lord's society. The rite of initiation into it was baptism. In this very simple act the convert was taught to recapitulate, as it were, the experience of the Lord. As the Lord had died and had risen again, so the initiate, disappearing below the surface of the water, made an end of his old pagan life, and then rose again, a new creature, " in Christ." It was the common practice, we gather from the Acts, for hands then to be laid upon him, with prayer that he might receive an endowment of the Holy Spirit of Christ. Thus, set apart from the world outside, and possessed by the Lord of the Church, he became a member of the Christian family. The term often used by St. Paul in addressing such members is that rendered in the English version " *the saints*," i.e. " *the dedicated*," people whose lives are dedicated to God.

The Christian, then, began his new life by entering into a new relation with the Lord of the Church and by receiving of his Spirit. All this, of course, presupposed the continued existence of that Lord in the spiritual world. He had ascended in triumph " into the heavenlies " : no Christian had any doubt of that. And more : with the world in the state in which it actually was, that triumph was obviously incomplete. But it would not remain so. At length, when God saw the time had come, Christ would finally be revealed as Lord of all. The glorious prospect shone before every Christian. He felt he was at the hour of dawn. The sky was brightening and giving promise of a perfect day. Never mind his immediate surroundings, whatever they were : he had an anchor beyond the sunrising. So each new member of the Church made the fresh start within the family relationship, uplifted by a new personal loyalty and a great hope, both independent of the changes and chances of mortal life.

We must not disguise from ourselves the plain fact that in trying to understand the experience of the first Christians we have to reckon with their reliance on the supernatural. They were confident that they had within themselves at least something of the Spirit of their unseen Lord. How was this confidence generated and sustained ?

GROUP-FELLOWSHIP

The psychology we have to deal with here is the psychology of a group. It was when they were assembled for fellowship and united worship that the Christians became specially conscious of a Presence and Power which they felt as the Presence and Power of their divine Lord.[1] There were often occasions of strange enthusiasm, when people seemed to lose the normal control of themselves and to come under the control of a spiritual force mightier than their own. Some would address the gathering in such language as normally they would never have been capable of using.[2] Once we are told that the very place in which the Christians were praying appeared to them to be shaken.[3]

The corporate worship included *prayers*, *teaching*, and *the breaking of the bread*.[4] From the evidence of the Acts we conclude that a gathering for " the breaking of the bread " took place on the first day of the week—at Troas on the occasion described in Acts 20 : 7, in the evening, presumably after the day's work : that it was natural for the leading Christian present actually to break the bread : and that the meal was a real hunger-satisfying meal. It is, indeed, simply as a fellowship-meal that it appears in the Acts. We further gather from what St. Paul says about it to the Christians at Corinth[5] that it was customary for people to bring with them the provisions for the meal : those who were rich bringing more and those who were poor bringing less, but all sitting down together and partaking of what was provided. The reserving of a portion for those who were absent is not mentioned in the New Testament, but

[1] Matthew 18 : 20.   [2] I. Corinthians 14.   [3] Acts 4 : 31.
[4] Acts 2 : 42, 46.   [5] I. Corinthians 11.

there is plenty of evidence that the needy were not neglected. A daily administration at Jerusalem of supplies to widows, for example, is recorded in Acts 6, and seven men were set apart and appointed to take charge of it. These seven are not called *deacons*, although in describing the ministry for which they were chosen the verb *diakoneo*, from which the noun *deacon* is derived, is actually used. Reference will be made a little later to the Communism that was for a short time established in the city.

To return now to the fellowship meal itself : " *the breaking of the bread* " is by no means just a usual expression for taking a meal. It refers to a particular action performed in the course of a meal, viz. the breaking of the flat loaf (still the staple article of diet in the Nearer East) in order that portions of it might be distributed to the assembled company. As used by the writer of the Acts, the phrase evidently looks back to his former volume, the Third Gospel, and especially to Luke 24 : 35, where two of the disciples tell the others on the evening of the first Easter Sunday how that at Emmaus the Lord had been " known of them in the breaking of the bread."[1] And this passage again certainly has in view the Lord's own action on the night before his crucifixion : " He took bread, and when he had given thanks, he brake it, and gave it to them, saying, *This is my body*."[2] The writer of the Acts does not himself in any way stress this connection, but it would appear to be latent in his use of the phrase.

We shall not be wrong, therefore, in associating with the weekly *breaking of the bread* the remembrance of what the Lord himself did on the night on which he was betrayed to death. It is indeed more than a remembrance ; it is in a sense a re-enacting of what then occurred. It is a dramatic re-presentation of what was itself a dramatic action. The night of the Last Supper was the night preceding the Jewish Passover. Next day the Passover lambs would be slain in the Temple. What the Lord did he did under a strong presentment of his own approaching death. As next day the bodies of the lambs would be lifeless, so too would his

[1] Cf. verses 30, 31.   [2] Luke 22 : 19.

body soon be lifeless; and he broke the loaf and said, "This represents what is about to happen to me": "*this is my body.*"

And this original drama was all the more impressive in that neither the disciples then present nor any who have pondered it since have ever felt that they have fully understood it. In so far as the rite which recalls it is effective, those who participate in it are brought to a sharing of the great mystery: not a mystery created or controlled by the word of an official, but the great mystery of life and death, of love and suffering and self-sacrifice.

It is not surprising that more than any other rite it caught the Christian imagination, and, when later on Christian buildings were allowed, it had a decisive effect upon their form and structure. The earliest Christian buildings are to be sought outside the Roman Empire. The Christian Church in Persia is said to have flourished as early as the second century. We hear of church buildings in Adiabene, beyond the Tigris, at a time when Roman Christians were still concealing themselves in catacombs.[1] All these churches, like all the later ones, have their holy table so placed as to indicate that the celebration of the Lord's Supper is the central act of Christian worship.

But we must go back to the earliest days. There is no evidence that every Christian meal of fellowship included the rite of *the breaking of the bread* with the special intention of making it a memorial act. Two later passages in the New Testament speak of a love-feast,[2] the relation of which to the Eucharist proper is not very clear. A very early Christian document, the *Didachè*, gives a prayer to be said over "the broken bread" at the Eucharist, in which there is no reference to Christ's broken body, but the thought is rather of the gathering together of the flour from the separate grains into one loaf: "As this broken bread was scattered upon the mountains and gathered together became one, so let thy Church be gathered together from the ends of the earth into thy Kingdom."

[1] J. Strzygowski, *Origin of Christian Church Art*, Eng. tr., p. 53.
[2] *Agapè*, Jude 12, II. Peter 2 : 13.

But love-feasts and non-memorial Eucharists gradually died out, and the church was left with the Lord's Supper as a memorial, and not a literal meal. The main idea expressed by the Lord's Supper at first was " the showing of the Lord's death till he come."[1] Very little, if at all, later we find other ideas associated with the celebration as well : those who partake, partake as receiving into themselves inestimable benefit from the Lord's sacrifice ; they feed on his love, they enter into intimate communion with him —with him in his supreme act of the offering of himself. The bread is his body : the Church itself is his body—the Christians, though many, " are one bread, one body "[2] : thus the Church's offering of itself in self-sacrificing service is associated with the Lord's own offering. And so on. Above all, the Lord's Supper continued to be, as from the first it was, a united expression of intimate personal loyalty and trust and of sure and certain hope, both directed beyond this present world.

THE PRAYERS AND THE TEACHING

The foregoing section on the fellowship meal has grown till it occupies rather a large proportion of this chapter, but that act of fellowship and worship so soon came to be such an important centre of the life of the Church, and it so enshrines the master-thought of the Christian religion, that it is only right to give it special prominence.

We pass on to the other elements mentioned in the summary quoted above from Acts 2 : 42, of the activities of the first converts in Jerusalem. " They continued stedfastly," we are told, " in the prayers." A hundred years later, Justin emphasises the corporate character of the prayers : " We all together rise and offer up our prayers." Much of the praying at first must have been extempore, and, even when set forms had to some extent been provided, persons who were regarded as spiritually gifted were encouraged to express themselves freely. So the *Didachè*, after giving a form of prayer for use at the Eucharist, adds, " But suffer

[1] I. Corinthians 11 : 26.   [2] I. Corinthians 10 : 17.

the prophets to give thanks in what words they will."[1]
The "prophets," of course, were held to be specially
endowed with the Holy Spirit, but they had no monopoly
of the Spirit. All Christians were baptised in the one
Spirit.[2] "If any man hath not the Spirit of Christ," St.
Paul writes to the Romans, "he is none of his."[3]

What, then, did the Christians pray for? It must suffice
to quote a sentence again from Justin, who speaks of the
"brethren" assembled together after the baptism of a
convert, "to offer prayers in common both for ourselves,
and for the newly enlightened, and all others everywhere,
with all our hearts, that we may be counted worthy, now
we have learnt the truth, by our works also to be found good
citizens and keepers of the commandments, that we may
be saved with the eternal salvation."

A similar moral enthusiasm characterised the early
Christian teaching. The sermons were practical. After the
reading of the records of the apostles and the writings of the
prophets, says Justin, "the president admonishes us by
word of mouth and exhorts us to the imitation of these
excellent things." All the New Testament Epistles contain
clear and incisive moral teaching. Some among the converts
had been rescued from the dregs of society, and the Christian
standards were unmistakably higher than those of the rest
of the world. That is why St. Paul so often issues his warning
against fornication, a practice made light of, or even condoned, in non-Christian circles. We further observe that
St. Paul prizes the gifts and fruits of the Spirit in proportion
to their social utility. He specially mentions: love, joy,
peace, patience, kindliness, generosity, good faith, gentleness, self-control[4]; and Hermas and Justin Martyr in the
next century quote very similar lists.

The greatest of all qualities is love: and the word St.
Paul uses is *agapè*—not infatuation, but true friendliness,
founded on consideration and respect. When Crito is trying
to persuade Socrates to escape while there is yet time, among

[1] Chapter 10.   [2] I. Corinthians 12 : 13.   [3] Romans 8 : 9.
[4] Galatians 5 : 22-3.

other things he says : " wherever you go, Socrates, men will love you " (using the verb *agapao*). That love, that affectionate regard, the Christian is to cherish towards all the world.

THE FELLOWSHIP IN PRACTICE

It is, of course, within the fellowship, within the Christian family, that the interchange of love is most readily and freely exercised. " Honour all men," writes the author of that beautiful little document known traditionally as I. Peter, " *love* the brotherhood." Within the brotherhood there must be a great comradeship, and there is no room for cliques. All the outward distinctions of rank or nationality, and even of sex, are transcended. All are one in Christ Jesus. [1] Many of the Christians were slaves, but before the end of the first century some were to be found in the highest circles at Rome. In all probability the writings of St. Luke have such educated readers directly in view. But, whoever he was, each individual had his own part to play for the well-being of the whole body. St. Paul delights in that metaphor of a body, and uses it more and more. Christ is the head, and the members in union with him all have functions to perform for the health and well-being of the organism as a whole. There must be no inconsiderateness of any kind. It would break the fellowship. The strong must not despise the weaker brother, but help him and protect him from stumbling. " To serve rather than to shine " should be the aim of every Christian, following the supreme example of Christ. [2]

AN EXPERIMENT IN COMMUNISM

Such being the spirit and tone of the Christian society, we need not be surprised to read that in the earliest days, while the society was still small, a form of Communism was adopted in Jerusalem. " All that believed were together, and had all things common ; and they sold their possessions and goods, and parted them to all, according as any man

[1] Galatians 3 : 28.   [2] Philippians 2.

had need."[1] This reminds us of the Essenes, a contemporary religious society in Palestine, who were organised in communities of a semi-monastic sort. But the Christians preserved the family of father, mother, and children as a unit within the larger family of the Church : the Essenes did not, and there are several other important differences between the two societies.

St. Luke, the author of the Acts, evidently regards this primitive Communism with admiration and approval. He notes that no less a person than Barnabas, " a good man and full of the Holy Spirit and of faith,"[2] " having a field, sold it, and brought the money, and laid it at the apostles' feet."[3] But St. Luke immediately goes on to tell of others who sold their possessions but kept back part of the price, and only brought a certain part and laid it at the apostles' feet.[4] The original sharing was spontaneous and entirely voluntary, and was the more natural in that the return of Christ from heaven to end the present order of things was commonly regarded as imminent. But some, like Ananias and Sapphira, were not wholehearted in their acceptance of the scheme, and were driven to subterfuge. Others[5] complained that the distribution was inequitable and unfair. And ultimately the experiment broke down and we hear no more of it. Human nature being what it is, *voluntary* Communism only comes within the range of possibility among those who are thoroughly imbued with such an enthusiastic spirit of brotherhood as that which marked the original community at Jerusalem. Even then it may prove to involve very serious practical difficulties. St. Luke shows how abuses were at once punished, and steps were taken without delay to correct defects in administration. But, even so, after a time the original arrangements were quietly modified ; and the early Church never thought it worth while to repeat the attempt (at least in that form) again.

[1] Acts 2 : 44, 45.   [2] Acts 11 : 24.   [3] Acts 4 : 37.
[4] Acts 5 : 1, 2.   [5] Acts 6 : 1, 2.

ORGANISATION AND DISCIPLINE

Something must now be said as to the organisation of a
Christian association and as to its method of discipline.
St. Paul in his letters from time to time refers to persons
who have responsibilities of oversight. We find both general
terms like " *governments*,"[1] and two particular kinds of
officials, named bishops and deacons.[2] The former could
also be called presbyters or elders.[3] St. Paul would have all
such leaders treated with respect and deference. So, for
instance, he writes to the Thessalonians : " We beseech you,
brethren, to know them that labour among you and are
over you in the Lord, and admonish you ; and to esteem
them exceeding highly in love for their work's sake."[4] But
though he claims to lay down rules for the Churches[5] and
an authority which the Lord gave him,[6] he would not be
thought " to lord it over " the faith of those who through
him had been converted.[7] And when he has a difficult case
of discipline to deal with he appeals to his readers to remember the " sweet reasonableness " of Christ.[8] There were, of
course, many Christians who fell far short of the Christian
standard of living ; and early Christian documents are
sprinkled with rebukes of various faults, especially anti-
social faults such as *whisperings, swellings, factions, jealousy*.[9]
Snobbishness, too, made its appearance early and is in-
dignantly exposed in the epistle that bears the name of
St. James.[10]

Discipline was exercised by leaders, like apostles, acting
in conjunction with the whole association,[11] the final punishment being exclusion from membership. And in the earliest
days the discipline of the society appears to have been
exercised with great wisdom. None were directly rejected
except those whose lives were flagrant denials of their
profession ; but by its devotion to the things of the Kingdom

---

[1] I. Corinthians 12 : 28.   [2] Philippians 1 : 1.   [3] Acts 20 : 17, 28.
[4] I. Thessalonians 5 : 12, 13.   [5] I. Corinthians 7 : 17.
[6] II. Corinthians 13 : 10.   [7] II. Corinthians 1 : 24 ; cf. I. Peter 5 : 2, 3.
[8] II. Corinthians 10 : 1.   [9] II. Corinthians 12 : 20.   [10] James 2.
[11] E.g. I. Corinthians 5 : 3–5 ; cf. Matthew 18 : 15–17.

of God the society attracted only those who were themselves seeking them and repelled those who were seeking its fellowship for meaner ends.[1] We should gather from the Acts that the officials were normally chosen, or at least approved, by the association, and set apart, or perhaps formally appointed, by the apostles and apostolic missionaries.[2] And Clement of Rome, looking back at the end of the first century, adds that the apostles " provided a continuance that if these should fall asleep, other approved men should succeed to their ministration."[3] Thus, while the evidence, recently cross-examined again very shrewdly by Dr. Streeter,[4] suggests—what is in itself very probable —that the details of Church order varied a good deal from region to region, the principle of the regular appointment of officials, approved and accepted by the association in which they were to minister, was everywhere adopted.

THE CHURCHES AND THE CHURCH

We must now go on very briefly to consider the relation of the Christian associations to one another.

From the point of view of organisation they soon came to present the appearance of being a federation of autonomous units. But to describe them merely as such would be to do less than justice to the strength of the spiritual bond which held them together. The local *ecclesia* felt itself to be the representative in a particular area of the *Great Ecclesia* of which it was an integral part. There was a good deal of coming and going between the Churches, and Christians carrying letters of introduction with them were sure of a welcome from their brethren wherever they went. Here, for example, is a perfectly charming note of St. Paul's, introducing Phœbe, a worker in the Corinthian Church, to the Christians at Rome : " I commend unto you Phœbe our sister, who is a servant of the Church that is at Cenchreæ : that ye receive her in the Lord, worthily of the saints, and that ye assist her in whatsoever matter she may have need

---

[1] Cf. J. Oman, *Vision and Authority*, p. 287.　　[2] Acts 6 : 3–6, 14 : 23.
[3] *Ad. Cor.* xliv.　　[4] *The Primitive Church*, 1929.

of you : for she herself also hath been a succourer of many, and of mine own self."[1]

It is very striking how anxious St. Paul was, in his own missionary work, to keep in living touch with the Christians of Jerusalem,[2] and how eagerly he threw himself into the task of raising a fund for their poor who, not for the first time,[3] were in need of relief.[4] The Body of Christ was for him, of course, the whole body of Christians throughout the world. There certainly were differing points of view within the one body—as, for example, between the Jewish and the Gentile Christians. But, as Professor C. H. Turner puts it : " There were links all along, from the right all the way to the left. There was nowhere any break, because all were united in something that transcended any difference : that is to say, in their loyalty to Jesus Christ, and their desire to spread his Kingdom."[5] Missionary enthusiasm was in the apostolic age, as so often since, a great unifying force.

THE CHURCH AND THE WORLD

Meanwhile the world outside, slow to understand the new movement, was suspicious and hostile. " Public life," as Professor Gwatkin says,[6] " was everywhere fenced with worship of the gods." It was therefore very difficult for Christians to take part in it. Their own form of worship was not a form recognised by the State : it was not an " allowed " form ; and so, at any time, proceedings might be taken against those who adopted it. Such proceedings were not, in point of fact, very often taken, for the Christians were quiet, law-abiding people, and it was no one's business to inform against them. Indeed, the better sort of magistrate discouraged informers. But still the Christians had to live without legal security, and were liable to suffer both from the malice of individuals and the violence of mobs. They gained a reputation for endurance—the noblest

---

[1] Romans 16 : 1, 2.   [2] Galatians 2 : 2, etc.
[3] Cf. Acts 11.   [4] II. Corinthians 8, 9, etc.
[5] Lecture on " Jewish Christianity," printed in *Catholic and Apostolic*, p. 242.   [6] *Early Church History*, I., p. 236.

of the emperors, Marcus Aurelius, called it obstinacy—and for standing by one another. It was said of them, " They love one another almost before they are acquainted."[1]

Walter Pater, in *Marius the Epicurean*, has an eloquent chapter describing the impression made on an earnest young Roman of good family by " the wonderful spectacle of those who believe." Gradually, very gradually, persons of that type as well as of all other types were drawn into the worshipping fellowship.

The social customs of the Christians themselves did not differ very noticeably from those of their neighbours. St. Paul was insistent, for example, that Christian women should obey the conventions of ordinary society. Outwardly therefore they were little more " emancipated " than other people. Nowhere else, however, outside the Christian society were women so fully recognised as, with their husbands, " *fellow-heirs of the grace of life.*" Christians continued technically to be slaves and the owners of slaves : but the relation between the two was in reality transformed when Philemon could receive back his runaway slave Onesimus " no longer as a slave but . . . a brother beloved."

An anonymous writer, probably of the second century A.D., sums up the position thus : " Christians are not distinguished from the rest of mankind by country or by speech or by customs. For they do not dwell in cities of their own, or use a different language, or practise a peculiar life. . . . Every foreign land is to them a fatherland, and every fatherland a foreign land. . . . They exist in the flesh, but they live not after the flesh. They spend their existence upon earth, but their citizenship is in heaven. . . . In a word, what the soul is in the body Christians are in the world. . . . The soul dwells in the body, and yet it is not of the body ; so Christians dwell in the world, and yet they are not of the world."[2]

[1] Cæcilius in *Minucius Felix*. [2] *Epistle to Diognetus*.

CONCLUSION

The stream of time runs only one way, and it is vain to attempt to reproduce the conditions of the New Testament period, or to reorganise our social and religious life by copying line for line the most primitive models. But if human fellowship is to be secured on the largest scale, and democracy, as Mr. Baldwin once said, is to be made safe for the world, it can only be through " the permeation of the whole by a regulative love."[1] That is *agapè*, the love which within a smaller area was actually and notably generated in the early Church : and there recognised as an endowment from God—" the love of God hath been shed abroad in our hearts through the Holy Spirit which was given unto us."[2]

" The religion of the Spirit," says Dr. Inge, " works always from within outwards," from the individual to society ; it follows what Matthew Arnold calls " the secret of Jesus," the law of victory through sacrifice : and it holds fast to an unconquerable hope, for it has heard " great voices in heaven " say, " The kingdom of the world is become the Kingdom of our Lord, and of his Christ."[3]

[1] Oman, *op. cit.*, p. 153.   [2] Romans 5 : 5.   [3] Revelation 11 : 15.

4. THE CHRISTIAN VIEW OF MAN AS SOCIAL

By J. S. BEZZANT, B.D.

THERE is a story that during the war an officer, in the presence of a chaplain, declaimed : " What does this fellow Wilson want to butt in for with his beastly League of Nations ? " (Here he knocked over his glass.) " Oh, damn ! Sorry, Padre. What I mean is, I can't stick all this blather about human brotherhood." Dr. Temple's comment runs : " The Chaplain, as representing officially the Church of God, was supposed to feel shocked at hearing the word ' damn ' ; he was entitled to an apology ; but it was not thought that he would expect an apology for blasphemy against the very heart of the gospel which he was commissioned to preach." The story is instructive, the comment apt. There is a definitely " Christian view of man as social " which will be set forth. The nature of this sociality is a brotherhood : its basis is the relation of all men to God in whose image they are and are being made—the God of whom the least inadequate human symbol is Fatherhood ; and this is " the very heart of the gospel." Men have sometimes spoken as though Jesus taught nothing else of vital importance. This, as anyone can see who will read the Gospels, is not a true opinion ; and many criticisms have corrected it. But such criticisms have frequently stated, and more often implied, that the doctrine of human brotherhood was no more than incidental in Jesus' teaching. This view is both perverse and foolish. A doctrine issuing from a conception of God and man, proceeding from an inner condition of spirit, and so determinative of all man's relations with other men (that is, of nearly the whole of human conduct in this life)—if it was taught or implied at all cannot be other than primary. If it be not the *whole* heart of the gospel it is so vital that without it that heart would cease to beat.

THE TEACHING OF JESUS

The essence of Jesus' teaching about the social character of man is not a total of isolated precepts. Of such precepts there are several. Man must love his neighbour as himself.[1] True greatness consists, not in lording it over other men, but in serving them[2] : he who would be first must be servant of all.[3] There must be no limit to the readiness to forgive[4] ; and " as ye would that men should do to you, do ye also to them likewise."[5] Conduct, inspired by such motives, is not to be limited to those who are " brethren " or " sisters " in a particular family or social group.[6] The parable of the Good Samaritan answers the question, " Who is my neighbour ? " and is made to follow immediately upon the statement that one's neighbour is to be loved as oneself.[7] Love is to extend even to enemies. And such sayings as " Come unto me, all ye that labour and are heavy laden, and I will give you rest," together with the Beatitudes and the Lord's Prayer, neither contain nor suggest any temporal or national limitations : they apply to all men and imply their unity.

But the Christian view of man's social nature is not an inference from such sayings and commands. Precepts, taken as such, are not the essence of Jesus' teaching. They issue from, and depend upon, something far more fundamental. This is a doctrine of man's relation to what is believed to be alone ultimately real and true. The dominating thought in Jesus' teaching is undoubtedly that of the Kingdom (better, the *Kingship*, or *Rule*) of God. This is the final reality, ultimately the only real power there is ; though it is not yet actualised on earth. The motive of Jesus' preaching is to prepare men for its coming, when God's will shall be done on earth as it is in heaven. This Divine

---

[1] Mark 12 : 31. This commandment, together with the " first of all " commandments (i.e. to love God with the whole being), are the two than which none is greater. Jesus thus combines two precepts from the Jewish Law (Deuteronomy 6 : 4, 5, and Leviticus 19 : 18). In St. Luke's form of the incident, it is the scribe who makes the combination, and Jesus approves.

[2] Matthew 20 : 25 ff.   [3] Mark 9 : 35.   [4] Matthew 18 : 21 ff., 6 : 14.
    [5] Luke 6 : 31.   [6] Mark 3 : 31 ff.   [7] Luke 10 : 29 ff.

Rule is a rule of love ; its symbol is Fatherhood. But it is a *Kingly* Fatherhood ; it claims the absolute surrender and obedience of man to its Rule. This means to love God ; to love him with the whole being is " the first commandment of all," out of which (and not otherwise) issues the right relations to men. If absolute obedience to God has precedence over all human duties, it is because it is indispensable to the right discharge of those duties ; the precedence is one of order, not of rank as between separable principles. There is no possibility of choice between alternatives. The combination of love to God and to man depends on, and implies, a common relation of men to God. But it also means that the fundamental and determining point of view is *religious*. Human virtues and brotherly acts inevitably flow from it, but these are not *commanded as a law* for man. The Christian view of man as social is, in Troeltsch's phrase, " the union of those who are united to God." The first essential is that purity of heart by which man may see God, who himself knows the secret thoughts of men, and who sees through all unrealities and hypocrisies. Every human soul is immeasurably precious in his sight : each is of more value than the gaining of the whole material world[1] ; of more value than the most sacred institutions, which exist for man not man for them[2] ; injury to that moral and spiritual life of man which is his Creator's image is more serious than injury to the body.[3] But this worth of man implies the importance of his welfare in the body here and now ; this may be seen from Jesus' actions among the sick and suffering, the poor and degraded, many of which, so far as we know, had no explicit connection with their specifically religious lives. It is not the will of the Father that one of his little ones should perish, and it were better to be dead than to cause one of them to stumble.[4] Acts of human kindness are done or not done to Christ according as they are done or not done to one of the least of his brethren, and they decide the eternal destinies of men.[5]

[1] Mark 8 : 36, 37.   [2] Mark 2 : 23–28.   [3] Mark 9 : 43–47.
[4] Matthew 18 : 6, 14.   [5] Matthew 25 : 40, 45, 46.

This supreme worth of man implies an equality of men ;
but it is a religious equality based on their common relationship to one Father. It is not that men have inherent equal
rights ; for they have *no rights* outside that relationship
which all have broken by their sin. When they shall have
done all that is commanded, they are unprofitable servants
still[1] ; they must beware of covetousness, for true life does
not consist in abundance of possessions.[2] Their equality lies
in a common need which only God can supply. Man is a
potential child of God and never ceases so to be, however
low he may fall. But sinful men have estranged themselves
from their true relationship to God ; when they repent
they may be restored to it, and the worth of each is such
that there is joy in heaven when the restoration of one takes
place.[3] Their potential eternal value can only be actualised
as they turn from all self-regarding motives for the sake
of the Rule of God. Then relationships with other men, and
the natural differences between them, are revealed in their
true proportions : the true relationship issues from a
changed condition of that inner heart whence all that is
good or bad proceeds. For as men are truly gathered into
the Rule of God, which is a creative will of love, they cannot but be inspired to actualise that loving will on earth.

Thus in one sense, and the deepest, the *individualism* of
the gospel is absolute : the appeal is always first to the
individual. Surrender to God's Rule is something which
each must needs do for himself : none can do it for him.
But because this loving will of God cannot be actualised
on earth except in human relationships with other personalities of equal immeasurable worth, this thoroughgoing
individualism is the basis of an absolute fellowship of love ;
for only individual surrender to the Rule of God can
actualise that fellowship of love among those who are
equally his sons ; and only as that love operates among
men can they be awakened to a true understanding of
God and of the way to him. In the common surrender to
God, individual natural differences (which it is flying in

[1] Luke 17 : 10.   [2] Luke 12 : 15.   [3] Luke 15 : 3–10.

the face of obvious facts to deny) provide the means for the increase of that love of which God is the Fount : he is the Father who draws all souls to himself in that true relationship to him in which alone they can be united.

THE PAULINE AND OTHER EPISTLES

With the rise and growth of the early Christian community, the social implications of the Christian doctrine were increasingly emphasised in their application within the Christian community. Christians must remember that there is no respect of persons with God[1] ; they are severally members one of another.[2] They are compared to the members of a physical body of which each member needs all the others and is implicated in their welfare or sufferings, though there are differences of function.[3] The basis of this conception is revealed in the immediately following famous hymn in praise of the heavenly love which beareth, believeth, hopeth, and endureth all things.[4] Love is the first of the fruits of the Spirit of God.[5] All commands which can be made to men are fulfilled by him who " loveth the other "[6] : " Love worketh no ill to his neighbour, and therefore is the fulfilling of the law."[7] In the one word " Thou shalt love thy neighbour as thyself " all is included[8] : it is " the royal law."[9] It is through love that Christians are to be servants one to another[10] in a unity in which there is " neither Jew nor Greek, bond nor free, male nor female," for all are one.[11] Where the Divine Spirit is and where Christ's law runs, each is ready to bear the burdens of others and equally ready to bear his own.[12] If there is any fellowship of the Spirit, Christians must " be of the same mind, having the same love ; doing nothing through faction or through vainglory, but in lowliness of mind each counting other better than himself ; not looking each of you to his own things, but each of you also to the things of others,"

[1] Acts 10 : 34 ; Romans 2 : 11.   [2] Romans 12 : 4, 5.
[3] I. Corinthians 12 : 12–27.   [4] I. Corinthians 13.
[5] Galatians 5 : 22.   [6] Galatians 5 : 14 ; Romans 13 : 8.
[7] Romans 13 : 10.   [8] Romans 13 : 9.   [9] James 2 : 8.
[10] Galatians 5 : 13.   [11] Galatians 3 : 28.   [12] Galatians 6 : 1–5.

after the supreme example of Christ.[1] To the peace of Christ, which is to rule in the individual heart, Christians are called in one body.[2] St. Paul feels no need to write at length about love to the brethren, " for ye yourselves are taught of God to love one another." [3] Even the great heroes of faith of the past cannot be perfect in themselves " without us "[4] ; and " above all things " Christians must be " fervent in their love " among themselves.[5] As in the Gospels, this love overflows to those who are not in the visible Christian community, though these are not primarily in view. Christians are to bless those who persecute them ; to " increase and abound in love one toward another and toward all men," [6] and to be " long suffering towards all."[7] St. Paul's teaching receives its final summing-up in the Epistle to the Ephesians. There is set forth the ideal of a Divine Society. Its unity is of a special and striking character : it is a unity in diversity existing in one body, primarily a unity of spirit. In this Society it is God's will that all shall be united on an equal footing under the Headship of Christ who has broken down the wall of partition which has hitherto separated them, in which barbarian, Scythian, bond, and free all enjoy the same privileges.

THE JOHANNINE WRITINGS

The same thoughts are fundamental in the writings attributed to St. John. In these, love is not only really but quite explicitly the whole content of the Christian moral law, which nevertheless clearly retains its religious basis. For the present purpose it is unnecessary to discuss the question as to what extent this Gospel may be regarded as a reliable report of the spoken words of Jesus. It is certainly evidence for the spirit of early Christianity which grew out of him and whose ideal was to grow up into him, and in that important sense it is evidence for " the mind that was in Christ Jesus." Here again the supreme value of human

---

[1] Philippians 2 : 1–8.   [2] Colossians 3 : 15.   [3] I. Thessalonians 4 : 9.
[4] Hebrews 11 : 40.   [5] I. Peter 4 : 8.   [6] I. Thessalonians 3 : 12.
[7] I. Thessalonians 5 : 14.

personality is not human nature taken just as it happens to be. Except a man be born anew (or from above) he cannot see the Rule of God.[1] To know God and to love him is to do his will[2]; and this is absolutely fundamental : " He that keepeth my commandments, he it is that loveth me,"[3] and the commandment is " that ye love one another, as I have loved you."[4] The washing of the disciples' feet is an object lesson of the humble service which there is all the more reason that they should do to one another because Jesus has done it to them.[5] In the final discourses, love for one another is described as " a new commandment " by seeing which all men shall know that they are his disciples.[6] They shall become one flock with one shepherd.[7] The prayer which Jesus prays in the great crisis of his mission contains the words : " Neither for these only do I pray, but for them also that believe on me through their word ; that they all may be one . . . that the love wherewith thou lovedst me may be in them."[8]

These same connected ideas are reiterated again and again in the First Epistle of St. John. " If we walk in the light, as he is in the light, we have fellowship one with another "[9] ; and " He that loveth his brother abideth in the light, and there is none occasion of stumbling in him."[10] Mutual love is a commandment both new and old. It gives the assurance of having " passed out of death into life."[11] We must love one another because " love is of God " who *is* love.[12] " If God so loved us we ought also to love one another " : only so can God's love be " perfected in us."[13] It is impossible to know God without love of the brethren : " He that loveth not knoweth not God."[14] Of the man who will not minister to the ordinary human needs of his fellows it is asked : " How dwelleth the love of God in him ? "[15] A man who claims to love God while hating his brother is

[1] John 3 : 3.   [2] John 14 : 15, 23.   [3] John 14 : 21 ; 15 : 10.
[4] John 15 : 12.   [5] John 13 : 12-15.   [6] John 13 : 34, 35.
[7] John 10 : 16.   [8] John 17 : 20, 26.   [9] I. John 1 : 7.
[10] I. John 2 : 10.   [11] I. John 3 : 14.   [12] I. John 4 : 7, 8.
[13] I. John 4 : 11, 12.   [14] I. John 4 : 7, 8.   [15] I. John 3 : 17.

a liar [1] : to hate a brother is to be a murderer and to have nothing of the life that is life indeed. [2]

THE RELEVANCE OF THE CHRISTIAN IDEAL

It is hard to exaggerate the extent to which the Christian view of man is a social view ; but it is easy to forget its essential and perennial spring. The basis of this sociality is the demand for absolute obedience to the Rule of God, a demand which must come as an individual appeal to every man. But that Rule is one of creative love for which all men are immeasurably precious and which never despairs of them. Submission to it is the indispensable condition of all that is best in human life. It creates a social life which is as thorough as the individualism, and nothing else can. It is the type of fellowship which alone can be lasting and can embrace all men, because it alone is rooted in what is the only ultimately real power in the world. It demands universal subjection yet confers universal freedom—the glorious liberty of the children of God which is utterly different from anarchical independence.

There can be little doubt that for Jesus and his early followers the Rule of God was conceived as something that would *shortly* be set up by the act of God rather than by human striving. That fact explains why the early Church seems to us to be hardly aware of the difficulties in the way of actualising its social ideal. It also explains why the early Church did not address itself directly to what we call social reform : the then existing forms of social life, organised otherwise than on the basis of the Christian ideal, were thought to be more transient than they have since proved to be. The same expectation explains why the particular rules of conduct which issue from the fundamental prin-ciple of man's relation to God were not always those which seem to us to flow from it inevitably. St. Paul does not abhor slavery ; his anxiety is that the old relationship between a master and his slave shall be transmuted into one of love. It was only as the Christian community

[1] I. John 4 : 20.   [2] I. John 3 : 15.

realised that its future in this world-order was to be longer than it at first thought, only as it expanded in the midst of a complex social order organised on bases very different from its own, that it realised how formidable were the adverse conditions in which its own social life had to be lived, and which it was called upon to influence and transform.

But the character of the first expectation of the time and manner in which God's Rule would be established does not in the least degree abrogate the truths of the conceptions of the supreme worth of personality, of how alone that worth is to be actualised, or of man's filial relation to God the Father of all. On the contrary, a truer apprehension that the full establishment of God's Rule must be a slow process, and that the obstacles thereto are more stubborn than early Christianity supposed, only serves to reveal the imperative need of the effective operation of those same truths ; only serves to demonstrate more clearly the impossibility of any social life, truly worthy of human personality, on any other basis. The existence of many huge social groups organised on bases other than Christian, the bewildering complexities of modern life and civilisation, immensely extend the field in which the influence of the Christian ideal has to spread. As the area of responsibility widens, the need of a social order which shall preserve and actualise the worth of personality (because built upon the recognition of that worth and of its source in God) only becomes more urgent.

THE SLOW PROGRESS OF THE CHRISTIAN IDEAL

When it is seen how little of the Christian ideal has been realised, and in how diluted a form, many are tempted to regard it as a vain dream. The slowness of its progress is largely due to the infirmity of human nature. The Christian ideal does not remain inoperative : it is not without increasing influence ; but the treasure is in earthen vessels. Hence the frequency of misunderstanding, prejudice, fear, hatred, and conflict between individuals and groups, between economic interests, between classes and nations. An important and humiliating contributory cause of the slow progress of the Christian ideal has been the failure of the Church to be whole-heartedly loyal to the ideal to which it is her primary mission to bear witness. This has often made Christians traitorously apathetic in the face of glaring social evils. To-day, multitudes feel that it is little use looking to the Church to do much to bring together nation and nation, class and class. Controversies about far less fundamental things than her primary message have obscured the Church's sense of proportion (though it is being slowly recovered), and hindered the realisation of the Christian social ideal. Politico-ecclesiastical interests, financial, dogmatic and ceremonial interests, have loomed larger than that message of God's Rule, and of man's relationship with man therein, without which all else is religiously vain.

But none of this invalidates an ideal which demands at the outset a radical change of heart as the *only* means to its realisation. The "natural man" cannot regenerate human society. Men desire human brotherhood, but they often will not have the Christian way of achieving it. Social life is largely what is is because men and the consequences of human action are what they are. A new social order can only be built up of new men and women, and such cannot be produced by organising them from without : they must be "born anew" from within. That multitudes are unconscious of this is the most gloomy, if not the most immediately serious, factor in the modern world-crisis. To build upon spiritual foundations will always tend to be slow work. Political alliances and economic plans, made by men as they happen to be, promise not only quicker but sufficient results. But human society, however organised, will continue to fall into disorder and distress if it aims only at material ends, pins its faith to secularist methods, and appeals only to utilitarian sanctions. Congresses, concordats, and protocols will remain but partially effective while the diseases whose symptoms and effects they seek to remedy remain untouched—until they are built on spiritual foundations comparable to the spiritual basis of human nature. It is true that when great evils and confusions have arisen through building on other foundations the mere proclamation of Christian ideals will not remove them. Nothing is more futile than the assertion that all modern difficulties would solve themselves if only men would become Christians. The Christian view of man, taken as the basis of practical action, is the only one which can mediate the spirit in which complex human problems can be solved ; but even if it existed in far larger measure than it does we should still need all the intelligence, knowledge, effort, and skill of men, which the Christian spirit can inspire and influence, for their wise solution. Nor may Christians (except by abandoning their ideal) refuse to co-operate in sincere attempts to improve the social order on the ground that such attempts do not proceed upon the conscious acceptance of the Christian ideal ; such refusal can only postpone the realisation of the ideal. For if men are nurtured in an order which continually suggests and impresses the need of selfishness, and the consideration of others only when it can be indulged without any cost to self, no amount of preaching will itself prevail against it. That there are conditions of living, and kinds of miserable poverty, which make a real Christian life impossible, and therefore also make impossible the actualisation of the Christian social ideal ; the importance of external aids to its realisation ; that a sound moral and spiritual life requires a corresponding basis of material and other environmental conditions—all this has been forced upon us by experience with an intensity unknown to the primitive Christian outlook. And it is no part of Christianity that the lessons of experience are to be ignored. Active participation in attempts to remove such adverse conditions, and to create such aids, is essential to the active love of the brethren which is fundamental to the Christian view of man ; and it is entirely compatible with the realisation and insistence that *by themselves* these methods will never suffice. In fact, changes in a Christian direction are constantly being made ; and their importance is nowhere more clearly seen than in the increasing sensitiveness to how much more must be done, and to the urgency of the call to do it.

THE TRUTH OF THE CHRISTIAN IDEAL

In spite of the obstacles (whether those inherent in human nature itself, or their external results) to the attainment of the Christian ideal, that ideal is grounded upon what no less really exists in the nature of man, by virtue of that divine image which is never wholly effaced. That there can be any agreement at all in human desires such as leads to collective effort towards a common end, depends upon the fact that, though men are never entirely alike, they are also never absolutely different. Communities have come to desire for social ends values which cut across the individual's selfish desires. It is the fact that human life must be lived in society which makes the individual the something more which constitutes him a person. Man is never an absolute egoist. Were it not that a capacity for self-denial and a feeling for others are implanted in human nature, conscience itself could never develop. Social life is possible only because tendencies which egoism would eradicate do in fact come to control egoism. Thus, as Dr. Tennant says, " that ' love is the fulfilling of the law ' is but the explication and amplification of what is written from the first upon the table of the heart." Human nature itself points to the Christian ideal, though that ideal cannot be actualised with any fullness without submission to the Rule of God, and the illumination and invincible power which come from it.

Man does in fact desire and value things which only self-sacrifice can win, and comes to value them more highly than things which are merely selfish. But the organisation of men for social ends is dangerous. Such ends always tend to care for the individual *only* in so far as he can be made to serve a common end. From this tendency there arises the danger lest the supposed demands of social welfare may be pressed to a point at which personality is desecrated, and man becomes a part of a complex machine. When that happens, the human material, out of which a worthy and satisfying social order can alone be made, is being mortally wounded. Hence the fundamental importance of that which keeps alive the sense of the supreme worth of personality; and this is the Christian conception of man as the child of God, made in his image. To make social life *an absolute end in itself* is to court a disaster just as real, if slower in operation, as that which must overtake the individual who would make himself an absolute end. Both deny reality. The true values, alike for the individual and for society, can only be seen and preserved in the light of a doctrine of man which does not find the whole of his significance or destiny in this world. Such a doctrine does not make for indifference to what is done in this world; rather it intensifies its importance. For temporal acts have eternal issues. " The life beyond is the inspiration and source of the ultimate value of the life that now is." The only ultimate power is the Rule of God; it is certainly not man's will, except as that is brought into captivity to obedience to God's Rule. As Mr. Barry writes : to make man the measure of all things is to ensure a loss of faith in man. It fails because it is opposed to reality; for man is not, and never will be, an irresponsible master in his own universe.

CONCLUSION

The essence of the Christian view of man could hardly be better stated than by Troeltsch : " Christian religious faith is faith in the regeneration of man who is alienated from God, a regeneration effected through the knowledge of God in Christ. The consequence of this regeneration is union with God and social fellowship so as to constitute the Rule of God." Christianity did not begin as a movement for social reform, and it can never find its *inspiration* therein. Yet its otherwise willing acceptance of varying social conditions must always end where these conditions hamper and maim personality and its inalienable values. Its spirit, though not inspired by social revolutionary programmes,

Hᴏ

will yet, so long as it does not atrophy and in proportion as it spreads, make for the abolition of evil conditions and for the foundation of better ones. But the personality which can rise above conditions of life and transform them can only arise and grow through the union of human life with God, its Source, and by the submission of the will to his Rule. An all-embracing divine love, and individual lives inspired and ruled thereby, can alone achieve a stable social condition worthy of human life. This alone can make harmony between the many social groups, large and small, which arise out of other more limited and often conflicting interests, and which are the concrete actualities called " Society." The Christian view of man inevitably issues in a social ideal whose influence must either wither or else slowly penetrate existing social groups and unite them in closer harmony. It enhances the importance of all social life because it makes sensitiveness to its conditions more acute, and because it extends their consequences far beyond the activities and the limits of life here and now. The eternal significance of all human effort is the true basis of its urgency. It is also at once the ground and the inspiration of that love which, as St. Paul said, is the first of the fruits of the Spirit, and which any social order, however justly organised, will still need ; for the deepest emotions and ills of life, sorrow, sickness, sin, suffering, and the last enemy, which will ever remain, require a love which is more than the justice which grows out of its roots.

5. CHRISTIANITY AND HISTORY:

A. *GENERAL DEVELOPMENT*

By MALCOLM SPENCER

THE NEED FOR CONSTRUCTIVE CRITICISM

THIS CHAPTER uses the record of Christian history as a quarry from which to hew stones for the building of the new social order that the age needs. This calls for both appraisement and criticism. There are moments and incidents in the past in which the essential truth and power of Christianity have shone out brilliantly. From these periods and incidents we may derive ideas of creative power. Equally, there are periods and passages of failure and shame from which there is nothing to be derived but warning. Generally speaking, the record is one of high principle too narrowly or too timidly applied. The greatness of the days when Christian truth was applied courageously, the shame of the days in which it was dishonoured, the sad mediocrity and decadence of the days when it was only feebly influential, all yield material for the social reconstruction Christianity must undertake immediately or incur still further calamity.

The practical purpose of the chapter limits its scope. There is no need to distinguish nicely between the contributions which came to society exclusively from Christian sources and those which came in part from other quarters. There is no occasion to defend Christianity from the blame of its failures or to set it in opposition to its natural allies. What is to the point is to see the power for social righteousness and peace that Christianity is capable of generating when its characteristic convictions are applied to that result.

At the same time, it would be absurd to approach this study in a mood of complacency. For the Christians of recent generations have undoubtedly taken over from the past such a conglomeration of Christian and un-Christian ideas and purposes that the society we were supposed to be leavening was bound to drift to the edge of terrible calamity as it has now done. For ages past the Christian gospel has not been generally expounded as a coherent and reasonable way to the salvation of the world from its collective ills. We need to feel the whip of history lashing our shoulders and to stand ashamed for this defective presentation of the faith.

The Sphere of Greatest Failure

The root cause of the present social crisis is to be found in the economic sphere ; and it is from this sphere of all others that Christianity has withdrawn its light for generations past. Offering itself as the Light of the World, it has not offered its light where the world has been stumbling in the greatest darkness. The moral standards it has approved or condoned in the economic sphere have not been its own proper standards at all. The philosophy on which the business life of the last two centuries has been based has been utterly alien to its own philosophy. Yet Christianity has not joined issue with that philosophy. The justification of this charge will appear as the argument unfolds. It is made here to account for the concentration of the present argument on Christianity's contribution, or lack of contribution, to the guidance of our economic life—albeit, it is a matter on which the Church's record is more broken and fragmentary and inconsistent than on any other.

Is it to be wondered that there is social chaos in a world that has allowed its social life to be the sport of any social change that might be economically profitable to some individual or firm ? Because Messrs. Manufacturer & Co. can add £1,000 a year to their profits by moving their works from Durham to Middlesex, fifty families may be uprooted from the county where all their traditions and affections are centred, the houses they lived in may become derelict, and the area they invade may have a new housing problem to face, whilst the social stability of an already staggering community may receive a further shock by their

departure. Even material values far more than £1,000
a year may be sacrificed, and the spiritual values sacrificed
must go uncounted. And all because the rules of the present
economic game have never been assessed by the Christian
moralists.

Is it to be wondered that there is moral chaos, when
many of our boys and girls, before their characters are
firmly established, go into occupations which are not even
honest, whilst most go into occupations where they cannot
conceivably serve God with all their heart and mind, or
serve their neighbour as they would themselves. Some are
engaged in work that is not honourable in itself, and others
in work which is not honoured by their fellows. Few indeed
have the opportunity of work that can call out their best
powers or command their inner allegiance. All such work
is unhallowed and profane, and a society in which it is
tolerated must lose its moral authority for its members.
Their morality is undercut. They are subconsciously initiated into moral irresponsibility and anarchy of soul.

Can we wonder at the intellectual revolt of many of the
more active minds amongst us ? It is impossible to offer
them a coherent moral and spiritual justification for the
way in which we now carry on the work of the world.
The affront to human dignity involved in continued unemployment, in the cutting out of business rivals, in the manufacture of second-rate goods, in the relentless dismissal of
surplus staff—these and many other such things are a deep
affront to the spirits of those who have once seen humanity
through the eyes of Jesus Christ. And the Christian teaching that does not recognise these evils, and offer a way of
escaping from complicity in them, is intellectually discredited. For Christianity, unlike many other religions,
does offer to empower men to make life on this historical
world-plane a humane and beautiful thing.

The Special Opportunity of To-day

Therefore the times require us to gather together the
inspirations that the past can yield and heed the lessons of

past defeats. Moreover, the development of the scientific method and habit of mind and the accumulation of historical knowledge make possible the critical survey that is required. Never before have men been so ready and so able as they are to-day to envisage their own past and learn disinterestedly from its successes and failures. The present chapter is an attempt to dig out this instruction from the periods of past Christian history which have most to teach us. Three main periods and two transition periods will be specially laid under contribution.

I. THE EARLY CHRISTIAN CENTURIES

The Gift of a Dynamic Ideal

The period of the New Testament and the generations immediately following have fixed for ever the Christian standards for personal and social life, and that is their main contribution to history. Within the comparatively narrow limits of their own community the early disciples of Christ exemplified a social fellowship which must ever command the allegiance of humanity. They manifested a type of personal character and social feeling which will stand in perpetual judgment of anything less sensitive to the things of the Spirit or less humane. They generated aspirations for liberty, equality, and fraternity ; motives of compassion, charity, and service ; sentiments of social responsibility and social justice ; an enthusiasm for humanity and a passion for fellowship that can never again die out of humanity's heart.

Compared with the wide community the whole Roman Empire which Christianity in later times essayed to leaven with its Spirit, the voluntary community of Christian people was a simple homogeneous social group. But in itself it was by no means simple or homogeneous. It embraced all the social and racial types of the ancient world. It gathered from all religions. It overstepped all the barriers of birth, sex, and prejudice which could then keep men apart. Roman and Jew, lettered and unlettered, freeman and slave, fisherman and patrician, harlot and merchant—

they were all represented in that many-hued fraternity, and they were all bound together in bonds of friendship and intimacy. The pictures in the catacombs, where men and women eat the love-feast together, portray the essential quality of universal friendship by which all less intimate and more exclusive companies stand condemned as deficient in humanity. In the first uprush of the Christian experience " they had all things in common." For, they said, " If we are fellows in that which is imperishable, how much more in things perishable ? "

The instinctive social enthusiasm and friendly feeling of the early Christians springs from the characteristically Christian closeness of association between the love of God and the love of man. It is impossible to contemplate Jesus Christ without the stirring and religious strengthening of affections and purposes which reach out immediately to every human being of whom one can make a neighbour. In the first creative period of Christian history the joy of sharing needed not to be taught as a duty ; it was discovered as an experience. There was a reason for it, but it was not induced by reason. " Wherein any can do good to his neighbours and does it not," he is " alien to the Lord's love." " For what we afford to our friends through affection, we should afford to strangers through humaneness."

The First Achievements and Failures

This being the social ideal of Early Christianity, it is something of a historic problem that the early Christians did not break more radically than they did with the social institutions of their time, and notably with slavery. It is clear that they were indisposed to tolerate wide differences of wealth or position. " To retain more property than we strictly need is a violation of a justice," they said. " It is a ' holding fast what belongs to others.' " Wealth was only excusable if it was socially used. Yet slavery was tolerated. Perhaps the political imagination of those days could not grasp the possibility of a different social order, but only the possibility of a change of personal relations within the existing order. Perhaps they were right if they judged that slavery could not be eradicated from the world till multitudes of slaves and multitudes of freemen had lived alongside one another for long periods in deep mutual respect and affection. Perhaps the general repudiation of slavery could only have led to bloodshed and anarchy. On the other hand, the long toleration of so un-Christian a basis of society may well account for the relative failure of the Church to leaven the Roman Empire with the principles when later the opportunity came to its hand.

But if the ideal was not fully realised, it was realised to such an extent that the most commanding personalities of the Roman Empire came to be convinced that Christianity was the religion which could create the character needed to save an empire threatened by social disruption. It was not the philosophy or the spiritual mysticism of Christianity that won the adhesion of the Roman mind : it was the social type to which Christianity gave rise. It was a time when economic developments were squeezing out the independent peasant farmer citizen on whom the empire had rested in the past, and multiplying the proportion of plutocrats, slaves, and unemployed freemen without the instinct or character for responsible citizenship. It was a time which has close parallels with our own, as Lord Eustace Percy has been pointing out. Moreover, the outlook of the responsible Roman rulers was not unlike that of the responsible leaders of our own time. Perhaps the same capacity of Christianity for inspiring responsible citizenship will again regain for Christianity the position it has to some extent lost in recent years. But there are other qualities elicited by later periods of Christian development that are equally necessary to the tasks of to-day.

II. THE TRANSITION FROM THE ANCIENT WORLD

We pass over very briefly the long period in European history between the establishment of Christianity as the religion of the Roman Empire and the Middle Ages, which is our next study, because this chaotic period, when the barbarians overran Europe, is not so relevant to our present times. It may be all too relevant if the lesson of history is not quickly learned and the crisis of our time prevented from issuing in calamity. But at the moment we are counting on the lessons being learned and the social evolution of our people maintained in peaceful paths. The only remarks, therefore, necessary about this intermediate period are two.

The Evidence of Creative Power

The first note to be made on this period is that it demonstrated to the full the capacity of Christianity for inspiring social ideals and loyalties that were strong enough to create a new order. This is not said to discredit the element of strength and vision that comes from the Roman partnership. All that was fine in Roman thought and life became tributary to this society-building power of Christianity, just as the strength and insight of the Greek appreciation of humanity had allied itself with the more enthusiastic humanity that Christianity inspired. But it was the unity of the common faith that created the unity of European culture, with no previous unity of custom or race among the warring tribes it subjugated to assist the process. It was primarily in the monastic centres that a social culture was maintained, and it was from the monastic bases that Europe was resettled and equipped with a Christian culture that ultimately embodied also many traditions of Greece and Rome.

The Limitation of the Working Ideal

On the other hand, we should note also that the social and political philosophy which was to underlie the great experiment of the Middle Ages was that formulated by Augustine in a period of impending political disruption, when Christian thinkers were new to the responsibilities of political life. This fact has a wide bearing upon the character and limitations of the later attempt at a Christian order of society made by mediæval Christians. It meant that the mind of the Middle Ages was formed at a time when the masses of mankind were peculiarly unfit for the appeal of reason, when the social life of the average man was particularly lax and licentious and when the governmental function was habitually exercised in arbitrary and autocratic ways. This gave an unhappy bias to the political and social outlook of Christendom for the next thousand years. It is accountable for a repressive, compulsive, overcentralised and autocratic temper in the governing thought of the Church.

What, then, did Christianity make of Europe when it finally triumphed and became the dominant influence in a settled society ?

III. THE MIDDLE AGES

Here again, as in the previous period, it is more important to see what ideal Christianity was able to maintain in the field of attention than to measure exactly how far the conduct of all men conformed to the ideal. We do not now know exactly how far the mediæval Christian teachers were able to exact obedience, for example, to their economic teaching ; but we do know that they were able to uphold the belief that God required of all men certain standards of economic conduct, and the Church was there to help and constrain them to conform their lives to that pattern. In that Christian vision and standard of social righteousness we shall find four points claiming notice.

1. *Their Strong Sense of Right*

The first characteristic note of the social conviction of the Middle Ages was the broad certainty that human laws should be the means of bringing men into harmony with the eternal order which is God's will for man. The well-being of society demands that in every sphere of conduct men should act under a high sense of duty to God and man, and should at least approximate to the Christian standard. No conduct was excusable if it was not reconcilable with the general interests of society. And the general interests of society included the ideal of a settled peace between the different estates or social groups into which society was divided. Rich and poor alike had their rights to the standard of life to which they were born and bred. It was, in this view, as wrong to violate a habitual right of that kind as it is in our view wrong to break a definite contract. Any kind of action which might lead to such action would have been condemned as a breach of justice.

Moreover, such justice was regarded not only as morally right, but as inexorably necessary. Any sin against justice must meet with calamity and lead to the undoing of society. The best thought of that period would therefore have been sure that any type of economic conduct that should deprive anyone of a steady share in the responsibilities and privileges of the work and wealth of the community (as does unemployment in our day) must be intolerable to God and doomed to judgment.

We pass then to consider how the mediæval Christian conviction about economic justice was expressed in two particular matters, viz. the Just Price and Usury.

2. *Their Control of Prices in Defence of Social Rights*

We can best understand the moral attitude of the mediæval Christian to unjust prices if we recall the wartime indignation against the " profiteer." A man who was known to profit much in a way that would involve as its correlative the privation of others or the obstruction of the national effort was felt to be doing something repulsive to all good feeling. The people of the mediæval period had the same feelings of abhorrence to those who at any time were greedy of gain. A large profit on any transaction was to them something disgusting. The spoils of war might be dignified by the risk of life and the display of manly strength involved in winning them, but the spoils of trade were mean and despicable things. And so we have the strenuous and complicated attempt of the period to prevent such gains, as much for the protection of a man against his own lower self as to protect society from his depredations —as we to-day might legislate to remove temptation to drunkenness from one who was too morally weak to stand against it.

The ins and outs of the working of the Just Price do not concern us here.[1] Its methods and results were necessarily approximate. The Just Price, wrote Thomas Aquinas, " is not fixed with mathematical precision, but depends on a kind of estimate, so that a slight addition or subtraction would not seem to destroy the equality of justice." The general result, as Professor Cunningham states it, was that " wages became the first charge on industry, and prices on the whole depended on them." The labourer was thus counted worthy of his hire, and no iron law could force down wages to a bare subsistence level (as has been usual in later times) except in days of plague and famine.

3. *Their Resistance to Unearned Wealth—The Ban on Usury*

In the same category as the unjust price the mediæval churchmen placed the taking of interest on money. It is not sufficiently realised in our day that their condemnation of usury was not confined to the taking of excessive interest on money ; it applied to the taking of any interest at all. The foundation of this attitude to interest was the observation that as a matter of fact in an agricultural community the man who was compelled by his necessity to borrow was rarely in a position at the best to do more than repay the original loan at its original total. It was this experience and concrete knowledge that gave weight to the specific teaching of the Old Testament, given under similar circumstances, to the same effect. Nor was it without weight for their minds that under the changed conditions of the New Testament the word of Jesus was equally strong against the loan that wanted " something again." It is beside the mark to trace the history of the process by which exceptions to the traditional teaching were so multiplied that it was emptied of almost all significance. What is rather to be

[1] The modern equivalent of the mediæval economic teaching is examined in a recent publication of the Christian Social Council, *The Just Price*, Student Christian Movement, 4s. 6d.

pondered is the fact that at a time of strong religious thinking on these questions it was generally recognised that the
taking of interest on money was fraught with great danger
to the moral life of the individual and to the general welfare
of society.

Every priest was therefore trained to understand how
readily " unreasonable covetousness " can show itself in
inequitable bargains between borrower and lender, buyer
and seller, landlord and tenant, master and servant. He
was required to give practical guidance on these matters
in his preaching, and in the confessional he was expected
" to ask barons, knights, mayors, and judges whether they
had always done justice, whether they had oppressed their
subjects by imposing undue taxes or exacting undue services. Merchants and shopkeepers were to be questioned
about usury (open or concealed), fraudulent sales, false
weights and measures ; farmers and labourers about theft,
withholding payments due to their masters, and encroach-
ing on their neighbours lands."[1] Thus even the details of
economic life were related with practical thoroughness and
common sense to the universal principles of the Christian
faith.

4. The Guilds

The instrument by which the Middle Ages strove to keep
its economic life in accord with its social ideal was the trade
guild. First on the field, the Merchant Guild enabled craftsmen and merchants in co-operation to establish their freedom of action outside feudal control, and to use that
freedom to maintain their standards of work and reward.
Therein they restrained the possible selfishness of unworthy
members who might otherwise gain advantage of one another by forestalling the rest in their buying or selling. The
Craft Guilds which followed served also the purpose of
maintaining the quality of the workmanship of each craft—
whether weavers, armourers, goldsmiths, or what not—that
in the words of the Newcastle Merchant Adventurers,

[1] *Historical Illustrations of the Social Effects of Christianity*, pp. 83, 87.

" honest and virtuous masters might maintain the feats of merchandise." By fines, imprisonments, and banishment (in the last resort) they sought to uphold a fair quality in the work, a fair price to the purchaser, and a fair livelihood for themselves and their journeymen and apprentices. By their religious character they brought higher sanctions to the support of their ideals. The proof of their sense of justice is the testimony of historians to the lot they secured for the worker. Thorold Rogers has in more than one place stated that the latter part of the Middle Ages was the Golden Age of the English labourer in respect of his material position. The dictum that " culturally the workman was his master's companion in ideas, beliefs, education, and tastes " was true of the privileged craftsmen, though not of the unattached labourer or of the vast peasant majority.

The foregoing description of the economic teaching of mediæval Christianity has endeavoured to bring out the features of it which were true to the spirit of Christianity in its classical form. Yet the economic ideal of that period broke down. That has to be remembered and accounted for. Has Christianity not the power to inspire conformity to its own ideal? Or was there some weakness in the Christian teaching of that particular age? There would seem to have been three elements of weakness that account for its downfall. In three respects it did violence to Christian principles of which the Christian consciousness of those days was becoming increasingly aware. From age to age fresh aspects of the Christian ideal come to be realised ; and as this comes to pass the ideas and practices formulated without appreciation of these newly emerging principles lose their hold upon the Christian mind and conscience and crumble away. It will be best, in the limited space available, to waste no words in describing the defects of the mediæval period, but to proceed at once to a description of the emergent convictions which became operative in the age that followed.

IV. THE BIRTH OF THE MODERN WORLD
1. *The Revolt from " Other-Worldliness "*

The first of the emergent Christian convictions that weakened the power of the mediæval Christian economics over the Christian conscience was the spirit of Christian humanism that came into power through the social and intellectual renaissance of the twelfth century and had its great exponent in St. Francis. Writing of this, Mr. Christopher Dawson has said[1] :

" The asceticism of St. Francis no longer involves the rejection of the natural world and the turning away of the mind from the created to the Absolute. . . . The powers of nature which had been first divinised and worshipped, and then in turn rejected by man as he realised the transcendence of the spiritual, are now brought back into the world of religion, and in his great canticle of the sun, St. Francis once more celebrates the praises of Mother Earth, Brother Fire, and all the other holy creatures of God. . . . Thus the Franciscan attitude to nature and human life marks the beginning of a new epoch of humanism."

From this newly realised joy in the natural delights the earth affords to man it was an easy step to the conclusion that it was good to be engaged in the work of making such things more plentiful and more accessible. The Christian consciousness was beginning to regard the life of trade and manufacture in a new light. It could no longer be regarded exclusively or mainly as a temptation. The old ascetic, repressive, and fearful attitude which inspired at least a part of the mediæval Christian restraint on wealth was undermined. Physical enjoyment in a moderate degree had become sacramental again, as it was to Jesus himself.

The impulse to develop and enjoy the riches of the world thus gained a footing among the things that the Christian

[1] In *Religion and Progress.*

might regard as good. And if these things were good and the Christian might rejoice in them with a simple, religious, childlike gladness, it was not possible for those who gave themselves to the activities of trade to defer as before to the restrictions which were dictated to some extent by the negative asceticism of an earlier day. The way was prepared for the layman to resent the impositions of the cleric in these matters. When, then, at the time of the Reformation, Luther and the Reformers, in their recoil from clericalism, required alternatives to the religious vocations of the monastic order, they could find these in the fields of trade. And so they did. Max Weber's study of the Protestant Ethic has made this convincing enough. The ascetic spirit in Protestantism took the form of industry, self-denial, and thrift.

2. *The Demand for Individual Freedom*

The second direction in which the Christian consciousness was awakening to a fullness of life not realised before was in respect of the rightful spiritual autonomy of every individual Christian man. The alliance of a monarchical Church with a feudal organisation of society had resulted in a limitation of the freedom of individual life that could not continue for ever. Persecution had become increasingly systematic and cruel ; freedom of expression had been silenced. But the age that discovered the joy of the natural life and took it as a gift of God was discovering also the power of the individual mind to think its own thoughts and go its own ways. Thomas Aquinas was extracting from the mine of Greek thought ideas about the rights of the human reason and the consequent autonomy of the sciences in their several domains which were bound to prove intoxicating to some. There were those who had evidence that a word of God was stirring in their own souls, and they chafed under the restriction of a rule of life that had been formulated in a period when man was less qualified for liberty and more in danger from the least manifestation of it. Liberty was now becoming possible, and the way was open for new experiments.

3. *The Claim to Progress*

Inspired with these new convictions, the only thing that could possibly have held the laymen of that period loyal to traditional guidance would have been its close adaptation to the rapidly changing circumstances of the social life of the time. But that was not to be. Perhaps inevitably, the Christian leaders of the transitional period were unable to detach the principles which inspired their teaching from the social conditions which were passing away. It was not so easy in those days as it is in ours to grasp the possibility of radical change in the structure of society. But radical change was coming inevitably with the opening up of communications, the increasing growth of cities and the replacing of the local by the international market. As Mr. Tawney has pointed out, under these circumstances a body of teaching could only hope to survive if it were re-thought ; but instead it was merely restated. Changing circumstances required the constant admission of qualifications and exceptions until the canon law of the Just Price had come to be like the schoolboy's definition of a net—" a lot of holes joined together by string." So the old body of teaching came rightly to be discredited though it may all the time have been enshrining principles that society could not afford to lose. Of the later phase of the process by which it lost all influence the Copec Conference volume of *Historical Illustrations of the Social Effects of Christianity* says :

" The doctrine that religion oversteps its province when it interferes with economic affairs would have been as unintelligible to most sixteenth-century Churchmen as to their mediæval predecessors. Where we see the movements of markets ebbing and flowing as irresistibly as the tides, they saw and lamented the failure to master economic appetites. Had they grasped the fact that particular acts of covetousness or oppression could be expressed in terms of general law, they would no more have regarded that fact as absolving the individual of his moral responsibilities than the modern statistician, who correlates the consumption of alcohol or the illegitimate birth-rate with the changes in the price of wheat, considers himself precluded from condemning intemperance or sexual immorality."

But the tide had set against the practice of the Christian teaching on these subjects.

" Increasingly disputed by practical men and gradually discarded by religious teachers, the conception that a moral rule is binding on Christians in their economic transactions gives way to the temper which asserts that no moral rule beyond the letter of the civil law exists. By the beginning of the eighteenth century the view that trade is one thing and religion another, if not explicitly asserted, is tacitly accepted. Could any intellectual revolution be more profound than one which substituted for a supernatural criterion one conception or another of economic expediency ? "[1]

The quotations cited above cover a long period, and that is as it should be, for the transition from the mediæval to the modern period was by no means abrupt. It is popularly supposed that the characteristic ideas of the Middle Ages remained largely unchallenged till Luther's appearance broke in upon a static situation. And even some who know the untruth of that view may feel surprise that the characteristic ideas of the modern period emerged so early and the characteristic ideas of the Middle Ages lingered so long. We come at last, however, to a period in which the full effects of both Renaissance and Reformation have been realised and the modern period is in its full stride. We may take the eighteenth and nineteenth centuries at any rate as fully illustrative of the modern spirit. We have then to ask of this period, How did the ethos of the period reach its

[1] *Historical Illustrations of the Social Effects of Christianity*, pp. 106, 108 and 109.

full development ? and : What did the Christianity of this period make of society and especially of its economic life ?

V. THE MODERN PERIOD

When we survey the outcome of the modern period, we find two curiously different but equally characteristic features for which the Church has to take praise or blame.

The Record of Social and Political Emancipation

In the first place the modern emphasis upon individual liberty, and the equality of men in regard to that liberty, has had vast and astonishing results. These are to be recorded alike in the religious, the political, the legal, and the social spheres. Undoubtedly the passion for religious liberty has been the driving-power of these great changes. But the fight for religious liberty and the discovery that it may easily be frustrated by political forces has called forth a powerful movement for political equality. Christian enthusiasm has passed over that point and flung itself into the fight for political equality. As a result it could be stated by Harnack, at a birthday celebration of George Washington in Berlin, that all the free political institutions of the world can be traced back to the Puritan reformation in England.

The wave of enthusiasm for liberty that created and was itself re-created by the struggle for political and religious liberty spent itself in its backwash upon the removal of the inequalities and other obstructions to individual rights that it found in the law of England. It is curious to note, however, how quickly the enthusiasm for a principle becomes an enthusiasm for a phrase. The idea of freedom is one of the easiest to invoke in an English mind. And it can be invoked for almost any cause. In the economic spheres the claim for freedom has in effect been the claim to immunity from interference when acting in ways that made others into virtual slaves. We are coming now to realise that the economic freedom of the rich and powerful means the economic enslavement of the weak and poor. We can see now that the " equality of opportunity " which so warmed the hearts of nineteenth-century Liberals is a ghastly travesty of equality so long as the social and economic opportunity to use opportunity varies as it now does—as Mr. Tawney has recently pointed out with inimitable satire in his book *Equality*.

But whilst the recognition of personal rights has been thus thwarted in the economic sphere, it has had many other manifestations in social life besides those already noted in the legal and political spheres. The political enfranchisement of women is but a feeble symbol of the social emancipation which has been accorded them. Children have for the first time in history gained the right to develop somewhat along the lines of their particular genius and not along the lines of their parents' wish or their teachers' prejudice. This period has also witnessed the rise of a great mass of philanthropies, animated by a very powerful sympathy for suffering folk. At the same time there has been a softening of the attitude toward prisoners, criminals, and every type of defective. This outburst of humanitarian feeling is far more than a mere sympathy for suffering. It at least desires to see the broken or bruised life made whole and strong. The missionary movement abroad and the genuine concern for child peoples evidence the same temper. Slavery has been largely, though not entirely destroyed by its power. Only the lust for economic gain can resist it.

The Record of Economic Enslavement

On the other hand, the spirit of humanity has, during this period, been ruthlessly subordinated to economic ends. It is truly astonishing to what depths of inhumanity men sank at the time of the Enclosures and the first decades of the Industrial Revolution, when we remember the high moral purposes with which the modern industrial development set out. The ruthless confiscation of the poor landworkers' privileges ; the heartless and savage treatment of those who resisted—exemplified by the transportation of the seven Tolpuddle martyrs " not for anything you have done, but as an example to others "—the relentless suction of the once independent worker into the factory and his degradation to the status of an ill-paid hand ; the callous cruelty to women and children in the early days of the factories when the owners were making fortunes ; the blighting of the countryside and its replacement by haphazard, hideous, inadequate, and insanitary towns—these things are told again in Mr. S. E. Keeble's *Christian Responsibility for the Social Order*. The story recalls the now almost unthinkable inhumanities of the slave traffic in ancient Rome or modern Africa or the Inquisition in the Middle Ages, and provokes the reflection how monstrous can be the action of men who once allow their humanity to be subordinated to a false economic or political theory which they have exalted to a law.

In its later developments, when its ruthless hurtfulness has been somewhat curbed by restrictive legislation, the free play of this philosophy and life has wrought remarkable results of very different kinds. On the one hand, it has produced prodigious material wealth, it has caused population to increase enormously, it has facilitated a notable rise in the standard of living of most classes of the community. It has greatly multiplied human wants. It has also greatly increased individual skill, initiative, invention, and resources in a thousand new directions, but at the expense of the more characteristically Christian virtues of gentleness and meekness. And it has trained the world in vast efforts of voluntary co-operation. On the other hand, it has torn multitudes out of the country, and exiled them in towns in which their old cultures withered, it has devastated whole countrysides by sudden change of economic process. It has ruthlessly exploited the resources and destroyed the ancient customs of primitive peoples, and now it has dealt unemployment to millions, anxiety and insecurity to millions more, and seems on the point of final collapse.

Mr. Christopher Dawson has recently worked out a parallel between the military exploitation and consequent destruction of the Roman world and the economic exploitation and threatened destruction of the modern world. Now as then we find the old standards of life, the old cultures, and the old agrarian economies everywhere broken up, and the peasants and free citizens becoming a smaller proportion of the whole community. Then when the vastness and rapidity of the development caused dislocation and reaction, the unified society proved too complex and its elements without sufficient vital and cultural reserves to make the necessary adjustments. In our own case the divorce from the soil and from the rhythm of nature, our excessive urbanisation, and the condition of high nervous tension induced by the speed and artificiality of life still further threaten us.

The Explanation of the Contradiction

If we seek the explanation of this spectacular defeat of the humanity of a people we may find it in part in the extraordinary fascination of an undreamed of opportunity for expressing personal power and securing personal gain. The earlier Christian moralists were proved right in their contention that covetousness is a sin that is literally insatiable. In part too, we may trace the sorry *débâcle* to the preoccupation of Christian peoples with their own quarrels. They were so busy persecuting and being persecuted, denouncing one another or defending themselves, that their energies were withdrawn from the leavening of the social life. These are partial explanations; but the main reason must be sought in the conflicting philosophies of life which inevitably arose out of the vast accumulation of new knowledge.

The Tardy Reassertion of the Christian Conscience

The main thing to the credit of the Church of this period, in this relation, is the continuance and ever-growing stream of individuals and movements that could not stay silent in the face of these iniquities. Mr. Keeble, in his *Christian Responsibility for the Social Order*, traces the course of the streams of Christian service and moral protest which ran in separate rivulets of personal action and protest of poets and artists, ministers and clergy, through the first half of the nineteenth century and broadened out into definite movements from the time of the Christian Socialists onwards. Towards the end of the century these movements are gaining a sort of semi-official recognition in most of the Christian denominations. By 1888 the Bishops at the Lambeth Conference exhort their clergy to set forth the true principles of society :

" The Christian Church is bound, following the teaching of her Master, to aid every wise endeavour which has for its object the material and the moral welfare of the poor. Her Master taught her that all men are brethren, not because they share the same blood, but because they have a common heavenly Father. He further taught her that if any members of this spiritual family were greater, richer, or better than the rest, they were bound to use their special means or ability in the service of the whole. . . . It will contribute no little to draw together the various classes of society if the clergy endeavour in sermons and lectures to set forth the true principle of society, showing how Property is a trust to be administered for the good of Humanity, and how much of what is good and true in Socialism is to be found in the precepts of Christ."

This was endorsed and strengthened by the Lambeth Conferences of 1897 and 1908. Indeed in each succeeding decade the voice of Lambeth has become richer and clearer in censure and counsel on industrial affairs.[1] Then, in 1891, Pope Leo XIII issued his Encyclical protesting against the injustice done to the working classes of Europe since and in consequence of the break up of mediæval corporate life, affirming the living wage as a " dictate of natural justice more imperious and ancient than any bargain between man and man."

[1] See especially the Archbishops' Fifth Report, *Christianity and Industrial Problems*.

We can thus look back upon the record of Christian effort and lack of effort to realise the Christian ideal in the sphere of social life from a point in time when the neglect of recent centuries has been dramatically repudiated and the task of working out a Christian order of society formally resumed. At the Copec Conference of 1924 the British Churches entered upon a new era in Christian history. The fourth large-scale experiment towards the establishment of a Christian community was then initiated. Since then the work of thinking out a new Christian sociology has slowly gathered strength. Later chapters of this book will tell the story of the resultant effort along the lines here under review. It remains in this chapter to ask the question : What are the constructive contributions to be won for to-day from the study of the past ? Can these be wrought into a coherent whole ? And is that whole sufficient for our present guidance ?

Behind this paper lies the conviction that the total inspiration of Christianity, scattered over Christian history, is sufficient for the modern task ; but only on condition that the very different inspirations of different periods are combined in one single whole. The early Church had not the power to establish the Christian order of society ; but it gave mankind a social impulse which drove the later centuries to make the attempt. The Middle Ages made the attempt on a considerable scale, and the attempt succeeded up to a point ; but was finally defeated by inherent defects in its understanding of the spirit of the Kingdom it sought to establish. The modern period has been more sensitive to some of the Christian values than any previous age, but has combined with its greater ambition for personal Christian freedom, a fatal surrender to the lure of material success. Only if we can count upon the rapid and widespread recovery of the convictions and impulses of all three periods have we reasonable hope. Is there any justification for that hope ?

The Gains of the Past

Take first the early centuries, with their deep humanity and enthusiastic goodwill. How much of the social qualities of those days remain to us ? Anyone who took his views of the modern Englishman from the reading of the English papers would suppose that the Christian character had disappeared from the earth. They largely address themselves to a community that is energetic, competent, resourceful, bent on superficial enjoyment, entirely indifferent to the demands of any absolute righteousness, and reliably selfish, save in so far as selfishness has learnt to take a class or national form. But as we mix with men we find the world is full of kindness, self-sacrifice, disinterested service, and eager good-will. Said a Japanese scientist visiting these islands for the first time, " What impresses me most about your country is the readiness of everyone I meet to show me kindness : Christianity must have entered very deeply into the character of your people for this to be so." It is at least a defensible proposition that the sentiment of those who count in this country is largely Christian still. In every rank of society the Christian heart beats strongly.

Take next, the dominant characteristic of post Reformation Christianity at its best. It is the sense of a personal calling to serve God in the work of life, and to put into one's service something unique and original. How much of these qualities remains to us ? Very much, in spite of all that the economic machine has done in the last hundred and fifty years to curtail the opportunities and crush the moral spirit of the mass of men. Professor W. G. S. Adams recently said that the outcrop of social initiative in new group activities in this country since the war is unique in history. The Vice-chancellor of Liverpool University recently testified to the unparalleled efficiency and devotion of our Civil Service. And is there not a very high degree of inflexible conscientiousness in the first rank, if not so much in the second and third ranks, of our leadership in industry and politics ? We have such high qualities, both for origination and for mutual assimilation and co-operation, that there is no reason for us yet to confess our experiment of spiritual democracy bankrupt. If only we had a more intellectual faith.

It is precisely in respect of those things in which the Church of the earlier Ages was strong that we stand in greatest need. We have so long disregarded the necessary co-ordination of truth. Fascinated by the modern discovery that the physical law is absolute and reliable in its own sphere, we have forgotten that the moral law and the spiritual law are absolute too. The society of man cannot be founded on physical science alone, though physical science is capable of enriching any society that is true to the whole law of its being. The Christian theology of the Incarnation is a child's fairy-tale unless it means that science will not serve the society that forgets the absolute demand of humanity upon men. The toleration of any practice that subordinates humanity to science must lead ultimately to social wreckage, as our economic science will do unless we quickly drive it back to its legitimate sphere. The rules by which man guides his economic life must not be those which merely multiply goods and the tools to make more goods : they must be those which promote the social relation and the spiritual culture which the science of the day makes accessible and humanity teaches man to regard as ideal.

Thus the early period of Christian history sets us the standard of society which must ever be our social ideal, and shows us the Church at work, through teaching admonition and discipline, holding its members loyal to that ideal. The Church of the Middle Ages witnessed the great experiment of a social order inspired by such conceptions of the Christian ideal as that age was able to appreciate, and backed again by all the Churches' forces for guidance and constraint. The Church of the later period has adventured a yet greater task. With a longer education in social progress and a greater wealth of individual development it has essayed, and so far deeply failed to bring men's social life into voluntary captivity to Christ. Shall we succeed where the immediate past has so signally failed ?

The Immediate Prospect

" Our problem is vastly larger than that which presented itself to the mediæval Church, but so also is our equipment for coping with it. . . . We are not in the dark to anything like the extent that the mediævalists were. We are far less compelled than were they to rely upon theorising and abstract reasoning in forming our conclusions ; and we know far more about the directions in which social institutions are capable of development and what consequences may be expected to follow for society and the individual.

" But probably the most important respect in which our problem has to be distinguished from what it was half a dozen centuries ago lies in the fact that in the meantime it has been upon his individual conscience solely that the faithful Christian has been driven to rely. The laying of such a burden upon the individual soul has helped to give us a tradition of ' conscientiousness ' that should add to our restored Christian teaching a quality of conscious co-operation far more splendid than any mere submission to a purely authoritative system, however pure the faith and devotion of those who offer it, could ever be.

" For all these reasons, then—and no doubt for many more—the Church, if she is to take up explicitly and corporately, as many of us feel she must, her challenge to worldly standards, will not be returning to any bygone phase of her history ; she will be entering upon a new one."[1]

[1] Quoted from *Social Discipline in the Christian Community* from a chapter by Maurice Reckitt, author of *Faith and Society*.

5. CHRISTIANITY AND HISTORY:

B. *SOCIAL PROGRESS AND THE CONTINENTAL CHURCHES*

By Dr. ALFRED E. GARVIE

THE Roman Catholic Church claims, not only temporal sovereignty for the Pope, but also moral guidance of the whole life of the faithful, besides the direction given in the confessional by priests trained to deal with questions of conscience ; and it is represented by the public pronouncements of the Pope on the issues of the day. These declarations, guided as they largely are by the traditions of the past, yet endeavour to apply the permanent moral principles of the Church to the varying conditions of the world. It is not to be in any way unjust to them to say that they incline to conservatism in the solutions which they offer to modern social problems. In accordance with its exclusive claims, Roman Catholicism refuses any official participation in any ecumenical movements among the Christian Churches.

THE ORTHODOX EASTERN CHURCH

The Orthodox Oriental Churches, while preserving a rigid attitude as regards dogma and ritual, being nationally organised, and laying stress on their autocephalous character, have not in recent years taken so exclusive an attitude, and have been represented at the Stockholm (*Life and Work*, 1925) and the Lausanne (*Faith and Order*, 1927) Conferences, as also in the World Alliance for International Friendship through the Churches, and have continued their co-operation in subsequent activities. While the more progressive leaders, who participate in these movements recognise the need and the duty of the Churches' witness and work in social matters, and are using their influence to stimulate interest and activity, yet, on the confession of some of them, it must be admitted that the rank and file even of the clergy have not abandoned an attitude of aloofness, and still confine religion to ritualism and mysticism. It must be remembered that the Greek and Balkan Churches were for centuries under Turkish sovereignty, oppressed and persecuted, with no opportunity for, and no obligations of, free citizenship, and that even now they are divided by national jealousies and enmities ; for their common inheritance of faith and order, to which they held very firmly, has not gained the mastery over their strong nationalism. Under more favourable conditions, and under the influence of the Western Churches, one may hope for a development of a more social Christian conscience.

THE PROTESTANT CHURCHES

Turning now to the Churches with which I am most familiar—the Protestant Churches of the Continent— a broad distinction, which is not adequately recognised in the English-speaking world, must be noted for a proper understanding of their social attitude—that between Lutheran (Evangelical) and Reformed (Calvinistic) Churches. The *Scandinavian* countries are almost entirely Lutheran, and represent an earlier phase of Lutheranism than the German ; in *Germany*, besides the politically influential Roman Catholic Church, both types of Protestantism exist, the Lutheran predominating. On political grounds, in some of the States, the two communions were, early in the last century, brought under one ecclesiastical administration, and are known as Union or Evangelical Churches, although the congregations are allowed to preserve their distinctive character. The Church of Prussia, the most influential of the twenty-eight territorial Churches, is a Union Church. In *Holland* the Reformed type prevails, but is sharply divided into " liberal " and " conservative." In the *other countries* of Europe, Protestantism, whether Lutheran or Reformed, is the faith of minorities. For the present purpose it is necessary as briefly as possible to mark a difference between Lutheranism and Calvinism.

LUTHERANISM

Luther remained essentially in the Middle Ages ; so long as hindrances to the individual's assurance of salvation, which the Roman Church in his judgment imposed, were removed, he was content to retain as much of dogma and ritual as was not inconsistent with the fresh experience of divine grace ; and, as regards the ordering of the Churches which sprang into life in the new movement, he committed himself to the princes rather than the people. The Peasants' Revolt so alarmed him that he wanted as little change as possible. In Germany, till the Revolution of 1918, the territorial Churches were so much controlled by the State that they could not develop an independent activity in social reform. One of the present leaders confesses that only now have they the freedom to fulfil their aims as Christian Churches. The historical Lutheranism recognises three spheres in which the Christian lives and works : the natural, the civic, and the religious or distinctively Christian. Each has its own laws of divine appointment, and in each the Christian submits to these laws in obedience to God. The Christian moral or social ideal cannot be transported into these other spheres. In the world the Christian must exercise his earthly calling, and ought to engage in philanthropy (*Liebesthätigkeit*) as expressing the divinely required love of the neighbour ; but the spheres of economics and politics are autonomous, and their laws must be accepted. Hence the acquiescence of the Churches of Germany, with little (if any) criticisms, in the policy of its rulers. The conception of the Kingdom of God, which in Great Britain and America has been the banner under which the struggle for social reform has been carried on, is in German theology for the most part regarded as eschatological—God's interventions in human history in his own way at his own time for his own ends. At Stockholm the attitude of the English-speaking section was condemned by many Germans as Anglo-American " activism," and it must be confessed that some of the English speakers did magnify the free activity of man, and minimise his constant dependence on God. By the end of the conference some of the German speakers did recognise that philanthropy was not enough, and that Christians might work as well as pray for a more Christian order of society.

CALVINISM

Calvin, in contrast to Luther, while accepting the doctrine of justification by faith as crucial in the controversy with Rome, made the sovereignty of God the guiding principle of his theology. He found the pattern for human society in the Bible, and in Geneva he essayed a theocracy, a social order in which civic authority must support ecclesiastical, in the endeavour to secure entire obedience to the law of God in the life of man. In the countries to which Calvinism spread—France, Holland, Scotland—the struggle for religious liberty forbade acquiescence in the existing social order ; and consequently the principles of Calvin have more directly influenced social development than those of Luther. But Calvinism soon came to be very closely associated with the development of capitalism, the beginnings of which go back to the thirteenth century. The Roman Church modified its prohibition of taking interest on loans as usury ; and this was one of the counts which Luther had against the Papacy. But Calvin recognised the new situation, and gave a much qualified assent to what he recognised was a necessity, if commerce were to be carried on. With Calvin, as Troeltsch maintains, began social reform as the conscious work of Christian society ; but the changes then effected were more in the interests of the middle than the working class. Weber has endeavoured to show a close connection between Protestantism and the spirit of capitalism, and has been followed by Troeltsch. Calvinism especially enjoined industry, economy, an abstention from worldly pleasures, and those who practised these virtues accumulated wealth, which they did not spend on themselves, but put back into business. Be this as it may, it is certain that it is in the countries influenced by Calvinism that the new industrial development found much of its support. During last century, and even in this, what may be described as a capitalist ethic has retained its influence among the wealthier laity of the Christian Churches.

GERMANY

But even before " Stockholm " there were opposing movements towards a more nearly New Testament ethic. Of the English-speaking countries it is not my task to say anything ; but the present situation in Germany and France may be described. The Social Democracy in both countries is definitely non-Christian, anti-Church. In Germany and Switzerland many of the trade unions are so definitely opposed to the Church that special Christian trade unions have been formed, and it was with difficulty that some of their leaders were persuaded that there was no need of a propaganda in this country for the formation of such organisations. It was in opposition to this Socialism that Stöcker, a Court Chaplain, started the movement now known as *Kirchlich-Sozial* (Churchly Social). This movement does advocate social reforms, and is very moderate in its demands. A more radical movement, due to Naumann is called *Evangelisch-Sozial*, and, while not committed to Socialism, is more progressive, and admits Socialists to its membership. Each of these movements issues a magazine bearing its distinctive name. A number of pastors are avowing themselves Socialists, but this action does not find general favour among the Church authorities. Since the disestablishment of the territorial Churches (now reduced from forty-one to twenty-eight), a federation has been formed for common action in common interests. This was officially represented at Stockholm, and continues to give generous support and valuable co-operation. A thoroughly equipped economist is supported by the German Churches as the Director of the Research Department of the Christian Social Institute at Geneva, and has made a thorough investigation of several social problems, most notably unemployment. In many districts of Germany there are " social pastors," qualified men set apart to look after the social activities of the Churches. It would not be just to German Protestantism not to add that the philanthropy has been most admirably organised in the " Innere Mission," which with its manifold institutions is in more immediate association with the Church organisation than are the benevolent institutions of our own land.

FRANCE

Protestantism in France is represented by a very small minority, but influential beyond its numbers. It is confronted with an aggressive, antagonistic Socialism, but among its pastors are many zealous for social reform, and a few even profess a Christian Socialism. The review, *Le Christianisme Social* represents a progressive advocacy of consistent and courageous application of the Christian principles of the Divine Fatherhood and the human brotherhood, and the consequent universal law of love, to the social order. Protestantism in the Latin countries, realising the small number of its adherents in lands of the Roman Catholic tradition, has formed an association for the advancement of these social principles, not in opposition to, but as independent co-operators with, the German and Scandinavian group, and the English-speaking group.

Each group has its own contribution to make to the common stock of Christian ideals and influences in the refashioning of human society in all lands, since the present crisis has shown that, following the old ways, in which economics and politics alike claimed an autonomy— freedom from all counsel and restraint by the moral principles of Christianity—human society has come to an impasse : poverty amid plenty, nationalism in a world which is increasingly becoming internationally dependent. I have not been able to refer to all the countries of the Continent where the new leaven of a Christianity, fully conscious of its social opportunity and obligation, is spreading. But enough has been said to show that, while there is still a great deal

Ic

of ignorance and indifference among Christian people, in all the Churches, there are leaders of vision and courage who desire to see human society, in all its interests, activities, and relations, transformed by the testimony and the influence of the Christian gospel, so that the Kingdom of God may come in fullness of blessing to all men, classes, nations, and races.

5. CHRISTIANITY AND HISTORY:

c. *THE STOCKHOLM CONFERENCE*

By Dr. GEORGE BELL, Bishop of Chichester

1. In the last few pages an account has been given of the character and work of the different sections of the Christian Church on the Continent, in isolation from one another. It is the object of the pages which follow to provide an outline of that movement for bringing them together in a common witness, which has found its most conspicuous expression in Stockholm.

2. The real obstacle to reunion is the ingrained habit of disunion. Christians have been divided in Europe for four hundred years ; and the Eastern Church has been sundered from the Western since 1054. And this fact, as Bishop Burge wrote in 1921, has more to do with continued separation than many apparently more important things. It is to be expected also that where this habit is longest established, in the Old World, Christian unity will be most difficult to secure ; indeed, without some overwhelming moral experience, perhaps impossible.

3. Before the world war there were various plans and projects for the union of the Churches. But those who took any but a limited interest in any one of them were very few. It is true that the great scholar, Professor Döllinger, in the sixties declared that union was " at once a supreme necessity of the Christian and a perfectly practicable achievement." In doctrine, even in ministry, perhaps an adjustment might have been made, on paper, between leaders untouched by the mental habit of disunion. But where could such leaders, and still more their followers, be found ? Before union is practicable after these centuries of disunion, some moral experience with suffering and tragedy must bring home to the Christian's conscience and heart that it is a " supreme necessity."

4. It is the world war that has made the difference. To

vast numbers of Christians in warring, as well as neutral countries, it came with a startling surprise : and to many it brought a deep moral shock. It was easy for the scoffer to deride the prayers of German, Frenchman, Briton—all calling to the one God to bless their rival arms : but the tragedy which lay behind those prayers sank deep in not a few Christian hearts. Amid the turmoil and hatred of nations, where was the Christian fellowship, where was the uniting power of the Cross ?

5. In November 1914 an appeal for peace and Christian fellowship was issued by a body of Church leaders in Scandinavia, Hungary, Holland, Switzerland, Finland, and the United States of America, on the initiative of the newly consecrated Archbishop of Upsala, Nathan Soderblom (who was given the Nobel Peace Prize in 1930, and died in 1931), containing these words :

" The war is causing untold distress. Christ's body, the Church, suffers and mourns. Mankind in its need, cries out, O Lord, how long ? . . . We, servants of the Church, address to all those who have power or influence in the matter an earnest appeal seriously to keep peace before their eyes, in order that bloodshed soon may cease. We remind especially our Christian brethren of various nations that war cannot sunder the bond of international union that Christ holds in us. . . . The strife of nations must finally serve the dispensation of the Almighty, and all the faithful in Christ are one. Let us therefore call upon God that he may destroy hate and enmity, and in mercy ordain peace for us. His will be done ! "

6. As the war went on, a desire for an international Christian meeting found expression—in Britain, where a British Council was formed to promote one ; in Sweden whence invitations were issued to Church leaders in the warring countries ; in Hungary, in Switzerland, and in America. No large international Christian Conference could

be held while the war lasted. But a declaration was issued from Sweden by Church leaders in the five neutral Protestant countries in December 1917 insisting on the underlying unity of Christians, and emphasising some principal points concerning the conduct of Christians in social life.

It began :

"When our Christian confession speaks of one Holy Catholic Church, it reminds us of that deep inner unity that all Christians possess in Christ and in the work of his Spirit in spite of all national and denominational differences. Without ingratitude or unfaithfulness to those special gifts in Christian experience and conception, which each community has obtained from the God of history, this unity, which in the deepest sense is to be found at the Cross of Christ, ought to be realised in life and teaching better than hitherto."

It continued :

"1. The Church, which has unfortunately not seldom laid more stress upon that which divides than that which unites, ought to enforce the ideal of Christian brotherhood, arouse and strengthen the judgment upon selfishness, and employ all its powers in the work for the removal of the causes of war, whether these be of a social, economic, or political nature.

"2. Christians ought to feel their share in the responsibility for public opinion ; they ought to serve the cause of truth and love in public national and international life as well as in personal relations, and to try to understand the assumptions that lie behind the utterances, thoughts, and deeds of others.

"3. The Church ought to educate the nations to a higher and higher degree of self-government.

"4. The Church ought to work for international understanding and the settlement of international controversies through mediation and arbitration."

7. The next step was taken in October 1919—at the meeting at the Hague of the World Alliance for Promoting International Friendship. Delegates from the Churches of the principal Western countries which had taken part in the war (save France and Russia) were present, in addition to those from neutral nations. It was a momentous meeting—the first time the Alliance had met since its birth, just as war broke out, at Lake Constance. Its Secretary was Willoughby (now Lord) Dickinson. The delegates listened to the statement made by Archbishop Soderblom about the place and programme of an Ecumenical Conference which he wished to be called if possible in 1920. One point he made very clear. This Ecumenical (Universal) Conference was not to be concerned with questions of creed and ministry, but with life and work. The three chief objects for which it ought to meet were suggested as follows : " (a) Common doctrine and endeavour as to international brotherhood and the organised Unity of Nations. (b) Christian principles and action for social renewal of society. Further, (c) A common voice must be created for the Christian conscience. ' I advocate an Ecumenical Council representing Christendom in a spiritual way.' "

8. The proposal was approved. The World Alliance did not see its way itself to arrange the conference, which was left to a small committee. In the end the date of the conference was fixed for 1925, to take place in Stockholm. Preparations went ahead with the active help of representatives of the American Churches, especially Dr. F. Lynch and Dr. Henry Atkinson, as well as Archbishop Soderblom and Church leaders from Britain and the European continent.

9. The relation of the Universal Christian Conference on Life and Work to the movement for a World Conference on Faith and Order (which began in 1910 and bore fruit at Lausanne in 1927) is best stated in the following letter of August 1922, from Archbishop Soderblom and Dr. Henry Atkinson, to Mr. Robert Gardiner, Secretary of Faith and Order :

" The realisation of the ideal of the Faith and Order movement must be comparatively remote, whereas the Christian communions can without difficulty unite here and now in the application of Christian ethics and the spirit of Christ to the problems of the present day. . . .

" We are concerned with service, and we believe that by serving the co-operation of the Churches we shall break down prejudices and create a spirit of fellowship which will render the accomplishment of the aims of the Faith and Order movement less difficult to achieve.

" Meanwhile, we are of the opinion that the two movements had better be kept distinct. Life and Work confining itself in the main to the co-operation of the Churches in the application of the Spirit and Teaching of Christ to social, national and international relationships, while Faith and Order devotes its attention to the ultimate but more remote goal of unity in Doctrine and Church Order."

10. Meanwhile, only a few months after the Hague meeting, the Eastern Orthodox Church awoke to the need of closer relations among the Christian communions. In January 1920 the Patriarchate of Constantinople issued an Encyclical Letter " Unto all the Churches of Christ, wheresoever they be." Its opening words were :

" Our Church is of opinion that a closer intercourse with each other and a mutual understanding between the several Christian Churches is not prevented by the doctrinal differences existing between them, and that such an understanding is highly desirable and necessary, and in many ways useful in the well-conceived interest of each one of the Churches taken apart and as a whole Christian body, as also for preparing and facilitating the complete and blessed union which may some day be attained with God's help."

The Encyclical noted the establishment of the League of Nations as making the proposal both " feasible and timely."

It suggested various ways of demonstrating such Christian fellowship, amongst them the convening of pan-Christian conferences to examine questions of common interest to all Churches ; and pointed out the many moral and social evils which all the Churches together should combat. Such a declaration from the centre of the Orthodox Church was most significant.

11. The obstacles in the way of the Life and Work Conference were immense. They were largely due to what has already been described as the ingrained habit of disunion. But in the end, and above all through the enthusiasm of Archbishop Soderblom, they were overcome. The conference met at Stockholm, August 19th–30th, 1925. Over 500 members attended. All the Churches of Christendom, save Rome (which refused), sent delegates. A weighty deputation came from the Orthodox Churches, headed by the Patriarchs of Alexandria and Jerusalem, and delegates from Rumania and Yugoslavia. Lutherans, Calvinists, Evangelicals of all kinds, Anglicans and Old Catholics, were present : and a large contingent from the Churches in the United States. Thirty-seven nations of the Old and New World were represented—China, India, and Japan, as well as the white races. The joint presidents were the Patriarch of Constantinople and the Archbishop of Canterbury (who appointed deputies), the Archbishop of Upsala, and Dr. Arthur J. Brown representing the Churches of America. The conference was unique. As Dr. Kapler, President of the German Evangelical Church Federation, said : " Since the days of the Council of Nicaea, the 1,600th anniversary of which Christendom is celebrating this year, no Ecumenical Christian Conference of this magnitude has taken place." On Sundays and week-days the members joined in prayer. And every day the speakers of the different Churches and nations gave their witness on the six main subjects before them : (1) The Purpose of God for Humanity and the Duty of the Church ; (2) The Church and Economic and Industrial Problems ; (3) The Church and Social and Moral Problems ; (4) The Church and International

Relations ; (5) The Church and Christian Education ; (6) Methods of Co-operative and Federative Efforts by the Christian Communions. There were of course difficulties. There was still the ingrained habit of disunion. There were strong national feelings after the war. And, perhaps not least, there was a cleavage of view as to whether the idea of the Kingdom of God was or was not to be kept apart from all earthly endeavours for temporal welfare.

12. At the close a message was issued by the conference, with four delegates alone dissenting. The opening sentences emphasised its origin and purpose :

> " The sins and sorrows, the struggles and losses of the Great War and since, have compelled the Christian Churches to recognise, humbly and with shame, that ' the world is too strong for a divided Church.' Leaving for the time our differences in Faith and Order, our aim has been to secure united practical action in Christian Life and Work."

The message continued with a confession of " the sins and failure of which the Churches have been guilty through lack of love and sympathetic understanding." It claimed that " The conference has deepened and purified our devotion to the Captain of our Salvation. Responding to his call ' Follow me,' we have in the presence of the Cross accepted the urgent duty of applying his gospel in all realms of human life—industrial, social, political, and international." It summoned " the Churches to share with us our sense of the horror of war, and of its futility as a means of settling international disputes." It emphasised the need of education, and acknowledged that " even Christian ideas and ideals cannot save the world, if separated from their personal source in the Father of our Lord Jesus Christ, and unless themselves taken up into the personal life of the believer." It appealed for the help of all Christians. In addition it appealed to the young of all countries, to all seekers after truth, and to the workers of the world, deploring " the causes of misunderstanding and estrangement which still exist." And it closed with the affirmation : " In the crucified and risen Lord alone lies the world's hope."

13. The Stockholm Conference was, however, " only a beginning." It had made a great new start in Christian fellowship. But how afterwards was the fellowship to be expressed and strengthened ? The conference, to meet this need, appointed a Continuation Committee, representing the various sections, both geographically and denominationally. The Continuation Committee met yearly, 1926–30, in Berne, Winchester, Prague, Eisenach, Chexbres. In 1930 it was reorganised as the Universal Christian Council for Life and Work—of 100 members with four joint presidents, representing the Orthodox, Continental European, British, and American sections ; each president holding office for two years. The presidents in 1933 are the Bishop of Chichester (acting chairman) ; the Metropolitan of Thyateira ; Dr. Kapler, President of the Evangelical Church Federation of Germany ; and the Rev. S. Parkes Cadman, D.D., President of the Federal Council of the Church of Christ in U.S.A. Since 1930 its headquarters have been at 2 Rue de Montchoisy, Geneva, where an International Christian Social Institute has been set up, with a research department and a general secretary. The director of the research department (Dr. Schonfeld) works in close association with the International Labour Bureau ; and the Council has the help of an official of the Bureau as liaison officer and member. The Council meets in alternate years ; its executive at least once a year ; and an administrative committee of five, under Dr. Adams Brown, more frequently. In 1932 a great step forward was taken by the appointment of H. L. Henriod, a Swiss, as joint general secretary of Life and Work, and of the World Alliance for Promoting International Friendship through the churches, at the same address. The budget of the Council is contributed by the four sections, in proportion, and collected by their secretaries from the Churches. In 1933 it is still under £5,000. A considerable amount of research work has already been done by the institute. It has

held conferences on Christian Sociology, the Economic Crisis, etc. It works in close touch with Christian social bodies in different countries. It seeks to inform public opinion on present-day problems, e.g. unemployment and the opium traffic. It publishes a quarterly " News Letter " in English, French, and German. In 1932 the Council was officially asked by the Secretary-General of the League of Nations to collect information from all the Churches (except Rome) as to their views on a Fixed Easter and Calendar Reform : the Council thus being recognised as the one authoritative organ in existence of a League of the Churches, outside the Roman Catholic. In addition, there are various international commissions, which meet from time to time—Theologians, Youth, Social, Press, etc., and the holding of a further World Conference in the next few years is kept firmly in view.

14. The Roman Catholic Church has steadily refused to have part or lot in the Stockholm movement. In 1928 the Pope issued an Encyclical (*Mortalium Animos*) in which the Stockholm movement was implicitly, and " these pan-Christians who strive for the union of the Churches " were directly, condemned. But though Rome stands aside, the coming of Jerusalem to Stockholm, and the fellowship of all non-Roman Western Christians with the Christians of the Orthodox East, is a fact not to be ignored.

15. The spirit which seeks union grows continually. And the vital point to emphasise is this : the Stockholm movement does not consist merely in organisation, merely in research work, or merely even in " practical Christianity." It is deeper than that : *Life* is more than *Work*, and being than doing. Stockholm stands for unity, and a life of unity with God and with the brethren. It started from the guilt of Christians fighting, and being made to fight, against each other in the war. Its creators longed for a Christianity whereby, and a time when, Christians in all countries could keep together and join hands in the future. Their disciples and successors do not suppose that discussion, or even working together for the solution of social questions, or

for a common faith and order, or for peace, will achieve such a goal. They seek its achievement rather through a much more central function of human life, and through powers far above human life : through the unity of worship, a unity which is there already, but is to be awakened and nourished more and more through common prayers ; through common services ; through common speaking of the greatest and most fundamental things in the Christian faith, of the Most High and of his works in Jesus Christ. As believers they already live in unity, however dim the appearance may have been, and they look for a strengthened unity and an increasing unity, as something growing out of that which they know they already possess.

6. UNITING THE CHRISTIAN FORCES

By EDWARD S. WOODS, Bishop of Croydon

THE MAIN contention of this book is that, faced with a world-crisis of unparalleled magnitude, Christianity has something commanding, something creative to say ; that, desperate though the world's ills may be, there is that in Christianity which can provide the remedy. The actual task of enlightenment, of transformation, of interpreting and practising the " Christian way " in personal, industrial, political affairs, must clearly be carried out, in this place and in that, in one country and another, by Christian groups, Christian " Churches," working with whatever wisdom and zeal may be theirs. But in every place and in every land these Christian forces, with stupendous forces arrayed against them, are gravely handicapped by one paralysing disability—*they are divided*. And " the world is too strong for a divided Church."

For long centuries such disabling divisions—which already existed a thousand years before the Reformation—were taken for granted. But to-day, with the dawning of a new hope that at least the first instalments of the Kingdom of God are, in the divine intent, to be realised on the scene of this earth, men everywhere are feeling a deep disquiet about these divisions, and are beginning to ask, rather sharply, how much longer we are to acquiesce in them. Whatever their original cause, have they any meaning or justification to-day ?

I. SOME BASIC PRINCIPLES

It seems clear enough that Jesus Christ, whatever detailed instructions he may or may not have given to his first disciples in the matter of organisation, did at least trust his followers to be sufficiently infected with his own spirit and ideals to express them in the midst of the common life of the world, and he evidently contemplated their doing this

by acting together in a real unity. No doubt he foresaw a
great variety within their unity ; but it cannot have been
his purpose that that variety should become disunion and
break up the organic life of the one body. The very idea is
forbidden by his fundamental teaching about the nature of
God. If God is what Jesus, by word and deed, showed him
to be, then there must be one fellowship of his people on
earth seen of men ; and it must be his purpose not only to
reconcile all men to himself, but to unite them to one
another in the Body of Christ. It was, and is, on the
Christian view, part of the divine plan that the earthly
life of Christ should be extended and fulfilled through a
human society. And, manifestly, any such " extension of
the incarnation " is disastrously impeded in so far as the
society is rent by internal divisions. Such division delays
indefinitely any complete revealing in and through human
life of the nature of God and the " values " of Christ. The
Christ in his wholeness is inexpressibly greater than the
attempted expression of him by any one group or Church ;
and in so far as the groups that bear his name are in fact
mutually suspicious and bitter and hostile, they express
to the world something quite other than the values of
Galilee.

When all has been said that might be said about " inevitable " historical reasons for disunion, about the varied
treasures of Christian faith and Christian life which have
been utilised and guarded by different Christian bodies, it
still remains true that the main cause for *perpetuating* these
divisions has lain in man's unconverted obstinacy and
pride ; in his natural aloofness, his unwillingness to forgive,
his reluctance to make friends, his jealousy of those regarded
as rivals, his sheer spiritual inability to see the work of God
in the unexpected and the unfamiliar. " None can doubt,"
confessed the bishops at the Lambeth Conference of 1930,
" that self-will, ambition, and lack of charity among
Christians have been principal factors in the mingled
process, and that these, together with blindness to the sin
of disunion, are still mainly responsible for the breaches of

Christendom. We acknowledge this condition of broken fellowship to be contrary to God's will, and we desire frankly to confess our share in the guilt of thus crippling the Body of Christ and hindering the activity of his Spirit."

II. REUNION AND THE WORLD'S NEED

The sense of guilt for Christian disunion may well lie heavy upon the Christian conscience, and not least when one contemplates the fact that the moral need of the world is most acute just at the very point where the Church itself is weakest. Everyone nowadays is keenly aware, often painfully aware, that the vast, complex, economic system of the world has completely broken down ; everyone knows also that there can be no recovery without the closest world-wide co-operation. All the nations are suffering together ; and if there is to be salvation, they will be saved together or not at all. The old order of things is passing away, and we are caught in the gigantic and prolonged birth-pangs of a new world-order. But, as is emphasised elsewhere in this volume, the coming of any new order of a more satisfying character will wait upon some drastic change in man's mental and moral outlook. Any vast economic unification, any satisfactory world-wide co-operation in the stupendous business of production and consumption, will hardly be possible without some underlying spiritual unity, some sense of fellowship strong enough to transcend selfish Nationalism ; and where shall there be found such a " soul " for the world's " body " save in that healing, reconciling, uniting power which is inherent in the very life of the Christian Church ? And how shall the Church reproduce that power on a scale and with a cogency adequate to a world's need unless within its own borders that power is operating to the utmost to mend its own disunion and fulfil the highest possibilities of its own fellowship ? A similar challenge confronts the Church no less imperatively in the matter of peace and war. With the fear of war still stalking like a spectre through the world, with the Disarmament Conference struggling for bare life at Geneva,[1] is the fellowship of the Church still too weak to make the world see the better way ? Or, alternatively, if world opinion against war, daily growing stronger, should prevail, is the world going to " discover " the way of peace before the Church has discovered that war is incompatible with the spirit of Christ ? And is the world going to struggle to improvise some hasty, patched-up, insecure fellowship before the Church is sufficiently united to demonstrate to mankind the nature and working of that God-given bond which is capable of uniting all nations and races in one brotherhood ? The only finally effective response the Church can make to the world's challenge, and the world's need, is to strain its will towards the actual practice of its Christian principles, and to show in operation the fellowship the secret of which, so it claims, has been divinely imparted.

We have, through long custom, learnt—to our shame—to take for granted our hampering divisions. If in this country, for instance, anyone becomes a Christian and wishes to join the Christian Church, he has to discover, probably with a shock, that all he can do is to join one out of several quite distinct Christian denominations. In the West we are accustomed to this state of affairs, but a similar situation in lands where the Christian religion is only just beginning to take root has damaging consequences. There are parts of Africa where a pagan who wishes to become Christian has got to make up his mind, before beginning to receive any instruction, which of six varieties of Christianity is right. That great Christian saint and missionary, Temple Gairdner, once wrote with real bitterness of heart : " It takes faith, believing in Christ, his Church and ministry, here in this Moslem city. But on my word, it takes more faith to believe in these when one thinks of the Church itself as it exists here—sect upon sect, each more intolerant than its neighbours, each practically excommunicating the others in the name of our Lord—and that in the face of an Islam which loathes all alike." " Four places of worship," said the Bishop of Dornakal,

[1] These words were written in March, 1933.

" stand within a hundred yards of each other in one of the cities of India, each barely half full at any ordinary service, all ministered to by underpaid ministers, each too often engaged in unceasing warfare, not against the sin and suffering all round, but each against the supposed defects in the beliefs and practices of the others." Let me adduce one more testimony out of an almost unlimited number which might be cited, this time from an able Chinese theological professor, Mr. Timothy T. Lew : " The non-Christian world to-day has an equal access to the facts of the history of the Christian Church, for the last 2,000 years, as we have ourselves. It sees for itself how we Christians have treated one another, and this is by far the strongest weapon it has by which to attack the very citadel of our endeavour." It is little wonder that those engaged in propagating the world mission of Christianity in Africa and the East feel that the dimensions of the task are so vast, and the difficulties so baffling, that nothing short of a complete unification of all the Christian forces in strategy, in prayer, and in sacrificial endeavour will meet the situation.

Another and closely related aspect of the same problem is that arising out of the success of missionary work, and the effective planting in non-Christian lands of indigenous Churches which are now beginning to emerge from their early stages and to grow towards manhood. These Churches have naturally derived their Christian life from the Church of the West, and inevitably what they have learnt has been coloured by the form, Anglican, Presbyterian, Baptist, or whatever it may be, in which it has been imparted to them. But while these younger Churches are still in their formative period, is their growth, like the rigid training of the fruit-tree along a wall, to be for ever tied to the lines marked out by the ancient divisions in the " sending " Churches, and with which these new Churches have nothing whatever to do ? It would seem sheer common sense to say that these indigenous Churches should be free to develop along lines best suited to their national character, unhampered by ecclesiastical divisions which to them are for the most part meaningless. Moreover, Christian converts in a non-Christian land, whatever Western Church gave to them their Christian life, are bound together so closely by their sense of common separation from the great non-Christian religions that their whole tendency is rightly and naturally towards the formation of one native Christian Church which shall present a common front to the non-Christians all round them. And if we in the West are slow to perceive this and, because of our own history and habits of thought place obstacles in their way, it is not at all impossible that in some lands they might break clean away from the historic Churches of Christendom, a course which would spell the gravest spiritual impoverishment both for them and for us, and would endanger the essential international character of Christianity.

III. THE REUNION MOVEMENT IN RECENT HISTORY

Through the centuries down to modern times the dream of Christian unity was never wholly lost ; but for long years the vision tarried. As long as men assumed in religion that a uniform opinion mattered more than a comprehensive fellowship, tolerant of varieties within it, unity was bound to wait. But with the gradual strengthening of the life of the Church during the last hundred years, and with a quickening of conscience about its world mission, the hope and desire for unity has revived, until in the present century it has at last begun to gain a place in the forefront of the thought of the Church.

It would probably be true to say that the modern movement towards reunion, more particularly in any organised form, had its inception, or at least gained a mighty new momentum, at the great inter-Church, international missionary conference held at Edinburgh in 1910. At that conference men saw quite clearly that the missionary task of the Church would remain impossibly difficult unless there could be achieved a far higher degree of co-operation between the different communions of Christendom. But, as this idea of co-ordination and co-operation gained ground, men began to ask themselves, Why not unity, not only in the Church's work and witness, but also in its faith and order? One man in particular, the gifted Charles Brent, Bishop of the Philippines—saint, scholar, and man of action—put this question very pertinently to himself and to his contemporaries on both sides of the Atlantic, pursued it with energy and persistency, and lived to see the reward of faith when there assembled at Lausanne, in August 1927—and under his own presidency—the historic World Conference on Faith and Order.[1] This conference, with representatives from all the Christian Churches in the world, including the Eastern Orthodox Church, though not the Church of Rome, carefully examining and recording points of agreement and of disagreement, accomplished an indispensable clearing of the ground preparatory to the actual planning and building of any united Christian Church.

Meantime, a few years before, another event, which meant much for unity, had taken place—the 1920 Lambeth Conference of Bishops of the Anglican Communion. Its famous " Appeal to All Christian People," together with the conference's resolution on reunion, was a great Christian gesture ; and the appeal found a responsive echo in hearts stirred and minds quickened by the world-shaking events of 1914–18. For the Anglican communion, through its accredited leaders and spokesmen, to say such things and in such a way was a new thing and a great thing in the history of the Church, and it did unquestionably inaugurate a new and more hopeful epoch of Christian fellowship.

The subsequent " Conversations " at Lambeth between bishops and leading Nonconformist divines, carried on in an admirably Christian spirit, began to consider in further detail how the agreed principle of " Unity with Variety " could be given practical expression in present acts, and in

---

[1] For a full account of this conference see the official report, *Faith and Order*, edited by Dean Bate (S.C.M.). Reference may also be permitted to a shorter, popular account, by the present writer, entitled *Lausanne 1927* (S.C.M.).

providing a foundation for a United Church ; and a
notable agreement was recorded that the Free Church
non-episcopal ministries should be recognised as " real
ministries of Christ's Word and Sacraments in the Universal
Church."

The next great impulse towards unity came from the
mission field. At the memorable international missionary
conference held at Jerusalem in the spring of 1928, the
representatives of the new and indigenous Churches of the
Near East and Far East insistently demanded, not only
that there should be a speeding up of the process of tackling
the reunion problem, but that they should be accorded, by
the Churches of the West, a reasonable freedom in building
up their own united Churches on national lines—a vital
matter for these " native " Churches, already referred to
in this essay. " Jerusalem " also endorsed the significant
agreement reached by " Lausanne " as to the content of
the Christian Gospel. " However much," said Lausanne in
effect, " we may differ on matters of Church order, at least
we are one in the message which we would proclaim as that
which alone answers the needs of sinning and suffering
humanity."

Lambeth 1920 ; Lausanne 1927 ; Jerusalem 1928 ; then
the next great milestone—Lambeth 1930. Ten years had
elapsed, and once again all the bishops—308 of them—
of the far-flung Anglican fellowship assembled at Lambeth.
And what did the conference accomplish for the reuniting
of the Church ? To begin with, it emphatically and solemnly
endorsed the great 1920 " Appeal to All Christian People "
and re-affirmed its principles. Then, further, it established
the principle that it is possible to achieve agreement on the
great fundamentals of the Christian faith while leaving
large freedom to the Churches concerned to express their
faith and order and worship according to their own national
instincts and traditions.

Proceeding on this principle, intercommunion with the
Old Catholics has already come into operation ; an
intercommunion which does not require from either

communion the acceptance of all doctrinal opinion, sacramental, devotional, or liturgical practice characteristic of the other, but implies that each believes the other to hold all the essentials of the Christian faith. A similar agreement has been reached with representatives of the Eastern Orthodox Churches, which are awaiting formal ratification by their due authorities.

Actuated by the same kind of motive, and pursuing a similar ideal, the conference gave its " general approval " to the great scheme for a United Church in South India, " rejoicing that one part of the Anglican communion would be found ready to make this venture for a corporate union with certain non-episcopal Churches," and recognising that, when the union is consummated, the United Church in South India, while being in full communion with the Church of the West, will not be an *Anglican* Church, but a new province of the Universal Church.

To the non-episcopal Churches in the homeland, the conference, animated by a deep and genuine desire for a closer fellowship, said, in effect, three things. In the first place, it pleaded for a much closer co-operation, specially as between the rank and file members of all the Churches, in doing the day-by-day work of God and in presenting to the British people our common gospel. Secondly, it gave approval, under certain definite restrictions and limitations, to occasional acts of intercommunion, an approval which has since been officially endorsed by the Bishops in the Convocations in this country. And, thirdly, it extended a cordial invitation to the Nonconformist Churches to enter once again into joint conferences with the bishops in order to explore the question of reunion. The invitation has been accepted, and the joint conference is at work and making progress.

So much for Lambeth 1930. To make this cursory survey of recent reunion movements at all complete, reference must be made also to the now reunited Church of Scotland, the great Methodist achievement of last year (1932), when all the Wesleyan and Methodist bodies formed one Church,

and the United Church of Canada. There is a stirring of
desire, which may before long become a " movement," to
see union between the Baptist, Congregational, and Presbyterian Churches in England. There are strong movements
towards the forming of a United Christian Church in
Persia and China and Japan, and in Northern and Southern
Nigeria, as well as in South India. And the Bishop of
Chichester's chapter on " Stockholm " (p. 259) shows
what strides have been made of recent years in achieving
co-operation in Christian work and witness as between the
Churches in our land with those on the continent of
Europe.

IV. THE PRESENT AND THE FUTURE

As the preceding pages have endeavoured to show, there
has been substantial, if slow, progress in Christian unity
during the last quarter of a century, and especially in the
last decade. What exactly, we may next inquire, is the
point now reached ? What hope is there of progress being
accelerated ? No one can reasonably doubt that if the
Christian Churches had the will to draw together into a
closer unity, there would be no insuperable difficulty about
the means. What signs are there to-day of such a will to
unite ?

Any attempt to answer these questions must, first, take
some stock of the position with regard to the proposed
United Church in South India ; for that proposal, novel,
carefully thought out, and far-reaching as it is, provides an
acid test of the attitude of the Churches towards unity.

South India

The essence of the South India scheme is as follows. The
uniting Churches are the Anglican Church of Burma,
India, and Ceylon, the South India United Church
(Presbyterian and Congregational), and the South India
Wesleyan Methodist Church. The basis of the scheme is
agreement on the fundamental matters of faith and order
as expressed in what is known as the Lambeth Quadri-
lateral (the Holy Scriptures, the Apostles' and Nicene

Creeds, the Historic Episcopate locally adapted), and agreement as to the general question of Church government. Within the framework of this general agreement there is to be freedom as to : (1) the exact meaning attached to the Historic Episcopate ; (2) the method of admission to the full membership of the Church ; and (3) the ordering of public worship (except for certain principles agreed on as to the service of Holy Communion). With regard to the ministry, all new ministers after the union will be episcopally ordained ; existing ministers who accept the scheme will be recognised without re-ordination as ministers of the Word and Sacraments in the new Church, but are not to be sent to minister to any congregation against the wishes of that congregation, thus safeguarding the position of congregations previously Anglican and who desire to retain the purely Anglican tradition. There are a great many Christians who feel that this scheme is the finest and most hopeful attempt at religious fellowship since the days of the early Church.

Unity in Great Britain

First of all, it is not as widely recognised as it should be what an impressive amount of unity between the Churches already exists. There is to-day among all the great Christian Churches a very large measure of agreement about the message of the gospel, the content of the Christian faith, and about Christian morals ; there are great groups of Christians who, though belonging to different denominations, are in fact closely united in Christian experience. For this existing unity there ought surely to be definite and regular thanksgiving in all the Churches, and there are many signs that it will find increasing expression up and down the land in joint work, social and evangelistic, for the Kingdom of God. The leaders of the Churches who meet round the table for negotiations at Lambeth (I speak from personal experience) invariably find themselves knit together in a really close spiritual fellowship.

There are many who are convinced—the present writer

among them—that the purpose of God for his Church will remain largely unfulfilled unless this existing unity can develop into some sort of visible organic union. That is to say, while leaving room (as in the South India scheme) for a very large element of variety, the union will be such that members of the united Church will have the privilege of receiving, and all ministers of the united Church the right of celebrating, the Holy Communion in Churches which before the union were in separation. Whether such a scheme is given the name of " Reunion " or " Federation " is unimportant ; it is the thing it really means that matters. Such a united Church will be more than a welding together of broken pieces. It will be in some sense a new revelation of the Church as it exists in the mind and purpose of God.

The lines along which such progress may be hopefully attempted are becoming already clear. The last two Lambeth Conferences and the Lausanne Conference have successfully traced out these lines, and the present series of " Conversations " at Lambeth are zealously continuing that work. As we have already seen, the Anglican communion is itself an object-lesson of a great unity based on intercommunion with large local and national variety. It is a " Commonwealth of Churches without a central Constitution ; it is a Federation without a Federal Government."[1] In the true and best British way, the ideal, and to a large extent already the practice, is that of organic unity without despotism or over-centralisation.

It is of course clear that an organic union with complete intercommunion for the uniting Churches cannot be had without a ministry which is universally acknowledged ; but there are many signs that the non-episcopal Churches would be quite prepared to accept episcopacy as the most suitable means for such a purpose. The sense in which such a ministry would be accepted by many members of the non-episcopal Churches can perhaps best be explained by quoting the description of such a ministry, very carefully worded, from one of the agreed statements at Lausanne :

[1] From the Encyclical Letter, Lambeth Conference, 1930.

" A ministry acknowledged by every part of the Church as possessing not only the inward call of the Spirit but also the Commission of Christ and the authority of the whole Body, and conserving all that the experience of the Church has found to be valuable in the Episcopal, Presbyterian and Congregational forms of Church Order." It is not out of place in this connection to recall that there is now a general agreement among scholars that in the primitive Church there was no single system of Church order laid down by the apostles. " During the first hundred years of Christianity the Church was an organism alive and growing, changing its organisation to meet changing needs . . . everywhere there was readiness to experiment and where circumstances seemed to demand it to change."[1]

It is true that there is considerable divergence of view as to the stage at which intercommunion should be generally permissible. There are many in the Nonconformist Churches who feel that, especially in view of the Lambeth declaration in 1925 as to the reality of the Free Church ministries of " Christ's Word and Sacraments," it is unreal not to encourage general intercommunion now. But most of us in the Anglican Church (though not all) hold the view that to attempt to establish intercommunion immediately would, apart from the immensely difficult questions of Church order it would raise, involve us in a certain unreality ; for to practise general intercommunion forthwith would be to pretend that we, the Christian Churches, enjoy a union which in fact we do not possess, and such a course might therefore stereotype existing divisions, and postpone indefinitely the day of real reunion. Meantime, let there be a large liberty for occasional intercommunion, a liberty already accorded by Anglican authority ; but for the other true and permanent intercommunion let us seek strenuously to deserve it and to win it, meantime accepting the pain and the guilt and the shame of doing without it.

There is another very large and very complex question

[1] *The Primitive Church*, by B. H. Streeter, p. 61.

which will have to be faced before there could be a united Church in England, and that is the whole question of the Establishment. In view of some of the tendencies and forces at work in the world and our own country to-day, it is more than probable—nay, it is practically certain—that there are bound to be large changes in the position of the Church of England as an Established Church. If nothing else raised the question as to the nature of these changes, it would inevitably be raised as soon as reunion began to come within the bounds of practical possibility. The dream that I dream (perhaps in this point in the chapter it may be well to slip into the first person singular) is that of a Church of the English people with a recognition of religion national in fact and not merely in name. In Wesley's day the English Church made a gigantic effort to become the Church of the people. With the coming of reunion that aspiration might be realised. For the Establishment to be ended, whatever the result might be for the Church, would in my view be a disaster for the nation ; but I see no really cogent reason why it should not be mended. No one can pretend that the Church of England nowadays is adequately representative of the nation on its religious side, and it cannot be wondered at if Free Churchmen, representing some of the best religious elements in the nation, feel keenly their exclusion from any right to participate in national religious acts and occasions. But if the nation continues to desire some sort of religious " Establishment," and if the various parts of the Christian Church in this land have as their first concern, not prestige, position, or properties, but lowly and self-sacrificing service of the nation for Christ's sake, then it ought not to prove impossibly difficult to find a way in which this great end might be achieved. There is no reason in the nature of things why Establishment should be incompatible with complete equality of religious bodies in the national life. It was for many of us a significant and welcome event when the Duke and Duchess of York acted as the King's representatives on the occasion of the inauguration of the great Methodist Union last year ; never before—so far so we are aware—has the Crown been formally represented at a Nonconformist official gathering. That there will have to be considerable alteration in the general Christian temper and outlook before great changes could be effected may be admitted. I should like to see the Church of England pave the way for such broadening of the Establishment by some really notable Christian gestures.

For example, we might express to the State our desire that, if they were so willing, Nonconformist representatives should be associated with us on the great religious state occasions such as the coronation. Another suggestion is that bishops should surrender their seats in the House of Lords, partly because in these days there are other and, in some ways, more satisfactory channels by which the Church can make its influence felt in the national life, and partly because of the danger of spiritual damage to the Church through that particular form of association of Church and State. Or alternatively, if it is felt to be desirable to retain bishops in the House of Lords, let them be fewer in number, and let places be given to representatives of the Free Churches. Then there is the drastic suggestion, which is worth something more than contemptuous dismissal made by the padre founder of Toc H, the Rev. P. B. Clayton, that instead of pulling down unwanted City churches we should, on receiving due assurance that they could be adequately used, give them to other Christian bodies. There must be many thousands of members of other Churches drawn Citywards by their work day by day, and it would appear that, apart from the old City churches, there are only two public places of Christian assembly within the City proper. If there are churches that we cannot use, could there be a more Christian way of disposing of them than this?

V. CONCLUSION

When one contemplates the monumental change of mind, change of religious custom, change of the " ingrained habit of disunion," which would be necessary if the Churches are to unite, one might well be tempted to regard the task as hopeless. But to despair thus would be to deny Christianity's most fundamental article of faith—that God is here, continually at work, and his Spirit can and does change men's hearts and minds and attune them to his own will and purpose. " The zeal of the Lord of Hosts will perform this." Of such movings of the Divine Spirit, of such renewal from above of the springs of our common life, there are many signs to-day. Our great hope—indeed, our only hope—lies in such renewal. A truly renewed Church, desiring only to give its life for the life of the world, would hardly need to regard reunion as an end to be painfully achieved : it would take it in its stride. We, the Christian Churches, could unquestionably come together in a corporate union within a very few years if we wanted to do so strongly enough ; the daily prayer of every Christian might well be that God's Spirit would increase and strengthen such desire and enable us to bring it to good effect.

And if, longing to serve the manifest will of God in this matter, the ordinary Christian of this or that Church asks what he can do, he might properly be urged, first, to get his whole outlook in the matter oriented aright and if necessary afresh. The Christian genuinely seeking unity will seek it in a maximum, not a minimum, corporate spiritual experience. He will cultivate the vision of a " large room," where no narrow domestic walls hide and separate. He will, at sacrificial cost, cultivate the spirit of absolute humility : the spirit which always asks, " What can I, holding only a tiny segment of the arc of truth, learn from these other Christian groups ? " He will cultivate a spirit of absolute unselfishness, the spirit which asks to share with fellow-Christians all it has of Christ. And, particularly in his own locality and neighbourhood, he will seek and make every opportunity to get to know his brother Christians in other Churches ; he will confer and study with them, he will try to understand their point of view, he will pray with them, he will work with them at many a local task of building the city of God.

If folk in the Churches think and act thus, their faith and love should at least make it possible for " things to happen " on a larger scale. Given any deep and sincere willingness on the part of the Church, the fire of God may descend ; and some of us may yet live to see a revived and united Church spending itself with sacrificial effectiveness for the salvation of the world.

7. WHAT THE CHURCH IS DOING: SOCIAL ACTIVITIES

By S. E. KEEBLE

IT IS NOT proposed in this chapter to attempt the practically impossible task of detailing the activities of the different Christian Churches. The several denominations are engaged in a thousand and one activities, spiritual, social, ecclesiastical, each after its kind, in ways commonly known. Many of them are in substance identical, and would involve wearisome repetition in enumeration. Those only are mentioned here which are common to them all, and especially those which are undertaken by them unitedly. It is these latter which will be indicated as the work of " the Church," that is of the whole Reformed Christian Church in this country.

I. THE NORMAL ACTIVITIES OF THE CHURCH

The Christian Church has been occupied in this crisis in the same manner as in every other crisis through which society has passed down the centuries. It has unceasingly pursued its habitual, perennial, and indispensable duties of proclaiming the Christian gospel, visiting the sick, poor, helpless, and forlorn within and without its fold, and ministering to their physical and moral necessities. Every day of every week it has cared for children, guided young people, comforted the infirm and the aged, and borne the whole community on its heart and in its prayers.

Let it not be said that all this is mere " Churchianity." It is more, it is Christian humanitarianism and religion's best ritual. " Pure religion ($\theta\rho\eta\sigma\kappa\epsilon\acute{\iota}a$) and undefiled before God and the Father is this : to visit the fatherless and widows in their affliction." This cannot be gainsaid. Without it, the community would pine apace, if not perish.

The normal activities of the Church are truly social. Worship is fellowship with God and with Men. Services, prayers, sacraments are not " dope " but fortifying, inspirational, elevating—a satisfaction to the highest and deepest human instincts. In pursuit of these activities the Christian Church has outlived more than one corrupt civilisation and may outlive this one.

The Evils of Intemperance and Gambling

In addition to its normal work, the Church is engaged in much social work of an ameliorative and reforming nature. There is *the Drink Evil*. The united Church has entered the cause of temperance reform. *The Temperance Council of the Christian Churches* was formed in 1916, representing fourteen denominations. Its four joint presidents were : the Archbishop of Canterbury, Cardinal Bourne, Rev. Dr. Selbie, and the General of the Salvation Army. That council has intervened in every General Election since 1916, not without effect. Recently five hundred delegates met at Westminster, under the presidency of the Archbishop of York, and ratified the council's legislative programme in ten familiar points.

It is public knowledge also that the Church's representatives upon the Royal Commission on Licensing were amongst its most efficient members, and that the evidence which came from the experts of the Church impressed the Commission and influenced its findings and recommendations. Since the war, gambling in old and new ways has seriously increased. The Church has unitedly endeavoured to abate this social and moral plague, damaging alike to society and the individual. It has done this in no puritanical spirit, but in the common interest. Its success has not been very great, but it has performed its social and Christian duty.

The Church was early in the field against the new gambling developments. In 1928 its *National Emergency Committee of Christian Citizens* sent a deputation one hundred strong to the Home Secretary to urge that power be given to localities to decide whether or not dog-racing tracks should be laid down in their districts.

Then the Church opposed the introduction of the

totalisator into this country, and proved that it had been a social bane in both France and Australia. In 1930 a protest was issued, signed by fifteen bishops and fifteen Free Church leaders, protesting against linking hospitals with sweepstakes. They objected, in the name of the *Council of Christian Ministers on Social Questions*, against the association of gambling with charity, as well as to the allurements such sweepstakes give to a gambling spirit already too fearfully prevalent.

The Church was active also over the Royal Commission on Lotteries and Betting. It presented documents of evidence to the Commission and twelve declarations by official bodies of the Churches. These were supported before the Commission by eleven witnesses of representative and expert capacity, headed by the Archbishop of York and the Rev. E. Benson Perkins. Their evidence so affected the Commissioners that their interim report, issued January 1933 unanimously accepted the hitherto unheeded affirmations of the Church on the matter. The report condemned " the exploitation for gain of the gambling instincts of the people," and unanimously recommended that the totalisator in clubs and on dog-tracks be brought to an end as soon as possible. Events have marched rapidly since then in the Church's direction.

The Protection of Sunday

The Church is, of course, vitally interested in the Sunday question. It has taken an energetic part, not always unitedly, in recent controversies and changes. Two schools have emerged, one leaning to greater latitude than the other, based upon different conceptions of the origin and nature of the day ; one school sternly upholding ancient Acts of Parliament in relation to the day, and the other, showing reluctance to impose upon masses of non-Churchgoers the desires and habits of a minority. This matter came to a head over the passing of the Sunday Entertainments (Regulation) Act relating to the Sunday opening of cinemas. The school which, whilst not itself desiring Sunday opening, yet felt that local communities should have the right to give or withhold permission, won the day and carried Parliament.

Nevertheless, the whole Church is united in contending that the day is a precious possession, and should be preserved for rest, worship, and Christian service. Since the passing of the above Act, the Church and other bodies have jealously watched its administration and have urged that the weekly hours of labour and the hours of opening should be protectively defined and limited. The London Churches also defeated a proposal of the London County Council to license Sunday afternoon openings, and that in the interests of the Christian training of children and young people.

The Church, then, is united in protesting against the exploitation of Sunday for private gain, against its utter secularisation, and its commercialisation. The Public Morality Council of London, which represents all the Churches, has been active in efforts to prevent the exhibition of films which violate decency and good morals. In 1927-8 an agreement was signed between Hollywood and the Council that the latter should be the British adviser or consultant in respect of moral questions affecting American films for England. It has resulted in a more careful scrutiny of sex and criminal elements in these films on both sides of the Atlantic.

II. THE PARTICULAR SOCIAL ACTIVITIES OF THE CHURCH

The Church is often charged with confining itself to criticism of the people's social habits, and scourging them for their dear delights. Its social work, it is said, is merely palliative or ameliorative—at the best, negative. It is admitted that the Church, being what she is, could not remain inactive in the presence of rampant evils, yet, it is held, she is dealing with effects rather than with causes, mostly with the sins of the people rather than with their wrongs and injustices—the sins of others.

In the not very distant past there was much truth in this

Kc

indictment, but it is not yet widely realised by the public that a distinct change has gradually taken place in the Church's outlook upon society, and in her activities. More and more the Church takes the whole community into its ken. It grows concerned with society as well as with the individual. It dare not, and ought not, to be less individual, for personality is precious to it, nor less ameliorative and palliative ; but it is more social and more reconstructive.

This change has been proceeding almost beneath the consciousness of the Church, due, in part, to the spirit of the age, and in part to the work of such pioneers as Thomas Carlyle, John Ruskin, J. M. Ludlow, F. D. Maurice, Charles Kingsley, and Vansittart Neale.

When the freshness faded from the messages of these great men, there came for almost a generation a lull in the Church's social interest. But later, in 1877, appeared a stirring in the dry bones with Stewart Headlam's *Guild of St. Matthew*, followed by the movements, from another Christian angle, of Andrew Mearns, Dr. Clifford, and Hugh Price Hughes.

This leaven spread in the Churches, and soon social-reforming groups appeared. *The Christian Social Union* was founded in 1889, under the inspiration of Dr. Westcott, Dr. Gore, and Dr. Scott-Holland, and did great work in the Church of England. Then, later, *Unions for Social Service* were set up in every other major branch of the Christian Church.

It is true that these all were worked by minorities in the Church, but they were responsible and instructed minorities, pregnant with the future of a great Church movement for social righteousness. For a score of years these organisations laboured by pen and speech, through pamphlet, platform, and pulpit, within and without the Church, exposing bad social conditions and injustices, such as ill-housing and " sweating," and calling for the social application of the teaching of Christ and of the Christian Church.

The Lambeth Conferences of 1888, 1897, 1908, and 1918 had made clear pronouncements upon social questions ; and after the war the Archbishops' Fifth Committee of Inquiry upon Christianity and Industrial Problems issued a report drawn up by Mr. R. H. Tawney, the Master of Balliol (Mr. A. L. Smith), the Bishops of Winchester, Peterborough, and Lichfield, and Mr. George Lansbury, with others. This, when published, had a sale of between thirty and fifty thousand copies. Few more drastic and thoroughgoing Christian-Social documents, based upon expert knowledge of both social conditions and Christian sociology and theology, have been published since. In 1912 the Christian Social Unions combined into what became known playfully as the " Panjandrum." It was a federation which met annually, a hundred strong, at Swanwick, under the secretaryship of Miss Lucy Gardner, for fifteen consecutive years. It manifested unity amidst diversity, embracing Anglicans, Free Churchmen, and Roman Catholics, who housed together harmoniously for a week at a time—all at one on the importance of social questions. Several useful joint publications were issued, on such subjects as *The Living Wage* (1913), *Land and Labour* (1914), *Christian Essentials of Social Reconstruction* (1919), *Christianity and the World Outlook* (1921), and *The Christian Order of Society* (1922).

After several failures to organise Christian laymen in public life and big business to take active part in Christian social reform, the " Panjandrum," in conjunction with the " Collegium," a small body of social experts which sprang from the Christian Student Movement, conceived in 1919 an ambitious scheme which took some years to develop but culminated in " Copec."

" Copec " and its Consequences

" Copec " was the famous conference held for a week in Birmingham in 1924, the letters standing for a " Christian Conference on Politics, Economics, and Citizenship." Fifteen hundred elected delegates from the Churches and other bodies declared at that conference the Christian mind on social questions. This was only done after five years of definite preparation, the last three of which were spent in intense, widespread, and organised consultation. Some two hundred thousand questionaires were circulated to Christian university students, to social study-groups in all the Churches, to outside bodies of many kinds, and then re-gathered and considered. Twelve commissions were appointed to explore beforehand such subjects as " God's Purpose for the World," " Education," " The Home," " The Relation of the Sexes," " Leisure," " The Treatment of Crime," " International Relations," " Christianity and War," " Industry and Property," " Politics and Citizenship," " The Social Function of the Church," and " Illustrations of the Social Effects of Christianity." These commissions sat for three years. Their findings were presented, discussed, and pronounced upon at meetings epoch-making for the Church.

At the very end, Bishop Gore confessed to a feeling of awe at the bold decisions of the conference. He heard the feet of those who had struck their tents and were already on the march. He solemnly asked if it were ready for the consequences—scorn, misunderstanding, hostility. He affirmed that the pomp, pride, and power of the world would rise against such Christian opinions and actions, with which he wholly agreed.

Nothing daunted, " Copec " calmly appointed its Continuation Committee, and published and sold thirty thousand copies of its twelve reports and added another on *Rural Problems*. It had a splendid Press, and soon praise and blame flowed freely. " Copec " had revealed to an astonished world that a remarkable change had come over the modern Church in relation to public affairs. It was evident that it would no longer remain a tame spectator of social evils and wrongs, nor accept with complacency anti-Christian theories and practices in industry and business. The march of the spiritual forces of society had begun.

In 1926 the General Strike took place. Before it occurred, and whilst it went on, influential representatives of the Church intervened with definite proposals in behalf of peace and conciliation. This was resented, even by some

Christian laity, although the interveners had been headed by Dr. Davidson, the late Archbishop of Canterbury. They were scorned and derided, and their proposals scouted. Ten bishops and ten Free Church leaders then entered the lists. They issued a reasoned defence of those proposals, and stated that it was their considered judgment that the substance of the proposals, which they enumerated, though not approved by the Government, " still held the field." The Church of Christ, however, was further disregarded, but the result of the encounter was to lead the Church to stabilise its organisation by increasing the number and making it still more representative. That organisation is known to-day as the *Council of Christian Ministers upon Social Questions*, which makes frequent appeals and issues periodical Christian statements upon the social problems of the day.

The Christian Social Council

The influence of the " Copec " meetings and reports continued to spread throughout the Church until the moment seemed ripe for the realisation of that which had long been desired and advocated, and which " Copec " had foreshadowed—a representative Council of the Christian Church in England and Wales upon social questions. Union for that purpose was accomplished in 1929 with the exception officially of the Roman Catholic Church, which continued its social propaganda alone, but in all friendly relationship. In the January of that year the Christian Social Council was launched in the Jerusalem Chamber at Westminster, after a Devotional Service in Henry the Seventh's Chapel in the Abbey, conducted by the late Bishop of Winchester and Dr. Garvie.

" Copec," although constituted mostly of delegates sent by the official assemblies of the Christian Church, was an *ad hoc* body which was meant to have but a temporary life. *The Christian Social Council* is a permanent representative organisation for expressing the mind of the Reformed Churches upon social matters. Its representatives, of which there are seventy-two, are elected in proportionate numbers by direction of the general assemblies and governing bodies of all the Churches. It works by a Quarterly Council, an Executive, and five Standing Committees. These latter are upon Social Research, International Co-operation, Local Co-operation, Social Education, and Youth. Already it has made world-wide contacts with other Christian Churches. It will be seen later that this council is vigorously expressing the Christian mind upon many matters of social concern in these difficult days.

It is doubtless quite correct to say that the *Christian Social Council* does not yet speak for the average member of the Churches, nor even for the whole Bench of Bishops and all Free Church leaders. But it certainly is official by appointment, and does represent the prevailing judgment of an important and growing section of the chief leaders of the united Christian Church, not a few of whom are expert economists and sociologists. Even if the rank and file of the Church are unaroused or inarticulate at present, it is inconceivable that they should long neglect the call of a body of their own respected Church leaders, whom they know to be trustworthy in other religious matters.

The young of the Churches are growing pathetically anxious, as well they may be, to follow wise and bold social leadership. This the Christian Social Council is now giving in its published books and leaflets. Some members of The *Oxford Group Movement*, who have rendered great service to the spiritual life of young people, have indeed revived the idea that " social " Christianity is inimical to " spiritual " Christianity. But this is due to a false distinction. There can be none of the latter without the former, just as there can be none of the love of God without the complete love of one's neighbour. Time will speedily deliver young Christians from a well-meant but out-of-date reversion to religious individualism and unscientific subjectivism.

The Church and Unemployment

Mr. Lansbury's dramatic appeal to the Churches " to do something for the unemployed " was either forgetful or uninformed. It is more than fifty years since the Church began " to do something," as her finances and her workers well know. Much has been done in London and the provinces. One chief Church spent £30,000 on plant alone a generation ago, and started new industries for the workless. The Rev. S. F. Collier, Bishop Russell Wakefield (as Mr. Lansbury has publicly acknowledged), Prebendary Carlyle, Commissioner Lamb, and many others have done yeoman work in that service.

Unemployment has always been indigenous to our economic system ; but unemployment is now vaster than ever. It is a world-problem, as well as a national one. It is due to the dislocations of the Great War, to its destructions, to its debts, its tariffs, and also to new technological inventions added to those inventions already in operation : it is a problem of the machine, of the financier, and of the statesman.

But though its solution is beyond the power and the province of the Church, its pitiful human victims have long been on the heart and humane conscience of the Church. In all the cities and large towns of the country hundreds of rest and recreation rooms, workshops for repairs and renovations, and near-by allotments have been provided by the Church, and, in addition, provision made for friendship, mental culture, discussion, and, when desired—and it often is—religious service.

At Brynmawr, in South Wales, the Society of Friends and others have helped the workless crowd there to transform their town into a pleasant place. By voluntary labour the dirt-heaps have been levelled and waste places turned into playing-fields for children and young men. Other improvements have been thus carried out, and much happiness created in place of depression. The Town Council rightly warns us that this use of the unemployed is not a *cure* for the evil plight of their town, which has lost its staple industry, but it is a welcome alleviation of their misery, and something wholly to the good.

At Tonypandy in the Rhondda, the Rev. R. J. Barker

has provided, by Christian help, for the use and comfort of the unemployed, a community house. There provision is made for every side of a man's nature—the physical, the intellectual, the æsthetic, and the spiritual. There can be found a resting-place, shelter, and friendship ; also books, pictures, music, and discussions. An interior chapel is also provided for quiet meditation and prayer, beautifully designed and furnished with symbols of love, sacrifice, service, and salvation.

The Local Councils of Christian Congregations and *Local Christian Social Councils* co-operate in many places with the municipal authorities, the Rotary Clubs, the Y.M.C.A.s, and other societies in the service of the workless. The Greenwich Christian Social Council, for instance, has opened the old Admiralty Trafalgar Tavern as an unemployed centre. The Christian Social Council itself, whilst preserving its own independence of method and work, co-operating when possible with the *National Council of Social Service* in its work of planting " Occupational Centres " up and down the land. But it makes it clear that it does not see in this device any cure for unemployment, or a satisfactory discharge of the duty of the Government. Something much more than palliatives is needed, or than subsidising private effort and charity.

The Church is watching with sympathetic interest the *Production for Use League*. This league seeks to organise groups of the workless to produce things, in their enforced leisure, for each other's use, and to exchange their products. Money is not to be circulated. There is to be no interference with existing markets. The scheme is one of primitive barter between individuals or groups, similar to the revival of barter now in process between some modern nations like Brazil and some American States, Russia and Canada and others. In 1930 one whole day's Conference on Unemployment was held in Westminster, summoned by the Christian Social Council, under the presidency of the late Bishop of Winchester. Sir Basil Blackett of the Bank of England, and a number of business men, publicists, and economists were present, with members of the organised unemployed. The conference considered and advised upon the position taken by the council in its printed productions.

The Church was indeed amongst the first to point out the real nature of this problem and the direction in which to look for its cure, and that at a time when the economists, financiers, statisticians, statesmen, and industrialists were urging wholly false remedies. It is not enough to say that it is an international problem—a world-problem. It is mainly a moral problem, and cannot be solved by the alms of the Church or of any other organisation. It is a call to face the real truth. It is a call for distributive justice to suffering millions.

The Church and the Slum and Housing Problem

It is a great moral blot upon the national reputation that, whilst re-housing upon a vast scale has been carried through for the middle classes and skilled artisans who can pay an economic rent, and for clubs, shops, banks, and hotels, the overcrowded and plague-provoking slums and tenements of the poorest have been left to fester and rot.

It was, of course, not primarily a Church matter, but a community and State obligation, which the latter have hitherto shirked. The Church knows the slums, and remembers perhaps how Bishop Basil of Cæsarea in the fourth century, in a pagan world, built his " New City," replete with such social amenities as were then unknown to the poor. Here, in the twentieth century, in three cities alone (London, Leeds, and Birmingham), there are about 100,000 dwellings which should be demolished and the inhabitants re-housed. In London, over 2,000 families of six persons and more are living in single rooms. The number living three or more to a room has actually increased. So long as we find money for many of the things for which we do find it, an *ad hoc* slum programme is a first necessity of the State. A practical impulse came to the Church at the " Copec " meetings, when a successful Belfast Church experiment was explained. Soon afterwards the *Church Army Housing Co.*

Ltd. was started, which has built some 300 houses for the poorest and re-housed 2,000 people.

Local Christian Social Councils, which engage in many kinds of united social service, have taken up housing work. They have held " Housing Weeks " and " Housing Sundays " in the churches, and thereby awakened interest and raised funds. *The Birmingham " Copec " Housing Improvement Society Ltd.* raised £10,000 at low interest, and has purchased and transformed some insanitary property. *The Bristol Churches' Tenement Association Ltd.* has done similar work. *The Manchester Housing Co. Ltd.*, co-operating with the City Corporation, raised £10,000, again at low interest, with which it has provided houses at 6s. 11d. per week, nonparlour, but with three bedrooms. *The Cambridge United Council of Christian Witness*, acquired, by similar means, a housing estate and built houses to let at 9s. 9d. per week, rates included, with six rooms each. *The Lambeth Housing Co.* (C.S.C.) has provided four blocks of six flats, each with three bedrooms. *The Market Drayton Housing Ltd.* raised £3,000 and bought twenty-eight slum houses to recondition or rebuild. These are samples of combined Church effort in slum housing. But the most successful effort hitherto has been that of *The St. Pancras Housing Improvement Society*, founded by the Rev. Basil Jellicoe. This society has transformed one of the worst slums in North London into a miniature garden city within eight years. It now holds the unencumbered freehold of the whole of the Sidney Street Estate, Somers Town. It has demolished notorious slum streets, built sixty-six flats, with a nursery garden-school, and has contracted for forty-seven more flats. The rents of these flats are the same or lower than those paid for the former hovels.

Yet this is but a drop in the ocean of distress. There are still three and a quarter millions overcrowded in England and Wales—that is, with more than two persons in a room. There are more than half a million occupying one-room tenements. And 100,000 are living in London alone in basements. One man re-housed at last by the Church at

Lower Edmonton had been living in a single room with a wife and seven children, and had sought in vain for decent accommodation for *twelve years*. Another applicant had waited for eighteen years.

The Church and International Peace

The Great War and its aftermath has moved the Church to review and revise its whole attitude towards war. It has, of recent years, in all its branches, declared that war is contrary to the teaching of Jesus Christ. The Lambeth Conference of 1930 affirmed that " war as a method of settling international disputes is incompatible with the teaching and example of our Lord Jesus Christ," and adds that " the Christian Church in every nation should refuse to countenance any war in regard to which the Government of its own country has not declared its willingness to submit the matter in dispute to arbitration or conciliation." The Methodist Conferences, the Congregational and Baptist Unions, and the Presbyterian Assemblies in England, as well as, of course, the Society of Friends, have done the same in similar phraseology. Hereafter practical action must harmonise with such statements. Yet there are difficulties even within the Church, and to meet these the Christian Social Council has issued a " message to the nations." It is entitled *Concord or Conflict*. It emphasises the slow progress of the Peace Movement. It is not that men want war, but their habitual pursuit of certain interests creates situations in which war is all too inevitable. The economic and psychological factors which facilitate wars are then examined. Nationalism, racialism, special interests, imperialism, the spirit of adventure as an escape from monotony, the desire for " glory," are among the motives which tend toward war. It may be said that " war arises from the failures of peace " when peace is inglorious, ignoble, avaricious, or apathetic. The function of the Church, it is said, is to guide the economic, social, and spiritual life of society into courses and modes of action which do not provoke conflict but induce concord. The Church's primary contribution is to secure that spiritual and social regeneration which will dissolve the passion for domination, replace fear by faith, and eliminate war-provoking economic conditions. The true way to peace is to find constructive methods by which men can achieve valid aims otherwise than by war. If this is unwelcome to unregenerate man it is the function of others to set the example, and to increase their own numbers.

For reasons best known to itself, the Press gives but little publicity to this work of the Church. Several large demonstrations in London and the provinces have been ignored or but meagrely reported. These were in support of the League of Nations, of disarmament, of international conferences related to peace. They were held in the Albert Hall, the Central Hall, Westminster, in Trafalgar Square, in the Free Trade Hall, Manchester, and elsewhere. One procession, headed by a thousand clergymen, ministers, and laity, shepherded by mounted police, which held up the London traffic, was hardly noticed by the Press. Yet this Press is eager to make a whipping-boy of the Church in times of crisis, while its teaching and appeals are all ignored. The fact remains that the Church is the strongest supporter of the League of Nations Union in this country. It is affiliated to it in thousands of active branches. It is also the mainstay, in every sense, of all the chief peace societies in existence. *Hitler is now in power!*

The Church and Industrial Questions

The Anglican *Industrial Christian Fellowship* is active in seeking to Christianise industry. It annually holds an " Industrial Sunday," preparing for it by the circulation of thousands of copies of an appeal from heads of firms, trade unionists, labour-leaders, and others for the application of the Christian ethic to industry and business. Its books and pamphlets on the subject are numerous. The brave work in connection with it of the late Rev. Studdart Kennedy (" Woodbine Willie ") will not soon be forgotten. The I.C.F. Crusades are visits in strength to large centres of population, with a thorough canvass of every section of the community in the interests of the permeation of life at every point with the Christian spirit and ideal. The Crusaders labour for a whole fortnight together, with some such slogan as " Bristol for Christ " pinned on each worker's breast. Free Churchmen are invited cordially to co-operate, and they eagerly enlist for the work.

The now united Methodist Church also, through its Social Welfare Department, is preparing an elaborate programme of Christian action relating to industrial matters.

A generation ago but few books and little literature of any kind on industrial questions issued from the religious Press. Now it is hard to keep in touch with the quantity poured forth. A perusal of the lists of the Student Christian Movement Press and those of any other leading publishers gives striking evidence of the change. Many of the books are written by Christians who are as competent economists and sociologists as they are theologians. These circulate in all the universities, colleges, and churches of the land. Does the ordinary man know of the leaflets, pamphlets, and question-aries which issue in tens of thousands on industrial and social questions from the Christian Church ? Does he know or value the hundreds of study-circles, groups, and con-ferences which elicit or study these publications ? The " Copec " reports alone still stand as a mine of Christian declarations and teaching.

Nor should the publications of the Roman Catholic Truth Society be overlooked—Leo XIII's Encyclical *Rerum Nov-arum* of 1891, Pius XI's *Quadragesimo Anno* of 1931, Devas's *Political Economy*, Mgr. Parkinson's *Primer of Social Science*, and also the Papal Appeal for a Jubilee Year of " peace, remission, and pacification." *The Catholic Land Associations of Great Britain* are making praiseworthy contributions to the present distress,

Another feature of the modern Church in relation to industrial questions is the number of social lectureships in existence. There are the John Clifford, the Scott-Holland, the Essex, the Swarthmore, the Halley-Stewart, the Hartley, the Beckly Lectureships in active operation. Lecturers of the highest qualifications deliver these social lectures on subjects of the day. Afterwards published, they circulate in thousands.

III. THE SOCIAL PRONOUNCEMENTS OF THE CHURCH

It is clear from the foregoing that the old evangelical individualism is passing even from its strongholds, and also that mere narrow " Churchianity," an exclusive ecclesiasticism, has been transcended. Both schools are increasingly conscious of the whole body politic as consecrated by the Incarnation.

The prevalent materialism of the time, and the scant respect to Christian ethics shown either in politics, economics, or social life, have combined to draw together all types of Christians for the defence, not only of Christianity, but of the life and well-being of society itself. The Church is now compelled to intervene in public affairs in a new way—in a united way—each denomination expressing itself also from its special point of view. It enters into politics, but is true to Coleridge's dictum, " There should be no party politics, but every church in England should resound with national politics."

It sends forth messages, manifestos, and declarations on the burning questions of the day. By these means democratic opinion can be expressed, and by them it is formed ; and public opinion finally rules the world. The Christian Church is now calling all men, and especially Christians, to look at modern social problems—in a scientific spirit truly, but also as they ought, directly in the light of the Christian religion. This is the modern world's wisdom and only hope. The problems have been regarded in the light, or darkness, of orthodox economic theories, of materialistic Socialism, of atheistic Communism, of national, imperial, and financial interests, of political shibboleths ; *and the world has grown worse*. The Church comes forward again and urges their consideration in the light of that religion which the majority profess. It seeks to help by its own new and numerous publications. In 1927, for instance, after nearly ten years of investigation by more than fifty Christian groups, accompanied by practical experiments in the application of Christian ethics in work and business, their final findings at Lady Margaret Hall, Oxford, were published as *The Kingdom of God in Industry*, an aid to troubled consciences.

The Cure for Unemployment

The Christian Social Council recently sanctioned the publication of two small volumes originated by its Social Research Committee, without committing itself to the exact views expressed, but as worthy of careful consideration. The first concerned the coal problem, and the second unemployment. Their titles were, *The Miners' Distress and the Coal Problem* (1929), and *This Unemployment* (1931).

In such books as these the economists, financiers, and industrialists are definitely arraigned for their attitude toward industry, business, and unemployment, both upon their own specific economic and financial grounds, and upon the principles of Christianity. Not for the first time in modern representative Christian literature, certain economic assumptions and practices are faced and challenged. It is not content with urging the relief of distress or indicating the cultural damage done and the bad human relationships set up by the present economic situation. It embarks upon a root-and-branch criticism.

The Church, through many such books and pronouncements, was among the first to draw attention to the tragedy of widespread poverty amidst plenty, both of goods and money. It declared that the present crisis was not one of production at all, but one of distribution, a technological and a financial problem. Since then the " Technocrats " have demonstrated the former, and the London Chamber of Commerce the latter. These pronouncements of the Council affirm unemployment as " both a personal affront and a symptom of social confusion." They allege that " economic experts are accepting theories for realities " and that " much alleged economic law is not economic law at all "—that a problem raised by the will and mind of man is capable of solution by the same. They declare that "bad science, bad logic, bad sociology, underlie the contradictory aims of modern industrialism," and adduces argument and evidence in support of this. The present problem is not a scarcity problem. It is fundamentally a problem of money—of more purchasing power wherewith to consume the surplus of goods which exists or may exist. They hold also that so-called " sound finance " is not sound economics ; and they lean to the view that " the social credit of the community is largely withheld from it." The evil cannot be cured by " such futile variations in monetary policy as deflation, inflation, and stabilisation." Nor, we might add, by " re-flation."

Thomas Carlyle once said that the " speaking man," whose value he realised, has wandered terribly from the point, and cried, " Could he but find the point again, take the old spectacles off his nose," and discover what " the real world-devouring devil now is." It looks as if he has this time discovered " the real Satan whom he has to fight "— human selfishness and wilful blindness perpetuating human misery. The council has also issued other pertinent books. Both the *Council of Christian Ministers on Social Questions* and the *Christian Social Council* have published reasoned manifestos, influentially signed, upon *War Debts and Reparations*, upon the *Means Test*, upon the *Present Economic Distress*, and others beside those already mentioned.

The Church and a Modern Christian Sociology

Individual Christians and groups of Christians have long been endeavouring to formulate some kind of Christian sociology for this industrial civilisation. This should have been done more than two centuries ago. Mediæval sociology attempted this for its own era. At the transition from medi-æval to modern times Calvin's keen logical brain assayed the task in his *Institutes* and his institutions at Geneva. Bishop Jewel and Richard Baxter in this country did their best. In modern times F. D. Maurice, Bishop Martensen of

Denmark, and others recently have expounded Christian social ethics. But the work remains to be systematically done by the modern Church if the world is to be saved from anarchy and destruction.

To meet this need, a new book is announced from the Social Research Committee, through the Christian Social Council, *God, Man, and Society*. It will be perhaps the first modern outline of a Christian sociology by the Reformed Churches. It is not likely at first to win the assent of a business world indoctrinated by education, custom, and habit with a set of non-Christian if not un-Christian principles and ideas which have brought the modern world to the edge of doom. For it will endeavour to state and work out the application of Christian principles to complex modern problems—an ambitious but an obviously and urgently necessary task.

We have shown that the Christian Church, despite her defects and shortcomings, is unceasingly active in administering spiritual aid to individuals of every kind and degree ; we have shown also that she is actively applying Christian remedies to social evils and communal troubles ; and we have indicated the intellectual work of a critical and constructive social nature in which the Church is engaged.

It may be said that she is not facing international Socialism, Russian Communism, European Protection, or American Technocracy. But that is not correct. The Church is well acquainted with them all. But it is her function to dive down beneath them to the nature of man, and to rise above them, to God as seen in Jesus Christ, and to set forth *The Christian Way*.

The Church cannot compel. It can only enlighten and persuade. In a rational and moral world that should suffice. Finally, it will suffice.

PART III

THE CHRISTIAN SOLUTION

1. PERSONAL AND FAMILY LIFE

By DR. A. A. DAVID, Bishop of Liverpool

1. CHRIST AND CONDUCT

THE FIRST purpose of this book is to study human life in the experience of to-day, with particular regard to human relationships, of man with man, man with woman, nation with nation. We suggest that the ills from which the whole world is now suffering may be traced to defects in those relationships. In the last issue the crisis is a personal crisis. We believe that in the revelation of God by Jesus Christ we know already how life should be lived in relation to other lives. We believe further that the same revelation has opened for us access to the directing and enabling power which can apply that knowledge in all stages of human effort to appropriate it. We have therefore a second purpose, namely, to show that the principles of Christ, rightly understood, offer not only an ideal way of life, but also effective guidance towards it at all times, and especially whenever mankind is conscious, as it is conscious now, of losing that way, and of having found no other.

This twofold purpose lays on us a double duty. In the first place, our survey of the present moral situation must be fearless and unprejudiced. We must face all the facts. And these facts we must seek not so much in statistics but rather in moral experience directly or indirectly available to us. There are large numbers of people in all classes of society who are questioning, ignoring, and even deliberately rejecting standards of personal conduct and relationships which previous generations regarded at least with respect. It is certain that no society of normally moral folk can dispense for long with conventions of some kind, tacit if not declared. What, then, are the new standards or conventions now being observed by those who declare that they have abandoned the old ones ? The question is important, because it may be that they are, perhaps unawares, basing their conduct upon a principle or an instinct of such a quality as to serve for a starting-point of a moral re-education. It was upon such a process of growth that our Lord himself relied. He began from the standards by which men were living, from what they already possessed. Taking this at its highest, he taught them how to raise it, and showed the ideal as the reason why that which they were using had been given them. He could do this because he understood them at the level they had attained. " He knew what was in the mind of man." Our first step, therefore, is to share this understanding. And this means an effort of sympathy and imagination which does not shrink from a calm examination of behaviour, however perverse it may appear, and of reasons for it, however inadequate they may seem to us to be.

Another duty laid upon us is to examine afresh the ideals of conduct set before us by our Lord, and especially to study the principles on which he would have them applied to life by successive generations as each sees life. It is possible—for it has happened before—that there is something defective in our expression of his mind as it is unfolded to the men and women of to-day. The language we use may not have been the best, the emphasis we lay may need readjustment. It is even possible that there are elements and directions in the way of life he taught, or in the methods he used in teaching it, which have been distorted, or overlaid, or taken too much for granted, or forgotten. These must be rediscovered if his revelation is to break anew with full effect upon the modern world, and men and women who have lost their way are to find it again.

In the present section of our survey it will be convenient to follow first the latter of these purposes. We shall face the situation of to-day in the sphere of personal and family morality with better hope if we begin by assuring ourselves that Christ's vision of the future allowed for it, and that he has already provided means to deal with it. We begin, then, by asking how he intended his principles to become effective, and, whenever that effect should be weakened, how he meant them to regain their power.

Did he intend us to accept his commandments as definite injunctions or prohibitions? It would have been necessary in that case to hand them down in writing, for this kind of law must be expressed and preserved in set terms. He took no such measures. It is true that some of his recorded sayings, if isolated from their context, might be understood in that sense. It is possible, for instance, to interpret what he said about marriage to mean that among his followers no marriage must in any circumstances be dissolved. But it is obvious that most of his precepts are not intended as rules to be blindly obeyed. Such imperatives as " Swear not at all," or " To him that would go to law with thee and take thy coat, leave also thy cloak," are not to be regarded as statutes. We might just as well attempt a legal embodiment of " Love your enemies." And to select some as binding in their literal meaning for all persons in all generations and circumstances, while accepting others as forcible expressions of ideals, would involve an entirely arbitrary division. If we regard them as a whole, and in the light of the spirit in which all Jesus' teaching was conveyed, we cannot escape the conclusion that they are not meant to be literally read. They are assertions of his moral authority addressed to beings so constituted that they can recognise it, and sufficiently endowed with the power of creative thinking that he is able to entrust them with the task of working out the applications of ideals for themselves. Jesus came to abolish legalism and to deliver religion from all rules except such as his disciples may make for themselves. He was not a legislator.

Thus he lays upon us a task more difficult than literal obedience. We are to think out our own solution of moral questions. This is the freedom for which Christ has made us free. It involves a heavy responsibility, and it is no wonder that many shrink from it. They would rather be told plainly whether this or that is right or wrong. They would like lists of things lawful and things unlawful. To such a demand our Lord gave no encouragement. Very seldom did he return plain answers to what the unthinking call plain questions. What he did was to offer the questioner materials which would help him to make his own judgment, and to set him in a position in which he could answer the question for himself. Among these materials we can discern two principles. One is that the moral character of every decision cannot be rightly assessed without consideration of the motive behind it. Has a man understood his own desire to act in this way or that? An early manuscript of the Gospel of St. Luke records that, seeing a certain man working on the Sabbath, Christ said to him, " Man, if indeed thou knowest what thou art doing, thou art blessed ; but if thou knowest not, thou art accursed, and a transgressor of the law." But this principle exercised alone is not enough. There is another to be fused with it. Conduct is not a purely individual matter. Most of my actions affect other free personalities around me, whether I am aware of it or not. Therefore when I have managed and judged my own motive, or oftener my own combination of motives, and made it as clean as I can, I must proceed to ask myself what will be the impact of my decision upon others. " Inasmuch as ye have done it unto the least of these my brethren " is a declaration which covers more than our acts of calculated benevolence. It points to the truth that my conduct of my life will ultimately be judged by its effects upon all whose lives touch mine—that is, upon my neighbours, and, through them, upon God, who is concerned for each and for all.

This concern is a personal concern, directed more to men themselves than to their actions, more to their characters than to the records of their conformity to rules and observances, more to the growth of their personalities than to their output of conduct. That is why Jesus describes God's relationship to us by the essentially personal word love. And it is the only word that can sum up all the requirements of our response to that revealed relationship. " Thou shalt love the Lord thy God " bids us cultivate not merely a particular emotion towards him. It enjoins an attitude of the whole personality (" with all thy heart, with all thy soul, with all thy mind "), which must issue in action (" with all thy strength "). And the field of our action is the whole body of other personalities, our neighbours. We are to " love " them—that is, not necessarily to be affectionately disposed to them all, but to care for their welfare equally with our own, and to think and act towards them constructively.

" There is none other commandment greater than these." He expounded them by illustrations in abundance, but never by enactments. To convert an ideal into a law would be to degrade the ideal and to make bad law. It remains true that men must make rules for themselves, and help to make laws and conventions for their communities. In both tasks Jesus left them free from the letter of any law in order that they may give new life and scope to the ideal in the changing conditions of each successive age.

2. A DIAGNOSIS

The challenge of the world to Christianity has never ceased, and never will. In every age afresh, Christians are required to commend their ideals, to defend their doctrines, to define their standards, and to justify the way of life enjoined upon them. As in each generation they renew this task they are called to take account of the new factors, intellectual and ethical, which distinguish the situation around them from that which preceded it. Life to-day is surrounded by conditions and forces which have sprung up so swiftly as to take us unawares. The new outlook on the world and the universe given us by science has profoundly influenced the thinking of the few who direct and shape the thinking of the many. New means of communication have increased our knowledge of other races and have greatly complicated international intercourse. The replacement of human labour by machinery will soon revolutionise industry all the world over. All these changes lie within the Christian concern. But there is another which is affecting human life and relationships more immediately, more deeply, and probably more widely, than any of the rest.

It is the change in public judgment of personal conduct.

That the morale of individual life has changed no one will dispute. There have, of course, always been tendencies to drift into a reckless disregard of conventional standards, and even to revolt from morality as such. Few, however, would deny that they are wider and stronger now than ever before. But the fact of most significance is that public opinion is so largely indifferent to them. Behaviour which not long ago would have shocked decent-minded people is now being tolerated by those who would not dream of conforming to it. They accept in others what in themselves they would condemn. Moreover, there are not a few who are genuinely perplexed as to what the Christian standard is. Has Christianity finally decided what is right and what is wrong, and, if so, on what grounds ? Such a situation may truly be described as chaotic. " Incomparably the most imperious challenge which to-day confronts Christianity is the moral chaos of our generation."

It is the fashion to ascribe most of our present difficulties to the effect of the Great War. Probably the explanation is too simple for many of them. But in those years of manifold tension we may certainly find one of the reasons, which some would call an excuse, for moral laxity. " After so stern and long a strain of every kind the nation must have its fling." But the process we are examining had begun long before 1914. What the war did was both to reveal and to accelerate it. While the war lasted almost anything was excusable except cowardice. And when it was over, certain old standards continued to be openly defied. It will therefore assist our diagnosis to describe as fairly as we can, and if possible to account for, the attitude and temper of people who were still young in 1920, and to suggest how this has affected the rising generation now.

It is not surprising that the war left the younger of those who had fought and worked in it disillusioned, resentful, and cynical. They asked themselves : Why should it have happened at all ? It seemed to them unfair that they should have suffered and toiled to clear up a mess created, not by them, but by their seniors. And who was the better for it ? What they wanted most was to forget the whole business. And the quickest way to forgetfulness lay through freedom to enjoy themselves. If the older generation disapproved, let it realise how far the war itself had deprived all elderly control of its title to respect. For the exercise of this liberty the readiest and most congenial opportunities were, as always, to be found in London, where the best and the worst in national life are growing side by side.

There they touched a relatively small but conspicuous set of people who had long thrown over all restraint, but with no excuse whatever except that they were rich and idle, and had found nothing better to do than freely to indulge their appetites. They had abandoned all standards. " What the rest of the crowd does is good enough for me." It is even doubtful whether they have any sense of loyalty to one another. When open disasters come, as they frequently do, the sufferer who has " crashed " drops out and is soon forgotten. The influence of such people would be much less mischievous than it is but for certain journals in which their most trivial performances are offered to the public interest. They enjoy and even take pains to secure such notoriety. And it encourages the impression that they are representative of aristocratic society. How far down the social scale their infection has spread it is difficult to say. It does not appear to have reached the working class. But few would doubt that it has been rapidly lowering conventional standards in the intermediate range, and there can be no question of its very marked effect upon the conduct of those who found themselves at a loose end in 1920.

Another factor to be taken into account is the new freedom won by women for themselves but not yet adjusted to the social whole. What does the equality of the sexes mean in terms of conduct ? In the first flush of their emancipation there has been claimed on behalf of women the same degree of liberty, even from sexual restraint, which tradition silently allows to men. There seems no doubt also that the drinking habit has greatly increased among women and girls of what are called the upper classes, with the inevitable effect of a further loosening of moral control.

It is always more difficult to generalise from experience actually surrounding us than from that of ten years since. When we look back, there has been time to correct first impressions, and to set what we remember in a truer perspective. But as we look around us we are in danger of seeing most clearly what we most desire to see. There is, however, one feature in the attitude of the younger generation of to-day which may be asserted with some confidence. Competent observers from different angles are agreed that they are growing weary of licence. Perhaps they have been a little frightened by its obvious effects. They have inherited something of the pessimism which grew out of war experience, and the depression has given them a second dose of it. They feel that chances of a settled life are against them, and the general insecurity has affected their moral sense. But they have also inherited the satiety which came to those who tried to drown their cares in hedonism. They are still impatient of authority. They cling to their independence, and are prepared to defend it, but uneasily, and no longer with that resolute *abandon* which distinguished the early post-war years. Still they ask : Why shouldn't I ? But the answer they expect, and half hope for, is one that will show them why they had better not. They are looking out for principles which might make sense of their freedom. They are ready for standards, and even for conventions, which seem to them reasonable—that is to say, which commend themselves to common sense. All this the younger among them desire for themselves, and the elder still more for their children. Even among the extreme libertines already described are parents who are pathetically anxious that the experience of their own youth shall not be renewed in their sons and daughters.

Here surely is the Christian opportunity. A whole generation is slipping into decadence, but is showing signs, faint but significant, of a desire for recovery. Jesus' story of the Prodigal offers to our imagination some hope beyond the assurance of his restoration. What will happen to the son of the Prodigal? We may assume that he will inherit his father's independent and adventurous disposition. But may he not be so trained and inspired that, while allowed to make mistakes of his own, he may yet be saved alike from his father's experience and from his uncle's priggish temper? The parable may well be the story of society to-day. Will such a sequel be the story of to-morrow? If so, the first task of an understanding Christianity is to seek, as our Lord did, those stable elements in human personality on which personal morale can be rebuilt. The following sections will attempt to discern three such elements, and to disentangle them from the clash of distortion and perversion in which they have been involved.

3. THE INSTINCT OF MODESTY

If in the present confusion there are indeed signs of a desire for moral direction, it is in the sphere of sexual relationships that we may expect to see them most clearly. Young people, and not these only, are confronted with a natural desire, almost universal, together with a new abundance of opportunity for its indulgence. On the other hand, they are conscious of a restraining instinct, equally normal, to which for the present we may give the name of modesty. How can they arrive at principles which shall bring the two into a working harmony with a sense of right and wrong, and at standards which shall keep that harmony at work?

There are some who hold that modesty is a primal instinct, a part of original human endowment, on the same level with sexual desire. Others would trace it rather to the restrictions with which that particular appetite has been surrounded for so long that the fear and shame of it now seems as natural as the desire itself. For our present purpose it is not necessary to decide how much of the truth lies in each of these views. Our point is that, whether it is primal or evolved, and whatever its origin may be, modesty is there. What is it? It is partly æsthetic, a protest against something ugly and disgusting, from which self-respect claims protection. In the morally normal person the first violation of modesty is accompanied by acute discomfort at the least, and is followed by an uprush of shame too strong to be due to nothing more than a consciousness of having offended against a convention. He feels, perhaps for the first time, that he is in the grip of an outside power that is using him, and he resents it. His personality has been outraged, and, though the sense of this outrage may soon weaken or disappear, the weakening comes by a progressive breaking down of that which held the person back, and he knows that a permanent mark has been left upon him. But it is not only himself that is involved. The exercise of his impulse must sooner or later affect other personalities. The instinct that limits it is based also on respect for them. It is notable that the words αἰδώς and *pudor* stood to the Greeks and Romans for a feeling not only of personal shame, but also of consideration for others. The words connote a complete sense of honour.

Christianity emerged through a race which upheld a higher standard in this respect than any other of that age. Spreading outwards, it encountered a civilisation which hardly recognised any standard at all. The early interpreters of Christ's revelation were engaged in a stern struggle against almost complete licentiousness. In their hands, as was inevitable, the whole subject was isolated and to some extent distorted. Sex itself became an unclean thing, and even marriage was often regarded as a kind of compromise, and therefore an inferior state. This attitude has coloured Christian thought on the subject ever since. To this day we can discern the suspicion, often unrecognised, that the sexual impulse is in itself sinful. It is assumed accordingly that motives tending to inhibit it should be strengthened by any reinforcement available, whether it be true or not. The result has been a corresponding distortion and isolation of the instinct of modesty. By adding artificial fear to natural shame it may appear to have been fortified, but it has also been twisted out of truth. Moreover, it has been concentrated on a negative aim. Thus the word " purity " is commonly understood as a characteristic produced by the suppression or elimination of this particular desire. But when Christ pronounced his benediction on the pure in heart he was thinking of a state less narrow and jejune. He had in mind a positive virtue exercising full control of every impulse which if misdirected may defile.

There is need for a renewed and fearless study of the mind of Christ and its bearing on this subject in the light of new vital factors unknown and undreamed of in his day. The new status of women has revealed possibilities, good and bad, of new relationships between the sexes. Some of these are diminishing the sexual tension, others are obviously increasing it. We have also an economic factor to face. The great bulk of young people to-day cannot afford married life till long after the age when they become ripe for it. Does true morality demand that they shall continue to inhibit a natural impulse up to the time when marriage sets them free to exercise it ? There can be no doubt about the Christian answer to this question. We are trustees of a standard which in the interest alike of the individual and the race we dare not relax, even if it involves a heavy demand upon some individuals for the sake of the highest social good. It has been asserted that sexual abstinence may be injurious to bodily or mental health. This is true only in the case of some men whose natural propensity has been increased by self-indulgence in other ways. Harder still is the lot of many single women, made for motherhood, who would undoubtedly be healthier in body and mind if they were married. But, with these exceptions, modern medical opinion is overwhelmingly in favour of the view that complete continence involves no ill effects. Reasonably sound and wholesome people have no more to fear from it than from any other means of attaining self-mastery.

It must be admitted that Christian teaching on the whole subject has not always been wise, and that offenders (especially women) have often met treatment in Christ's name which is not Christian. We have relied too much on fear. For most men and for many women chastity demands the hardest form of self-control. But it is a mistake to dissociate it from other forms by a direct and frontal attack. The surest way to it is indirect, and lies through the building up of a self-disciplined life, full of energetic interests. We know much more than our ancestors did about the growth and management of our emotional equipment. The knowledge is not yet ordered or established or safely available, but one day it will be. And we shall need it in the task that awaits us of handling anew this instinct of modesty, and giving it its proper function in the development of personality as a whole. We can count upon it as a stable element in the spiritual inheritance of women and of men. It may at times be overlaid, as now. But it survives, and we can build on it.

In the meantime we have begun to clear the ground, encumbered as it is with relics of mistaken beliefs and traditional prejudices. The Lambeth Conference of 1930 declared that " a new day has dawned, in which sex and sex matters are emerging from the mists of suspicion and even shame into the clear atmosphere of candour, honesty, and truth." The report adds the opinion that " the complete openness with which such subjects are discussed is on the whole to the good, for they have been taken from the obscurity of half-secret conversation and brought out into the cold light of knowledge and experience." And a significant step in that emergence was registered when the conference formally acknowledged that " intercourse between husband and wife as the consummation of marriage has a value of its own within that sacrament, and that thereby married love is enhanced and its character strengthened." Thus in one branch at least of the Christian Church has appeared a conviction that the way to a higher moral standard lies in promoting a saner, healthier, and truer attitude to the whole question rather than in multiplying prohibitions and safeguards at the risk of creating new sins.

4. THE INSTINCT TOWARDS MONOGAMY

The moral confusion of to-day is seen at its worst where it affects the general estimation of the married state. The principle of monogamy is being both secretly challenged and openly attacked on various grounds. One of these is the frequency of marriages that obviously fail. In how many married lives pledged to faithfulness are the essentials of happy union secured ? And does the Church's blessing make much difference ? We are told that there must be something wrong with an institution based on a contract which in so many cases is so imperfectly fulfilled.

Here again it is fair to remember that the whole question is in these days being discussed with a freedom which is still new. It is not surprising that the abandonment of all reserve in dealing with it should have had the first effect of disclosing a large number of unpleasant facts hitherto kept out of sight. Now that these are in the open, they may well have produced an exaggerated impression of failure, which would be corrected if the evidence of reasonably successful marriages were equally conspicuous. It is, moreover, not irrelevant to inquire into the background of the lives which have suffered matrimonial disaster. There is much evidence that failures are most frequent among people who have too much money, or too little interesting work, or both. At either end of the social scale it is the pressure of boredom that drives married people into discontent with themselves and with each other. It is self-pity that makes them eager for any kind of compensation for the dullness of their lives, and the readiest seems to them to be a change of partners. But it would be a mistake to generalise from such experience. There are great masses of people working for wages or salaries who have no inclination, and many of them no time, to be ever asking themselves whether they are as happy as they deserve to be, and, if not, who is to blame. It is possible, therefore, that what has gone wrong is not marriage itself, but the character and content of many married people's lives, and, to that extent, of modern life in

Lc

general. Nevertheless, the challenge exists and the problem remains. Is Christianity prepared to meet it ?

There are some who find a sufficient answer in the mere assertion that all marriages are indissoluble ; that Christians are bound, in loyalty to their Master, to reject separation, with right to re-marry, not only for themselves, but also as recognised by the State ; and that therefore they must oppose every attempt to reform the divorce laws, however immoral they may be, because they ought never to have been introduced at all. But here the modern critic will demand, " Are you quite sure that Christ, when according to his manner he threw his ideal into an imperative, intended you to apply it without discrimination as an enactment ? Even if he did, and you accept the rule for yourselves, have you the right to impose it upon all ? And, if you have, is that the wisest way of commending your ideal to mankind ? "

Others there are who, on the general grounds described in the first section of this chapter, would hold that in what our Lord said about marriage he intended something higher than to bind us by a law. He saw marriage as God meant it to be—a connection in which two personalities should grow into one relationship so close and stable that it can no more be severed than that of brother and sister. But he did not promise that God would create this relationship whenever certain words of his Son are pronounced over two persons who have pledged their intention to attain it. If by the fault or misfortune of one or both the intention cannot be fulfilled, would our Lord have us deny the possibility of a second chance for either ?

There is little doubt that the latter view will ultimately prevail. But the process will be slow to take effect, because in most religious communities it is exceedingly difficult to alter canons or rubrics bearing on this, or indeed on any, issue. What is happening in most of them is that " case-law " is allowed to redress the hardships threatened by rigidity. But in the meantime many Christians think it compatible with charity and wisdom to declare that any breach of written law is in itself a sin ; that a man who marries his deceased wife's sister, or a woman who, having been deeply wronged by a worthless husband, marries again, is to be accounted guilty of a moral offence. It is no wonder that many high-minded people outside the Churches, and some within them, hesitate to accept the Christian judgment of any moral question.

A further difficulty confronts those Churches which act as agents for the State in the contracting of legal marriages. Many people, for reasons sometimes quite irrelevant and inadequate, desire to be married " in church," although their actual attachment to any religious body is of the loosest. The " solemnisation " of such weddings is a duty often very distasteful to the clergy concerned. It would at least make for honesty if all marriages were contracted under State law, and afterward, if desired, blessed in a religious service. In that case a Church might confidently impose her own conditions, and secure some guarantee that the parties understood and were prepared to abide by them. Even now it may be suggested that the cause of Christian marriage is less well served by fulminating against divorce than by teaching people how they may make a success of married life, and why, for society's sake as well as for their own, that success is worth some sacrifice.

People who are in love with one another are apt to suppose that when they marry their love will of itself complete the spiritual union which their courtship has begun. But they soon discover that more is needed. Indeed, if their love itself is to grow, or even to last, it must call into its service a whole company of allies, such as intelligence, patience, humour, self-control, and, most of all, a watchful respect on the part of each for the character and temperament of the other. Marriage is an art, its material is personality, at first that of each, finding in the other new scope for its enrichment. Its final triumph is the blending of the two into an abiding harmony, a real sharing of one life. Like all arts, it is long and difficult, and may have its times of crisis. Writing to a friend at such a time, D. H. Lawrence, who cannot be suspected of prejudice in favour of old-fashioned morality, says : " One must learn to love, and go through a good deal of suffering to get it, like any knight of the Grail, and the journey is always towards the other soul, and not away from it. Do you think that love is an accomplished thing the day it is recognised ? It isn't. To love, you have to learn to understand the other more than she understands herself, and to submit to her understanding of you. It is damnably difficult and painful, but it is the only thing that endures. . . . Your most vital necessity in this life is that you shall love your wife completely and implicitly and in entire nakedness of body and soul. Then you will have peace and inner security no matter how many things go wrong. And this peace and security will leave you free to act, and to produce your own work, a real independent workman."

Most of those who are seeking to attain (by experiment) a new morality would give very different counsel in a case like this. They would accept the disaster, and say to each of the sufferers, " Your first concern is the development, through free expression, of your personality. Whenever your individual temperament demands fresh sexual experience you are at liberty to make it. But you must give equal freedom to your partner." Some of them would add, " And for the sake of the children you had better continue to live together and agree to conceal your infidelities even from one another." It is difficult to take such people (and their number is growing) quite seriously. They profess to aim at their own personal development. Do they really think that with such freedom they can grow at all in anything but selfishness ? The plain truth, amply confirmed by biological and social science, is that " no man liveth unto himself alone." All experience teaches that the personality which emerges from unlimited freedom is a poor and limited thing. If an individual is to grow to his full possibility he must be willing to renounce, and it is the creative power of love that will enable him. When love fails, it is the woman who suffers most. Disintegration in the sex-life means for women disintegration of the personality in a sense graver than for men. A hardened man may deny that he is conscious of it. But the woman, unless she is a prostitute, knows that she has given away a part of herself in exchange for a cruel pretence, and she can neither recover nor forget it. As for the children, it is idle to pretend that they are unscathed by the discovery, sooner or later, of so ugly a relationship between their parents.

Other and similar attempts are being made to adjust the institution of marriage to the conditions and the supposed demands of modern life. To some of these we may at least give the credit of sincerity. They are honestly directed to a constructive purpose of a kind. They aim at the maximum of happiness for the two partners, and therefore, it is claimed, for society at large. But they leave the children out of account. We have nowadays to reckon with a theory that the private family has done its work and must sooner or later give place to the State nursery. But far wider and stronger is a conviction rooted in the facts of life. The human child remains an infant much longer than the offspring of the lower animals. More even than the wife he needs the security and permanence of a home which provides him not only with physical support, but also with the only conditions in which he can naturally learn lessons of dependence, of responsibility, of confidence, and of obligation. Through ages of experience mankind has been guided to " a natural law of monogamy." It has often been obscured by adverse circumstance, but only to break through and reassert itself in whatever new conditions it may encounter.

One such has recently appeared in the discovery that conception can be controlled, and the size of the family determined at will. Those who would apply the mind of Christ to the conduct of their lives are called upon to judge for themselves whether married people are at liberty to make use of this new power. It is impossible in the present article to do more than to indicate the broadest of the principles on which this judgment should rest. Those who accept the view of their responsibility set forth in the first section will not be inclined to a wholesale condemnation of contraceptives. They will judge their use according to the purpose of those who use them. They will exclude at once the motive of avoiding parenthood altogether, except it be for the most compelling medical reasons. They will equally condemn contraception as a means to unrestrained indulgence. But they will recognise that the purpose of spacing births and limiting families is not only a worthy purpose, but also a duty, and that abstention from intercourse is no longer the only, and may not even be the morally best, method of fulfilling it. If they take a wider view of the question and apply it to the problem of an over-populated world, they may discern a reason why in this particular epoch mankind has been endowed with a new control of procreation. While it was uncontrolled, the human race was protected from too rapid multiplication by famines and pestilences, by warfare and a variety of barbarous practices. In modern times these checks have a constantly diminishing effect, and the death-rate in most countries is declining. There is more need now than ever that population should be regulated. But in future the regulation will come less from what are called natural causes, and more from man himself. We have entered upon an age in which, for good or ill, he has been entrusted with a new power of controlling his own natural increase. It is a duty of Christian moral leadership to handle that power with intelligence and a deep sense of responsibility, whatever the perils of misuse may be. Of these, the greatest arises from the indiscriminate advertisement and sale of contraceptive appliances. Restriction will be difficult, but there are obvious and urgent reasons why it should be attempted.

The subject of the foregoing paragraph is at the present time much in the public mind. But its relevance to personal morality may easily be exaggerated. Far more important and fundamental is the issue on which this section began. It may be technically incorrect to use the word instinct in connection with the principle of monogamy. Biologists may not yet allow us to call it a product of evolution, though it can hardly be questioned that in the development of the higher mammals there is at least a tendency in that direction. Students of social habit may tell us that human respect for it is based partly on a man's unwillingness to bring up another man's child, and partly on the ancient idea of a wife as a piece of property. But we have yet to account fully and reasonably for a deep-seated and almost universal conviction which shows itself even in those whose conduct belies it. Most men and nearly all women will acknowledge that a faithful marriage would be for them the best and happiest, if only they could attain it. The rescue, the re-education, and the encouragement of this conviction are the first and fundamental conditions of moral recovery in the sexual sphere, for upon this all the rest depends.

5. THE RELIGIOUS SENSE

We have seen reason to believe that in the normal human being there exists what for practical purposes we may call an instinct of modesty, and, connected with it, another which has come to recognise the monogamous family as an essentially desirable ideal. The value of these two senses has been almost universally recognised in the experience of the race, and declared in the conventions which humanity has made for itself in order to promote the good life of individuals, and to encourage such sex-relationships as shall minister to the happiness of the community. But is this recognition based only on utilitarian grounds, making its appeal merely to enlightened self-interest? Or can we assume in the attempted management of these and other motives a still more fundamental sense of responsibility to God?

If so, we must realise that the religious sense also is at all times exposed to adverse forces, tending to weaken and sometimes almost to extinguish it. And we must face the fact that we have been passing through an age in which such forces have been peculiarly numerous and strong.

The material side of life has rapidly become more interesting and more distracting. Cheap pleasures have multiplied. Religious observance and study are being crowded out. Hasty inferences from new discoveries have led many to suppose that God is an unnecessary hypothesis, and religion an optional extra to real life. To these obviously destructive influences must be added the more subtle effect of defective religious teaching. The last century inherited, developed, and presented to the young an attitude to religion which insisted on authority, especially where it forbids and denies. Such insistence can never be too strong, provided that it is balanced by teaching which inspires a child to recognise God as one who not only commands and prohibits, but also understands and shares ; to discover him in beauty as well as to accept him in truth ; to answer his call for our energy to work with his ; and, in the words of the Scottish Catechism, " to enjoy him for ever." This side of the whole truth about God was underemphasised in the old teaching, and is only now beginning to find its true place in the new.

Thus the first generation of the present century was standing midway between two stages of religious thought and practice. People were turning their backs upon the Victorian expression of the religious sense, seeing its weakness only too clearly, and not appreciating its strength. But as they discarded it they found nothing to take its place. So more and more they were ignoring religion altogether. In the midst of this transitional uncertainty they were caught by the war, and it found great numbers of them unprepared for so fiery a trial of faith. Indeed, it not only accelerated a general tendency to indifference, but converted it into something like a positive and deliberate rejection of all that side of life. Many of the men and women who came back in 1919—full, as we have seen in Section 2, of a grievance against authority—regarded religion as a part of that restraining influence from which they now claimed to be free. Their attitude is fairly described by E. F. Benson in *As we Are* :

" Many of these young men had a bone to pick with God. Such a statement of their intention may sound gratuitously profane, but no other expression seems quite to convey what I mean. To say in milder phrase that ' a wave of irreligion ' swept over the young generation in the years 1914–18 does not meet the case. For some years already a growing indifference to religious matters had been sweeping over them : it might be called a wave, or it might be called a tide. But there was no hostility about it, any more than there was when Darwin published his *Origin of Species*. Science then simply formulated certain incontrovertible conclusions which seemed to invalidate the first chapters of Genesis, but these conclusions were not designedly polemical. . . . But now there was something different. The fathers and mothers of most of these young men and women who were being targets to prove the efficiency of chemists, or were scrubbing floors in hospitals where the damaged targets were patched up again for future practice, had accepted Christianity as they accepted most other traditions and had brought up their children in a faith that to them was still a guide for life and a consolation in death. But the children, particularly those who thought, and whose already existing emancipation demanded the right to use their intelligence, began to find very serious objections to taking for granted any longer the code in which they had been brought up, and made of this an indictment for prosecution. They did not speak of it much, for that is not the English use, but many conducted, *in camera* within their own minds, a pretty cross-examination, and they found the answers of the defendant highly unsatisfactory. . . .

" I do not want to draw an unfair picture of this quarrel. There were thousands of young men, as padres at the Front would testify, in whom belief in God was an unshakable conviction, and who in danger, in bodily agony, and in death found peace and consolation in their undimmed faith. There were thousands upon thousands again for whom religion had always been a matter of indifference, and to whom it remained so. But there were also those, not negligible in point of numbers, and far from negligible in point of intelligence, who quietly thought about it all, and found that the faith in which they had been brought up was not reconcilable with the horrors that were their daily bread. About the reality of them there was no doubt : to see your friend turned to tripe or a dish of brains before your eyes was actual ; and they threw over the other, not with indifference, but with the savage contempt of those who have been fooled."

It would certainly not be fair to regard this temper as generally characteristic of those who returned from the war. But in the diagnosis of a disease we are bound to take account of its acutest symptom. Moreover, the attitude described by Mr. Benson undoubtedly infected others for a time. Intellectually it can be traced to an inadequate and, indeed, a grotesque idea of God (for which the Churches must take their share of blame) very common among those who have not learned to think about religion. It is that God is alone responsible for all misfortunes which cannot be immediately ascribed to ascertainable human agency ; that, for instance, he " sent " the war *ab extra*, or did not choose to stop it, which comes to much the same thing. Such a conception, even if held unconsciously, makes an impossible background for a gospel which presents him as entering human life itself and sharing the worst consequence of human perversity. The contrast of these two views is illustrated by an incident of the war. An officer had volunteered to repair an entanglement and to do it alone. Just before starting, he asked a padre friend to pray that he might come safe back again. The padre said, " No, but I will come with you." It was a blunt expression in human example of the truth that God shares from within, rather than manipulates from above, the course of all adventure. This is the central fact upon which the whole gospel of

Christ depends. Unless it is grasped, we can hardly hope for any abiding revival of religious faith.

Can any signs of such revival be discerned in the present generation? Not in statistics of increased attendance in church, even where there is definite evidence of it. Generally speaking, the desire and even the willingness to join in public worship is a comparatively late development of religious growth. But when we examine the attitude to religion of people in early life to-day, and compare it with that of their predecessors twelve years ago, we find some differences that are at least significant. The active hostility may have left its mark, but it has almost disappeared. It is true that there are some who see in religion, as presented to them, a positive hindrance to their own aspirations for mankind. But there are also great masses of ordinary men and women who are dimly aware that they need satisfactions other than physical if they are to " make sense " of their lives, and suspect that there may be a unifying principle which interprets life as a whole, and an enabling power ready to give satisfaction and security if only they can make touch with it. Professor Malinowsky represents many who have thought less deeply than he has when, " speaking not as a specialist but simply as a thinking and feeling man," he declares that " I am not able to deny the existence of God, nor would I be inclined to do so, still less to maintain that such a belief is not necessary. . . . But I am unable to accept any positive religion, Christian or otherwise. . . . I profoundly differ from the confident rationalist or disbeliever of the past generation or two. . . . The typical rationalist says, ' I don't know and I don't care.' The tragic agnostic would rejoin, ' I cannot know, but I feel a deep and passionate need of faith, of evidence, and of revelation.' "

How is the confession of this need to be explained? Does it merely express a feeling of helplessness in face of frustration and adversity? Or does it proceed from an innate sense that man was never intended to be completely at home in the material world, that he cannot live by bread alone ? If so, we shall here discern a new stirring of the religious sense. There is much other evidence to the same effect. It comes from publishers, who assure us that the demand for religious literature is second only to that for novels, and from the universities, where students are taking serious advantage of religious opportunities to an extent as yet unknown. They are not strongly moved in this direction by authority, nor by any appeal to be Christians for their own benefit. But the flippant disregard for " piety " once supposed to be characteristic of them is rapidly disappearing. When they are invited to join in the search for that which all men seek, they respond, and will readily listen to those who affirm their own assurances.

The course of this renascent sense is not in human control. It lies in the purpose of God, who implanted it, who watches as from time to time it sinks into latency, and meets it as it rises again into fuller life. At these times he " comes " to claim and use it. Just now it looks as if in this country the stage is being slowly set for such a coming. What we can do is to prepare his way, first by frankly revising current conceptions of God and substituting a truer idea of his nature and purpose, and also by initiating such a change of spirit in educational aims and methods as shall lead them into line with his. Education must sooner or later be set free from the miscellaneous tyranny of " subjects," each with its separate claim to all it can get of the pupil's time and energy. It must be re-directed from the beginning to the harmonious growth of all his gifts and powers into a whole personality. It is precisely this wholeness that Jesus had in view for us. And there is no other way to it but the way he taught. That way lies open to him who humbly accepts the only power that can knit together all that is within him into a whole, self-ordered and therefore free.

6. RECOVERY

Thus there can be no short cut to the re-establishment of the religious sense in the function for which it was given.

In the present confusion, all that can be done is to indicate how it may find its own way to its full work in the development of personality. That way begins in childhood. Already a step has been taken in the removal of obstacles which have obstructed it. In the last century the aim of the teacher was to present the truth about God to children in the forms prepared by the Churches for the adult mind. Great pains were taken to translate these forms into words which were seldom as simple to the child as they seemed to the teacher. And too often the approach to God lay through fear in its crudest form. Some verses introducing religion to the young in 1852 thus began : " Little children, pause and think. Turn away from ruin's brink."

During the last generation educational concern has been rapidly shifting from the teaching subject to the child that is taught. Interest has been already concentrated less upon our methods of presentation and more upon his reactions to the kinds of knowledge we think right to offer him, and the use he can make of each. " Religious instruction " is one of them. But hitherto we have studied these reactions separately. Now the time has come for a further step. We must consciously aim at the total health of the child as a whole. And in this synthesis we must first discern the natural expression of his spirit and relate it to the working in him of the Spirit of God. It is, of course, necessary to hand on to him the experience of the past. He must be *taught* from without. But we must also look to his own future. That is within him. The contact we desire between him and God is not a first contact. He is religious already. Our task is to lead him from God in life as he sees life to God in the life that waits for him. Only so can he be *educated* from within.

Because this education concerns the whole child, it cannot be compressed into a separate " subject." Its most vital moments are those in which all his faculties of memory, imagination, and will are concentrated upon a single act of his own. When the teacher's concentration is imposed upon him, the child may listen, remember, understand, but his whole self is not there. It is when he is engrossed in a sight which attracts, awes, and fascinates, or a chosen task which absorbs, that he meets his earliest experience of exaltation and of creative work. " All that is within him " begins its worshipful response to the glory and the energy of God. Soon also comes to him experience of failure, frustration, and helplessness. He is not sufficient for these things. He must depend on comfort, help, and understanding from outside himself, and this conscious reliance introduces him to that which lies at the heart of Christ's religion, namely, love. If he is fortunate, it is in this setting that he will realise his own wrongdoing, not as only a breach of rule or a defiance of authority, but as something proceeding from him which has marred a relationship. When he is forgiven, and finds himself trusted again, he learns how by love the relationship has been restored. And with the sense of being trusted comes new power to respond to confidence. Thus love proves itself in terms of human life, not without risk, and not without suffering whenever the risk has seemed to be taken in vain. And thus may the growing child become prepared by experience for the appeal of the beauty, the love, and the patience of God, so that when the time comes for an explanation of the relationship offered him in the language of the Church, he will have for that language a content of his own. For him the gospel will not be superimposed as an additional piece of knowledge or an arbitrary rule of conduct. It will prove its relevance to the facts of the life he has lived and shared already, and of that life as a whole.

But the recovery of the religious sense involves more than avoidance in the future of those educational defects which have assisted to submerge it in the past. Can those who are dimly aware of its existence within them be awakened to the possibility of its resurgence in spite of all that has obscured and still obscures it ? From the time of John Wesley onwards such awakening has been attempted by mass-evangelism through preaching based largely on fear, and with considerable success. This appeal has lost its power, partly, no doubt, for lack of great preachers filled with that particular conviction, but also because it is realised now, more clearly than before, that Christ made little use of the motive of self-preservation. He warns us, it is true, that God's law of cause and effect is inexorable in the spiritual as in the material sphere. He gives us a background of darkness, unhappiness, and destruction against which his light and life and peace are radiantly set. And his gospel sounds a note of urgency, for earthly life is short and its momentous opportunities must end with it. But his whole emphasis is laid not on escape but on achievement. He would fix our eyes not on what he can save us from, but what he can save us for. And that is life, namely, the harmonious and abundant exercise of all those gifts and powers with which a man is entrusted for use in creative activity. The first material for this creation is his own self. But, left to himself and being free, he blunders in the task. And he will go on blundering until he recognises that he can succeed in it only in so far as he accepts the creative purpose of God, and the power that belongs to it. The purpose was explained in the life, the teaching, and the death of Jesus Christ. The world, having blundered, was not to be left to itself. Creation had been checked but not frustrated. There is still the possibility of re-creation. To this end he called men to work again with God, as before, and on his terms, not on theirs, but with a difference. For now they understand those conditions as never before. One of them is that no man can create or re-create himself apart from his neighbours. " Whosoever shall seek to gain his life shall lose it." And by consequence the work involves cost in self-limitation, varying according to need and call from unselfishness in daily intercourse to acts of real and painful sacrifice. This is no arbitrary condition imposed *de haut en bas*. For God has laid it on himself. Mankind shall be re-created whatever the cost he must bear. There stands the proof that the purpose we are called to share grows out of a love so compact of faith and sympathy, of patience and self-giving, that its appeal to the highest in human instinct, and alike in human understanding, cannot for ever fail.

If this were all, we might indeed be drawn to wonder and even adoration by the love that gives and trusts and waits, and still be impotent to follow it. But Christ did more than expound and exhibit the God that is love. He admitted us to a share not only of his purpose, but also of the power that carries it into continuous effect. Proved once for all in his victory over human death, that power proves itself again in the deep satisfaction of those whose lives have been changed, whose personalities have been re-made, by contact with his own risen life.

That such growth is not manifest in the lives of all, or even of most, professing Christians does not invalidate the proof. In large numbers of them it has always been obvious, and it is so now in many who are living under conditions which to most of us seem highly unfavourable to it. As to the rest, it is not for human judgment to pronounce their witness to be of no worth because we discern in them defects of character and conduct. Often the reason is that they have not yet grasped the whole truth that is in Christ Jesus. They have selected some secondary element in Christian belief and practice which they distort out of its relation and proportion to the whole. And they pursue it so narrowly, and often so aggressively, that they are blinded to the great commandment of love. Thus they hinder their own growth. They are not wholly Christian because they are not wholly themselves. Yet it cannot be denied that in these also a constraining power is plainly at work. And it has reached them through their religious sense. As that sense is developed and trained to receive it, so will the power of the Spirit attain to its perfect work in a man, gathering his instinctive intuitions and desires under one control, and restraining them only that he may share the free creative life which is life eternal.

2. EDUCATION

By Sir CHARLES GRANT ROBERTSON

THE HYPHEN between this short contribution and the preceding chapters can be stated in a question. If the fundamental principles of the Christian faith are applicable to the needs of a " new " age, perplexed with intellectual difficulties affecting belief, and moral difficulties affecting conduct, what can or ought to be the contribution of education and, above all, of " religious " education (which is instruction in religion) to such a constructive solution ? " Is youth," asks a recent writer of authority, " in all countries altogether wrong when it yearns after a new conception of the world, a *Weltanschauung*, which will give a firm point of departure for the establishment of a new order, wherein man and matter alike may be brought under due control ? "[1] Note " a new conception," which is a matter of knowledge, and " control," a matter of morals and conduct—precisely the two fundamentals underlying, by agreement, the English tradition in education, and the ideals of the disciplines which that tradition embodies—the training of intellect and of character in a unified system.

In the history of education, new knowledge, leading to a new interpretation of the universe and man's place in it, has always, sooner or later, led to a reorganisation of the curriculum, so as to co-ordinate the principles of conduct in harmony with the new knowledge. It has always, also, raised the simple but vital issue : Is instruction in religion (religious education) an essential part of any sound educational system, without which the training, intellectual and moral, would be both incomplete and misleading ? For whether the answer be a clear affirmative, or a no less clear negative, instruction in religion cannot be placed in the category of luxury or optional subjects (such as music, dancing, drawing, etc.) which we ought to take, if we can afford to pay, or for which we are convinced that we have

[1] *The Universities in a Changing World*, p. 23.

some aptitude, or because they provide an additional and desirable accomplishment of social or cultural value, or the omission of which will be made good in some other way. Instruction in religion, broadly based on the Christian interpretation of the world-process and the Christian mentality in all problems and rules of conduct, will either colour all the other secular disciplines, or must be dismissed as a positive and falsifying obstacle to true knowledge and right conduct. The issue must, therefore, be squarely faced.

EDUCATIONAL DEVELOPMENT, 1820–1930

One of the main difficulties in squarely facing it to-day is the legacy of the remarkable educational development which began about 1820. The bitterest of the many bitter controversies raged round " religious education," mutilating and retarding progress and reform in the purely secular sphere, yet the parties in these controversies were not, as might have been supposed, for the most part two opposed hosts—Christians *versus* non-Christians—but two opposed camps of Christians, each of which regarded the Christian religion as the most fundamental element in life and conduct. In a word, the battle was between competing *denominations*, which, rather than surrender to, or acquiesce in, " a privileged monopoly " in favour of a rival, were ready to exclude the subject altogether, or water it down to a colourless and negligible " Bible teaching " plus a " conscience-clause." Even the famous Birmingham demand of 1870, that education must be provided by the State and must be " secular, compulsory, and free," was not really an attack on " religious instruction " as such, and was supported by hundreds of thousands of high-minded and devout Nonconformists. The denominational battles were, in addition, submerged in larger political issues, which fill our history books with their splendour, heat, and dust ; and beneath the fire on the surface, rival theories of the legitimate or illegitimate functions of the State glowed red and no less hot. In particular, it was passionately asserted, and no less passionately denied, that the State had as little " right " to spend a shilling of the taxpayers' money on teaching children the religion that their parents who paid desired as to spend it on teaching a form of religion which the parent and taxpayer repudiated. For the State was more than Gallio. It *ought* not to " care for any of these things."

The renaissance of science, with its emphasised antagonism to religion, and its confident prediction that a mechanistic interpretation of the universe, codified in " immutable laws," would reveal all the secrets of life, was followed by the renaissance of an economic sociology, which explained the evolution of social civilisation as a series of definable phases determined solely by the intrinsic nature and potency of the economic forces operating in a purely material world. The Christian religion, generated for the phase of society to which it had belonged, was now pronounced to be only a vestigial toxin, " Capitalist dope " or " State opium," for the proletarian masses, used to delay their accession to inevitable power, or to sap their mentality in the exercise of it.

But since the Education Act of 1902 and its codicil, the Fisher Act of 1918, and the extension of the franchise to women, some of the volcanoes which continuously erupted in the nineteenth century are plainly extinct : from the crumbling craters of others, smoke still drifts, and intermittent rumblings excite the curiosity of the educational tourist. Science no longer speaks with the pontifical dogmatism of forty years ago ; it stresses its limitations to the purely physical and mathematical, and, outside these, takes refuge in the ambiguity of the Delphic oracle which, however the event may turn out, will prove to have revealed the ultimate truth : psychology, enjoying both a renaissance and a vogue, more and more emphasises the crucial importance of personality and the connection, not yet precisely defined, between individual experience and conduct ; no less significant, the rival Churches, realising the results of two disastrous generations of internecine controversy, are at last moving towards agreement on what divides them least, and are finding a common front in the unity of a common faith in Jesus Christ and applicability of his teaching to every sphere of human activity. The lava has, indeed, cooled and the purely educational issue can now be tackled in a new atmosphere and on its merits. For outside the schools and the universities where formal education must be given lie human life and the universe. Those living in the present recall with an effort, almost with aversion, the old unhappy far-off things and the battles long ago. Our gaze must be fixed on the ground in front stretching till it melts in a horizon veiled in cloud above and with chill mist blotting out the sky-line : the secular guides, once so sure, are uncertain as to the route, nor can they say what awaits the traveller at the end of the long day's march when the sun goes down, as it will, and night folds all in the shroud of her wings.

THE EDUCATIONAL PROBLEM

Education in the strictly technical sense has felt the full force of the welter in which ethics, economics, science, and politics, and the fundamentals of belief have been submerged. The travail of man's intellect has grafted on to a vast inherited stock a new knowledge which is being added to all over the world every year : how are we to teach those born into this inheritance of expanding knowledge what is necessary to enable them both to use and to enjoy it, and make a sound intellectual discipline the instrument of the purposive ideals of a new social and economic organisation, based on righteousness and justice, and of a new international order in which both the big and the small national groups combine as equal partners and equal shareholders in a unifying and co-operative enterprise ? How to find in the inexhaustible treasuries of cosmic and terrestrial phenomena the purpose and the plan, the qualities of intellect and aspiration, the spiritual and coercive supremacy of will and love which man in his self-imposed struggle to rise upwards, ever upwards, has expressed in poetry, song, and prayer, and in noble buildings for worship, for study, or the public life of his nation—each and all witnesses to the beauty of truth and the truth of beauty—how to find the unifying link between this soaring human spirit, between creative brain and directive will and the perplexing and inspiring majesty of the cosmic system of which man's world is but a tiny fragment ; how to discover the eternal values which alone can justify the whole and every part of it ? On the one side, the illimitable universe, the miracles of creative intellect responding to the splendour of creative spiritual purpose—on the other, the miserable frailty of the human body, a pitiless environment, the anarchy and impotence bred by carnal appetites and passions, and alike for saint and sinner, the selfless and the selfish, the pure in heart and the rake, a brief span of living and then silence and the dust of physical mortality.

Education, in short, is confronted with the task of meeting the imperative demand : how can man equip himself by training from childhood onwards to understand the true nature of his environment and overcome the difficulties with which his passions and his appetites, his family and community life, the instinct of sex, the rivalry of individual with individual, of group with group, of nation with nation, daily confront him ? Knowledge and a disciplined brain ; vocational training and craftsmanship so that he may not starve ; the fundamental morals of citizenship so that the communal life may be broadened, deepened, and enriched ; decent standards of enjoyment for the bracing use of leisure—clearly, all these are indispensable ; and as knowledge increases and the potentialities of communal life are discovered, the intellectual and moral sides of training through education will be more and more sharply and insistently emphasised. But are these enough, and are they all that man must have ? Surely, the history of the past and the experience of the present combine to prove that the deepest human instincts and aspirations are not intellectual or even moral, but spiritual ; that the power of the unique illumination shed by the spiritual are to be found most completely in the sphere of the Christian religion, and that the greatest revolution in the evolution of the world began with the life, death, and Resurrection of Jesus Christ. And the essence of that revolution was concentrated in the individual revelation of a Person to each individual human soul and the unity of all individual souls in the single Fatherhood of God. It was a revelation of a truth—the Word became Flesh—and it came with the promise of a new power which brought the conduct of each human being into a new relation with revealed or purely secular truth. A metaphysic of ethics can truly say that, unless we know and love the right things, we cannot will the right things, and that we cannot do the right things unless we know, love, and have willed them ; that the right things imply " ought," and " ought " implies " can." The revealed truth of Jesus Christ added to this metaphysic that " can " always presupposes " ought," and promised the believer the power to prove it. That addition just made all the difference. And it is that difference with which a complete and efficient education must reckon.

INDISPENSABLE SUBJECTS IN EDUCATION

What makes a subject indispensable in any sound system of education ? Two restricting conditions have to be remembered—first, that the total number of years available is strictly limited, and, secondly, the total number of hours in each day for instruction is also limited. Even the cleverest can only learn a few selected subjects, the inclusion of which in the curriculum must be justified on the intellectual discipline they involve, on the indispensable character of the knowledge they impart, and on the help they give in the training of character and the principles of right conduct. The " educated " to-day go out into a " modern " world and they must be equipped, under the two restrictive conditions mentioned, to understand and master that " modern " world, to earn their living, to be decent members of their community, and to tackle the problems that life will thrust on them—problems above all, of conduct. No educational system can guarantee that the inclusion of essential subjects will automatically produce good men and women who will triumphantly overcome all the difficulties of life ; it can only guarantee that " the educated " will not become bad men and women or come to shipwreck because the essential equipment has been denied them. The most damning indictment of any educational system is when adult men and women discover gaps in their equipment and ask, with tragic bitterness, " Why were we not taught these things at school ? "

It is far too often assumed that the main reason for including religious instruction in a curriculum is to secure a flow of recruits for the Churches and to lay a basis for making good Anglicans, or good Roman Catholics, or good Wesleyans, or good Presbyterians. The controversies of the past are largely responsible for this educational fallacy. The educational argument proper is quite different from the argument for strictly denominational schools. The purpose of including instruction in the fundamentals of the Christian religion is not to make good Anglicans or good Wesleyans, any more than the purpose of studying history is to make good Conservatives or good Marxists, or of studying science to make good Darwinians—but to impart instruction which in itself can be a first-rate intellectual discipline and some knowledge, without which the learner will be imperfectly equipped for life. But let us note, also, that because a syllabus has been badly drafted, or the teachers are not properly qualified, or some learners fail to learn, are not good reasons for ruling out mathematics, for example, as an indispensable subject. To get the proper educational value out of any indispensable subject the syllabus must be drawn by those who know it, and the teaching must be given by teachers qualified in the subject. A syllabus of Latin, for example, drawn up by mathematicians and taught by those who know more French than Latin would be an educational fiasco. Religious instruction—to be of any value—therefore, must rest on a syllabus drawn up by the qualified and taught by the qualified (not the " parson " necessarily, by any means, but by lay teachers trained for the purpose, but, again, not exclusively for this purpose). If it is dumped into the curriculum because an odd " period " has somewhere to be found for it, and taught by those with inadequate knowledge, or to whom it is a bore to be got over somehow, or who do not believe in what they teach, its educational results will be nil and its moral results will be disastrous. In a word, all indispensable subjects must be treated with the equality of consideration and opportunity due to their indispensability, and must be taught with the maximum of skill available.

If without religious instruction as an indispensable the learner is imperfectly equipped, we may well ask : For what ? And the answer is : For understanding the world process, for life and for individual conduct. The real burden of proof lies on those who assert that you can (and, therefore, must) do without it.

SUMMARY OF THE ARGUMENT

Be it granted that to-day we are passing through a crisis which is both intellectual and moral. Such a crisis, however, is no new experience in man's history, and later on it will be repeated in different and therefore new circumstances. Previous crises—and there have been plenty—present the same synthesis of blended intellectual and moral needs, the same blended and inarticulate cry of individual brain and conscience—" What *must* I know, what *can* I do, what *ought* I to do ? " and have always led, educationally speaking, to the same answer ; which, briefly, is that the revelation of the new knowledge in the " new science " harmonises on a deeper examination with the revelation of the Christian religion ; that in the universe, as in human life and conduct, the spiritual is a more powerful and real force than the material ; that the power of the material can only be fully realised through the spiritual ; that there are " laws " in the operation of the spiritual as binding and as intelligible as those of the material and physical ; and that just as man can, by the right training, equip himself for the mastery of the material forces, so by the right training he can equip himself for mastery of the spiritual, for he shares his quality of spirit with the spiritual power operating in the universe and in the organised or individual life of men and women in a workaday world.

The proof of the efficacy of the fundamentals of the Christian faith lies deep in the history of the past and is verified in the individual experience of the living. The omission from the outlines of the evolution of civilisation of what is embodied in the Old and New Testaments, and of the revolution wrought by the Crucifixion and the foundation of the Christian society, would be both a worse suppression and a worse omission of truth than the omission of Greece and Rome.

Interpret the world of to-day and its needs in as modern terms as you please, stress as you like the imperative desirability of scientific knowledge for a modern generation and a new age, and deny the necessity of, or acquiesce in the omission of, religious instruction as an indispensable subject in the intellectual and moral equipment for life which it is the function of education to give, and the result will infallibly be that those so trained will go out into the modern life of their new age imperfectly equipped, and with gaps as serious in their knowledge as in their moral outlook, standards of conduct, and criteria of values. Life will find out the gaps and exact the penalty. It is easy to say, " I have done with God " : but what if " God has not done with us " ?

THE RESPONSIBILITY OF THE STATE AND THE CENTRAL ISSUE

The inclusion of religious instruction as an indispensable subject in schools wholly or partly provided by the State is still clogged with conflicting arguments about the " legitimate " functions of the State, the " legitimate " use of money raised by rates and taxes, and the " inalienable " rights of parents and so forth. " The rights " of the State are only too often confused with the *responsibility* of the State, and it is inferred that " rights " and " responsibility " are identical : so too " the rights of minorities " and of " the conscientious objector " are pitted against the " rights of the majority " in a democratic community.

All this polemical dialectic is not due merely to careless or woolly thinking but also to the change-over in the nineteenth century from a *laissez faire* to a " collectivist " theory of the State, in no sphere more clearly visible than in education—and to the national predilection for compromises which allow the vested interests under one theory to survive, provided that they do not collide too patently or too injuriously with the new practice of an opposed theory. The English mind to-day retains the general English aversion from logic and abstract principles. When it cannot clearly be shown that an extension of State " interference " has a balance of advantage in practical administration, the extension will not take place ; but when clearly it is the only way of securing the desired end, no question of legitimacy or of function will prevent the men and women, who make the State, from arming it with all the necessary powers, and the rights of minorities or of " conscientious objectors " will receive in such cases very short shrift. In a word, what a majority decide is a legitimate function will be acted on as such. If, then, a majority is satisfied that instruction in religion is indispensable, and to a much greater extent than it is at present, not much will be heard about the enormity of using public funds to do something which " the State has no ' right ' to do."

In education, as in many other spheres, the citizen to-day expects the State to do much that was formerly left to individual action, with the result that what was done by good fathers and mothers was left undone by the ignorant, the selfish, the vicious, or the thriftless. " The State " by its compulsory authority and its coercive powers, stepped in to relieve the good parent and to see that the children of the ignorant or the thriftless do not suffer—because it is dead against the interests of all that starved or undeveloped or sick or ignorant children should drag down the whole standard of citizenship and well-being. " Conscience," i.e. the sense of right as against wrong, was really the motor power, for we forget too often that conscience far more than " self-interest " has armed the State with its power to override the " sacred right " to do as one pleases.

The powers of the State, in fact, only reflect the interpretation of the responsibility of the State by a majority of the citizens, which is previously determined by the individual citizen's interpretation of his own personal responsibility. In the case of religious instruction, this will be the individual Christian conscience interpreting the obligations of the Christian faith.

Two points, at any rate, are fairly clear. The British people still accept the principle that their commonwealth is a Christian commonwealth ; they have rejected so far the principle that the education in " provided " schools shall be wholly and exclusively secular. It is no less clear that they have not asked what exactly a Christian commonwealth implies, if its Christian character is to be maintained ; nor have they decided whether the education in " provided " schools adequately carries out or hinders the maintenance of the Christian basis and character of the State that they vaguely assume and accept.

But there are not wanting signs that the real and fundamental issue may be squarely raised and have to be no less squarely answered. Great Britain may have to decide whether she wishes to remain a Christian State, broadly based on the Christian interpretation of life and the Christian code of morals and of conduct.

The indispensability of instruction in the Christian religion as a part of any sound educational system imposed and paid for by the community will not, in all probability, be decided on purely educational grounds, but on a major premise far more comprehensive in its scope and far more tremendous in its implications. For it will be the validity and value of the Christian faith, as an interpretation of the meaning and purpose of the world-process, and as an essential foundation of right conduct tested by experience, that will be the central issue.

Once that major premise has been decided—and not as at present left in the vague obscurity in which the British people love to leave great issues until they cannot be evaded—the practical consequences on our educational system will be so far-reaching as to bring about a drastic reorganisation. Two of these practical consequences may be briefly noted in conclusion. First, the time and place allotted to religious instruction in the curriculum will be as important as those assigned to any other indispensable subject, retained because of its intellectual discipline and its contribution to the training of character ; secondly, the instruction will be in the hands of *qualified lay* teachers, and not left to the unqualified, or to those qualified for every-thing but this " indispensable " subject.

That neither of these conditions prevail generally to-day is matter of common knowledge. That in certain areas and under certain educational authorities agreed and admirable syllabuses have been arrived at by a fine co-operative effort of the denominational Churches and the layman, and are being loyally and efficiently worked with admirable results, is the best proof that, despite all the unhappy controversies of the past, the thing can be done and done well. What is being done in some areas is therefore the best hope for the future in all areas, and for all schools.

3. THE SOCIAL AND ECONOMIC ORDER:

A. *THE BASIS OF EXCHANGE*

By Dr. HEWLETT JOHNSON,
B.Sc., Ass. M.I.C.E.   Dean of Canterbury

WE LIVE in a machine age. Steam and petrol replace muscle. Productive capacity multiplies. One man replaces ten, twenty, fifty. The spectacle of a modern gas or power plant alarms and inspires—vast buildings, ranges of retorts, the still hum of machines, and a fearful loneliness—the homes of a million heated and lit by robots, not man. There is a single modern turbine installation which has an energy output equal to that of nine million men.

The significance of these facts is hardly realised, but must be faced. We live in a new world. The soil was never more bountiful, with chemicals to increase its yield and tractors to till it. Raw materials exist in abundance, with implements of every class ready to transmute them into goods. A motor plant can turn out 10,000 chassis in a day at the labour cost of 208 men ; and, dividing the man-power formerly required by more than a thousand, a single electric lamp plant can supply every man, woman, and child in Manchester with a fresh bulb a day.

It is a marvellous world, and none need want in it. Yet men and machines stand idle at the very moment when many languish for the things they can produce. In an age of plenty we starve. Possessed of a machine which can supply every need, we see it running down before our eyes. Brains in the board-room plot to curtail production, and hands at the machine ca' canny. Wheat is fired in the field and coffee dumped into the sea. We look out upon a mad world.

What creates the real tragedy is that human life and happiness are at stake. Men are hungry and naked beside the machines that can clothe and feed them. Tailors with sodden shoes, and shivering boot-mechanics, meet year in and year out at the doors of the Labour Exchange, while the needle of the one and the last of the other are still. And so on and on—in this land ; in every land. Children reach the middle twenties and never know the joy of work, lacking means even to provide for their own employment. Where education should advance, it withers. Boys and girls in overcrowded classes breathe over-crowded air whilst their fathers—masons,perhaps, or carpen-ters—struggle to maintain them out of their dole, forbidden to build the rooms they need, and whilst teachers wonder where to get a job. Character deteriorates, lives rot, services languish, and war grows imminent. Our manufacturers must have markets for what we cannot buy. And as markets shrink —for the same conditions obtain in other lands as in ours— we and our competitors must fight for them.

The scientist looks on in despair and the engineer in anger —their labours wasted, their gifts returned with a curse ; the glorious industrial machine, the fruit of their hard think-ing, somehow prevented from distributing its bounties. Like a Rolls-Royce car condemned to jolt along at four miles an hour on an antiquated highway, it is being ruined by the track in which it runs. Industry operates in a financial system suited only to an earlier age, quite obviously unsuited to this. Saddest of all perhaps is the apathetic acquiescence of old and young (most tragic in the case of the young) in all the confusion and wastage around them, as something mad and foolish indeed but yet inevitable. The power to change it seems to lie so far away from their hands.

We must grasp firmly the nature of our problem. It is a prob-lem of plenty, not of scarcity. A commonplace to many of us ; but a commonplace needing repetition in face of repeated assertions that we are poor and must practise strict economy. We are amazingly rich in all that constitutes real riches ; for real riches lie in the capacity to produce the things we need. Such capacity is in no question. Even the war, which was said to make us poorer, left us with a greater productive capacity than before it was fought, and therefore richer in real riches : too rich, indeed, for we soon began to destroy what we had made. If we are poor, it is only financially poor, not actually poor. And that means that the financial system neither reflects nor implements our economic realities. It is unsuited to modern needs, and demands fresh and fearless re-examination.

Excuses are made for it in plenty by bankers, economists, and others, and many causes are suggested for its obvious collapse, such as tariff barriers, the mal-distribution or shortage of gold, limited raw materials, or the dole. America is the answer to all this. She is blessed with limitless raw materials, abundance of gold, and no dole. Yet so completely has her money system broken down, despite these supposed advantages, that desperate men, two million of them, plan schemes of barter entirely outside the current financial system. Such facts compel us to seek the cause further back, and drive us to examine afresh the money mechanism in which modern industry functions, refusing to be thwarted even when we are pontifically told that its workings are scientific, its laws inevitable, and that whether we like it or not we must operate within them. Very readily we grant that the laws of the present system inevitably produce certain results : it is just because those results are so diastrous that we challenge the system, and urge that financial as well as other systems are made for man and not man for systems. If a system inevitably brings disastrous results, it is surely up to us to frame another. New modes of transit generally demand new tracks, and it will not be strange if new industrial developments demand new financial roadways for their operation. So we turn to a closer examination of money, which is the mechanism of distribution and exchange, and probe for the causes of its failure to function with satisfactory results.

MONEY : ITS FUNCTIONS, ITS FORMS, AND ITS CREATION

Money exists to facilitate the production, distribution, and exchange of commodities or services. Originally men bartered goods for goods—a direct mode, but cumbrous. At length some substance was adopted, intrinsically valuable yet readily portable, such as gold or silver, to act as a medium of exchange ;

and in time a token with no intrinsic value has come to serve in place of gold. We are familiar with the banknote.

In its essence, then, money is merely a mechanism. It is not a commodity. Money tokens need have no value in themselves. This is a fact whose vast importance will become more apparent in later paragraphs, and when we speak of the gold basis.

So far we have referred only to tangible money, that money which can pass from hand to hand, our metal or paper currencies. But there is other money, far more important than the cash in our pockets, money familiar to us in the cheque and the bank deposit, which originated and developed in the following manner. For safety's sake, and for convenience, men in earlier days deposited their tangible money with the goldsmiths. On making a purchase, they would often send a letter to their goldsmith authorising payment against their store of money deposited. So cheques originated.

These goldsmiths came in time to be called bankers, and the growth of banking naturally was rapid, for payments through a bank proved extremely convenient. In course of time most ready money found its way into the bankers' vaults. There the bulk of it lay untouched, only a small amount at a time being withdrawn for current needs : a fact which led to a supremely important development. In the belief that they would never be called upon to pay up the whole of their deposits at any one time, the banks began to lend the greater part of what they actually held in trust.

Weigh carefully what that means. The banks were now actually creating money. For if A, B, and C each deposited £100 in the bank, and on the strength of that £300 the bank lent £100 each to D, E, and F, and perhaps several more, the new loans do not lessen the right of A, B, and C to their £100. A, B, C, D, E, and F each have now the right to draw up to £100. New money is thus created, and it is money as real, though it has no tangible existence, as if it had been coined.[1] Intangible money, created and

[1] Only recently has this immensely important fact become generally recognised. The Right Hon. R. McKenna, Chairman of the Midland

transferable by mere book-entry, it is nevertheless as real as the shilling in my pocket. A Crown function has slipped unawares into private hands. Something immensely vital to the community is created, controlled, or destroyed by a private concern. Jealously have we guarded the right to coin cash. Carelessly have we delegated the right to create credit. They are both and equally money, though banknotes and bank-credit together form approximately ninety-seven per cent of the whole of our money supplies. He who controls money wields sovereign powers.

There are self-imposed limits within which banks create money. They know from experience to what extent deposits are likely to be withdrawn in cash, and consider it safe to expand their deposits to nine or ten times their cash reserves. Part of these reserves being the deposits of the ordinary banks with the Bank of England, that concern can exercise complete control over the creation of money and over our economic destinies. Producing nothing, the Bank of England can control all production, wielding a power not less tremendous because exercised so silently. " The growth of the nation, therefore, and all our activities are in the hands of a few men," wrote President Wilson in 1916. Distinguished statesmen, from Gladstone onwards, have said the same, and it is more true than ever to-day. Even Governments are made to toe the financial line. The servant has become the master, and a despotic one too. We must regain our freedom and secure the following facilities :

THREE ELEMENTS OF MONETARY REFORM

1. *The Community must Control the Creation of Money*

First and foremost, we must insist upon regaining for the

Bank, and sometime Chancellor of the Exchequer, now acknowledges frankly that when a bank makes a loan to a customer in the ordinary course, the loan will be drawn upon the bank and paid into someone's credit at the same or another bank : " the drawer of the cheque will not have reduced any deposit already in existence, because we are supposing a case in which he has been given a loan. The receiver of the cheque, however, when he pays it into his own account, will be credited with its full value, and thereby a new deposit will be created."

Mc

community the right to create and control its own money. The banks must yield up their monopoly ; but perhaps it is unnecessary, in the light of the foregoing paragraphs, to add that this means neither disbanding, nor disorganising, nor even necessarily nationalising the banks. The banking system would retain, as it does now, its proper and admirably conducted function of accountancy. An appropriate department of State would perform the function of creating money, using the banking system simply as its agent.

2. *The Community must Create Money, not According to any Arbitrary Standard such as Gold, but According to Industrial and Economic Requirements*

Next, we must insist that money shall be created according to the needs of production and consumption. Methods of regulating the money supplies according to the amount of gold possessed may suit financial interests, but they ignore industrial needs.

Let us clearly understand what is meant by the gold basis, and why we must avoid it. To say that a country is on a gold basis used to mean that all the non-gold money in circulation could be changed on demand into gold. Nowadays it only means that the quantity of legal-trader currency in circulation is regulated in amount by the gold held in the vaults of the central banking institution. In practice, of course, this by no means involves the limitation of money to the amount of gold actually in possession of the banks, because experience has shown that all depositors do not desire to convert their money into gold at once. The banks in a gold-basis country are permitted to issue credit in excess of the gold supply, but are limited to a stipulated proportion. Hence the possession of gold regulates the amount of money in circulation. This imposes an absurd restriction. For gold is scarce ; it is fatal to tie up our productive system to something which constitutes so small a part of real wealth, cramping it, in order to conserve the precious metal, by the imposition of high banking rates, and causing money to be dear at the very moment when trade may demand that money shall be cheap. It ties industry to the chariot-wheels of finance.

Countries on a gold basis create money, not according to industrial need, but according to the quantities of a certain metal possessed by their banking systems. And that is an abuse of the essential character of money, for in its essence, as we have seen, money is a token and not a commodity. Regarded as a social mechanism, the creation of money should be regulated solely according to the actual real wealth of a country—that is, the country's power to produce the commodities its citizens need or desire. Finance must be made the servant, not the master of industry.

3. Money Must Reach Consumers in Adequate Amounts

It is useless for a community to create its own money, and to create it according to real requirements, unless it ensures that the money finds its way into the pockets of members of the community as consumers in quantities adequate to gain for them full access to what they make as producers. As consumers the public demand fair treatment. They should pay the just price for what they buy—that is, they should be charged only for what they actually consume. If the members of the community as purchasers are debited with all capital depreciation, they should, as a corollary, be also credited with all capital appreciation. And it is just here, it would seem, that the financial system breaks down so lamentably to-day. Analysis, as well as common observation, suggests that the financial system is as fundamentally unsuited to modern industry as Tudor roads to modern motor-cars. Debiting the purchaser with all depreciation without crediting the community with simultaneous appreciation leaves him helpless to claim what he can produce, for the total money he receives is not adequate to the task ; treating him unjustly, it also wrecks his industrial machine by inevitable stagnation.

In this connection some facts of common observation stand clearly out—inadequacy of purchasing power foremost of all. Consider, for a moment, the community under its two aspects—on the one hand as producers, on the other as consumers. As producers, they are waiting to hand over to themselves, as consumers, goods of every kind. But they can only do so on condition that a certain number of money tickets are handed back through prices. These money tickets must cover all the costs. Most obviously they are insufficient for the task. It is a commonplace to-day to speak of " the lack of purchasing power."

THE FUNDAMENTAL CAUSE OF INADEQUATE PURCHASING POWER

It has been suggested that there enters into the costs of commodities—boots, motor-cars, and the like—an element which is not available in spendable income; something which is charged into the prices of goods, but not distributed as wages, salaries, and dividends in respect of that particular cycle of operations which made them. The goods, thereupon, go into the market unaccompanied by the requisite number of money tokens. Tokens A, B, and C are charged. Tokens A and B only are distributed. Token C is short-circuited away from the pockets of purchasers, with the inevitable consequence that all the goods can never be claimed by the community which made them.

The fact of shortage of money on the buying side of the market is obvious. The foregoing explanation sounds reasonable. None other so adequately holds the field, and we are encouraged to proceed and ask : What then are these charges which enter into prices and are not met by distributed purchasing power ?

In these days monetary savings are no longer relied on to provide for the whole of industrial expansion, and new money is frequently created for that purpose by the banks in the way we have explained. Such money is accountancy money. It is created " out of the blue." Real money, indeed, but never existing in tangible form ; book-entry money, created on the strength of the real capacity of the works to produce goods and sell them.

This new money is the financial equivalent of the

community's appreciation in value, of its real and actual enrichment. By withdrawing it as if it were a loan, it ceases to function as purchasing power before all the costs have been met. Hence purchasing power fails to keep pace with prices.

Take for fuller elucidation of this thesis, and in further explanation of the shortage of purchasing power, an apt illustration supplied by Mr. V. A. Demant[1] :

> " A bank customer has enough money to pay direct production costs (wages, salaries, etc.), but wants to build an addition to his Kettle Factory. The bank creates £1,000 to pay for the extension, raw material, etc. £1,000 plus *production costs* are paid out and are included in the price of kettles. The equivalent of the total amount of money disbursed (£1,000 plus *production costs*) has to be recovered in the price of kettles. The cost of factory, £1,000, is repaid to the bank, who cancels the ' loan.' The remainder of the money recovered in the price is used again to pay further production costs of kettles—but the cost of factory is not wiped out though the community has paid for it (i.e. delivered bread, boots and films and cocktails to the builders of the factory in exchange for £1,000 now cancelled) ; a charge, such as a sinking fund or other arrangement for recovering £1,000 to replace the factory, etc., when worn out is included in the price of future kettles. So after the loan has been repaid the community receives only wages, salaries, etc., representing the production cost of kettles, but it has to meet in prices not only this cost for which it receives equivalent money but the cost of factory of which it does *not* now possess the financial equivalent. There therefore tends to be a gap between purchasing power and price which is roughly represented by the financial cost of capital equipment."

[1] pp. 123–4 in *This Unemployment : Disaster or Opportunity*, by V. A. Demant, B.Litt., B.Sc. Mr. Demant in this book, and in *The Just Price*, a series of essays edited by him, and contributed to the Research Committee of the Christian Social Council, published by the Student Christian Movement, has elucidated at length the " Social Credit " theme.

To Major Douglas lies the credit of originating the analysis we are now examining. As a civil engineer of world experience he was familiar with the problem of unutilised productive resources. As a costing expert for the Government during the war, and in other ways, he had first-hand opportunities for detecting the causes of the perpetual inability of the community to avail itself as consumer of what it made and could make as producer. The problem is essentially one of accountancy. That perhaps is one reason why economists have been slow to probe it ; why also perhaps their predictions have missed the mark as invariably as Major Douglas's have hit it. There is perhaps another reason, which I as a trained engineer have always felt to be weighty. Engineers, and they alone, realise the immensity of the unutilised power of the industrial machine and the magnitude of the hold-up. All the remedies I see suggested and the explanations given seem to suggest that the hold-up is infinitely smaller than it is and the possibilities less than they actually are. What they *promise* is totally inadequate to the potentialities of our present industrial powers.

We reach the same conclusion if we approach the matter from the other end and begin our thinking with the consumer rather than the producer. And here Mr. Hattersley will help us.[1] He reminds us of two things ; first, that every penny leaving the producing system for the consuming system—all the wages, salaries, and dividends—must be recovered from the consuming system again through prices. Secondly, that not every penny which leaves the consuming system and goes back to the producing system really goes to reduce the mass of unrecovered disbursements. Some is diverted and ear-marked for another purpose. So consumption is restricted and further production is held up. The producing system has to refuse goods to the consuming

---

[1] In *This Age of Plenty : Its Problems and their Solution*, by C. Marshall Hattersley, M.A., LL.B. (third edition), at p. 75. Mr. Hattersley's is the most lucid and comprehensive treatment of this difficult subject with which I am acquainted. Many of the obscurities of the " Social Credit " analysis have been removed by him and objections to it answered. I personally owe much to his restatement of the theme.

system : the necessary tickets are not available, as they have been surrendered already.

Mr. Hattersley puts it concretely thus :

" Let us by way of illustration assume an isolated and self-contained community in which consumers spend on the average £10,000 weekly on the goods they require and also invest in industry an average weekly amount of say, £500. To enable them to do this they must receive from the producing system an average weekly income of at least £10,500. There is thus, *ex hypothesi*, a constant flow of at least £10,500 per week from the producing to the consuming system, and consequently a weekly addition of at least £10,500 to the amount sooner or later to be recovered from the consuming public in prices. On the other hand, although each week £10,500 is recovered by the producing system through the two channels of price and investment, the average amount recovered each week *through prices* is only £10,000."

The unrecovered disbursements mount up and the average time required for the recovery of " costs " through prices lengthens out.

Facts say the same. Witness the colossal capital growth of registered companies. Indeed, when it is asked how, if there is a progressive disproportion between purchasing power and prices, we can account for the fact that the goods produced are actually bought, the answer is mainly because of fresh bank loans for future production, which indeed pours fresh money into the market, but only to leave the disabilities for the next cycle greater still. Export credits, bankruptcies, writing down of capital, hire-purchase debts, and so forth, have likewise taken their share and helped to hide the trouble, and postpone for awhile the inevitable stalling of the machine.

CONFUSION OF ORTHODOX ECONOMISTS AND FAILURE OF THEIR REMEDIES

It is more than a decade now since this trenchant analysis was first made. We have listened to the criticisms of financial magnates and orthodox economists, and have watched them yielding ground.[1]

But we have noted mainly their complete confusion,[2] their variance amongst themselves and the failure of their predictions. While Mr. J. A. Hobson urges that every five shillings saved puts a man out of work for a day, Sir Josiah Stamp calls the nation to greater investment, despite the fact that the trouble lies in lack of money to purchase the old, let alone the fresh production. Mr. J. Maynard Keynes, always versatile, at one moment adjures us, with Mr. Hobson, to spend, and at another, with Sir Josiah, to save. All alike seem singularly to miss the immense potential power of the machinery we possess and the possibilities of to-morrow, and its certainty of displacement of human toil : they still think in terms of scarcity and of finding " work." Those of us who spoke with Major Douglas when he first published his analysis recall now with wonder the almost uncanny, and certainly the terrible, fulfilment of his own predictions.

This analysis, if it is correct, explains the failure of many suggested remedies. The economy remedy, the cheapening of production by rationalisation, and the lowering of wages, mean at present less distribution of purchasing power. If the money distributed in the production of a car is less, the money available to purchase it is less in proportion, and more men stand idle. This very type of failure is highly significant.

THE JUST PRICE

But the analysis, if correct, has even wider moral consequence. It gives us the promise of securing that thing which the Church has always desired—the Just Price. It suggests how we may regain, by an automatic machinery and in an entirely scientific and unarbitrary way, the moral control of the financial system by which men live. We have boggled at dilution of commodities, at cornering of markets,

[1] As in Mr. McKenna's acknowledgment of the fact that banks create credit.
[2] See *This Unemployment*, V. A. Demant, pp. 79 ff.

or over-reaching of middlemen, and rightly so ; but because we gave the matter no thought, because we were more intent perhaps on " making " money than on understanding it, and because we were intimidated by the financial system, we have allowed the cost of the development of industry to be smuggled into prices and piled upon the consumer of ultimate goods : straining out the gnat and swallowing the camel. This, however unwittingly permitted, is injustice on the grand scale. The consuming public is charged with each addition to the increase of the nation's resources.

The remedy suggested for securing the Just Price, and setting the wheels of industry free to travel as they have never travelled yet, is simple enough in principle, and, when carefully examined, is less odd than it sounds. It asks for no violent upheaval, no forcible redistribution of property, no disorganisation of existing factories and banks. Its only obvious effect, if the analysis has been correct, would be a fall in prices beneficial to the consumer and without detriment as now to the producer or seller, the quickening of industry, shortened hours of labour, and increasing access of all to the things they need, with associated benefits too wide to enumerate.

Three propositions describe the process :

1. That consumers' goods should be offered to buyers at a proportion of their financial cost of production.

2. That this proportion should be calculated in accordance with industry's capacity to meet the increased effective demand.

3. That the Treasury or other public issue department should then reimburse to retailers the amounts they were consequently out of pocket.

Take these points in their order.

1. *That consumers' goods should be offered to buyers at a proportion of their financial cost of production.*

We must remember that financial cost is not the same

thing as real cost. Real cost is measured accurately in terms of consumption. The real cost of the goods produced throughout any period, for instance, is the total amount of goods consumed—from foodstuffs eaten to machinery scrapped—during that period. To make a correct national balance sheet we must weigh the total national depreciation—that is, goods consumed and exported—against the total national appreciation—that is, goods produced and imported, whether ultimate goods, such as motorcars, or intermediate goods, such as works to make them.

Seeing that to-day appreciation far exceeds depreciation, we must bear the fact constantly in mind and remember always that " the real cost of national production is national consumption—something much smaller. If the money system were a scientific reflection of actual realities, the aggregate prices of the goods produced during any period would amount to the financial cost of the goods consumed in that period. But this would mean selling below the financial cost of the goods produced."[1]

2. *That this proportion should be calculated in accordance with industry's capacity to meet the increased effective demand.*

" The proper cost, or the Just Price of an article to a consumer, bears to the financial cost of its production the same ratio as the gross depreciation bears to the gross appreciation thereof." The reasonableness of this becomes apparent on reflection. Let the nation cease work, then appreciation decreases. So prices would rise. Let the nation work, economise, invent, and labour-save ; appreciation increases relatively to consumption and prices fall. The common man would always have his finger, through price, upon the country's real position.

3. *That the Treasury or other public issue department should then reimburse to retailers the amounts they were consequently out of pocket.*

And just because the sellers can only sell at less than

[1] *This Age of Plenty* (third edition), at p. 212—a passage which amplifies and illustrates the arguments outlined here.

production cost if they are reimbursed, it is logical and reasonable to suggest that the Treasury should reimburse them the precise amount they are out of pocket by selling at the Just Price. This new money would be the token equivalent of the net appreciation of real wealth.[1] Money would be created by the community, according to the precise needs of the community, remaining in being exactly as long as the real values against it remained in existence, and placed automatically and scientifically in the pockets of those who needed it.

The effect would be natural, immediate, and beneficial. Prices would drop as they ought to drop, in reward for our industrial achievements. They would drop, as they ought to drop, phenomenally ; in the manner in which the engineer and the scientific inventor would expect them to drop, and in the proportion which the harnessing of steam, petrol, and water-power suggests as natural ; and they would drop, not as now to the detriment of the manufacturer, who would be compensated for all his costs automatically in the manner just suggested. The price paid by country and consumer to the manufacturer would remain up. The price drawn from the consumer would fall progressively and phenomenally. The industrial machine would at length show what it was capable of.

THE POSSIBILITIES AND PROBLEMS OF THE NEW AGE OF PLENTY

Doubtless other problems would speedily confront us. Leisure would increase. The demand for labour, rising at first because of the speedy and full operation of all our now idle machines, would begin soon to decrease as demands were satisfied and labour-displacement—now a blessing and not a curse—was devised and encouraged. Money would soon need to be distributed apart from work, the price-factor regulating and safeguarding the process.

---

[1] The banks, indeed, create money on the same basis to-day, but they call it debt and withdraw it, to the complete embarrassment, as we have seen, of the industrial machine.

Those who put their faith in compulsory work and the lash of necessity to make men moral will be in terror of a new era of idleness and mischief. But need there be terror ? Are people, even to-day, really so essentially idle ? I have seldom met the really idle boy or girl, if he or she possesses facilities for occupation ; witness only their eagerness to excel in games, a high form of technique. The generous and creative instincts would have freer scope. That which drives some to cultivate a garden or construct a wireless set would drive others to conquer disease and win fresh triumphs over nature. Some would be free to teach children in the way that only the children of the very rich can be taught to-day ; and others to preach the gospel both at home and overseas. With the present poverty, squalor, and despair removed, with the social services no longer starved, with parishes and schools and hospitals no longer under-manned and half-equipped, the surroundings of life for the new generation would totally change, and it is astonishing what boys and girls will do in any creative community freed from miserable surroundings and the drag of " ways and means." Struggle there would need to be. When one height is achieved the next becomes apparent. But it would be struggle on a nobler plane. And surely we ought never to avoid the obvious duty of the moment for fear of the consequences of our success. Far be it from Christian men and women to shrink from making productive machinery effective, from securing for the buyers a just price, from removing a primary incentive towards war, and from mastering instead of submitting to our money system, through fear that if they succeed they may demoralise men through plenty. It is a poor view of human nature which refuses to cure its ills for fear of its misuse of health. It is not, I am convinced, the view that will long appeal to the members of his Church who fed and healed without money and without price and with no conditions as to how the recipients should employ his gift.

3. THE SOCIAL AND ECONOMIC ORDER:

B. *CIVIC AND INDUSTRIAL REFORM*

By J. MORGAN REES

I. INTRODUCTION

THE WORLD crisis which broke upon us in 1929 was the result not merely of the aftermath of the War but was also a crisis in our social and industrial way of life. Great Britain has been in difficulties since the end of the short boom after the war—say since the winter of 1920. Our economic and social position improved until we went back to the gold standard in the spring of 1925, but since then, relative to that of Europe and the rest of the world, it grew worse from the economic point of view up to 1929.

We have never had fewer than three-quarters of a million of unemployed persons over and above the pre-war average of the number unemployed in any of these years since 1921. Since the slump began we have suffered more and more, until in the late winter of 1933 we had not far short of three and a half millions of people who, seeking work and willing to do anything, were unable to secure it.

Our problem in this section is to examine, briefly, what reforms on Christian lines of our civic and industrial organisation are likely to bring about a better standard of life for our people. Before we can discuss these questions adequately we must begin with a diagnosis of the situation. What are the essential changes required before our present social and economic system is carried out on New Testament principles?

2. WHAT CIVIC AND INDUSTRIAL ORGANISATION MEAN IN OUR PRESENT SOCIETY

In the first place, general agreement will be found on what we mean by democracy to-day: that organisation of

our political, social, and economic life which aims at securing the widest equality of opportunity to every man and
woman to give of their best to society and to receive the
best which society can give to them in return. It means
not merely from each according to his ability and to each
according to his need, but the widest possible scientific
organisation of the individual and his social life to secure
that all his capacity and character shall develop his personality to the utmost in order that he may have a full life
so that society and his fellows will be able to make the best
use of his abilities. This will enable society to give to each
member according to his need.

This meaning embodies to many of us the ideal of a
democracy on Christian lines. What is the form of our
present organisation ? How does it enable this ideal to be
achieved ? What is wrong with our civic life ? What is the
real cause of poverty in the midst of plenty ?

Over eighty per cent of our people live in towns, and
over half our total population is concentrated in five large
industrial centres—London, Birmingham, Manchester and
Liverpool, Tyneside, Glasgow and the Clyde. We are
obliged therefore to provide certain minimum services in
common ; and hence local government grew up as an organisation of our social common needs and services without
which we cannot live together. As these are linked up with
other needs, and also with the needs of neighbouring towns,
and as the local authorities are the agents of the national
State for carrying out certain duties, there is a close link
between civic structure, its purpose, organisation, and
functions with the form, structure, and purpose of the
modern State. But we cannot examine these functions in
this section except in so far as they depend upon our
economic or industrial activities. And what are these, and
how are they organised ?

Before the war most of these were organised unconsciously. " The most obvious economic problem which
confronts the inhabitants of any country or of the world as
a whole does not appear to be submitted to any deliberate

or conscious decision at all. That problem is to determine how the limited flow of savings, its limited equipment of human brains and hands, is to be allocated between the infinity of uses in which they are capable of yielding a harvest of enjoyment. In the main this momentous decision is left to the operation of what are vaguely termed " natural forces," acting through the desires and activities of disconnected individuals. . . . Value or price stands at the centre of this system or lack of system. . . . Various agencies, notably the powers of finance and of the State, are sometimes more concerned than would at first sight appear with the major problems of industrial government, the proper allocation of society's resources between different uses and occupations."[1]

It is this system—which worked automatically, as it were, before the war—which has broken down in our country and in the world. The unconscious adjustments which individuals made for their own gains and for a living are no longer adequate. And just as in the days of long ago the idea of the modern State arose out of the common needs of defence, justice, and order, so now our civic and industrial lines of change will lie in the direction of making conscious, deliberate, and planned, the means of our economic and industrial life. In local government we have seen the growth of social services ; in national government we have seen the pressure of problems of transport, finance, and other economic services, forcing the State to become more and more involved in planning instead of being merely regulative and neutral. In short, the State's functions are being changed from being that of a policeman to that of a Father Christmas, whose gifts do not come only once a year but every day in the calendar. These gifts are obtained more and more from our production of wealth and our services. From being merely a collector, a poacher, and a policeman the State is becoming rapidly transformed into a universal provider. Signs of these new functions were omnipresent during the

[1] Mr. D. H. Robertson—see Salter's *Economic Functions of the Modern State*, p. 145. Pitmans, 5s.

Great War ; some were retained into the peace, but the most recent developments of the Electricity Commission to generate a national system of electrical power, and the organisation of the British Broadcasting Corporation by the State to provide and to distribute news and entertainment, and, we hope, education, will readily occur to all of us.

3. INCOME—THE CENTRAL FACTOR IN INDIVIDUAL AND SOCIAL LIFE, FOR THE LOCAL AUTHORITY AND FOR THE STATE

Everyone lives by means of a money income in our complex, modern industrial society. The individual secures this money income by performing a service for others in return for which he is paid a wage or a salary which is spent on goods and services for himself and his family, or the individual secures this money income from the incomes of others by lending to them the use of his property or his capital, and for which he extracts his price. Now the difficulty in our present system is this : all production of goods and services is social and co-operative, but the proceeds of this production become the property of individuals from whom they must be bought by the expenditure of our incomes. The conflict in society, civic and industrial, arises just here at this very point. We produce goods and services socially, we buy them according to the extent, quantity, and distribution of our money incomes—except those goods and services which are also bought for us socially and distributed socially like order, roads, public libraries, public health, water in the tap, etc., etc.

The problem of poverty in the midst of plenty is due to the fact that science has been harnessed in the service of man to such good effect that the problem of the production of food and raw materials has been solved, as also the resultant manufactured goods ; but we have failed to arrange satisfactorily for the distribution of these, either among the various people of the earth or within any given territory, owing to the breakdown in the mechanism of exchange due to tariffs, prohibitions, quotas, and debts ;

in short, owing to the very breakdown of our price system which was supposed to regulate automatically the costs of production for the producer, and the utility or capacity to satisfy desire of the product to the consumer.

There are all sorts of reasons given for this breakdown of the price system, from the shortage of gold, and therefore of currencies based on that gold, to the intense political and economic nationalism of the post-war years. The reader will be familiar with the illustrations on these points given in dozens of books on these subjects. Although all these explanations have an element of truth in them, there is one fundamental assumption in them all, and that is, that it is possible to set our world to rights again if we cancel all international debts and restore an international gold standard ; that, if we get back to relatively freer trade without strangling world tariffs, everything will go on as before. But were things going on smoothly before the War for the wage-earning millions in our industrial civilisation ? Have we forgotten the thousands of wage-earners in our own country who were earning less than £1 a week and the hundreds of thousands more whose work was regarded as indispensable earning 25s. a week ?

Something has gone wrong with our economic system, and this has brought to the spotlight of publicity and the glare of public opinion its inherent defects. The most fundamental defect is the assumption that all that can be produced under this system of ours can be bought by the people who are organised economically and socially to produce it. Wages are a cost to the employer, but a living income to the wage-earner. If costs of production must come down because prices are falling and the producer finds he cannot produce to sell at a profit without cutting his costs, and he finds that he can do this most easily by displacing labour and installing a machine, or retaining the labour and paying reduced wages, it is as inevitable as the rising of the sun that total purchasing power among wage-earners will be reduced. According to economic theory it can be argued that in the long run this will not follow, because either the displaced labour will be absorbed into the same or some other occupation owing to the fact that wealth will increase and that demand will expand as prices fall, or it will be clear that if the labourers retain their jobs at reduced rates of pay, if retail prices fall as much in proportion as their wages, then they will be as well off as before. It is actually the case that this sometimes happens, but it takes a long time for these adjustments to work themselves out. So long as markets were expanding or new markets were to be discovered, and we had a monopoly of industrial skill and efficiency in the nineteenth century, this theory seemed adequate, but it is no longer a sound theory based on the real situation.

Labour is now being displaced by machinery far faster than it can be re-absorbed into any other industry—if at all ; we have seen a biological revolution in food production, for agriculture is being mechanised and we require fewer and fewer people on the land to grow a greater and greater quantity of food. The result has been a greater risk of maladjustment between production and consumption on an unplanned, basis until the world crisis has demonstrated conclusively that no longer will a balance be attained on the old methods. Even if savings equalled investment, there would be no assurance of a balance unless the investments were sound investments, and by sound is meant here not economically sound (i.e. that they will pay a normal dividend) but that the goods and services which will be brought into production by or through this " investment " will be such as to add to social welfare. At present there is no machinery to ensure this, nor is it possible under our system as it used to be organised.

There is a tendency inherent in the system of Capitalistic organisation to produce more than can be effectively consumed by the masses, owing to the fact that our laws of property and our assumptions of *laissez faire* make quick adjustments impossible. This is bound to be so, so long as goods and services are produced not according to needs but according to the possibility of paying a dividend on borrowed capital. This capital, in the form of money, may be withheld from the potential users unless it gets its market price ; and this price means a lien on the social product.

A lien on the social product will involve an individual claim to ownership of what is produced socially and co-operatively, and that means an unscientific distribution of the product, resulting in shortage of purchasing power or often in an excess of capital goods over consumption goods, or *vice versa*, or again in a too rapid obsolescence of fixed capital at a price which has to be paid by the community.

An income is not obtainable by the vast majority of people unless they are hired by an employer. If they are not hired they become unemployed, and the community has to maintain them at the expense of those in employment. The employer, in business to earn a profit, when he cuts costs by discharging labour and installing machines does not gain the whole of the difference between the cost of operating under the new and the old conditions ; but he is able to gain some of it, for the community shoulders the burden, except in so far as he contributes in taxation to the exchequer. The real difficulty arises because the burden is borne by a different set of people in the community, e.g. unemployment burdens are shared by the State, employers, and employed, and pooled, therefore the faster the displacement of labour by machinery the greater is the advantage to the firm which can do so most effectively, until all the firms in that industry have done the same. When this point is reached there will still be a gain to the firm which is the most efficient. The employing class will be wealthier because real costs of production have fallen, but unless the gains are used to employ the displaced labour and so released to produce additional wealth, labour will not be able to maintain its standard of living. Alternatively, unless we as a community deliberately maintain the standards of the labour set free, by employing it, using up in this way new savings, the community will have to pay the difference in the social bill of unemployment costs—total demands will fall and there will be grave danger of prolonged depression.

Income, then, is the central fact of our complex system. Profits are the income of entrepreneurs who decide what shall be produced and in what quantity. They control production or regulate it, but they cannot determine output at a price and demand at a price. That is, though they are able to place a commodity on the market at a certain price, they cannot compel consumers to spend their purchasing power on that output unless they (the consumers) secure an advantage (satisfaction) by doing so. There is thus competition between producers for that proportion of the income of the consumers which can be spent on a particular product as against other products, and also competition between producers in the same industry for the market in a product.

If for any reason profits cannot be made, industry slows down, men are turned off, unemployment increases, the total wage and salary aggregates shrink, causing purchasing power to contract and a depression.

The world crisis simply came because of a sudden contraction of money incomes in the world owing to the failure of our price, money, and credit system to adjust production to consumption all over the world. When incomes fall suddenly and fixed charges remain the same, deficits ensue both for individuals and for the nations. Before making a survey of civic and industrial organisation it will be well to note the incomes of individuals and the proportions which go to the different groups of people.

According to an estimate after the war, 94.5 per cent of persons have 56 per cent of the national income, leaving 5.5 per cent of persons with 44 per cent of the national income.

If we take ownership of wealth as a basis, we have 96.2 per cent of persons owning only 17.22 per cent of the national capital, while 3.8 per cent of persons own 82.78 of the national capital.[1]

A later examination of the national income does not substantially change these proportions. Wages make up

[1] See Henry Clay's *Address to the Manchester Statistical Society*, February 1925.

about two-fifths, salaries about a quarter, rents of landlords about one-tenth, while profits and interest come to
about a quarter of the national income.[1]

These figures refer to Great Britain and the facts they
reveal do not differ very greatly from those of the United
States of America in regard to the maldistribution of wealth
and so of incomes. Inequality is the keynote of our modern
society. There is a challenge here to our principles of
brotherhood and fellowship. So long as these conditions
remain we shall be faced with extraordinary difficulties of
adjustment even after this crisis has passed away.

4. A BRIEF SURVEY OF CIVIC AND INDUSTRIAL ORGANISATION

a. *Civic Organisation*

Having grasped the importance of income in our personal
and social life, we turn now to the civic organisation and
examine its income and how it is spent. In this way we
can most quickly see its structure, functions, and purpose.
Afterwards we can go on to consider industrial organisation
on the same lines.

The simplest form of civic organisation is that of local
government. If we live in the country, we belong to a
parish and probably therefore are governed in regard to
our social common economic needs by the rural district
council or the urban district council. If in a town, we are
ruled in these matters by the municipal borough or a county
borough. There is one form of organisation into which all
these fit, except the county borough, and that is the county
council.

The parish, rural, and urban councils and municipal
boroughs are all agents or subsidiaries of the county councils, which delegate certain functions to these or work
through them. In large urban centres the county boroughs
are the sole authority though, of course, they co-operate
with the county councils of their surrounding territories for
common purposes.

[1] See Colin Clark, *The National Income* (Macmillan 1932).

It is important to note that the parish is the unit in all of them, though now, to most of us, it has little meaning, yet at one time it was very important, as the inhabitants of the parish during the time of Elizabeth were charged with the duty of looking after the poor and of raising money through a rating assessment to pay for this and other services. We still retain this parish basis as our unit, though for economic and social purposes it has long ago lost its importance as a real scientific unit owing to the growth of population and transport, and the economic specialisation of to-day.

The county council and the county borough are practically identical in regard to their functions and powers. They are the largest, the most powerful, and the wealthiest unit in the organisation of our local government to-day, just as a small local parish council is the smallest.

It will be clear that all these forms of organisation have grown up from early days before industrial civilisation as we know it began. Many of their old functions have been superseded by other organisations, but linger on ; in other cases the units are too small for effective economic purposes, or too poor to carry out efficiently the duties laid upon them.

An examination of the figures reveals, roughly, that the income of the local authorities is spent as follows : Nearly half of the whole sum raised by local rates is spent on the social services (45.4 per cent), one-fifth (19.6 per cent) on roads and bridges, and the remainder on local administrative services, i.e. carrying out, efficiently, the work of providing means of living together locally.[1]

It would be impossible to exaggerate the importance of the work carried out by our local authorities to-day, and its significance for our well-being. An examination of the expenditure itself will indicate the extent of the work carried out on behalf of the citizen, work of which often he is entirely unaware except when the rate demand note comes round. Expenditure on corporate welfare by local authorities is conveniently divided into two kinds : (a) expenditure

[1] For year 1924–25. Later figures give more recent position.

on revenue account on rate fund services ; and (*b*) capital expenditure and outstanding debt. The expenditure is covered by a rate in the pound on the rateable value of assessments of property and by grants from the public exchequer. In 1929 the total revenue expenditure of local authorities in England and Wales on all services, except trading services, was £252,623,238 ; in 1930 it had risen to £262,352,203. Of these totals, grants from the State amounted to £89,022,042 in 1929, and £107,463,251 in 1930 ; i.e. 35 per cent and 41 per cent respectively. Expenditure out of capital grants is not included in the above.

This income was expended in the year 1929–30 as follows :

1. Education   £79,685,166
2. Highways and Bridges   £48,470,092
3. Public Health (including the sanitary
   services, lunacy and mental de-
   ficiency)   £42,678,884
4. Relief of the Poor   £31,457,884
5. Police   £20,899,587
6. Housing   £13,927,407

Capital expenditure is in addition to the above, and amounted in 1929 to a total of £96,407,691 and in 1930 to £102,303,213 respectively for all the local authorities. This capital expenditure is incurred on trading services like tramways, or on rate fund services like housing, and for house purchase or for other rate fund services. The net outstanding loan debt corresponding to these capital expenditures was for 1929, £1,109,261,627, and in 1930, £1,157,879,087.

The above figures give some idea of the large burdens incurred by the citizens to provide these services which are indispensable to-day.

Are these services adequate to our present social needs ? When we look at our slums and at our other housing needs, we have no doubt that the answer is in the negative. The burdens on local rates have increased so fast that many local areas are weighted down with debt, and are unable to provide the minimum requirements of housing or carry out their necessary educational and public health improvements. A good illustration of the inequality which exists between town areas in the incidence of rates is as follows : Merthyr in Glamorganshire, a town severely hit by the depression, a coal and steel centre, has to spend 13s. 10d. in the pound on public assistance, 7s. 8d. on education, and 2s. 7d. on public health, while Bournemouth, with its magnificent public services, has to spend only 10½d. in the pound on public assistance, 1s. 4d. on education, and 1s. 5½d. in the pound on public health.

Despite the recent changes in the direction of equalising burdens, including the Local Government (De-Rating) Act of 1929, the poor areas still maintain their poor, and the facts are clear that our local government, despite its magnificent record in some cities like Manchester and Bradford, is wholly inappropriate to the establishment of minimum conditions of health, housing, poor relief, and education. So long as such a large percentage of its expenditure is incurred on highways, bridges, and relief of the poor, its difficulties will continue. It is agreed by most students of the problem that more of these charges should be paid by the national Exchequer and that greater equality of burdens is essential as between the different areas. The scandal of the inequalities in treatment as between different areas in the administration of the Means Test is another illustration of this problem.

It should be noted that the Local Government Act of 1929 (the De-Rating Act) introduced far-reaching and revolutionary changes in the whole structure of local government. The financial relationship of the Exchequer and the local authorities was altered in such a way that the loss of revenue through the de-rating was made up in another way. " The Act provided an amount of what was called ' new money,' which was fixed at £5,000,000, and the three items, an amount equal to the loss of rates, an amount equal to the loss of grants, and the ' new money ' made up what was called the general Exchequer contribution, which was a consolidated block grant paid annually and fixed for what was described as the first grant period of three years. The scheme operated as from April 1930, in England and Wales, and from May 1930, in Scotland. This first grant period would terminate on March 31st next, after which we could embark on a second grant term to last for four years, and thereafter the grant period would be for five years. The amount in respect of loss of grant and rate to be made up by the general Exchequer contribution was a standard figure for all time—as long as the world remained.' (*Laughter.*) It was fixed according to the standard year 1928-29 and was a matter of ascertainable fact."

" The loss on grant and rate in respect of the first grant was £38,580,000, which with the £5,000,000 of new money made a total general Exchequer contribution of £43,580,000. The grant for the second grant period would amount to a total of £43,928,000."[1]

The changes in the machinery of local government set up by the Act have undoubtedly been fundamental. The Boards of Guardians were abolished and their powers taken over by the County Council Public Assistance Committees which in effect are a new machinery of poor law administration.

The most interesting change financially in administration is the provision in the Act for distributing the total sum between the local authorities on a formula based on population : the number of children under five (their proportion to the whole), rateable value per head of population, unemployment, its percentage, and mileage, its density of population to each mile of public road. A block grant took the place of a percentage grant based on the expenditure of the local authorities. While this is of advantage to the Treasury in that it is known what the burdens are to be on the Exchequer, it penalises a poor area which endeavours

[1] Mr. Shakespeare, House of Commons debate, Feb. 21st, 1933 : *Manchester Guardian*, Feb. 22nd, 1933.

to provide minimum services in respect of maternity, child welfare, tuberculosis, and other aspects of public health for large numbers below the usual standards, because the Exchequer contribution is fixed except for the small movable portion of five millions. Local authorities are being discouraged from providing services vital to the health and well-being of the people. The proportion of the contribution of the Exchequer to the total cost is less than half, and the Report of the Ray Committee on Local Expenditure[1] has made recommendations for drastic cuts in expenditure and a slowing down of all educational and public health better-ment. The chief recommendations of this committee were as follows : Wherever possible percentage grants to be replaced by block grants ; closing of redundant elementary schools ; reduction of school staffs, elementary and second-ary, by increasing the ratio of pupils to teacher ; closing of all secondary schools with fewer than 150 pupils ; immediate termination of the Wheatley subsidy for housing ; sub-stantial reduction of the subsidy for slum clearance ; an arrest in the development of the health services for some undefined " breathing space," as it is called ; and lastly economies in out-relief.

It is hardly necessary to point out that these recommenda-tions are a reversal of the engines in respect of the social services generally, and a drastic lowering of standards in regard to education and public health provision. The rate burdens of those areas which tend to provide minimum services in these directions are bound to be increased, quite apart from the problem of the distressed areas suffering from severe unemployment and so forced to provide relief from the rates to thousands of families in distress.

The tendency again is clear : to place upon the local authorities the duty of carrying out tasks which the growth and complexity of our social life throw upon the State, while at the same time limiting the expenditure of the State, and leaving the financial burden of the local authori-ties heavier than ever.

[1] Cmd. 4200, 1932. Price 2s. 6d. H.M.S.O.

b. *Civic Organisation and National Taxation*

The total national revenue from taxation and local rates is being increased at the time when our capacity to pay these charges is sorely diminished by the long depression and our falling income owing to the loss of trade and consequent increase in unemployment.

The following table gives a picture of the relation between national taxation and local rates.

Year	National Taxation[1]	Local Rates England and Wales	Scotland	Total	Total Taxation and Rates
	£	£	£	£	£
1913–14	163	71	8	79	242
1927–28	673	166	23	189	862
1928–29	664	166	23	189	853
1929–30	654	156	21	177	831
1930–31	681	149	19 (est.)	168	849
1931–32	710	148	18 (est.)	166	876
1932–33	732	—	—	—	—

National taxation has been multiplied four and a half times since 1914, local rates have rather more than doubled. During the five years ended 1931–32 national taxation increased by £37 millions. Local rates decreased by £23 millions, there being a fall both in the average poundage of rates and in the rates collected per head of population.[2] In the current year the Budget estimates for 1,282 (out of 1,755) rating authorities in England and Wales compared with the corresponding half year[3] in 1931 was the same in 162 areas, lower in 1,005 areas, higher in 115 areas."[4]

The increase in national taxation has been largely due to unemployment, the total contribution to this fund made by the taxpayer has increased from £11.8 millions in 1928–29

[1] Including Exchequer share of motor vehicle duties.
[2] See *Rates and Rateable Values England and Wales*, Ministry of Health.
[3] *Hansard*, Thursday, June 2nd, 1932, col. 1312.
[4] Royal Commission on Unemployment Insurance, Cmd. 4185, 1932, p. 350.

to £80.5 millions in 1932–33, exclusive of £38.2 millions paid by the employers and employed (1932–33). There will thus be expended in the current year £118.7 millions on unemployment.

There is a great cry for economy, and great pressure has been brought to bear to lighten the burden, but it is unsound economics and bad Christianity to achieve this economy at the expense of the poor, the helpless, and the distressed. To thrust the burden away by closing one's eyes to the distress, to economise at the expense of the unemployed, who will then be thrust further into utter despair, is not merely bad economics but bad humanity, and contrary to the elementary teaching of the Gospels. The working of the Means Test has been found utterly impossible, and large and responsible authorities have been forced to give up control to commissioners appointed by the Ministry of Health, who are evidently obliged to administer the law strictly regardless of the effect of it on poor suffering families. The obvious duty of an enlightened governing community is to remove the cause of the distress instead of economising pharisaically at the expense of the helpless.

It is time for our Christian conscience to protest at this recent trend of our time to make the helpless suffer for their helplessness, the children to be deprived of their right to education unless their parents pass a Means Test, the public health standards to be lowered because our system is groaning under the burden. The truth is that we are unwilling to face up to the ugly facts that underlie our cry for economy. We must put our house in order and increase our well-being by the reorganisation of our whole income-earning structure, or continue to pay out bread and circuses until the whole system collapses.

Let us examine, briefly, our national revenue for the current year. This is the State's income, and let us see how it is to be spent ; how much of it goes to civic needs and how much to other things, and we shall see at a glance how difficult the situation is which we must face.

The total inland revenue estimate of income for 1932–33

is £427,000,000 ; customs and excise come to £300,000,000 ; motor vehicle duties £5,000,000 ; post office (net receipts) £11,700,000 (Exchequer share); Crown lands, £1,250,000; receipts from sundry loans £4,350,000 ; miscellaneous receipts, £17,500,000—a total ordinary revenue of £766,800,000,[1] exclusive of the self-balancing revenue of £82,098,000, which is again paid out to the same amount to be spent by the post office (£59,188,000) and by the road fund (£22,910,000) respectively.

We propose to spend £276,000,000 on interest and management of the National Debt. Including other payments of like nature to Northern Ireland and other consolidated fund services the total is £286,300,000, leaving a total of £468,631,000 to be spent on the supply services, exclusive of the self-balancing expenditure. By supply services is meant the running of the business of the State, paying the civil servants, making grants to local authorities, maintaining order and defence, etc.

It will be noted that more than half of the colossal amount is paid out as interest and sinking fund on the National Debt. In the 1931 expenditure, out of every pound it has been estimated that 13s. 6d. was spent on interest on past wars, the effect of wars, or on preparation for war, while only 6s. 6d. was devoted to all other expenditure.

There is another disquieting feature which must be noted : if we take the whole of the national income and distribution account, in money value it was estimated at £4,060 millions in 1924[2] (including income from overseas

---

[1] The actual figures were :

Expenditure (excluding debt payment)	£748,114,000
Revenue	744,791,000
Deficit	£3,323,000

The payment to the United States of £28,956,000, brings the deficit up to £32,279,000.

The figures include £17,250,000 for Sinking Fund which satisfied all contractual obligations.

[2] Professor Bowley and Sir Josiah Stamp, *The National Income*, 1924, pub. 1927.

investment). An examination of the distribution of this income made by Mr. Joseph Kitchen gives us an analysis of 10 per cent of the total income spent on public debt service, 16.4 per cent on interest and rent, making our fixed money obligations 26.4 per cent. Other governmental expenditure came to 7.0 per cent, profits of enterprise 16.8 per cent, wages and salaries 49.8 per cent. Now, for every fall of 20 per cent in our level of prices, there is a rise of 25 per cent in purchasing power. As our price level falls, therefore, the amount of goods and services which the fixed money obligations take out of the national income increases very definitely. Since our wholesale price-level has fallen 48.8 per cent since 1924[1] (*Economist* index), the proportion of the national income accruing to the different groups of the nation alters appreciably in favour of the *rentiers* and fixed income groups. As public debt charges are the same in money reckoning (until the Conversion Loan was effected) it will be seen that the proportion of the national income going to these two groups changed from 10.0 per cent to 16.7 per cent for public debt service, and from 16.4 per cent for interest and rent to 27.2 per cent, making 43.9 per cent for these two groups instead of 26.4 per cent, because the general level of prices fell over 40 per cent from the level of 1924, leaving only 56.1 per cent of the total income for all other Governmental expenditure, profits, wages, and salaries.

The above is one explanation of the pressure of money in the banks awaiting investment, for the people who own this money are in possession of a greater proportion of the national money income than in the past, and, as their command over goods and services has been disproportionately increased, they are left with a surplus of purchasing power which they cannot use except to invest. As solvent borrowers are scarce there is a surplus of money. Those who need it to spend it on goods and services cannot get it unless they are employed for wages and salaries, and, as profitable industrial investments are scarce because of the lack of a

[1] Feb. 1933.

stable market, employment shrinks and our national position gets steadily worse.

c. *Industrial Organisation*

It will be unnecessary to go into any detail to describe the organisation of industry to-day. It is familiar to everyone. Let us therefore survey it briefly by stating that there are four chief classes or types of organisation in modern industrial life : the one-man business, working on his own or borrowed capital, comprising not more than five persons ; the private partnership—or the modern variant of this, the private limited company, confined to not more than fifty members ; the joint stock company limited ; and lastly, the modern concern which may itself be an amalgamation of several businesses like Imperial Chemical Industries, Limited. To this class belongs the public concern or semi-public-controlled undertaking like the Port of London Authority or the electricity power companies. These are more or less controlled by public boards with limited profits, and are mainly operated in the interests of the general public after a moderate return on the capital invested.

The above obviously does not exhaust the list, but it is sufficient for our purpose. Everyone works in one or other of the above groups, unless he is a public servant and so employed by the State or local authority or a public institution, or unless he is an independent worker serving his fellows directly by his labour or service, like the jobbing gardener, the dentist or the barrister.

All income is derived from work or ownership, or a combination of the two. By far the largest group is that of the joint stock company form, operating on capital supplied by the public or from its own reserves, and producing goods and services to sell in a market for a profit.

While it is evident that the field of the public concern is growing rapidly, yet the vast majority of our business undertakings are operated mainly for private profit in spite of the following exceptions : (1) national undertakings operated by the central Government itself, like the post office, tele-graphs and telephones, dockyards and manufacturing establishments of the War Department, the Office of Works, etc. ; (2) national undertakings operated by officially appointed *ad hoc* bodies, e.g. the British Broadcasting Corporation and the Central Electricity Board ; (3) the revenue-raising undertakings of the local authorities (gas, water, electricity, housing, etc.) ; (4) the local undertakings operated by officially appointed *ad hoc* authorities (docks, harbours, water boards, etc.) ; (5) companies under the Building Societies Acts and the Industrial and Provincial Societies Acts ; (6) semi-public undertakings established under Private Acts of Parliament and Provisional or Special Orders (railways, gas, water, electricity, tramways) ; (7) other independent undertakings not run for profit but to carry out public functions like the Ecclesiastical Commis-sion, the universities, schools, and City companies ; chari-ties, owning estates, property, schools, etc., and administer-ing them for the benefit of the general public or their members.[1]

It has been estimated that the above operate in round numbers £4,000 millions of capital, about a sixth of the whole national capital, so that the field is still largely oper-ated by private or joint stock concerns for individual gain.

An analysis of 70,000 companies for the Colwyn Com-mittee on the National Debt confirms this conclusion ; for 54,000 companies were private and 16,000 public, but the latter (i.e. public joint stock companies producing goods and services firstly for dividends and secondly for service) had three and a half times the capital of the former. Again, it was noted that three-quarters of the total of business profits came from corporate enterprise (public joint stock and private joint stock) as contrasted with one-man or other small individual enterprises. Of this three-quarters, 56 per cent came from public companies.[2]

[1] See *Britain's Industrial Future*, p. 61 (Benn Ltd., June 2nd, 1928). Report of the Liberal Industrial Inquiry.

[2] See *Economics of Modern Industry*, P. Ford (Longmans & Co. Price 4s. 6d.).

The reader is referred to other sources for further information, especially to the illuminating series of reports known as the Balfour Reports on Industry and Trade and other official documents and publications, but it is hoped that sufficient has been indicated for the general reader to grasp the general situation regarding the organisation of industry.

Employers' associations are organised locally and nationally to look after the interests of the owners as affected by the trade as a whole, such as, for example, the South Wales Siemens Steel Association or the National Federation of Iron and Steel Manufacturers. For trade and commerce again, we have similar bodies covering local chambers of trade to a national association. More centralised organisations are the Federation of British Industries, and the National Confederation of Manufacturers' Associations, the International Chamber of Commerce, etc. We do not know enough about them, for they are not compelled by law to register. We know all about trade unions, and their organisations among the various occupations and trades. Their central organisation is the Trade Union Congress General Council. There is no doubt at all that the trade union representatives and the representatives of the employers wield immense power in our national and social life, but the power of the latter is veiled and hidden, whereas there is plenty of publicity about trade unions. What is the amount of the subscriptions paid each year to the political parties by these employers' associations to defend their interests ? We do not know. We do know what the trade union sums amount to, and how they are spent. The same knowledge should be available for both.

5. AN EXAMINATION OF PROPOSALS FOR REFORM

As national and local government income and expenditure depend upon the prosperity or depression of our industries—our means of life—we propose to confine ourselves to an examination of the general principles upon which reform on Christian lines can be advocated for our industrial and social order, leaving any other detailed

Na

considerations or specific recommendations on the reform of national or local government to be inferred from the analysis of the general theory put forward on the main suggestions.

Most of the conclusions for the reform of British industry, or the organisation of our business, or an improvement in the industrial relations between employer and employed seem to go unheeded. For instance, that admirable report on *Britain's Industrial Future* published by Benn's, the Report of the Liberal Industrial Inquiry, is much more than a political document : it is a mine of facts and information and wise observations. So also are the dozens of Government reports on the various problems. For instance, the recent Report of the Royal Commission on Unemployment Insurance[1] makes far-reaching suggestions on the subject which, if adopted, will undoubtedly improve the situation for millions of our fellow-citizens. But all these suggestions are made on the assumption that the framework of the present industrial system and our structure of production remain as they are, or, at any rate, that the changes will be slow. Whereas, in fact, the real issue is not faced, namely that the Capitalistic system as a coherent whole has broken down, because men will no longer work it when they are mere tools for others' gain ; there is thus no free market where prices reach equilibrium easily and quickly ; there is no stability of prices ; there is, in short, no longer *laissez faire*, but, at best, a state of armed neutrality between two forces opposed to one another : the people who function, i.e. who live by work, and the owners who own, but do not control, the means of life. This is best seen in the realisation that, more and more in any industry organised on large-scale lines, there is a complete divorce between the shareholders who own and supply the capital, and the management who are generally salaried officials ; yet the *policy* or *planning* of the business may be in the hands of representatives of these functionless shareholders with little skill, no knowledge or efficiency. These are the representatives who

[1] Cmd. 4185, 1932, 7s. 6d.

live by owning, and they control the factors of production upon whose effective mobilisation and operation depend the livelihood of millions of our people. Decisions of moment are decided not by the general effect of a particular course upon the welfare of the workpeople or the interests of the nation, but whether a particular course will or will not result in a profit to shareholders. If it does, it will be adopted regardless of the influence on the nation as a whole. We must face the issue as Christians as well as neutrals.

We can no longer pay for the national or local social services and allow the system to be run as it is running now. Trade unionists cannot be paid a standard minimum wage in many of our export industries, if we allow a disorganised industry to pursue a policy of cut-throat competition for profits among one another at home behind a tariff, and a plea for a free hand abroad to win back non-existent markets at the expense of the general consumer at home. We cannot afford to pay more than half our national taxation revenue to functionless war debt holders and provide national housing schemes, slum clearances, and a high level of education. We cannot understand the United States insisting on the payment of war debts from Europe, and refusing to receive them except in gold, because she confuses gold and goods and tariff wall effects. We see clearly that the United States cannot be paid in gold ; but she can be paid in goods only if she lowers her tariff, and this means that she will have an excess of visible imports over exports. But we refuse to see the beam in our own eyes : that we cannot run a Christian social community with rising standards for all on the basis of the dictatorship of the Capitalist, directed mainly to one end—the extraction of the largest possible income for the owners of land and capital in the form of rent, interest, and profit. Only a small fraction of the community, the private owners of the means of production, exercise this government of industry through paid managing representatives, who sometimes climb into the ranks of owners themselves.

The difficulty of most of the reports, inquiries, and

commissions is that they ignore this vital assumption of the sacrosanctity of an order which is changing rapidly under our eyes—except the Liberals, who seem to think that they can go on making the best of both worlds for a long time yet, and that they are as Socialist as the Socialists, and as individualistic as the Conservatives. Even the final report on unemployment insurance has to record : " While our inquiry has extended over the whole field of national and local provision from public funds for the able-bodied unemployed, our terms of reference do not require us to make suggestions with regard to an industrial policy for the future. That is a more difficult as it is a more important question. The restoration of industrial prosperity, which alone can provide a permanent expansion of employment and the absorption of the employed, raises questions of general economic policy which are outside our field of inquiry. We have to take the facts of unemployment as we find them, and we have to assume, broadly, the continuance of our present system of economic organisation. Obviously, the type of provision against unemployment will vary with the type of economic system within which unemployment occurs. Our problem has reference to the present and to the immediate future of British industry and we seek to discuss it within these limits."[1]

In our view, we must transcend those limits and look to foundations in any suggestions of reform on Christian lines.

6. TESTS BY WHICH OUR INDUSTRIAL COMMUNITY IS JUDGED

There are tests by which an industrial community is judged in the light of Christian principles. Without in the least subscribing to the view that this Capitalist system of ours is being attacked, we must face the facts : (1) that it does not secure the maximum production of goods and services for our people ; (2) that it does not attain justice in its distribution of wealth ; (3) that it has failed to provide a tolerable existence for its producers when in our country

[1] Cmd. 4185, 1932.

to-day three millions are unemployed and thirty millions needy in a world of plenty ; (4) that it fails to secure the greatest possible freedom and stimulus to personalities and to social progress.

On the other side of the account, we must record the fact that our people are better off than they were one hundred years ago ; though that is poor consolation if the proportional distribution of wealth has not changed very much. It has banished famines from our industrial world : we refuse to allow the unemployed to starve to death. There is no doubt again, that, to those who have the purchasing power, this is a great and remarkable world with wonderful appliances for comfort, convenience, and health. Our public health and standard of sanitation have improved enormously ; and we have provided for knowledge and capacity in the means of the production of wealth which, if released, would astonish the world. Yet they are only released in time of war, for destruction.

On balance, the tests leave us a poor Christian community, judged by brotherhood and fellowship, when we urgently require one million working-class houses, which can never be built by private enterprise to let at economic rents, despite a pathetic belief to the contrary against all the facts. Our vital industries—coal, transport, iron and steel, textiles—are in drastic need of reorganisation to enable us to live. This cannot be done so long as they are run mainly for private profit. Why not say so then, everywhere ? Even if they are rationalised the problem is not solved, for we shall have technological unemployment.

All civic and, ultimately, all State reform depends on the possibility of altering our industrial structure, organisation, and functions in the direction of a scientific ordering of the community life. This cannot be done by " nationalising " everything ; but, though *laissez faire* is dead, we have yet to demand as Christians that we shall no longer tolerate a community life dependent on profit as the prior claim before existence or necessaries are first forthcoming.

7. THE TRUER CONCEPTS OF CITIZENSHIP

Communism is to-day challenging Christianity, both as a materialist economic system and as a religion. Our civilisation is in difficulties ; everywhere uncertainty, perplexity, economic chaos, and despair. There is plenty of food in the world, but we seem powerless to effect a bridge between our plenty and these wants. Unless Capitalism can improve its technique of marketing and of distribution, so that under-consumption and unemployment can be prevented, and unless the standards of living of workers in our Capitalistic world can be quickly and materially raised, our civilisation will pass away.

The challenge of Communism lies in this : it states that our modern Capitalistic system is based on tyranny and on the exploitation of man ; that it is rooted in selfishness and on the negation of personal freedom and liberty, which is based on economic freedom ; that it is unjust, and that, as Christianity, in the form of official religion, condones this or seems helpless to secure justice, its beliefs unconsciously make it a tool of the oppressing classes, and that, therefore, it is a sham or an unreal thing, and must be replaced by Communism, which, it is claimed, is a theory of life and value based on reality.

Let us examine this position. Christianity consists of three central propositions : God is a father, as taught by Jesus in the New Testament. If we accept this, it follows, secondly, that men are brothers ; brotherhood, or fellowship, therefore, is the second great truth. Lastly, as men are sons, and each one has a human soul in the image of God, this leads us to the third proposition of the highest value in life—the sanctity of personality. Out of these two arise the social implications. If personality is supreme and sacred, if men are brothers, then there is laid upon all Christians the duty of service to others in love and fellowship. We must realise the dynamics of these principles in the economic system by means of which we live. " The deeds that I do bear witness of me." The battle of the creeds has been left

behind. Now, as Christians, we are faced with the great
task of christianising the economic order in its foundations.
Christianity is not merely a contemplative religion : it
arouses men to act on the assumption that the best things
are possible. Faith is not enough, we are being judged by
our works, by our social and economic systems. These
truths are more and more being proved to be sound in the
economic world.

Man is a social animal. Individual and social conduct
cannot therefore be separated. We cannot judge a society
by its economic results regardless of its bases, or an
individual on his morals. The spirit which would divorce
economic activity from religious considerations is therefore
un-Christian. The New Testament points out clearly the
dangers in the pursuit of wealth as an end in itself. A
human being is not a means but an end in himself, not a
means for the production of wealth to shareholders. A
Christian community is morally responsible for the
character of its own economic and social order.

Whatever be the imperfections of our achievement—
and " a man's reach must exceed his grasp, or what's a
heaven for ? "—that is the reply to the Communists.

Judged by these principles, our society to-day is not
Christian, because in all the tests, despite bright gleams
here and there, and signs of change, it is not based on
service to others first, except in national and local government, and in the other forms of industrial organisation
noted previously. It is co-operative in production, but
individualistic in distribution, even of the primary needs of
food, clothes, warmth, and shelter. So long, therefore, as
the majority of the people are short of these essential
requirements of a minimum standard of the good life, how
can we, as Christians, support it even by acquiescence ?
We must be up and doing.

The truer concept of citizenship demands as a duty of
the Christian he should recognise that the present organisation of our society stands condemned. He must work to
change it peacefully and quickly, or it will perish. But we

must keep the business going while the shop is undergoing repairs. Yet no repairs will be scientific, and therefore adequate, which do not aim at making the system serve man in order to free human personality, and make wealth serve the ends of welfare. Passive contemplation will not effect this ; neither patriotism nor economic nationalism is enough, nor a belief in the virtues of the British Empire or British prestige in dealing with other people. There is plenty of good-will and fellowship in our society if we mobilise them and harness them to our purpose. Business men in charge of important affairs are not monsters of iniquity. They are usually average human beings grappling with difficult tasks, and as well-disposed towards their fellows as the average trade unionist. But they lack identity of aim, and both are the victims of circumstances which can be changed if we but will to do so. They both tend to identify their own interests with the general interest ; but, as there seem to be more trade unionists than business men lacking ordinary decent conditions of life in the wealthiest societies of the world, it seems necessary to be on the side of the worker in this conflict between labour and capital. Instead of labour hiring capital, the owners of capital hire labour. Capital has to bear the losses as well as the gains, but so does labour ; the former has a sinking fund and a depreciation fund, the latter has not, except after bitter struggles in Parliament to pay unemployment benefit.

8. CONCLUSION : OUR IMMEDIATE TASKS

In their summary of conclusions on the condition of British industry, the Liberal Industrial Inquiry says : " In many of our leading, old-established industries the organisation is too deeply embedded in nineteenth-century grooves. The essential weakness is not national, it does not lie in obsolete plant or in an antiquated lay-out of coal mines. It is rather psychological. It lies in a stubborn adherence to outworn methods, ideas, traditions, resulting in a general organisation of industry which fails to pass the test of twentieth-century conditions. Nor is it business organisation in the narrow sense that is at fault. Our industrial efficiency is gravely impaired by unsatisfactory relations between employers and employed, bursting out every now and then into wasteful conflict.

" But we have not only to adapt to new conditions the structure of some of our industries, we must be ready also to re-adapt the whole structure of our economic life. We must not continue to wait passively for something to happen which shall restore the peculiar balance of our pre-war industrial life. Rather should we extract compensation for the troubles of our export industries by turning our attention to what we have too long neglected—the development of our home resources. We should seize the opportunity to press on with housing, road construction, electricity, and the regeneration of agriculture and our rural life. These are the broad conclusions to which our survey leads us." [1]

This is an admirable programme with which we all agree.

But is it practicable without first establishing a principle : that our economic and industrial system must be transformed from one based on securing profit to functionless shareholders as the price of service, to one which puts service first always, and profits next at the cost of whomsoever it concerns ?

This means that a man's property is less important than the man himself. Competition for dividends does not automatically bring about a well-ordered and never-failing stream of goods and services. Supply and demand are human laws, and only operate within limits—severe and narrow limits. If a higher rate of gain will be secured by investing in new cinemas and new shops rather than in houses, then it is the business of a Christian community to see that houses are built first. And, if necessary, the State must do it, even if it means a National Housing Commission which alone will be able to secure capital at a low price. Private enterprise, it can be proved economically, will never do so.

[1] *Britain's Industrial Future*, pp. 454-5.

First things should come first. If our price system has collapsed we must manage our currency and our internal level of prices by a planned money policy. It is immaterial whether a re-organised Bank of England directorate does this or some other body. The bank acts in the public interest. It has moved from the individualistic private form to the responsible public form. Let us recognise it then. The joint stock banks are public institutions operating the public credit, firstly, in the interests of their shareholders and depositors, next, in the interests of the nation. A Christian demands that this order should be reversed, even if it means controlling the volume and the price of credit in the interests of British industry and the general welfare. In practice this would mean a better safeguarding of the deposits of the public than under the existing system, for their application would be directed in ways more conducive to social welfare. We do not ask for more bureaucracy. There may be a dozen methods of carrying these principles into effect. Power to legislate resides in the House of Commons, but it is powerless to control our national economics. Why not set up, then, a National Industrial or Economic Council to which could be devolved definite tasks ? Or, again, it could set up statutory commissions of the best, most expert people to carry out definite jobs, e.g. to put our vital industries in order. It is already trying to do this in some way by trying to get coal owners to amalgamate to close down some pits and work others full time. This will not do, unless the coal industry is treated as a national unit. Every economist knows that ; but if it is assumed that dividends must be paid at the cost of whomsoever it concerns, then our reforms will be patchy, anæmic, and ill considered. Similarly with cotton, iron, and steel.

We are not wedded to any scheme of State operation or State management. In our complex civilisation we have to preserve initiative, enterprise, and individual resource and freedom, but it is a mistake to suppose we are achieving these by our profit-making system. We must release personalities and arouse the best efforts of people, not by the whips of fear and unemployment, but by service and understanding.

As foundations, therefore, we believe that public ownership or control of the chief requisites of production should be insisted upon, whether of land or power, finance, and transport. The key is control of finance, even if it means setting up a National Investment Board with the power to indicate clearly its blessing or its disapproval of any new capital issues. It should itself, if necessary, initiate and carry through national schemes of betterment, or even of revenue-producing undertakings through appropriate commissions of the required type.

To begin with, this policy would mean state ownership of power (coal, electricity, oil, and transport, i.e. railways, air transit, canals, harbours, and shipping), but not necessarily state management. This cannot be carried out without the control of banking, currency, and credit in the public interest. Are we prepared to begin with these ? Do we agree that we cannot christianise our means of life until these are carried through ? It is no use any longer shirking the issues.

We must plan our society on these lines, or collapse. There is no single road to the Kingdom. There will always be large fields open to private enterprise—personal service, the one-man type of business, the thousand and one forms of our social life—but if there are large differential gains owing to the operation of economic law in our industrial system, they should accrue to the society, to be used by it to raise its standards, level down its inequalities and build up the new Jerusalem in our land.

There are pointers on the road. The National Government calmly sets up £150,000,000 to control foreign exchange ; it places an embargo on new issues ; it proposes scientifically controlling milk distribution by buying up if necessary all the milk. Logically, we must see to it that this is to go on under whatever political party which delivers the goods. Local government is sadly in need of repairs. Can they be carried out unless we arm local authorities with legal power to do all they require to do in the public interest without the necessity of seeking new powers for every change by Act of Parliament ?

These changes are on the way. May they come soon ! for time is short. Disarmament policies at Geneva are not enough. There must be economic disarmament within each State as well as international peace between the nations, for the latter will not be sound unless based on the former. May we forgive our debtors at home and abroad as we expect them to forgive us. We must persuade by thought and action all who oppose these ideas. Christians must gird themselves in this fight for the freedom of man and of the world. The time is short. We must not fail. Politics are vital ; so also is education. More than all is the aim and purpose of industry. We shall not improve our local government very much unless we first change industry from being a means of wealth to the few, to a means of life for all. This is the acid test of a Christian. What are our views of the social order ? We must refuse to profit by it. We must aim at service, not a career. A career will come through service, if business is made a profession, as it can very well be—but service first, anywhere, anyhow, to make better personalities, better Christians, and so a better world.

The alternative is a collectivised man with one religion— the religion of hate and strife to secure justice.

3. THE SOCIAL AND ECONOMIC ORDER:

c. *INDIVIDUAL FUNCTION AND THE COMMUNITY*

By E. C. URWIN

I. THE PROBLEM: INDIVIDUAL AND COMMUNITY

How, in the modern world, is the individual to find his place and function in the life of the community? The question is the touchstone of any vital view of society, as well as the test of the obligation the individual owes to the community and the quality of life offered by the community to its members. "There are no individuals," it has been said, "who are not social individuals, and society is nothing more than individuals associated and organised. Society has no life but the life of its members, no ends that are not their ends, and no fulfilment beyond theirs. . . . The quality of a society is the quality of its members."[1] All great societies can be tested by the quality of individual life possible within them, and no human society has yet arisen which satisfies the test. The ancient civilisations of Greece and Rome, no less than those of the Nile and Tigris–Euphrates valleys, rested on the broad, long-suffering back of the slave. The life of the free-thinking Greek citizen, as of the proud Roman patrician, had a richness and fullness of charm, doubtless, individually satisfying to those who participated in it: but it was a mere apex of human blessedness resting on a base of dull servitude and plebeian discontent.

The problem arises as acutely in our modern world. The social bond arises first of all because of certain rudimentary and organic needs: needs of food and drink, air and light, clothing and shelter, which are best secured by being pursued in common. Even in primitive society there springs up something like division of labour and diversity of function. Plato recognised that long ago when he sketched in

[1] Maciver, *Community*, p. 68.

graphic phrase the origin of community : " A husbandman
for one, and a housebuilder, and besides these a weaver
. . . a shoemaker, and perhaps one or two more people who
minister to our bodily wants." The division of labour has
gone far since then. It has added infinitely both to the
variety and the convenience of life, for the widening range
of need is met only by the extending range of service. The
intricate and complex processes of modern industry call
forth not only the sturdy qualities of the miner and the
metal-worker, but the skilled scientist and the careful
technician. Every new invention or discovery adds a new
region of specialisation, serving the community by added
convenience and delight. Human society becomes increasingly complex, requiring service ranging from a dustman
to a Prime Minister, from a milkman to an economic adviser
at the International Labour Office at Geneva.

Yet how far do the individuals composing our modern
society find their true function, or the material for a satisfying life ? A walk down a mean street in any of our great
cities will show us " the sordid sights inseparable from the
life of the poorest strata of a civilisation which does not
know what to do with its dregs." There the sharp edge of
our social evils will be found pressing " where the resistance
is weakest and the suffering greatest," " the results . . . of
forty million people on a small island, getting a living in
dirty ways from coal-pits and iron-mines and resulting
steam factories."[1] A vertical section through the gradations
of modern society from the base of the pyramid to its apex
will reveal the sources of our discontent. Three sharp-edged
considerations emerge, touching sensitive spots in the life
of society, viz. : (1) the relation of status to service ; (2) the
variations in the scale of living ; and (3) the fact of class.

1. *The Relation of Status to Service*

Status means " standing," recognised position, and accorded worth. Plato's Republic accorded a differing status
to Governors, Defenders, and Producers. In the modern

[1] Urwick, *Philosophy of Social Progress*, pp. 9–11.

State we are concerned with the differing status accorded to the capitalist, the professional man, and the wage-earner : and the acute problem is the status of the wage-earner. In antiquity, the slave did service, but had no personal status. He was a tool, an instrument, a chattel. In the modern State, the slave is replaced by the wage-earner. The wage-earner differs from a slave by having " freedom of contract." But, as the history of modern industry eloquently shows, it has been no easy task to give real effect to that status of freedom, so that it should result in a permanent enhancement of personal well-being. First, the human end was subordinated to the purpose of gain. " Profit " was the admitted motive on which the new economic order rested : the labour of the wage-earner was hired to that end. Second, there was his detachment from the means of production. He was employed to till ground that did not belong to him, at a coal face owned by another, at a loom or spinning-frame that belonged to someone else. His labour was his own, but not the material upon which he used it, nor the instruments he employed, nor the fruit of it when done. Third, in the estimation of his worth, society found it hard to throw off standards of judgment derived from the older slave economy and the condition of serfdom. The worker was a " hand," a servant, a hireling : his employer was " head," " master," " boss." Although the relations thus designated were often qualified by personal regard and human feeling, it is undoubted that the new status of freedom acquired by the worker was insufficient to ensure him fullness of personal worth and life. When the relations between him and his employer were depersonalised through the dominance of the instinct of acquisition and the motive of gain, a condition of service resulted that was not far removed from servitude. Even now, when industry is subject to State regulation, and " organised labour " confronts " organised capital," it is by no means clear that we are much nearer an adequate personal status for the worker commensurate with the function he fulfils. If we compare the care that is taken to recruit and equip men for " the

professions " with the casual and indifferent way we recruit
and equip men for industry, we have some measure of the
differing estimation in which they are regarded.

2. The Variations of the Scale of Living

Every thorough-going analysis of modern society calls
attention to the gaunt extremes of riches and poverty and
the differing rewards that accrue to those who serve community. Can we find any principle by which these variations can be justly regulated and wide divergences in the
standard of living be overcome ? The case can, of course, be
argued from several viewpoints. The service to community
varies : therefore reward should vary. But the difficulty is to
determine the value of the service : a purely economic test
may not assess real value or worth. Where varying rewards
are given, each will be tempted to strive for greater recognition of his own service, and depreciate the worth of that
of others. Some service will be estimated beyond its true
worth, and other below. The constant tendency to depreciate the worth of labour, the unceasing endeavour to
reduce wages, and the existence of so large a section of the
community on or about the poverty line, all seem to be
rooted in this unequal apportionment of reward to service.
Again, it is suggested that different callings require differing
standards of maintenance to sustain the personal interest
and self-respect needed to inspire effective and willing
service. Will the same standard of life content a railway
porter, an elementary school teacher, a doctor, and a civil
servant ? Yet it is not the largeness, but the certainty and
sufficiency of the economic reward, that are the determining
factors. The greatest fret in the industrial world has arisen
from the insecurity of livelihood, when labour is casual,
hired from hour to hour, or subject to a week's notice.
There is no more poignant expression of the worker's longing than the oft-heard cry " for something to come in
regular." This leads to the consideration of reward appor-
tioned to need. It is likely that in an age of increasing
plenty, made possible by the application of science to

industry and agriculture, together with the displacement of human labour by the machine, that more attention will have to be paid to this principle as the determining factor in distribution. What need for any to starve or go short, when wheat is to hand in embarrassing abundance, and only a corporate short-sightedness prevents us getting it to those who need it ? Less and less, it seems, will a man's title to a livelihood depend on the performance of dull and drudging labour. That is the function of the machine. Unforeseen difficulties may have to be faced as we admit this principle into the social structure as the determinant of reward, but admittedly the prospect of a more full and satisfying life should be opening to all the members of community, and not to a favoured few alone.

3. *The Fact of Class*

Our economic divergences in community lead us to another fruitful seed of social discontent : the fact of class divisions. A class is a group within the community held together by a complex of interests, of which the predominant one gives the class its name. By this complex of interests, the group is distinguished from other groups of the community, possessing different, and, maybe, antagonistic interests. " Thus we speak of governing classes, in terms of a predominant political interest ; of leisured classes, working classes, professional classes, agricultural classes, and so on, in terms of their respective economic interests. Or, again, we distinguish classes as upper, middle, and lower, in terms of social status."[1] Is the existence of classes in society a good or an evil ? In some sense it is inevitable, so far as groups within the community perform a common function for the whole. It is natural, and indeed justifiable and good, that men serving the same function in the community should associate in the furtherance of that function, as in the case of professional associations like the Medical Association and the Law Society : and inevitable that in the association a common mentality and outlook and standard of life

[1] Maciver, *Community*, p. 107.

should develop. If the trade unions had not been forced to grow up so much as defensive associations, they might have gravitated in the same direction, just as employers' federations might have become economic associations whose main object was the service of community. But when such associations pursue sectional interests at the expense of the wider good of the whole community, they become a source of evil and division. What is obviously needed is that in every class a strong sense of solidarity with the whole community should exist. Without this, an individual born into one class may take on the characteristics of that class without ever realising community with people of other classes. " Grave social evils result from the separation of modern society into classes which live largely apart from each other." These evils arise from the extreme inequality in the distribution of wealth, with its attendant sense of class conflict, accentuated by differences of upbringing, education, and social habit. The supreme evil is the subordination of community to class. " No class of the community is rich enough in imagination and sympathy to live this partitional life without forming wrong impressions of its own usefulness and erecting wrong standards for its own enjoyment, based upon wrong ideas of the meaning of life to other people, and of their character and work. Hence arise all manner of occasions for suspicions and strife between the classes, the more so since one class is so largely subject to another's will."[1]

II. SOME ALTERNATIVE SOLUTIONS

Our survey of modern society reveals no very satisfying opportunity for the individual to find his true place and function. By the accident of birth, he may find himself accorded a position of low status, of an indifferent and uncertain standard of livelihood, and separated from other sections of the community by more or less artificial barriers arising from differences of education and upbringing. What lines of solution are open to us ? Three alternative theories

[1] Malcolm Spencer, *Social Function of the Church*, p. 23.

of the relation of individuals to society are here examined, viz. : (1) economic equality, as exhibited in Communism and the dictatorship of the proletariat ; (2) necessity of classes : " many must be slaves that some may enjoy true culture " ; (3) difference of task with equality of status : " is it a dream ? "

1. *Equality : Communism and the Dictatorship of the Proletariat*

The history of modern democracy is strangely coloured by the effort to give expression to the idea of human equality. The word was one of the triple watchwords of the French Revolution. The American Constitution roundly declared that " all men are created equal." The idea has not been easy to define. " Equality of opportunity " is ambiguous, since it ignores differences of native endowment in physical fitness and mental capacity. Abraham Lincoln perhaps as nearly as possible expressed the only meaning the phrase can bear : " All men are born with an equal right to life, to happiness, and the fruit of their labour." Actually, the idea has served as a necessary corrective of the idea of freedom, and both have needed correction by the ideal of fraternity. Political liberty was worked out in terms of political equality, as in equal representation, or " one man, one vote." The problem in our time is that of economic freedom. Is economic equality the true solution ? This is the solution with which Communism confronts us. The evils that follow from according unbridled liberty to the individual to pursue his economic interest are too unmitigated to pass without restraint. They issue in exploitation of the weak, in aggrandisement of the rich and depression of the poor : in exaltation of mean motives and in consequent spiritual impoverishment. Social control of economic liberty is, therefore, inevitable both in the interests of equality and fraternity. Communism offers us a vast experiment in enforced economic equality. It endeavours to expunge the economic motive of gain, and enforces the motive of service for the community. We may recognise the spiritual exaltation which may follow from voluntary acceptance of poverty and community of goods, as in monasticism, to which a parallel is not wanting in the religious fervour of the Communist movement. But Communism also must be tested by the quality of individual life which it makes possible. The peril of every Communistic society is a dull repression of individual variety and richness of expression. This partly accounts for the dullness of monasticism : and over Communism likewise rests the shadow of the servile state, where individual worth is subordinated to a whole, which takes little reck of him, but has no end apart from him. The picture of the labour gang moving under guard to work on a collectivist farm fills us with no more enthusiasm than the picture of driven labour in the nineteenth century. Marxian Communism, with its doctrine of economic determinism, and its insistence on the class war and the dictatorship of the proletariat, exalts economic need at the expense of other factors equally necessary to human well-being. Nevertheless, underlying it is a conviction to which the modern world will do well to pay heed : that the economic possibility of fullness of life should be shared by all and not be accorded only to the few.

2. *The Necessity of Class*

But if enforced economic equality runs the peril of producing a dull and servile uniformity, are we compelled to perpetuate the distinctions of class resting on different economic status ? For if even Communism does not escape the peril of servility, neither does an aristocratic or plutocratic social order. Aristotle long ago called attention to the fact that advancement in culture only became possible with the emergence of a leisured priestly class, able to canvass and explore fertile new ideas. Mr. H. G. Wells[1] has recently ascribed a high significance to the social significance of the " priestly " class as the custodians of cultural ideas, while giving a wide extension to the meaning of the word. But is culture also to be the privilege of the few, and

[1] *Work, Wealth, and Happiness of Mankind*, pp. 309–314.

not the cherished possession of the many ? " Must many be slaves that some may enjoy true culture ? " So far in the development of human society we have never been able to find the solution of that harsh antinomy. It is staggering to reflect how the glory that was Greece, and the very pride of Rome, were sustained on a slave economy, no less truly than that Solomon's Temple, the pyramids of Egypt, and the wonders of Babylon were erected at the cost of the exceeding bitterness of forced and servile labour. A similar phenomenon greets us when we examine the social and industrial history of the nineteenth century. Victorian culture reached its highest expression amongst the middle and professional classes. There the attainment of wealth made an interest in learning, literature, art, and music possible. But over against that degree of culture, such as it was, we have the sorry picture of industry sustained by overdriven child and woman labour, and by the wearisome round of long hours of toil six days a week borne by the industrial section of the community. Yet there was many an indication that, given leisure and opportunity, nay, often in spite of the lack of these, the sons and daughters of labour were as capable of attaining and enjoying culture as those of the middle class. The educational system of Scotland showed that a love and regard for learning might be cherished by the children of the soil. In England and Wales, democratic movements in education, like the Sunday school, the day school and mechanics' institutes, were all indicative of the same awakening desire for culture. It was confined to no section of the community. Religious workers in Durham testify to the wide and instructed interest in books often taken by the Durham miner. In the textile workers of Lancashire and Yorkshire, as amongst the pottery workers of Staffordshire, a love of art and music was engendered ; and, often under the inspiration of religion, intellectual enthusiasms were awakened among East Anglian farm labourers and Cornish fishermen. Only the imperfect results of an educational system which still precipitates children on the labour market at too early an age, and the baneful effects of a commercialised Press and an instrument of culture like the cinema that too easily becomes the tool of a depraved art, blind us to the capacity of every class in the community to enjoy the highest culture.

3. A *Dream : Difference of Task with Equality of Status*

We thus reach a position of fruitful possibility. On the one hand, basic economic need must be met and satisfied. That is essential if the members of the community are to be liberated for the loftier flights of the human spirit and for a cultural life of the highest quality. But economic organisation, with the help of the machine, should now make possible the satisfaction of economic need with a minimum of human labour. Not that we escape from the necessity of drudging or even menial toil in the service of the community, though it is not necessary to suppose that it must be the same kind of drudgery in every case. The culture of the soil and the minding of machines are both exacting and fatiguing : so is the ward work of a hospital, and the medical examination of patients, and the visitation of a parish. No cultural enjoyment is possible except at the cost of drudgery to someone : the disciplined drudgery of rehearsal precedes a finished first-night theatrical production, to say nothing of the toil of producing a film-picture. Even callings directed to mental and spiritual culture exact their meed of drudgery. William James spoke expressively of the labour of spirit it cost him to give a lecture to his classes in deductive logic ! The work of scientific discovery involves long, laborious, and painstaking observation and experiment, often without immediate result. Such considerations must be borne in mind as we look forward to the thoroughgoing organisation of the work of a great community. The range of " productive " service may extend from the rearing of cattle and the tanning of their hides for shoe-leather, to the applied skill and science of a surgeon in an orthopædic hospital : from the production and distribution of food-supplies to serve physical need, to the training and development of character which is a teacher's productive task, and the nurture of faith and righteousness, which is the productive work of the Christian ministry. This surely is the true significance of " division of labour."

But should not " equality of status " go with " division of labour " ? Why not ? To say that " all service ranks the same with God " is not merely a religious sentiment, but affirms a true measure of social worth. Society is often arbitrary and capricious in its estimate of worth : but a safe moral principle, at any rate, is that any useful work well done according to the capacity of the doer is equally worthy, the dustman's with that of the sanitary inspector and the medical officer of health, only allowing for the difference of training, equipment, and sustenance necessary for the fulfilment of each function. But can economic reward be made proportionate to moral worth ? This might not be desirable even on moral considerations : though economic reward is now distributed on very unsatisfactory ground. It sometimes brings gain utterly incommensurate with the economic effort put forth, and sometimes denies to worthy effort the fruit of its labour. Nor is it sufficient to reply that this is the working out of natural and economic laws : it is the subordination of these to human ends and purposes that is the task as well as the problem of the hour. One way of subordination is for the community to ensure all possible fullness of well-being consonant with individual capacity to every one of its members culturally and economically. " The ultimate test of any democracy," wrote Bishop Gore, " is to be found in the demand that in its organisation of human society it shall so truly grant equality of opportunity to all who are born into its citizenship, as to encourage and enable them freely to develop the fullest richness of personality of which they are capable. "[1]

[1] *Christ and Society*, pp. 135–6.

Proposals for Approximating to this End :

1. *Reform of Education*

How can we approximate to this end ? Three proposals are here examined. First, reform of education. True culture can only be open to every class in the community if the same cultural discipline is open to all, and to supply this is the task of a national system of education. A common culture seems indispensable to community life. At present, some of the acutest divisions between different classes of the community are due to different standards of education. The degree of community possible between a child in a Hoxton Council School and a boy at Eton is not easy to compute. True, the range of cultural discipline may be wide and varied, allowing for great diversity of type as well as the vocational purposes to be served. It was the merit of the Hadow Report that it provided for this, as well as an extension of the school age. The last is imperative for more than one reason. There seems no legitimate reason why school education should be prolonged in some cases till sixteen or eighteen years of age, followed possibly by a university training, and it be considered sufficient in the vast majority of other cases to end at fourteen. Some curious illusion seems to regard this as fixed, or having psychological validity. Actual observation often shows a " lamentable deterioration " between the ages of fourteen and eighteen when school life terminates at the earlier age and the immature adolescent is rudely precipitated on to the industrial market, so that only a small proportion of what he learned at school is retained or becomes ultimately fruitful. The wastefulness of modern education is seen most palpably here. Nor is there longer any industrial necessity that work should begin at fourteen. The likelihood of lessened demand for labour which the machine makes possible removes this ; and the prospect of a longer school life for the eventual worker looms in view. What this might mean in lifting the tone and quality of industrial life cannot easily be reckoned. Factory and workshop life is often coarsening and hardening ; but more finely equipped mentality in those entering upon it might conceivably make it no less " a career for gentlemen " than entering a bank, without being less robust or verile. In any case, the faculty of appreciation for other things than work would be vastly enhanced, and the way to a richer cultural life made possible.

2. *More Equal Distribution of Wealth*

This inevitably forces us back on the problem of the unequal distribution of wealth. It is not necessary, even if it were possible, to consider the idea of economic equality, for it is doubtful whether it would ever remain a stable condition of society for long. But a communal spirit that puts wealth at the service of need proffers a truly Christian solution. The experiment of the " social services " indicates the possibilities that open to us. Youth can be given a rich and worthy physical, mental, and spiritual equipment for life. Age can receive its due meed of happy and contented leisure. The labour, physical and mental, by which the needs of community are met can be asked from, and will be given by, manhood and womanhood in its strength. Let it not be said that this means the many living at the expense of the few, democracy reversing the aristocratic principle. Even now, a population of forty millions is being sustained by the labour of much less than half that number ; dependants, mostly wives and children, outnumber the actual wealth-producing members of the community. Nor is the spirit of self-respect and sturdy independence thereby undermined. Scholarship children are chiefly drawn from the homes of the most self-respecting of the families of the workers. Old age pensioners and widows achieve a new dignity as the fret and fear of haggard and ignominious poverty are removed. Nor does this redistribution of the national income necessarily involve any retarding of the increase of national wealth. It chiefly means a redistribution of the national spending power, and thereby a heightening of the standard of well-being for large numbers whose life would otherwise be depressed.

3. *The Rising Standard of Life : Increasing Leisure and its Use*

Thus a new social order looms before us, carrying with it the possibility of a still rising standard of life, of increasing leisure for cultural enjoyment, and fresh advances of the human spirit. To these even the struggles of the nineteenth century were steadily bringing us nearer. Continually did the machine replace the human labourer, though we were slow to harness the fruitage for the general good. By dint of conflict, hours of labour were steadily reduced. Housing, though still woefully deficient, showed signs of improvement, and the amenities of life softened, manners grew gentler, and the level of culture heightened. Even so, it is dubious whether the full advance possible was really made ; and once the possibilities of the present are really grasped, and the causes of world depression mastered, as they can and ought to be, a much larger, more rapid and comprehensive advance, affecting the whole community, should be registered. The problem of the future, it is widely recognised, may be the use of leisure rather than the organisation of the communal industry. Gloomy forebodings are sometimes expressed of a dull and uninspiring round of athletics and social festivities, and a bored and unemployed populace desperately waiting for some new interest to turn up. Need it be so ? Doubtless the peril is there, but only if we fail to equip ourselves worthily for the new age. Nor is the outcome of the battle so sure that we may yet fear the issues of the ensuing peace ; the task of evolving a worthy social order will test the spirit of mankind for many a generation to come.

III. IS THIS CHRISTIAN ?

How far is this line of argument in keeping with Christian conviction ? Is the social order to which our thought has moved a Christian order ? We can only test it by principles emerging clearly from the New Testament. In the New Testament there are twin conceptions of the relation of the individual to community. One is that of the sanctity and worth of the individual, as one " for whom Christ died." The other is that of the individual finding his true life in fellowship with, and exercising different functions in, the Christian community. " We are members one of another." The idea of a Christian democracy has always found its springs in a radical and thoroughgoing application of these two conceptions, taken side by side. A sharper edge has been given to them by the German writer Troeltsch,[1] in his description of the Christian Church as primarily an association for worship based upon the religious equality of its members before God. The impact of Christianity upon human society has arisen from the persistent, always implicit, often explicit, impulse to transfer this religious equality into the region of social relationship. Even if its action has been slow and conservative, its eventual result has always been to undermine the unjust institution, and to give greater place to freedom, brotherhood, and equality.

So there has arisen the persistent Christian responsibility of criticism of the existing social order, as the Church found it, in the light of these two conceptions—individual worth, and fellowship in a society of equals exercising different functions. In no age has the criticism been entirely wanting, though the force and direction of it have varied, and sometimes the spokesmen of the Church have too complacently identified the Church's teaching with continuance of the existing order. But through all the vicissitudes of Christian history Christian men have cherished the vision of " a new heaven and a new earth," and in the light of it have tested the world about them.

The responsibility is ours also. Our survey of modern society reveals profoundly disquieting features. Neither by unregenerated capitalism, nor by enforced Communism, can we guarantee individual worth or a rich, free communal life. Nor is the responsibility one of criticism alone. It is also that of action, both by individuals and groups, in the direction of establishing a Christian order. There is a new outlook to be exhibited, and there are concrete

[1] *Social Teaching of the Christian Churches.*

proposals to be examined and tested. We recall the late Bishop Gore's almost passionate plea for " a special association, intellectual and practical, for Christian social propaganda," " groups of men, inspired probably by prophetic leaders, who have attained to a true vision both of the source of our evils and of the nature of the true remedies ; and who have the courage of faith to bind them together to act and to suffer in the cause of human emancipation until their vision and their faith come to prevail more or less complete in society at large." And all this because " Christianity is a life before it is a doctrine, and that life a fellowship "—" not just an individual discipline," but " a brotherhood."[1]

[1] Gore, *Christ and Society*, p. 164.

3. THE SOCIAL AND ECONOMIC ORDER:

D. *LABOUR AND LEISURE*

By DR. A. MAUDE ROYDEN, C.H.

IT HAS come to be generally believed that unemployment is due to the enormous development of labour-saving machinery and its widespread use in industry. This, it is said, has resulted in over-production, and, because we have produced and are still producing more wealth than we need, we can no longer employ those whose work was once necessary and profitable.

This view surely has only to be stated in order to be seen in its naïve absurdity. There is no country in the world in which everyone has all he wants even of the ordinary decencies—not luxuries—of life. There are vast numbers of human beings who live in a state of extreme poverty and almost of destitution. While millions perish from undernourishment or actual starvation in China, and millions more live below the poverty line in India and elsewhere, it is fatuous to talk as though the world had as a whole produced more wealth than it could use. The discussion of the use of leisure must moreover appear irrelevant to the masses of people who are at this hour overworked to the point of exhaustion. Heated discussion (for example) of the beauty or ugliness of pylons carrying electric current all over the country is not appreciated by women in whose cottages there is at present not a single labour-saving device. In this country especially, labour-saving in the home has made but very little progress, and the over-burdened housewife is uninterested in the question of the use of leisure, since she has none. In the labour market the conditions are much the same. There are hundreds of thousands of workers who work not too little but too much. Their problem of leisure is not how to use it but how to get it.

I. THE PROBLEM

It is, however, probable that we shall in course of time learn not only to produce but to distribute our wealth. From that point it will be a short and easy step to a state of things in which we shall all have enough material wealth to begin cutting down hours of labour for the great mass of workers. The question of the right use of leisure will then indeed be with us, and it is right to look and to plan ahead now. Already we are told that : " World production of foodstuffs and raw materials rose by about seventeen per cent between 1913 and 1925, whereas world population rose only by six per cent. Between 1925 and 1929 there was a further rise of eleven per cent in production and of only four per cent in world population. In North America production rose by over twenty-six per cent between 1913 and 1925 and population by nineteen per cent. Up to this point Europe was hardly more than keeping pace in production with the rise of population. For Europe's population is estimated to have risen by one per cent, and production by only two or three per cent over this period. But at this time Europe was still suffering seriously from the immediate after-effects of the war ; and between 1925 and 1929 there was a significant change in the situation. The population of Europe (excluding Russia) rose by about three per cent in these years, whereas production rose actually by nineteen per cent. In America the rise between 1925 and 1929 was much smaller, and population actually rose almost as much as production—by about six per cent in both cases. These figures relate only to the production of foodstuffs and raw materials, as there is no ready way of measuring over the world as a whole the rise in the output of manufactured goods. But it can be confidently stated that the rise in the output of finished goods was even larger than the rise in the output of foodstuffs and raw materials."[1] . . . " This conclusion is borne out by the movement of the indices of productive activity published in these

[1] G. D. H. Cole, *The Intelligent Man's Guide Through World Chaos*, p. 27.

days by most of the leading nations. Between 1925 and 1929, according to these indices, industrial production rose to an extraordinary extent. In Poland the rise was thirty-eight per cent, in Canada fifty-four per cent. France increased her industrial production by thirty per cent, Sweden by twenty-seven per cent, and Germany by twenty-two per cent. The United States with fourteen per cent increase and Great Britain with thirteen per cent lagged behind these spectacular advances, but even their progress would have been regarded as remarkable in itself. The U.S.S.R. over the same period, starting of course from a very low level, more than doubled its output of industrial goods."[1]

In some places and at some times, mass production on this scale has already been accompanied by a shortening of the hours of labour. Not only is the Communist experiment in Russia based on this very principle, i.e. that as soon as the point of " over-production " is in sight the workers in the industry reaching that point will have their hours shortened, but in America Henry Ford has set an example which has had its effect throughout the United States and perhaps beyond, though unfortunately the accompanying " drive " of the worker during the hours of work has also been carried to a pitch which makes it probable that he has, on the balance, lost rather than gained. In any case, the essence of the problem is to be found, not in conditions which have affected a comparatively small number of workers in special circumstances, but in the fact that everywhere in the world the enormous increase in material wealth now made possible by applied science is bound in the end to lighten and decrease labour ; consequently to increase leisure.

We are, by a melancholy coincidence, confronted in the first instance not with wanted but unwanted leisure. We have to consider the plight not of men and women released from excessive toil so much as of men and women completely unemployed. Long before science and industry have

[1] *Op. cit.*, p. 29.

conspired to lift us all above the poverty line, our senseless methods of distribution have created leisure for many who do not desire it and who are made painfully to feel that it is theirs, not because their labour has been of a value unparalleled before, but because they and their labour are not wanted. In a word, we are called upon to grapple with the problem of leisure in the most deplorable circumstances imaginable, and we are likely to be discouraged by difficulties which would not have arisen if it were really the progress of applied science which had given leisure to all. Nevertheless the problem is here and cannot be ignored. It is at least possible to plan for the future and to make experiments now.

II. TWO KINDS OF WORK, AND OF WORKER

Let us first of all clear our minds of a certain confusion. Some people think of shorter hours of labour and longer hours of leisure as the ideal at which the whole of society should aim and against which there can be no possible objection to raise. Others angrily complain of the laziness of such a state of mind, decry the demand for shortened hours of work, and exalt the gospel of labour. Such people are accustomed to declare (and quite truly) that they do not want an eight-hours day and only wish to be allowed to work as long as life and strength permit.

It ought to be realised at once that there are, in fact, two kinds of work and two kinds of worker ; and that these differences will remain and ought to remain. We shall get no further if we persist in arguing as though our own sort of work and worker constitutes the whole world of men. Broadly speaking, the difference is between the artist and the mechanic, and between creative and repetitive work.

Obviously this is a very unsatisfactory definition. There are many kinds of work which share the nature of both creation and repetition, and there are probably no workers who are not sometimes artists and sometimes mechanics. The " artist " is not only a painter, poet, or actor : he may put into the organising of a great industry or the driving of a powerful machine the same creative delight that a poet would in writing a great epic. The quality that is present in both is the quality of creativeness and the delight that goes with it. This is the real distinction between what for convenience—I fear a very clumsy convenience—I shall call the " artist " and the " mechanic." Many a mechanically minded man or woman takes an enchanted joy in the inventing, tending, or driving of an engine : but it remains a fact that quite outside such joy—a joy essentially creative —there is being developed more and more the kind of mechanical industry which is merely repetitive, uninteresting, and, as far as may be with human beings, automatic.

We have all heard of the miserable wretch who spends his life giving half a twist to a screw and knows nothing of the finished product of his deadening and intolerable toil. We have not heard, or heard with incredulity, of the man who *likes* such work and is perfectly content with it, preferring it indeed to any other. We have supposed that if such a monster really exists he must be sub-human—mentally deficient to the verge of idiocy—and we have looked with horror at a future which, it cannot be denied, seems certain to offer more and more such work to more and more such " nit-wits." What could be more deplorable, ask the artist, the inventor, the organiser, than a generation of men and women who take no interest in their work and whose eye is always on the clock ? Whose demand is for more and more time to waste the moment the clock has struck ?

This is a very real misunderstanding. It is true that to some their work is so absorbing that it is their life. These do not watch the clock, or, if they do, it is because the hands hurry on all too fast for their desire. For such workers the day is too short for all they want to do, and perhaps it may be said that they are the fortunate ones, life's favourites to whom is given the greatest of all boons—a work which is their life. Yet even they have their temptations ! Such a worker is apt to be incapable of using leisure and to find himself, when work is over, at a very loose end indeed. Who has not met men and women who, when their powers

Oc

fail and the tide of life begins to slacken in their veins, feel that they might just as well lie down and die, so little are they able by a diffusion or variety of interests to use their leisure ? The least imaginative of the workers of the other sort, whom the " artist " so readily despises, is as well able or better able than he to be at leisure when work is done. Those, moreover, who have met some of these " nit-wits " who are clamouring for shorter hours know them to be by no means invariably sub-human but a very distinct and necessary type of worker. They may be people of various tastes and interests such as do not lend themselves to exploitation for wages or gain. To them (and they are often highly intelligent and very attractive persons) the ideal life would be a short period during which they should discharge their debt to the community by doing some of its least interesting but very necessary labour, while the rest of the day remains free for their vagrant fancy to indulge in any kind of hobby or interest that they choose. Is this really such an abominable way of living as to merit our criticism or contempt ? I cannot admit it.

III. LEISURE FOR BOTH KINDS OF WORKER

Let us then plan the leisure of a society which consists of the artist and of the mechanic ; of the man whose work is his life and the man whose life must be found outside his work. Let us reflect that the artist's work can never be done by machinery, *and* that there are many kinds of work which are utterly odious or completely dull and that these *ought* to be done by machinery. I cannot now define the limits of these two kinds of work, even if I had the capacity to do so— which I have not : let me only pause to say that if those who have the requisite power of discernment would try to guide us in these matters it would be more profitable and wiser than mere indignation at the spectacle of a mechanised world. To take extreme cases, about which surely very few people have any doubt, we ought to recognise, on the one hand, that truly creative work, and especially the creation of beauty or life, cannot be done by machinery, and, on the other, that some very necessary work can never be enjoyed by human beings. To try to produce beauty by any system of mass production, or to turn our beauty-loving and fastidious eyes from the more disgusting kinds of toil and ignore the fact that they must be done by someone, are equally mistaken policies, although those who take the latter part and speak with loathing of the mechanisation of society are generally apt to think themselves superior merely because they are horrified. To my mind, the work of transport, the work of wringing from the depths of the earth the raw materials of our wealth, and the task of cleanliness, whether it is the scavenging of our streets, the removal of our refuse, or the washing up of our dishes and plates, ought to be done as far as possible by mechanical means. " To take the burden of toil from the shoulders of men and women and lay it on steel " is in these matters right. In how many more I do not know, but I believe that when we have cleared our minds on this matter we shall be better able to find some guiding principle. Meanwhile the artist's interest in leisure, although it be indirect, is no less than that of the mechanic. The mechanic works for him and does those necessary jobs which he would loathe doing and yet, if he will be honest with himself, he knows must be done ; but *the artist also works for the mechanics*, and without that great mass of people whose lives will increasingly lie outside and not inside their hours of toil, he would be working in a void.

We must accept the fact that the increased use of machinery does mean an increase in uninteresting work. It is true that machinery is intensely interesting to the man with the mechanic's genius and that the invention and improvement of machines is a fascinating business to him. But because this is true he does not fall into the purely mechanical class but is an artist, at least in his degree. His very inventions, however, will demand for their success an enormous number of people who are content—like our typical example—to give half a turn to a screw for several hours in the day. What then ? We cannot be content with a world in which the great mass of the workers are contented to do such uninteresting and unskilled work merely because they are not fit for anything better. Quite the contrary. We must aim at an education which will create, in this type of worker, the demand for much leisure and the ability to make excellent use of it.

I was once present at a discussion during which a speaker described the pitiful position of a young man engaged in some unskilled repetitive type of work. At the conclusion of the speech a man arose in the audience and declared himself to be one of such workers and to be in no need of our pity. " I learnt my job in a very few hours," he said, " and from that time have been able to do it automatically. My mind is now released from the necessity of attention and is able to range at large. I find a number of other workers near to me, engaged in the same task and with minds equally free. We discuss all manner of things, including politics, our various forms of entertainment, and sport. Finding ourselves interested, we attend meetings of various kinds, get books and study them, are in several cases keen politicians or interested students of the marvels of modern science. We envy no one. We are perfectly aware that the work that we do is necessary, and we are also aware that we ought to do some work. We have, however, a variety of interests, and we should not mind having our work hours shortened and our leisure hours increased ! "

IV. THE USE OF LEISURE

This young man and his friends were by no means so unusual as the " artist " may suppose. During the boom period which came soon after the end of the war, the International Labour Office issued a questionnaire on the subject of the use of leisure by those whose shortened hours had made the question a live one ; and in the following year (1924) reported on the replies. They were in some respects disappointing, since they showed a rather languid interest in the matter on the part of some Governments, and but few original or illuminating proposals on the part of others.

Nevertheless the report is worth studying, both because some valuable suggestions were made and because of the information given about the use of leisure already enjoyed by the workers in various countries. Contrary to the expectation of the pessimist, " it has been ascertained that excessive drinking has become less frequent in those centres in which the working day has been shortened. Excessive drinking is frequently the result of overwork, since the workman, tired by the continuous effort required by long working hours, is tempted to seek relaxation by going from the workshop to the public-house. . . . It is clearly shown by the general tenor of the evidence given and the declarations made by representatives of employers' and workers' organisations, by secretaries of provincial councils, by industrial employers, etc., that not only has the new system failed to produce any increase in intemperance but that, on the contrary, it has been one of a number of other important causes of the marked decrease in drunkenness which is attested by fiscal and judicial statistics. . . . The worker welcomes the opportunity of improving his home and taking exercise in the open air. Workers' gardens and sports clubs have increased in number, and sport has a beneficial effect upon health and character."[1]

Elsewhere we read that " In all countries the introduction of the eight-hours day has resulted in increased attention to sport on the part of workers. The movement for physical development is rapidly gaining ground amongst them. In many cases the workers' organisations themselves take the initiative of founding sports clubs. This is particularly true in Great Britain and the United States. In Germany also, according to information supplied by the Commission for Physical Training (*Reichsausschüss für Leibesübungen*), the number of members of the chief sports clubs increased from 1,586,000 in 1914 to 2,955,000 in 1922. The number of members of workers' associations exclusively devoted to sport and athletics increased from 186,000 in 1914 to

[1] Questionnaire 1, International Labour Conference 1924 : *Development of Facilities for the Utilisation of Workers' Leisure*, p. 16.

382,000 in 1920."[1] But this is not all. There are innumerable "institutions intended to interest the workers in the various aspects of the political and social life of the nation and to develop in them a sense of their responsibilities as citizens. As has been already stated, this was a point to which attention was drawn in the manifesto issued in February 1923 by the General Council of the Trades Union Congress. All the various kinds of institutions of this class cannot be enumerated here, but mention may be made of workers' clubs, study circles for political, economic, and social questions, public lectures, etc."

With regard to suggestions for the use of leisure, the various Governments seem rather unnecessarily alarmed lest they should appear to be dictating rather than suggesting. One may however find here and there light on the situation. In Holland, for example, we learn—"diamond workers who have had the benefit of the eight-hour day for a number of years highly appreciate the long afternoon's rest which enables them to take their dinner at home. This is certainly an excellent utilisation of leisure, of very great value from the point of view of family life." And again—"experience in Finland has proved that free institutions founded in various towns and industrial centres for the education of the workers attract year by year an ever increasing number of workers eager for instruction. . . . Among pastimes which attract the workers and contribute to the improvement of their health mention may be made of physical culture, including gymnastics, and various sports. The form of amusement offered to young workers has a special educational value."[2] And in the summary at the end of the report we read—"far from increasing intemperance, legislation on the eight-hour day has definitely reduced drunkenness by preventing the workers from becoming overtired, encouraging them to live in the suburbs, and giving young persons the opportunity of devoting themselves to sports, which greatly contributes to physical and moral hygiene."[3]

[1] International Labour Conference, as above ; p. 21.
[2] *Ibid.*, p. 45.   [3] *Ibid.*, p. 92.

V. FURTHER PROPOSALS

A great deal of work has been done in this country ; and it has met with a wide response. Dr. Jacks even suggests a National College of Leisure Craft, and now writes—" just such a college has been started in Leeds through the help of the Carnegie Foundation." In a recent number of the *Listener*, Mr. S. P. B. Mais describes a number of experiments in the use of leisure by the unemployed, including the learning and practice of various handicrafts, listening to lectures, reading books, gymnastics, concerts (given by the unemployed themselves), debates, amateur theatricals, and visits of inspection to places and sights of interest. Meanwhile, without waiting to be unemployed, the *Listener* reports, " all over the country there are to-day groups of quiet, socially inclined folk who like to spend their leisure time at classes or lectures, listening to wireless talks, belonging to film societies, studying music or the arts, or talking over current affairs among themselves. They do this, not under the ægis of any one society, but through dozens of varied bodies, religious, recreational, political, and literary. . . . A thousand discussion groups have been formed in various parts of the country to listen to broadcast educational talks." This in spite of a howl of rage from less intelligent listeners who did their best at one time to convince the B.B.C. that there was no public at all for such a programme ! They were wrong, and so are the pessimists who believe that shorter hours of work can only lead to increased drunkenness, chambering, and wantonness. " We are most of us disappointed bunglers in the art of life through sheer lack of knowledge and practice. The higher pleasures are acquired and cultivated tastes. The enjoyment of music, painting, and literature has come to most of us through a lucky accident. The new generation, therefore, must be taught how best to enjoy its increasing hours of freedom."

When in the United States (before the economic slump), I found the belief that the advance of science must greatly diminish the amount of manual work required, and therefore increase leisure, was almost universally held, and the prospect accepted as good. When I inquired if such leisure would be well used there was equal optimism. I was assured that the high standard of living already common among the American working classes had had fine results. Young people were kept at school and at the university for long years before they entered the labour market, and, when work began, short hours and long holidays were used for motoring into the country—often in family parties—camping in the open air, making or improving wireless sets, and so on. Certainly there was also an enormous public for the cinema, good and bad, and the standard of taste in these matters was not high. To this point I shall return later and here will only say that nation differs from nation in its gifts, and the typical American is on the whole more interested in science than in art. It will be admitted moreover that it will take a very bad cinema indeed to have a worse effect on the American citizen than the speakeasy or the pre-war saloon ! I was convinced from my own observation that the increasing sobriety of the American citizen was far more due to the leisure which enabled him to get out into the open air and enjoy himself than to any virtue of prohibition. It seems that America herself begins to agree with me.

Let us then cease to complain of the growing mechanism of the world. It cannot be avoided. It can be made the blessing that its enthusiasts proclaim. It can " take the burden of toil from the shoulders of men and women and lay it on steel." It can release the consciences of those who depend upon the toiling masses for every necessary of life from another kind of burden, which they ought to feel a great deal more intolerable than some of them do. All the sentimental talk in the world about the "dignity of labour" will not make it agreeable to be a night-soil man, a stoker in a great ship depending on coal for its steam, or—let us be rid of sentimentality altogether—a harried housewife whose work is never done.

Let us think then, in terms of human beings, of those who are to have leisure. Who are they ? Not the artistes,

for they neither desire it nor can be compelled to take it :
but the others, who are the greater number.

Their leisure should ideally be spent in physical as well
as intellectual or spiritual occupation. For this they are at
present often too tired. Shorter hours will remedy that. They
will now be still fit and fresh when the day's task of work is
complete. The tramping holidays of the young and energetic,
already enormously enjoyed by hundreds, can be much
more, and more commonly, enjoyed by men and women,
boys and girls, who are able to keep themselves in good
trim all the year round by physical exercises of all sorts,
boxing, fencing, dancing, and games, as well as " physical
jerks " and drill.

Allotments and gardens will keep thousands in the open
air in all sorts of weathers, and give scope to the creative
powers which are rarely entirely absent from any human
being even if, on the balance, he belongs rather to the
mechanic than to the artist class. Dancing will give balance
and rhythm, and become the means of self-expression to
others. Dr. Jacks's plea for the development of this side of
education is full of point and significance when he observes
that he is sorry for anyone " who is trying to produce a
disciplined mind in an undisciplined body."

VI. A NEW PUBLIC FOR THE ARTIST

There is no *asceticism* in the narrow sense in the teaching
of Christ, but there is much room for *athleticism*, that is to
say, a discipline imposed upon oneself for a desired and
inspiring end. The monotony of the factory and its often
cramped movements, or almost absence of movement, will
be compensated by the physical training and exertion
undertaken in the worker's leisure. He can be interested
in most things that make that leisure interesting and de-
lightful. The modern man is not content to listen in ; he
will put together, adapt, and improve his own wireless. He
cannot afford merely to drive his cheap little car, he must—
and generally he wants to—understand it, take it to pieces,
put it together, bring it up to date and carry out all its

running repairs. He will (we hope) go to the theatre and the cinema, but with the zest and interest of the untired body and mind. It is not possible yet to measure the effect on artistic production of a public such as this. It is probably true that there is an irreducible minimum of imbeciles who prefer imbecile entertainments to any other, but I believe that most of us like a show that makes no demand whatever on our intelligence simply because we are too tired when evening comes to respond to such a demand. I remember the time when I felt nothing but indignant scorn for older people who showed a tendency to shirk a performance of *King Lear* or *The Trojan Women* in favour of something that was pretty to look at, amusing to hear, and sufficiently remote from reality to demand no great intelligent or emotional response. Alas ! how readily I understand them now ! How easily I can understand why great plays have but a short run and a limited public ! But if the vast public which crowds the cinema and cheaper theatres came to them untired and full of vitality ? Imagine an audience for actors— a public for artists, writers, and painters—of men and women who have done enough mechanical labour to make them eager for something more interesting at the end of it, but not so much as to destroy energy and interest alike ! The sheer silliness and the intolerable sex obsession of much of our art and literature to-day would be no longer desired. We like silliness because we are too tired for sense : we like sex-appeal for this is the one nerve which will still respond when the others are deadened : but if those who cater for us in these respects could count on our intelligent response to something less one-idea'd or un-idea'd, how enormous would be the gain for them !

It has been said that the reason why Greek sculpture reached such unsurpassed heights of beauty long ago was that every Greek knew a good statue when he saw it. It is no less true that one reason why our theatre in the Elizabethan age reached such a height of greatness was that every Elizabethan knew a good play when he saw it. The intelligent use of leisure by those not primarily gifted with creative genius, but nevertheless possessing their little share of it, will lead to that higher appreciation of all arts and crafts which belong only to those who share, in however humble a way, in its creation. Amateur dramatic societies, amateur orchestras, and choral societies, sketching clubs, wireless listeners can all help in creating that kind of public which insists on receiving from the artist his best. And in return for that best, the people who are not artists in the first sense will do for the community its uninteresting, necessary, disagreeable toil, in hours as short as the communal sense and the genius of mechanical science will make possible. Once more we are all—artists and mechanics alike—driven back to the Christian ideal. Once more we must learn that we are all members one of another and that if one member suffer all the members suffer with it. The artist cannot afford to be indifferent to the hours of work or the employment of leisure of the mechanic : the mechanic must render that service to the community which is necessary and which he alone can give. Learning from one another, we shall be able to make out of this much dreaded machine-made civilisation, which is the civilisation of the future, an order of society which will release for us the greatest powers of the artist, and nobler understanding of their work by the mechanic, and at last a clearer understanding as to which part of life's work can and should be mechanised and which part must for ever be kept free from machinery.

3. THE SOCIAL AND ECONOMIC ORDER:

E. *THE REBIRTH OF THE VILLAGE*

By Sir W. BEACH THOMAS

THIS ENGLAND was founded on the village community ; and in spite of changes that have caused some few villages, as in Wiltshire, wholly to disappear—church, farm, cottages, and all—and have robbed almost every village in certain districts of a large percentage of its inhabitants, the village keeps its ancient place. Indeed, a bundle of new activities open out. It remains a society—the only society—where the classes and professions coalesce into a friendly and natural relationship, where kindness is not regarded as either patronage or charity (in its vulgar and narrow sense) nor service as a humiliation ; where wealth recognises its privileges and obligations ; where religion is central and centralising. True communal feeling exists in its most fruitful form where classes are most distinct. The community of the village is wholly uncommunistic. More than this : the light and learning that were the privilege of the town have become available in the remotest hamlet.

WHERE THE LAND DIES

The decay of the village is obvious and general, nevertheless ; and in spite of the likelihood that it will be even more influential than ever in history ; and the causes are not obscure. The land on which they are built has died. Their modern story is *La Terre qui meurt*. Much of the land on the high land above Marlborough was sold early in this century at £4 an acre freehold. Land not very much better is *rented* in Scandinavia for the same price. In Huntingdonshire, a property of 2,000 acres was valued two generations ago at £36,000. It could be bought to-day for £5,000— that is, for a sum much below the value of the houses on it. The value of the land is put at −o. The derelict camps you may see at Ballarat or any deserted mining area have relapsed to misery for exactly the same reason as a Huntingdonshire village which had a population of 800 in 1885 and has now 180 : the wealth of the soil is no more. The mine, though not worked out, is abandoned.

With the fading away of the traffic on the land, its one industry, life in the village was felt for the first time to be desperately dull. There was an exodus as well as degeneration and sterility. These negative causes are still at work to-day. Rectories and schools are being closed, as tilth goes down to grass, and the members of a village no longer served by one clergyman or possessed of its own school, loses something of its pride of individuality. The depression of the country house has helped to destroy that sense of ownership with each member of the community felt in what was best in the village, to whomever it belonged. " *Our* children " was the standard phrase of an old man who tended the stock on the glebe or in the park. He meant, of course, his employer's children. The poor owned the possessions of the rich in a real sense ; and the rich did not so much give as give back.

WHAT THE VILLAGE CAN GIVE

This sort of feeling, which those who do not like it call feudal (as if, incidentally, the perpetual feu was not the best form of landlordism ever designed by the wit of man), has been whittled away, and something must be put in its place. If we desire, as all desire, to re-establish village life, we wish also to re-establish the community feeling where difference of status does not foster either jealousy or condescension. We all know (as M. Herriot hinted, foretelling the collapse of Britain because it has neglected this truth) that in a healthy State the urban and the rural minds must balance one another, as well as rural and industrial economics. Those born and bred in the country still possess —in spite of the Sidney Webb view of the future State— certain qualities essential to the health and well-being of humanity. The Happy Countryman is real, is founded on first principles ; and it is out of neglect of first principles that the unprincipled are bred. Simplicity, the source of most genius as well as of general stability, is lost in the hurly-burly of the secondary phenomena which are the commonplace appearances of the town. We must keep our villages and revivify them, if we are to keep our spiritual as well as our economic solidity and vitality. In the west of England, which is as sharply contrasted with the east as if they were different countries, the almost contiguous home-steads are in some measure a substitute for the village, for the hamlet ; but we may group them and their place of worship with the village. What is true of one community is in the large true of the other. Let this, then, be granted ; let this, indeed, be integral to our political creed, to our moral and social creed : that vigorous and healthy villages are as vital to the national organism as healthy and vigorous cells to the individual body.

NOT A GARDEN CITY

It must be understood that the problem is not one of preservation. We do not wish to preserve the village as we preserve an old building—that it may proclaim the beauty of an extinct art. The village is not just a relic of the Saxon community enclosed within a hedge for the care of both defence and individuality, though it draws strength from the forces of its long descent. It must fit itself to the rhythm of the *step* of accelerating progress. We may see the birth of a new sort of rural community, a collection of people and houses that is neither town nor village. Those already in existence are known as Satellite Towns or Garden Cities ; and the real thesis of their founders—though the point is sometimes forgotten—is devolution. They desire to see the factory removed from crowded areas into spaces so empty that the workers may live in a circle round the factory and not lose the rural atmosphere. The ideal is good, though it is proving difficult of fulfilment. The Garden Cities remain in some measure the " dormitories " that no one wishes them to be. In any event, they will not be a substitute for the village, and their problems are different, are almost alien, though the village may learn a good deal about their theory of devolution, of carrying out in rural surroundings some of the arts and crafts that have been migrating to the towns. However much we may admire the Garden City and idea, we must not confuse the essential problem of reviving the village by any imaginary feeling that it may develop into a city of a new type. I suppose that the most salient fact in the world at present is the rapid and thorough progress in the mechanism of civilisation, coinciding with a sudden and complete collapse in its control and management. We can produce wealth without the sweat of our brow, we can overproduce at a moment's notice, but we fail to make the wealth available. The value of life falls as wealth increases. In some degree we see this contrast, this absurd, illogical contrast, in the village. The mechanics of village life have improved out of reason. No village is isolated. The aerials beacon, even to the unobservant passengers in a streaking car the plain fact that the village too has the freedom of the ether, can listen to the accent of the Antipodes or the immortal music of the past. The distances have shrunk. The once-distant town is a quarter of an hour away and the journey easy and merry and cheap. If some gracious valley and austere downs are outraged by strange poles and wires, the offences at least point to the near presence of the greatest of boons, withheld from the cottage through the ages. Light and heat and power are at the door of the humblest dwelling, if they do not, as yet, enter. The engines of progress are at our elbow in the village not less than in the town. The problem is just this : how to make use of the new powers, how to convert them into wealth, into comfort, into happiness, and, it may be, into spirit. It should be an easier task in this island than the management of a like problem among nations, separated by distance and language and prejudice. We have a straight and simple thing to do. Let us do it.

LIGHT AND THE HOME

It has sometimes been presumed, as if it were an established fact, that the ideals of Socialism and Christianity are contrary in this regard : that Socialists see progress in the bettering of material conditions, and Christians in the advance of spiritual perception : " the heart is its own place." The contrast is, of course, essentially false. On one side the spirit has been hampered by evil conditions and on the other the chief trouble of the world is that material progress has outrun the spirit. Which ever side of this twin progress is emphasised, it is felt by all that the home matters supremely. It is doubtless true, as Max Müller said on a famous occasion, that " much may be done in a hovel " ; but dark and crowded rooms are agents of spiritual degeneration as of material discomfort and ill health. The village home matters supremely ; and the rural slum is as bad as the city slum, though it may be more picturesque. Cottages have improved, and are improving ; rural slums are less common and less sordid ; but it is still a general truth that it is very difficult in most cottages to be *librement occupé*, to be idle in a pleasant and wholesome manner. The use of leisure is more than half the problem. It is especially difficult to read ; and for the most part no reading is done. Many young people, even to-day, almost forget how to read and write between the ages of fourteen and seventeen. What matters perhaps more than anything is light. The villages are full of Goethes demanding " more light " ; and, as with that most famous of dying prayers, no one can quite decide whether the plea is wholly material or in part symbolic. Light is available, and some experiments in cheapening the supply and distributing it to the smallest houses are in operation. The best is in the neighbourhood of Bedford, and we may get from there—and perhaps from Aylesbury—a model for imitation. Nevertheless, in spite of such examples most of the cottages of England are as dark as ever they were, and likely to be in many districts. It is the deliberate and cynically confessed policy of some of the distributing companies, especially those with urban names, to refuse to supply either cottages or farmhouses and homesteads. The argument—perfectly sound as far as it goes—is that such distribution would not at first pay a sufficient dividend ; and the definite policy has been adopted of never extending the benefit except where a lucrative return is immediately guaranteed.

A SWEDISH EXAMPLE

Is such a policy, which dooms the cottage to darkness and the farm to the loss of power, a policy that can be countenanced ? An analogy may be quoted from Sweden. When the telephone (which owed much to Swedish inventiveness) became sufficiently developed the Government said in effect : " This is a heaven-sent means of educating our people and bringing the most isolated dweller into touch with the life of the nation and within the circle of Swedish culture. Whatever the capital cost, we will extend the telephone to the outermost stations of our peninsula, and thus extend to all the benefit of our national culture and our national ideals. An incomparable agent of spiritual civilisation as well as of economic development is put into our hands. Not to use it would be a ' sin in the soul.' " We cannot enjoy rural development in this island if we refuse to recognise such spiritual obligations as moved the Swedes in the matter of the telephone—the voice from afar. Nationally we do take exactly the contrary view. We say in effect : " These heaven-sent agents of civilisation are meant to be a source of profit for those who seek an investment for their capital. We will not allow a ray of light or an atom of power to any house or homestead which cannot give us a satisfactory return for our money." While such purely commercial policies hold the field, we have to confess that the regeneration of country life—that necessary preface to health in any state—is impossible : the State is in opposition to the State ; there is war in the members. In any case, the health of the village is not a case of cunning adaptations, of dodges, of little arts and artificial crafts, or even of local leadership. It is dependent on a large policy, a serious purpose. To return to the detail of light, it is impossible for the life of the village to be vital, as it should be, or for the home to be the centre of culture that it should be, when a company with a Government monopoly can write and say in effect : " We cannot supply your line of fourteen cottages and small houses with light and power, though the cable is at their doors, because the return would not be sufficient. As to supplying the farm just beyond, that is quite out of the question." A radical change in outlook and intention is necessary before reform can be as much as thought of. If populous villages thirty miles from London suffer such deliberate deprivation, what hope is there for the remoter hamlet, the isolated homestead ?

WHAT OXFORD DOES

Electric light and power are new gifts. They are perhaps the flourish set on the home, though they come to be essentials. Not all cottage homes, or even small farmhouses and buildings, are ready. The village slum is not yet purged. No body of workers for reform have collected more information or suggested better remedies than the Rural Community Council of Oxfordshire. Many other such councils have wasted both money and energy on vain and ignorant abstractions recorded on endless sheets of foolscap, covered with half legible typescript. The Oxfordshire printed pamphlets are " breeders "—to use a botanical term : they give a summary of facts, hard to discover by the general worker, and record the wise initial endeavours to set things right. In one of these pamphlets,[1] the prime evil is briefly touched upon by way of preface to an account of local details. " One of the worst features of the housing position in Oxfordshire is the extent to which overcrowding exists and the number of insanitary and dilapidated cottages which remain in occupation. This fact is emphasised by most of the Parish Councils from whom communications

[1] *More Houses*, Barnett House, Oxford, 6d.

have been received and is not denied by the local housing authorities. Its existence has been forcibly impressed on members of the Enquiry Committee who have made personal inspections in various parishes." The sharp contrast between the newer County Council cottages and the old often disturbs the mental as well as the material balance of the village. In a number of Hertfordshire villages the new cottages have been supplied with water and with light. The inhabitants of older cottages cheek by jowl with them have been allowed neither water nor light. They must draw their water (in some places from a depth of 200 feet or more) by a bucket, and the wells are some distance apart. More than this, the methods used for supplying the new Council houses with water are likely to retard the bringing of water to the older cottages. The village, in short, is being organised by the Councils themselves in a partial and prejudicial manner. In some villages this tends to create a spiritual lack of unity as well as narrow jealousies.

THE HOME FIRES

Country people, even the poorest, are very ready to pay for genuine benefits. One of the leading authorities in England writes as follows to a private correspondent : " I entirely agree with you on the subject of raising conditions of life in agricultural districts by installing electric light, and there is no question that, after the possibilities of cheap transport introduced by the motor-bus, electric light is the greatest humanising influence. . . . In the country districts, where fuel is a much more serious business than in the towns, consumers are willing to pay for electric cooking rates a penny a unit higher than in the towns. *If this particular development catches on, it might make a dramatic difference in the whole situation.*" The cottage has been cold as well as dark. Men have set out to work from a house where the fire was lit too late and was of too small dimensions to provide adequate heat either for comfort or for cooking. The difficulty and labour and cost of fuel have complicated life and robbed it of decent leisure. The workman who in

winter left his home in the dark and cold returned in the
dark ; and every coal that had helped to banish the chill
was regarded as a heavy subtraction from the spare money.
The change may indeed be called dramatic if the labour
and delay and cold can be banished by the click of a
switch ; and experiments now nearing a conclusion suggest
that the cost of electric cooking and heating may be much
below the cost of coal, which is always dear in country
districts ; and the more remote the hamlet and smaller the
cottage, the dearer the fuel and the harder to procure.
A cottage badly built of bad material standing on land
else valueless is not necessarily cheap. In some villages the
worst cottages, for which least is done by the proprietor, are
more heavily rented than the best. The reason lies in the
ownership. It is the custom of local tradesmen, innkeepers,
and the rest, to invest their savings in cottage property. The
investment is a good one only if the highest possible rent is
charged and the least possible amount spent on repairs.
The health, happiness, and progress of the community are
adversely affected by the prevalence of this sort of ownership. Condemnation of such cottages by local inspectors is
ineffective, because it means eviction of the cottagers,
which is not desired even by those whom it is desired to
benefit. The remedy of this evil is one of the " conditions
precedent " to social and moral progress.

LEADERS OF THE REVIVAL

We may, then, take it as undeniable that the mechanics
of civilisation have reached such a point that the rural
unit, even in the less populous places, may enjoy most of the
material advantages of the town and many of its intellectual
advantages : the omnibus, the wireless, and electric power
have annihilated distance. The village, at the same time,
enjoys its peculiar virtues, denied to the town ; its air, its
gardens, its individuality, its humane solidarity, its native
beauty. Where the old darkness and dullness and discomfort remain, the fault lies with the human control. Since
the war the attempts to improve the control, to secure for

country folk their share of amusement and culture, have multiplied and intensified. The formation of the Council of Social Service (though its presence is often unheeded) marks an advance in idea, if not in practice, almost comparable with the Education Act of 1870 ; and its activities are happily free from the evils of ill-designed and urbanised education. The men's clubs took a new breadth and activity from returned soldiers. The Service organisations, the Boy Scouts, and especially the Women's Institutes, gave and give a social stimulus. An offshoot of the report of the Social Service Council was the Rural Community Council, which was to pool and direct the various clubs and societies just as the Council for the Preservation of Rural England has pooled, and most successfully directed and enlivened, the work of a score of constituent societies. Many of these Community Councils have failed dismally ; but not all. One at any rate—and that the first to be formed—has done work, has set an example, has given a model that may yet influence our rural civilisation root and branch. The pamphlets of the Oxford Community Council, and indeed of several others, including the Hertfordshire quarterly, *The Village*, are full of the right practical and indeed spiritual ideas, and record a succession of achievements that suggest the discovery of the authentic philosophy. First the Council pools information. Any villager in any doubt or difficulty can consult a particular expert at particular hours. It does not matter what the subject ; and sheer ignorance is the cause of many maladies, even to the paying of exorbitant rents. This Community Council does for Oxfordshire very much what the Council of Social Service, a beneficent association of which much more will be heard, does for the country in general. You cannot revivify rural life without some central organisation. To leave villages in the hurly-burly of a muddled circumference, without reference to a " creative centre," is to sacrifice the cause. Local leadership may of course do much in isolation. For example, almost every woman in the village of Hunsdon has become an expert at some village craft, from needlework to carpentry, to the despair of competitors from other Women's Institutes. But a village has as many needs and activities as a town ; indeed, more, for it must to some extent provide its own amusements by co-operation.

THE COMMUNITY COUNCIL

Now the Oxford Rural Community Council (the Ork, as it is familiarly known) has an active Health Committee that concerns itself with the whole subject : nursing federation, regional planning, sanctuary provision, the disposal of rubbish, and the rest ; and its voluntary work has been valuable to local councils, burdened with the unfamiliarly new duties in regard to water supply, inspection of food and milk, nuisances, child welfare, and the rest. One of the most deadly failures in the village has been the virtual abandonment of the boy whose education is completed (save the mark !) at fourteen. The reason why boys' clubs fail—and hardly any succeed over a long continuous period —is that the boys have nothing to do, nothing that encourages their more laudable desires and instincts. There are of course beneficent organisations which do much, such as the Boy Scouts, and here and there the wholly admirable Young Farmers' Clubs. The Community Council has not only been able to increase these clubs and to enlarge the recognition of the Young Farmers. It has in general provided all sorts of local leaders with schemes of a definite character. It has also stimulated the movement for the building of village halls, which are of prime importance for village unity and for the corporate sense.

All who have watched the advance, the real progress in the villages of Oxford, of Nottingham, and of Somerset—to quote perhaps the three best examples—have a real confidence that in the Council of Social Service and the Community Councils affiliated to it has been found a form of organisation that may completely reorganise the village, both in material and spiritual progress. The encouragement of the arts goes on concurrently. Rural theatricals are already a lively influence and interest. Concerts and community singing grow in favour. The guilds of black-smiths in Hampshire and Kent are some evidence of the real revival of the rural craft.

THE NEW FARMING

All this gives good ground for hope ; but the first essentials for rural revival are better homes and better husbandry. Out of these may well emerge a peasantry able to stand on its own feet and exert its own and proper influence in the progress of the nation, in the manner, if not in the degree, of the rural population of Denmark. Husbandry will revive. How and when are questions that cannot be answered, even allusively, in this place ; but we may remember that in one of the best books on rural revival, *The Soul of a People*, it was associated with co-operation, with the common effort of the rural producer to farm better, live better, and sell better. A very rapid transition in agri-culture is in progress within Britain ; and the new farming will help social progress. The biggest change is the sudden socialisation of both distribution and production in their mutual relationship. Producers will produce individually as before, and the present distributors will remain ; but in some of the commonest, most essential products—especially pig products and dairy products—a standard sale price will be assured in return for a standard product ; and the new Commissions will use their power also as an excuse, an occasion, an opportunity for education. The Empire Marketing Board has set in motion a rural policy that far transcends the particular and technical things with which it deals.

The enemies of mechanisation have their objections. They fear the reduction of workers, but labour saving, though it may go too far, has the virtue of its defect ; it produces and encourages the labour that is intelligent and must be well rewarded. In one of the most successful experi-ments—by Mr. Henry Ford in Essex—men were receiving more than twice the standard wage. Small changes as well as big are helping the village and the small intensive

cultivator. Sale of fruit, vegetables, and eggs by the roadside is now on a very large scale. A farmer at Kingston
Bagpuize sold in twelve months over £700 worth of this
sort of produce at the side of the road. Naval caterers in the
south-east of England send a car out daily to buy their
fruit and vegetables and poultry produce at the roadside.
A Women's Institute in Hertfordshire built a spacious hall
for the most part out of money accumulated by the sale of
fruit and flowers from their small village gardens. The
astonishingly successful scheme of " Collective County
Markets " tried out at East Grinstead, and likely to spread
widely, has given new scope to the small intensive producer ;
and he is the man who seems likely to multiply. Women's
Institutes, again, have prospered beyond all expectation
with their market stalls, which have earned £2,000 within
the year in a single county. If that desirable consummation
is reached, villages situated in any of the more fertile areas
will increase their independent vitality. An ideal, already
realised, is to be seen at Badsey and Pershore, where a
co-operative factory and distributing agency secures better
prices for its members and, more than this, promotes
corporate spirit and furthers technical education.

CALL OF THE REMOTER HAMLET

Now there are wide spaces—the wolds of Lincolnshire,
the clays of Northampton, the chalk of Wiltshire, the hills
of Westmorland, the upland of the East Riding—where
any intensive cultivation is not to be dreamt of. Just as
husbandry has chiefly waned on the worse soils (though
part of East Anglia, where the soil is good, is an exception),
so the life of villages in these outer places has lost vigour.
Parishes are amalgamated and schools closed, and the
diminishing hamlets are passed by with the deliberate
cruelty of the Levite, because there is no money to be
extracted from them. Leadership is harder to discover, and
has much less to stimulate its energy. To repeat the Swedish
analogy, it is in such districts that the use of modern
apparatus will do most good. Such villages most need—

and are at present least likely to be given—motor service, light and power, a water supply, the telephone, and the wireless. One Community Council finances several motor-cars, whose chief work is to take out lecturers and organisers to hamlets otherwise hard to approach—hard to bring within the cultural circle of the nation. It may be forcibly argued that such remoter spots should be specially considered by the central authorities, by the county—indeed by the nation. Farming itself cannot flourish in isolation. Perhaps the provision of cheap light would do more for product, on than many grander and more direct schemes, than quotas and Produce Boards and all Government devices. Light, which has special uses for poultry-breeding, has attracted many country women to an industry less repulsive. As a rural, social, and, in essence, an economic influence, the provision of light to remoter farms and villages would pay big dividends, though the outlay would probably be uneconomic, in the narrow sense, perhaps for a number of years. Something of this has been realised by the more rural and more far-sighted distributing companies, such as the companies that supply Gloucester, Worcestershire, and Herefordshire, who are doing good service for rural revival. An exactly contrary policy is favoured by such urban-minded companies as the North Metropolitan. The promotion of the longer policy is worth the action of the Ministry of Transport, under whom the distributing companies have been placed. A definite rural policy is needed.

THE CENTRAL CHURCH

Since the Reformation, as before it, the Church has been the centre of the village. The architectural grace and strength of most English village churches has remained a symbol of unity and aspiration. In smaller and remoter hamlets the parson has been the centre of village life, materially as well as spiritually. He has organised coal clubs and clothing clubs, distributed charities, and made himself the information bureau for a people singularly ignorant of their rights, opportunities, and claims. The new village possesses another central organiser. Especial attention should be paid to the Information Bureau, as organised in Oxfordshire. It is much used. Anyone who pleases may write inquiries or visit the office to seek information about pensions, rent, insurance, nurses and child welfare, education, or any other points concerning local, public, or social services. Village Community Councils joined to the County Community Council, as that is associated to the Central Council of Social Service, are being successfully formed. The object of such a council (elected by Church, chapel, Women's Institute, Mothers' Union, men's club, Parish Council, cricket club, and so on) is to bring all village interests together without regard to politics or religion. It is a superficial view that such common action weakens in any way the influence of the Church or of religion. It should strengthen both. It is easier to leaven one lump of dough than many differently compounded lumps. It should mean that there is more leisure, more energy reserved for the diffusion of the religious spirit. When a variety of agencies are brought together co-operatively, each of these has a better opportunity of carrying on its own work fruitfully. As a farmer in a co-operative group may, to his greater profit, rid himself of the burden of personal marketing and condense his energies on production, so may the Church in a spiritual and the club in a social reference. As was written in *The Happy Village*,[1] the fault with religion is that it has not spread its influence as it might among the common concerns of life, the work, the leisure, the games. Saturday has mattered too little, and Sunday perhaps too much. The ardent co-operation of all groups in a village is itself an expression of a religion that will most surely be Christianised if the Church throws itself into the service of such unity.

[1] *The Happy Village*, by W. B. Thomas. Benn. [*Ed.*]

THE HAPPY VILLAGE

We have a chance to establish " The Happy Village," where houses will be lit and reading become possible, where villages in common council shall work their own salvation, where produce of farm and garden shall have its mart, where music and drama and crafts shall be a common pride, where youth can learn and playing-fields be substituted for " the loafer-burnished wall," where religion may grow almost automatically because the organism is healthy and fulfils the natural instinct for thanksgiving and prayer.

Even at its worst the village, with its natural humanity and its neighbourliness and sense of individuality, can give our civilisation something that the town cannot. It is essential to the complement of national life ; and for this reason alone its reconstruction should be a definite aim in the national policy. Whatever the immediate cost, it should be given light and opportunity, and its share of " the deep power of joy," on which Wordsworth relied.

4. THE STATE AND CONSTRUCTIVE CITIZENSHIP

By Professor W. G. S. ADAMS

I. THE GROWTH OF STATE SERVICES
1832–1870

THE HUNDRED years which have just closed since the first Reform Act was passed, have seen in this country an amazing growth in the functions of the State. It is well to recall how meagre was the range of State action at the beginning of this period. The poor law placed on local bodies the relief of the local poor, but while Parliament might enjoin duties there was little or no administrative control from the centre. Poor law was the only social sphere in which the State had required provision by the community for the needs of its most distressed members. State education, State assistance in public health were practically unknown. The opening of the nineteenth century had seen in 1802 the first Factory Act dealing with the health and morals of apprentices. But if we look at England in 1832, we see a community in which the State has as yet hardly begun to make any social provision, save for the protection of the life and property of its citizens from aggression from without or disturbance from within. If we keep the two pictures in our mind, of the State in 1832 and then of the State in 1932, we get some impression of the progress which has been made to build up in the last hundred years the status of citizenship with its rights and its duties. But progress was often slow and very tentative. The first State grant for education was in 1833, and was for a sum of £20,000 ; 1833 saw also the important Factory Act of that year which made provision for inspection, a very notable step ; 1834 is remembered for the Act which set up the Poor Law Board, and the Report of the Royal Commission which led to its establishment must be regarded as one of the great historic documents which made men think in a new way about the sphere of the State and its methods of administration. In the next decade important steps were taken in the field of public health (the Public Health Act of 1848 is a landmark like the Poor Law Act of 1834). Sometimes the way was pioneered by progressive local authorities like Liverpool. If we let our mind traverse the period between 1832 and 1870, we can see many signs of the coming of a new idea of the State. But it is still a period dominated by the doctrine of *laissez faire*, and Mill's great pamphlet on *Liberty* is a fine expression of the best thought of the times. It was an age which preached initiative and self-help, and which felt strongly the value of personality. But it was an age of gloomy surroundings, of conditions, especially in the cities and towns, which told the tale that individual effort was not enough, and that the State, central and local, had to gird up its loins for collective action if there was to be a good citizenship.

1870 to 1905

The years from 1870 to 1905 may be usefully regarded as the second period. It was marked by great developments of a comprehensive character in legislation and administration. The Education Act of 1870 ; the Irish Landlord and Tenant Act of the same year, which opened a very important chapter in land legislation ; the Act of 1871 establishing the Local Government Board and bringing under its control, poor law, public health, and local government ; the Trade Unions Act of that same year ; the Public Health Acts of 1872 and 1875, marked the new lines of advance in several great spheres of State action. Again, in the eighties the growth of municipal services, the Municipal Corporations Act of 1882, the establishment in 1888 of the county councils, and a number of other measures extending the powers of local authorities, marked the increasing activity of the State in the local sphere, where the daily life of the citizen is most directly affected by government and in which also a larger group of citizens can take an active part in the direction of the affairs of the community. The Housing Act of 1890, though not the first of its kind, is a much more far-reaching measure of State action than had hitherto been attempted, and prepares the way for the still more comprehensive measures of the twentieth century. The great Factory and Workshops Act of 1901 consolidated the long line of factory legislation since the Act of 1802, while in 1902 the Education Act provided a compromise in the church- and board-schools question, completed the national framework of elementary education, and laid the foundations of a much more adequate system of secondary education. Finally, the Unemployed Workmen's Act of 1905 ends the period and directs attention to the problems which were to engage the State much more earnestly in the years which stretch from 1906 to the present day.

Looking back over the period from 1870 to 1905, we see a wide extension in the scope of State control over the life of the community. There is some exaggeration in speaking of it as the age of Socialism or of collective action, but it is a great constructive period in which the foundations of modern democratic government, both local and central, were laid, and in which at least the policy of municipal Socialism, in the form of extended ownership and operation of public services affecting the health and comfort of the citizen, is becoming firmly established. There is in this period a gradually deepening sense of the obligations of civic life. The character of the State is changing. It is becoming more conscious of its purpose as a great moral instrument for the realisation of the good life. The teaching of T. H. Green, especially in the *Principles of Political Obligation*, is the most profound and influential expression of the trend of thought in this period. The contrast between the conception of the State as seen in Mill's *Liberty* and in Green's *Principles* gives an index of the change in outlook. The emphasis by Green on the functions of the State as providing the conditions which make possible the good life, points the direction in which men were feeling their way. But the scope of State action was still, at the end of this period, very limited as compared with the developments which followed in the years after 1905.

1905 to 1914

It is in the third period from 1905 onwards that we get the much fuller revelation of the nature of the modern State. The years from 1906 to 1914 will stand out in history as one of the most creative periods in our community life. Many of the measures passed were only the first beginnings of a new movement of social control. Thus in 1906 and 1907 the short Acts which provided for the feeding of school children who were improperly nourished, and for medical inspection in the schools, mark the growing importance of the school as an instrument of social control. The " Choice of Employment " Act of 1910, which enabled the education authorities to give guidance to those leaving school in finding suitable employment, is another evidence of the movement to relate the school to the social and industrial life of the community. Again, the Children's Act of 1908 and the Housing Act of 1909 embodied a much deeper sense of social duty and control than had been expressed in the earlier Acts for the protection of child life and the development of healthy homes for the people. There is thus a widening view of the nature of community action. The idea of planning the life of the community begins to be felt with town planning and, later, country and regional planning. So also, in another direction, the Trade Boards Act of 1909, which dealt with the sweated industries and unorganised trades by providing for minimum wages and for representation of workers and employers, followed by the minimum wage legislation in 1912 affecting the miners; and, later, in wartime and after, the extension of wages regulation to agriculture and an increasing number of trades are each significant of the changing attitude of the State towards industry. In another direction, the establishment of Labour Exchanges in 1909, the National Insurance Act of 1911, providing a system of wide-spread insurance against sickness and at least the beginnings of the provision for unemployment insurance, and the development of machinery for arbitration and conciliation in labour disputes are steps towards the better organisation of our industrial life; while the provision for old age pensions in 1909 is in itself another evidence of the new social endeavour to build up standards of security and independence.

The War Period

The years 1906 to 1914 mark the first period of the twentieth century. We can usefully divide up the remaining years into two periods, the years of war and the post-war period. The war years are deeply significant in the development of the State and in their influence on citizenship. In war the State is writ large, but in the late war this was especially true. To an extent hitherto unknown the whole resources of the nation were mobilised. The State took control in varying degrees over the greater part of the industry of the country, including its transport. It called out, however, not only great administrative State organisation, but a wonderful development of voluntary effort and a new spirit of social service. Among the many forms of State action in this period, we may note some which are of particular significance from the point of view of a more permanent public policy. First, the recruiting statistics directed fresh attention to the unsatisfactory physical condition of the nation. In 1918 the Local Government Board was replaced by the Ministry of Health and Local Government. Second, the importance of better industrial conditions was recognised, particularly through the development of welfare work in factories and workshops. Third, the growth of the remarkable War Savings Movement, which has been carried on in the National Savings Movement, helped to stimulate thrift and saving, and associated in this work a great army of volunteers not only amongst the general population but in school and factory. Fourth, a new policy with regard to agriculture was as formulated in the Corn Production Act of 1917 and in other measures relating to the development of the land, the regulation of food supplies, the control of prices, and the establishment of a

Consumers' Council. These and other movements in this period make the war years of deep permanent significance in the organisation and development of the community. But the period was no less remarkable for the fact that before the close of the war there had been formulated a great new educational programme embodied in the Education Act of 1918, while under the Ministry of Reconstruction nearly every aspect of national life was being reconsidered, and plans laid for the future. Notable amongst the reports of the committees of the Ministry of Reconstruction was that on Adult Education; nor should it be forgotten that the last of the great Franchise Acts extending the vote to women was carried before the conclusion of the war. We recall these aspects of the war period because it is important to recognise their significance in the building up of constructive citizenship. And it should also be remembered that there were wider aspects of national policy which were arousing interest. War drew together the different parts of the Empire and widened our horizon. A new chapter was opening in our relations, not only with the self-governing Dominions, but with the Empire of India; and the Montagu–Chelmsford Report of 1918 marked another stage of progress in our imperial citizenship.

The Post-War Period

If it is not easy to measure in any brief compass the social significance of the war period, it is still more difficult as yet to appraise the significance of the post-war years. On the one hand, there was the desire to throw off the wartime restrictions and even to abandon the constructive policies of that period ; on the other hand, there is a great extension of the lines of policy which had been laid down in the years 1906 to 1914. Public health, housing, town and country planning, the extension of old age pensions, and the provision of widows' and orphans' pensions, are amongst the subjects of legislation and administration which mark the extension of the pre-war policy. But most important of all were the developments in connection with the problem of

Pc

unemployment. In 1920, there was a great extension of the provision for unemployment insurance, and successive measures during the twelve years following have focussed, to an increasing degree, public attention upon the great question of employment, production, and distribution. In 1932, the report of the Royal Commission on Unemployment drew attention to the change which had come over this problem. Post-war unemployment has grown to such dimensions and has proved so continuous, and, in certain areas, so concentrated that it differs almost in kind from any pre-war experience that the community had had of this evil. In the eleven years from 1921 to 1931, the average percentage of unemployment had reached 13.04 per cent and in no month had unemployment fallen below 8.6 per cent, while in the end of the period it had risen and maintained a level of over 20 per cent. There was nothing comparable to such continuous and intense unemployment in pre-war experience. But this great problem has itself entered on a new phase in the last three years since 1929, when not only has unemployment in this country remained steadily over 20 per cent of the registered insured workers but other countries throughout the world have been suffering severely, and, in some cases, even more acutely than this country. Nevertheless, it was realised that, whatever might be the defects of the system, unemployment insurance had enabled us to carry through a period of great depression with a far less degree of distress and unrest than if there had been no such constructive provision available. Yet with this unabatement of the evil, and with the prospects of its continuing still for a considerable period, the public mind has become seized with the importance of more effective action in dealing with a problem of such magnitude and urgency.

But if we are to understand the problems of the post-war period, we must note the great contrast between the war years and after. In wartime the problem was one of production. Every effort was directed to planning and increasing output. Man-power was economised in every possible way, woman-power was brought into service on a scale hitherto unknown. Demand everywhere outran supply. In the post-war period the growing problem has been to maintain demand rather than supply, and to control distribution rather than increase production. The great impulse given to mechanisation in wartime and to the means of saving labour, the sense, also, of the magnitude of the problem of reconstruction, and, therefore, of what seemed at the time an unlimited demand in the years immediately following the war, all stimulated the productive side of things. Furthermore, wartime itself had developed new fields of supply throughout the world. It is not, therefore, surprising, after the end of the waste of war and when the first great stage of reconstruction had been passed, that production outran demand and that the problem has become, in an increasingly acute form, one of distribution and consumption. The post-war period is of such complexity, that its analysis is as yet far from complete. The problems of reparations and war debts, the confusion caused by instability of currencies, and the rapid developments in the policy of economic nationalism have contributed to the complexity of the problem. All these factors have been making a heavy demand on statesmanship and on the development of State policy and action. Yet, whatever the shortcomings of statesmanship, this period will none the less stand out as one in which there is a great trend towards State and Community planning, even when compared with the constructive period immediately preceding the war. It was, in part, a consequence of the experiences of wartime, but it also marks the progress of a social trend which was already evident before the war. Thus, in this country, the Railways Act of 1921, the Coal Mines Reorganisation Act of 1925, the Electricity Supply Act of 1926, and the Agricultural Marketing Act of 1931 stand out as very notable provisions in national planning, just as in another field we have the establishment in 1925 of the British Broadcasting Corporation. What characterises this development as a whole is the attempt to provide national organisation without nationalisation. Production is still left in the hands of private enterprise, but to an increasing extent there are controls of output and regulation of distribution. The most striking example of this has been the development of the quota system, which in coal mining has regulated both production and distribution, while in its latest field, the agricultural industry, it is developing an important imperial and international aspect of quantitative control affecting the exchange of commodities between countries. It is clear that the State has entered upon a new phase not only of national but of international reconstruction. This tendency has been greatly accentuated by the fact that supply has outrun demand and that in consequence there has followed an unparalleled period of unemployment of world-wide character. The magnitude of the problem of unemployment and the prospect of its continuance have made necessary State and Community planning. It is no longer possible to leave things simply to adjust themselves. The problem of conscious direction, and of securing the co-operation of the Community in assisting the Government in its undertakings, has never been so urgent. Thus, however difficult it may be to assess its character, we are conscious that the post-war period is shaping the character of the Community and of its citizenship in ways which are different from either the period of war or from that which preceded it. There is one other index of the magnitude of the change which has been taking place, to which at least a brief reference must be made. Each year a return is now made to Parliament of public expenditure, national and local, on the social services. These services include expenditure on unemployment insurance, national health insurance, widows' and orphans' and old age pensions, war pensions, education, health and housing, and public assistance. Expenditure on these and kindred services in Great Britain was in 1900, £36,000,000 ; in 1920, £306,000,000 ; and in 1930, £463,000,000. No statement could show more clearly the magnitude of the change in the sphere of the State during the three decades of the twentieth century.

II. THE STATE AND CONSTRUCTIVE CITIZENSHIP

We have seen, then, how great has been the growth of the State in the past 100 years. This amazing development is yet far from having reached its climax. But gradually out of the complexities of the present there seem to be emerging two great trends of thought. On the one hand, there is the idea of society dominated by a plan which is largely imposed from above. It is a plan in which the State is supreme, and in which there is only a very subordinate place for all other associations. The Church, the family, the trade union, and other social organisations are subordinate in the conception of a society which seeks to control the life, liberty, and property of the individual to a degree hitherto unknown. On the other hand, there is the idea of a Community much less dominated by plan, much more free and flexible in its nature, which seeks to develop the individuality of groups and to build up an ordered society in which the State leaves a large place of freedom to the family, the Church, the trade union, and other forms of association. It is based on the conception of the rights of the individual to life, liberty, and property, and on the rule of law expressed through a system of free representative government. At such a time it is necessary to rethink and restate the fundamental ideas which seem to us to underlie a true society. Thought becomes clearer through this conflict of ideas. Yet there are many things which may be found to be common between the two great trends of development, and each may in due course deeply influence the other. For the great experiments which are taking place in the modern State in Soviet Russia, and in another direction in Fascist Italy, have in them lessons of real significance for the communities which are based on the rights of the individual and the rule of law. Let us consider the view of the good society which is revealing itself more fully in our minds, and the principles which underlie this type of society.

1. *The Good Life of the Individual*

First, the aim of society is the good life of the individual. Kant said " Treat every man as an end and not as a means only." Freedom of thought and of speech, freedom of association and of worship, the conception of property which seeks to distinguish where property should be common and where it should be private—these rights are fundamental to our idea of a good society. If a community denies to its citizens freedom of speech, of association, and of worship, it can never satisfy mankind ; and a good State cannot be built on unsound foundations. We believe, therefore, that the greatest element in constructive citizenship is the maintenance of these fundamental rights of man. All rights imply duties. As Mazzini said to the workmen of Italy, " Every right you have can only spring from a duty fulfilled." But the basal conception of society must be one which sets out clearly as its end the realisation of the good life for all its members through the maintenance of these fundamental rights. It is in the daily exercise of these rights and duties, and in the opportunities which the State affords to the individual of developing his faculties, that constructive citizenship is built up.

2. *The State as a Moral Agency*

Second, we conceive of the State as a great moral agency. To recall the famous definition of Aristotle, " It comes into existence to make life possible, it continues to exist to make life good." As the end of the State is the good life, so the State is justified in doing anything which contributes to that good life. There is thus no limit to the sphere of the State, save as experience may prove that State action checks rather than aids the attainment of goodness. Thus experience has shown that if the State seeks to impose belief in, and conformity to, this or that religion, it hinders rather than helps the attainment of a good life. The State can do wrong as well as right, and a good State will be ready to recognise its error and to give up powers as well as to take them. But we can set no other limit to the activities of the State, and the more our politics are moralised and our morals socialised the higher becomes the Community and the freer its life.

3. The Community

Third, the Community is greater than the State. The State may be regarded as in a sense the architect of the Community. It has a position which no other association within the Community holds. But other associations as well as the State have their rights, and the good State recognises the place of these other bodies and their freedom within the community. There may seem to be a paradox in speaking of the rights and the freedom of other associations when the State is sovereign ; but the true nature of sovereignty lies in realising the good life of the Community and of its members. The good State does not seek to determine the policy of the different associations within the Community and to regulate their proceedings, but rather gives them liberty to develop their individuality so that they may serve their members in the way which suits them, as long as this liberty does not inhibit the opportunities of others to enjoy freedom. Western society is discovering more and more fully how the sovereignty of the State can be reconciled with the freedom of the individual and of the groups and associations within the State. In this sphere one of the greatest advances has been made in the relations of Church and State. The good State does not seek to drive religion outside the Community, nor, on the other hand, does it seek to impose a conformity of belief amongst its members. In a society where the majority is in favour of a particular Church being associated with the State there is no reason why this should not be confirmed and established by the State, but on one condition, that there is permitted to others the free opportunity for the exercise of their religious practice and communion, so long as that does not disturb the freedom of others within the Community. It is this recognition of freedom which constitutes the condition of good constructive citizenship. For the more we think seriously for ourselves and make our choice and witness to our loyalties, the more real and full becomes our individual life. The Church of Scotland Act 1921 is perhaps the most striking example of this liberty which the State accords to all beliefs while at the same time recognising the national will that one Church should be regarded as the national Church. It marks the community sense not only of the religious character of society but of the relationship between State and Church. The Church is not subordinate to the State, the State must not interfere with the doctrines and practices of the Church so long as the Church does not claim for itself any jurisdiction or authority over those who are not its members. It is in this large atmosphere of freedom that we develop good citizenship. And so also with the Trade Unions. The right to associate for the purpose of collective bargaining and of advancing and protecting common interests affecting the welfare of the body of workers is, as experience shows, essential to the good life of the community. We should not wish to go back to the state of individualism and of the struggle for the survival of the strongest which the old unorganised individualistic system involved.

And there are many others forms of association which the good State recognises and safeguards. The State, as so conceived, is becoming the architect of the co-operative community, seeking to develop a rich variety of associations within it, and giving to those associations the greatest measure of freedom and opportunity for self-development. In all this work it is creating the conditions which make possible a good citizenship. But, while we recognise this vital importance of the freedom of the groups and associations within the Community to develop their individuality and their particular services to the society, we recognise no less clearly the unique position of the State : that it is the representative of the whole society ; that the will of the majority must be accepted by the minority ; that the State alone has the duty of determining the relations of groups one to another, and their place in the Community ; and that in a free society it has to be the guardian not simply of the rights of the majority but of the right which belongs to the minority—the right to convince the majority. The goodness of our modern society thus depends in a great measure on the growth of all kinds of voluntary organisations alongside of the State ; and we see before us, more and more clearly, the vision of a community in which we have the voluntary and the statutory agencies working in harmony one with another, discovering how each can help the other, and contributing in their partnership each to the development of the other. For the extent of good State action has depended and will depend upon the development, alongside of it, of voluntary action ; and good voluntary action in turn requires the co-operation and support of the State. There has never been a time in which voluntary societies were seeing so clearly their relationship not only one to another but to the State, and in which, on the other hand, the State was seeing so clearly the nature of the services which the voluntary societies could render in assisting the discharge of the functions of the State. We are in this way more conscious of the place of the State within the Community, and of the nature of the relationship between the State and all the other voluntary organisations.

4. *Local Government*

Fourth, the State is growing, not only in its central but in its local government, and, beyond these, also in its membership of the international commonwealth of States. The roots of democracy lie in local government. One of the greatest factors in the building up of good citizenship is the exercise of the rights of local government, and the interest which members can take in the development of their own local affairs. Hence it is that all over the world to-day we see greater attention being paid to the study of this subject and to the problem of the relations of central and local government. Even in this sphere we are witnessing the growth of international co-operation.

The periodic international conferences of local government authorities show how one State is comparing its experiences with another, and how we are learning one from another and helping one another. It is out of this atmosphere of conference and co-operation that we are building a new constructive idea of citizenship. Society is being rebuilt from its foundations in local affairs. The good society is not one in which the will is imposed from above with little consideration of the views of those who are governed. It requires the development of strong local self-government related to, if not represented on, the central government, while that central government is in turn related to and represented on international government. We see therein a growth which is enabling the individual citizen to share in a life which is not only local and national but international, and to discover that one loyalty does not interfere with another ; that in being a good citizen of his own town, he can help his country and beyond that the community of nations. It is in the exercise of these loyalties that we call out the quality of citizenship.

5. *The State and other Societies*

Fifth, the State, with the co-operation of other associations in the community, has to provide the conditions which make possible the good life of the individual. The great significance of the development of State action in the past century, has been the attempt to lay the foundations of standards of work and life, to protect the hours of labour, to secure at least certain minimum standards of wage, to make provision against unemployment, to provide standards of housing which make possible better home life, and, in many other ways, to help towards a good life. But of all the factors which contribute to the development of good citizenship, the greatest is *education*, a province in which the State has entered increasingly during the past sixty years. Yet whereas in other countries it has been the claim that the State should control the system and matter of education, in England, above all countries, there has been the tradition of toleration and of variety of expression in our education. This may seem to make it lack system. But what it loses in system it gains in spontaneity, in richness and variety, and in character.

This is a very great and very precious tradition which must be jealously safeguarded. The Act of 1902 has proved itself to be a broad foundation on which different elements can join together in building up our national education, and the State through the Board of Education has shown in an increasing measure the desire to recognise the value of this variety so long as the standards of efficiency were not impaired. The State thereby has proved itself to be broadminded and tolerant. Uniformity is an evil thing in education as well as in religion. There has been, accordingly, a rich growth of experiment both in dealing with the years of infancy at the one end and in the development of adult education at the other end of the scale. Our national system has been enlarged by this freedom to experiment. But even in that part of the field which has been more purely the domain of the State—elementary and, to a lesser degree, secondary education—there has been a growing elasticity in our system and a much more earnest endeavour to relate education to life. We may be still far from achieving this, but slowly and patiently, by trial and error, we are getting nearer to it. It is becoming more and more clear how valuable the school is as a centre of social control and of building up the character of the community. But great efforts are required to make our educational provision more complete and more effective in training and moulding the rising generation. To-day the most urgent problem is the development of the resources of education in dealing with the adolescent period. The Fisher Act of 1918 stands out as a direction post, though the advance towards it has been checked. But just as everywhere social effort must be directed to eliminate waste, which is not only an individual but a great social sin, so particularly is this needed in the training of the body, mind, and spirit. For the great majority of our youth there is the post-school gap, with reactions which have come from the relaxation of discipline.

We have not yet worked out the way of stopping this waste

and developing the human resources which are at present so largely unused. Great as may be the need for the conservation of the wealth of the soil, still more urgent is the conservation and development of the wealth of the body and the mind. The school has to be the great centre of opportunity. It must provide an increasing variety of training in the spirit of self-help and of co-operation among its members. Voluntary movements—especially the club movement in its various forms—have played and are playing a great part in this work. But we can reach out to something which keeps the club spirit and joins with it the training of the school, or which links with it the experience of industry and trade. In this respect, one of the most hopeful and valuable developments in the last ten years has been the growth of the Young Farmers' Club movement. It has taken a deep hold in Canada and the United States. But there are encouraging signs of its growth also in this country. The Young Farmers' Club provides most valuable lessons not only in the proper management of crops and stock and in the business of keeping accounts and acquiring the habit of co-operation, but it is a means of calling out the spirit of self-government and the capacity to manage affairs. There is nothing more hopeful to-day in rural England than the advance which has been made amongst the younger generation in this training of their interest in the land. We must not judge things by their quantity but by their quality, and the work which can be seen at the competitions of the Royal Show and at the National Dairy Show, or in the functioning of a club in its local home, proves what a valuable instrument of rural-life education and citizenship this movement can be. Or, again, in the field of physical training : those who are interested in this work are seeing how much more can be done, while not losing the splendid quality that games have given to us, by closer attention to the training and development of the body, and the principles of health. Fitness is part of Godliness in the Pauline tradition.

There is thus wide room for variety of experiment in

developing associations of one kind or another, above all with a large element of self-government in them, on lines which afford training in industry, in commerce, and in scientific work for the adolescent generation. And there is nothing more worth while than a great concentration of effort in developing this field of our educational life. But behind and through all must lie the idea of training for citizenship. The good citizen, as Aristotle said, must be educated in the spirit of the Constitution. A great deal more is being done than was done, but still how far short do we fall ? The adolescent stage is a very critical period in the education of democracy, and the preparation which is done there will determine in a large measure the quality of the citizen body on which the government of the State has to rest.

The problems of adult education were examined by a committee appointed by the Ministry of Reconstruction in 1918 under the chairmanship of the late Master of Balliol. It issued a report which even to-day should be studied by all who are seriously interested in the subject of adult education. This country has given a great lead to the world in that field. But we have not to be content with the good start made, nor is it enough to spread the movement far and wide. We require to think out and plan our educational provision with a realisation of values. Adult education should first of all be an education for citizenship, to enable the individual to discharge his duties better as a citizen, to exercise his judgment on political, economic, and social questions, to take his part in local if not in national affairs, and to have the satisfaction of the interests not only in national but in world affairs. Everywhere we are realising how much peace and progress depend on an informed public opinion. The making of this can only be done by the quiet steady work of groups all over the country, and by the intercourse which these groups can have one with the other. The resources of modern civilisation are infinitely greater in this respect than anything which was dreamed of even at the beginning of the present century. Just as printing opened out a new age, so broadcasting has made possible a new era in national and international thinking and education. It is thus a most precious instrument in the making of civic life. But even here we have to recognise the dangers. Doing, it has been said, is better than listening. Individual thought and individual expression must be consciously provided for and exercised. The planning of life, and the right use and not the waste of time, is needed for the individual as well as for the nation, and this can only be realised if we have a community of members who are trained in self-help and self-reliance and who do not look simply for orders and instructions to be given. It is the more necessary because of the mechanical character of much of our production and of the rigid concentration and discipline which is required in this work. We have to look, therefore, to education as the great instrument in the building up of our citizenship, in the care of health, in the training for industry, in the cultivation of the arts and the appreciation of nature, in the application of reason and judgment to the affairs of the community, and in the thinking out as an individual of the foundations of belief and of the principles of conduct. In these different elements of education which make for developed individuality, we have the great road to constructive citizenship. From this will flow different policies which are required to secure the better development of the resources of the community, the regulation of its economic order, and the relations of the community to other communities.

In all this constructive work, the Churches and the groups of Christian people who have much in common in their fundamental thinking should be able to give a great lead in the Community. There was never so great an opportunity nor a time in which there was so deep a hunger not simply for the material, but for the spiritual things of life. Nor was there ever a time in which one nation could do so much to influence another, not only among nations which are near one to the other and often akin in blood. East and West are coming nearer together, however much discords at the moment may seem to keep them apart. The East needs to understand better the best of the West, and the West needs to understand the best of the East. For out of this alone will come true world citizenship. And that must be the end of constructive citizenship. Nothing short of a conception of loyalty which reaches from the home and the village or township up to the Commonwealth of Nations can satisfy the human spirit.

III. UNEMPLOYMENT

The past three years have been a period of deepening crisis in world affairs. There is no parallel in the records of history to what has been happening. The disturbances and depressions in the economic world have been affecting not one but all States. There is unemployment on a scale unprecedented, and the world is groping for a way out of its difficulties. In such a position we must get back to fundamentals and try to restate them in a way which will give us some guidance for our future course. We have to form a picture in our minds of how we think the good community is to be realised. That good community must, we have seen, give more true liberty and not less. It must bring security to the individual as regards the means of earning his livelihood. It must also give the opportunity for leisure. The problem is largely one of distribution. John Stuart Mill once said that the laws of production were like the laws of Nature but the laws of distribution were human and under human control. We have been wresting from Nature her secrets, and have been conquering the problem of production, but we are still far from solving the problem of distribution. And the problem of distribution lies behind the problem of security for the worker and of a proper measure of leisure for all. Face to face with the great new changing economic and social conditions, we have to build up more securely the foundations of a good society, and, in so doing, there are two main objectives on which attention should be directed.

The first of these is to make real the right to work ; the

second, to develop the good use of leisure. The experience of the present century is very eloquent. The State has made far greater efforts than ever before to deal with the problem of unemployment. Reference has been made to the Unemployed Workmen's Act of 1905, which seems to end one period and mark the beginning of a new attitude to the problem of unemployment. It was a serious effort to harness the statutory authorities and voluntary agencies in relieving distress amongst the unemployed and providing work, and yet it proved entirely inadequate. It revealed more clearly than ever before the need for a new analysis of the problem, and for new methods of attempting its solution. It was realised then that we must get down to the analysis and measurement of the causes of unemployment, and to the attempt constructively to build up machinery of State and of voluntary service, which would reduce, if it could not remove, the causes of this great social evil. It was seen that there were three great elements which were contributing to unemployment. The first cause is the maladjustment of supply and demand. The study of cyclical, as well as seasonal, fluctuations of trade was undertaken on a scale hitherto unknown by governments but still more by individual researchers in this and other countries, with a view to discovering how these fluctuations could be reduced. The second cause of unemployment is stoppage of work due to strikes and lockouts. The third cause of unemployment is the inefficiency due to such different factors as the prevalence of sickness and ill health, the lack of training, and the defects of our industrial organisation.

A systematic attack began to be made on all these different factors contributing to unemployment. More careful measurement of our national output was first provided by the census of production in 1907, while a much more adequate record of unemployment was made possible by the establishment of the Labour or Employment Exchanges in 1909 and by Part II. of the National Insurance Act 1911, providing for unemployment insurance, at first limited to a few industries and later on extended until it covers over more than two-thirds of wage-workers. The establishment of the Industrial Council of Conciliation in 1911, and of the Whitley Councils during the war period, was also amongst the efforts which our society has made towards the control of this complex question. And if the State has not succeeded in solving the problem, it has at least advanced a long way in recognising and making provision for the maintenance of the worker through the periods of unemployment. But the present crisis has brought it home to the nation that the provision of mere subsistence is not enough, and that the great problem is how the right to work itself shall be made real. The right to a living wage or to compensation for unemployment is only a second best. Alike, the interests of the community as a whole, and the safeguarding of the individual against the deteriorating effects of unemployment, have made us realise that nothing but a great effort of community planning and persistent community co-operation can hope to solve this baffling problem. Let us approach the consideration more definitely of the right to work, and see what is involved in this claim and its obligations.

First, the right to work springs from the fact that the individual cannot have a satisfying life unless he has an independence which comes from his own efforts and not from the bounty of others. Work is a satisfaction, because it is the exercise of an energy which is in the individual and which can only be satisfied by work. It exercises the faculties of the individual, and provides the natural means by which he is able to support himself and those who depend upon him. It is, therefore, a good in itself for the individual, while it is at the same time contributing to the enrichment of the community. The satisfaction of the individual depends upon this conscious or sub-conscious feeling that by his work he is helping himself and also others. It is this privilege of and right to work which is the healthy desire of men, and which society must seek to satisfy if it is to merit the title of a good society. It is a perfectly natural and sincere demand of the great majority that what they want is not relief or even insurance, but work. However difficult may be the problem of making real this right and of securing work to all who are willing to work, if we can get the resolve in ourselves and in our fellow-members of society that we must so plan life as to make this right real for ourselves and others, we have made a step forward. To-day we see an all-powerful State which directs, like an army, the battalions of the workers into the different fields of community service, and which controls the production of society and distributes the product among the members. That is the ideal which the Union of Socialist Soviet Republics is endeavouring to realise, and it has a great lesson for society. What we have to ask is whether there is not a better way of achieving this end, and whether we cannot, by the combination of State and voluntary effort, make real the right to work at a lesser sacrifice of individual initiative and individual choice than the Communist system requires.

In this great and difficult undertaking there are two aspects which can be distinguished. First there is the direction and planning of work, by individuals and groups, with or without State assistance. This effort is based on the maintenance of private enterprise and private property. If we believe that there is a quality in private property which not only enriches the wealth of the community more fully than publicly controlled and owned enterprise, but also fosters the exercise of social virtues, and gives to society a spontaneity and variety, and a richness which it would otherwise lack, then we must see to it that the institution of private property is made as good as it can be. Aristotle long ago answered an argument of Plato in a way which has seemed, to many, convincing ; and, less than a century ago, Mill wrote that the institution of private property has never yet received a fair trial. Men, he said, have made private property of things which should not be private property and they have had property without conditions when it should have been conditioned. If, therefore, we wish to leave to the individual the opportunities of enterprise and the choice of employment, rather than to make a society which moves like an army under orders from above, we must create conditions and rules which control to better social purpose the institution of private property and the system of private enterprise which is built upon it.

But the problem of unemployment is so deep, so difficult and so slow of solution that the available work must be better distributed. To this end there is needed the co-operation, above all, of organised labour. It is a delicate and difficult subject. Organised labour, by the reduction in the number of hours, has been able to provide for a better distribution of work. The fact of international competition makes this problem, as we have recently seen, one of great difficulty. But every effort must be made by the regulation of hours to distribute work throughout the community rather than to have two great divisions—those who have and those who have not work. It is a sacrifice, but also an insurance on the part of the worker, and it should be possible so to evolve a system as will have in it the elasticity enabling it to extend and contract the hours of work in response to the contraction or expansion of demand. The Government cannot do this except with the co-operation of organised labour; but behind these two powers in the State must be the supporting and directing force of a public opinion which is determined to make real for all the right to work.

There is, however, a second aspect to the problem. When private enterprise fails, public action must step in. We are getting a new vision of a well-organised community. The State, central and local, as the great architect of the Community must think out what work there is in the service of the Community which can be carried out when private enterprise fails. We are all deeply conscious of the fact that there are great needs of the community which remain unsatisfied, work upon housing, lighting, draining, and the better equipment of the community in village and town in a wide variety of ways. Unemployment is not only a great individual but also a great social loss. It is not merely the work given but the satisfaction achieved in building up the better equipment of the community, which can result from good planning of public work against unemployment. In this, not only the State but a great company of voluntary associations, which exist not for private profit but for the advancement of public well-being, can play their part in providing work. We have as yet only touched the fringes of this problem ; but if there is the will to make real the right to work, we can create a far happier and richer community than we have to-day. And, in thinking of this, let us seek to organise to the full extent the resources which contribute to the independence of the individual home. The movement for settlement on the land as the sole or main means of subsistence is strictly limited. But there is an almost inexhaustible reserve of social economic value in the land. We can equip the home with its garden or allotment which provides the means of giving work in times of shorter hours, of supplementing the family resources in ways which contribute to the health and amenity of life, and also of providing satisfaction for leisure with that rich variety which nature alone can supply. In the same way, the establishment of village and town workshops, where, by co-operation, tools and materials can be economically supplied, makes possible the use of spare hours, or of leisure, in occupations that may assist the work of the allotment or the comfort of the home. Every step in mobilising our resources in this way is calling out constructive citizenship.

Leisure

The second great question is the use of leisure. This subject has been treated elsewhere in this volume, but it may be permitted to revert briefly to the subject in connection with our present approach to the Community problem. The end of war is peace, and the end of work is leisure. A good Community will be judged in no small degree by the use which it makes of leisure. If much work must be, by the nature of our industrial system, mechanical and of a routine character, it is to the use of leisure that we must look for the relief which comes from monotony of repetition and for the fuller development of the faculties.

Leisure is the sphere in which the individual has his liberty; and the right use of leisure must depend upon the will of the individual so to use it. But a great deal can be done by the State, and by other associations in the Community, to assist the individual in the enjoyment and profitable use of leisure hours. The experience of the past year has revealed all over the country, in town and village alike, how valuable leadership is in the use of leisure, and how much organised community self-help can do towards stimulating a much more active and profitable use of leisure. Man is a sociable being, and if there are facilities available in allotments, in village workshops, in study groups, in physical training and organised games, the opportunities so provided stimulate the spirit of self-help ; and out of the free efforts of self-constituted and self-governing groups, there comes a variety of recreation and opportunity for self-improvement which is impossible where no steps have been taken to develop this side of community life. We must not spoil the quality of leisure by over organisation. One of the most precious things in calling out individuality is the cultivation of the capacity for being alone. *Nunquam minus solus quam cum solus.* In the cultivation of the habit of meditation lies the secret of the development of the richest personality. Our modern life is so full of distractions and so highly organised that there is a very real danger that we miss the deepest cultural and spiritual exercises which can only come from seeing and reading and reflecting and doing by ourselves. We need both sides of life, our own personal communion and our communion with our fellows.

But there is another consideration to keep in view. The old learning might be narrow, but it had often a sense of values which is in danger of being lost in our modern education. There is so much that is good that we may lose sight of the better and the best. The work of selection and guidance is one of the great services which is to be performed by our teachers and thinkers. We do not wish the strict censorship which a Plato would impose upon his ideal community, but we need more and more the service of those who are thinking about, and expounding for the consideration of their fellows, the idea of values. There is so rich a field both in the study of nature, which can appeal to the scientific and to the æsthetic instincts of men, and in literature, music, and art. And there are other riches that can become more and more the heritage of all. The opportunities for physical recreation and enjoyment, with the safeguarding of our open spaces and the provision of playing fields, and the facilities for travel make possible a share in the good things of life which can far outweigh the dangers to personality that result from the mechanisation of industry. Yet, in all this potential wealth, there is a new significance in the warning, " What doth it profit a man if he gain the whole world and lose his own soul ? " The unexamined life is not life. The aim of leisure must be, above all, to help the individual to the clearer sense of his duties, and to an appreciation of the mystery and reverence without which life cannot give us the best of its riches. It is towards this development of the free community that we have to strive, and we know that the road cannot be found if there is not the freedom of adventure. The State itself can create a larger freedom ; that is the lesson which we are finding from the study of the State in relation to the many voluntary associations, economic, social, cultural, which have come up in answer to our common human needs. It is because our Western, and, above all, our Anglo-Saxon, society has developed this tradition of freedom—but a freedom which is under the rule of law, and it is because it calls out the spirit of constructive citizenship, that we must seek to understand it more fully and make it understood amongst our fellows as something far richer and better than any system of life which is imposed upon us from above, and which denies to the individual his freedom of thought, of association, and of worship.

5. THE WORLD OF INTERNATIONAL AFFAIRS:

A. *CHRISTIANITY AND THE LEAGUE OF NATIONS*

By LORD DICKINSON, P.C.

IT IS WELL that Christians should take part in discussing the crisis; for it is evident that from whatever point of view one approaches this subject one arrives at the conclusion that, to a very great degree, the present chaos in politics, finance, industry, and general social conditions all over the world may be traced to the fact that Christianity has not yet acquired the power over the world which it is capable of exerting.

Christ's teaching is the surest guide not only in spiritual matters, but in everything that concerns mankind; and if it has not operated in the business life of nations, it is not by reason of any deficiency on its part but because the so-called Christian nations do not put it into practice.

The crisis has been described by other writers. They have shown how our political institutions have been disorganised, how our systems of international finance and commerce have become unworkable, and how the social requirements of vast aggregations of men and women have strained the resources of government to breaking-point. All these facts are beyond dispute, and the questions which remain are, firstly, To what are these evils due? and secondly, By what means can they be removed?

The main cause, in my opinion, is the world war. It is true there have been other processes going on which, sooner or later, would have disturbed the ordered course of events. We have seen the rapid supersession of men by machinery, the shortage of gold, and the increase in the productivity of the soil; but none of these of itself would have knocked the world off its balance. The real cause of our present trouble is the war, and men must be brought to recognise this ; otherwise they will repeat the folly of 1914 with results still more disastrous than those we are experiencing. It was the war that threw away millions of useful working lives, that destroyed vast quantities of accumulated wealth, wrecked economic systems, left nations involved in debt from which there seems to be no escape, and divided up the world into watertight compartments where each nation lives in fear of its neighbours and strives to get the better of them. It was the war that poisoned international relations, leaving the world under a dense cloud of mutual distrust and suspicion.

Of all these evil legacies the last was the worst ; for the prosperity of the modern world depends upon men's faith in one another. The marvellous growth in our international trade could not have come about were it not for our elaborate machinery of credit. Commerce cannot thrive except on confidence, nor can prosperity prevail except in peace.

Men might have learned this lesson out of history, since a like knowledge was to be gained after the Napoleonic Wars. But just as those events have been forgotten, so will these be very soon, and history will repeat itself, unless we devote our energy at once to rooting out the prime cause of our trouble, namely war and the fear of war.

In doing this we ought to be greatly assisted by our present experiences ; for the sufferings of to-day, which are mainly felt in Christian countries, are the lessons of the war. May it not be that God sends them in order to make Christians understand that their first duty is to rid the world of war ?

THE LEAGUE OF NATIONS

Some progress in this direction has been made ; but, unfortunately, not enough to restore confidence or indeed to counteract the tendency of public opinion to regard the return of war, some day or other, as being inevitable. The institution of the League of Nations in 1920 struck the imagination and sent forth a bright ray of hope throughout the world. That ray, however, has become dimmed by the fact that despite fourteen years of work the League has not yet constructed any permanent bulwark against war. Although delegates from all nations have met regularly at Geneva this has not made the peoples of the world more friendly to one another. Individual statesmen have, indeed, learned to know one another, and this is a real step forward on the road to international understanding ; but this very fact has given rise to suspicion amongst their own people at home, and we have often seen the deliberations at Geneva followed by violent criticism and dangerous repercussions in one country or another which have worsened international relationships rather than improved them.

All this arises from lack of confidence amongst the nations—a lack of confidence in each other, a lack of confidence on the part of the public in the League, and, conversely, on the part of the League in the public. So long as this continues it is impossible to make any progress towards the reconciliation of Europe. We must discover a way whereby to lead public opinion back to the position it occupied in 1919 when there was a universal desire for co-operation in lieu of competition. We must re-invoke the spirit which made the creation of a League of Nations possible and inspired the statesmen who signed the Covenant of the League.

THE SPIRIT OF THE COVENANT

In order to remind ourselves of what that spirit was, I will quote the preamble to the Covenant. It runs as follows :

" The High Contracting Parties, in order to promote international co-operation and to achieve international peace and security
   by the acceptance of obligations not to resort to war,
   by the prescription of open, just and honourable relations between nations,

by the firm establishment of the understandings of
international law as the actual rule of conduct among
governments, and

by the maintenance of justice and scrupulous respect
for all treaty obligations in the dealings of organised
peoples with one another,

Agree to this Covenant of the League of Nations."

The twenty-six articles that follow on this declaration
of purpose provided a good workable machine whereby the
nations, if they had been earnestly desirous to co-operate,
and willing to incur some sacrifice of their own national
interests, could, by now, have elaborated effective methods
of " achieving international peace and security." Unfortunately, one obstacle after another proved too great for them,
and gradually the spirit which prompted the Covenant
lost its hold upon the people.

SHORTCOMINGS OF THE LEAGUE : DISARMAMENT

Let me cite two instances in support of this contention.
By Article VIII. of the Covenant there was laid upon the
League an obligation to bring about a reduction in the
national armaments, and also to advise how the evil
effects attendant upon the manufacture by private enterprise of implements of war could be prevented. When the
Allied statesmen at Versailles imposed disarmament upon
Germany and the other defeated foes, M. Clémenceau
informed them that the reduction of all other national
armaments was to be " one of the first duties of the League."
Fourteen years have elapsed since that declaration and yet
no decision has been reached on either of these questions.
Germany is still in a position of inferiority ; more money
is being spent by the other nations upon armaments than
before the war, and private firms are still carrying on the
trade in munitions unchecked by any kind of international
control.

It is true that the Council of the League has been confronted by difficulties, but by none that might not have

been surmounted, had there been sufficient courage on the part of the Powers to insist upon settling this question. But for a long time they were afraid to recognise the claim of the defeated States to be restored to a position of equality with themselves. They have now accepted this principle ; but the acceptance is ten years too late. In the meantime, smarting under a sense of injustice, the German people have grown more and more resentful. Had the principle of ultimate equality in respect of armaments been acknowledged (as it should have been) when Germany entered the League of Nations, we should never have witnessed the revival of German militarism which now constitutes so great a danger to the peace of Europe.

MINORITIES

A similar lesson may be drawn from the experiences of the League in relation to the minorities. The treaties signed in Paris in 1919 imposed upon the League its first real administrative duty. It was to ensure that various rights and privileges promised to racial and religious minorities in certain countries should be enjoyed by them. The Powers at Versailles made the League the " guarantor " of these rights, and, when the League accepted this responsibility, it declared that it would not only investigate individual complaints of a breach of the treaties, but also would " ascertain that the provisions of the treaties for the protection of minorities are always observed." The Council, however, has never carried out the latter part of its duties, notwithstanding the widespread dissatisfaction which constitutes a continuing menace to the peace of Europe. This inaction on the part of the League is due to the objection raised by the States affected by the treaties to any procedure which might give to the Council a power to interfere in their local affairs whilst other States are exempt from such liability. On grounds of equity it is difficult to resist this contention ; but, unfortunately, the exempted States include the Great Powers, and these refuse to accept restrictions which they have not hesitated to impose upon their neighbours.

So long as this feeling prevails, the present unequal arrangement will remain and the minorities will continue to suffer. Seeing that there are some thirty millions in Europe subjected to the rule of foreign races, it is certain that, if there were to arise any general disturbance, these people would seize the opportunity of freeing themselves from a yoke which has become more and more galling through the reluctance of the League to exercise in full its powers under the treaties.

A STUPENDOUS PROBLEM

And it is not only in relation to these subjects that the reluctance of the League to grapple with urgent international problems has stood in the way of re-establishing normal relationships. There are many sore places in the great body of the human society which have required attention. There was the question of the Far East, where intervention by the League five years ago would probably have warded off the present conflict between China and Japan. There are the questions of the Polish Corridor and of the frontiers of Hungary, Italy, and other countries, where the settlement of 1919 has proved to have been impolitic and unjust. There are the tariff walls erected for the purpose of destroying a neighbour's trade. There are questions relating to the revision of treaties, the adjustment of international disputes, the methods whereby decrees of an international authority may be executed. In short, all the problems that each nation has slowly solved for the conduct of its own affairs are now thrown upon the chessboard of the world where the pieces are not men, but vast aggregations of men whose will it is far less easy to curb, and whose desire it is vastly more difficult to ascertain than are those of the individuals that make up a nation.

Here we have a stupendous problem. How shall we attack it ? Attack it we must ; for, if we fear to do so, civilised society will go under. Along what course shall we steer, so as to reach an ordered, righteous, and effective system of world administration ? Surely along the lines that Jesus

Christ has indicated : those of love, justice, self-sacrifice, readiness on the part of all to put the common good before everything else. It may be extraordinarily difficult to apply these principles over so wide a field of conflicting interests, beliefs, and customs ; but there are none other which meet our requirements. Let us therefore keep them firmly in mind when considering how to erect our new edifice of international co-operation.

A WORLD PARLIAMENT

Amongst plans for reform there is first that for establishing one world-state, legislated for and governed by one Parliament—a " Parliament of man." This may look well in poetry but to the practical politician the prospect of setting up a single Government for the whole world is not attractive. There are many almost insuperable difficulties that present themselves. There are the questions : How shall such a body be constituted so that it will represent, fairly, two thousand millions of people ? What powers shall it possess ? Shall its jurisdiction extend into every corner of the globe ? Shall it regulate the life of every human being ? These questions must be seriously answered before anyone can adopt as a policy for the new world the institution of a single supreme Government. The idea, I think, is not only impossible of realisation, but, even if it were possible, would not be desirable. I see no advantage in forcing either men or nations, creeds or languages into one mould. God has made them different, has given them different tongues, colours, and characters. The remedy is not to be found in welding the nations into one soulless mass, but so to shape the relations between them that they may discover of themselves the road whereon they may travel together in friendship and security. This is what Christianity is able, and indeed is specially fitted, to accomplish. It has been doing this, to some extent, within the British Empire. Our Commonwealth of Nations could not have grown to its present state had not its course been guided by Christian men and women. In addition to the religious influence exercised by generations of missionaries, both in their special sphere and in their semi-political activities, we may point to many a great British administrator who has shown what Christian character and example can do in reconciling men who, but for that influence, would still be enemies. There is no rigid bond that binds together the British Empire ; nothing but a common interest and a family feeling. It should not be impossible to develop a similar bond of union for the world. When this is accomplished, we shall possess a far more effective organisation for peaceful co-operation than would result from the creation of one unmanageable authority bearing sway over the entire globe.

A "UNITED STATES OF EUROPE"

Another proposal that is attracting attention is one for a " United States of Europe." Apart from the fact that neither the United States of America nor the United Republics of Soviet Russia has yet proved to be a perfect instrument of popular government there is the further question whether by creating a few big groups of nations one will advance the cause of peace ? It is not improbable that if we were to organise great units of government for Europe, Asia, America, etc., we should find that the rivalries between these groups would lead to war. The League of Nations is based upon the conception of the unity of mankind, and it is this we must strive after. Even in its present truncated condition, with North America and Russia outside, it is the richer for having amongst its members the growing Republics in South America and the ancient States of Asia. I believe that to create the " United States of Europe " would be a step backwards on the road towards the Brotherhood of Man.

INTERNATIONAL POLICE FORCE

A third proposal, equally objectionable in my opinion, is to make the League of Nations a policeman. Peace is to be enforced by means of armies on land, sea, and air, directed from Geneva and constituted of men who will be sworn to execute the behests of the League. By these means it is thought that the League will be able to compel compliance with the Covenant, and will thereby become more effective as a guardian of the peace.

Even if we admit that the use of force to defend the victim of aggression, or to assert the demands of justice, is not contrary to Christian doctrine, it is doubtful whether Christians could support a League which, whilst out-lawing war, would, nevertheless, be busying itself constantly with preparing for war, training men to kill each other, and inventing engines capable, by their destructiveness, of terrorising the whole world.

Some people would put up with these objections in the belief that the influence of the League for peace would be enhanced. I doubt if this belief is well-founded. In our own country we purposely abstain from placing lethal weapons in the hands of our police, and their influence is all the greater for this reason. It will be the same with the League. Under the present arrangement, the Powers which constitute the League have set it up as a means whereby their joint influence may be used to prevent war and ensure justice, and it lies with them to make it capable of fulfilling this purpose. If they are not prepared to place at its disposal their own forces when circumstances render this necessary they would probably also decline to allow an international army to operate. In either case the League would be broken up ; since, if loyalty to it and to each other fails, no armed force at Geneva, however well-disciplined and equipped, would be of any avail.

A REFORMED LEAGUE

We are, I believe, driven to the conclusion that whatever system of administration we have must be loosely knit together. It is both impolitic and impossible to weave a net within which all races shall be drawn together by a single string. Nations must remain free to move and to develop in accordance with their respective habits and mentalities.

This is the principle on which the League of Nations is constructed; and our policy should be to maintain the League and mould it into such form as will remove its defects and make it capable of meeting the increasing demands of the people for international progress.

In the first place the League must be completed so that it shall embrace all the nations of the world. Here we are met by the difficulty that neither the United States of America nor the Union of Soviet Republics has been willing to enter the League. This does not imply that they will not take part in any international body, and it is by no means impossible that before long we shall see a change of opinion in both these countries. The best thing that we can do is so to re-fashion our machinery that it may be more acceptable to them, when they realise that they must, in one way or another, find their way into the general international movement of the time. There are already signs that in America thinking people see the error that was made when their country rejected the great ideas of President Wilson.

RESPONSIBILITY OF ALL

But, secondly, even if it be impossible to include these two great nations in our League, we must go on with our process of reconstruction, making use of such materials as we have. There are fifty-seven States now in the League; and if they could ensure that these will act together when a crisis arises, the League will acquire an immense moral power even though it may not exercise physical force. In order to reach this position, it will be necessary that all members shall undertake to give a definite minimum of actual assistance to the League when called upon by the Assembly. Such an undertaking must be furnished by every member, so that when a sacrifice has to be made it shall be made by all. The smaller nations, in particular, must be brought in. It has been too readily assumed hitherto that the task of supporting the League would fall only upon the Great Powers. The lesser States are equally interested in peace, and must take their share in enforcing it.

For this purpose, each of them must be not only willing but ready to fulfil its duty, and to ensure this the Covenant shall be completed. This was attempted by the proposed convention, known as the " Geneva Protocol," which was abandoned chiefly because our Government refused its consent. The Protocol was merely a scheme of preparedness, and experience in relation to the Sino-Japanese conflict has shown that the world cannot afford to be without some arrangement of this kind. A well-thought-out plan of sanctions is indispensable, and it must be based upon common action by the entire League.

Thirdly, there must be a means of arriving at a decision by the Assembly. At present the rule requiring unanimity renders it impossible to test the opinion of the League. Even if a vote becomes inoperative by the refusal of certain States to accept it, it will have a great moral value. The world will know what the majority of the League thinks, and ways may be found to carry its decision into effect.

Fourthly, it must be made clear that it should be the constant duty of the League to concern itself with every question that threatens to disturb good understanding between nations. These are the words of Article X. of the Covenant ; but they have never been acted upon in time to be of service. Had the League proceeded under this article it might have prevented the conflict in Manchuria, have satisfied the minorities, and have brought about adjustments of frontiers without much injury to any State. The fault of the League has been that it has not felt strong enough to exercise its own powers. A definite mandate should be given to it to see that justice is done and injuries rectified before the situation becomes dangerous.

REVISION OF TREATIES AND INTERNATIONAL JUSTICE

Fifthly, this entails some better facilities for the revision of treaties. I mention this word with some fear seeing that it always gives rise to heated discussion. There are some men who assert that the peace treaties are sacrosanct and no letter in them can be changed ; whilst there are others

Qc

who demand that the entire post-war settlement be over-hauled. Both sides are wrong, and it needs only cool heads and common sense to reach a reasonable solution. No treaty can be regarded as everlasting. Nothing in this world is everlasting. All that God has made he changes from time to time. Human society demands a continuous process of adjustment which in civilised communities is effected through their Parliamentary or other system of legislation. For the adjustment of international affairs there is, as yet, no such system except by the cumbrous method of conventions. The organs of the League are well qualified to perform this function. All they need is authority to undertake this task.

Sixthly, it will be necessary to reconsider the present system of international jurisprudence. The institution of the Permanent Court of International Justice at The Hague has proved to be a long step forward in the march of civilisation. It has already justified its existence by a series of fine decisions and the settlement of many international disputes. It is gradually accustoming the world to accept peaceful adjudication in lieu of war. The late M. Briand once said that, on hearing that France had lost her case before the Permanent Court, he felt more proud of his country than he would have been had she won it upon a field of battle.

But this view is by no means universally accepted, and much work needs to be done before nationalistic sentiment will bow to an adverse decision by a foreign court; and in this direction especially that Christians can render assistance, since their principles involve submission to the dictates of justice.

It will also be necessary to extend the existing system so as to embrace, if possible, disputes that are not strictly juridic in character. Methods of compulsory arbitration will have to be devised whereby the right and wrong in every difference that may arise between the nations shall be ascertained and adjudicated upon. When this has been accomplished, the world will find itself in a new position, a position in which war will be excluded by becoming unnecessary ; and the peoples will recover confidence and regain prosperity.

THE MOTIVE POWER

All these reforms are necessary if we are to have any effective instrument of international co-operation ; but however perfect the machinery we set up may be, it will be useless unless we apply to it the right motive power. Where shall we find this so surely as in the Christian religion ? Notwithstanding the many shortcomings of those who have professed, it there is no creed in the world so constructive in nature, or so well suited to the needs of the human race, as is that which Jesus Christ has offered to men for their salvation. Time after time in history its power has proved to be irresistible ; time after time its adherents have failed to utilise it. We have now an opportunity to bring it to a triumphant issue, since it furnishes a means—I believe, the only means—whereby the political machinery of the League can become effective and nations can labour together for the welfare of mankind. This is a goal that is worth striving for, and one which it is not impossible to attain if we advance with determination and with faith.

5. THE WORLD OF INTERNATIONAL AFFAIRS:

B. *THE CRISIS AND THE EAST*

By Professor J. B. RAJU

1. WHAT IS THE EAST?

Geographically considered, East and West are purely relative terms, having a varying application in different localities. For example, what are known as the " Far Eastern " islands of Japan are themselves situated to the west of the United States ; while the American continent in its turn lies farther east of Asia. Similarly, the various countries that lie in what is known as the " Near East," like Turkey, Iraq, Arabia, and Persia, are all situated considerably west of India and China. Though there be no hard and fast line of geographical demarcation between East and West, yet such a distinction has actually come to be made historically within the compass of the Ancient World, which was not aware of the existence of a New World beyond the seas ; and this distinction has survived to our own day in spite of all the interchange that has taken place between the two throughout the ages.

Long before the dawn of history, great emigrations had already taken place from the heart of Asia into various parts of what we now know as Europe and Northern Africa ; and be it remembered that, in spite of the separation, differentiation, and endless intermixture with other stocks that has subsequently taken place, there survives in the background, to this very day, a substantial racial identity between the several nations of modern Europe on the one hand and the vast masses of people that still dwell in Asia and Northern Africa. In the dim beginnings of historical times we find the enterprising activities of Phœnician mariners and merchants linking in fruitful exchange of commodities distant parts of Asia and Africa with the coasts of Europe ; and throughout later historical times there has been a more or less constant interchange of ideas, practices, commodities, and peoples between these various regions. But until the advent of the modern era, with the notable exception of the great Hellenistic and later Roman impacts upon Asia and Africa, the East has generally been the aggressor and on the whole exercised a more potent influence for good and evil upon the life and destiny of the West than the other way about. Oriental religious and secular conceptions and influences from Egypt and Carthage in Northern Africa and from several parts of Asia like Asia Minor, Mesopotamia, Arabia, Persia, India, and distant China, have penetrated westwards into Europe throughout the centuries and profoundly affected the trend of European thought and life. Christianity itself, which has taken root as the universal religion of Europe, is of Asiatic origin, and remains as an enduring witness of the triumph of Asia over Europe. Towards the latter part of the Middle Ages, in Europe, the Arabs ruling over Spain, the Turks conquering Hungary, and the Mongolian hordes pouring into Russia, were all but the vanguard of a triumphant East overflowing into the West. The influence of Arabic learning was one of the potent factors in producing the European Renaissance and ushering in the modern era in the Western world.

Since then the tables have been turned, and Europe has wakened into life and activity, while the ancient countries of Asia and Africa sank into sleep and remained dormant for centuries. At the beginning of the nineteenth century the impact of modern European influences wakened the ancient peoples of the East from their slumber. Towards the latter half of that century it seemed as if the whole world, including Africa and Asia, would be divided up and absorbed under the dominion of different European nations ; and that Western ideas, methods, and institutions, economic, social, political, and religious, would overwhelm all countries and peoples. By the end of that century, Europe appeared as not merely the conqueror, but the teacher of the whole world. The phenomenal success and prosperity of European nations fired the imagination of Oriental peoples. At first the impact and influence of modern Europe was confined to a few pioneer individuals and progressive people in the prominent maritime regions of Asia and Africa. But it has rapidly spread in ever-widening circles to the remotest inlying regions of those continents, until now no part of Asia or Africa remains unaffected by European ideas and methods, customs and manners, ideals and activities in religion, government, commerce, and industry. The whole East is pulsating with new life, and there is a growing desire and effort on the part of its many peoples both to imitate and out-rival the successful nations of the Western world.

So, for present purposes, we may accept the historic distinction between the older countries of Asia and Africa on the one hand and the modern countries of western Europe, with their still more recent numerous off-shoots in American soil and elsewhere. Herein " the East " must be understood to comprehend the continents of Asia and Africa, in which more than two-thirds of the entire human race dwell. By this is meant not so much a huge, more or less contiguous geographical area as the many different racial groups inhabiting that area, the several more or less distinctive cultural types that have come into being therein, ranging from the primitive negroid tribes of tropical Africa right up to the more advanced Semitic, Aryan, or Indo-Iranian and Mongolian peoples of Asia, who are all now being stirred to their very depths by powerful modern Western influences. In spite of the fact that these many peoples are in different stages of development, and differ from one another in endless ways, they may truly be said to be all alike in so far as their life and institutions are still authoritarian, i.e. externally governed rather than self-determined. Consequently they lack freedom, spontaneity, initiative, enterprise, and control over their environment, and are still primitive and mediæval in outlook as the peoples of Europe were centuries ago.

II. THE CRISIS AND ITS EFFECTS UPON THE EAST

During the last three decades more phenomenal changes have taken place than in the whole span of the preceding three thousand years. We are apt to think that the Great War, the outstanding event of recent times, is the root cause of this subsequent upheaval and confusion. But it would be untrue to think that the present crisis is simply the aftermath of the Great War. The war has certainly accelerated and accentuated changes that were already germinating, but it did not create them. As a matter of fact, the Great War was itself the result of pre-war conditions and tendencies, and has in its turn given rise to other and far-reaching consequences which are discussed in other chapters of this book. The enormous insight into the workings of nature that has been gained in recent times, and the tremendous power and control in harnessing and utilising natural resources that such insight has given man, have roused the expectation of endless possibilities and produced unbounded confidence in human nature. The narrow domestic limits within which men and nations were circumscribed throughout past ages have suddenly disappeared, and distance is annihilated by the use of steam, electricity, motor-transport, aircraft, and the wireless in our day. The demarcation line of countries have shrunk to the dimensions of counties in the Middle Ages.

The issues involved in scientific advance, and the consequent invention and perfection of efficient mechanical appliances, are not merely economic and political, but profoundly cultural and moral. Already radical changes in the life and habits of many lands, in the mutual relations of different classes of people living within the same territory and of various countries to one another, have come to pass. Organised production, that has developed to huge proportions in the industrialised countries of western Europe and America, is dependent not only upon the nature and extent of the demand on the part of consumers, upon the vast investments of capital, and upon the supply of skilled labour, but also upon raw materials made available for modern industry by the toil of primitive peoples living in backward countries, more especially those situated in the tropical regions of the world. The merchant ships and looms of Lancashire await the harvest of humble tillers of the soil in far-off sun-baked lands. The very complexity of organisation involved in modern industrial advance has raised in an acute form the fundamental issue of what is not merely economically profitable or politically expedient, but morally right in the relation between producer and consumer, supply and demand, capital and labour.

Nations which were till now mere consumers or suppliers of raw materials are themselves rapidly becoming industrialised, and the situation becomes aggravated as rivalry and competition increases. Different countries resort to various devices, such as boycott of foreign goods or tariff duties, in order to protect their own industries or to affect adversely those of their rivals. This is a fruitful source of friction not only between different States, but between producers and consumers within the same State. Besides, while industry and commerce have by the very nature and necessities of their development become international, and dependent on the activities and conditions of many peoples in many lands, sovereignty has remained rigidly national and confined within territorial limits. The high hopes raised by the establishment of the League of Nations at the end of the Great War largely remain unfulfilled because, by the very nature of its constitution, the League is only an assembly of independent States each of whom is jealous of its own sovereignty, while co-operation between different States across frontiers has become imperative. What power can break this vicious circle ?

It is clear that what this generation needs is not increase of material resources or knowledge and skill, but the motive and the will to utilise them not selfishly for the profit of some, but unselfishly for the good of all : how is this to be achieved ? The whole temper and trend of this generation is to hope for this to be brought about by the gradual growth of a spirit of enlightened self-interest among people which will teach them to realise that the interests of each, can be best realised only in harmony with those of all others. This is the essence of the modern gospel of secularism, as in Soviet Russia. The same secularist spirit now animates the activities of others in all lands even though they may not consciously repudiate religious sanctions. It is the expression of unbounded confidence in human nature to effect its own reformation and ultimately its salvation. This is in radical opposition to the fundamental teaching of religion in general, and more especially of Christianity. The opposite point of view stressed by religion is that human nature is utterly incapable of achieving its own moral reformation and salvation without supernatural aid. Unless there is the vision of God and eternity, there is no adequate motive for unselfish conduct, and no reason why people should not pursue their own immediate interests ruthlessly, indifferent to what it may cost others. Organised religion is following its traditional course without waking up to meet the urgent need of this generation for a new vision of God and eternity which will transform human motive and regenerate the world. Such is the real need that the crisis has revealed ; and how is this to be met ?

Before coming to grips with this fundamental question, let us briefly take a survey of the effects of modern Western influences upon the life and outlook of the ancient peoples of the East. Originally it was the desire for wealth that impelled European nations to exploration and adventure in foreign lands ; and European merchants first went to the markets of the East in quest of rarities like porcelain, tea, muslin, ivory, and spices. With the advent of machinery and the dawn of the Industrial Revolution in the Western world, the character of Western overseas trade changed and European merchants began to seek in Eastern lands not only valuable raw materials for their home industries, but also new markets for the sale of their cheap machine-made goods and industrial products among the vast populations of Asia and Africa. The introduction of modern machinery and large-scale production has not only created acute unemployment in the industrialised lands, but it has thrown out of work large numbers of hereditary craftsmen in non-industrialised countries who were unable to compete with machine-made goods. Besides, the use of machinery and modern facilities for transport, and the higher standards of life that go with it, could not long remain a European monopoly ; and they are coming to be adopted in Asiatic and African lands as well. Ancient Oriental economic systems are rapidly crumbling to pieces everywhere before the advent of modern industrialisation and wholesale production. The old aristocracy of hereditary landlords, warriors, and priests is rapidly being displaced by a new generation of prosperous merchants, lawyers, bankers, and schoolmasters, who are everywhere the champions and leaders of the new nationalist movements in Africa and Asia. What happened during the Renaissance in the fifteenth-century Europe, and later during the Industrial Revolution in the nineteenth century, is now happening simultaneously all over the East, liberating people everywhere from ancient prejudices and generating new hopes and ambitions. The underlying motives in the new life stirring among non-European peoples are the same everywhere : namely, rivalry to Europe, the desire to beat Europe back with its own weapons, and to make Oriental lands self-contained and independent of European capital, industry, merchandise, and control in any shape or form, ruthlessly indifferent to what the ultimate effects of this will be not only to Europe, but to themselves and the world at large.

III. THE REACTION OF THE EAST TO THE CRISIS

The response to European influence has naturally been different in the case of those Oriental peoples who did not possess a highly developed civilisation and culture of their own and those who did. So we must distinguish between the more primitive and more advanced countries of Africa and Asia in estimating the response to modern influences. The lands inhabited by primitive people have largely come under the control and dominion of one or other European Power—Spain, Portugal, Holland, Belgium, Germany, France, Russia, and Great Britain. Of all these, British interests and commitments in Asia and Africa are the largest, and British influence has been greater than that of any other Western Power. Great Britain, more than any other European Power, introduced its ideas and ideals of education, nationalism, and democracy into all her overseas possessions. The best example of its effects upon primitive people is provided by British West and South Africa, where a numerous class of negroes has entirely assimilated British manners, customs, speech, education, religion, and mode of life, and is aspiring to the right of political freedom and national self-determination. Similar changes have taken place under the influence of France in the Levant and Indo-China, and of Holland in the Dutch East Indies. But European influence is not confined to territories actually under European dominion. On the contrary, it has been even greater in entirely independent Oriental countries like Japan in the Far East, and Turkey in the Near East. Perhaps their geographical position at the two extremes of the Oriental world, and their lack of any ancient and highly developed traditions of their own, may have contributed to the extreme Westernisation of these two countries. A similar process to a lesser degree is taking place in the independent sovereign States of Arabia, Iraq, Persia, and Afghanistan.

But in China and India there are old and highly developed civilisations which have prevented rapid Westernisation. British influence in India has been the largest and most potent of all European influences, and has given rise not only to economic changes, but to social and political aspirations and to cultural and religious revivals. Tsarist Russia never succeeded in producing similar cultural results in its Asiatic possessions, perhaps because it itself savoured too much of an Oriental despotism to evoke any far-reaching changes. But with the advent of the Russian Revolution in 1917, the influence of the Soviet Republics introduced a new and seriously disturbing factor into the life of Asiatic peoples and their relationship to European nations. Though Soviet policy in Asia as in Europe has been throughout naturally determined by its own needs, interests and desire for expansion, yet it has been put forward in theory and carried out in practice in the name of an international ideal which recognises no barriers of race or creed whatsoever. But the secularist aim and economic ideals of the Soviet have not found favour with the ancient peoples of the East and are not making any serious progress. This provides an opportunity especially for a Christian Power like Great Britain to demonstrate in her dealings with these peoples the intrinsic superiority of genuinely Christian principles to the merely secularist policy of enlightened self-interest pursued by the Soviet.

To sum up, European influences, operating on the several peoples of the Eastern world, have produced the paradoxical result of a revolt against the West simultaneously with an attempt to imitate and assimilate Western methods and achievements. In the midst of this dual process that is taking place in varying degrees in different parts of Asia and Africa, the present crisis, with all its heart-searchings, perplexities, and anxieties, has come as a blessing in disguise to East and West alike. It has made the West self-conscious and critical of its own life and methods, and has led it to probe into its presuppositions and implications as never before. The nations of the East which have till now been under the glamour of the success and prosperity of the West, seeking to follow her example and copy her methods, will now cry a halt in their blind race for Westernisation and begin to scrutinise and evaluate everything for what it is intrinsically worth. In East and West alike it is increasingly coming to be realised that scientific discoveries, mechanical inventions, modern conveniences, social upheavals, and democratic institutions have none of them proved to be an unmixed good. Both increased knowledge and increased power have proved a double-edged sword in the hand of man, that can be wielded for good as well as evil. They are not ends in themselves, but only the expressions and instruments of

the human spirit ; and what we need is not more knowledge or greater organisation and control, but a fundamental change of spirit, a new sense of values, with a firm
hold on realities. If earthly life is the sum and substance of
human existence, if there be no God and no eternity, then
indeed it is hopeless ever to effect any thoroughgoing reformation of human nature in any sense adequate to the
measure of our necessities, and there is no way out of the
present chaos ; for there is no power on earth potent
enough to prevent the abuse of increased knowledge and
power for self-interest and destructive purposes. On the
other hand, if we are not creatures of time but heirs of immortality, predestined to be shaped into the very image
of the Divine Perfection, then it will radically transform all
our motives and values. In short, the task confronting our
generation is religious in the broadest sense of the term, and
involves the revaluation of all hitherto accepted values
and the achievement of a fresh orientation of the world
and human destiny.

IV. THE MEANING AND MISSION OF CHRISTIANITY

In the gigantic task of reconstruction that confronts this
generation, the several peoples of the Eastern world, each
with their distinctive heritage and specific endowments,
will make their contribution, along with the nations of the
West, to the commonwealth of humanity. The modernisa-
tion of the Orient cannot mean the destruction of what is
intrinsically individual in Africans, Arabs, Persians, Hindus,
or Chinese. It will no more make them less of what they
really are, and are capable of becoming, than it has made
Englishmen, Frenchmen, or Germans to be less of what they
really are. After all, what is individual to men and nations
is not their backwardness or ignorance and impotency. As
they gain knowledge and power, it will not destroy or
conceal what they really are, their special aptitudes and
peculiar gifts, but clarify and sublimate them. That this is
really so is evident from the influence that these many
peoples are already beginning to exert on the trend of

modern development. Negro music and dances have already spread far and wide in the Western world, and their plastic art is coming to be appreciated. It is not easy to estimate as yet what contributions the negro race may make towards our knowledge of the world and of human nature and other future achievements. But it is incredible that their experience and special gifts should fail to enrich our insight into, and control over, things. If such be the case with backward African peoples, there is ground for far greater expectation from the ancient and cultured peoples of Asia. The chivalry of the sturdy Arab desert-dwellers, the art, poetry, and refinement of the Persians, the intellectual subtlety and contemplative gifts of the Hindus, and the immemorial patient heroism, stoic morals, and practical genius of the Chinese, as well as their distinctive artistic and cultural traditions, are all bound to enrich in as yet unsuspected ways the knowledge, powers, and artistic appreciation of the world culture that is yet to come into being.

Apart from this, there survive in the world of to-day four great religious systems—Hindu, Buddhist, Muslim and Christian—which embody the hopes, dreams, visions, experiences, and ultimate beliefs of countless generations of people. Their contents stand in urgent need of being evaluated not only with reference to one another, but with reference to the experience and the knowledge of our time and the elemental needs that the present crisis has revealed. Of these, Hinduism is a confused mass of beliefs, speculations, rituals, and mystical practices that have historically grown up in the religious experiences of Hindu India, and till now withstood the onslaught of many waves of foreign influence. Under the stress of modern conditions it has wakened with new-found missionary ardour, and aspires to cease to be a mere national cult and become a universal religion. Amidst all its conflicting beliefs and practices it has certain outstanding features that are not only of interest to the scientific student of comparative religion, but may prove of real value to the religious needs of the world of our day. The most distinctive feature of Hindu religion, shared in common by all its many rival sects, is its extreme and impressive emphasis on Divine Immanence, i.e. a vivid and all-pervasive consciousness of the indwelling omnipresence of the Deity in the phenomena of the material universe as well as the vicissitudes of human life. This is the fundamental religious heritage of Hindu India ; and it stands in vivid and startling contrast to the genius of Islam, which has laid firm hold of precisely the opposite truth of Divine Transcendence, i.e. a deep-rooted conviction that God is infinitely higher than the highest we know, and that nothing, not even the best in nature or human life, is good enough to be identified with the Divine Perfection. In opposition to this, the Hindu firmly holds that nothing, not even the meanest thing, can fail to reveal the ultimate reality in which it is rooted and has its being. This radical difference in point of view explains why it is so natural and easy for Hindu India to practise idolatry and to believe in endless incarnations of the Divine, while Islam has remained throughout fanatically iconoclastic and bitterly opposed to any idea of divine incarnation. The very uncompromising exaggerations of these two great historic faiths, which have got a firm hold of opposite sides of the ultimate truth, makes it appear as if there were no possibility or chance of their ever coming to a mutual understanding, and this lies at the root of the bitter age-long Hindu-Muslim conflicts in other spheres of life.

How then do the other two great historic faiths of Buddhism and Christianity stand in relation to this fundamental antithesis which reveals itself between the Hindu and the Muslim ? Buddhism, by the very accident of its historical origin as a protest against Brahminical sacerdotalism, turned away from all theological and metaphysical speculation and has confined itself to the practical task of finding a way of life, a code of conduct for mankind, and so has no contribution to make to this ultimate question. Christianity, on the other hand, reveals in its historic development a surprisingly balanced hold of both aspects of this sublime truth in its distinctive doctrine of the deity as a Trinity in Unity. There is nothing that the most extreme Muslim has stressed about Divine Transcendence which is not included in the Christian conception of God the Father, the First Person of the Trinity, the Creator and Fountain-head of all things, himself eternally distinct from, and transcending, all that he has willed into being. At the same time there is nothing that the most extreme Hindu has stressed regarding the opposite truth of Divine Immanence which does not find room in the Christian doctrine of God the Son, the Eternal Logos, foreshadowed in all creation in diverse ways and measures and in the fullness of time finally incarnated in the unique life and person of Jesus Christ. Besides these two, there is the Holy Spirit, distinct from, and yet indissolubly one and consubstantial with, the other two in the Unity of the Godhead. Such is the nature of the Divine as revealed through the life and message of Jesus Christ which Christian Europe has cherished as ultimate truth for nineteen centuries ; and it is seen to hold the key to the ultimate reconciling and superseding of both the antithetical Hindu and Muslim points of view. This is an invaluable contribution that Christian Europe can make to the religious future of the Hindu and Muslim worlds. On the other hand, though Christian Europe has laid firm hold of the truth of the Divine Being as a Trinity in Unity, yet it has largely tended to regard this as an unintelligible mystery baffling human comprehension. It is precisely here that the intimate study of the sharp antithesis between Hinduism and Islam will prove of value in rendering this sublime mystery intelligible.

Passing to the other great question of religious interest, namely the problem of human conduct and destiny, what do we find ? Hinduism and Buddhism alike have stressed impressively, in their well-known doctrines of Karma and rebirth, the great truth of the discipline of consequences for the purification and perfection of human life. No power in heaven or earth can break the chain of causation or interrupt the operation of the inexorable law of action and consequences ; and these not only survive after death, but persist before birth, determining the nature and trend of successive embodiments of individual beings till they attain enlightenment, and cease to be born, or die and become one with the All. In radical contrast and opposition to this, Islam, which has apprehended the Divine, not as " the All " but as " Higher than the Highest we know or can conceive of," has stressed the opposite truth of the omnipotence of divine grace in transforming human life and modifying the consequences of human actions in its impressive doctrine of the efficacy of divine forgiveness. Here also, surprisingly enough, the Christian doctrine of Atonement, stressing both elements of truth at once, holds the key to the ultimate reconciliation of the rival points of view of the Hindu and Buddhist world on the one hand and of the Islamic world on the other. Christian Europe, in keeping a firm hold of both aspects of this truth, has, at the same time, emphasised the burden and privilege of vicarious suffering and the corporate nature of human destiny as against the simple individualism of Hinduism, Buddhism, and Islam. Here also, while Christian Europe has firmly held to the truth of the doctrine of the Atonement, it has tended to regard it as an unintelligible mystery, baffling human comprehension. Once more the intensive study of the opposite elements stressed by the ancient faiths of Asia will throw a flood of new light in rendering the sublime mystery of the Atonement intelligible to the best thought of this and future generations.

In spite of the radical contrasts considered above, there is a common feature underlying all the diversities in doctrine and practice of Asiatic life, and that is a beautiful sense of other-worldliness, a deep-rooted conviction that this world of change and all it contains, including the age-long drama of successive generations of human beings, is insignificant, and counts for nothing as contrasted with the timeless self-contained reality of the Infinite. In striking contrast to this point of view, the key-note of European life is an intense belief in the reality of this world and the present life ; a deep-rooted conviction that, whatever other worlds there may be in the infinite scale of being, what we are supremely concerned with is our life here and now, and that what we each make of our opportunities will make the biggest difference to us, as well as to others besides us. Modern secularism is but an extreme development of this typically European belief in the reality of the actual – in vivid contrast to the characteristic Eastern view which holds that the actual visible world, with all its feverish activities and varied scheme of values, is but the unsubstantial shadow of an invisible world of changeless reality. This is the key to the contrast between the Oriental ideal of the contemplative life and the Western ideal of strenuous activity. Here again it is profoundly significant that Christianity has succeeded in keeping a firm hold of both these opposite truths which have been exaggerated separately by East and West in opposite directions to the point of error. There is room for both points of view within the Christian scheme, and the amazing thing is that they are held together without contradiction. To the Christian, as to those of other faiths, this world and the present life are but a prelude to other and more enduring life elsewhere, and yet our motives and actions here and now are held to be so intensely real as to count for time and eternity in settling our destiny. Once more this provides ground for holding that in the new interchange between East and West that is already dawning upon us, Christianity holds the key to a balanced inclusive view that would reconcile the conflicting claims of the here and hereafter of time and eternity embodied in the till now typically Western and Eastern points of view.

When all this is pointed out, it must not be forgotten that Christianity is neither a mere system of doctrine nor a code of ethics, nor a body of rites and practices, though it includes all these elements, like other faiths. But above and beyond all these, fundamentally it is a life of loyalty to a unique Person, in whom, by whom, and through whom has come to the world a final revelation of the very heart of reality and of human destiny, which not only comprehends all that prophets and sages have taught throughout the ages, but also fulfils all that the restless human spirit has sought and found in its age-long hunger and thirst after reality. The essence of this revelation is that at the heart of reality is deathless Perfection, in relation to which all things and values become intelligible, and which is itself responsive to human aspiration and co-operates with human endeavour in transforming the whole vast and varied scheme of actual existence into the Kingdom of God. The sublime simplicity of this profoundest of all messages cannot be better expressed than in the immortal words of the Christ, who said, " Love the Lord thy God with all thy heart, with all thy mind, and with all thy strength ; and thy neighbour as thyself. On these two commandments hang all the law and prophets." When asked pointedly as to " Who is my neighbour ? " the reply was given for all time in a parable—that of the Good Samaritan. Those who regard it as a graphic object-lesson in charity miss the whole point of its message, which is brought home by the rhetorical question with which the parable concludes, namely, " Which of these, think ye, was neighbour unto him ? "

So the Christian message to the world may be said to be a call to a life of love to God realised through willing service rendered to needy humanity. " Whatsoever ye have done to the least of these, ye have done it unto me." What profounder message or mission can there be for men and nations, in this or in any age, than this ? The only way, now or ever, in which men and nations can attain to the fullness of their stature is through giving themselves to the uttermost in the service of others for the glory of God and the establishment of his Kingdom of Righteousness ; and human life and all its powers and possessions alike are only a trust committed to us for this sublime end. There is nothing ancient or modern, Eastern or Western, about this. It is broadly, tenderly, profoundly human, and for all time and all people. How utterly unlike is this to the ideas and ideals of the autocracies of the earth, with their narrow schemes and short-sighted methods. The supremely amazing thing about Christianity which comes home to one with special vividness, in contrast to other historic faiths, is the fact that it does not merely teach an all-comprehensive doctrine, or prescribe a sublime code of conduct, or practise a superb ritual, or point to the most impressive and inspiring example of him whose name it bears, but that it contains the promise and pledge of his immediate indwelling presence and enabling strength in the actual life and endeavour of all who choose to avail themselves of it. Solitary individuals of all nations and tongues and peoples, who have tasted of this fountain of eternal life, have testified to its reality throughout the centuries. It remains yet for men and nations to enter into this inheritance. Meanwhile, the co-operation of East and West will help to reveal and appropriate the as yet hidden resources of the Eternal Christ as the one enduring hope of a sorely tried and needy world.

5. THE WORLD OF INTERNATIONAL AFFAIRS:

c. *DISARMAMENT*

By THE ARCHBISHOP OF CANTERBURY

The substance of the following sermon was preached by the Arch-bishop at a service, preparatory to the meeting of the Disarmament Conference, held in St. Paul's Cathedral on December 15th, 1931. Some passages have been omitted and some phrases altered which specially referred to the situation existing when the sermon was preached.

THE CLAIM of the old evil maxim, " If you wish for peace you must prepare for war," has been for ever shattered. The lesson of the Great War has been written large— in letters of blood—that great armaments can only lead to war. It is as certain as anything can be that it was the enormous growth of armaments, and the sense of insecurity and fear which they caused, which made the Great War inevitable. Most rightly, therefore, the nations, our own included, who signed the Covenant which is part of the Treaty of Peace declared that " the maintenance of peace requires the reduction of armaments to the lowest point consistent with national safety and the enforcement by common action of international obligations."

Well, more than ten years have passed. Yet still, in spite of all the reductions achieved by the Naval Conferences at Washington and London, the level of armaments remains as high as ever. The world is spending on them no less than £2,000,000 a day ; we in this country £200 a minute. Truly the time has come when a deliberate attempt must be made by international agreement to remove this intolerable burden, this continuing menace, from the peoples of the world.

Further, let it be not forgotten that in this matter there lies upon the nations who signed the Treaty of Peace an obligation of honour. Here are its terms—" the Allied and

Associated Powers wish to make it clear that their requirements in regard to German armaments were not made solely with the object of rendering it impossible to resume her policy of military aggression. They are also the first step towards the reduction and limitation of armaments which they seek to bring about as one of the most fruitful preventives of war, and which it would be one of the first duties of the League of Nations to promote." Thus national stability and national honour alike demand that a serious endeavour should now be made to stand by these declarations.

This, then, is the task of the fateful conference which is now in session—to effect a progressive reduction of armaments by general agreement. There is no question of one-sided disarmament. The essence of the problem is a general agreement to disarm. Our own country, we may honestly say, occupies at the conference a position of strong moral authority. She has already made more substantial reductions than any other country. Indeed, there are many who think that she has already reached the lowest point consistent with her safety and obligations. This very fact creates a difficulty which her representatives at Geneva have to face. It may not, e.g., be possible for them to accept some general reduction by a fixed common percentage. But within classes of armaments there are possibilities of reduction which she must be willing to offer. Our representatives are making every effort to bring about at least a true and honest beginning of general disarmament.

For assuredly the consequences of failure cannot be contemplated without dismay. It might mean the withdrawal of Germany from the League ; even her determination to begin the increase of her own armaments. It would certainly mean a most serious blow to the authority of the League and to all its efforts to hold the world together by an international rule of reason and justice. It would be a setback to the hopes of a period of settled confidence essential to the recovery of the world from its present confusion and distress. God in his mercy grant that a calamity so grievous may be averted !

Yet we cannot shut our eyes to the immense difficulties which stand in the way. These difficulties call not only for the patient efforts of statesmen meeting in conference, but even more for the powers which are latent in the public opinion of the peoples of the world themselves. Armaments, as the Secretary for Foreign Affairs has said, are but the symptom of a disease. It is well indeed to attack the symptom, but it is the disease itself which must ultimately be reached and healed. And that disease is Fear. The spirit of fear is still haunting the nations. It is this which makes them cling nervously to their armaments. And yet since the war a great structure of arbitration treaties, some 300 in number, has been built up. Nay, sixty-one nations, and among them all the most powerful, have bound themselves by the Pact of Paris to renounce war as an instrument of national policy and have agreed that the settlement of all disputes, of whatever nature or origin they may be, which may arise among them shall never be sought except by pacific means. Are not such solemn pledges enough to banish fear ? If they are not, the question arises whether these States are to be trusted to mean what they have said and to stand by their pledged word. If there be any doubt as to the answer, the very grave and ominous question remains, Has civilisation itself the strength of will, of conviction, of courage, to maintain the ideals on which its very existence depends, or must it still, and always, give way to the old untamed competitive instincts of primitive mankind ? These are questions which only the public opinion of the peoples can answer. Is there among them not a wish only, but a settled and resolute will for peace ? Here sounds the call to Christian citizens in every land. To them the renunciation of war as an instrument of national policy must be a matter not of mere aspiration, but of loyalty to the mind and spirit of the Lord whom they profess to serve. They must be everywhere a strong leaven steadily strengthening the lump of national life. Then, if the nations can trust one another to keep their word, if civilisation proves that it has within it the will to maintain the ideals which are its very life, there can be no place for fear. And, if fear be banished, the reduction of armaments will follow.

Further, there is another and kindred disease of which armaments are a symptom—the disease of a selfish nationalism which moves one nation to press its own advantage without regard to the needs of others. This is the ultimate cause of the vast economic depression which has come upon the world. All the perplexities, apprehensions, confusions, which surround the words reparations, war debts, tariff walls, armaments, are growths which spring from this same root of a self-seeking Nationalism. Yet the very distress which binds the whole world in bondage is a proof that the world is now one community of nations in which the welfare of one member means the welfare of all, and the calamity of one member brings calamity to all. It is the consciousness of this that has led to the proposal for a world conference which, accepting this fundamental truth, will endeavour by international co-operation to stay the distress and hasten the recovery of the world's economic life. Assuredly the only hope of rescuing civilisation from its present plight is to make the fact which that very plight proclaims—namely, the oneness of the whole body of nations—the ruling principle of international life. Then, so far as this problem of disarmament is concerned, the question of each nation would be, not what armaments does it need to maintain its own position but what contribution can it make to the armaments needed to defend the unity of nations against any aggressor who would try to break it.

It is in the translation of this ideal of the community of nations into terms of national policy that the hope of the future lies. But mere ideals are apt to be vague and transitory. They need a strong faith to give them power and persistence, the faith that they correspond with the ultimate Purpose which shapes the destinies of men or, in the old great words, with the will of God. It is this faith which the citizens of our own and other nations who profess and call themselves Christians are most clearly called to bring now to the succour of the world. For in these ideals—that we are all members one of another, that each must look, not only on his own things, but also on the things of others, that we must love our neighbour as ourselves—that is, show towards him a sincere will for his good—in these ideals they must discern the mind and will of him to whom they owe their loyalty. They are the laws of his Kingdom, of that Rule of Eternal Values—that City of God—which gives light and healing to the nations of the world. By the evidence of patent facts it is now made plain that they must be the basis of practical policy. The condition of the world to-day proves that it is only by seeking first the Kingdom of God that all those things which a perplexed and despondent world needs can be added unto it.

5. THE WORLD OF INTERNATIONAL AFFAIRS:

D. *A CHRISTIAN PEACE POLICY*

By E. N. PORTER GOFF

THE IMAGINATION of anyone who is brave enough to consider the probable character of the next war is revolted at the thought that such should be the end of all our hopes and strivings. The reaction of any man of decent feeling must be a resolve that he will play no part in the perpetration of such devilry ; he may well feel that the attitude of the conscientious objector is the only possible one for him.

Such considerations have probably determined the attitude of those who in our universities have declared that under no circumstances will they fight " for King and Country." The choice of these last four words has not been accidental. They embody ideas the existence of which are one of the greatest obstacles to the abolition of war. Deep down in the national consciousness war is associated with high ideals. The call to take part in a war to defend one's country—and every war is so described by both sides— appeals to the very best that is in a man. The last war did something to expose the unreality of this romantic appeal ; knowledge of the character of modern warfare should do more. But until the public faces the truth about war, and ceases to think in terms of the Horse Guards' Parade, the war-makers will have an easy task in rousing the nation by appealing to its best feelings.

On the other hand, the taking of an individual pledge that under no circumstances will one fight is unlikely by itself to do much to stop war. The next war will not be averted by individuals deciding what they are going to do when it breaks out. It must be stopped by the corporate action of large bodies of people *now*.

THE LAMBETH RESOLUTIONS

Most Christian bodies in England, and some in other countries, have already declared themselves to some extent. The Lambeth Conference of 1930 affirmed " that war as a method of settling international disputes is incompatible with the teaching and example of our Lord Jesus Christ." That such a declaration has been made is a great thing. But how far is it the considered opinion of the rank and file of the Christian Churches ? Does the fact that this declaration has been made in the name of the Anglican communion, and has been endorsed by other Christian bodies, mean that the Governments of what are known as Christian countries can no longer rely upon the help of a large section of their people in the prosecution of war ?

Some such result was evidently foreseen by the Lambeth Conference. Resolution 27 reads as follows :

" When nations have solemnly bound themselves by Treaty, Covenant or Pact for the pacific settlement of international disputes, the Conference holds that the Christian Church in every nation should refuse to countenance any war in regard to which the government of its own country has not declared its willingness to submit the matter in dispute to arbitration or conciliation."

Here a situation is visualised in which, in certain circumstances, the Church will find itself unable to support a war. The acceptance of such a resolution by the bishops of the Anglican communion may be regarded as a great advance from the pacifist point of view. It is at any rate an attempt to apply a general principle to particular circumstances. But its practical value is likely to be slight. A Government embarking upon a war, even in defiance of its treaty obligations, will take care so to present its case that it can put the blame for the conflict upon its enemy. What constitutes willingness " to submit the matter in dispute to arbitration or conciliation " ? We have had recently two instances of the difficulty of giving a clear answer to that question. In the dispute between the British Government and that of the Irish Free State over the land annuities, both sides have declared their willingness to submit the dispute to arbitration or conciliation—and both have embarked upon an economic war because they cannot agree as to the method of arbitration to be employed or the conditions of conciliation by direct negotiation. A similar readiness to seek a peaceful way out was professed by Japan in her dispute with China. But she resorted to force nevertheless, because, while China wished to employ the machinery of the League of Nations, Japan insisted upon direct negotiations. Something more, therefore, than the line of action envisaged by the Lambeth Conference is required.

THE LEAGUE OF NATIONS

What positive policy, based upon Christian principles, is it possible for the Churches to adopt ? First of all, they can state definitely and authoritatively that they will support all efforts to uphold the League of Nations. The League, whatever its defects, and however faulty its Covenant, provides the best machinery of international co-operation in the world to-day. Through its regular meetings it gives the statesmen of the world opportunities of encountering one another without incurring suspicion and speculation as to their purposes. Under the Covenant, nations are pledged never to go to war until they have exhausted all the means of averting war which Articles XII.–XV. of the Covenant afford. Under Article XII. the States members of the League agree that, if there should arise between them any dispute likely to lead to a rupture, they will submit the matter either to arbitration or judicial settlement or to inquiry by the Council, and that in no case will they resort to war until three months after the award of the arbitrators or the judicial decision or the report of the Council. Articles XIII.–XV. describe the machinery of arbitration, the competence of the Court of International Justice, and the means by which the Council of the League can deal with disputes which are not considered suitable for arbitration or for submission to the Court of International Justice. The League thus provides nations with machinery by which they can settle their disputes without having recourse to the arbitrament of war, and the members of the League are pledged to use this machinery. However little a nation may respect this pledge, the fact that it has been taken makes it more difficult to strike a quick blow. It would be still more difficult if the other members of the League were to make it clear that they would abide by their obligations under the Covenant and sever all relations with the offending State. It was the failure of the States members of the League to do this in the case of Japan, even after they had in the League Assembly accepted the report of the League's own Commission which condemned Japan, that increased the sense of insecurity in Europe and made France still more apprehensive of the effect upon Europe of the Nazi control of Germany. The world is one, and a failure to uphold justice in one part speedily reacts upon other parts. As these words are being written the British Prime Minister and Foreign Secretary are trying to save the Disarmament Conference in Geneva, while in the capitals of Europe the date and place of the next war is being discussed. Had a strong League policy been pursued in the Far East eighteen months before, the outlook for peace in Europe would be brighter to-day.

THE OBLIGATIONS OF THE COVENANT

That leads us to the second point of a positive Christian peace policy, namely, that we should support our Government in fulfilling its obligations under the Covenant, with this proviso—that the Articles of the Covenant stand or fall together. We are, for example, under Article X., pledged to " preserve as against external aggression the territorial integrity and existing political independence of

all Members of the League." But morally we can only
be held to the fulfilment of this undertaking—and of a
similar undertaking in the Treaty of Locarno with special
reference to France and Germany—when the other
articles of the Covenant have been observed. Article VIII.
pledges the members of the League to disarmament.
Article XIX. pledges them to the revision of treaties
" which have become inapplicable " and the alteration of
" conditions whose continuance might endanger the peace
of the world." Only when these articles have been observed
can any moral obligation rest upon a State to fulfil its
obligations under Article X. Christian people should declare
that they will take part in no war of which the object is to
defend the present provisions of the Treaty of Versailles or
to preserve, even against aggression, the territorial integrity
of a country which has brought about the outbreak of
war by its reluctance to agree to any real measure of disarmament by international agreement. It would be a great
contribution to world peace if the British Government were
to declare that it will fulfil its obligations under Article X.
of the Covenant and the Treaty of Locarno only in a
disarmed world, and that as long as each nation is seeking
to provide for its own security it must expect no assistance
from us.

THE WAY OF CHRIST

If Christian public opinion were to demand the translation into action of these two points, a great deal would have
been done to clear the international atmosphere and Great
Britain would have gained the moral leadership of the world.
But one point more must be emphasised. While we believe
in international co-operation and in the fulfilment of international obligations, we must under no circumstances
countenance the putting into operation of the modern war
machine. Philosophical discussions as to whether force is
ever justified are irrelevant here, and in any case there is
little prospect of agreement on the subject. But Christians,
or indeed anyone of decent feelings, must surely agree that

nothing can justify the bombing of defenceless cities from the air and the loosing upon civilian populations, men, women, and children, of gases which bring about a horrible death, or of germs for the spread of plague and disease. No considerations, no obligations, even the so-called " sacred right " of self-defence, can justify a nation in embarking upon such warfare. And yet such tactics are regarded by the experts as providing the only means of defence. We must, we are told, hasten to annihilate our enemy before he can annihilate us. Young men are being trained for this purpose in our own and other countries to-day. It is high time that those who profess the name of Christ should call " Halt ! " and refuse to have such things even contemplated by the servants of a Christian nation. That we may not, as yet, be able to get other Powers to agree to the abolition of Air Forces cannot alter our duty as Christians. Christ did not preach a conditional morality ; he did not tell us to live the good life only if we could be quite certain that our neighbours were going to do likewise. The Devil cannot be fought with his own weapons. Our way of life, if we are true to our profession, must be Christ's way of life. It may lead to a cross—a crucifixion of a defenceless nation by cruel and powerful enemies. But the cross is not the end. " My Kingdom is not of this world ; if my Kingdom were of this world, then would my servants fight."

* * * * *

EDITOR'S POSTSCRIPT

The following statement, which appeared in the Press on March 18th, 1933, has received general agreement :

The Church and War Peril

At a private meeting of some fifty leading representatives of the Christian Churches this morning, there was discussed the problem of the Christian attitude towards the present war peril.

After the meeting the following statement was issued :
We are convinced :

(*1*) *That God at this time is calling the nations of the world to learn to live as one family ;*

(*2*) *That the machinery of international co-operation provided by the League of Nations, while not yet perfect, affords the best available means of applying the principles of the gospel of Christ to stop war, to provide justice, and to organise peace ;*

(*3*) *That the application of these principles constitutes the only practical politics at the present time ;*

(*4*) *That Christian people should pray, and resolve that, by these means, faith shall be kept, confidence restored, and there shall be no more war.*

6. IS THERE AN ALTERNATIVE?

A. *SCIENTIFIC HUMANISM AND RELIGIONS OF LIFE*

By H. G. WOOD

IN WHAT faith and with what hopes are we to face the present crisis? What guiding principles will enable mankind to bring some satisfying order out of the present world-chaos, and turn their grim necessities to glorious gain?

A large number, perhaps the majority, of those who pride themselves on being progressive, and who claim to interpret or create the modern mind, would unhesitatingly reply: " Put your trust in science and have confidence in yourselves." This is the faith of scientific humanism, the faith, we are sometimes assured, of all educated persons under forty.

It is, of course, realised that science is concerned with means rather than ends, that it places at our disposal powers of control over nature which may prove disastrous unless mankind develops morally, and can thus cope with the crisis. For that reason, in addition to faith in science, we need faith in human values, confidence in our social ideals. Some moderns are doubtful about the appeal and authority of social ideals, if such aims are merely human, and they suspect that there may be something ineradicable in man's desire to devote himself to something higher than himself. They are doubtful whether humanity will quite serve as the object of devotion, but they think they see in the life-force the kind of reality-higher-than-man which may give meaning and purpose to human existence. So the simpler faith of the scientific humanist may be enlarged to include reverence for life and devotion to life's purposes.

POSITIVE ELEMENTS IN SCIENTIFIC HUMANISM

With much that is positive in scientific humanism the Christian can and should cordially agree. The Christian

Rc

believes, or should believe, with John Robinson, the Pilgrim Father, that " all truth is God's truth, from whatever source it comes." We have no refuge but in truth, and our only hope is to use to the full the knowledge we have, and fearlessly to extend the realm of science. Whatever changes may come in our world-outlook, and whatever adjustments may be required in social organisation and moral convention, let knowledge grow from more to more. We should not reluctantly accept the necessity for intellectual and social reconstruction, but welcome the advance in science and the new opportunities and responsibilities which it brings in its train.

If the Christian shares the humanist's faith in science, he shares also his faith in humanity. That men should entertain a high respect for themselves, that they should use their talents and not bury them in napkins, that they should trust one another and live and work in hope—all these are commonplaces of the Christian faith. The humanitarian sentiment, which most modern humanists uncritically accept, is, in its present form, largely the outcome of the influence of Christ. There is a sense in which the Christian, like the humanist, bids men have confidence in themselves.

Nor is the modern theme, which Ortega y Gasset defines as an emphatic assertion of the value of existence here and now, altogether alien from the Christian outlook. When Julian Huxley attempts to summarise the meaning of humanism, and to define its aims and its scale of values, he adapts the language of the Fourth Gospel. " One sentence to my mind really contains them all—to have life, and to have it more abundantly." It is strange how the gospel anticipates while it corrects our modern mood ! One object of Christ's coming is to fulfil the life-aims of the humanist.

If we try to define these aims more closely, the Christian and the humanist need not part company. When Bertrand Russell defines " the good life " as " one inspired by love and guided by knowledge," the Christian will gladly assent, however distasteful it may be to Mr. Russell to find a mere

Christian in agreement with him. When Olaf Stapledon outlines the social ideal in the following terms : " We want everyone to live fully according to his capacity. . . . In short, we want the whole world of men and women to be a thing of beauty, cherished by all, served by all, fully organised, but allowing plenty of freedom for everyone," the humble Christian may say, Amen, as well as Aldous Huxley in the columns of the *Referee*. When H. G. Wells organises an open conspiracy to further a world-economy so planned as to secure peace and co-operation among nations and to end the curse of degrading poverty, the Christian can heartily approve, even if his superstitious beliefs disqualify him for membership in Society Z. However much they may differ in detail, Christian and humanist may agree and might co-operate over many of their this-world objectives. But the Christian cannot conceal his conviction that this-world objectives are not enough, that neither scientific humanism nor religions of life can generate the courage or provide the guidance needed for this or any other crisis.

THE PREJUDICE AGAINST THE SUPERNATURAL

The most obvious and most fundamental characteristic of scientific humanism is its antipathy to any idea of the supernatural. When Will Durant writes on philosophy and social reform, he thinks that we can learn quite a lot from Plato, but we must of course ignore his absurd theory of ideas. In essence, as Julian Huxley sees it, " Scientific humanism is a protest against supernaturalism. The human spirit now in its individual, now in its corporate aspects, is the source of all values *and the highest reality we know*."[1] Professor H. Levy phrases the protest even more emphatically. " A Rationalist denies the efficacy of Heavenly aid in the solution of Earthly problems. . . . Rationalism asserts that supernaturalism can find no place in a civilised World Theory. For the practice of mankind has shown that there is no human activity that achieves its purpose by ' Divine ' intervention. . . . The history of

[1] *What Dare I Think?* p. 174. (Italics mine).

human progress is the history of the emancipation of man from supernaturalism."[1]

This rejection of the supernatural is regarded as essential to the scientific outlook. Science compels us to take a unitary view of the world. To the scientist, or at least to the Rationalist, " the universe is a closed system, a continually changing matrix of events, embracing the celestial bodies, Man, and his social system."[2] " The universe," writes Julian Huxley, " is not divisible into regions, or compartments labelled natural and supernatural, material and spiritual, scientific and non-scientific and so forth, as the surface of the globe is divisible into land and water. . . . There are not two regions of reality, one of which is accessible to scientific method and the other inaccessible. Rather there is a single reality, but scientific and other ways of approaching it and treating it. Man's poems and religions, his values and hopes, are part of this single reality, just as much as are the chemical elements or the geological strata."[3] This is the constant refrain of the scientific humanist, man a part of nature, to be described and explained by the same laws and on the same principles as the movements of the heavenly bodies or the combinations of chemical elements. " Man is a part of Nature, not something contrasted with Nature. His thoughts and bodily movements follow the same laws that describe the motions of stars and atoms."[4] So Bertrand Russell begins his " Confessio Fidei " in *What I Believe*. Mr. Stapledon states the same position for children and their parents in the following terms : " Man, it seems, is a tiny thing and has only just begun. He grew out of an animal which grew out of simpler animals. And all has grown out of the stuff of a star. So men are not something utterly different from the rest of things. Man is all of a piece with his world. His nature is just a rather complicated bit of stuff of the world's nature."[5]

To admit the supernatural in any shape or form is to

---

[1] *R.P.A. Annual*, 1933, p. 55.   [2] Levy, *op. cit.*, p. 55.
[3] *Op. cit.*, pp. 139, 140.   [4] *What I Believe*, p. 9.
[5] *Outline for Boys and Girls*, p. 748.

betray the scientific outlook. The scientific humanist does not simply surrender beliefs of an other-worldly or transcendental order ; he sternly rejects and even fiercely combats them. To believe in a God who is personal and transcendent, to believe in an eternal world of values, to believe in personal immortality, to believe in Jesus as Lord, is to commit one's self to a series of " transcendental perfidies." " God and immortality, the central dogmas of the Christian religion, find no support in science." If, then, men believe them, they sin against reason, for they determine their beliefs in accordance with their desires and not in accordance with the evidence. Casual expressions of this attitude of mind are often more arresting than more considered statements. Thus it is suggestive that Harold Nicolson, reviewing T. R. Glover's *Greek Byways* in the *New Statesman and Nation*, felt obliged to qualify his enthusiastic praise of the book by a protest against Mr. Glover's *outrageous* monotheism ! It makes the scientific humanist angry that anyone in these days of enlightenment should believe either in God or in a future life. So it comes about that the seventh of the seven broad principles which H. G. Wells lays down for the guidance of the Open Conspiracy is the denial of personal immortality. The corollary to the supreme duty of subordinating the personal career to the creation of a new world-order is " the admission therewith that our immortality is conditional and lies in the race and not in our individual selves."[1]

The whole-hearted acceptance of this point of view will, it is assumed, issue in a concentration of thought and energy on scientific progress and social reconstruction. It seems obvious that the less men think of another world, the more they will think of this. Let us, then, cease to ask the questions that science cannot answer, and cease to indulge in speculations that science cannot test. We must eliminate illusion and phantasy from men's outlook. Instead of daydreaming about heaven, men should return to earth, their true home and fatherland.

[1] *What Are We to Do with Our Lives ?* p. 113.

Wisdom in the guise of neo-Positivism will not only enable us to make the most and best of life in the sense of securing to us the maximum of health, wealth, and happiness, so far at least as the latter depends on the first two, but it also opens the way to the realisation of the highest ethical ideal, namely, the entire surrender of ourselves and of all enduring hopes for ourselves in the service of others. Middleton Murry has come to the conclusion that true disinterestedness, intellectual and moral, can only be realised by the acceptance of *complete* materialism. The desire for survival after death, it is thought, is only a refined spiritual selfishness, perhaps the religious counterpart or prolongation of the acquisitive, possessive spirit of the West. "But now we are beginning to feel that the desire to live for ever as a little self is, after all, not a very alive kind of desire : in fact, it is not what a man ought to desire." So scientific humanism makes room for the highest form of self-denial.

DOES NATURAL SCIENCE SUPPORT HUMANISM?

At first sight this faith seems so sensible and so noble that it is inevitably attractive. It is adopted and advocated by so many eminent men of science and so many novelists of repute that its vogue is easily intelligible. All we need to do is to lift up the banner with the legend " For Science and Humanity," and we can advance to the conquest of happiness and the building of the brave new world. But while this thought-structure looks at first view well built and weather-tight, a closer inspection reveals some disquieting gaps and fissures. It seems simple to trust science and to have confidence in ourselves, but do the two articles of our faith really support one another ? Does science establish our confidence in ourselves, and does our knowledge of ourselves confirm our trust in science ? Is there not a tension between science and humanism which can only be resolved by trust in something higher than both, a quarrel between our love of knowledge and our love of our fellows which can only be decided on appeal to a higher court ? Does science permit us to retain our respect for human nature, and, if we are to retain our sense of human worth, shall we find that science, like patriotism, is not enough ?

Some scientific humanists seem to falter where once they firmly stood. The advance of science is depicted by Llewellyn Powys as a succession of humiliations for man. " The human race has suffered three grave humiliations : when Copernicus showed that the earth was not the centre of the universe ; when Darwin proved that man's origin was not the result of a direct creation ; when Freud explained that man was not the master of his own thoughts and actions. It must endure an increment of ignominy before it will be prepared to temper its demands."[1] Julian Huxley, indeed, asserts that the human spirit is the highest reality we know. He takes his stand on the fact of the evolutionary process, on " the tendency . . . of living matter to progress to ever higher levels of achievement, into forms which have more internal harmony, more external control, more intensity of mental life. And man, with his scale of values, is the culmination of this second trend."[2] But humanists who let their judgments of value be swayed by astrophysics rather than biology take no such view of man's worth. Here is the closing sestet of a sonnet of Eden Phillpotts, entitled " Consciousness " :

> *Clown in the travelling circus of a sun,*
> *By learned souls with piety perverse,*
> *Declared the victor in a race not run,*
> *Proclaimed the acme of the Universe,*
> *Man struts, while aged stars in mercy mild*
> *Doubt the majority of such a child.*[3]

It is true that the poet recovers from this rather dismal mood in two admirable sonnets on " Reason " and " Hope," but to Bertrand Russell this estimate of man is sober truth. " Vitalism as a philosophy and evolutionism show . . . a

[1] *The Pathetic Fallacy*, p. 126.   [2] *What Dare I Think ?* p. 264.
[3] *R.P.A. Annual*, p. 19. It is interesting to find a Rationalist poet resorting to the pathetic fallacy. " Science " does not permit us to attribute mercy or doubt to the stars, however aged. What a pity ! But, after all, poetry is wiser than science.

lack of sense of proportion and logical relevance. They regard the facts of life, which are personally interesting to us, as having a cosmic significance, not a significance confined to our earth's surface. . . . All such philosophies spring from self-importance, and are best corrected by a little astronomy."[1] Evolution, according to Mr. Russell, is a long, wearisome story with a very poor point. It resembles a tedious anecdote related by a doddering old gentleman. " Moreover, the ' point ' of the anecdote, even when it is reached, appears hardly worthy of so long a preface. I am willing to admit that there is merit in the tail of the fox, the song of the thrush, or the horns of the ibex. But it is not to these things that the evolutionary theologian points with pride : it is to the soul of man. Unfortunately there is no impartial arbiter to decide on the merits of the human race ; but for my part, when I consider their poison gases, their researches into bacteriological warfare, their meannesses, cruelties, and oppressions, I find them, considered as the crowning gem of the creation, somewhat lacking in lustre. But let that pass."[2]

At this stage Mr. Russell, it must be admitted, fails not merely to appreciate the point of the story, but also to meet the point of the argument. A gem that lacks lustre is still a gem, and may still be a crowning gem. But if Mr. Russell is justified in doubting whether the mind of man is anything better than the tail of the fox, and if this doubt is widely entertained, faith alike in science and in man must collapse. Perhaps this kind of passage is not to be taken too seriously. Mr. Russell is more in earnest when he questions whether there is anything in the process of evolution that demands the hypothesis of a purpose, whether immanent or transcendent. So when Julian Huxley appeals to evolution, and describes man as the highest reality we know, Mr. Russell would dismiss him as an evolutionary theologian, " a learned soul with piety perverse." There is not, in fact, a single agreed scientific outlook, or view of the universe. A personal equation always infects the scientific

[1] *What I Believe*, p. 23.   [2] *The Scientific Outlook*, p. 127.

outlook as defined by any scientist. The physicists and biologists are not agreed, and those biologists who seek a religion of life in the facts of evolution are roughly handled by the physicists. Yet the claims that the biologist makes for man are after all modest. Julian Huxley will remind us that " man is a limited and partial creature, a product of material evolution. He is a relative being, moulded by the struggle to survive in particular conditions on a particular planet. We have no grounds for supposing that his construction is adapted to understand the ultimate nature or cause or purpose of the universe, and indeed every reason for supposing the contrary. Quite apart from that, we can be sure that there are whole realms of knowledge which he has not yet discovered."[1]

So evolutionary science combines with astronomy to keep us humble. Can we really have much confidence in ourselves ? Apart from the findings of particular sciences, we have to face all those disconcerting facts which dim the lustre of nature's crowning gem, all that sad record of human failure which convinced Newman of the truth of original sin, and which prevents Bertrand Russell from recognising any assured progress in the course of evolution. For the scientific humanist with a positivist outlook there is further the spectacle of the appalling waste of rational powers and spiritual energy in the vain pursuits of metaphysics and religion. Faith in man ? It calls for courage !

DOES HUMANISM PERMIT FAITH IN NATURAL SCIENCE ?

If science shakes our faith in man, this in turn shakes our faith in science. A scepticism " painful and barren," a scepticism generated by the skill of men of science,[2] is now

---

[1] *What Dare I Think ?* p. 242.
[2] *Scientific Outlook*, p. 104. Mr. Bertrand Russell asserts this scepticism as an essential feature of an intellectually honest outlook. He thinks it may be a temporary phase. For him at least it is very temporary. He commits himself to scepticism at the end of Part I., chap. iv., and reaffirms an unyielding rationalism with a robust faith in knowledge at the close of chap. v.

undermining, not religion, but Rationalism ; it is destroying our confidence in science as the pursuit of truth. The lengths to which this scepticism is at present carried by some humanists are rather bewildering. Thus Aldous Huxley assures us that " Science is no ' truer ' than common sense or lunacy, than art or religion. It permits us to organise our experience profitably, but tells us nothing about the real nature of the world to which our experiences are supposed to refer."[1]

The logic by which this conclusion is reached is no less bewildering than the conclusion itself. The chain of reasoning is as follows. " The only facts of which we have direct knowledge are psychological facts. . . . One fact cannot be more of a fact than another. Our psychological experiences are all equally facts. There is nothing to choose between them. No psychological experience is ' truer,' so far as we are concerned, than any other." " The criterion of truth and falsehood must always remain internal, psychological. To talk about truth as a relationship between human notions and things in themselves is an absurdity." How does Mr. Aldous Huxley come to commit himself to fallacies so patent ? If he is right, there is no such thing as a criterion of truth and falsehood, and to talk about truth at all is waste of time. As all experience consists of psychological facts, and as all such facts are equally facts and equally true, there is no such thing as falsehood. Consequently, there is no such thing as truth. This follows at once from Mr. Huxley's principles. All judgments are psychological facts. The judgment, " Mr. Aldous Huxley is writing arrant nonsense," and the judgment, " Mr. Aldous Huxley has discovered a profound mystical truth," are both internal, psychological. Being psychological facts, one is not more a fact than the other. There is nothing to choose between them. They must, therefore, mean the same thing. In other words, neither of them means anything. This conclusion applies to all judgments, those of Mr. Huxley included.

If Mr. Huxley had left out his reference to lunacy, he

[1] *Do What You Will*, p. 2.

would have said something worth saying. There is a sense in which the judgments of the scientist are not " truer " than the judgments of common sense, or the judgments of the artist and the saint. But this can only be the case if common sense, art, and religion represent independent, or at least distinct, contacts with external reality. It cannot possibly be based on the mere circumstance that all judgments of any kind are psychological facts. If " to be true " means only " to be psychological fact," this criterion swallows up the distinction between truth and falsehood as well as between science, common sense, lunacy, art, and religion. Then there can be no distinction between a false hypothesis and a true one in science, no distinction between proverbial wisdom and old wives' fables in common sense, no distinction between good and bad art, no distinction between faith and superstition in religion. Indeed, it is an insoluble mystery that we are able to make any distinctions at all, if " all psychological experiences are equally facts and there is nothing to choose between them." Why distinguish science from common sense, or from lunacy, or from art, or from religion ? The only academy in which Mr. Huxley's philosophy would win applause or command assent is a lunatic asylum.

Bertrand Russell is almost as extreme. He does not indeed regard science as no better than lunacy, but he does hold that it gives us no reliable information as to the nature of the external world. Science, it was supposed, had established the view that the world is a unity. The unitary view of the universe is, as we have seen, the first article in the creed of the scientific humanist. But the acids of scepticism are at work on this faith in science. With regard to the belief that " the world is a unity," Mr. Russell writes : " The most fundamental of any intellectual beliefs is that this is rubbish. I think the universe is all spots and jumps, without unity, without continuity, without coherence or orderliness or any of the other properties that governesses love. Indeed there is little but prejudice and habit to be said for the view that there is a world at all."[1] Mr. Russell has rather a contempt

[1] *The Scientific Outlook*, p. 98.

for governesses, and one almost expects him to make them responsible for originating the superstitious belief in the universe as an ordered whole. But it seems the responsibility lies, not with governesses, but with their youthful charges. In *Education and the Social Order*, Mr. Russell rightly argues that children get bored with uncharted freedom, and that some regular routine in the nursery is not only good for them, but fits in with their preferences. He suggests that our faith in the uniformity of nature may be nothing more than the projection of our childish liking for routine in the nursery ! But of course Mr. Russell would not rest too much weight on this argument. " To speak seriously : such orderliness as we appear to find in the external world is held by many to be due to our own passion for pigeon-holes, and they maintain that it is quite doubtful whether there are such things as laws of nature."[1] " Of unity (in the universe), however vague, however tenuous, I see no evidence in science, considered as a metaphysic." " In metaphysics, my creed is short and simple. I think the external world may be an illusion, but if it exists, it consists of events, short, small and haphazard. Order, unity and continuity are human inventions just as truly as are catalogues and encyclopædias."[2]

It must be admitted that this radical scepticism about science is very disconcerting to the faith of scientific humanism. In this sweeping attack on belief in the unity of the world, Mr. Russell thinks he is routing Parmenides, academic philosophers, theologians, clergymen, journalists, and governesses. He is really undermining the position of the scientific humanist, and stultifying himself. What, for example, becomes of the statement that nature has produced everything, from stars to Mr. Russell's philosophy, in accordance with laws which the physicist is beginning to discover ? This statement, instead of being the sober embodiment of scientific truth, is now found to be a speculation whose rashness borders on extravagance. " Nature ! " There is very little but prejudice and habit to be said for

[1] *Scientific Outlook*, p. 99. [2] *Ibid.*, p. 99.

the view that nature exists at all. Laws which the physicist discovers ? " Invents " is what Mr. Russell should have said. There are no laws of nature, only the projections of our human desire for orderliness.

Again, what becomes of Mr. Russell's appeal to the scientific view of the world to justify the rejection of theism ? " The progress of biology, physiology, and psychology has made it more probable than it ever was before that all natural phenomena are governed by the laws of physics ; and this is the really important point." Is it ? I should have thought Mr. Russell's view of the status of laws of physics was not unimportant. If intellectual honesty compels him to deny that order, unity, and continuity belong to the external world, he cannot appeal to the laws of physics to justify the belief that the world, whose very existence is doubtful, is a closed system of rigid mechanical necessity. But, in any event, the whole idea that an appeal to physical laws can settle the problem of theism is a piece of confused thinking. It is ridiculous to say that physics and the physical sciences have produced no evidence, however vague, however tenuous, in favour of belief in a world of order, unity, and continuity. But when it comes to deciding the nature of order, unity, and continuity, physics offers, and can offer, not a shred of evidence in favour of materialism rather than idealism, or of naturalism rather than theism.

The intelligent Christian will not be stampeded into the scepticism of Bertrand Russell and Aldous Huxley. The Christian ought to have a firmer faith in science than these brilliant but erratic moderns. We are living in God's world, and it is not a huge deception. If there is a bare possibility that nature is quite other than science leads us to suppose, the Christian, with Julian Huxley and most scientists, will embrace the faith in the unity and rational order of the world on which science depends and to which science points.[1] He will agree, too, with the same author in regarding science as a function or activity of human nature, prompted by the desire to know and by the desire to control

[1] *What Dare I Think ?* p. 126.

external nature for our advantage. Scientific discoveries are not discoveries of exact or absolute truth, but approximations to truth which are convenient ways of ordering and enlarging our experience. Even Bertrand Russell and Aldous Huxley agree that science is *working* satisfactorily. Like the negro preacher who in a mixed company of Fundamentalists and Modernists was asked the crucial question, " Do you believe in the inspiration of the Scriptures ? " and who wisely replied, " I think the Scriptures are sufficiently inspired for all practical purposes," Mr. Russell and other sceptics think science is sufficiently near the truth to achieve great practical successes. But the limitations of the natural sciences are undeniable. When Professor Levy declares his belief in nature as a closed system, he is speaking as a Rationalist and not as a scientist. When Mr. Russell says, " Nature has produced our desires, hopes, and fears in accordance with physical laws," he exceeds any brief supplied to him by the sciences. At least the sciences cannot and do not tell him what nature ultimately is. The conclusions of the natural sciences do not of themselves form an adequate account of the unity of which men and the stars form parts.

NATURE AND VALUES MISUNDERSTOOD BY SCIENTIFIC HUMANISM

The difficulties, intellectual and moral, in which scientific humanism is involved, all spring from overvaluing and misinterpreting the conclusions of the natural sciences. They assert, quite correctly, that the natural sciences point to a unitary view of the world—i.e. the world is an ordered whole. They assert, again quite correctly, that we men belong to this ordered whole, we are part of it. Then they assume that the true fundamental character of the universe is disclosed to us in the natural sciences, and pre-eminently in physics, and to their own amazement they find they cannot fit man into the unitary view of the world derived from physics. The world of nature as conceived for the purposes of the physicist is a world without values. Man is a creature whose behaviour is apparently determined in some measure by ideals, by what might be as well as by what is, by concepts of what ought to be, and of what he ought to do. From the standpoint of the scientific humanist, the disconnection between man and " Nature " is complete, yet he is sure that his concept of " Nature " is right and that man is nothing but a complicated part of " Nature " so conceived. The only rational way of bridging the gulf is to recognise the reality of the supernatural, in this sense at least—that we recognise that there must be something more in the universe than nature as presented to us in the physical sciences. No concept of " Nature " derived from physics or biology can describe or explain conscious behaviour. No such concept of nature can account for value-judgments. If physics disclosed to us the whole truth or the most fundamental truth about " Nature," science itself would be impossible. Nature and man can only form part of one whole, if physical energy and ideal values are derived from the same source, a reality greater than nature and higher than man. Theism is the only way by which the unity of nature and man, which the scientific humanists assert, can be maintained and interpreted.

The scientific humanist will not, of course, look at this way out. Three different solutions, or types of solution, of the problem of values are offered to us by leading humanists, and none of them can survive a critical examination. The first is to regard values as purely human. Nature has nothing to do with values. Man is the only source of values. We are asked to believe that the dualism between nature and man is absolute, and at the same time that the unity of nature and man is complete. Bertrand Russell is the best exponent of this simple self-contradictory faith. The second is to regard values and the consciousness of values as purely natural, as parts of an essentially physical order. Values are either an illusory, shadowy accompaniment of a physical reality whose true character is to be understood through the physical sciences, or else they are themselves tenuous, refined physical forces, or peculiar qualities curiously attached to physical forces, and again the whole truth about them will be disclosed to us in the laboratories of the physicist and biologist, and the psychologist who confines himself to the methods of observation and experiment employed by the physicist and biologist. This is the view advocated by Professor Levy, Professor L. T. Hogben, and, I judge, Professor J. B. S. Haldane. The third solution is to regard values as biological. We can adopt the conception of the life-force as getting us nearer to the reality of nature than the electrons and protons of the physicist. If the concept of the life-force is thus dominant, we can attach religious significance to it. We can interpret evolution as the movement of life towards the embodiment of values. Then we arrive at the religions of life, and we shall find our prophets in G. Bernard Shaw, H. G. Wells, Julian Huxley, and Middleton Murry.

No one of the solutions to the problem of values offered to us by scientific humanists is intellectually defensible. If any one of them were true, values would lose their power to control and inspire conduct. Since each is irrational, youth, if once it is critically awakened, will seek other guides than the scientific humanists through the present chaos.

VALUES AS PURELY HUMAN

Of the three types of solution, the first seems intellectually the shoddiest. " The philosophy of nature is one thing, the philosophy of value is quite another. Nothing but harm can come of confusing them."[1] This is obviously not true, *if nature and value form part of one system.* A philosophy of nature which ignores values is simply not true. A philosophy of value which takes no account of nature is necessarily false. " Undoubtedly we are part of nature, which has produced our desires, our hopes and fears, in accordance with laws which the physicist is beginning to discover."[2] " It is we who create value and our desires which confer value. In

[1] *What I Believe*, p. 22.   [2] *Ibid.*, p. 23.

this realm we are kings, and we debase our kingship if we bow down to Nature. It is for us to determine the good life, not for Nature—not even for Nature personified as God."[1] Undoubtedly, if nature produces, and so determines, our desires, and our desires create values, then it is nature and not ourselves that creates values and determines the good life. We cannot debase our kingship, for we do not possess it. If nature produces our desires, hopes, and fears, and these create values, the philosophy of value is only part of the philosophy of nature. On this issue, the second type of solution is intellectually more honest and more defensible than the first. Bertrand Russell ought to have the courage to throw up monism and naturalism if he really believes that " we are ourselves the ultimate and irrefutable arbiters of value and in the world of value Nature is only a part. Thus in this world we are greater than Nature."[2] For he believes in the supernatural, even while he confines the supernatural to man. He is himself evidence of the reality of the supernatural. When, for example, he compares " this very unpleasing universe " to " a bottle of very nasty wine,"[3] he is clearly greater than nature. No mere part or product of nature could pass such a severe judgment on the universe. Only a child of God, and a spoilt child at that, could have conceived and pronounced a verdict so asinine.

Though Bertrand Russell is still the most popular exponent of a vacillating half-hearted dualism, all humanists who regard man and not nature as the source of values are beset with the same difficulty. Julian Huxley, whose outlook differs profoundly from Mr. Russell's, is nevertheless mired in the same fallacy. Thus, he holds that " man's poems and religions, his values and hopes, are part of this single reality just as much as are the chemical elements or the geological strata." But, in spite of this, man's poems and values tell us nothing about the world external to us ; they tell us only something about ourselves. Beethoven's music produced something new in the world. " It is not new knowledge of the external world as Mr. Sullivan in his

[1] *What I Believe*, p. 25.   [2] *Ibid.*, p. 24.   [3] *Scientific Outlook*, p. 123.

Beethoven would wish us to believe, but knowledge of new capabilities of the human spirit, new experience."[1] Here again Mr. Huxley cannot have it both ways. If the external world and ourselves form parts of a single reality, the nature of the external world cannot be determined apart from ourselves. Beethoven's music conveys knowledge, not simply of our capabilities, but of that single reality in which we and the external world are united. We cannot determine the nature of the single reality by the knowledge of the external world gained through the physical sciences. The divorce implied in Julian Huxley's criticism of Mr. Sullivan is quite inconsistent with the unitary view of reality with which he started. Humanism is unable to save the unitary view of the universe which science seems to imply, whereas theism accepts this unity and attempts to do justice to it.

VALUES AND CRUDE NATURALISM

The second type of solution of the problem of values insists that values will turn out to be a form of physical reality, or at least so dependent on a purely physical reality as to be determined by it and understood through it. The exact position which writers like H. Levy, L. T. Hogben, and J. B. S. Haldane wish to maintain is certainly not clear to their readers, and I doubt whether it is clear to themselves. Sometimes they appear to be arguing for the view that consciousness is a mere ornament, a useless accompaniment of a physical process which is the real thing. It may even be suggested that consciousness does not exist. In any case, free-will is an illusion. We suppose ourselves to be active and responsible in choice and decision, in examining ideas, framing judgments, testing arguments, and planning experiments. But all this is superficial by-play. The reality is that a physical stimulus sets up measurable, calculable, predictable movements in our nervous system, which responds in measurable reflex reactions, and these take place whether we are conscious of them or not, whether we will them or not. Much of what

[1] *What Dare I Think?* p. 154.

Professors Hogben and Levy write seems to imply this conclusion. If they do not intend to convey this meaning, they convey no meaning at all. If this is their meaning, their position is the old epiphenomenalism, which assumes that consciousness makes absolutely no difference to the physical reality which it mysteriously accompanies. This is one of those propositions which Mr. C. D. Broad rightly characterises as so silly that only very clever men could pretend to believe them or try to defend them. At other times these writers appear to be arguing that human willing, deciding, reasoning, planning, make a difference, but must be a kind of physical force or energy, or at least qualities attaching to a physical reality. There may be— nay, there must be—physical occurrences exhibiting such characteristics as truth and purpose.[1] This second position, unlike the first, is at first sight compatible with common sense and science, and in so far as the activities of the human mind have a physical side which can be observed from without, it is all to the good that this view of consciousness should stimulate research into what may be called the physical or, better, the physiological aspect of mental processes. But unfortunately this does not bring the scientific humanist to his desired haven. He wants consciousness to be part of a system whose nature is completely revealed by physics. The physical occurrences which exhibit truth and purpose may turn out to be measurable and observable from without, but these characteristics can never be known in that way. Whereas physics may tell us the whole truth, or the whole truth accessible to us, about electrons and protons, it can never tell us all that we need to know about the physical occurrences which exhibit such peculiar characteristics as truth and purpose. We are still face to face with the supernatural, if we draw our concept of nature from the physical sciences. The scientific humanists who are working on this line imagine that if it is possible to observe from without the physical side of a psychophysical process, this is tantamount to proving that the

[1] *R.P.A. Annual*, 1933, p. 15.

psychical side is either non-existent or ineffective, and that the psycho-physical process is in fact purely physical. They also assert that no knowledge of a psycho-physical process can be scientific, unless it is founded on observation of the physical occurrences from without. In other words, they have no use for introspection.

Mr. Hogben maintains this particular standpoint. " Materialism implies the conviction that the only genuine knowledge is that which can be gained by pursuing the method devised by scientists for the study of what are ordinarily called material objects."[1] Tennyson stated the same erroneous theory of knowledge more succinctly when he wrote, " We have but faith, we cannot know ; for knowledge is of things we see." Materialism is the maintenance of the adequacy of this outworn mid-Victorian theory of knowledge. Mr. Hogben deduces from this that in genuine knowledge there is no room for introspection, introspective concepts, or the introspective method. He is simply reviving " the fundamental fallacy of Comte's system, his rejection of the validity of ' inner observation ' and with it of all psychology."[2] To oppose " the method devised by scientists for the study of what are ordinarily called material objects " to introspection, and to rule out introspection as unscientific, is to show that you have never reflected on the nature of scientific method. Aldous Huxley is certainly right in saying that we must all start from psychological facts, and psychological facts can only be known by introspection. Unless something occurs in the consciousness of the scientist, and unless he observes and interprets the content of his consciousness by introspection, he cannot devise any method by which he can know anything. All scientific methods are absolutely dependent on introspection at every stage. Introspection is in fact and in logic prior to observation from without. The latter would not be possible without the former. Solipsism is sheer lunacy, but it is common sense

[1] *Nature of Living Matter*, p. 16.
[2] *Life of P. H. Wicksteed*, p. 187 ; a valuable and penetrating criticism of Comte.

compared with materialism. To suppose that psychological facts will some day be resolved into purely physiological or physical facts is to surrender to a phantasy.

Nor is it legitimate to impugn the introspective method in psychology while admitting introspection as the essential foundation of methods of observation from without. No one disputes the difficulties and limitations of the introspective method. No one wishes to rely on inner observation alone, where results can be checked by methods of observation from without. But no one who knows what has been accomplished in psychology by the use of the introspective method will have any doubt as to its scientific value and validity. Contempt for the introspective method is not a sign of scientific enlightenment.

The absurd lengths to which the prejudice against introspection can be carried may further be illustrated by an example from Professor Levy's pamphlet *Science in Perspective* (pp. 13 and 14). In a trial for murder, the jury will discount what the prisoner says about his motives and intentions, his state of mind. They will judge his intentions, if they can get the evidence, by what the prisoner was observed to have done, by his actions, by his physical behaviour observed from without. Professor Levy actually thinks that the prisoner's evidence is discounted because he is using the introspective method, and because we all know that the only valid evidence must rest on the method of external observation. Professor Levy then deduces : (1) that introspection tells us nothing trustworthy about " intentions " ; (2) that intentions can only be discovered through external observation of essentially physical behaviour ; and (3) since this physical behaviour can be described in purely physical terms, intentions either do not exist or make no difference in an essentially physical causal nexus. I need only point out : (1) that the prisoner's evidence is discounted, not because he is using the method of introspection, but because to save his life he is strongly tempted to lie ; (2) that to deduce intention from physical behaviour you must know intentions and their relation to physical behaviour by introspection ; and (3) that the third proposition is an obvious fallacy in logic and an obvious error in fact. It is hardly necessary to add that no jury would ignore personal statements as to intentions and feelings, and no intelligent lover of truth would reject introspection.

The conflict of materialism with science is inevitable. Science depends on " rationally planned experimentation " ; i.e. on voluntary conscious behaviour which makes a perceptible difference in the succession of events. Materialism, according to Hogben, hopes that ultimately we shall discover in our own behaviour nothing conscious, nothing voluntary, but only complicated combinations of physical reflexes functioning automatically in a causal nexus marked by calculable necessity. What a hope for a scientist !

The very progress of science depends on the emergence of men of genius. Professor Levy says of the outstanding names of those whose advances broke away from the track of the scientific herd, " they were men with a flash of genius, and there is no scientific criterion for genius."[1] This is surely right. The advance of science is neither within the range of scientific prediction nor subject to human control. The progress of science itself is a sufficient disproof of materialism and incidentally of Professor Levy's Rationalism. There is no way of bringing mind within the compass of Naturalism. Once again we must believe in the supernatural if we are to do justice to values.

VALUES AND THE LIFE-FORCE

Humanism, the view that values are an exclusive concern of men, fails to preserve the unitary view of the universe which science demands. Naturalism or materialism only preserves the unitary view by denying the reality of values, including science, or else it feeds its devotees on wind, on the idle hope that some day the physicists may produce such a thin, volatile concept of matter that it will include mind. If pure humanism and refined materialism give no

[1] *The Universe of Science*, p. 199.

satisfactory solution of the problem of values, there is still the method of associating values with life. The study of evolution shows us progress as a fact. Man's consciousness, and his rational and ethical standards, have developed in and for the struggle for existence. " Man, in virtue of his fundamental and unique *biological* property of possessing general ideas, is thereby at a bound provided with abstract standards."[1] It is at least better to speak of the possession of general ideas as a biological property than to regard truth and purpose as " characteristics of certain physically specifiable occurrences."[2] Granted that this unique property of man is biological in so far as it has been developed in the struggle for existence, and in so far as it enables man to carry on the course of biological evolution, can it possibly be regarded as purely or mainly biological? The term " life " is itself ambiguous. If we include in it all that is meant by spiritual life, man's poems and music and religions, for example, it is no longer purely biological. If we do not include all these elements in the term " life," and stick to a strict biological definition, then the faculty of possessing general ideas is not exclusively, and perhaps not mainly, concerned with biological ends, and cannot rightly be described as biological. Put more concretely, biological ends might include health and strength, physical and mental, but cannot rightly be held to include more than that. We may also admit that these are goods in themselves, and not merely means to other ends. But no biological ends can in themselves be adequate objectives for humanity. Given greater capacities, to what ends shall we devote them? A purely biological programme would resemble the advice given by Lord Rosebery to the Liberal Party to clean its slate and write on it the single word, " Efficiency." The question at once arises, efficiency for what? And though it is safe at all times to promote better health and higher capacity in general, we could not be sure even of what we really meant by efficiency unless we were sure of our ulterior objects. When biology has done its best, we

[1] *What Dare I Think?* p. 210.　　[2] *R.P.A. Annual*, p. 15.

should still be looking round for something which would
" our little lives with purpose fill."

No, the problem of values is not exclusively a biological
one, and cannot be solved in terms of biological evolution.
History is not simply a continuation of a biological process.

SCIENTIFIC HUMANISM CAN NEITHER DIRECT NOR INSPIRE SOCIAL PROGRESS

No form of scientific humanism is intellectually satisfying
in dealing with values. Whether humanism assigns values
to a world of imagination where men's tastes and fancies
range unchecked by nature and objective standards, or
whether it treats values as strange miraculous characteristics
of physical occurrences, or whether it finally associates
values with the life-force, it is clear on reflection that none
of these taken separately account for values, and that all
three taken together fail utterly to explain either the existence of the categories " ought to be " and " ought to do,"
or the actual part played by particular value-judgments in
human experience. It is not likely that a philosophy so
shallow will meet the demands of the present crisis.

As a matter of fact, the humanists do not expect that it
will. Walter Lippmann depicts without exaggeration a
scientific humanist world that has lost heart. With old traditions corroded by the acids of modernity, men are asking
everywhere : Does it really matter what we do with our
lives ? H. G. Wells warns us against the habit of " everydayishness," the habit of just breezing along with the breeze,
the habit so easy to acquire and so difficult to break, so easy
to deplore and so difficult to counteract. Aldous Huxley,
writing in the *Referee*, regards the social ideal as quite
obvious to any rational person, but, unfortunately, though
" the greater number of us perceive it, we do not choose in
practice to do anything about it." " The incentive to action
provided by our scientific reason is not strong enough in
most cases to counteract the pull of our lower impulses towards immediate gratifications which are incompatible with
the pursuit of the higher, but more distant, ends." Mr.

Llewellyn Powys does not exactly deplore this. He seems rather to welcome it. What we really ought to do is to cultivate the natural happiness we share with animals and with such of our African cousins as have not been contaminated by " civilised " whites.[1] Perhaps the social ideal is not quite so obvious from the standpoint of scientific reason as Aldous Huxley supposes ! In any case, Llewellyn Powys represents an inevitable trend in the humanist ranks towards " everydayishness," or towards the old Cyrenaic philosophy of living for the most exquisite sensation of the moment, and this pursuit of natural happiness will never salvage civilisation.

Indeed, Aldous Huxley is quite mistaken in thinking that social ideals are self-evident or are simple rational constructs. The social ideal suggested by Olaf Stapledon appeals to Aldous Huxley and the intelligentsia of to-day as obviously rational, but so did faith in progress seem to the intelligentsia of yesterday, and Aldous Huxley now has nothing but contempt for the faith that seemed supremely reasonable to his predecessors. He describes faith in progress as the creed of industrialists, financiers, and prosperity-mongers, but he has read Bury's splendid book on the *Idea of Progress* in which Bury proudly and justly claims for Rationalists the credit of elaborating this creed. It is true that the motto of the book might almost have been, " I come to bury progress, not to praise it," and it showed the complete failure of Rationalism, divorced from Christianity, to establish a reasonable faith in progress. Still, faith in progress was a fashionable creed among the intelligentsia, the Aldous Huxleys, of the last century. They found they could not believe in progress apart from Christianity. Neither can Aldous Huxley prove the reasonableness of his social ideal apart from Christianity.

RELIGION INDISPENSABLE

If scientific humanism cannot frame a social ideal without Christianity, can it hope by itself to sustain and direct social

[1] *R.P.A. Annual*, pp. 21 and 24.

purpose or generate social enthusiasm ? Aldous Huxley
admits that it cannot. " The appeal to reason has always
been without general response. It has, therefore, been necessary to invent non-rational motives for the compassing of
the most supremely reasonable ends. Hence mythologies
and religions. etc." " One great obstacle stands in the way
of the acceptance of Humanism. This philosophy of reason
has not yet been interpreted in those terms of picturesque
and exciting unreason which alone have power to move the
minds of men." Aldous Huxley has produced a noble
rational philosophy : will someone kindly invent an irrational religion to get it across to the multitude ? Professor
Morris Ginsberg, in a most valuable article on " Aspects
of Moral Development," finds the greatest obstacle to the
spread of moral universalism in " the comparative failure
of reason to inspire that passion without which nothing
great or noble can be achieved."[1] The need for religion is
undeniable.

Nor is it only to inspire enthusiasm for social progress
that religion is essential. A society dominated by a scientific
technique will exploit not only nature, but man, ruthlessly.
To this kind of development Mr. Russell says, " It may be
thought that religion and sentiment will always succeed in
opposing an immovable veto." He adds, " I wish I could
think so." It would be a good thing, from Mr. Russell's
point of view, if Christianity could maintain its conviction
of the importance of the individual soul, and so stem the
development of a new ethic " which will be ruthless and,
according to traditional ideas, immoral." Since the sense of
individual worth depends on the Christian faith, it would
seem that Christianity is the religion we need, and that
Christianity alone can save us from the possible inhumanities of a one-sidedly scientific society.

And science itself needs not simply religion, but Christianity in particular. As the sense of " something beyond "
decays, and faith in the supernatural declines, the utilitarian
view of science tends to prevail, and it is fatal to science

[1] *R.P.A. Annual*, 1933.

itself. Bertrand Russell deplores the tendency to pursue knowledge for the sake of power instead of for the sake of truth. Without religion this tendency is likely to increase. " Bourgeois scholars speak of any branch of learning with mysterious awe, as if it were a thing produced in heaven, not on earth. But any science grows out of the demands of society or its classes. *No one takes the trouble to count the number of flies on a window-pane or the number of sparrows in the street, but one does count the number of horned cattle. The former figures are useful to no one ; it is very useful to know the latter.*"[1] Unless some sense of the sacred is attached to reason, science is in for a bad time when it falls into the hands of the Philistines.

RELIGION AS PURE EMOTION IRRATIONAL

The need for religion is manifest and confessed. Science and humanism are not enough. What then are we to do ? Can we retain religion as an emotion and an experience without assuming any object corresponding to it ? This is the rather naïve suggestion of H. G. Wells. He recants " God, the Invisible King." There is no such God. " If there is no sympathetic impersonal leader outside us, there is at least in us the attitude we should adopt towards a sympathetic personal leader."[2] Julian Huxley toys with the same idea. Religion is a function of human nature, and the mere exercise of the function is worth while in itself. Mystical experience involves no knowledge of or communion with a God external to ourselves, but the experience is valuable in itself. " It is a way of combining thought and feeling, inner and outer, which gives satisfaction in its own right just as does feeling well, or making a scientific discovery, or looking at a beautiful landscape."[3] Julian Huxley's religion at least complies with Aldous Huxley's conception of religion as irrational. We cannot go on indefinitely feeling awe and reverence when no worthy object of reverence exists. We cannot maintain an attitude of loyalty to a sympathetic personal leader if there is no sympathetic personal leader

---

[1] Bukharin, *Historical Materialism*, p. ix. (Italics mine.)
[2] *What Are We to Do with our Lives ?* p. 30.   [3] p. 251.

to whom to be loyal. Awe and reverence certainly imply an object, or they are meaningless. To indulge in the sense of the sacred when nothing is really sacred, or to concentrate our religious emotion on an imaginative substitute for reality, would be to share the melancholy fate of the young man in one of Dickens's novels who fell in love with a barber's dummy. Religion without revelation is a hopeless proposition. Religiously man cannot live except on words which proceed from the mouth of God.

Of course, this is not Julian Huxley's consistent attitude. He realises that the individual seeks and needs sanctions and supports outside himself, greater than himself, and such sanctions are to be found in the evolutionary process. We are in the van of a movement which is outside ourselves, and so greater than ourselves. But unfortunately the life-force as expressed in natural evolution is only greater than ourselves in a physical sense. The human spirit is the highest reality we know. The fact of progress in evolution can give us some support, but no sort of sanction, no object of reverence. If the life-force be regarded as the source of values, as a reservoir of possibilities, and not simply as a blind striving to be, it would be genuinely greater than ourselves, and we might worship it and feel that we were serving purposes not simply our own. But this is to admit the supernatural once more, to assimilate the life-force to the God of theism, and Julian Huxley will have none of this. So he cannot offer the individual the kind of sanction which he says the individual *inevitably* seeks. We might pity a poor blind striving *élan vital*. If we pretend to worship it, we are worse than the heathen in his blindness, for he, even in his blindness, attached some supernatural significance to wood and stone, and we are consciously reverencing something which we know to be spiritually and morally less than ourselves.

Similarly, Olaf Stapledon suggests that we may link up our labours for the Kingdom of God on earth with the movement of evolution. " Remembering that man is all of a piece with the rest of the universe, we may feel that this effort of his is really in some way an effort of the universe itself to wake. And if man should, after all, fail, we may still hope that somewhere else this great awakening may occur."[1] Can Mr. Stapledon give any rational meaning to his faith, or any rational justification for his faith and hope, without going beyond the limits of scientific humanism? Is there any scientific reason for preferring wakefulness to sleep, consciousness to unconsciousness? Will the universe thank us for waking it up? Doesn't the value of being awake depend on what we are awake to? In *Vice Versa*, Paul Bultitude awakes to the dismal absurdity of his position. Suppose the universe awakes only to realise that it is no better than a bottle of nasty wine, would it not have been kinder to let it sleep? If, on the other hand, the universe awakes to the realisation of something good, what is the use of that, if science assures us that the eternal sleep of cold death is the ultimate end, not only of the individual and the race, but of the universe itself? Why awake the universe to a tantalising experience which must end in the sorry wisdom of Omar Khayyám and Ecclesiastes?

Then is there any sense at all in speaking of the universe as waking, unless life and consciousness are latent throughout it, unless there is an *anima mundi* asleep in the world? But this takes us beyond physics and biology. Mr. Stapledon's feeling is just as definitely an instance of the pathetic fallacy as Christianity, and less defensible, less inspiring. It is worth while and truer to reality for children to think of themselves as part of a universe which is essentially a sleeping beauty, gradually awakened by the kisses of a fairy prince. There is some sense in such a myth. It might lead to the realisation of the truth of Henry Vaughan's lines :

> *But life is, what none can express,*
> *A quickness which my God hath kist.*

There is, indeed, only one way forward, a way indicated by Bertrand Russell at the close of his *Scientific Outlook*. There he says that science is not the only form of knowledge.

[1] *Outline for Boys and Girls*, p. 749.

" The desire for knowledge has another form, belonging to an entirely different set of emotions. The mystic, the lover, and the poet are also seekers after knowledge—not perhaps very successful seekers, but none the less worthy of respect on that account. In all forms of love we wish to have knowledge of what is loved, not for purposes of power, but for the ecstasy of contemplation. ' In knowledge of God standeth our eternal life,' but not because knowledge of God gives us any power over Him."[1] Russell is right, and Hogben quite wrong. The knowledge acquired by methods devised by the physical scientist is not the only genuine knowledge, nor is it the form of knowledge of which we stand most in need in the present crisis. For that higher wisdom we must turn to the mystics, lovers, and poets, and above all to the prophets. As a group, the scientific humanists are brilliant and attractive, stimulating and even at times progressive. But fundamentally, scientific humanism is bankrupt. It can sustain neither our faith in science nor our hopes for mankind. If we are to find our way through our present difficulties and steadily walk therein, we must live by a faith that is in closer touch with a more enduring reality.

[1] *Scientific Outlook*, p. 270.

6. IS THERE AN ALTERNATIVE?

B. *INDUSTRIAL SECULARISM*

By MAURICE B. RECKITT

THE END OF AN EPOCH

ALL DIVISIONS of historical time are to a greater or lesser degree arbitrary. Every age can claim to be in some measure " an age of transition," and contemporaries are always in danger of exaggerating the significance for civilisation of the movements of their own day. Historians may take this self-conscious and apprehensive " post-war world " less seriously than it takes itself. Yet the widespread impression that it marks the end of an epoch has more than a mere habit of neurotic introversion to justify it. For, faced with an unprecedentedly rapid acceleration of technical development and potentiality, with its accompanying accentuation of noise, strain, and nervous exhaustion, making its ever-mounting demands on mind and body, amidst every sort of human discouragement, from world war to world slump, the spirit of man is reacting to events in a manner unparalleled for more than four centuries. For the first time since the Renaissance, man has become aware rather of the frailty than of the solidity—or even the validity—of his communal achievement. The creative myth of progress seems at last to have exhausted its impulse. It can no longer avail against the facts of to-day—still less against those of to-morrow, now casting their huge shadows before them. Man is losing his nerve, and the civilisation of humanism is dispiritedly surrendering the initiative to the " trend of events."

The assumptions upon which all reformers have proceeded for two hundred years, that an answer could be found for all social problems, and that, when found, men would be ready to welcome it, are assumptions which sociological writers can no longer take as granted by those whom they would address. In the eighteenth century, the rational character of man being assumed as a bedrock principle, it was a short step to belief in his rapid perfectibility when the appropriate political technique had been discovered. Nor was there thought to be much mystery about that. " Politics," said Sieyes, " is a science I believe myself to have completed." Men swallowed such a statement as this, for experience had accumulated no material to arouse suspicion of it. Government had been the prerogative of kings and priests, who were assumed to be some sort of sub-human monsters ; and it was with perfect logic that the revolutionaries of 1792 evolved a new calendar and dated it " The Year One." In the nineteenth century, things began to look rather different. The developing science of the enlightenment seemed to suggest that perfectibility might take considerably longer than had been expected. There was an unforeseen biological substratum to progress ; yet it was progress none the less, for evolution was always upward, and we could faintly trust the larger hope. With many of us the trust was anything but faint, and the hope very large indeed.

The eighteenth century believed, the nineteenth hoped, but the twentieth does neither. A huge disillusion and an enveloping discouragement have overtaken society, and are nowhere more evidently triumphant than among the young, whose vitality has not availed them to resist it. Even the " decadence " of the nineties has zest and gusto when we compare it with the " barren leaves " and " vile bodies " presented to us by our bright young authors of to-day. Disillusion is easy to account for, and is not wholly attributable to the war—or even to the peace. But the discouragement of to-day is more menacing and more significant, for even the prospect of a roseate future would not dispel it. Nay, it might even deepen it, and there are signs that it is doing so ; for that prospect is before us and men are afraid to look upon it. The resources of civilisation, say our professional comforters, are not exhausted. Indeed they are not. But our vitality is exhausted in face of the most bracing and emancipating challenge a potential civilisation has ever offered to mankind.

Men look before them and see two alternatives—depression and free leisure. Both terrify them. For both threaten the persistence of that employment which, however little its particular form might be welcomed, has provided in its character of creditable routine a shelter from the challengers of full and responsible living. So long as progress offered a rationale for social effort, and employment an automatic medium for it, life had only to be endured, it did not have to be faced. The war offered to the vast majority in heightened form occasion for praiseworthy but irresponsible effort. We had to do our bit, and for few of us was there any difficulty in finding the bit to be done. We piled up armaments or learnt to use them—as the Russians are now piling up tractors and learning to use them—for the sake of the new world that was to come afterwards. But the fundamental social problem is not the attainment of a new world of plenty and distributed opportunity, but the development of the will and the capacity to live in such a world. For the new world makes new demands even while it brings new gifts, indeed because it brings them. If we flee from the gifts because of the demands, we must see society wither away in want, envy, confusion, and a depression that is even more sinister in its spiritual than in its material effects. If we are to enter into the heritage of leisure and abundance promised us within a generation, we must develop new qualities to match the opportunity.

For this is not only a crisis for society, it is a crisis for the human spirit. We cannot go on as we are, for, as we are, we are losing the will to go on at all. It is a remarkable fact that amidst an unparalleled glorification of the physical— of sex, of bodily culture, of every form of gymnastics and athleticism, and of the pre-occupations of the beauty parlour—this age, for all its emancipation from the shackles of the past, from marital obligation to petticoats, is exhibiting not an exuberance of vitality but a decline of it. Even passion is not preserving its illusions. " I feel that this is the

Sc

beginning of something rather heavenly," says one of Mr. Evelyn Waugh's " vile bodies " to his paramour on the morrow of their first night together. " Nothing really heavenly ever happens," she replies. " All for love," perhaps ; but the world is not well lost, for the world is not worth losing. Is life in such circumstances worth keeping ? How many answer this question in gas-ovens and beneath tube trains our papers tell us, for suicide has not yet ceased to be news. But it has ceased to be rare, and it is losing the tragic dignities of its tradition. Men do not commonly, as of old, shoot themselves in the cause of honour, nor women drown themselves for love ; they " give up " because " they can't go on " ; kill themselves in temper for a whim, or from fear of a reduction in some bourgeois standard of living. The crisis of an insane world-economy is doubtless responsible for much of the despair that leads to these things, but it does not tell the whole story. Men with a real hold upon life, with a genuine appetite for the multiform variety of human experience, do not let go so easily. It would seem that Stevenson is wrong, and that the world is not so full of a number of things that we can be as happy as kings. The number of things has indeed been miraculously expanded in this century by human ingenuity, yet are we not as happy as kings. We are not even as happy as men.

THE RESPONSIBILITY OF RELIGION

The recovery of faith is the pre-condition of effective moral energy. Man at the height of his material achievement has had the confidence, which he never needed so much, sapped by secular doubts of his moral autonomy and spiritual significance. Mechanistic philosophies and Behaviourist psychologies have stolen from him the conviction that he is the master of his fate, and have left him with nothing but a *psyche* over which to attain to a precarious captaincy. However much faith there may have been in the " Honest Doubt " of a Victorian generation with security enough to indulge in such luxuries, it is something at once more resolute and more rational which is needed to pull things round in the extremities of to-day. It is no use hoping for a faith equal to the emergency which does not draw its strength, consciously or unconsciously, from the faith of the Christian community, effectively explicated and exemplified by those who nominally profess it. The recovery of human initiative over events will never spring from the dissemination of a purely sub-lunar optimism, for which, indeed, there are scarcely more grounds in reason than there is support in the contemporary mood. Faith in a Divine Reason independent of the universe it has created and sustained ; in a living God identifying himself with the fate of his human creation ; belief that the creature thus redeemed has eternal significance, that man is not inevitably the slave of events or of technique, and that a rational solution for human problems exists *and can be found*—these are the conditions which can alone recreate the energy of spirit and mind sufficient to save civilisation from a new Dark Ages.

Religion, then, must lead the rescue party upon every plane of human need. In particular, it has to recover from secularism, the bewildering jungle of modern industrialism, making paths in that wilderness, and planting anew landmarks now long overthrown. It is an oft-quoted dictum that Christianity has not failed ; it has been found difficult and left untried. However this may be true of Christianity in general, it is conspicuously the case with Christian sociology in particular. It was the ever more bewildering character of the *terrain* which, more even than any weakness imposed by its developing internal divisions, brought about the standstill and ultimately the defeat of the Christian sociology which had dominated and largely moulded the mediæval synthesis. Religion did not evacuate the position from any growth of the conviction that it had no right to occupy it. This conviction came much later, and was, in fact, the rationalisation of an apostasy. As Mr. Tawney has declared—and definitively established—what requires justification is not the claim that social problems should be regarded as within the provinces of Christian concern and guidance, but the relatively recent affirmation that they should not.

This affirmation, let it be repeated, has not derived its strength from principle, but from a spirit of defeatism originally implanted by the enlargement of the scale of the problem. This enlargement was, indeed, formidable enough, and it came about far more rapidly than is generally appreciated. While the mediæval façade lingered substantially unaltered through the fifteenth century, and even into its successor, vast changes were taking place behind its traditional elevations. In particular, economic relations were ceasing to be predominantly the sphere of direct transactions susceptible to a code of primarily individual ethics. The later mediæval schoolmen and doctors might, on the whole, strive eagerly and honestly to expand and modify that code to fit the facts of an expanding economy. But the facts went too fast for them. Complexity began to obliterate responsibility, as it has ever increasingly done down to our own day, in which " world causes " have begun to be presented by the politicians, into whose hands the control of economic events affecting millions has nominally fallen, as a pretext on which they may absolve themselves for their incapacity to make any impression upon them.

Yet however difficult Christian sociology may have been found, it must assuredly be no longer left untried. It is precisely the expansion of social problems beyond the scope of the individual conscience, and even understanding, which so urgently demands the exemplification afresh of the prophetic office of the Church. For the complexity of contemporary social phenomena has reached such a pitch as to produce in individuals a sense of fatalism about the economic circumstances of their lives. The " Intelligent Man " may conscientiously work his way to the end of a " Guide through World Chaos," but his studies are more likely to impress him with the magnitude of chaos than with the efficacy of intelligence. Moreover, he may find himself suspecting that intelligence is not enough ; that something more akin to divination is needed, some power which will exhibit a capacity to disentangle the essential from the contingent, and teach men afresh what are the primary ends of human order now concealed behind the false axioms of financiers and commissars. Such must be in every age the responsibility of religion, and, until its spokesmen plainly reassume it, men will continue to feel that events are for ever now beyond their control, that nothing they may attempt to strive for in their social relations will make any effective difference, and that industry and commerce have ceased to be a sphere of moral significance. It is no rhetorical flourish which describes as soul-destroying an outlook which is spreading more widely with every apparent new confirmation of it.

THE CANONISATION OF ECONOMIC ACTIVITY

Hence we find conspicuous in the economic sphere that discouragement which is now the characteristic of a civilisation dominated by an exhausted humanism. It is moreover a striking, if by now a familiar and unchallengeable, fact that no objective justification for such discouragement exists. We are weary by this time of having it demonstrated to us that we live in an age of plenty. As has already been suggested, such demonstrations actually tend with many people to enhance the discouragement they should logically dispel. For they threaten the restoration of that pre-war normality of assured and praiseworthy routine in which toil, however aimless, was consoled for by security, and a respectable gloss was cast over occupations which exacted from those who followed them the minimum of intelligent effort and moral energy. Duty was done and automatically rewarded ; the requirements of virtue were thus fulfilled, and nothing more could reasonably be expected. This utterly sub-Christian conception, indifferent alike to the claims of vocation and the call to the perfecting of every human faculty, was the product of that social apostasy of religion already described. This development culminated in the unhallowed union of Puritanism and Capitalism, which, for all its superficial religiosity, was the real source of industrial secularism. As a result thereof, economic activity, as such, regardless alike of end and of means, became established as a guarantee of moral integrity which no man might venture to impugn. Profit could thus be regarded as a barometer of worshipful energy, and, whether avarice or true enterprise were the dynamic of it, became, even for religion, an irrelevant consideration. But while the opportunity for profit was not for every man, the obligation of a maximum of economic activity was not to be escaped by any. For the masses it involved the imposition of a relentless assiduity, accelerating with the acceleration of technique, and the distortion of the ancient Christian sanctions for work into the Capitalist compulsion to employment.

From the tyranny of this inhuman and increasingly irrational pressure we have scarcely begun to escape. It dominates our mental habit; it prejudices our every effort to handle the emancipating opportunities of a power age. A century and more ago it gave to the Industrial Revolution that peculiar combination of self-conscious rectitude and social brutality which acute minds have perceived to be lingering in the assumptions and operation of contemporary sound finance. As mechanisation developed, the great engines came to embody in concrete form the idea of worshipful energy, crushing out beauty from the earth, recking naught of the worker's needs as a skill-hungry animal, and clogging the world with goods which the laws of their being forbade them to distribute. For it is economic activity in production which alone may be rewarded according to the canons of industrialism. So we must watch mechanisation spreading with an aimless voracity, stimulated by the assumed necessity of putting money into circulation solely through the channels of producer-income in a world which is rapidly eliminating the human agent from routine industry. And finally, to bedevil the situation, we find the whole process of multiplying the economic assets of society requires to be initiated by loan credit from the banks.

accounted into prices as debt, and withdrawn by cancellation from the purchasing-power of the community.

It falls to other hands to analyse these developments more minutely and to suggest correctives of them demanded by a fresh application to economics of the requirements of reason and a reviving Christian sociology. What this section is concerned to establish is that this development, which seems to have reached in our day a supremely menacing culmination, has come about as the result of a complete surrender of initiative by religion to the unrestrained power-striving of Mammon. All the traditional controls characteristic of a Christian economic—the regulation of price by the objective reality of justice ; the restraint of usury as a practice inevitably involving exploitation ; the imposition upon individual enterprise of a functional organisation with religious sanctions—all these were set aside in order that man might have his head, and, economically speaking, do his damnedest. As a result, human order has been submerged, and the purpose of industry obliterated in the blind intensification of it. The perversion of thrift into avarice by a gigantic system of investment has laid up a vast treasure upon earth which the moth and rust of modern financial theory are corrupting into a dead weight of debt. We have taken so much thought for the morrow that millions are in dire need to-day of what they shall eat and wherewith they shall be clothed. The canonisation of economic activity has ended in a world of unnatural passivity in which not only are man's engines falling silent and the wheels thereof ceasing to revolve, but even Nature's workings are suspended over fields in which wheat and barley grow no more.

THE DYNAMIC OF INDUSTRIAL SECULARISM

Deadlock and scarcity might seem a singular outcome of a process which had set so much store on the expenditure of energy and devoted itself so whole-heartedly to the accumulation of material things. Absorption with these ends has led to the familiar charge against our civilisation that it is materialist, an accusation which has been particularly in favour with Christian critics thereof. The indictment is certainly not without substance so far as some of the second-ary manifestations of a plutocratic society are concerned. But as an ultimate analysis it is inadequate, and not free from suspicion of being based upon a superficial antithesis of spirit and matter as essentially good and evil which is far closer to Manicheism than to Christian orthodoxy. " The enemy of Christianity to-day," Mr. V. A. Demant has acutely observed,[1] " is not materialism but a false re-ligion." We are the victims of something far more subtle and more powerful than mere greed and indulgence, rather is the root evil " an inexorable and very ideal philosophy."

" To make things in order to enjoy them was the ' in-fantile ' and sane motive of our pre-industrial era. Now we are not gross enough for that—we make things in order to sell them. We may enjoy a few things by the way, motor cars or crépe rubber soles, but the true ideal of a modern industrial state is to sell abroad more things than it buys—a favourable balance of trade—which in practice has come to mean, we make things in order to get other nations into our debt. This is called ' economic solvency.' . . .

" The heart of the modern social system is not in material things but in money as the symbol of power. Not the fields or factories, but the bank is the holy of holies. Money is an idea ; now wanted not so much for what it will buy as for what it signifies in the way of prestige, security, creditorship, political power—and is the dy-namic power which now often over-rides all the personal, spiritual, and social values to which Christianity is com-mitted. When in the name of human dignity and free-dom the system is challenged, the reply of its upholders is that the complainants are materialistic-minded people

[1] In an article contributed to *Stockholm* (1931, No. 1), entitled " Is Modern Civilisation Materialistic ? " from which the passages here quoted are taken.

who would sacrifice an ideal of economic stability for a mess of pottage. It is those who protest against the achievements of industrialism who are making a material claim, and a just one ; its sponsors and experts are far above that level in their anxiety to maintain certain ideas of economic soundness—and this while a few millions are starving in the world and there is more power to produce necessities and luxuries than the producing countries know what to do with. If industrial society is materialistically minded it is making a very bad job of it as far as the greater part of its population are concerned."

The truth seems to be that pride rather than greed has been the fundamental dynamic of industrial secularism. But the goal of pride is power, and power cannot preserve its prerogatives in a world of widely distributed abundance and opportunity. It presupposes scarcity, and all that threatens to end such scarcity is, whether consciously so recognised or not, its enemy. However our economic world-order may appear to have escaped the control of human agency, it is as a fact controlled to a remarkable degree by the centralised interest of financial power—a power at issue with the realities of human achievement no less than with the clamant demands of human need. We witness (as for example in the half-stifled claims of American " Technocracy ") what Oswald Spengler has called " the despairing struggle of technical thought to maintain its liberty against money thought." We witness man first robbed of his human status to become an epiphenomenon of industrialism as an employee, and then thrust out as redundant to society altogether in his new character of " unemployee." The wheels slow down, the ships rot in the ports, and the corn ceases to grow. Even gold no longer performs the strange function allotted to it of measuring and activating, within its narrow and artificial limits, the real wealth of mankind. But finance preserved its soundness and its masters their power.

THE NATURE OF CONTEMPORARY ACQUISITIVENESS

It is surely small wonder that we see in such a world a corrosive and wholly unnatural fixation upon gain. Contemporary acquisitiveness has been well defined as a misdirected search for security. In every stratum of society men are moved to grasp for more as the only way that seems open to them to maintain themselves where they are. Avarice has almost ceased to be recognisable as a temptation in a social order which presents it rather as a condition of self-preservation. Men who cannot find either in the practice or in the theory of their economics environment, illumination, or even common sense, drift into accepting as normal a ruthless, self-regarding struggle against deprivations which are plainly without any justification in the nature of things. Moreover, fidelity to duty being no longer rewarded even by secure employment, and less still by any opportunity to rise, the masses are tempted more and more to break out of the crowded compound of destitution by imitating—through indulgence in gambling, and, still more significantly, in " banditry "—methods analogous to those by which the most conspicuous figures of plutocracy have climbed to power. It is unrealistic, and even pharisaical, for the Churches to meet these tendencies by nothing but a campaign of prohibition directed against those whose imprisoned lives offer no natural opportunity of relief from drab monotony and destitute idleness. The Tote Club and the greyhound track, the " racing special " and the gigantic sweepstake, are not mere unnatural cancers upon contemporary society which, were they ruthlessly cut away, could regain its health. They are symptoms of deep-rooted disease in the body politic, and those who fail to diagnose, to stigmatise, and to treat them as such are ignorant of the realities of their age and of the maladies that inevitably breed in it.

The truth that has to be faced is that the withdrawal of religious control over social development, and even of any religious understanding and judgment of it, has made the very appreciation—to say nothing of the practice—of virtue so unnaturally difficult for thousands that power to discriminate the true and the good is being obliterated in modern civilisation. " The world," as M. Maritain has declared, " will presently become uninhabitable for anyone but saints. The rest will drag out their lives in despair or fall beneath the level of man." It has long ceased to be a question of whether the Church has a right to any say in social affairs. It is rather a problem of how society can go forward at all without the illumination, the discrimination, and the power of resistance to every kind of falsehood of theory and value which the Church should be pre-eminently fitted to give. Nor is this a problem which will wait indefinitely for its solution. Industrial secularism has brought Western civilisation very near to an abyss of material ruin and spiritual despair. It is only the prophetic leadership of a religion revitalised by a sense of its vast responsibility which can achieve the rescue of humanity by the redirection of its footsteps.

THE TASK OF A CHRISTIAN SOCIOLOGY

What is involved in such a leadership ? Something far more definite and more distinctive than the majority of Christian people have been accustomed even to imagine. The effect of Christianity upon society has generally been conceived as being exercised either indirectly through the individual example and influence of the faithful, or by corporate religious exhortation to purity of motive and ethical idealism. But a true Christian sociology—to adopt a term now rapidly gaining recognition, and even some degree of understanding—necessarily pre-supposes something much more fundamental. It rejects as wholly inadequate any conception of " christianising the social order " which confines itself to a process of infusing individuals with pure motives and benevolent intentions while leaving the aims and purposes of economics and industrial organisations unquestioned. It is vital for religious people to realise that upon our plutocratic society an increasing determinism is being imposed as a result, not of any

Marxist theory, but of the operation of the scarcity " principles " of financial orthodoxy. Within these imprisoning limits there is ever less opportunity for even the most respectable motives to exercise any beneficent effort. The employer cannot be generous to his workpeople while he is forced to trade on a cumulative deficit ; the worker cannot for ever accept sacrifices which undermine his physique and threaten to break up his home. Religion will never get anywhere by trying to make the false assumptions (" we are a poor country ") and the unreal objectives (" finding more work ")—so largely taken for granted by contemporary thought—produce morally satisfying results. For religion is concerned with something more fundamental than any system of ethics. It must be concerned with the validity and rationality of what men are seeking to do before it can usefully assess the fidelity with which they seek it.

A Christian sociology, again, will have to be something much deeper than a religious dynamic for individual reformation. Its quest will not be for expedients, whether ethical or practical, for keeping a misdirected and purely secular industrialism from falling into dissolution by feats of moral heroism on the part of its victims. It will refuse to regard the industrial system as intended to be either an organ of social discipline, or a sort of moral obstacle-race by perseverance in which a proportion of the competitors may qualify for an ultimate salvation. " Social good, is good," it has been well remarked, " because it has intrinsic value in the sight of God, and not because it provides opportunity for moral activity." The social function of religion is something deeper than the satisfaction of the individual conscience or the prosecution of humanitarian reform. Its aim is nothing less than social redemption, and its true purpose the elucidation of standards by reference to which human society can be brought back to its authentic purpose as a sphere in which God's will for perfect reason and justice and love can be expressed without encountering inflexible obstacles in the objectives and institutions which men take for granted in the secular philosophy of their day.

It is essential for Christian opinion to appreciate that, while the fullest respect has to be paid to the material assembled (if not always to the conclusions reached) by the social sciences, he can never accept a purely secular approach to the problem of human order as truly realistic. For that problem is not merely a matter of social mechanics ; it is the problem of a being with a spiritual nature and an eternal significance. The first postulate of a Christian sociology, then, must be the primacy of supernatural ends, as the second will be the rational validity of social objectives. Assessed from this standpoint, the culmination of industrial secularism, as exemplified in its contemporary deadlock, will reveal not only the bankruptcy of a self-regarding economy, but the absurdity of the contradictions in which it has involved itself. The scientific effort to eliminate redundant human labour, clashes inexorably with the assumed social necessity to multiply employment. The " prosperity " presumed to be bound up with the dispatch of goods for export (a universal goal of industrialised communities in a world of artificially limited markets) co-exists not only with a deplorable lag between real and effective demand at home, but with an actual embarrassment caused by imported commodities from overseas. Many more such contradictions could be suggested, and will indeed have been illustrated in earlier sections of this volume. If organised religion is to offer any leadership whatever in the moral and intellectual confusion of to-day, its spokesmen must discipline themselves to think and speak in complete independence of hypotheses, the validity of which they have for too long been unwilling to test or examine with any seriousness. The Church can never interpret its own truth in the terms of the world's falsehood.

THE PROSPECTS OF INDUSTRIAL RELEASE

The Christian message, then, must be plainly disengaged from all the fallacies and distortions, whether of consolation or prevarication, to which men resort in order to " by-pass " the need of facing the essential issues of the moment.

One can detect, for example, a sinister tendency to borrow moralistic phraseology in order to reconcile man to the endurance of deprivations based on dubious, if not actually invalid, propositions. The noble Christian conception of the call to personal sacrifice is invoked to induce participants in every stage of the industrial process to accommodate themselves to the requirements of no objective reality, but to the Procrustean demands of financial monopoly. Hallowed by the description " sacrifices all round," these unnatural deprivations offer a consoling glow of virtue to those who are falsely taught to believe that they suffer in humanity's interests. It is more than time that Christian opinion freed itself from the hypnosis of such verbiage, and restored the validity of the idea of sacrifice by relating it to reality on the one hand and human volition on the other. The obligations of personal asceticism, the give and take of family relations, the disciplining of self-will in the innumerable contacts of social life—such are a few of the characteristic directions in which sacrifice will be abundantly called for in the life of all faithful Christians. It is for every reason deplorable that such calls to voluntary self-surrender should be confused with the enforced and unjustifiable impositions of an oppressive economy.

It is indeed essential that the Church should no longer evade the challenge of a world in which, with the capacity to overcome enslaving poverty and toil now actually at hand, the basic spiritual problems of life can emerge, not for a leisured few, but for the whole of every community of Western man. Religion has to take its primary share immediately in what is perhaps the largest spiritual and intellectual adaptation ever demanded of mankind. As Mr. J. B. S. Haldane has graphically stated, " To-day the external conditions of life in civilised communities differ more from those of 1829 than the conditions of 1829 from those of Noah's flood." It is entirely useless, even if it were morally justifiable, for Christian people to lament that so much potential plenty should have been vouchsafed to all in a world where but a few have hitherto regarded themselves as having any right to it, or to wring their hands over the moral havoc they postulate for populations no longer safely locked up in factories for eight and more hours a day. Assuredly the prospect of leisure opens up its problems, as does the appropriate handling of that enormous power-mechanism which now opens the way for it. I have dealt at some length with these matters elsewhere,[1] and others treat of them in this volume. But the magnitude of such problems must not intimidate the Christian realist into an evasion of them which will prove as impossible in practice as it would be spiritless in principle.

The Christian sociologist will not be likely to pour out any indiscriminate benediction upon either the development or the technique of industrialism. Under the impetus of plutocracy it has in innumerable ways mangled the body and maimed the spirit of man. It still does both. None the less, its achievement, and still more its latest developments, most especially perhaps in the potentialities of electric energy, offer to us now a manifold opportunity of release, and not from material anxieties only. For, by a paradox, the significance of which is not always perceived, the implementing of abundance, for the postponement of which there exist to-day only artificial causes, so far from plunging society into materialism, is likely to reduce the unnatural pre-occupation with money and all that is bound up with it in a world of induced scarcity. That an idolatry of material success exists to-day, and exercises a devastating effect on the human spirit, is indisputable. Its manifestations range from the savage ruthlessness of avarice through every kind of insatiableness (the *pleonexia* stigmatised by St. Paul) to the degrading snobberies inculcated by the publicity-monger, to whose interests our popular newspapers are so largely dedicated. Consider the implications of such an advertisement as the following :

" ' It's smart to own a ——' says the man who knows !
' If a man who opens the doors of many hundreds of

[1] *Faith and Society*, pp. 359–73 and 342–58 (Longmans, 1932).

cars a day doesn't notice the kind of cars the doors belong to, he isn't what I call an observant man. Now take me. *Do I know what a man is by the car he drives up in ?* Do I know what cars the real swells buy ? Well, I ought to and I do. And I'll tell you this. Every day I open more —— doors. And the people in them ? They're what I call the new poor—used to luxury, you know, and what's what, but a little short of what you might call ' the treacle.' Of course they buy these new ——, how else could they get what they're accustomed to, without paying—— Excuse me, Sir. Good morning, Sir Charles —— What did I tell you, Sir ? ' "

We must, it seems, revise our familiar proverb and say that to-day a man is known not by the company but by the car he keeps.

A lady once told the writer that in speaking to a neighbour of some newly arrived visitors to her town, she remarked that she had heard that they were very nice people. " Have you heard that ? " was the reply ; " *I* heard that they hadn't a penny to bless themselves with."

Such are the not unnatural values of a financial civilisation. The deceitfulness of riches, of which our Lord spoke, not only betrays the few who enjoy the indulgence of them but dazzles and distorts the vision of the multitudes who gaze hungrily on a spectacle in which they can never hope to share. There will never be a time, one must suppose, when no such possibility of deceitfulness will exist to parade in some form its fatal temptation to the soul of man. The allurements of avarice and envy will not be finally exorcised by any form of social reconstruction. But it is surely reasonable to conclude that in a society in which normal human needs are met upon a normal scale, the tendency to canalise natural aspirations into a wholly unnatural absorption in material success, and the sordid and often ruthless means to its attainment, will be halted and reversed. If it is true, as many of our most profound social critics are now contending, that we have not to-day to put down the mighty from their seat as a means to exalting the humble and meek, but vice versa, it is surely more than probable that the levelling up of human security and opportunity, which a released abundance will render possible, will rather undermine than strengthen the mingled envy and sycophancy which the harassed many have exhibited towards the seemingly so fortunate few.

There can be no doubt, moreover, that the plutocracy in which industrial secularism has culminated has gravely distorted the motive for human co-operation in work and the basic Christian principle of vocation. It is quite spontaneously assumed as axiomatic by many professing Christians that economic success is the primary object which men will consider when selecting an occupation for their children and when following one for themselves. It is time that Christian opinion was awakened by its leaders to the fact that such an attitude is not merely sub-Christian, but actnally anti-Christian. It exemplifies that " covetousness which is idolatry " and as much a sin deadly to the soul as adultery, cruelty, and cherished hatred. It is indeed a principal part of the indictment which Christianity has got to draw against the economic order which its own apostasy has contributed to develop, that it cramps and stifles the possibility of vocation at every turn, squeezes the square peg into the round hole, and encourages men to compensate themselves for their thwarted aspirations by turning their economic tasks into a hunt for mere profit or a yet more destructive struggle for personal power.

THE OPPORTUNITY OF FAITH

The essence of industrial secularism is the exaltation of economic activity at the expense of social purpose. It gained its first initiative over the restraints of a Christian social philosophy in a world of peasants and craftsmen labouring with some measure of spontaneity and responsibility to fulfil functions clearly recognised and understood. It has attained its culmination in a world of proletarians and " unemployees " wandering bewildered in a maze of universal depression. Under its influence, industry has ceased to be a natural mode of human energy and vocation, and become a breeding-ground of pride and avarice for the successful, and of apathy and discouragement for the remainder. It is important to appreciate that this is not the upshot merely of the developed technology of the Industrial Revolution. That huge enlargement of economic opportunity would have had results very different from those that have developed from it had it not taken place in a world from which the saving principles of Christian social tradition had been long expelled. The nearest thing to a social principle to which the new Capitalist philosophy could aspire was the gratuitous assumption that the general good would accrue from the complete unleashing of enlightened self-interest. By what considerations self-interest was to be enlightened did not appear ; but it was confidently claimed that the new plutocracy would at least deliver the goods. But financial power, which has been in reality dominant ever since usury escaped from restraint some four centuries ago, has subordinated technical potentialities as ruthlessly as it has trampled upon human ones. Capitalism can no longer deliver the goods, it can only accumulate them ; and the waves of plenty beat helplessly against the dam of sound finance.

The liquidation of commercial prosperity, most recently and most significantly in the United States, where its consolidation had been most universally assumed, presents a fresh and morally inescapable opportunity for religion to return to the task of social interpretation. We have reached the end of optimism ; the world will belong to those who believe and understand, and do not merely hope. The degrading superstition of regarding acquisitive success as an index of individual significance and social value is withering at last in the blizzard of world depression. The secular religion of the modern world gains much of its force from its rejection of this base idolatry ; for, Communism, spiritually blind and ruthless as it is, has witnessed to the reviving conviction of mankind that private advantage at the general expense is not the purpose of human order. But, in exalting secular collectivity above human personality, it falls into an error as destructive of true social values as the perishing philosophy which it opposes with so much prospect of success. In a conflict of falsehoods, staged in a world of deadlock and drained vitality, no authentic recovery can come, save from the divine society which must interpret what it worships—the Way, the Truth, and the Life.

Such is the call to the Church of this generation. But the call carries no guarantee of success with it, even if the response be faithful. It is not for us to imprison God's purposes within human horizons, or to demand that religion shall recover in a lifetime what it has been so largely content to surrender for centuries. We may be entering upon a new Dark Ages of social confusion, world upheaval, and racial war. But the lesson of the Dark Ages is that the faithfulness of a few may restore what the recklessness of millions has seemed to obliterate for ever ; and a study of those centuries is a revelation of the inadequacy of evolutionary hypotheses and materialist philosophies of history. The man born in 880 might have died in despair of every Christian value and every human hope. But fifty years after his death the assured foundations of mediæval Christendom were laid. The man born in 1880 may die in a similar dismay. Yet from his fidelity may spring the Christendom of the new world, which, without it, may be halted for generations.

It is indeed impossible to exaggerate the significance which attaches to the illumination which even a few, faithful to the light vouchsafed to them by their belief, may shed upon a world suffering more perhaps from the darkness of bewilderment than from a hardness of heart. Indeed, the paradox of accelerating crisis with a really widespread good-will, reveals that the conventionally Christian efforts to solve social issues exclusively on the plane of motive are inherently and necessarily inadequate. Something more profound is needed, and that something religion is already, though belatedly and insufficiently, stirring itself to supply

—a Christian judgment not merely on the actions of men within the social structure, but upon the validity of that social structure itself. The task is urgent, for men are less unready for such a judgment at this moment than at any time since the rise of industrialism, if only by reason of the exhaustion of their hopes of it. They are sated with achievement which brings with it no solace ; and we may apply to this generation, not without hope, the words of George Herbert :

> *Let him be rich and weary, that at least*
> *If goodness lead him not, yet weariness*
> *May toss him to my breast.*

6. IS THERE AN ALTERNATIVE?

c. *COMMUNIST SECULARISM*

By NICOLAI BERDIAEFF

I. CHRISTIANITY AND COMMUNISM IN RUSSIA

CHRISTIANITY in our times has to live in the midst of a completely new and unfamiliar reality. Much in the world has moved away from religion, or has become indifferent or hostile to it. Christianity is challenged from all sides. But those questions of the modern age which take the form of hostility to Christianity cannot always be lightly turned aside by a Christian conscience as products of evil, as deeds of Satan. By such a simplified attitude Christians relieve themselves of responsibility and refuse to fulfil their proper duties. The challenge offered to Christianity by the opposing forces is a stimulus to Christian thought and creative effort.

Among the forces hostile to Christianity, doubtless the most powerful and threatening in the world is Communism. Communism declares war on all religion. It considers all religion " opium for the people " (the expression was first used by Karl Marx in his *Introduction to a Critique of the Philosophy of Hegel*). Communism appears on the scene not simply as a social and economic system which might be religiously neutral, but as a religion—a new religion with its own " opium for the people," an opium with a powerful effect on the consciousness of the masses. The pretensions of Communism are thoroughly religious in their nature. Communism pretends to give answers to all the questions of human life. It offers an integral comprehension of the world (*Weltanschauung*) easily comprisable in a brief catechism ; it combines theory and practice ; it attempts to control the human spirit to its very depths ; it wishes to be not only an organised society, a State, but a Church as well, judging the conscience of men. It includes within itself a Messianic faith, it teaches the salvation of mankind. And as a religion, as a doctrine of salvation, as a discipline for the human spirit, it clashes cruelly with the Christian faith and conscience. Hence comes the fanaticism of Communism, its intolerance of all religion, of any other system of thought ; hence come its anti-religious propaganda and anti-religious persecution. This is inherent, not in the economics and the politics of Communism, but in its religious nature.

It is very difficult for the West to understand Russian Communism. Neither those who wish to unite against it as a threat to the existing social order, not those who, attracted by the power and scale of the experiment, are interested in its novelty, quite understand the Communism of Russia. It is hard to understand because it quite fantastically combines two elements—the international and the national. The international element is bound up with Marxism, which the West understands, but which in the West never produced anything like Russian Communism ; the national element is connected with the past of Russia, with the Russian character, the formation of the Russian spirit, with its maximalism, its Messianism, with the absence in the Russian consciousness of the Roman concept of property. Russian Communism is of the East, the Communism of a partly Asiatic people. There need be no sense of inferiority in this phrase ; for the European type of culture is not the only one extant. But it must be distinctly said that only the upper cultural layers of the Russian people were in contact with western Europe ; for western Europe never touched the masses. The spirit of the Russian people was cultured by Eastern Christianity—Orthodoxy ; and this produced a quite distinct type of soul. Like all revolutions, the Russian Revolution bears a universal idea, but it is revealed in the Russian national elements. The English and French Revolutions both had a universal idea, but in both cases this idea passed through the prism of the national types involved. In the universal idea of the Russian Revolution there are unrecognised Christian elements ; but they are submerged by the anti-Christian ideology of Marxism, they are directed into conflict with Christianity.

We have here to deal with a curious regeneration of a religious psychology. The religious energy of the spirit, result of many centuries of Christian education, can be turned into another channel and directed into the service of anti-Christian aims. Communism is a militant challenge to Christianity ; it competes with Christianity, attempts to replace it. Communism wants to set up the Kingdom of God on earth, only without God.

In many phases Communism is a caricature of Christianity, a perversion of ideas, which in their origin are Christian. Whence does Communism derive its idea of the equal worth and brotherhood of all men, so foreign to the aristocratic cultures of Greece and Rome and of Renaissance Europe? Whence does Communism get its supernationalism, its universalism, so foreign to civilised nations and cultures of our time, or that concept of life as the service of some super-personal purpose which is so rapidly fading from the consciousness of people of the modern age ? Or, finally, whence comes the idea of the communion of men as in one body, an idea foreign to the individualism of Western civilisation ? All this is taken from Christianity, but perverted and distorted into a caricature. All this is to be realised by terrible violence and cruelty to man, because it is to be attained in the spirit of materialism, apart from all spiritual values. But we must remember that every time such a challenge is offered to Christianity in the form of a realisation, even if distorted, of that which Christianity proclaimed but has not realised, this challenge is a reproach and a reminder, the putting of a question which demands an answer. Such is the challenge of Communism.

The Communist experiment in Russia is in one sense the Russian Revolution as defined and formed by Russian historical conditions. In this quality, it is a political revolution finally ending the absolute monarchy, and an agrarian revolution, liquidating the remnants of Russian feudalism and giving the land to the peasants. The specific qualities of the Russian Revolution derive from the fact that it took place in an atmosphere of war, when the army was breaking up and when military methods were transferred from the front to the interior of the country. All revolutions have a military character, the English and the French Revolutions included, but the Russian Revolution was military to the maximum degree : it was accomplished by a people which had been turned into an army and had received a military training.

In the Russian Revolution we find Asiatic features, foreign to western Europe. In it there is no sign of the spirit of citizenship which played such a rôle in the French Revolution. On it there lies the seal of the unique humility of the Russian folk, its capacity to bear suffering in meekness. Under the conditions of the time, Bolshevism was the only destructive, and at the same time organising, power which could control the situation, could satisfy the instincts of the mass and deal with the actual combination of forces. Bolshevism made use of everything : the lack of desire for war and the impossibility of carrying it on ; the lack of social discipline amongst Russian peasantry ; the religious structure of the Russian soul, ever seeking social justice, inclined to mysticism and maximalism and capable of almost endless sacrifice ; the subconscious Russian Messianism, held in a way peculiar to Russia, and quite different from that of the West. Bolshevism made use of the Russian people's lack of an individualistic concept of property, and of Russian collectivism, which has its roots in Christianity. It corresponded with the Russian tradition of a despotic Government from above, of the enormous rôle of the State in promoting culture. It made use of the Russian's capacity for faith, his lack of scepticism. Even the Nihilists were always men of faith and dogma. Contrary to the opinion widely held among Russians, the Russian Revolution has a peculiarly national character. And even if it is characterised by internationalism instead of nationalism, this is in reality only an ancient Russian trait, the old dream of a universal mission. Here we approach the

Soviet Communist experiment from another side. It bears in itself a universal idea—wishes to be a world-revolution and to have a world-significance. But Russian Communism represents a danger to the world ; because other groups base on it their hopes for the beginning of a new world-epoch and the building of a new society. Russian Communism interests us from just this world viewpoint.

II. THE TYRANNY OF THE COLLECTIVE

Communism wishes to create a new way, to be a new stage in anthropological development. Its pretensions in this regard are very large. The new man will bear no resemblance to the European individualistic man as he is revealed, beginning with the period of the Renaissance. The new Communist man is no apotheosis of the individual, autonomous, endowed with individual initiative and boundless yearning—no Faust of modern history, no atom possessing exactly the same formal rights as every other atom, though not at all equal in actual power or material possibilities. It was this individualistic man of modern times that created humanist culture, with science and capitalism as well. But neither is the Communist man the Christian man who still remains, although suppressed, in the lower levels of the modern individual. The new man of Communism is a social man, socialised to the depths of his spirit, with a socialised consciousness and conscience, socialised thinking and activity. It is incorrect to say that the Communist man has lost all sense of the difference between good and evil, that he is amoral. In a certain sense he is submitted to a very rigid standard, a severe moral discipline, but one quite different from that of either Christianity or humanism.

This morality is that of the social *collective*, and the subject of moral evaluation is no longer a person, but the collective. For this morality everything necessary to the realisation of a perfect Communist society is possible, but not at all that which is needed for individual human aims. This morality demands of man great sacrifices, but it offers an almost mystic joy of submergence in the collective life, in which the tragedy of the life of the individual disappears, as well as the fear of death, the fear of failure, and of the difficulties of life. Man lives in the whole, in the collective, as in the brightest reality and the abundant life. For the new man, life in the collective replaces that life in God which the Christian considers the highest aim of life. And just as, for the Christian, life in God is to resolve all contradictions and difficulties, so for the Communist they are to be solved by life in the collective, and by collective labour, as the sole reality of existence.

The new social man is not at all a man of economics, the *homo economicus* of classic political economy ; he is in complete contrast to such a conception. The economic man was an individualist ; he was motivated by personal interest, and depended on personal initiative and the exercise of his power in competition with others. For him, economics was separated from the rest of life and subject to its own laws. The new social man is indeed concerned with economics and technology, almost exclusively engaged in economic and technical activity. But economics itself has a completely new meaning for him. Economics and collective effort are not for him differentiated parts of life ; for him they take on a spiritual character, replace spiritual life itself.

This is why we are astounded at the enthusiasm which the Five Year Plan arouses in Communist youth. The purely economic and technical achievements of the Five Year Plan are not very great ; in comparison with America they are insignificant. But it is as a spiritual phenomenon that this plan of economic and technical construction astonishes us. We are surprised at this almost religious faith in the economic and technical building of a new world, a new life, this complete self-devotion to the titanic idea of construction. Every young man considers himself a re-builder of the world, constructor of a new life. He is serving, not himself, but the whole of society, the collective. He is engaged, not in the ordering of his own individual economic life, but the organisation of the world. This is the attraction and the temptation. Although the individual man desired expansion, although at the height of his development he was an initiator and inventor, still his possibilities were limited. The new social man is omnipotent ; he receives his power from the collective, which is divinity. Communism cramps and limits the individual man, but to the social man it gives boundless possibilities. Individual consciousness, individual thinking, individual moral values—all these were born of class society and class contradictions. All ideology, all theories of the past, arose from the sharp distinction between physical and mental labour, and the emergence of privileged groups which had leisure for abstract thinking and contemplation, but were separated from social activity. In a classless Communist society, knowledge, thought, even the structure of thought, will be joined with the collective process of labour. And in this collective process there will be no barriers for the social man. Human energy has been expended on the mutual social conflict of classes, producing anarchy. In the classless Communist society, organised according to plan, developed by social reason, man will not be weakened by conflict with other men, and his power will be greatly increased. This is the Communist faith and hope. The new Soviet philosophy, developed during recent years, is the basis for a social titanism. The titan is not a separated herd-man, but a social man, a man of the collective. With this comes the pathos of the Five Year Plan, the faith in the possibility of the industrialisation and mechanisation of an enormous agricultural country by the magic of the Communist idea.

It is sometimes thought that Communism denies God and confesses a militant atheism because it has deified man. This is not entirely true. Not man is deified, but the collective in which the individual is dissolved. Thus Communism is equally hostile to both Christianity and European humanism. The Communist idea conflicts not only with the idea of God, but with the idea of man. Communism permits a cruel, even merciless attitude toward the concrete, living individual, for the sake of the social collective —the perfect society which is to come—for the sake of the power of the social man. But the positive significance of Communism is that it puts the question of society and community as an independent problem, one which Christianity has not solved. We believe in the existence and the value of the individual man, but the social man also exists ; man is also a being called to live in society, and called to the ordering of society on the basis of justice and love. Man is called to social activity, and this, too, ought to be permeated by Christian influence.

Communism demands the utmost activity in man's relation to nature and to society. Man is to conquer the elemental forces of nature ; he is to organise, regulate, rationalise the life of society ; and, in order to direct the whole of man's activity to this end, the inner, spiritual life of the human personality is denied. It is held that spiritual problems distract from social activity. The whole man belongs to social action ; he must devote to it all his powers. Therefore the central organ of society—of the collective—must be on guard lest man's energies be wasted uselessly on so-called spiritual life, on meditation, on religious services, on the metaphysical considerations, on fine art—all of them socially unfruitful. Man's mental powers must be devoted to the social process of labour ; they must serve the cause of production, of the remaking of the world.

But here we encounter the basic psychological contradiction of Communism. The realisation of all these grandiose aims, the attainment of Communism, demands the religious energy of the spirit, postulates the capacity for self-sacrifice in the service of a super-personal purpose. Where shall this spiritual energy be obtained, this capacity for sacrifice, this ability to devote oneself to high causes ? When the religious springs of life are finally dried up, when under the influence of anti-religious propaganda the religious energy of the spirit is quenched, the realisation of Communism will become impossible, for no one will care to make the terrible sacrifices necessary, or to serve a super-personal aim. Although it is so hostile to Christianity and to religion in general, Communism is utilising the results of the Christian training of the spirit, the Christian formation of the soul. All the movements in the world, even when they take anti-Christian forms, are utilising the results of centuries of Christian influence. If these results were to be finally eradicated from the spirit of man, it would put an end to all his capacities for any sort of unselfish social effort ; it would mean reducing man to the level of the beasts. No matter how much European Communism denies Christianity, it is living unconsciously on Christian elements. The recognition of the worth of each individual, the value of each human soul, freedom of conscience—all these truths are drawn from the Christian revelation. Once complete Christianity is denied—the Christian doctrine of man—there can be no argument against a return to slavery, against man's exploitation of man ; nothing can prevent the apotheosis of unbridled force, quite merciless in its attitude toward the weak. And inasmuch as Communism breaks completely with Christianity, it permits the enslavement of man in the Communist State ; it leaves room only for the strong, and is merciless toward the weak. But even for the realisation of its own anti-Christian purposes it needs the enthusiasm and unselfishness aroused by super-personal ideals. Communism is concerned with man ; it must be realised by men ; it demands not much, but all of man's powers. But in setting its aims it forgets about the individual and considers him as simply an instrument, just as in the capitalist system.

The denial of all spiritual life for the sake of a social purpose is based on the fact that man is transformed into a machine, a mechanism, capable of producing the maximum for society in the minimum of time. Man is given no time to think, to concentrate on the meaning of his existence. The capacity of man for great sacrifice and unselfish service is discovered to be the capacity of a perfect automaton. Communism desires to create a more perfect society, and it is justified in this desire ; but in Communism the question of society completely replaces that of the individual. In man there is left no trace of an inner centre, no inner life which is his own, and is directed not toward nature and society, but toward God. Man is a function, an instrument of society.

When the enemies of Communism, partisans of the older forms of society based on sharp inequalities, accuse Communism of denial of individual personality and of debasing the quality of personal life, they are only partially right. The problem is more complex. Communists can reply that the privilege of being a highly developed personality, with high qualitive content, belonged only to those of a comparatively small ruling class, assured of leisure for that purpose. The labouring class never had this possibility : in them personality was oppressed and enslaved and given no chance to express itself. Communism elevates personality, personal worth, and personal opportunity in the labouring classes, and this is more important than its debasement of personality and limitation of opportunity for the privileged groups. Perhaps the remnants of the old intelligentsia feel themselves oppressed in Soviet Russia, but the masses of workmen and peasants feel much better for it.

There is some truth in this retort. The positive value of the Russian Revolution is that it has raised the level of life for the masses of workers and peasants. But the important question is : What principle has inspired it ? Does it affirm the intrinsic worth of every individual worker, of every human individual, his right to an abundant life, his true freedom, or does it deny the value, the right, and the freedom of all personality, because it denies the principle of human personality in general ? By virtue of its ideology, while protecting the personalities of the oppressed classes, Communism inclines to deny personality in general.

III. ETHICS AND THE MYTH

The basis of Russian Communism is Marxism. And it is Marxism which gives Russian Communism its fundamental moral contradictions. Marx considered himself in principle amoral. He refused to recognise independent significance in moral categories and estimates. He denied that any

difference exists between good and evil. For him, moral
values were determined by economics and by the class to
which one belonged. He considered his Socialism as not
ethical but scientific. Socialism is the necessary result of
economic development, he claimed ; it will be born of the
necessities of the process of production itself. Socialism will
be born out of violence, and will be good because it will be
necessary, because it is the last stage of the social process,
and not at all because it is just or right in the realm of
human relationships.

Marx despised moral values and considered them
" bourgeois." No other moral existed for him than that of
class. And at the same time Marx failed to realise how constantly he made use of moral values, or even misused them.
For Marx, evil did exist, even the genuine idea of original
sin. This evil, this original sin, is the exploitation of man by
man, of class by class. But exploitation is a moral, not an
economic category ; exploitation is a morally reprehensible,
evil attitude of man to man. Marx, and after him all Marxists, are continually in a state of moral indignation against
the exploiters, the bourgeoisie, against " those blood-
suckers," against rich farmers, against profiteers and
counter-revolutionaries. But whence this moral indignation ?
How can it be justified ? If we are to consider social phenomena from a completely amoral point of view, and to make
no unconditional distinction between good and evil, then
it is incomprehensible why exploitation is such a bad thing,
or why anyone who has the power should not oppress his
neighbour. The bourgeoisie is a necessary outgrowth of the
economic process of production ; all its qualities are determined by economics. Why such indignation against the
bourgeoisie ? A Christian should condemn the exploitation
of man by man, but why should a materialist ? There is a
startling contradiction here.

And here lies the theoretical weakness in the principles of
Communism. Communists greatly misuse moral indignation
against the bourgeoisie, against imperialists, against
counter-revolutionaries and the like. All the reviling which

fills Communist literature is of a moral nature. It is all moral qualification and moral evaluation. For Marxism, the bourgeoisie of the world and the world's materialism are not necessary products of economics, but rather moral crime, injustice, and oppression. The basis of the Marxists' philosophy, however, gives them no right to take such an attitude. That they do, simply shows that man cannot escape from good and evil, cannot easily throw off moral values, that the element of the moral, even in a distorted form, is natural to man. If the Communists say that they are judging the bourgeoisie from the viewpoint of proletarian morality, this is possible only because what they consider as proletarian is the all-human moral element which has existed since the beginning of time.

The same kind of contradictions exist in Marxism as regards the perception of truth. Marxism considers all ideology, all theory, to be a reflection, an epiphenomenon, of economic actuality, a superstructure on a materialistic base. This is the sheerest relativism. But what is the ideology of Marxism itself, its doctrine of the historic process, of surplus value, and the like ? Marxism will never agree that it is just as relativistic as other ideologies, that it is the reflection of a definite economic reality and of economic interests. Marxism is convinced that to it the real secret of the historic process has been revealed—the secret of social life. But this confidence in its own truth undermines its very basis, which demands relativism. Whether we see in Marxism a revelation of truth or a relative reflection of economic reality, either undermines the basis of Marxism itself. Marxism has smuggled into itself both absolute good and absolute truth ; and from the heights of this good and this truth it passes judgment on the world.

Communism is social titanism. But it replaces the problem of man by the problem of society. The problem of man is of central importance in the criticism of Communism from the Christian point of view. For Marx, class replaced the individual. He could not see man for the class to which he belonged ; behind each individual he perceived his class.

The whole man, the very depths of his soul, were determined by the class of which he was a member. There is nothing in man which is not determined by the social order. For Marxism, the man of the bourgeois class is not a real man ; his nature is deformed, perverted by the sin of exploitation ; truth and justice are not revealed to him ; his ideology is false and hypocritical. There is no light in him.

But the real man, nevertheless, appears in Marxism. This genuine man is the proletarian. The proletariat is no longer merely a class ; it is the real, the only humanity. This class is free from the sin of exploitation ; to it the truth is revealed ; by its very nature it desires justice ; it is the liberator of mankind. Marxism denies the existence of a human nature in general, which both Christianity and humanism have recognised. According to Marxism, it never existed in the past, but it will appear in the future as the nature of the proletariat. Marxism relativises and makes valueless all human history, but it makes an absolute of the proletariat, the Messianic class.

This faith of Marx and the Communists in the proletariat is truly a religious faith, the religious side of their doctrine, a peculiar experience of a secularised form of ancient Messianic expectation. There is absolutely no scientific basis for this belief in the Messianism of the proletariat. Here Marx is a creator of myth. He produces a genuine myth of the proletariat, a myth at once dynamic and active. The proletariat of Marx fails to coincide with the empirical proletariat which does not possess such exclusively Messianic qualities, which is composed of many types quite different in interests and psychology. Marx's proletariat is a New Israel, a sort of chosen people of God. The universalism of the proletariat is a caricature of Christian universalism and the Christian Church.

More than others, Russian Communism has adopted this religious, Messianic, mythical side of Marxism, and the Messianism of the proletariat has become fantastically joined with the old Messianism of the Russian people. This explains much of the psychology of Russian Communism.

Tc

The scientific aspect of Marxism plays a very small part— actually it is contradicted by the very nature of Russian Communism. Marx never foresaw the possibility of a proletarian revolution and a dictatorship of the proletariat in a country industrially backward, in a country chiefly agricultural, with a large mass of peasants and a very small industrial proletariat of the factories. Here Russian Communism is a living, actual confutation of the materialistic concept of history ; it has a clearly idealistic character. The idea has proved stronger than the reality ; it can rule over and define reality.

The central committee of the Communist Party, permeated by this Messianic idea of the proletariat, is omnipotent. It can and it does determine the economic development of an enormous country, instead of being itself determined by this economic development, as it should be, according to Marxian theory. This proves once more how much Russian Communism is a religion instead of a scientific theory or a method of politics. He who fails to see this cannot understand the power of Russian Communism, its capacity to inspire and engender enthusiasm. But just in its character of religion it conflicts sharply with Christianity. Christianity cannot consent to the identification of mankind with the proletariat, which means the denial of humanity in every other form. Christianity believes that in every man there is the image of God, even though this image may be distorted or mutilated by class interests or class psychology. There is much that is true and quite acceptable to the Christian consciousness in the Marxian idea of the distortion of human nature in the bourgeois class. But Christianity cannot accept class hatred, the denial of the oneness of all humanity, even if it be sinful and perverted. Communism puts the question, in a form distorted into caricature, of the unity of humanity, of a human community which shall exclude domination and exploitation. And the more Communism denies the oneness of all humanity, the more it demands that all humanity be united. Christianity must accept this challenge.

IV. GODLESSNESS IN CAPITALISM AND COMMUNISM

A certain economist once remarked to me : " We economists are all atheists ; ours is a godless science." Although this was said in jest, it contains a serious truth. An economy which is completely autonomous, which recognises only its own laws and bows to no spiritual or moral principle, is an economy truly atheist. And the capitalist world is an extreme expression of just such a godless economy. What capitalistic society of the nineteenth and twentieth centuries understood as economic freedom is complete economic autonomy, its isolation from any spiritual or moral principle. In a society founded on such an atheistic economy, man exists for economy, and not economy for man. The worth of man, his dignity and value, cease to be guiding principles in such an economic system.

But the moment you bring forward the value of the human individual, you limit the autonomy of economy and submit it to spiritual and moral principles. Communism is on the one hand a product of this godless economy, and on the other a protest against it. Marx himself spoke of the influence Ricardo and the economics of his day had on his own economic doctrines. He derives most of his theory from the godless economy of the contemporary European society. Marx even believed himself that a godless economy, guided exclusively by the interests of profit, was the eternal basis of society and of culture. But for Marx and for Russian Communists, economics has a completely different significance from that which it had in bourgeois capitalistic society. The militant atheism of Marxism makes economics sacred. The Communist economic system is no longer neutral, godless : it becomes divinity itself, true being, the better life, the transfiguration of the world.

The Communist economic system is no longer autonomous, separated from all other sides of life. But on the other hand it cannot be said that it is a system subject to a higher spiritual order. It has itself been transformed into a higher spiritual order, which directs the whole of life,

Hence it has again become a holy system, but in a sense quite anti-Christian. The " holy " Communist economic must be regarded as anti-Christian because at its centre, instead of the individual and his worthy existence, there stands the Communist society. Just so is Capitalism godless, because at its centre is godless industrial development instead of man and his right to live a worthy life. The individualism of Capitalist society recognised, instead of the supreme value of human personality, the supreme value of the economic man, of an individual guided by personal interest and the profit motive in economic development. Communism has this great advantage over Capitalism, that it makes the problem of economy a " holy " problem —that is, something not completely automatic, anarchic, separated from the rest of human life.

The Christian idea of economics differs chiefly from both the Capitalistic and Communist in the fact that at its centre there must be the living individual, and that the organisation of society must have in view the happiness, the value, and the dignity of every man, the dignity and sanctity of human labour. But in its statement of the problem Christianity is nearer to the Communist economy than to that of Capitalism. And it must be admitted that in the economic psychology and ethic of mediæval times, condemning the taking of interest on money loaned, and subjecting economics to a religious principle, there was more of Christian justice than in the economic psychology and ethic of Capitalist society of to-day.

This autonomy in economic life which produces licence and anarchy is inacceptable because the very existence of man on the earthly plane, in our sinful world, depends upon economics : it is the elementary basis of life. Economics is connected with material, that is, with the lowest level of being, and this lowest level of being cannot be granted complete freedom. Its freedom must be limited by the value of the higher levels of existence. The higher we go in the hierarchy of levels of being, the greater the freedom ; the lower we go, the less liberty we find. The maximum of freedom is found in the life of the spirit. Marxism reverses the hierarchy of values. It asserts the economic basis of life as the supreme value, and subordinates spiritual values to economics. Christianity must restore the hierarchy of values to their proper order, subordinating the lower to that which is higher, and thus attaining the original order of life.

The only eternal inequality which Christian conscience can recognise is not that of " higher " and " lower " classes, but the natural qualitative difference in the spiritual, mental, moral, æsthetic qualities of people themselves, the inequality of powers and gifts. But this inequality has no relationship with class distinctions, and does not even correspond to them. This does not mean that the orientation of the whole social order from the living man, his good and his values, is the setting up of a utilitarian ideal. Man is a consumer ; he cannot live otherwise ; but his value is determined by the fact that he is a producer and a creator. And every man should have the opportunity of realising his calling to create, to utilise his productive energy.

The partial success of Russian Communism is unquestionable. People may speak of certain technical and economic achievements of the Five Year Plan. I am not an economist, and therefore cannot enter into a discussion of this question. But in my opinion Communism's greatest success is not economic, but psychological. The economic realisation of Communism in an agricultural country with a retarded industrial development has proved very difficult. The food-situation in Soviet Russia has remained very serious, and at the moment seems to be becoming worse. People are starving. The partial successes of Communist industry are largely isolated examples—demonstrations. To build a few model factories or a few enormous buildings is of small significance in the vastness of Russia. But what has succeeded is the arousing of enthusiasm in Soviet youth in the *Komsomol* (Communist Youth Association).

This youth group is the principal ideological support which Communism has. Here Communism succeeds in creating a new spiritual structure. The conquest of the spirit is proceeding much faster that the conquest of economics. Communism shows greater spiritual prosperity than material. For the time being, Communism in Russia demands far greater sacrifices than it offers goods, and this implies a spiritual attitude capable of renouncing privileges and making sacrifices for the sake of the Communist idea. This bears witness once more to the fact that the materialism of the Communists is a very naïve philosophy, with a really spiritual tone. Matter replaces spirit, but somehow becomes spirit itself.

Viewed from the standpoint of the sober, realistic concept of economics held in the West, the Soviet attitude looks like extreme idealism—or even like a phantasmagoria. The attitude toward itself demanded by the Five Year Plan is an attitude almost mystical. It is an attitude which, in the past, only religious objects have demanded. For men of everyday life, and for their nourishment, such an idealistic, mystical attitude toward economics is very difficult. The idea threatens completely to smother the living man. But Soviet youth is carried away by this idea. This is the psychological success of Communism.

And for Christianity the psychological success of Communism is more alarming than its economic success would be. The economic sphere of life might be religiously neutral : one might imagine a combination of Communist economy with Christianity. But the psychological success means winning souls for the anti-Christian idea ; it means lives re-directed in a manner which the Christian conscience cannot view without alarm. The very sacrificial willingness of the spirit of Communist youth, its capacity of devotion to super-personal aims, has its source in Christianity, but it is directed to ends completely anti-Christian. This conversion is not only forgetting God ; it forgets man as well, his spiritual essence, his inner life. And because of this, the final success of Communism is impossible. Man cannot finally forget himself, his image, his existence : he cannot cease to exist. But when man, his inner life crushed out, finally ceases to exist, so does Communism. This deep contradiction is fatally undermining the Communist system.

Communism gives the human soul a substitute for spiritual life, it does not give him real food for the spirit. For the grace emanating from God, the source of life, there is substituted the grace derived from organised society, from the social collective. But this social collective is the creation of man himself. We find ourselves in a vicious circle.

V. THE TASK OF CHRISTIANITY

The greatest conflict between Christianity and Communism occurs in connection with one problem, the deepest which human nature knows—the problem of death. Man's fate, man himself, depend on his attitude toward death. And in the face of death all human titanism is pitiful and negligible. Materialistic Communism wishes to paralyse in the human soul the very rise of the problem of death, to extinguish the thought of death itself, and hence to destroy all relation, all connection, with past generations. The soul which is submerged in the constructive effort of the collective partakes of the collective's immortality. For this soul the question of death does not exist. The " red " funerals in Russia are a glorification of the collective ; they have no connection with the deceased. Communism wants to kill the memory of the past, of those who are dead ; it looks only toward the future. Here Communism is completely opposed to Christianity. Christianity envisages a resurrection, believes in the resurrection of all who have died. Therefore it is a religion of eternal life.

The religion of Communism knows no victory over death —does not even desire such a victory. This is because the Communist religion has no interest in personality. And it is only in connection with personality that the full significance of the question of death arises. Communism recognises only one inequality in principle, and desires to make it permanent : the difference between the generations who have passed on and those of the future. For the one, eternal darkness and death ; for the others, light and life. But Christianity can never be reconciled to such inequality. It remembers all past generations, their calling to eternal life ; it treasures its contact with them. Therefore, the Christian Church, which working for greater light and joy in the future, affirms the communion of all human generations.

Facing Communism as a world phenomenon, the task of Christianity is not at all that of conflict with every social movement of our times, but rather the spiritualising and Christianising of those movements, bringing into them a new spirit, the education of human souls for a new social life, a new community of men. It is not enough to preach the spiritual regeneration of men and to ignore social life. Such preaching gives an impression of hypocrisy and the desire to defend the *status quo* by hiding it under high-sounding phrases.

The spiritual regeneration of the individual man cannot but express itself in social change. An unjust, godless society, or unjust and godless social relationships, always give proof of inner, spiritual evil, of the spiritual debasement of men. There must be a spiritual regeneration of both personality and society, the realisation in society of the commands of Christ. In the future we must strive toward a society in which his very social position man cannot be an exploiter or an oppressor.

To be sure, there will always be the expression of evil will in social life. But the remedy lies in the sincere determination of Christians to war against the social expression of evil. Communism intends, by means of the compulsory, external organisation of society, to produce a juster social order, which is the good in Communism ; but in endeavouring to attain an inner communion of men, a brotherhood, by this external compulsion, Communism enters an evil path leading it straight to tyranny. A new social order must be created, one which eliminates man's oppression of man and the unbearable inequality of to-day ; but inner brotherly communion is a spiritual task. It is a Christian task, which transcends the limits of a legal organisation of society. Communism's challenge to the old society and to Christianity faces the whole Christian world with these problems, with the necessity of building a new society, a new Christian community.

7. THE CHURCH IN THE WORLD : FAILURES AND OPPORTUNITIES

By F. R. BARRY

I. WHAT IS THE CHURCH FOR?

JOHN WESLEY once described himself as a man sent by God to persuade men to make Christ the centre of their fellowships. It would be hard to find a better description of the tasks and functions of the Christian Church. It has not fulfilled its mission in the world when it has persuaded a number of people to add the habit of going to church or chapel to their other habits, but without changing them ; it is here in order to train men and women to experience life from a new centre, and, because it does so, to transform the world. " The Kingdom of God is at hand," proclaimed Jesus : " change your minds and believe in the good news." The result of his mission was the Christian Church. Controversy has raged for many centuries about the nature and character of the Church and its system of ministry and organisation. Christians have wasted a tragic amount of energy in debating what (or where) is the true Church, and in trying to un-Church one another in terms of their differing answers to the question. The various Christian " denominations " have stood, in the past, for real differences in emphasis or religious experience. They are complementary to one another, and each has preserved something of real importance which others have been in danger of forgetting. Each has stood for a positive contribution to the whole faith and practise of Christianity. To regard these differences as unimportant, or due to mere quarrelsomeness and faction, is a superficial reading of history. Nevertheless, it has been sheer disaster that such divergences of interpretation should have been allowed to harden into sects which have broken up the Christian society. It has meant a deplorable weakening of Christian forces. The Catholic Church in which we profess belief—the universal

Uc

Church which is yet to be—will not merely tolerate, but welcome, the richest possible variety of interpretation and expression in one living and organic unity.

So long as we ask : Which of all the Churches is to be regarded as the true Church ? we are holding back the hope of such unity. We are asking a question to which there is no answer, and can merely debate " about it and about." For hitherto men have attempted to answer it by scrutinising the records, examining the lines of tradition, and trying to reach a conclusive definition from their reading of the Church's past history, in New Testament times or in the early centuries. But such inquiries lead into a blind alley. No mere historical investigation can decide what is the nature of a living Church. The nature of anything that is alive must be defined in terms not of its origin, but of the goal towards which it is moving and the purpose which it is organised to serve. If the Church is indeed a living society, inspired by the Spirit of the living Christ, then all discussion about its true nature and the right ordering of its life and system must be teleological rather than archæological. For structure is relative to function. Thus the right question to ask about the Church is not : What has it been ? but : What is it for ? And if the question is raised in that form, it lifts the discussion out of the shifting sands of ecclesiastical or sectarian controversy on to the rock of ultimate Christian faith in the nature of God and his purpose for the world. For the Church exists that it may be the instrument of God's work, through Christ, in human history. It is in the world in order to redeem it. The true task and function of the Church as an organised society in the world is the redemption of the social order.

This book as a whole rests on the conviction that the world-order can be reconstructed by that which Christianity offers to bring to it. But no individual inspirations can carry through a task so tremendous. It can only be achieved by a society which is living the kind of life that it proclaims. We have argued that the present world-crisis is ultimately spiritual and moral. The political and economic chaos is connected with causes which lie far deeper down, and reflects a confusion still more disastrous in the sphere of men's motives and convictions. It is surely true that the misery and anxiety which are grinding down the life of civilisation, the suspicions, conflicts, and antagonisms which are making the world a nightmare of fear, are traceable in the last resort to the atrophy of vital conviction in a righteous Purpose sovereign in history, in being conformed to which both men and nations find alike their fulfilment and their freedom. The disorganisation of the world is largely due to the fact that it is not organised by any conscious acceptance of a purpose other than the immediate self-interest of the individuals and groups within it. So that our economic interdependence, which should be the outward and visible expression of our fundamental unity one with another, becomes but a fresh occasion for conflict, or of such attempts to assert our independence as are bound, in the nature of things, to be self-defeating. The *débâcle* of economic Nationalism is, in fact, a relentlessly searching commentary on the fragmentariness of our social order, unrelated to any common world-view. It vindicates, in the sphere of economics, that essential community of interest which none without disaster can seek to evade. The conflicting interests of the various classes, the racial and national antagonisms, illustrate with what fatal ease, and (too often) with what disastrous consequences, human groups come at cross purposes for lack of belief in a unifying Purpose.

Civilisation is attempting to meet the gravest danger that has yet threatened it, sustained by no coherent philosophy. When we act at all, we act departmentally, like an army without a higher command, in which the various services and departments are in no communication with one another. The fundamental trouble with the modern world is that politics, economics, and morals are in no proper relation to one another. The political organisation of the world is in defiance of economic reality ; and notoriously our economic systems are treated as though they existed in their own right, and have not been brought under any such control as would make them the servants of real human welfare ; which is what would be meant by making them moral. It is but the merest truism to assert that the one essential problem of modern politics is the moralisation of economics. For what has been said so often about armaments is equally true of production and distribution : if man does not master economics, economics will master man. That is happening at the present moment ; and the Marxian philosophy becomes true so soon as man abdicates his sovereignty and allows financial policy to control him. But we cannot bring industry and finance or the organisation of society under the control of human purposes without some vision of what the world is for and what *is* the purpose and destiny of mankind.

That is precisely the Christian contribution. Christianity rests on faith in a divine purpose, operative in the history of the world, in the sharing of which man's life is fulfilled. That purpose it called the Kingdom or Realm of God—the perfect society of persons in fellowship with God and with one another. This does not remain in the sphere of mere " ideals." It is to be realised in the life of men, " on earth as it is in heaven." Christianity is the only great religion which takes economics quite seriously. The material bases of human life are of the utmost importance to it. It cannot ignore the claims of the physical. For its faith is in God, who became incarnate in the psycho-physical life of Jesus Christ. And as it believes that God has been manifested, and is at work in mankind through him, so it believes that the whole range of activities which make up the actual lives of men are to be redeemed by his Spirit, brought into conformity with the divine purpose, and made organic to the " Body " of Christ—the outward manifestation of his Spirit and the instrument of God's will for man. That, in essence, is what we mean by the Church. It is to be the Body of Christ in the world. That is to say, it is to be the society through which God is revealed in the social order—all its interests and occupations being consecrated to the Father's purpose, and its whole life organised and directed by God's will for the human race as declared and mediated by Christ Jesus.

This makes it clear, incidentally, that the " preaching of principles " is not enough. A principle, after all, is a poor ghost unless expressed in concrete material. It is merely sentimental to speak of principles which are not embodied in economic realities and the organisation of society. There were fine principles in plenty before the coming of Christ to the world, as there are still, apart from Christianity or in circles which it has indirectly influenced. But the Christian faith in an Incarnation means that the Spirit of God in Jesus Christ laid hold upon the actual life of a man, with its instinctive and material basis, as the instrument of his perfect purpose. By his work in the hearts of men through Christ, that is to be, and is being, realised throughout the whole order of human life.

The Christian redemption of the social order is offered the world through a redeemed society, in which " Christ is the centre of men's fellowships." But the only way in which this can be achieved is through an actual society consciously directed by that purpose and expressing it in the quality of its life, so that the Spirit of Christ may become incarnate in the world's social and economic order. No human society is wholly " secular." There is no form of human association which does not reveal, in its own degree, something of that life of love or fellowship which has its source in the being of God. But no existing human associations completely realise their ideals. They are limited by their own limited aims, or spoiled by the selfishness of their members, or come into collision with one another. Every human group as we know it, just so far as it is self-centred, at least falls short of the glory of God, and may—as we know too well—become something which impedes and impoverishes fellowship. It can realise its full possibilities only when it is brought into relation with a life and a purpose higher than its own, and becomes a sharing in the Divine Society. That can be verified in any home ; it is just the meaning of the Christian family. It has yet to be verified in politics and human association on the big scale. When Christ is the centre of men's fellowships, they can be redeemed from whatever mars them, and made a true community of the Spirit.

II. REVOLUTION OR RELIGION

A well-known writer has recently raised the question whether the movement begun by Jesus Christ was indeed a world-revolution, or nothing more than a religion. The question implies that if it is a religion it will have no bearing on practical politics, or, if it has, will provide the inspiration for the preservation of the existing order. That was scarcely the judgment passed upon it by the Roman imperial Government, or the general feeling in the popular mind. " Men who have turned the world upside down " was a description of the Christian missionaries. There have, no doubt, been versions of Christianity which have played into the hands of reaction, and the Church in Russia is paying a terrible price for it. But Christianity first appeared in the world as a new, revolutionary way of living, and wherever it has been true to its own genius it has had within it a dynamic power of social reconstruction and renewal. But this is precisely *because* it is a religion, and upon this depends its whole effectiveness. It is perfectly fair to urge against the Churches that Christianity is a way of living much more than a system of theology, and that Christians have at some times forgotten this. But it is a God-centred way of living, wherein life is seen from a new centre and man's course is set by a new pole. It is this new Godward orientation, this conviction that man's life in time is only fulfilled in his eternal purpose, which is the secret of its transforming power in morality, politics, and economics, and the whole structure of society. Apart from that it has nothing to say to the world, and would soon degenerate into another name for the average moral opinions of the West.

But the Church is to be the " school of Christ," educating mankind in this changed way of living. It follows that

worship is, and always must be, its primary and most characteristic activity. It is the submission of all human standards and the consecration of all human activities to the
God who claims us in Jesus Christ. That is what it is in the
world for. Hence the rather absurd popular criticism that
the Church is inept because it is " otherworldly," when it
should be concerning itself with social programmes, altogether misses the real point at issue. Just in so far as the
Church knows its business, its centre of gravity cannot be in
this world, though it is in this world that its task is to be
performed. Its mission is to bring the order of this world—
with all its social and economic systems—into conformity
with the divine ideal of it. The Christian life is by no means
fulfilled in specifically religious activities ; that is the mistake of the pietist at all times. Yet it certainly falls below the
Christian level, and becomes sterile and ineffective, if it is
conceived only in terms of conduct, unlit and unwarmed by
worship at the heart of it. What the Christian religion is,
essentially, is the consecration by the Spirit of Christ, and the
offering in worship to the Father, of all human interests and
concerns, whether of thought, emotion, or conduct. St.
Paul said that " God was in Christ reconciling the world
unto himself."[1] That involves far more than making all
men religious ; and more, even, than the forgiveness of sins.
It means no less than the reconciliation of all personal and
social purposes, to God's perfect purpose of love through
Christ's redemptive work in the hearts of men. And as
every purpose must be embodied (as " the Word was made
flesh " in Jesus), it implies the organisation of our lives and
of our social and economic systems as sacramental expressions of that purpose. Thus the so-called " secular " activities are as essential to the Christian life and the realisation of
the City of God as our inward faith and our religious exercises. All attempts made by men and women, whether as
parents, teachers, or artists, whether in politics, industry,
or science, or any other legitimate occupation, to mould the
conditions of human living to the service of spiritual

[1] II Corinthians 5 : 19.

purpose, are part of God's reconciling work, part of his redemption by Christ.

The Church, as the worshipping society and the Body of Christ in the world, is to be the means of that reconciliation. This is the proper business of Christians. Therefore worship " in spirit and in truth " ought to mean a continual conversion of our thought, our standards, and our aims ; and it must result, in direct proportion to its vitality, richness, and sincerity, in a moral and social revolution. It follows that the justifiable criticism would be not that the Church puts worship first, but that such big areas of its life in the world are still unpenetrated by the spirit of worship. Many Christians fail to relate what they say and think in church on Sunday morning with what they say and think, as sincerely, when they read the paper on Sunday afternoon.

III. WHAT IS THE CHURCH DOING ?

Always in times of public anxiety the question is asked : What is the Church doing ? Those who ask it imply the answer : Nothing. It is taken for granted in much current literature that the Church, at least as a moral force in the world, is hopelessly effete and discredited. And it must in all candour be admitted that the one really formidable argument against the truth of the Christian religion is the record of the Christian Church. Again and again it has betrayed its Lord, fought against truth, and denied his teaching, and supported abuses which he died to rectify. Again and again it has failed in the hour of crisis. When we look back at its crimes and its infidelities, when we look now at its weakness and disunion—that is real challenge to faith. Nevertheless, the striking fact is that at almost any period of history in which the Church has seemed to be dying, and its dissolution has been predicted, it has risen again vital with new life, and proved once more its inherent creativity. It was so, for example, after the eclipse in the grey twilight of the Age of Reason. All that men say now about the Church, and its apparent inertia and decay, was said with equal confidence and dogmatism by the contemporaries of Joseph Butler (1692–1752). Yet the immediate sequel to that period came in the form of two sweeping revivals (the Evangelical and Tractarian Movements), the foundation of the missionary societies, and the almost unbelievable expansion of the Church throughout the world in the nineteenth century. Indeed, this is the daily renewed miracle. If we think of the Church as an organisation akin to a State or a political party, it may appear to be feeble and ineffective, and even, at times, sub-Christian in its standards. If we think of it in terms of its inward life in the minds and hearts of its members, it is always alive and always active as the leaven leavening the lump. There may not be much for the onlooker to see ; he may ask : Look we for another ? Yet, wherever it is, the lame walk, the dead are raised up, and the poor have the gospel preached to them.

There is one obvious criterion by which the effect of the Church can be estimated. What would have been the course of social history, let us say since the Industrial Revolution, and what the hope of social redemption, if the Christian Church had not been there ? This was what Marx, for example, overlooked. The " inevitable " course of history has not, in fact, turned out as he predicted ; the emergence of an unnoticed factor has disturbed his economic calculations just as unseen, unsuspected stars may falsify the predictions of astronomers. That factor has been the rise of a social conscience, with the consequent growth of social control, which has intervened to protect the proletariat from the incidence of crude economic law. If the subsequent history of Capital has not conformed to the Marxian patterns, it is due primarily to a moral factor. And behind it there lies that enlightenment of conscience and sensitiveness to the claims of personality which has been the effect of the Christian Church in the lives of thousands of unknown men and women. The " social movement " is the child of the Church. It is true, no doubt, as the Hammonds love to point out, that the original Methodists and their followers were interested only in " saving souls," and that they, like their Tractarian successors, had little direct concern with the social problem. It is equally true of St. Francis of Assisi. Yet he was the father of the friars, and has been the patron saint and inspiration of widespread movements in art and science, and the real founder of political democracy. So it was also with the evangelical movements. Despite their apparently narrow range of sympathy, they did evoke out of average men and women, who now saw their starved, impoverished lives against the background of an eternal destiny, a new recognition of the rights of man and a new concern for the sacredness of humanity. They made Christ the centre of men's fellowships ; and the power of this compelling allegiance began to transform the external conditions of life. The slightly dejected " saints " of the Clapham sect may have seemed, and would probably seem to us, prim, narrow-minded, and reactionary. Yet it was they who with dauntless tenacity, and in the teeth of embattled vested interests, forced through Abolition and the Factory Acts. The Church is not dead and effete when such things happen !

For the Church can act, it must be borne in mind, only through its individual members. Why, we are asked, did the Church do nothing to protest against the iniquities of the slave trade ? The answer is : It did much more than protest ; it abolished them—in the person of Wilberforce. How could the Church sit still and remain inactive while the cry of the victims of mines and factories " came unto the ears of the Lord of Hosts " ? The answer is that the Church did hear their cry and delivered them—in the person of Lord Shaftesbury. And still to-day the claim can be fairly made that wherever you find constructive effort at work for social and personal regeneration, you will find that in nine cases out of ten there is Christian inspiration behind it. Such a claim scarcely needs argument if we look beyond Western civilisation and watch the inherent Christian dynamic exhibiting its moral resources in the redemption of non-Christian cultures and the education of new peoples.

The Christian Renaissance in tropical Africa, both in Uganda and on the West Coast, is one of the startling chapters in history. Not less spectacular have been the achievements of the Christian mission in the Indian villages. Kagawa's work in industrialised Japan can only be described as miraculous. The fact is that there is in Christianity an innate moral and social creativity. It may be, and frequently is, inhibited by corruption, cowardice, and false teaching ; but wherever there are men and women brave enough to trust it, it proves itself. Wherever the authentic tree grows, there it is known by its fruits.

If at a time of demoralisation such as that in which we are now living, when everywhere standards are tumbling down and men losing faith, hope, and courage ; if at such a time there are " seven thousand in Israel " who have not bowed to false material values and whose hearts remain untouched by the corrosions of scepticism, selfishness, and despair—that may not be a spectacular achievement, but it shows that the Christian Church is still the salt saving civilisation from going bad.

Nevertheless, when all this is said, it remains true (and must be frankly admitted) that the Church does not count for half as much as it might in the reconstruction of post-war society. There are many weaknesses and inconsistencies which expose us to justifiable criticism ; and such criticism will not be resented by a Church which is true to the mind of its Master. But the fundamental weakness of the Church now is its lack of moral courage and realism. It has been far too ready to come to terms with the false gods of crude, insensate nationalism, which to admit is an ultimate betrayal. It has been, and is, too much on the side of property. It is not nearly as brave as it ought to be about armaments and slums and exploitation. What it needs at present most desperately is that moral sincerity and passion which is the best gift of the rising generation.

The constant danger of " organised religion " is to become self-centred and introverted, more concerned with its own preservation than with the redemption of society.

The Church to-day is not secure against this. It tends to be asking : How can we save the Church and strengthen it against hostile forces ? But it ought to be asking the very different question : How can the Church save the world, even at the cost of its own life ? Hence it is in danger of becoming preoccupied with the maintenance and extension of its system, too little concerned with the purpose for which it exists. On such terms Church membership degenerates with appalling ease into a dead conformity, and even triviality and sentimentalism. Compromise and timidity beset it, and it rapidly forfeits the allegiance of the younger and more vigorous elements, to whom moral candour and sincerity are the absolute values in religion. Some of those who are outside the Church take moral issues more searchingly than some of us who are inside its fellowship. The Church abdicates its moral leadership if its members draw dividends from armaments, or in other ways acknowledge complicity with abuses which they are pledged to destroy.

A church that is true to the mind of Christ, outward-looking upon the world's need and its moral and spiritual mission to it, has before it a task and an opportunity such as has not been given to it for centuries. Never before has the world been so willing to accept an authoritative moral leadership. Seldom before have average men and women, oppressed with a sense of futility and despair, of false values and ambiguous standards, been so disposed as they are to-day to receive convincing spiritual guidance. The Christian Church has everything before it—a world to win and only its chains to lose. But it must be honestly willing to lose its chains.

What weakens its moral witness at present is not that its members are insincere or their lives consciously inconsistent. It is rather, I think, our fatal readiness to sentimentalise Christianity. And this, I suggest, is not unconnected with our appalling incontinence of preaching. We have let ourselves form the disastrous habit of assuming that ceaseless exhortation—which we carry to the point of a vice—is the same thing as moral reformation. It becomes an emotional substitute for action. Moreover, it tends to defeat its own object, for lack of realistic analysis. To exhort people to " be good " is futile—for wherein does goodness consist ? What, in fact, *is* the " Christian ethic " in the circumstances of twentieth-century life ? That we have scarcely begun to think out ; and this uncertainty and hesitation weakens the whole life of the modern Church. I am not thinking only of " pronouncements " made by accredited leaders and official bodies. It is even more true of the pastoral ministry exercised by the rank and file of the clergy, and by parents, teachers, scoutmasters, and so forth. All efforts at training Christian character and helping people in moral perplexity are inevitably impeded and weakened by the sense that we do not know with sufficient clearness what *are* the demands of the Christian way of life, whether in public or private action, in the chaotic conditions of our time. Hence a pint of Christian moral research would be worth many gallons of exhortation.

But moral research, if it is to have any value, can never be merely theoretical. No theories about religion are worth having unless they are put forward by people who themselves practise religion from within. Nor can any views about Christian conduct command serious consideration unless they arise out of a society which is attempting to put them into action. Thus the great task before the Church is to learn how to " practise what it preaches "—not only by training individuals in personal rectitude and integrity, but by discovering in its own life and exhibiting in its corporate activity the vital patterns of a social order baptised into the allegiance of Christ.

That task is at present frustrated by sectarianism and disunity. A Church thus divided and anatomised is a standing denial of its own creed. If anywhere we can hope to discern the will of God for our day and generation, if at any point in our experience we can hope to perceive the leading of the Spirit, it is in the yearning of the human race for a unity which transcends our differences, and an international society which shall enfold mankind in one family without suppressing its local associations. The Church has it in it to create that unity, if it will begin to put first things first, and esteem Christ's purpose and command above even the most precious traditions of men. Christians daily profess their belief in one holy Catholic Church. It does not yet exist, but they believe in it. They are pledged to help it come true on earth. There is nothing, however rich and venerable, which we can afford, in this hour of crisis, to allow to stand in the way of its realisation.

8. THE CONCLUSION OF THE MATTER

By THE ARCHBISHOP OF YORK

CONCERNING the trouble in which the world now finds itself, there are as many theories as there are students. It is due to tariff walls and the nationalism that builds them ; it is due to a monetary system based on gold ; it is due to productive capacity outrunning distribution or effective demand ; it is due to prodigal expenditure on the part of Governments ; it is due to niggardly thrift on the part of Governments and citizens alike. So our authorities teach and bewilder us. And between such theories the Christian is no more competent to judge than anybody else. There is justifiable irritation at the attempt to give the dignity of religious sanction to any speculation in this field. The gospel contains no illumination concerning the rights and wrongs of bi-metallism, or social credit, or " techno-cracy." For Christ did not come to save us the trouble of accurately observing facts, and of drawing correct inferences from our observations. Christianity has no programme for the restoration of prosperity ; it is not even greatly interested in prosperity. But it is greatly interested in human welfare, and has a great deal to say about it.

For while it is true, and most important, that the gospel provides no policy, it is also true, and at least equally important, that it does provide principles, and declares that any policy inconsistent with those principles must lead to disaster. For it claims to disclose the character of the eternal God, so that whatever is in conflict with its principles is in conflict with ultimate reality. The declaration that " God is Love " is not only a consolation to the over-burdened, but is a judgment upon the self-centred. If God is Love, selfishness must always be, even from its own standpoint, a mistake. That is why Christ could say that to act on his teaching was like building on a rock.

If, then, we really want to estimate the relation of Christianity to the crisis, we must consider how far the action of men and nations in the nineteenth century and first quarter of the twentieth were in accord with the principles of the gospel ; for any relevant discrepancies that are observable may well be part of the cause of the disaster into which the world has fallen. We must make this search in two main fields of inquiry—the international and the economic.

THE INTERNATIONAL PROBLEM

There are some Christians who hold the view that Christianity forbids any Christian to fight. I respect that view, and, though I do not share it, I rejoice that there should be many who hold it. If " pacifism " is an error, as I think it is, at any rate it is the best error, and is invaluable as a makeweight against the more pernicious errors of uncriticised and unchecked nationalism. To me it seems that circumstances may arise when not to fight is even worse than to fight. But such circumstances ought not to arise, and would not arise if the nations followed Christian principles in the conduct of their affairs. Those principles involve the ordinary pagan virtues of justice and veracity, and the supreme ethical rule that each nation should regard the welfare of other nations equally with its own, and never seek an advantage for itself to the detriment of others. In other words, they involve the recognition of nations as constituting one commonwealth or family. The establishment of the League of Nations represents the first definite attempt to give actuality to this ideal. Till then, the relation of civilised nations to one another had been that of individuals to each other in Hobbes's state of nature wherein, as he justly observes, the life of man is " solitary, poor, nasty, brutish and short." No one, reading the international history of Europe in the nineteenth century would find himself impelled to the conclusion that most of the inhabitants of Europe believed in the Christian gospel.

Part of the trouble about all discussions of this subject is that people always take the standpoint of their own country, and proceed to assert its perfect integrity and innocence, while condemning its enemies with a righteous indignation which is pernicious in proportion to its sincerity. This is a symptom of the essential disease. We do not believe in any family of nations. And the first necessity for a Christian is to escape from the nationalist standpoint and take up that of Christendom or of the commonwealth of civilised nations. For even though circumstances may arise in which a Christian should fight, yet the occurrence of such circumstances is proof that somewhere at least there has been treason to the Kingdom of God.

In the Treaty of Versailles the victorious nations imposed upon the chief vanquished nation an assertion that this nation was the only real culprit. Even if that were true concerning the controversy immediately preceding the war, it was a disastrous thing to do. It was disastrous because it was bound to create in Germany a festering sore of resentment—as has in fact occurred. It was still more disastrous because it based the structure of international relationships for the period of the peace then inaugurated upon a division of nations into innocent and guilty which has hindered any serious inquiry into the ethical roots of the war. Consequently Europe as a whole has still not become conscious of the vast divergence between its course in the nineteenth century and the principles of Christianity. It has not seriously begun to think about the matter. All hope of recovery turns on a radical repentance ; and there is nothing but self-justification.

It is of vital importance that the nations engaged in the Great War should cease to plead the justification for whatever policy they severally adopted, and, taking the international standpoint, ask what was wrong with the civilisation that led to the war, and what was their own share in that wrong. There is no need to deny the justifications so commonly alleged ; what is needed is to cease attending to them and look at the other side of the picture. Our own country, for example, intensified the nervousness of nations and " speeded up " the race in armaments by building the *Dreadnought*. Judged by the standards of policy then commonly accepted, that was justifiable ; but the welfare of the world depends on our adopting for the future standards of policy by which it would be condemned.

For the present acute distress is largely due to lack of mutual confidence ; and that in turn is due to the exaggerated nationalism which leads every country to look on its neighbours rather as potential enemies than as partners in the common enterprise of civilisation. Both views have a foundation in fact. But, as so often in human affairs, the direction of attention to one or other of two alternative possibilities has a great influence in determining which of those possibilities is actualised. If we regard each other first as potential enemies, we shall soon be real enemies ; if we regard each other as colleagues, the risk of hostility will dwindle away. The plain fact is that national sentiment is lagging far behind the economic realities. The world is now commercially a single unit ; if one member suffer, all must suffer with it. No doubt that was always true in the last resort, because it is necessitated by the spiritual constitution of the world. But now it is apparent to the most casual observer. Commercial facts reinforce Christian doctrine ; yet still we cling to a nationalism which has no foundation except in sentiment, and the strongest advocates of this pose as realists, condemning as sentimentalists those who call attention to manifest facts. Anyhow, in so far as the Christian principles always point to fellowship and co-operation, there can be no doubt that they now point the way to restored prosperity.

THE ECONOMIC PROBLEM

The special distress of our time is that of stagnant trade and unemployment. This is increased by the international tension, friction, and suspicion to which reference has been made. But that is not the only source of it, and, as we have asked whether there is anything in the recent international tradition of which Christians must repent, so we must ask the same question concerning recent economic developments.

When the great industrial expansion began in the later part of the eighteenth century, the new opportunities were exploited with quite scandalous neglect of the human interests primarily involved. The treatment of all workers, but especially of children, has become a very legend of horror. No one now disputes the statement that Christian principles were, in the Industrial Revolution, flouted on every side. The people of that time were taken by surprise. Change had hitherto come gradually. They were not accustomed or prepared to consider how far any modifications of what they had known for generations were consistent with beliefs which through the same generations they had held with varying degrees of personal apprehension. We have no such excuse. Partly because of the evils that then grew up through inadvertence, we have had prophets and teachers in plenty to warn us of the hypocrisy and futility in which we are involved, if we do not perpetually criticise social facts and tendencies in the light of our Christian principles.

Now it is perfectly certain that in the great expansion of industry in the nineteenth century the desire to accumulate wealth—not always for self, but for family or country—completely overshadowed desire to let the wealth accumulated enrich the human life of citizens at large, and bind them in social fellowship. The true ends of life were relatively neglected while attention was concentrated on the means of attaining them. And that has produced its logical result, for one reason for our poverty to-day is that we produce wealth so easily. Modern devices turn out what the world needs in such profusion that the pressure of competition, complicated by reparations and war debts, drives down the price below the level at which it is profitable to produce at all. The Christian, as such, is not concerned with the technical aspects of the problem thus presented, except to insist that the best thinking available be directed to them. But he is very much concerned, precisely as a Christian, to insist that economic wealth is a means to human well-being, and that any action or policy must be wrong which tends to increase the former while diminishing the latter. And he will have an initial sympathy with those lines of thought and suggestion which start with the consumer, and ask how he is to be able to obtain what he desires or needs to consume, because it is in consumption that the human value—the end for which all economic processes exist—is found to reside. So the Christian welcomes the " dole " in principle, even if he recognises a necessity in present conditions to restrict its amount ; he welcomes it because it gives power to consume to a large number of people ; and he notices with satisfaction that it has in fact done much to keep alive our home market.

In like manner the Christian, starting from the principle of free personality freely expressed in fellowship, can only regard Communism as at best a temporary makeshift. As an ideal it is falsely based, for it ignores the freedom of personality and the absolute worth of every individual person. But the Communist may justly retort that in practice our existing social order is guilty of the same offence. No doubt our existing order does not make this offence into a principle ; but the Christian view of life will only prevail over this redoubtable antagonist if it is able to secure a fuller expression of its own principles than is visible in our great industrial centres to-day. Whether we call our social policy Distributivism or by some less repellent name, a Christian social philosophy must meet the denial of the rights of property with something more effective than a bare assertion of those rights. It must assert the excellence of property, and the natural right of every civilised man to some property so far as the available wealth of the community allows. If this involves some new monetary system with a new basis, so be it ; but with that suggestion, we pass entirely beyond the region of Christian principle, unless, indeed, it can be shown that some clear moral consideration is involved in our own or any other monetary system.

Some will say that we have been beyond it in most paragraphs of this essay ; they hold that there are economic

" laws " like the laws of physical nature, which the Christian should study, because otherwise he may act disastrously through ignorance of them even when his intentions are the best possible ; but he must not presume to suppose that he can alter them, any more than he can alter the law of gravitation, whatever that may ultimately turn out to be when Einstein's successors have done for his theory what he has done for Newton's. Now there are some economic laws of this kind ; they are such as consist solely of applied mathematics. But most so-called economic laws are generalisations from the observed behaviour of men. The Christian knows, as all men know, that the behaviour of men can be modified not only by the radical method of spiritual conversion but also by the use of sanctions designed to promote some ideal end. The mediæval guilds existed partly to prevent the free play of the forces of competition and secure society against certain evil results expected to ensue if those forces were not checked. The methods of the guilds became unsuited to changing conditions ; but few would maintain that the release of the forces of competition from restraint was purely or predominantly beneficial ; indeed before long Parliament was passing laws to impose restraint in new ways. The notion that economic laws are like the laws of physics, and unalterable by any activity of the human will, is very natural and partly true ; but it is also partly and disastrously false. These so-called laws are in a very few cases nothing more nor less than applied arithmetic, and these are no doubt unalterable. Thus, for example, you cannot distribute wealth unless it is produced—which was once a very relevant consideration, but seems to lack relevance in a world where the chief problem is to find consumers for what has been produced. Most economic laws are (like the laws of physics) generalisations from the observed behaviour of economic forces, and would at once be altered if a new direction were given to those forces. Thus the law of supply and demand arises from the assumption—commonly justified—that sellers and buyers are always concerned to make the best bargain that they can.

But a seller does not always charge the highest price that he can get ; he sometimes charges less than this because he is satisfied to make what seems to him a fair profit on his outlay and would definitely prefer not to make more. The price charged in such a case represents the requirement of his conscience and not any law of supply and demand. If all men came to " seek first the Kingdom of God and his justice," the law of supply and demand would be found to operate far less extensively than it does to-day. And even to-day it is by no means absolute or universal in its operation.

Of course, it is true that this result is not to be brought about by a few people desiring it. The law of supply and demand is a sufficiently accurate generalisation from actual facts to be accepted as a guide to what now takes place, and will continue to take place until men's outlook is substantially altered. To ignore it, while men's motives are unchanged, is certainly to court disaster, as surely as to ignore the law of gravitation is to court disaster. But this does not mean that it is no more subject to human volition than is the law of gravitation ; for it is a summary of human choices, and men might choose otherwise. Nor is there any reason to fear catastrophe if they did choose otherwise, though, if only one, or only a few, conduct business on other principles they may under certain conditions be driven from the market. If the aim of all men were a just price for their goods and a fair reward for their services, to the exclusion of any additional advantage to be gained by exploiting scarcity or need, trade and commerce would unquestionably thrive better than they do to-day ; already to a great extent they are conducted on this basis, and a great deal of the world's work is carried through on the same basis. If men universally adopted what are now the standards of the best, the laws of political economy would be found to have changed considerably. But we cannot alter the laws except by altering the people of whose behaviour the laws are summary descriptions.

Commerce and industry did not first become predominantly selfish in the principle of their organisation at the Industrial Revolution. Like every other human activity they had exhibited this character in greater or less degree throughout their history. But the temptations presented by the new processes of manufacture were overwhelmingly great and the infection of commerce and industry with the poison was correspondingly pervasive. Commercial and industrial England was very far, in the nineteenth century, from seeking first the Kingdom of God and his justice. We have to repent of our ingrained habit of putting means in the place of ends and preferring economic wealth to human well-being.

HOW TO BEGIN

This kind of discussion may do more harm than good if it suggests to those who read it that the great need is for someone else to do something, or that the proclamation of Christian principles will alone make any real difference. What is called for is personal practice of the Christian religion, with an expectation of illumination in reference to these problems. Expectation is an integral part of vital faith, and it is through our faith that Christ heals our ills. It would not be fitting to turn this essay, at its close, into a sermon. And yet it is that guidance which is appropriate in a sermon for which the situation clamours. Every politician and every journalist is prepared to tell us that we can make our contribution to the remedy of the world's distraction by showing public spirit in place of selfishness, by substituting confidence for anxiety in our outlook, by trusting others and inspiring trust in them by our trustworthiness. But there they stop ; and just there the Christian Church begins.

The call is the old one—" Follow me." We can do all those things which wise men recommend to us, if, and, broadly speaking, only if, we live in the companionship of Christ, expecting to find in him the Way to tread, the Truth to act by, the Life to sustain us, in political and economic, as in all other matters. We must use his mind and spirit to test our policy, our ambition, our admiration, our condemnation. For the world is God's world, and the only plans that can in the long run succeed in it, are those which are parts of his.

Does anyone still ask what is the gospel or good news which the Church is commissioned to give to our world ? It is the same which the Lord proclaimed : " The Kingdom of God is at hand ; repent and believe the good news." For to repent is to alter one's way of looking at life ; it is to take God's point of view instead of one's own. It is only through such repentance on the part of a sufficient proportion of men to control policy, commerce, and industry, that our political and industrial ills can be cured. Nor is there any practical hope of such repentance until men effectively believe and act on the good news concerning God which was given to the world through Christ.

INDEX

16q) God